Palgrave Handbook of International Trade

D1086954

Palgrave Handbook of International Trade

Edited by

Daniel Bernhofen
American University, US

Rod Falvey
Bond University, Australia

David Greenaway
University of Nottingham, UK

and

Udo Kreickemeier
University of Tübingen, Germany

First published in 2011
First published in paperback 2013 by
PALGRAVE MACMILLAN

Palgrave Macmillan in the UK is an imprint of Macmillan Publishers Limited, registered in England, company number 785998, of Houndmills, Basingstoke, Hampshire RG21 6XS.

Palgrave Macmillan in the US is a division of St Martin's Press LLC, 175 Fifth Avenue, New York, NY 10010.

Palgrave Macmillan is the global academic imprint of the above companies and has companies and representatives throughout the world.

Palgrave® and Macmillan® are registered trademarks in the United States, the United Kingdom, Europe and other countries

ISBN: 978–0–230–21727–0 hardback
ISBN: 978–1–137–35180–7 paperback

This book is printed on paper suitable for recycling and made from fully managed and sustained forest sources. Logging, pulping and manufacturing processes are expected to conform to the environmental regulations of the country of origin.

A catalogue record for this book is available from the British Library.

A catalog record for this book is available from the Library of Congress.

Contents

Part C Special Topics

Tables

Figures

Contributors

James E. Anderson is the William B. Neenan Millennium Professor of Economics at Boston College, where he has spent his entire career. He was born in Cleveland in 1943, received his BA from Oberlin College and his PhD from the University of Wisconsin, supervised by Robert Baldwin. He has made numerous contributions to the theory of international trade and trade policy. In the last decade he has focused on index numbers of trade policy. (How high are trade barriers, understanding that there are thousands of them?) His book with Peter Neary *Measuring the Restrictiveness of International Trade Policy* (2005) integrates and extends this work. Most recently he has focused on inference about other forms of trade barriers that are implicit in trade patterns, drawing on his earlier economic theory of gravity (*AER*, 1979). For a recent account of developments in the gravity model, see his essay in *Annual Review of Economics*, vol. 3 (2011). A related line of research focuses on insecurity and its implicit effect on trade.

Kristian Behrens is Professor of Economics at the Université du Québec à Montréal (ESG-UQAM), where he is holder of the Canada Research Chair in Regional Impacts of Globalization. He is affiliated with the Centre interuniversitaire sur le risque, les politiques économiques et l'emploi (CIRPÉE) and the Centre for Economic Policy Research (CEPR). His research focuses on international trade (impacts of trade integration, trade frictions), on regional economics (spatial distribution of economic activity, changes in spatial structures) and on urban economics (spatial sorting, agglomeration economies). He earned his PhD in economics at Université de Bourgogne, France, and has been a postdoctoral and Marie Curie fellow of the European Union at the Center for Operations Research and Econometrics (CORE), Belgium. He is currently editor of the *Journal of Economic Geography*.

Jeffrey H. Bergstrand is Professor of Finance in the Mendoza College of Business Administration and a Faculty Fellow at the Kellogg Institute for International Studies, both at the University of Notre Dame in Notre Dame, Indiana. He received his BA in economics and political science from Northwestern University and his PhD in economics from the University of Wisconsin at Madison. He worked as an economist at the Federal Reserve Bank of Boston from 1981 to 1986, conducting research and providing policy advice on international and macroeconomic issues. He has authored over 50 papers on international trade flows, the gravity equation, free trade agreements, foreign direct investment, multinational enterprises, exchange rates, and international currency substitution for, *inter alia*, the *American Economic Review, Economic Journal, Review of Economics and Statistics, Journal of International Economics* and *Journal of International Money and Finance.*

Daniel M. Bernhofen is Professor of International Relations at the School of International Service at American University in Washington DC. Prior to moving to Washington, he was Professor of International Economics and Director of the Globalisation and Economic Policy Research Centre at the University of Nottingham (UK). He was educated at the University of Ulm (Germany) and Syracuse University (USA) and started his academic career at Clark University (USA). Daniel has published widely on the theoretical, empirical and historical aspects of international trade. He is best known for his rigorous tests of general equilibrium trade theory in the context of the 19th century opening up of Japan. His research papers have appeared in *American Economic Review*, the *Journal of Political Economy*, the *Journal of International Economics and Economic Theory.*

Brian R. Copeland is Professor of Economics at the University of British Columbia. He grew up in British Columbia, attended UBC as an undergraduate, and has a PhD from Stanford University. His research has focused on developing analytical techniques to study the interaction between international trade and the environment. He has investigated the role of environmental policy in affecting trade flows, the design of environmental policy in open economies, the interaction between trade in goods and trade in pollution permits, and the effects of trade liberalization on renewable resource management and on environmental outcomes. His work has appeared in journals that include *American Economic Review, Quarterly Journal of Economics, Journal of International Economics,* and the *Journal of Economic Literature*. He and Scott Taylor are authors of the book, *Trade and the Environment: Theory and Evidence* (2003). He was previously coeditor of the *Journal of Environmental Economics and Management* and is currently an associate editor at the *Journal of International Economics.*

Carl Davidson is Professor of Economics and current Chair of the Department of Economics at Michigan State University. He has published widely on many topics, most notably the influence of labor market structure on issues related to international trade and the development of models of oligopolistic behavior designed to help us better understand how firms with significant market power interact. His work has appeared in such publications as the *Journal of Political Economy, Review of Economic Studies, Economic Journal, Rand Journal of Economics, International Economic Review,* and the *Journal of International Economics*. He is also author, with Stephen Woodbury, of *Recent Economic Thought in Search Theory and Unemployment* (2003), and, with Steven Matusz, of *International Trade and Labor Markets: Theory, Evidence, and Policy Implications* (2004).

Peter Egger received a PhD from the University of Linz in 2001. He served as a researcher at the Vienna Institute for Comparative Economic Studies and thereafter at the Austrian Institute of Economic Research. He then held an assistant professorship in economics at the University of Innsbruck. He was professor of economics at the University of Munich between 2004 and 2009 and a department head at the ifo Institute of Economic Research at the same time. Since 2009, he has been professor of economics at ETH Zurich and is a department head at KOF there. He is also a fellow of CEPR and, jointly with John Whalley, a director of the Global Economy Area of CESifo.

Wilfred J. Ethier received his PhD from the University of Rochester. He has been a professor of economics at the University of Pennsylvania for many years. He is a former editor of the *International Economic Review* and a fellow of the Econometric Society.

Rod Falvey is Professor of Economics at Bond University. Before that he was Professor of International Economics at the University of Nottingham, UK. He has held academic positions at the Virginia Polytechnic Institute, Tulane University and the Australian National University and was at Nottingham from 1996 to 2010. The focus of his research interest is international trade theory. He has published extensively in refereed journals, including the *American Economic Review, Quarterly Journal of Economics, International Economic Review, Journal of International Economics* and the *Economic Journal*. At various times, he has held visiting positions at the University of Auckland, Institute of International Economic Studies at Stockholm and the Economic Policy Research Unit in Copenhagen. He has been an associate editor of the *Review of International Economics* and a member of the Editorial Advisory Board of *World Economy*.

Joseph Francois is Professor of Economics (with a Chair in economic theory) with the Johannes Kepler Universität Linz. He is Fellow of the Centre for Economic Policy Research (London) and the Tinbergen Institute (Amsterdam/Rotterdam), Director of the European Trade Study Group and the Institute for International and Development Economics, research fellow with the Vienna Institute for International Economic Studies, and a board member of the Global Trade Analysis Project. He serves on the editorial board of the *Review of Development Economics*, and the *World Trade Review*. He is a member of the policy advisory group TradePartnership. He was previously professor of economics at Erasmus University Rotterdam, research economist for the World Trade Organization, and chief of research and acting director of economics for the U.S. International Trade Commission.

Noel Gaston is the Principal Research Adviser at the Productivity Commission, the Australian Government's independent research and advisory body on a range of economic, social and environmental issues. He is also an Adjunct

Professor of Economics at Monash University and the Founding Director of the Globalisation and Development Centre at Bond University in Australia. He completed his PhD at Cornell University and has worked at universities in the United States, Canada, Germany, South Korea and Japan. His main research interest is in examining the impact of various dimensions of globalisation on labour markets. He co-authored *Measuring Globalisation – Gauging Its Consequences* (2008) and coedited *Globalisation and Economic Integration: Winners and Losers in the Asia-Pacific* (2010) and has published in such journals as the *International Economic Review, Journal of International Economics* and *Oxford Economic Papers*.

David Greenaway is Vice-Chancellor of the University of Nottingham and Professor of Economics. He was the founding director of the Leverhulme Centre for Research on Globalisation and Economic Policy. From 2004 to 2008 Greenaway was university pro-vice-chancellor, having previously held this position between 1994 and 2001. He was dean of the faculty of law and social sciences between 1991 and 1994. His research interests lie primarily in the fields of exporting and productivity; cross-border investment and international trade and economic development. Current projects include work on exports and productivity and spill-overs from Foreign Direct Investment. He has published extensively in peer reviewed journals including the *Economic Journal, European Economic Review, Journal of International Economics, Journal of Development Economics and Canadian Journal of Economics*. He is also Managing Editor of *The World Economy*.

Richard Kneller is Professor of Economics at the University of Nottingham, a Research Fellow in GEP and CESifo. His research in international trade has focused on firm adjustment to globalization and has considered questions on the determinants of firm export behaviour as well as firm strategies towards offshoring. He is currently an associate editor for *The World Economy*.

Carsten Kowalczyk is Associate Professor of International Economics at the Fletcher School of Law and Diplomacy at Tufts University, and Honorary Professor at the University of Aarhus. He has also taught at Harvard, Dartmouth and Penn State. He is the editor of *Economic Integration and International Trade* (1999) and *The Theory of Trade Policy Reform* (2001), and has published in such journals as *American Economic Review, Economica, International Economic Review*, and *Journal of International Economics*. He is the book review editor of the *Review of International Economics* and a member of the Scientific Board of the *Midwest International Economics Group*. He has consulted for the WTO, the World Bank and *Microsoft Corp.* He received his Cand. Polit. (economics) from the University of Copenhagen, and his MA and PhD (economics) from the University of Rochester.

Udo Kreickemeier is Professor of Economics at Tübingen University. Previously he was Associate Professor in the School of Economics at the University of Nottingham. He is an External Fellow of the Leverhulme Centre for Research on Globalisation and Economic Policy. His research interests lie in the field of International Trade Theory and Policy. In particular, he is interested in models of trade in the presence of labour market distortions and unemployment.

Pravin Krishna is Chung Ju Yung Distinguished Professor of International Economics and Business at Johns Hopkins University (School of Advanced International Studies and Department of Economics) and Research Associate at the National Bureau of Economic Research (NBER). Professor Krishna's fields of research interest are international economics, political economy and development. He has published articles in a number of scholarly journals including the *Journal of Political Economy*, the *Quarterly Journal of Economics*, the *Journal of International Economics* and the *Journal of Development Economics*. He is the author of *Trade Blocs: Economics and Politics* (2005).

Professor Krishna holds a BA in engineering from the Indian Institute of Technology, Bombay, and a PhD in economics from Columbia University. He has previously held positions at Brown University, the University of Chicago, Princeton University and Stanford University.

Dermot Leahy obtained his BA from Trinity College Dublin and his Master's from University College Dublin (UCD). He obtained his PhD in economics in 1994 from UCD. He was a lecturer in economics at the University of Birmingham (1994–95), UCD (1995–2007) and is currently a senior lecturer in economics at the National University of Ireland, Maynooth. His main research fields are international trade and industrial organization. He is especially interested in the following topics: outsourcing, cross-border mergers, trade and intellectual property rights, trade and labour standards, trade and industrial policy, trade and foreign direct investment, strategic investment under uncertainty.

James R. Markusen is a US native and also holds EU citizenship. In 1990, he moved to the University of Colorado, Boulder, where he now holds the rank of University Distinguished Professor. Markusen's principal interests are in the field of international trade. His research for the last 15 years has concentrated on the location, production and welfare effects of large-scale firms and multinational corporations. He is credited in particular with developing the 'horizontal' model of the multinational firm.

Will Martin is Manager for Agricultural and Rural Development in the World Bank's Research Group. His recent research has focused primarily on the impacts of changes in trade policy and food prices on poor people in developing countries. Earlier research has also examined the impact of major trade policy reforms – including the Uruguay Round; the Doha Development Agenda and

China's accession to the WTO – on developing countries; implications of climate change for poor people; and implications of improvements in agricultural productivity in developing countries. He trained in economics and agricultural economics at the University of Queensland, the Australian National University and Iowa State University, and worked at the Australian Bureau of Agricultural Economics and the Australian National University before joining the World Bank in 1991.

Steven J. Matusz earned his doctorate at the University of Pennsylvania in 1983. He has been on the faculty at Michigan State University since that time, currently holding the rank of professor. He has been an external research fellow at the Leverhulme Centre for Research on Globalisation and Economic Policy since 2001. His research focuses on the interaction between globalization and labour markets. His published works have appeared in leading refereed journals, including the *American Economic Review*, the *Journal of Political Economy*, the *Quarterly Journal of Economics*, and the *Review of Economic Studies*.

Danny McGowan is a Postdoctoral Research Fellow at the University of Nottingham, from which he obtained his PhD in 2010. His research interests are primarily in the fields of industrial organization, with a particular focus on firm productivity, entry and survival, and international trade. His PhD thesis addressed a number of issues related to the impact of multinational ownership on plant survival, as well as the impact of globalization and macroeconomic factors in shaping entry and exit rates in a cross-country setting. Currently, he is engaged in two research programmes, one that focuses on the interaction between taxation and outcomes at the firm level and another that looks at the effects and determinants of trade costs.

Chris Milner is Professor of International Economics, currently head of the School of Economics, and a research fellow in the Leverhulme Centre for Research on Globalisation and Economic Policy (GEP) at the University of Nottingham. He has published extensively on trade and development issues, and has considerable advisory experience on trade policy issues for national governments in Africa and the Caribbean and for international agencies such as the World Bank, Commonwealth Secretariat and UNCTAD.

Peter Neary is Professor of Economics at Oxford University and a Professorial Fellow of Merton College. Educated at University College Dublin and Oxford, he was professor of political economy at University College Dublin from 1980 to 2006. He is the author, with Jim Anderson, of *Measuring the Restrictiveness of International Trade Policy* (2005) and of various scholarly articles, mainly on international economics. He is a research fellow of the Centre for Economic Policy Research in London, a fellow of the Econometric Society and the British

Academy, a member of Academia Europaea and the Royal Irish Academy, and a past president of the European Economic Association.

Doug Nelson is Professor of Economics in the Murphy Institute and the Department of Economics at Tulane University, and an External Fellow of GEP. His current work focuses on international migration, political economy of international trade and the interactions between corporate governance and trade.

Gianmarco I.P. Ottaviano is Professor of Economics at the London School of Economics and Political Science, Associate of Centre for Economic Performance and Vice-Director of the Paolo Baffi Centre on Central Banking and Financial Regulation at Bocconi University Milan. He is research fellow of the Centre for Economic Policy Research London and Fondazione Eni Enrico Mattei Milan as well as non-resident senior fellow of Bruegel Brussels. He is a co-editor of the *Journal of Regional Science* and associate editor of the *Journal of the European Economic Association, Journal of Economic Geography, Regional Science and Urban Economics, Spatial Economic Analysis*. His research interests span international trade, urban economics and economic geography. His recent publications focus on the competitiveness of European firms in the global economy as well as the economic effects of immigration and offshoring on employment and wages.

Stephen J. Redding's research interests include productivity growth at the firm and industry level, international trade and economic geography. He is currently a professor of economics in the department of economics and Woodrow Wilson School at Princeton University, a coeditor of the *Journal of International Economics*, a research associate of the International Trade and Investment program of the National Bureau of Economic Research, a research fellow of the Centre for Economic Policy Research, an international research associate of the Centre for Economic Performance (CEP) at the London School of Economics, and an international research fellow of the Kiel Institute for the World Economy.

Raymond Riezman is the C. Woody Thompson Research Professor of Economics at the University of Iowa. His research focuses on customs unions and regional trading arrangements, climate change agreements, political economy, voting theory, outsourcing and experimental economics. His PhD is from the department of economics at the University of Minnesota and he did his undergraduate work at Washington University. He is an external research fellow at GEP, Nottingham, research fellow at the Center for Economic Studies – Institute for Economic Research (CES-ifo), Munich, associate editor of *Economics Bulletin* and is founder and director of the *Midwest International Economics Group*.

Roy J. Ruffin is the M.D. Anderson Professor of Economics at the University of Houston. His articles have appeared in the *American Economic Review, Review of Economic Studies, Journal of Economy Theory, Journal of International Economics* and others. His research has centered on trade theory and oligopoly theory. He has taught at Washington State University, the University of Iowa and Carleton University, but has been at the University of Houston since 1977. He has been a visiting professor at the University of Wisconsin, the University of Chicago and Rice University, and the Bundesbank professor at the Free University of Berlin.

Paul S. Segerstrom is Tore Browaldh Professor of International Economics at the Stockholm School of Economics. His main research fields are international trade and economic growth. Recently, he has been studying how multinational firms respond to changes in intellectual property rights protection. He is best known for developing the first model of endogenous growth with a quality ladders structure (published in the *American Economic Review* in 1990) and for developing a model of endogenous growth without scale effects (published in the *American Economic Review* in 1998). He received his BA (mathematics and economics) from Brandeis University, his MA (economics) from Brown University and his PhD (economics) from the University of Rochester. He was a professor at Michigan State University from 1984 to 2000, has been at the Stockholm School of Economics since 2000 and has recently served as economics department chair.

Alan Woodland is currently Scientia Professor of Economics and Australian Professorial Fellow in the School of Economics within the Australian School of Business at the University of New South Wales. He was previously a professor at the University of Sydney and at the University of British Columbia. Woodland is a fellow of the Econometric Society, a fellow of the Academy of the Social Sciences of Australia and a recipient of the Distinguished Economist Award of the Economics Society of Australia. He is an associate editor of the *Review of International Economics* and is on the editorial boards of *Empirical Economics*, *International Journal of Economic Theory* and the *Economic Record*. Woodland's primary research interests are in international trade theory, applied econometrics and population ageing. Within the area of international trade, research has included work on higher dimensional trade theory, the welfare implications of trade policies, the design of Pareto-improving trade policy reforms, illegal immigration, climate change and the endogenous formation of customs unions and free trade areas.

1
Editors' Introduction

Daniel Bernhofen, Rod Falvey, David Greenaway and Udo Kreickemeier

When Palgrave approached us with the proposal of editing the *Handbook of International Trade* targeted at the beginning postgraduate student, their rationale was the existence of a market niche supporting the teaching of the economics of international trade at either the masters or beginning doctoral level. Existing handbooks and surveys in international trade were primarily aimed at a research-oriented readership. When we contacted potential contributors we were encouraged by their willingness to join us in this endeavour. We are now delighted to introduce the finished product to teachers and students.

The organization of the *Handbook* reveals the several objectives that we had in mind. First, we aimed to be comprehensive by covering what we viewed to be the major sub-literatures of international trade. But, inevitably some topics have been left out and others will have received less attention than some readers will feel they deserved. Second, given our target audience, we opted for covering this material in a single volume. Each chapter was intended to provide a balance of knowledge that has stood the test of time and work that is at the current frontier. Being faithful to the concept of comparative advantage, we left it to the contributors to strike this balance, which has resulted in some heterogeneity in chapter designs. Since the chapters have been written with masters students in mind, the content should be accessible to students with a very good undergraduate training in economics. Although the *Handbook* has not been targeted specifically at doctoral students, we hope that beginning doctoral students find the chapters complementary to existing textbooks and a guide to the journal literature in the respective fields.

Before guiding the reader through the individual chapters, let us briefly reflect on the intellectual developments we aimed to take into account in editing the *Handbook*. It is well known that international trade is the oldest subfield in economics; with the practice of international trade going back to the dawn of civilization, and the analytical approach having its genesis in Ricardo's 1817 formulation of comparative advantage. However, the last few decades have witnessed a remarkable broadening of both the subject matter and analytical approaches. Until relatively recently, the main questions in trade evolved around its determinants and welfare effects (in goods) and their applications to trade policy.

The deeper integration of the world economy has expanded the subject to the study of economic globalisation in all its manifestations. This expansion in scope has created new linkages between trade and subfields such as labour economics, environmental economics, economic growth, geography and regional economics, and political economy. The analytical approach has broadened in two dimensions. Up to the late 1970s trade was, with a few notable exceptions, a pure theory field dominated by the $2 \times 2 \times 2$ Heckscher–Ohlin–Samuelson model. The last few decades have witnessed many theoretically rich and empirically relevant extensions of both the competitive and new trade theory frameworks. The general equilibrium approach has expanded to incorporate a range of different modelling strategies regarding market structure and agent heterogeneity, while still maintaining the distinctive features that define trade as a field. Broader access to data (especially at the disaggregated micro level), increased computing power and advancements in empirical methodologies have transformed trade into an empirically oriented field. While a decade and a half ago Leamer and Levinsohn were lamenting that empirical studies had limited value and impact, we can now see a body of empirical work with credible claims on verifying existing theories, stimulating new theories and providing plausible estimates of the impacts of globalisation.

This *Handbook* is organized in three parts: 'Foundations and Modelling Frameworks' (Part I), 'Policy' (Part II) and 'Special Topics' (Part III). The 'Foundations' section begins with a brief history of the intellectual development of trade theory, which also provides useful context for the remainder of the volume. This is followed by an overview of competitive general equilibrium trade theory. While this approach may not currently be at the frontier of trade research, its history and versatility keep it at the heart of the field. The various empirical approaches aimed at confronting the competitive framework with data are then discussed. The remaining chapters in Part I are devoted to the industrial organization approach to trade which departs from the perfectly competitive market structure. This discussion begins with 'new trade theory', which assumes monopolistic competition and its extensions. This approach has been shown to be a fruitful framework for incorporating firm heterogeneity and product differentiation in general equilibrium. The related empirical literature, which also helped inspire the theory, is then examined. The final two chapters survey the small-group, or strategic modelling, approaches to international trade and the theory and empirics of multinational activity.

Part II begins by reviewing the positive theory of price and quantitative trade restrictions in both competitive and monopoly settings, before moving on to the issues associated with general trade policy reform. The following two chapters provide an overview and assessment of the political economy literature which focuses on the deeper determinants of protectionism, and a survey of the different approaches to the measurement of protection. A prominent feature of the trade policy landscape since the 1990s has been the proliferation of preferential trade agreements (PTAs). The emergence of PTAs has stimulated research on their effects on the welfare of member countries and on the process of multilateral liberalization via the WTO. This work is surveyed in the final two chapters of Part II.

Part III of the *Handbook* contains topics that have grown sufficiently in importance to constitute a sub-literature and to deserve separate treatment. The links between trade, trade policy and unemployment have been neglected in the past, and the first chapter surveys the small but growing literature that focuses on the effects of trade on national labour markets. Environmental concerns, both national and global, are increasingly prominent, and the second chapter provides an extensive overview of the modelling approaches and central questions pertaining to trade and the environment. Up until the late 1970s the trade literature treated countries as single entities and largely abstracted from trade costs within or between countries. The new economic geography literature, which is reviewed in the following chapter, illustrates how the interaction between increasing returns to scale and trade costs are central to explaining the allocation of economic activity across space. The theoretical foundations and empirical applications of the gravity equation, which has evolved to become the main framework for the empirical explanation of trade flows, are then reviewed. This is succeeded by a discussion of the use of large-scale computable general equilibrium models to assess the effects of policy reforms on international trade flows and national welfare levels. The next two chapters focus on the links between international trade and economic performance over time; namely the role of trade in affecting long-run growth and the role of trade and trade policies in economic development. The *Handbook* concludes with a survey of the literature on trade and migration viewed from a trade perspective.

1   Part I: Foundations and Modelling Frameworks

Being the oldest subfield of economics, international trade has a distinguished intellectual history. In chapter 2, Roy Ruffin provides an overview of the historical evolution of international trade theory. He takes the reader on a historical journey which starts with David Hume's eighteenth century intellectual response to mercantilistic arguments against free trade and ends with a discussion of the most recent developments of the new trade theory models under imperfect competition. In his treatment of classical writings, Ruffin points out that Ricardo's original formulation of comparative advantage was both more subtle and general than is presented in textbooks. Ruffin's historical narrative of neoclassical trade theory focuses on the evolution of the characterization of a trading equilibrium. The narrative highlights how the 'intellectual movement' towards low-dimensional general equilibrium formulations opened the path for both the development of comparative statics predictions and the use of graphical analysis to obtain an intuitive grasp of these predictions. Overall, this chapter provides a tribute to the policy roots, the scientific progress and to the pioneers who established the foundational structures of the field.

In chapter 3, Alan Woodland provides a thorough overview of competitive general equilibrium trade theory. Woodland starts his survey with the classic Arrow–Debreu characterization of a competitive general equilibrium. He uses simple geometric illustrations to illuminate one of the most fundamental insights of general equilibrium trade theory: that free international trade yields an equilibrium that is Pareto optimal. After introducing the modern duality representation of the general competitive framework, he takes the reader through the fundamental general equilibrium relationships in the classic setting of an open economy with fixed resource endowments and exogenous goods prices. He examines the effects of changes in factor endowments on factor prices and outputs (the Rybcynski Theorem) and the effects of exogenous goods prices on factor prices (the Stolper–Samuelson Theorem), both in the two-good, two-factor model and in higher dimensional formulations. When perturbations yield changes in the international terms of trade, the general equilibrium approach can yield startling insights – like the transfer paradox, the Metzler paradox and immiserzing growth – which would have been impossible to detect from a single market framework. Woodland concludes his survey by discussing the principal submodels of international trade that isolate either technological differences (the Ricardian model) or factor endowment differences (the Heckscher–Ohlin model) as fundamental determinants of international trade. This prepares the path for a discussion of the empirical literature which has focused on how these subtheories hold up to empirical scrutiny.

In chapter 4, Daniel Bernhofen reviews empirical applications of the general equilibrium model. He highlights the changing positions that have occurred on both the empirical and theoretical sides in the quest to link theoretical frameworks to the empirics. The apparent tensions between the Heckscher–Ohlin model and Leontief paradox as well as the phenomenon of 'intra-industry' trade have been resolved. Bernhofen stresses that the competitive and new trade theory models should be viewed as complementary rather than competing explanations for international specialization. Modelling approaches aimed at relaxing the symmetry assumptions of the Heckscher–Ohlin–Vanek framework have shown that this framework is quite compatible with the pattern of the factor content of international trade. Theoretical advancement of

the Ricardian model has expanded its application beyond an 'undergraduate classroom tool' to a general equilibrium framework capable of structural estimation. The Ricardian framework is capable of providing predictions about the parameters of gravity equations as well as firm heterogeneity regarding export activities. Bernhofen emphasizes that the competitive trade model distinguishes itself from the monopolistic competition trade model by linking production specialization to economic fundamentals rather than postulating that such specialization is arbitrary. The exploitation of a natural experiment confirms the various predictions of the competitive trade model at the individual product level.

Chapter 5 by Kristian Behrens and Gianmarco Ottaviano, is devoted to the monopolistic model of international trade. Much of the literature in this field has built on Krugman's Nobel Prize winning formulation of monopolistic competition. Krugman's application of a Dixit–Stiglitz type specification of demand has proved to be a highly tractable framework to examine the role of increasing returns to scale in a variety of contexts. Behrens and Ottaviano present this strand of the literature in detail, carefully pointing out the simplifications that result from the CES assumption, but also the limitations that result from using it. The survey stresses that this framework was a giant leap forward towards making firms visible in general equilibrium. Behrens and Ottaviano point out that the recent extensions aimed at relaxing the empirical straightjacket of cost symmetry has brought to light the versatility of the monopolistic competition framework for analytical guidance on a host of empirical questions that are discussed in more detail in chapter 6. This includes the modelling of fixed and variable trade costs as well as firms' choices on products and organisational forms.

The exploration of plant-level data sets, which started during the 1990s, has led to robust empirical regularities regarding the size and productivity of firms and their engagement in foreign markets. Because these regularities could not be linked to any existing trade theories at the time, they motivated the new modelling approaches on firm heterogeneity discussed in the previous chapters. In chapter 6, David Greenaway, Danny McGowan and Richard Kneller survey the empirical literature on firms' internationalization strategies. The authors start out by reporting the stylized facts that exporters tend to be larger, more productive, and more capital intensive than non-exporters. They then survey the empirical attempts aimed at isolating the underlying determinants of the strong performances of exporting firms. One of the key issues with which the literature has wrestled is whether more productive firms self-select into exporting, or exporting provides a vehicle for productivity improvements. The existing empirical evidence favours the self-selection hypothesis. In the second part of their chapter, Greenaway et al. provide an overview of recent empirical work on multiproduct firms and on firms' decisions on international outsourcing and offshoring. The overall conclusion of the literature is that more productive firms self-select into various internationalization strategies, with the type of strategy depending on the characteristics of the industry in which a firm operates.

In chapter 7, Dermot Leahy and Peter Neary survey the second strand of 'new trade theory': the oligopoly modelling of international trade. Leahy and Neary take the reader through the core features and recent extensions of the reciprocal-markets model. This framework was launched by Brander's fundamental insight that if economic profits in an industry are large enough, firms will penetrate into each other's national markets, resulting in intra-industry trade, even if their products are identical. This provided a new causal theory for the existence of trade and also emphasized a new welfare aspect of trade in the form of a reduction of firm market power. The second part of the chapter discusses strategic trade and industrial policy in the context of the Brander-Spencer 'third market' oligopoly model. After discussing the classic findings that strategic trade policies are sensitive to the strategic assumptions, they review more recent modelling approaches which yield more robust welfare predictions about industrial policies in the presence of industrial spillovers. The final part of the chapter addresses the perennial criticism that the strategic approach to international trade neglects potential cross-market or general equilibrium effects. Leahy and Neary first review the obstacles that arise from embedding oligopoly into general equilibrium and then discuss a recent approach aimed at overcoming these modelling difficulties.

The growing empirical importance of foreign direct investment calls for a modelling framework involving multinational firms. Chapter 8 by James Markusen concludes Part I by discussing the main empirical regularities, conceptual frameworks and modelling approaches relating to multinational firm activity. Markusen points out that the 1970s 'pre-new trade theory perspective' of treating foreign direct investment (FDI) as an international capital movement capable of being explained by the Heckscher–Ohlin framework was at odds with the empirical facts. He also points out that the early modelling of multinational firms in international trade theory borrowed insights from the business literature, which emphasized the necessity of firm-specific assets that could successfully be exploited within the firm's boundaries, but outside the country where its headquarters are located. This line of thought made it clear that the modelling of multinational firms needed to be rooted in imperfect competition. Markusen illustrates the trade-offs facing a firm by setting up a simple partial equilibrium model of location choice which allows one to distinguish between vertical and horizontal multinationals. He then covers the early general equilibrium models from the 1980s, which typically featured either horizontal or vertical multinationals, but not both; before moving on to the canonical knowledge capital model, which can accommodate both types of firms in equilibrium. The last part of the chapter discusses the trade-off between producing abroad in-house (thereby becoming a multinational firm) and international outsourcing.

2   Part II: Policy

In chapter 9, Rod Falvey and Udo Kreickemeier give an overview of the traditional theory of trade policy and reform. The organizing principle of their chapter is to analyse as many issues as possible in a partial equilibrium setting, moving to a multi-sector general model only when the issues demand it. Since trade policy under oligopoly has already been covered in chapter 7, they begin by examining the effects of tariffs and quotas under monopoly and perfect competition. These results serve to highlight the importance of market structure to policy outcomes. The second-best problems arising in the context of trade policy reform are presented in a framework with multiple import goods, necessitated by the need to distinguish between the level of protection in a specific sector and the overall structure of protection across sectors. Traditional results of the piecemeal policy reform literature are presented alongside more recent results on the interaction between welfare and market access effects.

While the traditional theory of trade policy focuses on the effects of protectionist policies, the political economy of trade policy is concerned about the fundamental determinants of protection. In chapter 10, Wilfred Ethier provides a critical assessment of the political economy literature in the context of unilateral and multilateral policy settings. Ethier employs a simple analytical framework to illustrate the strengths and weaknesses of different modelling approaches regarding unilateral policy. He points out that there are significant differences between what appears to be important in practice and what turns out to be significant in the economic modelling. This is reflected in the relative unimportance of tariff revenue in practice and its relative importance in obtaining interior solutions in the models. Although Ethier applauds the theoretical literature in stimulating empirical work, the empirical evidence to date has been unable to discriminate between different modelling approaches. The second part of the chapter surveys the two motivations behind the political economy of international trade agreements. The terms of trade externality approach, which has received the most formal attention, views these agreements as aiming to resolve the prisoner's dilemma that arises from countries' mutually destructive attempts to exploit monopoly power on world markets. The alternative approach assumes that trade agreements are motivated by improving access to export markets. Although their explanations are quite different, both approaches give very similar predictions regarding the broad features of trade agreements. Ethier argues that the specific features of the GATT/WTO system are more consistent with the market access approach.

While the previous chapters examined the determinants and effects of protection, chapter 11 by James Anderson discusses its measurement. Two questions arise. How is protection measured at the sector level? And how are the sector-level measures aggregated to an economy-wide index? Since protectionist activity is difficult to observe directly, Anderson discusses methods that have been used to infer sector-level protection from data on prices and trade flows. Assuming accurate measurement at the sector level, an aggregated protection index is then a weighted average of the sector-level measures. The crucial and non-trivial task is to find appropriate weights. The second part of this chapter focuses on tariffs as the instrument of protection and starts with the illustration that the popular practice of relying on a trade-weighted average tariff is undesirable. Anderson then presents the model-based approach developed by himself and Neary, where the aim is to find an index number that is equivalent to a given tariff structure in respects defined by the researcher. He then provides a detailed discussion of three particular index numbers: the single tariff rate that is equivalent in welfare terms to an existing tariff structure (the trade restrictiveness index); the single tariff rate that leads to the same import volume as the existing tariff structure (the mercantilist index of trade policy); and the single tariff rate that leads to the same rents for sector-specific factors (the effective rate of protection).

The last two chapters in this section of the *Handbook* pertain to preferential trade agreements. Chapter 12 by Pravin Krishna provides a brief and accessible primer on the economics of PTAs, supported by reference to the major empirical studies in the literature. Because PTAs are a discriminatory form of trade liberalisation, the analysis of their welfare effects involves consideration of the second-best. Krishna uses the classic concepts of trade creation and trade diversion – introduced by Viner in the 1950s – to demonstrate the generally ambiguous welfare effects of discriminatory trade liberalisation. He then discusses extensions of this work which try to determine the characteristics of trading partners most likely to generate trade creation. Krishna concludes that trading arrangements involving geographically proximate partners are no more likely to be welfare improving a priori than PTAs involving distant partners. The Kemp–Wan Theorem on Customs Unions and its extension to Free Trade Areas, which lay down the sufficient conditions for a PTA to be Pareto improving, are used to motivate consideration of the GATT/WTO requirements on PTA formation. Krishna also discusses the role and potential misuse of rules of origin in trade agreements.

In chapter 13, Carsten Kowalczyk and Ray Riezman extend this analysis by surveying the theoretical literature on the welfare effects of preferential trade (broadly defined) in competitive general equilibrium models. They begin by demonstrating that the welfare effects of trade policy changes (small or large) can be decomposed into two components – a terms-of-trade effect and a volume of trade effect. They then demonstrate how small countries may gain more from preferential trade with a large country than they would from unilateral liberalisation. The implication is that large countries may end up in PTAs with many small countries, resulting in a proliferation of overlapping PTAs that will not seem unfamiliar. Kowalczyk and Riezman emphasise the constraint that PTAs be self-enforcing, and note the importance of side payments to compensate for terms of trade losses. They also consider the welfare effects of gradual trade liberalization in a multilateral context, which complements the corresponding discussion on unilateral trade liberalization in chapter 9.

3 Part III: Special Topics

In chapter 14, Carl Davidson and Steve Matusz present an overview of the literature on trade and labour markets. They discuss the 'traditional effects' of trade on factor returns, which result from frictionless models with perfect competition in all markets, but devote a large part of the chapter to the discussion of models that incorporate labour market imperfections into otherwise standard models of trade. Once labour market distortions are taken into account it becomes possible to discuss the link between trade and unemployment that has long been assumed away in the theoretical trade literature. Davidson and Matusz's survey of this literature starts with Brecher's seminal minimum wage model and then, drawing on the authors' own extensive work in this area, discusses a large number of more recent developments, which all feature microfoundations of unemployment in general equilibrium. The chapter concludes with a survey of the emerging literature which considers heterogeneity of both firms and workers.

In chapter 15, Brian Copeland gives a comprehensive overview of the theoretical and empirical literature on trade and the environment. Copeland develops his chapter by incorporating environmental constraints in a standard neoclassical trade model and uses this framework to address key questions, such as whether trade is good or bad for the environment. Copeland points out that the effects of trade liberalization on the environment depend on sometimes-complex interactions between market driven forces and policy responses. In reviewing the empirical literature he notes the difficulties in identifying the role of trade relative to other factors in affecting environmental outcomes. On the conceptual side, Copeland stresses the growing importance of the notion of 'environmental capital', which recognizes the negative effect of pollution on productivity. On the policy side, Copeland surveys the various modelling approaches regarding the interactions between trade and environmental policies and their implications for the design of trade agreements and global policy harmonization.

In chapter 16, Stephen Redding surveys the theoretical and empirical literature on economic geography that developed – under the label 'new' economic geography (NEG) – following Krugman's path breaking paper in the early 1990s. In the theoretical section, Redding focuses on the original Krugman model, carefully describing the key equations and derivations, as well as the economic agglomeration and dispersion forces that are by now familiar as recurring features of economic geography models. The crucial role of transport cost and the possibility of multiple equilibria are discussed. The empirical section provides evidence on some of the key predictions of NEG models. Here, the survey covers such questions as the measurement of agglomeration, the empirical role of market access for wages and location choices, and the evidence for multiple equilibria.

The gravity equation is one of the most widely used empirical specifications in applied economics. In chapter 17, Jeffrey Bergstrand and Peter Egger provide a comprehensive overview of the history, theoretical foundations and various applications of the gravity equation. Since the gravity equation is the principal framework used to conceptualize economic frictions, Bergstrand and Egger launch their survey with a general discussion of 'how to think about' frictions in the world economy. After discussing the historical roots and early empirical applications, Bergstrand and Egger provide an overview of the micro-foundations of the gravity equation. They observe that the more serious engagement, during the last decade, with economic and econometric theory and the increased use of longitudinal data sets has led to better inferences across the domain of empirical applications. While the gravity framework continues to play a dominant role in estimating the effects of economic integration agreements, the domain of applications has been broadened to include the economic effect of infrastructure projects, geography, and political and institutional factors, as well as explaining the determinants of foreign direct investment and migration.

In chapter 18, Joseph Francois and Will Martin provide an overview of multi-sector computational general equilibrium (CGE) modelling in international trade. The authors introduce the reader to the literature by specifying a canonical constant returns to scale model with a representative household. They then discuss specific modelling strategies that arise in matching a static general equilibrium framework to real world economies with heterogeneous households that are involved in inter-temporal savings and investment decisions. The authors explain how the 'more mature' modelling frameworks from the new trade theory literature have already been incorporated into the CGE framework and discuss the challenges that arise from incorporating insights from the heterogeneous firm literature. The authors stress the prominent role CGE models have played in the policy debate about the benefits of multilateral and regional trade agreements. Increased concerns about the global environment and globalisation's effects on it have provided new application domains for computational models.

In chapter 19, Paul Segerstrom provides an introduction to the literature on trade and economic growth. He begins with a brief overview of the theoretical and empirical literature, noting that most of the early growth models treated the rate of technical change as exogenous. The theoretical analysis of the effects that trade or trade policies had on the long-run rate of growth awaited the development of endogenous growth models in the 1990s. In these models the steady-state rate of growth depends on the rate at which profit maximising firms choose to innovate. Policy interventions (such as trade liberalization) then influence the growth rate via their effects on the costs and benefits of innovation. Since these include both relatively straightforward direct effects and less obvious indirect effects through commodity and factor markets, a dynamic general equilibrium model is required for their analysis. Because the analysis can be quite challenging, Segerstrom opts to introduce the reader to the relevant theoretical literature by developing, in some detail, a relatively simple model. The assumptions are designed to give tractability, while still illustrating the essential issues. The model shows that a reduction in trade costs leads to a (temporary) increase in the global innovation rate.

Economic growth is central to economic development, and in the past the appropriate role for trade and trade policy in the development process has been a particularly contentious issue. Advocates of market-based strategies for development emphasized the dangers of policy failure and benefits of competition in the domestic market, and they recommended active participation in international markets. Advocates of more centrally planned development strategies emphasized the existence of pervasive market failures and structural rigidities in developing countries, and they recommended that international trade be tightly controlled. The relevant theoretical and empirical literature around these issues is discussed by Chris Milner in chapter 20. The persistence of market failures in developing economies means that policy analysis continues to be constrained by the theory of the second best, and optimal intervention analysis remained relevant, even after governments recognised the benefits of trade reform. Most developing countries adopted programmes of unilateral trade policy reform at some point in the last quarter of the twentieth century. Since a one-shot movement to free trade was never contemplated, managing the shift towards freer trade from a typical import-substitution regime with a high average tariff and wide tariff dispersion raised interesting issues in piecemeal trade policy reform. Milner illustrates the difficulties that arise in adjusting trade policy in an inter-temporal context and emphasizes that extracting the greatest benefits from trade and trade policy reform in practice depends on adopting a range of complementary policies.

In chapter 21, Noel Gaston and Doug Nelson review the literature linking trade and the migration of workers. Research in this area has focussed on two main questions: Are trade in goods and factor services complements or substitutes? What are the effects of migration on the wages of native workers? A main concern has been to explain how much international labour flows contributed to rising wage inequality observed in advanced countries in the 1990s. This issue has been addressed by both trade and labour economists. However, the different modelling strategies undertaken lead to rather different quantitative conclusions. After reviewing the, by now, quite extensive literature, Gaston and Nelson conclude that, whatever approach is adopted, the general pattern of results is that the wage effects of immigration seem to be 'quantitatively unimportant'. As to whether international factor (in this case labour) and commodity movements are substitutes or complements, they find that the empirical evidence generally supports a conclusion that migration has a positive effect on trade flows. Migrant networks can provide channels of information that reduce the problems of asymmetric information likely to hinder exchange between countries with quite different cultures, institutions and histories. These networks may also create a potential market for exports from the migrants' source countries.

Part A

Foundations and Modelling Frameworks

2

The Development of International Trade Theory*

Roy J. Ruffin[†]

Trade theory is the oldest branch of economics. The reason may well be that the central economic fallacy prior to Adam Smith had to do with international exchanges: the mercantilist doctrine that the only way for a country to prosper was to run an export surplus. When Adam Smith and David Hume exploded this fallacy, the way was set for a paradigm shift. Thus, the revolution in trade theory occurred very early when David Ricardo stumbled onto the law of comparative advantage. As fate would have it, the paradigm shift was sort of a family affair. James Mill, the father of John Stuart Mill, had convinced Ricardo to write a book explaining economics. It was during the writing of that book the essential revolution occurred; and John Stuart, who of course knew Ricardo as a child, completed the paradigm shift when he presented the Ricardian model as we know it today – a model which still flourishes in the modern literature as a vehicle for exploring difficult issues.

In this chapter, I will try to provide an exposition of trade theory that pays considerable attention to its historical roots, a task that is made easy by the fact that trade theory has had such a remarkable development. Indeed, trade theory has always been told from an historical perspective.

We begin with the transition from mercantilism to classical trade theory, culminating in the classical works of David Ricardo and John Stuart Mill. Classical trade theory emphasizes the productivity of labour across industries and between countries. Unlike classical trade theory, neoclassical trade theory (Marshall and Edgeworth) emphasized the general structure of trade models without production details. In the middle of the development of neoclassical trade theory, the Heckscher–Ohlin model, with its emphasis on questions of distribution and the role of factor endowments, began its slow ascent until it dominated trade theory for more than half a century. Finally, I briefly enter the modern era of models of imperfect competition and what they add to the story but leave the detailed telling to other chapters in this handbook. But in more ways than one, trade theory has never left its Ricardian origins.

15

1   Classical trade theory

The quintessential mercantilist, Thomas Mun (1571–1641), believed that all trade was a zero sum game and so the only way a country could win was to sell more to other countries as a whole than its purchases from them. David Hume (1711–76), in his essay 'The Balance of Trade' (1752), punctured the mercantilist arguments that policy should be directed towards achieving an export surplus.

Hume asked: why had not the supply of gold in England disappeared over the previous 20 years when the country had been repeatedly warned of impending disasters from trade deficits? Hume combined the quantity theory of money with the basic principle of the gold standard that allows the natural inflation or deflation from the movements of gold from country to country to correct any imbalances. This cleared the way for an understanding of what is really involved in international trade: countries are trading exports for imports, and so there are likely gains from trade as goods move from low valued areas to high valued areas.

As we will see with Adam Smith, prior to the work of David Ricardo it was well understood that it costs more to make some things at home than to buy them from another country by exporting other things. Jacob Viner (1937, 440) called this the 'eighteenth century rule'. The gain from trade was even more clearly shown as early as 1701 by the anonymous author of 'Considerations of the East India Trade'. The author was later identified as one Henry Martyn. It was also Martyn who suggested that trade allowed people to enjoy the fruits of the world in a single location and use the 'spices of Arabia' without the disadvantage of living under a scorching sun or 'drink of the vineyards which we never planted'. If asked about the basic cause of trade, those who probed more deeply than generalizations about diversity of conditions on the earth would probably have embraced the absolute advantage theory, most clearly expressed by Ricardo's contemporary, Robert Torrens (1780–1864). As shown by Ruffin (2005), throughout Torrens's *Essay on the Corn Trade* (1815) the idea is expressed that in order to achieve gains from trade, it is necessary to export goods that require less labour and capital at home to foreign countries that use more labour and capital for the same goods:

> When any given portion of capital can, in England, fabricate a greater quantity of cloth, than in Poland; and can, in Poland, produce a greater supply of corn, than in England; then, the absence of regulation is all that is necessary to establishing between the two countries in active and mutually beneficial commerce. (Torrens, 1815, 297)

This is the perhaps the classical statement of what, in modern textbooks, we mean by absolute advantage. It is ironic because Torrens has been sometimes mentioned as one who anticipated Ricardo. But bad history dies hard.

It is interesting that Adam Smith himself did not fall into the fallacy of absolute advantage, though many textbooks allege that he is the responsible for the theory of absolute advantage. When, on superficial reading, Smith appeared to discuss absolute advantage, he did not lapse into Torrens's error, and coolly made a correct argument that the gains from trade result from devoting fewer home resources exporting other goods to pay for imports:

> By means of glasses, hotbeds, and hot walls, very good grapes can be raised in Scotland, and very good wine too can be made of them at about thirty times the expense for which at least equally good can be brought from foreign countries. Would it be a reasonable law to prohibit the importation of all foreign wines merely to encourage the making of claret and burgundy in Scotland? But if there would be a manifest absurdity in turning towards any employment thirty times more of the capital and industry of the country than would be necessary to purchase from foreign countries an equal quantity of the commodities wanted, there must be an absurdity, though not altogether so glaring, yet exactly of the same kind, in turning towards any such employment a thirtieth, or even a three hundredth part more of either.

Whether the advantages which one country has over another be natural or acquired is, in this respect, of no consequence.

Notice, he did not say that it took 30 times the labour and capital used to produce grapes than in foreign country, but that it may take 30 times the expense of acquiring the same wine from abroad. He then said the same argument holds for a number significantly smaller than 30 times. Thus, he was just really talking about the gains from trade. This is the eighteenth century rule in all of its glory.

Ricardo's law of comparative advantage is a deeper theorem that probes into the linkages between productivity and wages so that we can say that countries more advanced in everything will still profit by importing goods from less advanced countries with lower wages.

Ruffin (2002) tells the story about how Ricardo discovered the law of comparative advantage. Briefly, from the exchanges of letters of Ricardo with James Mill and Thomas Malthus we know that he had just adopted the labour theory of value in March 1816. When Ricardo turned to the chapter on international trade in September 1816 this caused him to question that theory of value. After two weeks of intense concentration, during which he forgot a lunch with Malthus, Ricardo realized that it was necessary to assume labour is immobile between countries in order to explain why the domestic labour content of exports did not correspond to the foreign labour content of imports. Remarkably, during the same period of time, he wrote a letter to Malthus outlining a factor price equalization world! In October of 1816, Ricardo sent the chapter to James Mill. A month later there is a letter from Mill that congratulates Ricardo on proving what is now called the law of comparative advantage as well as a version of Hume's specie flow mechanism. Thus, we know when and how Ricardo developed the law of comparative advantage. It was Ricardo himself who, later in his 1817 *Principles of Political Economy*, coined the phrase, comparative advantage.

Ricardo's proof was quite ingenious because the logical structure did not depend on the number of goods or countries, as has sometimes been asserted. Instead of starting with resource endowments and labour inputs per unit of each good, he started with the terms of trade and the amount of labour contained in a trading bundle rather than labour per unit of output (Ruffin, 2002; Maneschi, 2004). I will adopt the logical structure of his argument. Ricardo of course assumed that labour can move from industry to industry, but not from country to country. Now suppose X units of wine trades for Y units of cloth or Z units of corn. Then if England uses less labour to produce the Y units of cloth than the labour required to produce X wine or Z corn, it will export cloth: if Portugal uses less labour to produce X wine than the others, it will export wine; and if Poland uses less labour to produce Z corn, it will export corn. All of this is independent of the absolute quantities of labour in each case; so, say, 100 units of British labour can trade for 60 units of Portuguese labour or 200 units of Polish labour.

The next stage in the development of international trade came at the hands of Mountifort Longfield (1802–84)in his 'Three Lectures on Commerce' (1835). He was probably influenced by Nassau Senior (1790–1864), whose 'Three Lectures on the Cost of Obtaining Money' (1831) contains a homespun account of comparative advantage, with special attention paid to wages and productivity. Senior gave the wonderful similes that protectionism was like using surgeons to cut hair or racehorses to plow fields! Longfield's extension of the Ricardian model to the many commodity case is his most valuable contribution.

> If English labour is, on an average, three times as productive as French labour, those kinds of labour in England, which are four times as productive as the corresponding French labour, will be cultivated in England, to the exclusion of France from the market of the world; and those kinds of labour which in England are twice as productive only as the corresponding kinds in France will, in turn, be cultivated in France, to the exclusion of England from the market of the world. Neither high wages, nor low productiveness of labour, can render commerce disadvantageous to a country, or can place its industry in need of protection. (Longfield, 1835, 56)

The multi-commodity Ricardian model using Longfield's insights is still one of the most useful frameworks for studying international trade. Let a_i and a_i^* denote the constant home and foreign labour costs of producing a unit of good i; then $1/a_i$ and $1/a_i^*$ are the home and foreign labour productivities (marginal and average). If w and w^* are home and foreign wages in international currency units, good i will not be produced in the home country if $wa_i > w^*a_i^*$ with perfect competition and zero transfer costs.

Next, assume that the goods (1–N) are numbered so that

$$a_1^*/a_1 > a_2^*/a_2 > \cdots > a_N^*/a_N \tag{1}$$

so that the home country's largest productivity advantage, measured by the ratio of its productivity to foreign, is in good 1, then good 2, and, lastly, in good N in sequence.[1]

To prove the Ricardian law of comparative advantage we need only note that if (i) $w/w^* > a_1^*/a_1$, then the home country cannot compete with the foreign country in *any* good; and if (ii) $a_N^*/a_N > w/w^*$, then the foreign country cannot compete with the home country in *any* good. If (i) holds, the ratio w/w^* will fall because there is no demand for home labour and the home currency will depreciate under flexible exchanges; and if (ii) holds, the ratio w/w^* will rise because there is no demand for foreign labour and the home currency will appreciate. The Ricardian law of comparative advantage follows: the ratio of home to foreign wages must be trapped between the home country's highest and lowest productivity advantages:

$$a_1^*/a_1 \geq w/w^* \geq a_N^*/a_N. \tag{2}$$

Thus we explain Longfield's insight: 'Neither high wages, nor low productiveness of labour, can render commerce disadvantageous to a country, or can place its industry in need of protection.' Which goods are exported by the home country depends on reciprocal demands; a greater demand for home goods will raise w/w^* and allow the home country to pay for more imports by exporting *fewer* goods as w/w^* marches up the scale in (1). When these ideas are coupled with demand conditions, the multi-good Ricardian model is still a vibrant and useful model for analyzing a range of issues from transport costs to technology transfers (Dornbusch, Samuelson, and Fischer, 1977; Eaton and Kortum, 2002; Jones and Ruffin, 2008; Ruffin, 2009).

It was John Stuart Mill who coupled the above analysis with demand and supply conditions to arrive at the equilibrium solution for the case of two commodities. Mill laid out the paradigm for trade theory and general equilibrium: specify the resources, the technology, demand, and then solve for the equilibrium. His solution can be expressed as follows. Let b_i denote the share of income devoted to good i in both the home and foreign countries. If both countries are specialized, then collapsing (2) for the two commodity case requires $b_2wL = (1 - b_2)w^*L^*$, where L and L^* are home and foreign labour supplies. That is, the value of home imports of good 2 must equal the value of its exports of good 1. Thus: $w/w^* = L^*(1 - b_2)/Lb_2$. As L^*/L rises (or falls), the foreign (or home) country will eventually produce both goods because w/w^* rises (or falls) until $wa_1 = w^*a_1^*$ (or $wa_2 = w^*a_2^*$). Mill then pointed out that the large country gains nothing from free trade and the small country reaps all the gains. However, with two or more factors or three or more countries, the Mill theorem disappears (Ruffin, 1988).

2 Neoclassical trade theory

Ricardo's assumption of a single factor of production obviously calls for some generalization. Alfred Marshall's 'Pure Theory of Foreign Trade' (1879) marks the beginning of what is called 'neoclassical trade theory.' Marshall described the useful concept of offer curves, and showed how they could be used to analyze basic questions of trade theory involving stability, uniqueness, and comparative statics. The offer curve shows export supply for any given import demand. Any movements along one 'should be considered as attended with rearrangements of internal trade; as the movement of the hands of a clock corresponds to considerable unseen movements of the machinery (F. Y. Edgeworth, 1894b, 424–25)'. Offer curves work well to describe comparative statics between two trading countries with respect to what happens to the terms of trade.

But neither Marshall nor Edgeworth described the production possibility set, and as such they backtracked from Mill's specification of production functions and labour supplies. The internal rearrangements matter a great deal. According to Abba Lerner (1932), it was Gottfried Haberler in 1930 who first suggested that opportunity costs in international trade can be described by the production possibility frontier (PPF). This approach was carried to its logical conclusion in James E. Meade's *Geometry of International Trade*. Here, the key is that one merely couples group preferences with a general specification of technology. There are no explicit assumptions about production functions or resource supplies other than concavity of production functions in order for the production possibility set to be convex. If X_i is the output of good i, the PPF can be denoted by the implicit function, $T(X_1, X_2) = 0$. If a mobile factor, call it labour, L, is transferred from good 1 to good 2, then if MP_L^j is the marginal product of labour in commodity j and since $dL_2 + dL_1 = 0$, $dX_2/dX_1 = dL_2 MP_L^2/dL_1 MP_L^1 = -MP_L^2/MP_L^1$, the marginal rate of transformation of good 2 into good 1 is MRT $= -dX_2/dX_1 = MP_L^2/MP_L^1 = p_1/p_2$ because $p_1 MP_L^1 = p_2 MP_L^2$.

Note here we have the full employment assumption. This assumption is proper when emphasis is placed on the net gains from trade because trade economists maintain that there is no link between the pattern of trade and generalized unemployment in any intermediate or long-run sense. However, this is no comfort to those who are lost in the shuffle and must search for a new job after losing one in an import competing industry. This search process is a legitimate area of inquiry (but see *Handbook* chapter 14).

The neoclassical theory of international trade can now be expressed very sim-ply (Leontief, 1933; Lerner, 1932). As a purely didactic device, assume there is a community or group utility function $U = U(C_1, C_2)$ with a marginal rate of sub-stitution MRS $= U_1/U_2$, where $U_i = \partial U/\partial C_i$, that is, the marginal value of good 1 in terms of good 2. The case of free trade for a single country is illustrated in figure 2.1. Profit maximization by competitive firms leads to point X where the MRT $= p_1/p_2 = p_1^*/p_2^*$. The line XC extended is the terms of trade line as well as the budget line facing consumers; hence, consumers maximize utility at point C where MRS $= p_1/p_2 = p_1^*/p_2^*$. The base of the *trade triangle* XAC is imports of good 1 and the height is the quantity of exports of good 2.

The Arrow impossibility theorem implies there are great difficulties in the concept of group preferences (Samuelson, 1956). Trade economists often get around this problem with the assumption of identical and homothetic tastes. However, in terms of basic theory, this is not really legitimate. A better way is to interpret the indifference curve U as the famous Scitovsky frontier, the efficient set of all national commodity bundles consistent with prescribed levels of utility for each consumer in the economy (Samuelson, 1956).[2] As an indifference curve for a representative consumer, it is clear that autarkic utility (tangent to PPF) is lower than free trade utility. As a Scitovsky frontier, figure 2.1 demonstrates that moving to autarky cannot make everyone better off, and someone or all must be worse off. There is a fundamental asymmetry involved in moving from free trade to autarky and moving from autarky to free trade. The former must hurt some consumers; the latter must benefit some consumers (Samuelson, 1962).

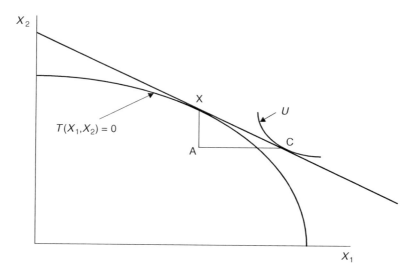

Figure 2.1   Basic trade diagram with free trade.

Now we can express the equilibrium conditions for two countries, Home and Foreign, where foreign is described by '$*$'.[3] Instead of assuming free trade, as in figure 2.1, assume that the home country puts a tariff of t_i on each good expressed as a percentage of the foreign price rather than the point of origin price (as in Lerner, 1936) with the foreign country adopting free trade.

Thus $p_i = (1 + t_i)p_i^*$. With this convention, a positive tariff on exports is a negative number and an export subsidy is a positive number.

$$\text{MRS} = (1+t_1)p_1^*/(1+t_2)p_2^*; \quad \text{MRS}^* = p_1^*/p_2^* \tag{3}$$

$$\text{MRT} = (1+t_1)p_1^*/(1+t_2)p_2^*; \quad \text{MRT}^* = p_1^*/p_2^* \tag{4}$$

$$p_1^*(X_1 - C_1) + p_2^*(X_2 - C_2) = 0; \quad p_1^*(X_1^* - C_1^*) + p_2^*(X_2^* - C_2^*) = 0 \tag{5}$$

$$\Sigma(X_i + X_i^*) = \Sigma(C_i + C_i^*) \tag{6}$$

$$T(X_1, X_2) = 0; \quad T^*(X_1^*, X_2^*) = 0.$$

Equations (3) and (4) are the private optimizing conditions for consumers and firms. We only need one of the market clearing equations (6) because of the budget constraints (5), so there are 9 equations in the unknowns X_i, X_i^*, C_i, C_i^*, and the price ratio p_1^*/p_2^*. Notice that the assumption of free trade in the foreign country means that the home country's budget constraint (5) is in terms of the p_i^*'s because the home country must pay world or foreign prices given zero transport costs. This also implies that tariff revenue is redistributed lump sum to consumers, an assumption without which anything can happen. Lerner (1936), for example, showed that if tariff revenue is entirely spent on imports (or if the imported good is sufficiently inferior), a higher tariff can lower a country's terms of trade. But this is not in any way paradoxical because one is diverting income towards imported goods.

A true paradox is the Metzler (1949) theorem that a tariff may not protect even if tariff revenue is redistributed lump sum. The economics is that at a constant import price, tariff revenue increases domestic demand but the falling foreign price can increase foreign supply if the supply curve is backward-bending. If the foreign supply increases by less (or falls) than domestic demand at a constant price, the tariff will protect. With an upward-sloping foreign supply curve of exports, a tariff by the home country must protect domestic demand increases and foreign supply decreases. What is valuable about the Metzler theorem is that its development summarizes the basic structure of tariff theory.

The key tariff theorem is Lerner's symmetry theorem that a uniform export duty has the same real effect as a uniform import duty on all imports at the same rate, or that a uniform import duty can be fully offset by a uniform export subsidy on all exports (see Ruffin, 2008, for the many commodity case and intermediate goods). This theorem is easy to prove in a two-commodity setting: If $t_1 = t_2$, the solution is the same as if there were no tariffs because an export subsidy on all exports at some rate just offsets an import tariff on all imports at the same rate or, equivalently, a uniform export tariff has the same real impact as a uniform import tariff (Lerner, 1936). Ricardo himself anticipated this result (Ruffin, 2002).

Let $p = p_1/p_2$ and $p^* = p_1^*/p_2^*$. If good 1 is imported, the difference between p and p^* can be considered the specific tariff. The change in a country's welfare is $dU = U_1 dC_1 + U_2 dC_2$ or, following Jones (1967), let $dy = dU/U_2 = pdC_1 + dC_2$ when utility is maximized (3). Equation (4) above implies that $dX_2/dX_1 = -p$ or $pdX_1 + dX_2 = 0$. Using the economics of maximization, the effect a marginal change in a tariff on a country's welfare can be obtained by differentiating the budget constraint for the home country:

$$X_1 dp^* + p^* dX_1 + dX_2 = C_1 dp^* + p^* dC_1 + dC_2.$$

Add and subtract pdX_1 to the left side and pdC_1 to the right side and we can write:

$$dy = pdC_1 + dC_2 = -(C_1 - X_1)dp^* + (p - p^*)(dC_1 - dX_1). \tag{7}$$

Equation (7) uses the condition that $pdX_1 + dX_2 = 0$ along the PPF. The first term is the terms of trade effect of a marginal change in a tariff and the second term is the volume of trade effect. Thinking of good 1 as imported, for a large country a higher tariff will depress p^*, and so the first term will be positive, and the second term will be negative if imports fall and $p > p^*$.[4] It follows that starting from free trade $(p = p^*)$, if a small tariff depresses p^* (the cost of imports), then an incipient tariff will make the country better off since the second term is zero. At the other end, starting at autarky, the first term is zero and expanding trade from lowering the tariff will also make the country better off. Hence, for a large country, there is a finite tariff that will maximize a country's welfare (the optimum tariff). It should be pointed out that at the optimum tariff, the foreign supply curve for its exports must be upward-sloping. If the supply curve were in a backward-bending range, the home country would have still an incentive to raise the tariff because not only would p^* fall (a positive terms of trade effect), but volume of trade would increase as well and so the second term in (7) would also be positive.

The optimum tariff argument, of course, assumes non-retaliation by the foreign country. In what is still a very good read, C. F. Bickerdike (1906) is the classic statement of the advantages of an optimum tariff. It is really an argument for tariff revenue $R = (p - p^*)(C_1 - X_1)$. Thus, substituting

$$dR = (p - p^*)(dC_1 - dX_1) + (dp - dp^*)(C_1 - X_1) \tag{8}$$

into (7) yields: $dy = dR - dp(C_1 - X_1)$. $\tag{9}$

At the optimum tariff, a small change in the tariff increases both R and p (by the Metzler theorem) by offsetting amounts. Since a higher tariff raises p, then at the maximum revenue tariff $dR = 0$ an increase in the tariff must make the country worse off, so the tariff that maximizes revenue exceeds the optimum tariff. Francis Edgeworth said of 'Mr. Bickerdike's particular scheme for taxing the foreigner, ... let us admire the skill of the analyst, but label the subject of his investigation POISON (Edgeworth, 1908, 554–56)'. The main grounds for this shared opinion by Mill, Marshall, and Edgeworth was the very real possibility of foreign retaliation (see Edgeworth, 1908).

Bickerdike (1906) also emphasized that the tariff must be small or 'incipient' because if it is too high the optimal tariff can backfire. An increase in a tariff that lowers tariff revenue must lower welfare by equation (9).

The stability issue was first clearly raised by Alfred Marshall; his conclusion was that the sum of the home and foreign elasticities of demand for imports must exceed unity. This is, of course, true; but it is a matter of arithmetic. The best approach is to follow Eugen Slutsky and J. R. Hicks with income and substitution effects. Let us assume free trade, so $p = p^*$. Define:

$$E_i(p,y) = C_i(p,y) - X_i(p); \quad E_i^*(p,y^*) = C_i^*(p,y^*) - X_i^*,$$

where, for example, $C_i(p,y)$ is the home country's compensated demand curve. Equilibrium requires

$$E_1^0 = E_1(p,y) + E_1^*(p,y^*) = 0,$$

where the real income levels y and y^* are themselves functions of p. Stability simply requires that $dE_1^0/dp < 0$. There are three things to consider: the substitution effects in consumption and production and the income effect. If p rises, the country that exports good 1 is better off, and the country that imports good 1 is worse off. Since $dy + dy^* = 0$ at the free trade solution, the income effects wash out if the marginal propensities to spend on good 1 are symmetrical. Thus, all that remains are the substitution effects in consumption and production, where $\partial E_1/\partial p$ and $\partial E_1^*/\partial p$ must be negative since $\partial C_1/\partial p < 0$ and $\partial X_1/\partial p > 0$. Instability can only happen if the country exporting good 1 has a sufficiently higher marginal propensity to consume that good than the country importing good 1 to offset those substitution effects.

The neoclassical model can also be easily amended to include intermediate goods and the concept of effective protection (Wilfred J. Ethier, 1977). The effective tariff rate on a good is then the increase in domestic value added caused by the tariff structure divided by the free trade value added (W. M. Corden, 1966). Ruffin (2008) argues that effective protection should be the centerpiece of tariff theory because of the web of input–output relationships in an economy makes it impossible to examine the effects of a single change in any nominal tariff or quota without estimates of the input–output table of the economy. Ruffin

(2008) shows that (7) must be modified as follows:

$$dy = \Sigma [(p_i - p_i^*)dC_i + (v_i^* - v_i)dX_i + X_i dv_i^* - C_i dp_i^*],$$

where v_i and v_i^* are domestic and free trade value added for good i. Note that every good in the economy becomes relevant for any tariff change. The first term is the value of the changes in consumption; the second is the value of the changes in production; the third and fourth terms are the gains in the values of current outputs minus the increase in the costs of current consumptions.

2.1 The development of Heckscher–Ohlin

Eli Heckscher (1919) pointed out that it is important to examine the cause of international trade in a general equilibrium setting. The role of factor endowments in international trade was probably intuitively understood by Ricardo himself and other classical writers (Viner, 1937, p. 504). But why the Swedish economists? The answer is simple: the great Knut Wicksell (1851–1926) was Swedish. It was Wicksell who invented the mislabeled Cobb–Douglas production function. As Heckscher (1919) tells the story, Wicksell wrote a suggestive book review that apparently made it clear one should begin with production functions involving several factors of production. So Heckscher asked the basic question: if two countries have identical production functions, what determines comparative advantage? Heckscher's student and future Nobel prize winner, Bertil Ohlin (1933), then filled out the general equilibrium details of such a model and as such set trade theory on its course for the next half century. Only simplicity was absent. Stolper and Samuelson (1941) constructed the two sector, two factor model with constant returns to scale and showed how the expansion of the labour intensive industry would result in higher real wages and lower real returns to the other factor.

Heckscher and Ohlin discussed a tendency towards factor price equalization. In what is probably the best single paper introduction to the factor endowment approach to trade theory, Paul Samuelson in 1948 showed that the Heckscher–Ohlin tendency to factor price equalization becomes a complete equalization of factor prices between two countries, sharing the same constant returns to scale production functions and facing the same prices, provided only that their factor endowments are sufficiently close. Upon reading this 1948 paper, Lionel Robbins sent Samuelson a copy of Abba Lerner's 1933 graduate student essay (Lerner, 1952). This led Samuelson to a somewhat clearer 1949 version and probably to Samuelson's great 1953 paper. I want to compare the way Samuelson (1948; 1949) expressed trade theory with the way it was expressed in Lerner (1952), Samuelson (1953), and the most popular version, Ronald W. Jones (1965).

Let $\lambda X_j = F^j(\lambda L_j, \lambda K_j)$ be the constant returns to scale production function for any positive λ and inputs of L_j and K_j of factors named 'labour' and 'capital.'

The intensive form of this production function is to let $\lambda = 1/L_j$ and so:

$$X_j/L_j = F^j(1, K_j/L_j) = f_j(k_j),\tag{10}$$

where $k_j = K_j/L_j$ is the capital/labour ratio in industry j. In this setup, the marginal product of labour is $\partial X_j/\partial L_j = f_j(k_j) - k_j f_j'(k_j)$ and the marginal product of capital is derivative $f_j'(k_j)$. The extensive form of the production function is obtained by setting $\lambda = 1/X_j$ so that:

$$1 = F^j(L_i/X_i, K_i/X_i) = F^j(a_{Lj}, a_{Kj}),\tag{11}$$

where a_{ij} is the amount of factor i used in a unit of good j.

The Samuelson (1948, 1949) approach to describing the production side of the model is to use the intensive form of the production function. The wage of labour and the rent on capital must equalized between sectors and there must be full employment. Let $k = K/L$ be the factor endowment ratio in a country facing the price ratio p for good 1:

$$p[f_1(k_1) - k_1 f_1'(k_1)] = f_2(k_2) - k_2 f_1'(k_2) = w\tag{12}$$

$$pf_1'(k_1) = f_2'(k_2) = r\tag{13}$$

$$L_1/L + L_2/L = 1\tag{14}$$

$$k_1(L_1/L) + k_2(L_2/L) = (L_1/L)(k_1 - k_2) + k_2 = k.\tag{15}$$

The first thing to notice is that the factor market arbitrage equations (12) and (13) may potentially be solved without looking at (14) and (15). This is the factor price equalization property of the Heckscher–Ohlin model. Two problems arise here: there may be more than one solution to (12) and (13) due to a factor intensity reversal, so the factor market clearing equations (14) and (15) are necessary to choose one of these; and if, say, only one solution, but (14) and (15) does not satisfy the constraint that L_i/L be nonnegative so that all labour and capital would be in a single industry. Samuelson (1948, 1949) popularized the equations $w/r \equiv \omega = f_i/f_i' - k_i$, the ratio of (12) and (13). Since ω and k_i are always positively related, we can write $k_i(\omega)$ for the cost minimizing capital–labour ratio. Figure 2.2 shows the Samuelson representation of the cost minimizing capital–labour ratios, where it is assumed that $k_1(\omega) > k_2(\omega)$ for all ω. Given k, figure 2.2 shows that the conceivable range for the ω's is $[\omega_1, \omega_2]$; for any higher or lower ω will cause either an excess demand or supply of capital in the factor market. The logic is that some price ratio, say p_0, determines ω_0, and thus the capital–labour ratios that must bracket the ratio k, as in figure 2.2. Given k and the k_i's, one can then solve for L_1/L. It is easy to show with this diagram that if $k_1(\omega)$ intersects $k_2(\omega)$ any number of times, there cannot be a factor intensity reversal for a given factor endowment.

The advantage of the Samuelson structure is that, with just a smattering of economics and inspection, the four basic theorems of the Heckscher–Ohlin model

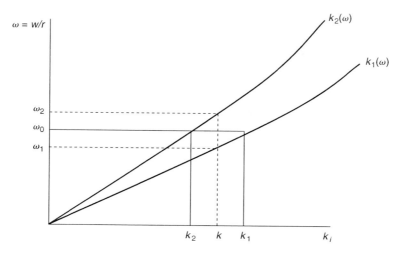

Figure 2.2 The Samuelson diagram.

become transparent. They show the value of an explicit general equilibrium model as opposed to a partial equilibrium approach. First, factor price equalization is possible because from conditions (12) and (13) given p there are four equations and four unknowns (w, r, k_1, k_2). Thus, it may not be necessary to know K/L. Two countries with the same constant returns to scale technologies, but different factor endowments, can have the same factor prices if they face the same commodity prices.

Next, the Rybczynski theorem follows from equation (15) and the factor price equalization property (Rybczynski, 1955). If K/L rises holding p constant factor prices remain the same so the optimal capital–labour ratios remain the same. Thus, if say $k_1 > k_2$ so that good 1 is capital intensive, then it must be that L_1/L must rise in order for the weighted average to rise given constant k_i's. This means that if L is constant, that the output of good 2, the labour intensive good must fall and the output of the capital intensive good must rise. The Rybczynski theorem gives the foundation of the Heckscher–Ohlin and third theorem that, given identical and homothetic tastes, the country with the largest ratio of K/L must export the capital intensive good simply because it produces relatively more of that good and demands the same proportion as the rest of the world.

The fourth theorem is the Stolper–Samuelson theorem that a rise in the price of the capital (labour) intensive good must raise the real return to capital (labour) and lower the real return to labour (capital). If the relative price of the capital intensive good rises, labour will move into that good so L_1/L must rise. If $k_1 > k_2$, the second form of equation (15) implies k_2 and by symmetry k_1 must both fall to keep the weighted average constant because heuristically for a small enough change in L_1/L the gap ($k_1 - k_2$) is positive constant. Since both k_i's fall, the law of diminishing returns requires the marginal product of capital to rise and the marginal product of labour to fall in terms of either good. This tells us that $r = pf'_1(k_1)$ must rise by more than p. Thus, the real return to capital increases regardless of how consumers spend their incomes. This nicely dovetails into the consistency of decentralized incentives: when resources shift from a labour intensive industry to a capital intensive industry, at constant factor prices an excess demand for capital and an excess supply of labour is created, causing the rent/wage ratio to rise, inducing industries to economize on capital.

The Samuelson set of equations is very easy to discuss but, ironically, difficult to analyze mathematically (see Kemp, 1964, chapter 1). The reason is that when one differentiates the system for any parametric change, one has to continually economize by carrying along the marginal conditions. Fortunately for the rapid development of trade theory, Lerner (1952) and Samuelson (1953) took another route that suggests the use of duality theory. Lerner used unit value isoquants and cost minimization together with prices equal to average costs to prove the factor price equalization theorem when factor endowments are sufficiently close. This may have led Samuelson (1953) to reformulate the production side of the Heckscher–Ohlin model along Lernerian lines. Here was the beginning of the duality approach to trade theory, culminating in Ronald W. Jones (1965) for the case of two sectors and the full and elegant use of duality theory.

Lerner (1952) invented what is now called the famous Lerner–Pearce diagram that if two countries with the same constant returns to scale production functions face the same output prices, they will share the same factor prices if their factor endowments lie in the same *cone of diversification*, that is, the set of all factor endowments consistent with a single set of factor prices.[5] Lerner's insight was to compare the isoquants of two industries with the same free trade value. In figure 2.3, $X_1 = 1/p_1$ and $X_2 = 1/p_2$ are the unit value isoquants. Lerner exploited the fact that, with constant returns to scale, any isoquant represents the entire isoquant map. Given p_1 and p_2, if both goods are produced both isoquants must be tangent to the unit value iso cost line with intercepts $1/r$ and $1/w$. The cone of diversification is formed by the two expansion rays, labeled Ok_1 and Ok_2. The endowment K/L ratio must be in between Ok_1 and Ok_2 if both goods are to be produced. Figure 2.3 establishes at a glance the factor price equalization theorem that factor prices merely depend on commodity prices if the factor endowment is inside the cone of diversification. Equations (14) and (15) above show that the capital–labour ratio in the economy is a weighted average of k_1 and k_2 or, geometrically, the vector (K, L) is the sum of the vectors (K_1, L_1) and (K_2, L_2) lying on the rays Ok_1 and Ok_2, as shown by the parallelogram in figure 2.3. Notice that Rybczynski follows easily here because if one increases K, holding L constant, the point (K_1, L_1) moves up and the point (K_2, L_2) moves down.

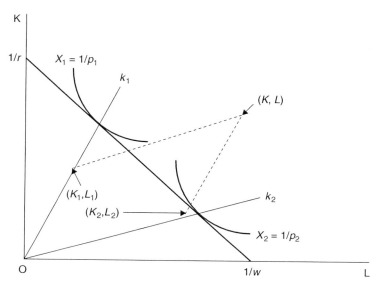

Figure 2.3 Lerner–Pearce diagram.

Since price equals cost of production, and there is full employment of resources, Jones (1965) made popular the following system of equations:[6]

$$wa_{L1} + ra_{K1} = p_1, \tag{16}$$

$$wa_{L2} + ra_{K2} = p_2, \tag{17}$$

$$a_{L1}X_1 + a_{L2}X_2 = L, \tag{18}$$

$$a_{K1}X_1 + a_{K2}X_2 = K. \tag{19}$$

The a_{ij}'s are the cost minimizing input requirements per unit of output. Equations (16) and (17) are the competitive price conditions in which the price of each good equals the minimum average cost of production consisting of the labour costs, wa_{Li}, and capital costs, ra_{Ki}. Given p_1 and p_2, equations (16) and (17) can be solved for w and r just as in figure 2.3 as long as there is no factor intensity reversal. Equations (18) and (19) are the full employment conditions, where $a_{L_i}X_i$ and $a_{K_i}X_i$ are L_i and K_i, respectively. If the resulting a_{ij}'s from (16) and (17) satisfy (18) and (19) with non-negative outputs, we have a solution.

Jones (1965) used the envelope theorem or Shepherd's Lemma that any changes in p_i would induce changes in w and r such that for small changes the a_{ij}'s can be treated as constants in the vicinity of the cost minimizing values where $wda_{Li} + rda_{Ki} = 0$. This makes it easier to study (16)–(17) with the calculus because one is essentially looking at the linear equations of motion in the vicinity of the equilibrium.

$$a_{Li}dw + a_{Ki}dr = wa_{Li}(dw/w) + ra_{Ki}(dr/r) = dp_i$$

Dividing by p_i and defining the distributive shares $\theta_{Li} = wa_{L_i}/p_i$ and $\theta_{K_i} = ra_{K_i}/p_i$ we obtain:

$$\theta_{Li}(dw/w) + \theta_{Ki}(dr/r) = dp_i/p_i \quad i = 1, 2. \tag{20}$$

Since $\theta_{L_i} + \theta_{K_i} = 1$, (20) can be used for a more fundamental proof of Stolper–Samuelson. Equation (20) implies that the relative change dp_i/p_i is the weighted average of the changes dw/w and dr/r and is, thus, trapped between those extremes. If you subtract equation (20) for $i = 2$ from $i = 1$ and eliminate θ_{Li} we obtain:

$$(\theta_{K_1} - \theta_{K_2})(dr/r - dw/w) = dp_1/p_1 - dp_2/p_2. \tag{21}$$

This shows that an increase in the relative price of good 1 must increase $(dr/r - dw/w)$ or r/w rises if $\theta_{K_1} > \theta_{K_1}$. Since the difference in the θ's is a fraction, the commodity price change has a magnified impact on factor prices. This is the Stolper–Samuelson theorem. Another way of showing Stolper–Samuelson is to assume the price of good 2 is constant. When p_1 rises, (21) demands that r/w rise when $\theta_{K_1} > \theta_{K_1}$. But (20) for $i = 2$ implies that w must fall because costs must remain constant, so r increases by a larger percentage than p_1 according to (20).

The Stolper–Samuelson theorem clearly depends on non-joint production. If mutton and wool are land intensive and produced by labour and land, a 1 percent increase in the price of wool may not increase the rent on land by more than 1 percent unless the price of mutton also increases by 1 percent.

Jones (1965) can be considered the two good, two factor comparative static analysis of the general system that Samuelson (1953) developed. Suppose $a_{ij}(w_1, \ldots, w_r)$ is the input of factor i per unit of good j for factor prices $\mathbf{w} = (w_1, \ldots, w_r)$. Define A as the $r \times n$ matrix of a'_{ij}s. Then if all n goods are produced and $\mathbf{p} = (p_1, \ldots, p_n)$, we must have:

$$A'\mathbf{w} = \mathbf{p}, \tag{22}$$

$$AX = \mathbf{V}, \tag{23}$$

where $\mathbf{X} = (X_1, \ldots, X_n)$ and $\mathbf{V} = (V_1, \ldots, V_r)$ are the vectors of outputs and factor supplies. Samuelson showed that since the 'GDP function' $Y = \Sigma p_j X_j = \Sigma w_i V_i$, profit maximization and cost minimization implies the envelope results that $\partial Y/\partial p_j = X_j$ and $\partial Y/\partial V_i = w_i$. Differentiating these envelope results shows two very useful theorems: Samuelson duality, $\partial X_j/\partial V_i = \partial w_i/\partial p_j$; and Samuelson reciprocity, $\partial w_i/\partial V_k = \partial w_k/\partial V_i$. The first is where Rybczynski effects meet Stolper–Samuelson effects; and the second where any two factors are mutual friends or enemies. These basic theorems do *not* depend on $r = n$ and merely depend on non-joint production. Equations (22) and (23) dramatically show that many models, such as Ricardo or Heckscher–Ohlin, are special cases; thus, resolving historical controversies over opportunity costs versus Ricardian labour cost theories. Ricardo is $n = 2$ and $r = 1$; the simple Heckscher–Ohlin model is $n = 2$ and $r = 2$. If $n < r$, then factor price equalization must break down because (22) cannot possibly be solved without adding (23). Samuelson (1953) showed that with $n > r$, the PPF has a ruled surface. This follows from the fact that if (22) is satisfied as an equality with $n > r$, there are an infinity of linear combinations of the X_i's for any set of commodity prices. Thus, the straight line Ricardian PPF is just an example of this general result. Samuelson's GDP function was fully exploited in Avinash Dixit and Victor Norman (1980) and Alan Woodland (see chapter 3).

Finally, in one of the most important consequences of the Lerner-Samuelson-Jones reformulation of Heckscher–Ohlin, Jaroslav Vanek (1968) showed how to calculate trade in factor services implicit in goods trade. With the assumption that even for $n > r$, one could have factor price equalization in a world of identical technologies, then for the world economy (23) is:

$$AX^\mathrm{o} = V^\mathrm{o}. \tag{24}$$

But if preferences are identical and homothetic in the entire world, the vector of consumer demands in the home country $C = sX^\mathrm{o}$, where s is the home country's share of world income. Thus, if we define the trade vector as $T = C - X$, we can multiply both sides by the matrix A and obtain:

$$AT = AsX^\mathrm{o} - V = sV^\mathrm{o} - V. \tag{25}$$

This is the Heckscher–Ohlin–Vanek equation and quantifies the trade in factor services (Helpman and Krugman, 1985). This has stimulated enormous empirical research (see chapter 4).

2.2   Modifications of Heckscher–Ohlin

A standard and tiresome criticism of trade models is that they assume too much mobility of factors domestically and too little internationally (John H. Williams, 1929). However, those assumptions are just simplifications and can be modified. There are many factors of production. Some factors can be immobile between industries; factors such as coal mines, oil fields, and rice paddies may be quite specific in the sense that rents would have to fall very low to switch them to other uses. Moreover, even though certain kinds of skilled labour and capital may be extremely mobile between countries, there are lots of other factors of production, such as land, and many kinds of labour that seldom leave a particular country! Thus, the two most important modifications of the Heckscher–Ohlin model are the specific factors model in which some factors are domestically immobile (Jones, 1971; Samuelson, 1971); and the Kemp–Jones model in which only capital is completely internationally mobile (Kemp, 1966; Jones, 1967). More generally, in the Kemp–Jones model there are two factors of production, with only one factor of production, mobile internationally.

To capture the tendency of factor prices to be equalized rather than full factor price equalization, the specific factors model assumes that each sector has a factor of production that cannot be moved to another industry, but otherwise shares all of the assumptions of the Heckscher–Ohlin model. This has the advantage of relaxing the strong assumption made in Heckscher–Ohlin that all factors earn the same return across all industries. As a consequence, the factor price equalization theorem fails but there may still be a tendency towards factor price equalization (Samuelson, 1971). Another advantage of the model is that one is not put in the Heckscher–Ohlin trap in which a country may not produce all of the goods if the number of goods exceeds the number of factors. This can be seen in a slight modification of Figure 2.3. Add more goods, and in order to produce all the goods the unit value isoquants would all have to be tangent to the same isocost line. This is highly unlikely. Jones (1971) presented the most popular version of the specific factors model:

$$a_{Li}w + a_{Ki}r_i = p_i \quad i = 1, \ldots, n,$$

$$\Sigma a_{Li}X_i = L,$$

$$a_{Ki}X_i = K_i \quad i = 1, \ldots, n.$$

In this model, wages are the same across sectors, but the returns to the specific factor, called capital, differ across industries. One loses factor price equalization because the price equations cannot solve for factor prices without the remaining equations. But one gains a richer model for investigating the impact of commodity price changes on wages, the mobile factor. Say the price of good k increases, then labour is attracted to that industry. Wages must rise because in other industries the marginal product of labour must rise due to the law of diminishing returns, but wages rise by a smaller proportion than the price of good k because $w = p_k MP_L^k = p_j MP_L^j$ with MP_L^j rising ($j \neq k$) and MP_L^k falling. Under neutral conditions real wages will rise if good k is exported, simply because consumption is less than production (Ruffin and Jones, 1977).

The Kemp–Jones model has not received the attention it deserves, but it is based on a Heckscher–Ohlin production structure with perfect mobility of factors internally as well as capital between countries. That such an assumption does not do violence to the law of comparative advantage has been conjectured for more than a century: 'Let it be granted that capital and perhaps business power is free to flow to all parts of the earth. Yet labour cannot be conceived as flowing so freely' (Edgeworth, 1894a, 35). The Kemp–Jones model returns to the Ricardian assumption that technologies differ between countries. If capital is perfectly mobile so that the returns are equalized between countries, one still has the brute fact that wages are widely different across countries. If two countries have the same rate of return on capital, but one has higher wages due to higher productivity, then the high wage country will have a comparative advantage in capital intensive goods simply because its relative price of such goods must be lower. This is just a matter of arithmetic. The higher wage country will find that compared to the low wage country its labour intensive goods are relatively more expensive than its capital intensive goods; thus, it should export capital intensive goods since only relative prices direct the pattern of trade. This would have been obvious to Ricardo, who discussed how higher wages would increase the price of labour intensive goods relative to capital intensive goods in chapter 1 of his book.

The model has at least three ramifications (Jones and Ruffin, 1975). First, the Kemp–Jones model shows that Edgeworth's intuition that capital mobility does not affect the law of comparative advantage is quite correct. As long as all inputs are not traded, absolute advantage takes over to explain the flow of mobile inputs and comparative advantages (as partly influenced by the former) explain the flow of goods (Jones, 2000). A concrete example of absolute advantage in mobile inputs is professional golf; where golfers from all over the world compete in each country for the same prizes. Second, the model shows that capital flows do not necessarily substitute for international trade but can magnify relative cost differences and, thus, may complement international trade. Third, just as higher relative prices for capital intensive goods translate into magnified effects on the return to capital, so too a differential productivity advantage in capital intensive goods has a magnified impact on the return to capital (beyond what would have happened in a one-good world).[7] Thus, capital might paradoxically flow from capital poor countries to capital rich countries that have strong productivity advantages in capital intensive goods.

3 Monopolistic Competition and Intra-industry Trade

The standard model does not account for the fact that in many developed countries intra-industry trade (i.e., exporting and importing goods in the same industry) is more important than inter-industry trade. Thus, the most important development since Heckscher–Ohlin has been the Dixit–Stiglitz model of monopolistic competition (Dixit and Stiglitz, 1977). Krugman (1979, 1980), Dixit and Norman (1980), and Helpman and Krugman (1985) applied the model to intra-industry trade. Here, one simply makes two assumptions that are common to trade theory: the Heckscher–Ohlin assumption of identical technologies and preferences, and the Ricardian assumption of a single factor of production, labour. It is then assumed that each industry consists of n different monopolitically competitive varieties. It is usually assumed that the production function for each variety involves the same α fixed labour costs and same β marginal costs.

Each variety faces the same demand and price elasticity $\varepsilon(n)$, so the output of each variety, x, and price, p, will be the same. It is usually assumed that the numeraire is the wage rate equal to unity. Average cost for each firm is then $\alpha/x + \beta$. The model consists of three equations for the price markup over marginal cost, the free entry condition that price equals average cost, and the labour supply is absorbed in all n varieties:

$$p = \varepsilon(n)\beta/[\varepsilon(n) - 1), \tag{26}$$

$$p = \alpha/x + \beta, \tag{27}$$

$$L = n(\alpha + \beta x). \tag{28}$$

Equation (26) represents profit maximization for each variety with the price reflecting the markup over marginal cost depending on the elasticity of demand. Krugman (1979) assumed that the elasticity of demand facing each variety was a declining function of per capita consumption. Dixit and Stiglitz (1977) and Krugman (1980) assumed the elasticity of demand was a constant equal to the elasticity of substitution between varieties. However, neither simplification is necessary, and it can be argued that it is more realistic to simply follow through with the implications of a constant elasticity of substitution (CES) utility function that shows that the elasticity of demand facing each variety increases with the number of varieties (see W. Michael Cox and Ruffin, 2010). The second equation is forced by free entry of new varieties until profit is zero; and the last equation is just the full employment equation. If you combine (27) and (28) to eliminate 'x' we can derive the price or cost of production as a function of the number of varieties.

The model nicely explains intra-industry trade between two identical countries because each specializes in particular varieties, but consumers in each country purchase all varieties (Krugman, 1979, 1980). It easily proves that the smaller country gains more from free trade than the larger country because it receives a bigger boost in the number of varieties and a larger decrease in prices compared to autarky.

This model has served to stimulate a great deal of theoretical (Cox and Ruffin, 2010) and empirical research (Feenstra and Kee, 2008) in intra-industry trade and the gains from trade. The Melitz model adds Ricardian rents to the familiar Dixit–Stiglitz model (Melitz, 2003; Montaegna, 2001). The purpose of this model is to reflect the fact that productivity differs between firms that export and firms that do not export.

4   Oligopoly and Trade

The classic paper by Dixit and Stiglitz (1977) has also led to the general equilibrium analysis of the role of oligopoly. Oligopoly may be considered a situation in which there is not free entry, giving rise to economic profits. The nature of the controversy over the role of oligopoly in trade policy questions has been more or less settled because the policy critically depends on strategic assumptions (chapters 8 and 9), but the impact of oligopoly on general equilibrium trade theoretic questions is still in its infancy.

J. Peter Neary (2003) and Ruffin (2003) use the convenient assumption that oligopolistic firms are small in the economy but large in the industry. It may have been felt that such an assumption may be appropriate for monopolistic competition, but not for oligopoly. The justification for this assumption is the basic observation that oligopolistic firms compete with the entire economy for factors of production but only with firms in their industry for product pricing. Oligopoly raises three trade issues: does oligopoly change the pattern of trade away from compare advantage? Does oligopoly expand or contract the volume of international trade? How does oligopoly affect the question of the gains from trade?

Following Ruffin (2003), the above three questions can then be answered as follows. First, oligopoly probably cannot change the pattern of trade away from comparative advantage unless the degree of oligopoly power across industries is uncorrelated across countries. Oligopoly serves to restrict output of a particular industry. But if this is roughly the same across countries, then one should not expect the pattern of trade to change. Oligopoly is likely to restrict the volume of trade because oligopoly pricing serves as an umbrella over costs of production, and thus the possibility that firms that could not compete under perfect competition can compete under oligopoly. Thus, there might be less specialization. Accordingly, the gain from trade to the economy might be less. But Ruffin (2003) proved the theorem that if labour is the only factor of production, opening trade must benefit labour more under oligopoly than with perfect competition simply because more competitors lowers prices of both exports and imports in wage units. This follows from an equation like (26) for imperfect competition: with more firms, the elasticity of demand facing each firm increases, so the price must drop. It is straightforward to show that international competition can either increase or lower domestic oligopoly profits, depending on the strength of comparative advantage and the tightness of the oligopoly: the stronger a country's comparative advantage and the weaker oligopoly power, the more likely profits will increase.

5 Conclusion

This chapter has tried to show how trade theory has developed from the simple Ricardian one-factor model and Heckscher–Ohlin multi-factor model to models of imperfect competition. The following chapters tell the rest of the story. It is interesting, perhaps, that trade theory often returns to its Ricardian roots of a single factor of production when more important matters take center stage, such as the study of heterogeneous firms (Melitz, 2003), transport costs (Eaton and Kortum, 2002), technology transfers (Jones and Ruffin, 2008), or imperfect competition as discussed above. Thus, while the circle of trade theory has widened, the center has remained remarkably stable.

Notes

* I wish to thank Ron Jones and Edwin Lai for highly beneficial comments without thereby implicating them.
† M.D. Anderson Professor of Economics, University of Houston.
1. According to Viner (1937), Hans von Mangoldt (1824–68) was first to discuss the ranking in (1). But the economics of the multi-commodity case are exceptionally explained in Frank W. Taussig (1927).
2. The Scitovsky frontier must be convex because it is the lower boundary of the sum of convex sets of each consumer, which contain the commodity bundles at least as good as the prescribed levels of utility.
3. The first use of starred variables for the foreign country was evidently in Murray Kemp (1964).
4. This sentence assumes that the good imported by the home country is a normal good or, at least, not too inferior and that the foreign supply curve of exports is upward-sloping.
5. I. F. Pearce came up with a similar diagram independently of Lerner (S.F. James and I. F. Pearce, 1951–52, p. 111n.). See also Pearce (1959) for interesting imagery in more than two dimensions.
6. James E. Meade's *Trade and Welfare* (1955), together with its mathematical supplement, played a role that must be considered in a detailed history of trade theory rather than in an historical exposition such as this.
7. See Robert E. Lucas (1990) for the one sector case.

References

Bickerdike, C.F. (1906) 'The theory of incipient taxes', *Economic Journal*, 16(64): 529–35.

Corden, W.M. (1966) 'The structure of a tariff system and the effective tariff rate', *Journal of Political Economy*, 221–37.

Cox, W. Michael, and Roy J. Ruffin (2010) 'Variety, globalization, and social efficiency', *Southern Economic Journal*, 76, 1064–1075.

Dixit, Avinash K., and Joseph Stiglitz (1977) 'Monopolistic competition and optimum product diversity', *American Economic Review*, 67 (3), 297–308.

Dixit, Avinash K., and Victor D. Norman (1980) *Theory of International Trade*, Cambridge: Cambridge University Press.

Dornbusch, R., S. Fischer and P.A. Samuelson (1977) 'Comparative advantage, trade, and payments in a Ricardian model with a continuum of goods', *American Economic Review*.

Ethier, Wilfred J. (1977) 'The theory of effective protection in general equilibrium: effective rate analogues to nominal rates', *Canadian Journal of Economics*, 10, 233–45.

Edgeworth, F.Y. (1894a) 'The theory of international values, I', *Economic Journal*, 4(13): 35–50.

—— (1894b) 'The theory of international values, II', *Economic Journal*, 4(15): 424–43.

——(1908) 'Appreciations of mathematical theories', *Economic Journal*, 18, 541–56.

Feenstra, Robert, and Hiau Looi Kee (2008) 'Export variety and country productivity: estimating the monopolistic competition model with endogenous productivity', *Journal of International Economics*, 74, 500–18.

Heckscher, Eli (1919) 'The effect of foreign trade on the distribution of income', *Economisk Tidskrift*, 21: 497–512.

Helpman, Elhanan, and Paul Krugman (1985) *Market Structure and Foreign Trade*, Cambridge: MIT Press.

Jones, Ronald W. (1965) 'The structure of simple general equilibrium models', *Journal of Political Economy*, 73: 557–72.

——(1967) 'International capital movements in the theory of tariffs and trade', *Quarterly Journal of Economics*.

Jones, Ronald W. (1971) 'A three-factor model in theory, trade and history', in J. Bhagwati et al. (eds), *Trade, Balance of Payments and Growth: Essays in Honor of Charles P. Kindleberger* Amsterdam: North-Holland.

——and Roy J. Ruffin (1975) 'Trade patterns with capital mobility', in M. Parkin and R. Nobay (eds), *Current Economic Problems*, Cambridge, 307–32.

——(2000) *Globalization and the Theory of Input Trade*, Cambridge: MIT Press.

——and Roy J. Ruffin (2008) 'The technology transfer paradox', *Journal of International Economics*, 75 (2): 321–28.

James, S.F., and I.F. Pearce (1951–52) 'The factor price equalisation myth', *Review of Economic Studies*, 19 (2): 111–20.

Kemp, Murray (1964) *The Pure Theory of International Trade*, Englewood Cliffs, NJ: Prentice-Hall.

Krugman, Paul R. (1966) 'The gain from international trade and investment: A neo-Heckscher–Ohlin approach', *American Economic Review*, 56 (4): 788–809.

——(1979) 'Increasing returns, monopolistic competition and international trade'. *Journal of International Economics*, 9 (4), 469–79.

——(1981) 'Intraindustry specialization and the gains from trade', *Journal of Political Economy*, 89, 253–66.

Lancaster, Kelvin (1980) 'Intra-industry trade under perfect monopolistic competition', *Journal of International Economics,* 10, 151–76.

Leontief, Wassily W. (1933) 'The use of indifference curves in the analysis of foreign trade', *Quarterly Journal of Economics*, 47 (3): 493–503.

Lerner, Abba P. (1932) 'The diagrammatical representation of cost conditions in international trade', *Economica*, 37: 346–56.

——(1936) 'The symmetry of import and export taxes', *Economica*, New Series, 3 (11): 306–13.

——(1952) 'Factor prices and international trade', *Economica*, New Series, 19 (73): 1–15.

Longfield, Mountifort (1835) *Three Lectures on Commerce and One on Absenteeism*, Dublin: Publisher.

Lucas, Robert E. (1990) 'Why doesn't capital flow from rich to poor countries', *American Economic Review*, 80 (2): 92–96.

Maneschi, Andrea (2004) 'The true meaning of David Ricardo's four magic numbers', *Journal of International Economics*, 62, 433–43.

Melitz, Marc (2003) 'The impact of trade on intra-industry reallocations and aggregate productivity', *Econometrica*, 71, 1695–1725. Reprinted in Rod Falvey and Udo Kreickemeier (eds), *Recent Developments in International Trade Theory*, Brookfield, VT: Edward Elgar, 2005.

Metzler, Lloyd A. (1949) 'Tariffs, the terms of trade, and the distribution of national income,' *Journal of Political Economy*, 57 (1): 1–29.

Montagna, Catia (2001) 'Efficiency gaps, love of variety, and international trade', *Economica*, 68 (269), 27–44.

Neary, J. Peter (2003) 'Globalization and market structure', *Journal of European Economic Association*, 1: 627–49. Reprinted in Rod Falvey and Udo Kreickemeier (eds), *Recent Developments in International Trade Theory*, Brookfield, VT: Edward Elgar, 2005.

Ohlin, Bertil (1933) *Interregional and International Trade*, Cambridge, MA: Harvard University Press

Pearce, I.F. (1959) 'A further note on commodity-factor price relationships', *Economic Journal*, 69: 725–32.

Ruffin, Roy J., and Ronald W. Jones (1977) 'Protection and real wages: the neoclassical ambiguity,' *Journal of Economic Theory*, 14: 337–48.

Ruffin, Roy J. (1988) 'The missing link: the Ricardian approach to the factor endowment theory of trade', *American Economic Review*, 78 (4): 759–72.

——(2002), 'David Ricardo's discovery of comparative advantage', *History of Political Economy*, 34 (4): 727–48.

Ruffin, Roy J. (2003) 'Oligopoly and trade: what, how, and for whom?' *Journal of International Economics*, 60 (2): 315–35. Reprinted in Rod Falvey and Udo Kreickemeier (eds), *Recent Developments in International Trade Theory*, Edward Elgar, 2005.

——(2005) 'Debunking a myth: Torrens on comparative advantage', *History of Political Economy*, 37 (4): 711–22.

——(2008) 'A rehabilitation of effective protection', *Journal of International Trade and Economic Development*, 17 (3): 333–42.

——(2009) 'The gains from specialization and population size', *Economic Letters*, 105: 76–77.

Rybczynski, T.M., 1955. 'Factor endowments and relative commodity prices', *Economica*, 22, 336–41.

Samuelson, Paul (1948) 'International trade and the equalisation of factor prices', *Economic Journal*, 58: 163–84.

——(1949) 'International factor-price equalisation once again', *Economic Journal*, 59: 181–97.

——(1952–53) 'Prices of factors and goods in general equilibrium', *Review of Economic Studies*, vol. 21, 1–20.

——(1956) 'Social indifference curves', *Quarterly Journal of Economics*, 70 (1): 1–22.

——(1962) 'The gain from international trade once again', *Economic Journal*, 72: 820–29.

——(1971) 'Ohlin was right', *Swedish Journal of Economics*, 73, 365–84.

Stolper, Wolfgang, and Paul A. Samuelson (1941) 'Protection and Real Wages', *Review of Economic Studies*, 9, 58–73.

Taussig, Frank W. (1927) *International Trade*. New York: Macmillan.

Torrens, Robert (1815) *Essay on the External Corn Trade*. London: J. Hatchard.

Vanek, Jaroslav (1968) 'The Factor Proportions Theory: The N-factor case', *Kyklos*, 21 (4): 749–56.

Viner, Jacob (1937) *Studies in the Theory of International Trade*. New York: Harper and Brothers.

Williams, John H. (1929) 'The theory of international trade reconsidered', *Economic Journal*, 39: 195–209.

3

General Equilibrium Trade Theory*

Alan Woodland[†]

1 Introduction

Since the inception of the study of international trade, the most common modeling framework has been that of perfect competition and of general equilibrium. While the recent development of what has been called the 'new trade theory' has led to the analysis of trade issues in models involving imperfect competition, including monopolistic competition and oligopolistic competition, the perfectly competitive equilibrium framework continues to be a dominant force in international trade theory.

The purpose of this chapter is to outline the main features of the perfectly competitive equilibrium framework as it has been applied in international trade. Such a survey cannot do justice to competitive equilibrium in international trade, since it constitutes the primary methodology in almost all areas of the subject. To fully survey the topic would involve virtually surveying all of the areas of international trade. Such a task is beyond the brief for this chapter and will clearly not be attempted.

Even within the brief for the chapter, I will not attempt to provide a comprehensive review of the literature. Rather than provide many references to the literature, I will be selective and attempt to provide the essential content of what I see as the main aspects of general competitive equilibrium analysis within international trade.

The first task of the chapter is to provide an overview of the concept of general competitive equilibrium. This task begins with an introduction to perfect competition, whereby agents are price takers and prices are determined to clear markets, and then to general equilibrium, whereby markets are connected for the whole economy under consideration. General equilibrium has not only been important for a whole range of economic analyses, but especially so for the study of international trade. Brief consideration is given to the existence and stability of equilibrium, topics that have occupied the minds of many general equilibrium theorists but which, although relevant, have not been central to international economics. To complete this topic, the two fundamental theorems of welfare economics, establishing the important connection between competitive equilibrium and Pareto optimality, are also discussed.

The second main task is to specialize the general competitive framework to the 'standard' model used in the international trade literature. Of course, there are many versions of competitive models in international trade so there is no one standard model. Rather, I present a model that provides the essence of such models. This model has the feature that while final products are traded internationally, factors of production are not.

Having constructed this model, the next section deals with the fundamental relationships that exist. These include the famous Stolper–Samuelson theorem on the relationship between product and factor prices, the Rybczynski theorem on the relationship between output levels and factor endowments, and the factor price equalization theorem on the relationship between factor endowments and factor prices. Not only are these relationships of direct interest, but they are central to many analyses of issues in international trade.

One of the main topics dealt with in this chapter concerns the use of the generic model to explain various theories of international trade. Such theories focus on particular differences between countries as the cause of international trade. While there are many such theories and variations, I focus on the main theories. These include the Ricardian theory, which is based upon international productivity differences as the basis for trade. The traditional specification in terms of just two goods and two countries is supplemented by the extension to a continuum of goods as undertaken by Dornbusch, Fischer and Samuelson. The second main theory is the Hecksher-Ohlin-Samuelson formulation of a model in which countries are identical except for their factor endowments, leading to the factor endowments theory of trade. Again, the traditional specification is followed by an extension to the case of a continuum of goods.

The final section of the chapter offers some concluding comments.

2   Competitive equilibrium framework

2.1   Perfect competition

Perfect competition is an abstraction of reality in which individual firms and consumers are sufficiently small to be unable to influence the price of any good through their actions. They are price-takers in the sense that they assume (correctly) that the price is exogenously given and they make production and consumption decisions given prices. Of course, this is a limiting argument. With finite numbers of firms and consumers, each may have a tiny effect upon aggregate supply and demand and, hence, a tiny effect upon prices. As the numbers of firms and consumers approach infinity, any such effects approach zero and so can be ignored.

Under the price-taking assumption firms and consumers choose their outputs and demands for a good. This behaviour yields (aggregate) supply and demand functions, which describe the aggregate quantities supplied by all firms and demanded by all consumers for the good as price varies parametrically. The perfectly competitive equilibrium is established at a price at which the aggregate quantities supplied and demanded are equal. This price is an equilibrium price since there is no market pressure for it to change; at this price buyers are willing to consume exactly the same amount that producers are willing to supply.

This brief description of perfect competition concerned the market for a single good, which is an example of a partial equilibrium analysis. It is termed partial, since it ignores the rest of the economy and so implicitly assumes away any effects changes in the market for this good may have upon the prices for other goods or incomes and, further, assumes away any feedback (general equilibrium) effects that such changes might have on the market for the good under consideration. While such partial models are useful, it is normally the case that these general equilibrium feedback effects are important and warrant being taken into account.

Accordingly, if the context is now extended to include many commodities (used as a general terminology for goods, factors of production, etc.), there are many prices and markets. A general competitive equilibrium then occurs if the prices of every commodity are at levels such that every market is in equilibrium in the sense that the quantities supplied and demanded of every commodity are equal.

Issues of existence, uniqueness and stability of equilibrium arise. The former issue relates to the possibility that there may be no price for which the quantities supplied and demanded are equal. The literature on general competitive equilibrium comprises many studies providing conditions under which an equilibrium exists. The second issue concerns the possibility that there exist more than one equilibrium price or, potentially, an infinity of equilibrium prices. If there are several discretely separated equilibrium price vectors, then the question of which equilibrium will be observed is important. The third issue arises from the idea that there is some mechanism for prices to change if they do not constitute an equilibrium, and that such changes may or may not lead the economy to the (or an) equilibrium. Again, much effort has been spent modeling dynamic adjustment out of equilibria and determining conditions under which convergence of prices to equilibrium is guaranteed. If these market forces are such that an out of equilibrium price converges to the equilibrium price, the adjustment mechanism is said to be stable.

These are issues of economic theory. The international trade literature has been largely content to skirt around such issues, recognizing their importance but not treating them as fundamental issues to be analyzed at the expense of questions of concern in international trade. There are some exceptions. There are some papers that have dealt with these issues in models in which trade between countries provides special structure.

2.2 General equilibrium

The basic idea of general equilibrium theory is now briefly discussed. The aim is not to do justice to the voluminous literature based largely on Debreu's (1959) seminal book, the *Theory of Value*. Nor will I be very rigorous in the exposition. Rather, the aim is to present enough to place the competitive theory of trade in context.

Suppose there exist firms with production sets Y^j ($j \in J$) defined over the set of commodities, where J is the set of firms. By convention, a production point $y^j \in Y^j$ represents the vector of net outputs; if the kth element has the sign $y^j_k > 0$ then commodity k is an output (a good), while if $y^j_k < 0$ then commodity k is an input. This same convention applies to other quantity vectors defined below. The firms take the price system defined as a price vector $p \in P$ (the unit simplex, meaning that prices are non-negative and sum to unity) as given and choose a production $y^j \in Y^j$ to maximize revenue. This yields the vector of supply functions for firm j as

$$y^j(p) = \arg\max_y \left\{ p'y : y \in Y^j \right\} \tag{1}$$

and the profit function

$$\pi^j(p) = \max_y \left\{ p'y : y \in Y^j \right\}. \tag{2}$$

The assumption of constant returns to scale ensures that profits are zero.[1] The aggregate supply function is $y(p) \equiv \sum_{j \in J} y^j(p)$.

Consumers have consumption or demand sets D^i ($i \in I$) defined over the set of commodities and preferences described by utility functions $u^i(d^i)$, where I is the set of consumers. They have initial endowments of commodities given by v^i. Aggregate endowments are $v \equiv \sum_{i \in I} v^i$. Consumers choose consumptions (demands) $d^i \in D^i$ to maximize utility subject to being in the consumption set and subject to a budget constraint. This yields the demand functions

$$d^i(p) = \arg\max_d \left\{ u^i(d) : p'(d - v^i) = 0, \, d \in D^i \right\} \tag{3}$$

and the indirect utility function

$$U^i(p) = \max_d \left\{ u^i(d) : p'(d - v^i) = 0, \, d \in D^i \right\}, \tag{4}$$

where the dependence on initial endowments has been subsumed. The aggregate demand function is $d(p) \equiv \sum_{i \in I} d^i(p)$.

Market equilibrium requires that the price system $p \in P$ be such that there is no excess demand for any commodity. Excess demand for the economy is defined as $z \equiv d - y - v$, which is aggregate demand minus aggregate supply minus aggregate initial endowments. Thus the excess demand function is $z(p) \equiv d(p) - y(p) - v$. Market equilibrium requires

$$z(p) \leq 0, \quad p'z(p) = 0. \tag{5}$$

This condition means that there can be no excess demand for any good. It also means (using the second part and the non-negativity of prices) that a strict excess supply for some good k ($z_k(p) < 0$) is consistent with market equilibrium only if the price of good k is zero ($p_k = 0$). If a good k has a positive price, then this market equilibrium condition requires the market for good k to clear; that is, if $p_k > 0$ then $z_k(p) = 0$ is required.[2]

In summary, a competitive equilibrium comprises productions $y^j \in Y^j$ that maximize revenue, demands $d^i \in D^i$ that maximize utility subject to the budget constraint and a price system $p \in P$ such that markets are in equilibrium. At the equilibrium prices, no consumer wishes to change her consumption/demand choice and no producer wishes to change his production choice. Moreover, these choices are consistent with market equilibrium so there are no market pressures for prices to change. The economy is in general competitive equilibrium.

In contrast with general equilibrium, partial-equilibrium analyses consider only parts of the economy and assume that some endogenous variables are constant. For example, one could undertake a partial-equilibrium analysis of a particular good 1. In that case, only the first component of the market equilibrium condition (5) would be relevant, namely $z_1(p_1, p_2, ..., p_N) \leq 0$, $p_1' z(p_1, p_2, ..., p_N) = 0$. The analyst ignores the markets for all other goods and assumes that their prices $(p_2, ..., p_N)$ are exogenously given. The effects of any change in the market for good 1 upon the prices of other goods and the consequent feedback effects on the demand or supply of good 1 are ignored. As a second, and important, example one could undertake analysis of the production sector alone (as is often done in the trade literature as discussed further below). In this case, the focus is on the aggregate supply functions, $y(p)$, taking the product price vector as exogenously given. The analyst may be interested in how the output vector responds to changes in prices or to shifts in the technologies and in doing so ignores the possibility that the outcomes are inconsistent with a full general equilibrium or that they might alter prices endogenously and have feedback effects. Similarly, one might focus solely on households and the aggregate demand functions, $d(p)$, ignoring general equilibrium and feedback consequences. Trade theory is replete with instances of partial-equilibrium analyses. They may be useful in their own right, when the general equilibrium feedback effects are reasonably small, but are typically stepping stones towards a full general equilibrium analysis. Instances illustrating this point will become evident further below.

Before leaving this general review of general competitive equilibrium, it is important to point out some properties of the price system and the excess demand functions. The first property of special note is that the demand functions, supply functions and, hence, the demand supply functions are homogeneous of degree zero in prices. For example, a doubling of all prices would not change a household's consumption choice, nor would it alter a producers choice of inputs and outputs; only price ratios matter. It is for this reason that some normalization of the price vector is needed. In the above model specification, the price vector was assumed to be on the unit simplex requiring prices to be non-negative and to sum to unity. This is only one of many possible choices of constraint on prices. In many applications of general competitive equilibrium, including international trade theory, one good is singled out to be the numeraire with its price set to unity. Then the prices of the other goods can be interpreted as the amount of the numeraire that a unit of the good in question is worth on the market. This choice requires assurance that the numeraire good will never be of zero value, of course.

The second important property of note is that the excess demand functions obey what is called Walras's Law. This means that if $N-1$ markets are in equilibrium, then market N must also be in equilibrium, where N is the number of commodities (markets). This is evident from the market equilibrium condition (5) above, the second part of which may be written as $\sum_{k=1}^{N-1} p_k z_k(p) + p_N z_N(p) = 0$. If the first $N-1$ markets are in equilibrium then the summation on the left hand side is zero, meaning that the last term must also be zero and hence the market for good N is in equilibrium. The condition $p'z(p) = 0$ for all p arises because individual producers' choices imply that $p'y^j(p) = 0$ and individual household choices imply that $p'[d^i(p) - v^i] = 0$ and, hence, in aggregate $p'z(p) = 0$.

These two properties are, of course, related. Because of Walras's Law only $N-1$ market equilibrium conditions need to be solved (once they are the last one automatically holds). Because of price homogeneity only $N-1$ prices can be determined (once they are the last price is automatically determined). Thus, while the model above has N market equilibrium conditions to solve for N prices it can be expressed in a smaller dimension. That is, eliminating one market equilibrium condition and normalizing the price system the model reduces to one requiring $N-1$ market equilibrium conditions to be solved for $N-1$ normalized prices. Once solved, the Nth price is determined from the normalization rule and the Nth market automatically clears.

2.3 Fundamental welfare theorems for competitive equilibrium

There are two fundamental theorems of welfare economics that play an important role in international trade theory, as well as in virtually every area of economics.

The first fundamental theorem informally states that any competitive equilibrium is Pareto efficient. This means that it is not possible to alter the allocation of resources to make any one consumer better off without necessarily making some other consumer worse off in terms of welfare. If this were not the case, then a re-allocation of resources would allow someone to gain in welfare without anyone else suffering a loss of welfare, which is called a Pareto improvement. If we consider all possible allocations of resources and determine the resulting utility levels for every consumer then we can construct a utility possibilities set in utility space. The upper boundary of this set is called the utility possibilities frontier – the set of Pareto efficient points. The first fundamental welfare theorem states that a competitive equilibrium puts the economy on this frontier.

The first fundamental theorem of welfare economics is an important concept because it highlights the 'apolitical' benefit of a competitive equilibrium – Pareto efficiency. Note, however, that Pareto optimality implies nothing about the distributive properties of equilibrium that may be deemed more important by society than efficiency. For example, a competitive equilibrium may be characterized by extreme inequality of income or welfare (or complete equality) even though it is Pareto efficient. If society considers the distributive characteristics of a particular equilibrium undesirable, redistributive economic policy can be employed to access alternative equilibria along the utility possibilities frontier (necessarily implying that some consumers gain at the expense of others), or even inside the frontier, that have more socially desirable distributive properties. The second fundamental theorem of welfare economics addresses the issue of distribution directly. It states that any resource allocation that is Pareto efficient can be obtained as a competitive equilibrium by a suitable reallocation of initial endowments amongst consumers, via lump sum transfers for example.

In the context of international trade it is readily established via the first fundamental theorem of welfare economics that free international trade with competitive markets yields an equilibrium that is Pareto optimal; starting from such an equilibrium no consumer can be made better off without some other consumer being made worse off in terms of welfare. Thus, free trade is efficient (though it may yield distributional outcomes that are not socially desirable as explained above). Within the context of international trade the second welfare theorem means that a different Pareto optimal outcome (perhaps one more socially desirable) could be achieved through a reallocation of endowments, provided that this can actually be done and through means that do not create distortions (such as taxes that discourage effort) in the process.

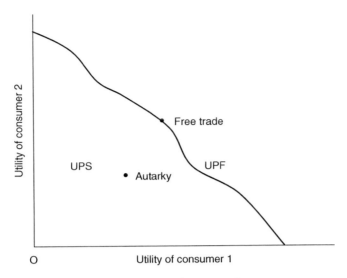

Figure 3.1   Utility possibilities frontier with two consumers.

The utility possibilities frontier for the case where there are two consumers (households) is illustrated in figure 3.1. The frontier is downward-sloping, reflecting the requirement that consumer 1's utility can only increase if that of consumer 2 falls. The region inside and including the frontier is often referred to as the utility possibilities set. In the international trade context, free trade is Pareto optimal or efficient and so yields a point on the frontier. This is depicted in the figure with the two consumers being the only households in the respective countries. Under autarky (no trade), the consumers and producers in the two countries face different price ratios and this results in a utility point that is Pareto inefficient from the world point of view, and hence inside the utility possibilities set, as also depicted in figure 3.1.[3]

2.4   Geometric illustration of general equilibrium in international trade

Before developing the standard international trade model, it is expositionally useful to present the essential ideas of competitive equilibrium in a simple model of trade. To this end, I consider trade in two commodities between two countries that have exogenously given endowments of the commodities (no production) and a single (representative) consumer in each country. Equilibrium in such a world can be geometrically expressed in terms of the famous Edgeworth-Bowley box diagram.

Figure 3.2 depicts a rectangular box whose dimensions reflect the world endowments of the two products. Point *A* is the allocation of the world endowments between the two countries, Home and Foreign. Home's endowments are

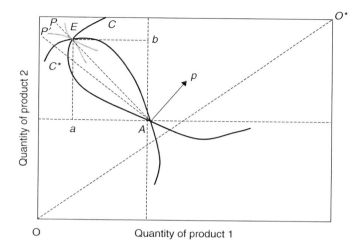

Figure 3.2   Competitive equilibrium with international trade.

shown with point O as the origin while Foreign's have point O^* as the origin, so Home has endowment vector OA while Foreign has endowment vector O^*A. Consumption vectors can be similarly represented, with world endowments OO^* being allocated between the two countries via a competitive equilibrium.

The competitive equilibrium world price vector, p, yields the budget constraint line passing through points A, E and P; for Home it is measured relative to origin O, while Foreign's is relative to origin O^*. At point E, each consumer is maximizing utility subject to being on the budget constraint (the highest indifference curves attainable for the two countries being depicted tangent to the budget constraints). Point E constitutes an equilibrium consumption allocation since, at the price vector p, each consumer is solving her constrained utility maximization problem and the products markets both clear (world consumptions equal world endowments).

At this equilibrium, Home imports Ab units of product 2 and exports Aa units of product 1 with Foreign doing the reverse. There is a balance of trade since the value of imports for each country is matched by the value of exports at the equilibrium price vector, p. The trade vector is indicated by AE.

If the world price vector is varied, the price line rotates through the endowment point, A, and the countries' consumption choices trace out the consumption paths labelled C and C^*. Treating A as the origin for these curves means that they become paths of trade offers (import and export quantities) and are called 'offer curves' in the international trade literature.

The equilibrium point E is stable under an assumed price adjustment mechanism. If the price of product 2 was higher than at E then the price line would be flatter (depicted by AP') and there would be an excess world supply of product 2 and a world excess demand for product 1. This induces, by assumption, a reduction in the price of product 2 – a process that continues until point E is reached. Geometrically, the equilibrium is stable because of the way the curves C and C^* intersect. It is easy to construct examples where the curves cross three times (say) so there are multiple equilibria, two of which are unstable.

It is evident from figure 3.2 that the consumers in the two countries gain from free trade, since their free trade indifference curves are higher than their autarky indifference curves (not shown) passing through point A. These utility outcomes under free trade and autarky have been already depicted in the utility possibilities diagram, figure 3.1.

3   The standard competitive trade model

The standard model that has served as the vehicle for the analysis of international trade issues in the context of perfectly competitive behaviour comprises countries that have fixed factor endowments and trade only final goods. Within the context of the general competitive equilibrium model described briefly above, this is a very special case. Nevertheless, it has been, and worked well as, the framework for much of the analyses of international trade issues undertaken over at least the last half-century.

In the following, this model is formulated within a multi-nation, multi-factor and multi-product framework. The literature has mostly concerned itself with smaller dimensional versions of the model, which are also given attention during the exposition. The literature has also dealt with many extensions and assumption relaxations, such as the consideration of intermediate inputs, variable factor supplies and international flows of labour and capital. In the interests of brevity, these extensions are given only cursory treatment here.

In the following, I consider in turn the production and household sectors in a partial equilibrium context, taking prices of goods and income as given. Then these are combined through the determination of income and this constitutes a model of a small open economy, which also takes world prices as given. Allowing for such economies to be large enough to influence world prices, the general equilibrium model for the world economy is then constructed by requiring world market equilibrium conditions for goods to determine world prices. Finally, I provide brief consideration on introducing governments.

3.1   Production

The production sector of a typical country produces a vector of net outputs of final goods given by $y = (y_1, y_2, ..., y_M)$ using a fixed endowment vector $v = (v_1, v_2, ..., v_N)$ of factors of production, constrained by net outputs being in the production possibilities set, $y \in Y(v)$. Constant returns to scale are assumed.

As is well known from the seminal work by Debreu (1959), the competitive equilibrium outputs may be obtained as the solution to the revenue maximization problem

$$y(p,v) = \arg\max_{y} \{p'y : y \in Y(v)\}. \tag{6}$$

The solution to this problem also yields the revenue function

$$R(p,v) = \max_{y} \{p'y : y \in Y(v)\}. \tag{7}$$

This has often been dubbed the gross national product or gross domestic product function, since it is the value of all goods and services produced in the economy.

In the competitive equilibrium framework, this revenue function summarizes all that is relevant about the production sector. Duality theory establishes a one-to-one relationship between the revenue function and the production possibilities set.[4] That is, under certain conditions on the production possibilities set, duality theory establishes the implied conditions on the revenue function and, moreover, shows that the production possibilities set can be reconstructed from knowledge of the revenue function alone. In addition, any function satisfying the properties of a valid revenue function has an implied production possibilities set that can be obtained. This result is of great theoretical and practical importance, since it means that any theoretical or empirical analysis can begin by specifying a valid revenue function; the production possibilities set need not be specified, but can be obtained in principle if needed.

In the theoretical literature on international trade some authors use the primal approach that is based on production functions and first order conditions for cost minimization or profit maximization, while others use the dual approach that is based on cost or profit functions, which have cost or profit optimization embodied. Strategically, it is best to use whichever approach is most directly appropriate for the task at hand. Dixit and Norman (1980) and Woodland (1982) provide early expositions of the dual approach, which has become standard.

The revenue function also has interesting properties (including homogeneity of degree one in prices and in endowments, convexity in prices and concavity in endowments) that can be exploited in comparative statics and other analyses. Of particular interest is the result that, under suitable differentiability,

$$y(p,v) = \partial R(p,v)/\partial p,$$
$$w(p,v) = \partial R(p,v)/\partial v, \tag{8}$$

where $w(p,v)$ is the factor price function, showing how factor prices depend upon commodity prices and factor endowments. This result shows that the output supply and factor price functions ($y(p,v)$ and $w(p,v)$) can be easily obtained from the revenue function by differentiation with respect to output prices and factor endowments respectively. The output supply functions are homogeneous of degree zero in prices and homogeneous of degree one in endowments, while the factor price functions are homogeneous of degree one in prices and homogeneous of degree zero in endowments.

Moreover, if the revenue function is twice differentiable, then the comparative statics effects of changes in product prices and factor endowments upon product outputs and factor prices can be readily obtained from the matrix of second derivatives. That is, under twice differentiability the comparative statics results are given by the elements of the symmetric matrix

$$
\begin{bmatrix} \partial y(p,v)/\partial p' & \partial y(p,v)/\partial v' \\ \partial w(p,v)/\partial p' & \partial w(p,v)/\partial v' \end{bmatrix} = \begin{bmatrix} \partial^2 R(p,v)/\partial p \partial p' & \partial^2 R(p,v)/\partial p \partial v' \\ \partial^2 R(p,v)/\partial v \partial p' & \partial^2 R(p,v)/\partial v \partial v' \end{bmatrix}. \tag{9}
$$

This partitioned matrix summarizes all of the comparative statics effects in the production sector. The blocks in the first row show the effects upon production levels of changes in product prices (left block) and of factor endowments (right block), while the blocks in the second row show the effects upon factor prices of changes in product prices (left block) and of changes in factor endowments (right block). Interestingly, the symmetry property means that $\partial w(p,v)/\partial p' = [\partial y(p,v)/\partial v']'$, meaning that these two effects are equal as first pointed out by Samuelson (1953–54). That is, $\partial w_i(p,v)/\partial p_j = \partial y_j(p,v)/\partial v_i$ – the production sector equilibrium effect of a unit increase in the price of product j upon the price of factor i is numerically precisely the same as the effect of a unit increase in the endowment of factor i upon the output of product j.[5] This result arises from the full competitive equilibrium for the production sector and highlights the importance of interactions involved in competitive equilibrium.

Convexity and homogeneity of the revenue function in prices implies that the matrix of second derivatives of R with respect to prices $\partial^2 R(p,v)/\partial p \partial p'$ is positive semidefinite such that $p'\partial^2 R(p,v)/\partial p \partial p' \equiv 0$. Similarly, concavity and homogeneity of the revenue function in endowments implies that the matrix of second derivatives of R with respect to endowments $\partial^2 R(p,v)/\partial v \partial v'$ is negative semidefinite such that $v'\partial^2 R(p,v)/\partial v \partial v' \equiv 0$. Finally, the homogeneity properties imply that $p'\partial^2 R(p,v)/\partial p \partial v' \equiv 0$ and $v'\partial^2 R(p,v)/\partial v \partial p' \equiv 0$.

In terms of the supply and factor price response functions, these properties are repeated as follows. Convexity and homogeneity of the revenue function in prices implies that the matrix $\partial y(p,v)/\partial p'$ is positive semidefinite such that $p'\partial y(p,v)/\partial p' \equiv 0$. Similarly, concavity and homogeneity of the revenue function in endowments implies that the matrix $\partial w(p,v)/\partial v'$ is negative semidefinite such that $v'\partial w(p,v)/\partial v' \equiv 0$. Finally, the homogeneity properties imply that $p'\partial y(p,v)/\partial v' \equiv 0$ and $v'\partial w(p,v)/\partial p' \equiv 0$. These constitute the complete set of comparative statics results that are implied by the general model (under differentiability). Any more precise results require more precise structure being

imposed on the model; however, such results will be consistent with, and special case, of the general results presented here. Details of the above matrices for
very general models were developed by Diewert and Woodland (1977), Jones
and Scheinkman (1977) and Chang (1979).

The above formulation is quite general in that the technology can involve
intermediate inputs and joint outputs. If a researcher wishes to be very general, the use of the revenue function and its properties is all that is needed.
On the other hand, researchers may wish to have more specific model formulations, which involve special cases of the technology. There are two approaches
to obtaining special cases. First, additional structure may be imposed on the
revenue function such as some separability or other general functional restrictions or a specific functional form. Second, and more commonly, one can begin
with specific assumptions about technologies for individual goods (specify $Y(v)$
in detail) and then construct the revenue function by explicitly maximizing
revenue (solving (7) above). This second approach is now used to produce a
commonly used special case.

If attention is restricted to final goods (without intermediate inputs or joint
outputs), we can provide a disaggregated set of equations describing equilibrium in the production sector. To this end, assume that good j can be produced
with production function $y_j = f_j(x_j)$, where x_j is the vector of non-negative factor
inputs used by industry j. Equilibrium in the production sector then requires
that each industry j chooses the inputs of factors and output to maximize profits and that the prices of the factors of production are determined to satisfy
factor market equilibrium. These requirements may be conveniently expressed
in terms of the industry unit cost functions $c_j(p) \equiv \min_{x_j}\{w'x_j : f_j(x_j) \geq 1,\ x_j \geq 0\}$,
which have the property (Shephard's Lemma) that the optimal input vector per
unit of output is given by $a^j(w) = \partial c_j(w)/\partial w$.

Using the unit cost function and Shephard's Lemma, the production sector
equilibrium is described by

$$c_j(w) - p_j \geq 0 \leq y_j, \quad j \in J \tag{10}$$

$$\sum_{j \in J} a^j(w)y_j - v \leq 0 \leq w \tag{11}$$

or, more compactly, by

$$C(w) - p \geq 0 \leq y \tag{12}$$

$$A(w)y - v \leq 0 \leq w, \tag{13}$$

where $C(w) = A(w)'w$ is a vector of the unit cost functions, $c_j(p)$, $A(w)$ is a matrix
of input output coefficients $a_{ij} = \partial c_j(w)/\partial w_i$ and the double inequalities denote
complementary slackness conditions.[6] The first expression (10) provides the
profit maximization condition for each industry j. If product j is produced, then

the requirement is that there are zero profits earned, meaning that unit cost equals price, $c_j(w) = p_j$; otherwise a positive profit would induce entry into the industry. The second expression (11) provides the market equilibrium condition for factors. If factor i is positively priced, then the requirement is that the market for this factor clears, meaning that demand equals supply, $\sum_{j \in J} a_{ij}(w)y_j - v_i$.

This formulation makes clear that not all products need be produced in equilibrium; indeed, $c_j(w) > p_j$ implies that $y_j = 0$. In a similar vein, but less relevant, the model allows for some factors to be free; if $\sum_{j \in J} a_{ij}(w)y_j < v_i$ then $w_i = 0$. On the other hand, as stated above, if good j is produced then zero profits must ensue ($y_j > 0$ implies $c_j(w) = p_j$), while the factor market for factor of production i must clear if its price is positive ($w_i = 0$ implies $\sum_{j \in J} a_{ij}(w)y_j = v_i$).

As a final comment on the production sector model, it is noted that the dimensionality of the model is important. If there are equal numbers of goods and factors then the profit maximization conditions (10) are sufficient in number to fully determine factor prices without regard to factor endowments (ignoring the possibility of multiple solutions, which are discussed later). Once factor prices are so determined, the input–output coefficients are determined and so the factor market equilibrium conditions (11) completely determine the output levels. This is the standard case considered in the literature. However, if the number of goods exceed the number of factors then factor prices are 'over-determined' by (10) if all goods are produced, while (11) has more unknown output levels than equations. The upshot is that there is indeterminacy regarding output levels (and the production pattern). It can be shown that the number of goods produced need be only as many as the number of fully used factors in equilibrium. Finally, if there are more factors than goods, factor prices are not fully determined by the profit maximization conditions and the system of conditions (10) and (11) have to be solved together to obtain the equilibrium outputs and factor prices.

3.2　Consumption

The standard, but not particularly appealing, assumption about the household sector is that it comprises a single household (person). This consumer has a direct utility function $u(d)$ expressed in terms of the consumption vector, d. The consumer faces prices p and obtains income $r = R(p, v)$ from the production sector. The consumer obtains the optimal consumption vector as a solution to the constrained utility maximization problem

$$d(p, r) = \arg\max_d \{u(d) : p'd = r\}. \tag{14}$$

The solution to this problem also yields the indirect utility function

$$U(p, r) = \max_d \{u(d) : p'd = r\}. \tag{15}$$

Again, the indirect utility function summarizes all relevant information and can be used for analyses.[7] The consumption vector can be obtained from the indirect utility function via Roy's Identity (under suitable differentiability) as

$$d(p,r) = -\frac{\partial U(p,r)/\partial p}{\partial U(p,r)/\partial r}. \tag{16}$$

If preferences are homothetic, as is sometimes assumed (somewhat against empirical evidence), then the indirect utility function takes the form $U(p,r) = r/e(p)$ in which the unit expenditure function $e(p)$ is interpreted as the consumer price index. In this case, the demand functions take the simplified form

$$d(p,r) = r\gamma(p), \tag{17}$$

where $\gamma(p)$ is the vector of demands per unit of income and the budget share vector (proportion of income spent on each good) is $s(p)$, which depends only on price ratios (homogeneous of degree zero in prices). That is, the budget shares are $s_j(p) \equiv p_j d_j/r = p_j \gamma_j(p)$, $j \in J$; in addition, the elasticities of demand with respect to income are all unity.

If there are many consumers, the above modelling needs amendment. First, the income from the production sector needs to be allocated to H households according to some factor ownership rule. Second, consumption needs to be aggregated over households.[8]

3.3 Trade

In a small open economy that faces a given world price vector, p, and has an endowment vector, v, the net import vector is given by

$$m(p,v) = d(p,R(p,v)) - y(p,v), \tag{18}$$

which is the difference between the national consumption and production vectors. The early literature devoted much attention to the properties of the net import function.

This completes the model formulation for a small open economy. Given world prices and factor endowments, the production consumption and net import vectors are determined as $y(p,v)$, $d(p,R(p,v))$ and $m(p,v)$. The factor price vector is then given by $w(p,v)$. These equilibrium solutions for output levels, consumption levels, net imports and factor prices clearly depend upon the exogenously given world prices and factor endowments. These solutions will generally change if the exogenous variables change. Importantly, these solutions also depend upon the nature of the technology (underlying the revenue or cost functions) and the nature of consumer preferences (underlying the utility, indirect utility or expenditure functions). Finally, it is important to remember that the solutions depend upon our assumption of perfectly competitive behaviour on the part of all participants.

Variations of the model and its specification are, or course, possible. First, if the model is formulated in terms of the expenditure function on the household side, then the Hicksian demand system is $\tilde{d}(p,u) = \partial E(p,u)/\partial p$ and the compensated (Hicksian) net import functions are $\tilde{m}(p,u,v) = \tilde{d}(p,u) - y(p,v)$. The model is completed by including the budget constraint $E(p,u) = R(p,v)$, which serves to determine the level of utility, u. This specification is particularly useful in welfare analyses when the main variable of interest is the level of utility.[9] Specifically, this specification of the model may be written as

$$\tilde{m}(p,u,v) = \tilde{d}(p,u) - y(p,v) \tag{19}$$

$$E(p,u) = R(p,v). \tag{20}$$

Second, the model is easily extended to allow for non-traded goods in addition to the factor endowments, which are assumed to be non-traded internationally. This is achieved by partitioning vectors into traded and non-traded components (if the partition is predetermined) and adding the market equilibrium condition for non-traded goods, $m^n(p^n, p^t, v) = 0$, which determines the price vector for non-traded goods, p^n.[10]

Third, the production sector specification of the model may be altered to yield what has been referred to in the literature as the 'specific factors model', due initially to Viner. In this specification, there is one factor of production that is mobile between production sectors and other factors that are each specific to a particular sector. This restricted factor mobility leads to different results concerning the effects of product prices and endowments upon outputs and factor prices than obtained when all factors are mobile. The specific factors model has been treated as a short run version of the mobile factors model discussed above, as for example by Neary (1978). Eaton (1987) develops a dynamic specific factors model.

3.4   Markets and equilibrium

The model described above refers to a single country. Now assume that there are K such countries distinguished by the superscript k. Thus, country $k \in K$ has revenue function $R^k(p,v^k)$, indirect utility function $U^k(p,r^k)$ and budget constraint $r^k = R^k(p,v^k)$. The indirect trade utility function is obtained by combining these as $\tilde{U}^k(p,v^k) = U^k(p,R^k(p,v^k))$. Net import vectors are given by $m^k(p,v^k) = d^k(p,R^k(p,v^k)) - y^k(p,v^k)$ as the difference between the national consumption and production vectors.

Markets comprise domestic markets for factors of production and international markets for final goods in the standard trade model. Since the former markets are automatically in equilibrium in our model specification, only international market equilibrium conditions need be specified here. These are

$$\sum_{k \in K} m^k(p,v^k) = 0. \tag{21}$$

These market equilibrium conditions determine world prices, given by vector p, as functions of the international distribution of the endowments of factors of production. Thus, the world price vector may be expressed as $p = P(v^1, ..., v^K)$. Other important determinants, subsumed in the notation, are the technologies and preferences of the various countries and, of course, the assumption of perfectly competitive behaviour. Thus, world prices summarize all these primitive aspects of countries. Variations in preferences, technologies or endowments will lead to variation in the equilibrium solutions for world prices and, hence, supplies, demands, factor prices and consumers' welfare in every country. In short, we have a general equilibrium.

Once the world price vector $p = P(v^1, ..., v^K)$ has been determined, all national variables can then be obtained. These include the national output vectors $y^k(p, v^k)$, consumption vectors $d^k(p, R^k(p, v^k))$, net import vectors $m^k(p, v^k)$, factor price vectors $w^k(p, v^k)$ and utility levels $U^k(p, R^k(p, v^k))$.

In short, this describes the competitive equilibrium for the world economy. World prices are determined to ensure world market equilibrium in final goods trade. In each country, consumers choose consumption vectors to maximize their utility functions subject to their budget constraints taking prices and incomes as given, producers choose input and output quantities to maximize profits taking prices as given, and factor prices are determined to ensure that all national factor markets are in equilibrium.

3.5 Government

In the above model of world trade, governments do not exist. In an extension, the governments of each country could be imposing taxes on consumption, production and trade to raise revenue to fund the purchase of factors and goods to produce a public good or to undertake income redistribution.

For example, suppose that governments only impose taxes and/or subsidies on international trade. If country k imposes a vector of specific trade taxes, t^k, on net imports then the domestic price vector becomes $p^k = p + t^k$. It is now this domestic price vector that enters the expenditure and revenue functions, since this is the price vector that is faced by consumers and producers.

It is often assumed in the literature that tariff revenue $t^{k'}m^k$ is distributed to the consumer in a lump sum manner, in which case consumer income is $I^k = R^k(p^k, v^k) + t^{k'}m$. Thus, net imports are implicitly determined from $m^k = d^k(p^k, R^k(p^k, v^k) + t^{k'}m^k) - y^k(p^k, v^k)$ as a 'reduced form' function $m^k = M^k(p^k, t^k, v^k)$.

Alternatively, it may be (more realistically) assumed that the tariff revenue is used to fund the production of a public good, as in Diewert, Turunen-Red and Woodland (1989) and Abe (1992), who develops the properties of the revenue function with public good production, for example. Tariff revenue may be supplemented by production or consumption taxes. Accordingly, assuming that there are no lump sum transfers, an increase in tariff revenue would then require lower domestic tax revenue or greater production of the public good to ensure satisfaction of the government budget constraint. In either case, there are now two budget constraints to be satisfied: the household and the government budget constraints.

4   Fundamental relationships

In this section the relationships between product prices and factor endowments on the one hand and outputs and factor prices on the other are developed and discussed in the context of the final goods model. For a small open economy product prices are given exogenously as world prices determined in world markets, which the small open economy is, by assumption, too small to influence. Thus, I focus on parametric changes in product prices, ignoring the fact that they are endogenous in a broader setting. I will come back to this later.

In the following, the first four topics deal with the production sector, which tends to get much greater treatment than the consumption sector in the international trade literature. The final topic combines the production and consumption sectors and concerns the properties of the net import functions. In each of these topics, the relationships that are discussed arise from the competitive equilibrium for the production sector and involve the connections between markets for factors and of profit maximization by firms.

The approach is to begin with general results and then move on to the traditional two-factor, two product model specification. Comparative statics results for higher dimensional models of the production sector have been developed by various authors, thereby extending the generality of some of the basic results discussed below. These extensions include work by Ethier (1974), Diewert and Woodland (1977), Jones and Scheinkman (1977) and Chang (1979). Ethier (1982) provides a very illuminating approach to some of the relationships discussed using the mean value theorem to establish inequalities interpreted as correlations.

4.1   Endowments and factor prices

At a general level, the relationship between factor prices and endowments can be expressed as an inequality that rises from the property that $G(p,v)$ is the minimum factor income subject to the factor price being in the factor price set (Woodland, 1977; Woodland, 2010). Since factor prices minimize factor income, it follows that $(w^1 - w^0)'(v^1 - v^0) \leq 0$, where w^i is the factor vector when the endowment vector is v^i and v^0 is the initial endowment vector. This establishes a negative correlation between endowment and factor price changes; the two change vectors form an obtuse or right angle. It implies that an increase in the endowment of factor j alone will decrease, or leave unchanged, the price of factor j. This result occurs since the above inequality may then be expressed as $\Delta w_j \Delta v_j \leq 0$, implying that $\Delta w_j \leq 0$ if $\Delta v_j > 0$. This is the generalized law of supply.

Assuming differentiability, the dependence of factor prices upon endowments is also expressed via the property of the revenue function given by $w(p,v) = \partial R(p,v)/\partial v$ and by the comparative static property that $\partial w(p,v)/\partial v'$ is negative semidefinite such that $v'\partial w(p,v)/\partial v' \equiv 0$. In the following, the focus is on the standard trade model, which has more structure.

If product prices are given along with factor endowments, the prices of factors and the outputs of goods are determined by conditions (10)–(11). Let it be assumed that the solution for these endogenous variables is unique. In general, not all goods need to be produced (there is specialization in production) and not all factors need to be positively priced. I ignore the latter possibility in what follows by assuming that all factors are positively priced (fully used). However, allowance is made for specialization in production and J^+ denotes the (endogenous) set of goods that are produced.

Let it be supposed that the number of produced goods is at least as great as the number of (fully used) factors of production so that the production sector equilibrium conditions are

$$c_j(w) - p_j = 0 < y_j, \quad j \in J^+ \tag{22}$$

$$c_j(w) - p_j > 0 = y_j, \quad j \notin J^+ \tag{23}$$

$$\sum_{j \in J^+} a^j(w)y_j - v = 0 < w. \tag{24}$$

The zero profit conditions (22) are sufficient in number to completely determine the factor price vector without direct consideration of endowments, since it is assumed that the number of produced products is at least as great as the number of factors. Consequently, $A^+(w) = [a^j(w), j \in J^+]$ is a constant matrix and the factor market equilibrium conditions comprise a set of linear equations in $y^+ = [y_j, j \in J^+]$ given by $A^+(w)y^+ = v$. Variations in the endowment vector, v, that do not alter the list of produced goods therefore affect production levels but do not affect factor prices. The set of all endowment vectors that are consistent with this outcome constitute a cone of diversification.

Figure 3.3 illustrates cones of diversification for the case of two factors of production and two or three (depending on the interpretation below) products. Consider three products whose unit value isoquants (isoquants for producing a dollar's worth of each of the three goods) are illustrated by the dashed curves and labelled I^1, I^2 and I^3, defined for given product prices. The economy-wide unit value isoquant is the curve ABCDEF, which shows input vectors that produce one unit of revenue for the production sector.[11] In the portion AB only product 1 is produced, along segment BC goods 1 and 2 are produced, along CD only

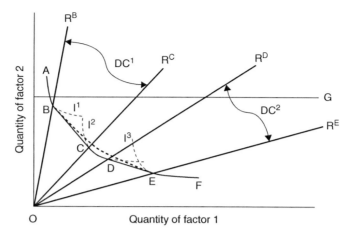

Figure 3.3   Factor endowments, diversification cones and factor prices.

product 2 is produced, on segment DE goods 2 and 3 are produced and on EF only product 3 is produced. The rays passing through points B, C, D and E divide the factor endowment space into five regions and form two diversification cones labelled DC^1 and DC^2. Any endowment vector within cone DC^1 will yield a factor price vector normal to the segment BC and involve production of both products 1 and 2. Similarly, any endowment vector within cone DC^2 will yield a factor price vector normal to the segment DE and involve production of both products 2 and 3. Variations of endowments within one of these cones will not alter factor prices, and will not alter the list of produced goods (though the output levels will alter of course). The invariance of factor prices to changes in endowments within a cone of diversification is an important aspect of the structure of the model, and is captured by the property of the revenue function that $\partial^2 R(p,v)/\partial v \partial v' = 0$ (i.e., that $\partial w(p,v)/\partial v' = 0$).

If endowments venture into the other regions, then specialization in production occurs. For example, in the specialization cone R^{C}OR^D only product 2 is produced and small variations in endowments within this cone are accompanied by changes in factor prices, relative factor prices being equal to the slope of the unit value isoquant depicted by CD.

Figure 3.4 depicts the relationship between the price of factor 1 and the endowment of factor 1 as endowments move along the horizontal line labelled G in figure 3.3. Noting that the relative factor prices are given by the slope of the unit value isoquant ABCDEF, it is observed that w_1 at first falls (AB), then remains constant (BC), falls again (CD), is constant again (DE), and then declines as the endowment continues to increase (EF).

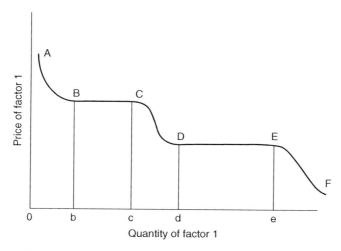

Figure 3.4   Factor price as a function of factor endowment.

As a final point, figure 3.3 can be reinterpreted as involving just two products if the unit value isoquant for product 1 is given by the dashed curve ABEF and that for product 3 is ignored. This illustrates the case where the zero profit equations $p_1 = c_1(w_1, w_2)$ and $p_2 = c_2(w_1, w_2)$ have two solutions for (w_1, w_2). Thus, even knowing that diversification occurs, product prices alone cannot determine factor prices; knowledge of factor endowments is needed. This reinterpretation of the figure makes it clear that the non-univalence (multiple solutions) of the zero profit conditions and having more goods than factors have essentially the same implications. Nevertheless, within each cone of diversification the pattern of production and factor prices are invariant to changes in factor endowments.

4.2   Endowments and outputs – Rybczynski Theorem

The Rybczynski theorem (Rybczynski, 1955) established a very clear connection between the outputs of goods and the factor endowments for a small open economy for the case where there are two goods and two factors of production. The theorem states that an increase in the endowment of one factor will lead to a proportionately greater increase in the output of one good and a reduction in the output of the other. Moreover, the good whose output increases is the one that uses the increasing endowment relatively intensively. This will be demonstrated within the context of more general results.

A general inequality relating endowments and outputs is

$$(v^1 - v^0)' A(\overline{w})(y^1 - y^0) \geq 0, \tag{25}$$

where y^i is the output vector when the endowment vector is v^i, v^0 is the initial endowment vector and $\overline{w}$ is an appropriate factor price vector possibly distinct from the price vectors w^0 and w^1. This arises from use of the mean value theorem (Ethier, 1982). This inequality establishes a sort of correlation between endowments and outputs and applies whether or not there is factor price equalization; under factor price equalization, $\overline{w} = w^0$. Thus, higher endowments of particular factors tends to be associated with higher outputs of particular goods.

An alternative general result can be obtained as follows. Assuming that the number of produced goods is at least as great as the number of (fully used) factors, it has already been established that the factor prices are locally independent of endowments. Therefore, the factor market equilibrium conditions (24) completely determine the output vector. Thus, a change in the endowment vector that does not change the pattern of production will not change the factor prices and so the change in outputs must satisfy the condition $A^+(w)\Delta y^+ = \Delta v$. This condition may be expressed in (discrete) percentage change terms as

$$\sum_{j \in J^+} \lambda_{ij}\widehat{y}_j = \widehat{v}_i, \tag{26}$$

where $\lambda_{ij} \equiv a_{ij}y_j/v_i$ is the proportion of the endowment of factor i employed in the production of good j and the hat denotes percentage change. This states that a weighted average of output growth rates equals the growth rate of factor i.

If the endowment of factor 1 increases while others remain unchanged, it follows that

$$\sum_{j \in J^+} \lambda_{1j}\widehat{y}_j = \widehat{v}_1 > 0,$$

$$\sum_{j \in J^+} \lambda_{ij}\widehat{y}_j = \widehat{v}_i = 0, \quad i \neq 1, \ i \in I^+. \tag{27}$$

Since the λ_{ij} are shares, the left-hand sides are weighted averages of output quantity changes. The first equation in (27) then implies that the weighted average for factor 1 must equal the percentage increase in endowment and, hence, that at least one industry's output must increase by a greater percentage; thus $\widehat{y}_j > \widehat{v}_1$ for some good j. Similarly, since the remaining endowments experience no increase, weighted averages of output growth rates must be zero to retain market equilibrium for factors $i \neq 1$ and, hence, at least one output quantity must fall; thus $\widehat{y}_k < 0$ for some good k.

This is the essence of the Rybczynski theorem and is what Jones (1965) called the 'magnification effect'. When a factor endowment increases, some output increases by a proportionately greater amount and some output actually falls. This simple, general argument leading to the magnification result cannot say how many factors will be in each category, nor which factors. To be more specific, one needs to examine the nature of the λ (or A) matrix in more detail.

In the special case of just two goods and two factors, equations (27) become $\lambda_{11}\widehat{y}_1 + \lambda_{12}\widehat{y}_2 = \widehat{v}_1 > 0$ and $\lambda_{21}\widehat{y}_1 + \lambda_{22}\widehat{y}_2 = \widehat{v}_2 = 0$. Thus, $\widehat{y}_1 = \lambda_{22}\widehat{v}_1/|\lambda|$ and

$\widehat{y}_2 = -\lambda_{21}\widehat{v}_1/|\lambda|$, where $|\lambda| = \lambda_{11}\lambda_{22}(a_{22}/a_{12} - a_{21}/a_{11}) = \lambda_{22} - \lambda_{12} = \lambda_{11} - \lambda_{21}$. If good i uses factor i relatively intensively $(a_{22}/a_{12} > a_{21}/a_{11})$ then $|\lambda| > 0$ and $\lambda_{22}/|\lambda| > 1$. Thus, $\widehat{y}_1 > \widehat{v}_1 > 0 = \widehat{v}_2 > \widehat{y}_2$, which is Rybczynski's theorem. That is, if the endowment of factor 1 increases, then the output of product 1 (which uses factor 1 relatively intensively) will increase by a greater percentage and the output of product 2 will fall.

The Rybczynski theorem is illustrated in figure 3.5. This figure depicts the initial endowment of the two factors at point C within the diversification cone AOB. At this initial endowment factors are allocated optimally in amounts a_C and b_C to the production of goods a and b. If the endowment of factor 2 increases from C to D, factor prices are unaffected and so the factor ratios used in production are likewise unaffected and the optimal allocations change to a_D and b_D. It is clear from the figure that the output of good a expands (by a greater percentage than the increase in the endowment of factor 2) while that of good b declines. This is the Rybczynski outcome; the output of the good using relatively intensively the factor whose endowment increase expands by a greater percentage and the output of the other product falls.

If the endowment vector increases further to point E then this production adjustment eventually results in complete specialization in product a. Further increases in the endowment to a point such as F takes the endowment vector out of the diversification cone so that the factor price vector changes to ensure cost minimization at F. Nevertheless, output of good a expands but now the output of good b is unchanged; Rybczynski's outcome is essentially preserved with amendment.

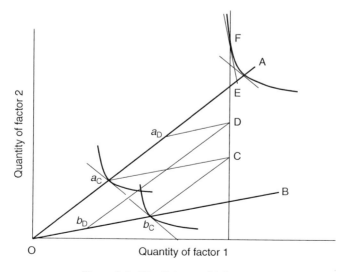

Figure 3.5 The Rybczynski theorem.

Attempts to extend this result to many dimensions have taken various forms, typically focusing on the properties of the matrix $A(w)$ of input–output coefficients. Specifically, this early literature attempted to establish conditions where there was a one-to-one connection between goods and factors; for example, if the endowment of factor i rose, then the output of product i would rise by a greater percentage and outputs of all other products would fall. See, for example, Uekawa, Kemp and Wegge (1973) and the survey of higher dimensional issues in trade theory by Ethier (1984).

4.3 Product and factor prices – Stolper–Samuelson Theorem

One of the most famous and useful theorems in international trade is the Stolper–Samuelson theorem (Stolper and Samuelson, 1941), which provides a clear relationship between the prices of products and the returns to factors used in their production. Within the context of a model with just two products and two factors of production, the theorem states that an increase in the price of one product will raise the real income of the factor used relatively intensively in the production of that product and reduce the income (nominal and real) of the other factor. This result has important implications for the effects of product price changes upon the distribution of income in an economy. Again, I begin with some general results and then deal with the two-dimensional case.

Similar to the treatment of the Rybczynski theorem, a general inequality relating factor and product prices is

$$(w^1 - w^0)' A(\overline{w})(p^1 - p^0) \geq 0, \tag{28}$$

where w^i is the factor price vector when the product price vector is p^i and p^0 is the initial product price vector. Again, this expression arises from use of the mean value theorem (Ethier, 1982) and establishes a sort of correlation between factor and product prices that applies whether or not there is factor price equalization. Higher product prices tend to be associated with higher prices for some factors. For example, if the price of good one (only) is increased by Δp_1, then $(w^1 - w^0)' a^1(\overline{w})\Delta p_1 > 0$ implies that some factor prices must rise.

Alternatively, further structure in the general case can be specified as follows. Suppose that the number of produced goods is at least as great as the number of (fully used) factors of production so that the production sector equilibrium conditions are given by (22)–(24) above and consider a change in the product price vector. If the price of a product experiences a discrete change, it is possible that the pattern of production alters. Assuming that the price change is small enough to retain the same production pattern, attention can be restricted to the comparative static analysis of the zero-profit conditions

$$c_j(w) - p_j = 0 < y_j, \quad j \in J^+. \tag{29}$$

Differentiating these conditions and converting to percentage changes, the comparative static equations may be expressed as

$$\sum_{i\in I}\theta_{ij}(w)\widehat{w}_i=\widehat{p}_j, \quad j\in J^+,\tag{30}$$

where $\theta_{ij}(w)\equiv a_{ij}(w)w_i/c_j(w)$ is the share of factor i in the cost of production of product j.

Jones's (1965) magnification result follows directly from these equations. If the price of good 1 increases while others remain unchanged, it follows that

$$\sum_{i\in I}\theta_{i1}(w)\widehat{w}_i=\widehat{p}_1>0,$$

$$\sum_{i\in I}\theta_{ij}(w)\widehat{w}_i=\widehat{p}_j=0, \quad j\neq 1,\ j\in J^+.\tag{31}$$

Since the θ_{ij} are shares, the left-hand sides are weighted averages of factor price changes. The first equation in (31) then implies that the weighted average in industry 1 must equal the percentage increase in price and, hence, that at least one factor's price must increase by a greater percentage; thus $\widehat{w}_i>\widehat{p}_1$ for some factor i. That factor must experience an increase in real income measured in terms of any good, since income has increased proportionately more than the price of good 1 and no other product price has changed – the first half of the essence of the Stolper–Samuelson theorem. The second set of equations in (31) imply that weighted averages of factor price changes in other industries must be zero to retain zero profits and, hence, at least one factor's price must fall; thus $\widehat{w}_k<0$ for some factor k. This factor must experience a fall in real income measured in terms of any good, since product prices have either risen or remained unchanged and the factor's income has fallen – the second half of the essence of the theorem.

There may be other factors whose prices rise by less than the increase in the price of good, in which case their real incomes may increase or decrease depending on their consumption patterns. This simple, general argument leading to the magnification result cannot say how many factors will be in each category, nor which factors. To be more specific, one needs to examine the nature of the θ (or A) matrix in more detail.

In the special case where there are just two goods and factors, the original Stolper–Samuelson result follows. In this special case, equations (31) become $\theta_{11}\widehat{w}_1+\theta_{21}\widehat{w}_2=\widehat{p}_1>0$ and $\theta_{12}\widehat{w}_1+\theta_{22}\widehat{w}_2=\widehat{p}_2=0$. Thus, $\widehat{w}_1=\theta_{22}\widehat{p}_1/|\theta|$ and $\widehat{w}_2=-\theta_{12}\widehat{p}_1/|\theta|$, where $|\theta|=\theta_{11}\theta_{22}(a_{22}/a_{12}-a_{21}/a_{11})=\theta_{22}-\theta_{21}=\theta_{11}-\theta_{12}$. If good j uses factor j relatively intensively ($a_{22}/a_{12}>a_{21}/a_{11}$) then $|\theta|>0$ and $\theta_{22}/|\theta|>1$. Thus, $\widehat{w}_1>\widehat{p}_1>0=\widehat{p}_2>\widehat{w}_2$, which is the Stolper–Samuelson theorem. That is, if the price of product 1 increases, then the price of factor 1 (which is used relatively intensively in the production of product 1) will increase by a greater percentage and the price of factor 2 will fall. This means that the real income of factor 1 increases, while that of factor 2 falls independently of preferences.

The Stolper–Samuelson theorem may be simply illustrated in figure 3.6, in which the zero profit (unit cost equals price) conditions for two goods are depicted in the factor price space for two factors. The initial equilibrium factor price vector (corresponding to the world price vector) is at point A, where product 2 is factor 2 intensive in production. If the price of product 2 increases, the zero profit curve for good 2 shifts outwards proportionally with price, resulting in a new equilibrium factor price vector at point B provided that this factor price vector is consistent with diversification. It is clear from the geometry of the figure that the price of factor 2 has increased by a greater percentage than the increase in the price of product 2, and that the price of factor 1 has decreased. Thus, the real income of factor 2 has increased (no matter what the consumer preferences, provided both goods are consumed), while that of factor one has decreased – the Stolper–Samuelson result.

As with the Rybczynski theorem, attempts to extend this result to many dimensions have typically focused on the properties of the matrix $A(w)$ of input–output coefficients.[12] Specifically, this early literature attempted to establish conditions where there was a one-to-one connection between goods and factors; for example, if the price of good j rose, then the real income of factor j would rise and the real incomes of all other factors would fall. See, for example, Uekawa (1971), Uekawa, Kemp and Wegge (1973) and the survey by Ethier (1984).

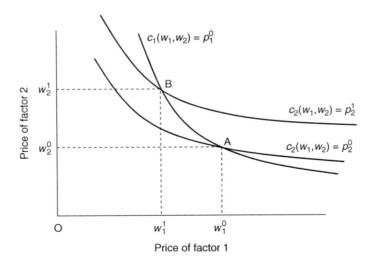

Figure 3.6   The Stolper–Samuelson theorem.

4.4 Product prices and outputs

The effects of product price changes on output levels can be determined at various levels of generality.

First, since outputs are chosen to maximize revenue on the production possibilities set it must follow that $(y^1 - y^0)'(p^1 - p^0) \geq 0$, where y^i is the output vector when the price vector is p^i and p^0 is the initial price vector. This establishes a positive correlation between output changes and price changes; the two change vectors form an acute or right angle. It implies that an increase in the price of good j alone will increase, or leave unchanged, the output of good j. This result occurs since the above inequality may then be expressed as $(y^1 - y^0)'(p^1 - p^0) = \Delta y_j \Delta p_j \geq 0$, implying that $\Delta y_j \geq 0$ if $\Delta p_j > 0$.

Second, it is known that optimization implies that the revenue function is convex (and linearly homogeneous) in product prices. If the revenue function is twice differentiable, then this convexity implies that the second derivative matrix $\nabla^2 R(p, v) \equiv \partial^2 R / \partial p \partial p' = \partial y(p, v) / \partial p'$, which shows how outputs change along the production possibilities frontier as prices change, is a positive semidefinite matrix such that $p' \partial y(p, v) / \partial p' \equiv 0$. In general, this is the complete implication for the matrix of responses of outputs to a differential change in the price vector. To obtain more concrete results, more structure on the model is required.

4.5 Net import functions

Having discussed the decisions of the production sector about what to produce and how much, the consumption decisions by households and the connection between the household and production sectors through income distribution, it remains a small step to specify the net import functions for an open economy. The net import functions, $m(p, v)$, were specified above as (18) and may be obtained from the compensated net import functions, $\tilde{m}(p, u, v)$, in (19) together with the budget constraint (20) that determines the endogenous level of utility, u.

Just as the price effect on consumption can be decomposed into the sum of a pure substitution effect and a pure income effect (the Slutsky decomposition), so too can the price effect on net imports. This decomposition may be expressed as (with r denoting consumer income)

$$\partial m_i(p, v) / \partial p_j = \partial \tilde{m}_i(p, u, v) / \partial p_j - m_j(p, v) \partial d_i(p, R(p, v)) / \partial r. \tag{32}$$

The first term on the right-hand side of this decomposition is the pure substitution effect that describes the movement around the production possibilities frontier and the indifference curve (equivalently, around the 'trade indifference curve').[13] In view of the properties of the separate production and consumption substitution matrices, the trade substitution matrix (equal to the difference) is negative semidefinite such that $p' \partial \tilde{m}(p, u) / \partial p \equiv 0$. This is a valuable property that can be exploited in comparative statics analysis of trade models. The second term on the right hand side of the Slutsky decomposition is the pure income effect. Assuming that each good i is normal in consumption, then $\partial d_i(p,r)/\partial r > 0$ and so the sign of the second terms depends on whether the good whose price has changed is imported. If good j is imported ($m_j > 0$) then the income effect acts to reduce net imports of good i; a higher price for imported good j reduces real income and so consumers reduce consumption of all goods, including good i. On the other hand, if good j is exported ($m_j < 0$) there is a positive income effect and so net imports rise.

4.6   World market equilibrium

The preceding discussions within this section have developed the effects of changes in national factor endowments and world prices for traded goods upon the outputs levels and factor prices for a small open economy. These effects are characterized as important features of the model and can form the basis of analyses in the broader context of international equilibrium. In this subsection, I discuss the role played by the general equilibrium aspect of the world market equilibrium, emphasizing the feedback effects that can play important roles in comparative statics analyses. Specifically, I briefly discuss the nature of the enormous literature on the analysis of this model through three particular examples where general equilibrium effects are prominent and then consider in detail just one specific issue – factor price equalization – that fits more closely with the rest of the chapter.

4.6.1   *General equilibrium price effects*

International equilibrium is established by specifying the world market equilibrium conditions as already done in (21). As explained earlier, these conditions determine the world prices as a function of the national endowment vectors, along with the national technologies and preferences. As should be clear, the model can be enhanced in many ways by, for example, including governments and policy instruments. These might include trade taxes (including import tariffs and export subsidies), trade quotas and income transfers between countries.

The literature on the analysis of this model or variations of it in the context of competitive equilibrium is enormous and covers a wide range of international economics. It would be pointless to try to summarize this literature and virtually impossible to provide a detailed account of the many issues and results involved. Here, I simply and briefly mention several areas to give a flavour of the literature and the role of general equilibrium.

The first issue is that of what became known as the 'transfer paradox'. In the context of a small open economy a transfer of income from one country to another unambiguously raises the welfare of the recipient country's household, since income rises and domestic prices are unchanged, and reduces the welfare of the donor country's household. However, in the context of a trading equilibrium with large economies the terms of trade effects of the income transfer arising from the need for markets to clear need to be taken into account. The paradox arises because it is possible, in various models, for the terms of trade effects to override the income effects to yield the outcome that the recipient country suffers a loss in welfare, while the donor country gains. The recipient country may have a high propensity to spend income on a range of goods, thus increasing world demand and inducing higher world prices for these goods. The consumer price index may rise by more than income, thus reducing real incomes for the recipient household – a paradox. This outcome cannot occur in the case of two goods under market stability but can occur with more goods or with several countries, for example. The transfer problem literature thus highlights the role played by general equilibrium market adjustments.

A second issue that further highlights the importance of world price adjustments in general equilibrium is provided by the analysis of the welfare and protective effects of tariffs. For a small open economy the imposition of a tariff on imports raises the domestic price of the import competing good and so encourages greater production of this good (as explained earlier in the context of effects of price changes on production) and a drawing away of resources away from production of the export good. The import competing sector is protected by the tariff. In addition, in the context of just two goods and factors, the domestic price change raises the real income of the factor used relatively intensively by the import competing sector and reduces the real income (ignoring the tariff revenue accruing to this factor) of the other factor of production. This is the Stolper–Samuelson theorem in operation.

Now consider the situation where the country is sufficiently large to affect world prices through its tariff policy. In the context of a trading world, it is clear that the reduced demand by this country (Home) for the import good and the reduced supply of the export good will require an increase in the relative price of exports (an improvement in Home's terms of trade due to the tariff) to clear world markets. The reduction in the relative price of imports will, after adding the tariff, lower the price of the import competing good thus moderating the protective effect of the tariff on the import competing sector and the real income gain of its intensively used factor. Even assuming that world markets are stable, it is possible for the terms of trade effect to be so strong that it generates the paradoxical outcome that Home's domestic price of the importable good is actually lower than before the tariff was imposed. If this turns out to be the case, then we have the paradox that a tariff imposed on imports and designed to protect the import competing sector and to raise the real income of its intensively used factor actually does the opposite; the tariff discourages production of the import competing good and encourages resource allocation to the export sector and, moreover, reduces the real income of the import competing sector's intensively used factor. This is the so-called Metzler Paradox (Metzler, 1949). Again, this example emphasizes the importance of general equilibrium world price consequences of policy changes.

The third and final example has been dubbed as 'immiserizing growth' by Bhagwati (1958). If a small open economy experiences an increase in its endowment of a factor the production possibility frontier shifts outwards and the welfare of the (single) household in the economy is enhanced. If the household has a strong propensity to consume the importable good there will be a strong excess world supply for the exported good. In the context of a trading world, the country's terms of trade may turn strongly against it. The upshot may be that the terms of trade deteriorate so much that the real income of the household may decline as a result of the endowment increase, since the consumer price index rises by more than income. This detrimental welfare outcome from the growth of the economy through an endowment increase leading to the term 'immiserizing growth' arises because of the general equilibrium effects of growth upon world prices.

4.6.2   *The factor price equalization theorem*

That the factor price vector may be locally unaffected by changes in the endowment vector, as demonstrated earlier, is the fundamental basis for the famous factor price equalization theorem. The factor price equalization theorem states that, subject to conditions, free international trade in goods leads to the prices of factors of production being the same in every country. This outcome is remarkable since factor markets are, by assumption, national markets and they are not directly connected. Rather, free international markets in goods alone suffices for the prices of factors in separated markets to be equalized. In this sense, free international trade in goods is a substitute for international mobility of factors.

Of course, the theorem requires strict assumptions for its validity and these occupy many pages in the international trade theory literature. Using the earlier discussion, some sufficient conditions become apparent. If all countries face the same world prices, have the same technology and produce the same goods given by set J^+, and the number of produced goods is at least as great as the number of fully used factors in every country, then the same set of profit maximization conditions (22) applies to every country and determines the factor price vector as a function of world prices, p, alone. This arises because equations (22) are equal in number (number of goods produced) to the number of factor prices to be determined. Thus, so the argument goes, every country has the same factor prices 'independently' of its endowment vector v^k; factor price equalization occurs.

This simplistic account of the factor price equalization outcome must be qualified in at least two very important respects. First, a simple counting of the numbers of zero profit equations for produced goods in (22) and the numbers of factor prices to be determined and finding these equal is not enough to ensure that the solution for factor prices is unique. Indeed, in figure 3.3 it was demonstrated geometrically that there may be more than one solution for the factor price vector and, consequently, more than one diversification cone. In this case, knowledge of world prices alone is insufficient to determine factor prices. Knowledge of factor endowments is also needed to determine which diversification cone and which factor price vector is consistent with equilibrium in the production sector.

Second, this simplistic account of factor price equalization must be qualified by recognizing that the endowment vectors, although not mentioned directly, play an important role behind the scenes in determining the complete general equilibrium for the world economy. That is, factor price equalization is a feature of the general equilibrium for a world economy and it is perhaps best to examine that equilibrium rather than focus on a country's production sector, conditional upon some assumed production pattern that is, in fact, endogenous. Put another way, although the above argument involves some primitive assumptions, such as identical technologies, there are other assumptions that are not primitive but restrict the nature of the equilibrium. Thus, while instructive, the above argument is deficient. Clearly, the list of produced goods in each country may not be the same, nor is it necessary that the number of produced goods be at least as great as the number of fully used factors (or that this list, in turn, is the same for every country) in every country. Preferences and the distribution of endowments may, and generally do, matter.

These observations are behind Dixit and Norman's (1980) integrated equilibrium approach to the factor price equalization issue and its graphic illustration recently discussed by Dixit (2010). The idea is to begin with the world endowment vector and then find the set of allocations of this world vector between two countries that would yield factor price equalization. Specifically, we can consider the closed equilibrium for the world as a single country which determines an equilibrium factor price vector. That vector will remain the common factor price vector in two countries formed by dividing the world endowment into two, provided the resulting endowment vectors remain in the cone of diversification for that factor price vector.

Figure 3.7 illustrates the two factor, two product case. The point O* represents the world endowment vector. The integrated world equilibrium factor price vector determines the optimal factor input rays given by OA and OB, which form the diversification cone AOB. The equilibrium allocation of factor inputs to the two industries are given by points A and B for industries 2 and 1, indicating that industry 2 is factor 2 intensive relative to industry 1.

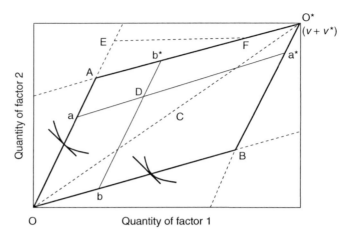

Figure 3.7 Integrated equilibrium and factor price equalization.

Now consider dividing the world factor endowment into two countries, which have the same technology and preferences. To this end, the point O* is the origin for country 2 and the endowment allocation is some point within the endowment box. Points such as C allocate the endowments such that one country is simply a multiple of another, so they are identical with each other and the integrated world except for size. Clearly, nothing has changed, so the two countries experience the same factor prices. Now consider a factor allocation such as at point D. If world prices for goods and factor prices were to remain unchanged, the home country would allocate its endowment OD to the two industries in amounts Oa and Ob, while the foreign country would allocate its endowment O*D in respective amounts O*a* and O*b* (measuring its factors from origin O*). However, will world product prices remain unchanged given that market equilibrium for goods has to occur? The answer to this question is 'yes', since this allocation of world factor endowments between the two countries leaves the world supply of goods and, hence, incomes unchanged and so supplies will still match the unchanged world demands. This is because the amounts of factors allocated to the production of each good under the integrated equilibrium (OA and OB) is exactly the same as under the disaggregated equilibrium (Oa + O*a* = Oa + aA = OA and Ob + O*b* = Ob + bB = OB). Thus, the disaggregated trading equilibrium is essentially the same as the original integrated world equilibrium; the only difference is the allocation of the same world production between the two countries. Factor price equalization occurs for these two countries.

The same argument applies for any allocation of world endowments between two or more countries within the parallelogram OAO*B. Within this region there will be factor price equalization. However, a factor endowment allocation outside this parallelogram cannot have factor price equalization, as it will generate world price changes and either production specialization or production diversification within different diversification cones, as explained by Dixit and Norman (1980). Outside the parallelogram it may be possible to have an equilibrium with diversified production in each country (if the cost-price equations have multiple solutions, meaning univalence does not hold) but factor price equalization will not occur.[14] This is of no consequence, however, and illustrates the value of taking the integrated equilibrium rather than diversified production and univalence of the cost functions as the starting point for the analysis.

The factor price equalization theorem is a famous and useful result, with a long and involved discussion in the literature. As the above brief discussion suggests, the conditions for its validity are strict, and so its application needs to be undertaken cautiously. Again, the above discussion highlights the important role played by general equilibrium considerations.

5 Theories of international trade

5.1 Comparative advantage and theories of international trade

In the above specification of the model of world trade, the equilibrium world price vector was determined as $p = P(v^1, ..., v^K)$. This formula explicitly includes the factor endowments of the K countries as determinants of equilibrium world prices, but implicitly included are the preferences and technologies of the K countries as well. Thus, world prices, and hence the pattern of trade, are determined by the primitive assumptions of the model – endowments, technologies and preferences.

Within the competitive equilibrium framework that is under consideration in this chapter, theories of trade focus on particular aspects of endowments, technologies and preferences that determine whether countries trade and, if they do, what pattern of trade ensues. One way to think of theories of trade in this context is to make assumptions under which there will be no international trade, even though it is allowed, and then to relax these assumptions sufficiently to generate trade as the equilibrium outcome. Clearly, the assumption that all countries are identical in endowments, technologies and preferences is sufficient to ensure that no trade is the equilibrium outcome. To see this, it is sufficient to show that the autarky (no trade) equilibrium prices for every country will be the same; then the opening up of the possibility of international trade will see no incentive to trade since no country has a price advantage in any good. In the terminology of Ricardo, there is no comparative advantage. Trade will only occur if autarky prices are different.[15]

Theories of trade can thus be based on any national difference that generates different autarky prices for tradeable goods. Autarky prices might be different because of national differences in technologies. The Ricardian model of comparative advantage is based upon national differences in the amount of labour needed to produce wine and cloth, that is, differences in technology. Alternatively, national differences in relative factor endowments between two countries can lead to different autarky prices and hence to international trade, as in the famous Heckshler-Ohlin-Samuelson model. Finally, differences in preferences for goods by consumers can also generate national autarky prices differences and hence trade.

In the following, I develop and discuss the main competitive equilibrium models that emphasize productivity and endowment differences between countries as the cause of trade. In each of these, the trade pattern is the outcome of the general equilibrium for the relevant model specification.

5.2   Ricardian (Productivity) models

The Ricardian model of comparative advantage emphasizes differences in technology as the primary reason for international trade. The classical version of the model is a special case of the general model outlined above, obtained by assuming just one factor of production (labour), two goods and two countries.

In this case, the constant returns to scale technologies can be described by the constant input–output ratios, given by a_j for the production of good j in the home country and by a_j^* for the foreign country. The production sector equilibrium conditions (22)–(24) for the home country then become

$$a_j w - p_j \geq 0 \leq y_j, \quad j \in J = \{1, 2\} \tag{33}$$

$$a_1 y_1 + a_2 y_2 - v \leq 0 \leq w, \tag{34}$$

where v is the labour endowment and w is the wage rate (both scalars now). An analogous pair of conditions apply to the foreign country. It is assumed that $a_2/a_1 < a_2^*/a_1^*$ so that the home country has a comparative advantage in producing good 2; these are also the autarky price ratios if it is further assumed that both goods are always demanded. Thus, in this case the autarky relative prices are such that $p_2/p_1 = a_2/a_1 < a_2^*/a_1^* = p_2^*/p_1^*$ meaning that the relative price of good 2 is lower in the home than the foreign country.

If world prices are equated in free trade, then the equilibrium world price ratio must lie between these two autarky price ratios, in which case specialization in production occurs. The home country produces good 2 while the foreign country produces good 1, implying that $a_2 w = p_2$ and $a_1^* w^* = p_1$ and, moreover, that $a_1 w > p_1$ and $a_2^* w^* > p_2$ (hence, production of good 2 is unprofitable). Thus, the world price ratio and the wage ratio are related by $p_2/p_1 = (a_2/a_1^*)(w/w^*)$.

Assuming identical and homothetic preferences for simplicity, the share of income allocated to each good (the budget share) is independent of income and is a function of price ratios. Thus, the budget share functions for the goods are expressed as $s_j(p_2/p_1)$. Income is $r = wv$ in the home country and $r^* = w^*v^*$ in the foreign country. The market equilibrium condition for good 2, expressed in value terms, is $p_2 y_2 = s_2(p_2/p_1)(wv + w^*v^*)$. Combining these, we have that $(w/w^*) = [s_2(p_2/p_1)/s_1(p_2/p_1)](v^*/v)$.

Thus we have two equilibrium conditions

$$(w/w^*) = (a_1^*/a_2)(p_2/p_1)$$

$$(w/w^*) = [s_2(p_2/p_1)/s_1(p_2/p_1)](v^*/v)$$

that can be solved for w/w^* and p_2/p_1. If preferences are Cobb–Douglas then the budget shares are constants and so the solutions become very simple; the second equation determines $(w/w^*) = [s_2/s_1](v^*/v)$ and then the first determines $p_2/p_1 = (a_2/a_1^*)[s_2/s_1](v^*/v)$.

Equilibrium in this model determines a world price ratio in between the two autarky price ratios, which are equal to the ratios of input–output coefficients.[16] Each country specializes completely in production, each producing the product in which it has a comparative advantage (lowest autarky relative price) and exporting it in return for imports of the other product in which it has a comparative disadvantage. Both countries gain from the exchange since the world attains productive efficiency.

Equilibrium in the Ricardian model of trade may be depicted in figure 3.8. The figure depicts the two production possibilities sets $Y(v)$ and $Y^*(v^*)$ together with their sum $Y(v) + Y^*(v^*)$. For simplicity only, the figure assumes common, homothetic preferences. The autarky equilibria are at A and A* with different relative product prices (given by the slopes of the production frontiers) and diversified production. The competitive free-trade equilibrium determines relative prices between the autarky relative prices, as depicted. Production is at y and y^* with Home specializing in product 2 and Foreign in product 1, while the consumption vectors c and c^* yield utility levels u and u^*. Both countries specialize in the production of the product in which they have a comparative advantage and gain from international trade.

This equilibrium can be thought of as an integrated equilibrium. Point E is the world production (and consumption) vector obtained by summing national vectors. It also represents the equilibrium for a closed or integrated world economy, being the best production point in the world production set at the price that ensures that the world household's consumption choice clears the market. In this sense, the Ricardian trade outcome is efficient from a world viewpoint.

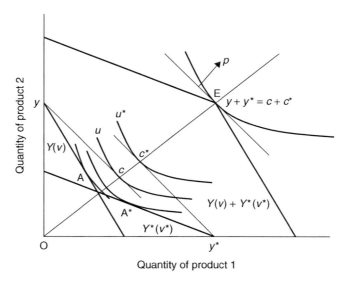

Figure 3.8 The Ricardian equilibrium in product space.

The crucial importance of Ricardo's principle of comparative advantage as the reason for beneficial international trade is that it is *comparative* advantage and not *absolute* advantage that is crucial. Home may have an absolute advantage in the production of both products ($a_1 < a_1^*$ and $a_2 < a_2^*$) but this, by itself does not determine the pattern of trade (and certainly Home does not therefore sell both products to Foreign). Home with have a comparative advantage in product 2 when $a_2/a_1 < a_2^*/a_1^*$, and this could occur whether or not it also has an absolute advantage in both or one product, or in neither. More generally, this crucial distinction was important in highlighting the importance of relative, not absolute, prices in models of general competitive equilibrium in trade.

The simple Ricardian model can, and has been, extended in various way. Maintaining its linear production structure it can be extended to multiple goods, multiple countries or both as in the Graham model discussed by McKenzie (1954). For other related references, see Bernhofen (2010) in this volume.

5.3 Dornbusch–Fischer–Samuelson Ricardian model

Dornbusch, Fischer and Samuelson (1977) produced a continuum of goods version of the Ricardian model presented above. In this extension, goods are indexed by $z \in [0, 1]$ and ordered such that $A(z) \equiv a^*(z)/a(z)$ is decreasing in z, where $a(z)$ and $a^*(z)$ are the labour requirements per unit of output of good z. Thus, there is a continuum of goods ordered with decreasing comparative advantage for the home country, in contrast with just two goods in the Ricardian model. It turns out, not surprisingly, that there exists a marginal good defined by $\bar{z} \in [0, 1]$ such that the home country will produce goods with $z \in [0, \bar{z})$ in which it has a comparative advantage, while the foreign country will produce the remaining goods with $z \in (\bar{z}, 1]$ in which it has a comparative advantage.[17]

In this continuum of goods case, the production sector equilibrium conditions (22)–(24) for the home country become

$$a(z)w - p(z) \geq 0 \leq y(z), \quad z \in [0, 1] \tag{35}$$

$$\int_{z\in[0,1]} a(z)y(z)dz - v \leq 0 \leq w. \tag{36}$$

The first equation is the profit maximization condition for the continuum of goods, while the second is the market equilibrium condition for labour. A similar set of conditions apply to the second country, of course.

The critical value of z, $\bar{z}$, defining the good that can be produced by both countries facing the same world prices, is obtained by solving the two profit maximization conditions $a(z)w = p(\bar{z})$ and $a^*(z)w^* = p(\bar{z})$. The solution is implicitly given by $A(\bar{z}) = \omega \equiv w/w^*$. Since $A(z)$ is assumed to be a decreasing function, $a^*(z)w^* > a(z)w$ for all $z < \bar{z}$ and so the cost of production in the foreign country is too high for production to occur; thus the home nation produces goods for which $z \in [0, \bar{z})$. For goods with $z > \bar{z}$, the cost of production in the home country is too high for production to occur; thus the foreign nation produces goods for which $z \in (\bar{z}, 1]$.

Homothetic preferences, the same for both countries, imply that the budget shares, $p(z)c(z)/I$, depend only on relative prices and, assuming Cobb–Douglas preferences, may be expressed independently of prices as $s(z)$.[18] The market equilibrium condition for goods produced by the home country is $p(z)y(z) = s(z)(wv + w^*v^*)$, and for other goods it is $p(z)y^*(z) = s(z)(wv + w^*v^*)$. Integrating the first of these, the budget constraint for the home country may be expressed as

$$wv = \int_{z\in[0,\bar{z}]} p(z)y(z)dz = \int_{z\in[0,\bar{z}]} s(z)dz(wv + w^*v^*) \equiv \upsilon(\bar{z})(wv + w^*v^*).$$

Simplifying this expression and repeating the supply side equation gives

$$\omega = [\upsilon(\bar{z})/(1 - \upsilon(\bar{z}))]\,(v^*/v)$$

$$\omega = A(\bar{z}).$$

These two equations may be solved for $(\bar{z}, \omega)$ to obtain the equilibrium for the model. The first describes an upward-sloping curve in $(\bar{z}, \omega)$ space, while the second describes a downward-sloping curve; the intersection defines the equilibrium.

Although this model rests on rather stringent assumptions about preferences and the technology, it has the appealing feature that equilibrium determines the range of goods that each country produces and hence exports. In this model, a country produces and exports the range of goods in which it has a comparative advantage, and imports its total consumption of the other goods. Furthermore, changes in any of the primitive assumptions about the technology, preferences and endowments will alter the ranges of goods produced (i.e., the pattern of production and trade). The inclusion of transport costs or tariffs into the model creates a wedge between product prices faced by producers in the two countries and this generates non-traded goods. That is, the inclusion of these wedges determines two critical z values rather than one, thus dividing goods into those produced by the home country alone, those produced by the foreign country alone and those produced by both countries and not traded internationally.

The Ricardian model, in both its discrete and continuum versions, has been influential in the international trade literature, with various extensions. Such extensions include contributions by Wilson (1980), Ruffin (1988), Eaton and Kortum (2002) and Matsuyama (2007). Matsuyama (2008) provides a short account and survey of this model and literature.

5.4   Heckscher–Ohlin–Samuelson (endowment) models

In the Heckscher–Ohlin–Samuelson (HOS) factor endowments model of trade, the only difference between countries is the relative factor endowments. When there are just two countries, two goods and two factors of production, the outcome is that trade occurs if there are differences in relative factor endowments and, moreover, that the country with a relative abundance of labour (say) will export the relatively labour intensive good and import the relatively capital (say) intensive good. In this case the predictions of the model are very clear and help to explain the popularity of the Heckscher–Ohlin–Samuelson model in the literature of the last half of the 1900s.

Before dealing with the standard two-dimensional Heckscher–Ohlin–Samuelson model that has previously been the workhorse for many analyses in the international trade literature, I briefly consider the general case of the model. To this end, let it be assumed that there are two countries with identical technologies and identical, homothetic preferences. The only differences between the two countries is in their factor endowment vectors, v and v^*. Their autarky prices for goods will therefore differ and reflect the endowment differences (provided the endowment vectors are not proportional to one another). The production sector equilibrium conditions (10) and (11) for the home country determine output levels, hence national income, given product prices. These solutions are denoted by $y(p,v)$ and $G(p,v) = p'y(p,v)$. Under homothetic preferences, the national demand vector is $\gamma(p)G(p,v)$. For the foreign country, these items are written as $y(p,v^*)$, $G(p,v^*)$ and $\gamma(p)G(p,v^*)$. The world market equilibrium conditions are then expressed as

$$y(p,v) + y(p,v^*) = \gamma(p)\left[G(p,v) + G(p,v^*)\right]. \tag{37}$$

These conditions determine the equilibrium world price vector as a function of the national endowment vectors, v and v^*.

It should be clear from this general formulation for the model that the countries differ only in their factor endowments and that this gets reflected in differences in free trade productions and, hence incomes. The production differences completely determine the pattern of trade, since the common homothetic preference assumption implies the same consumption patterns (ratios) in each country.

At this stage, the assumptions of the model do not preclude an equilibrium with specialization or national factor price differences. To focus on the equilibrium with diversification and factor price equalization, appropriate further assumptions are made. If it is further assumed that there are equal numbers of goods and factors and that all goods are produced, then the profit maximization conditions simplify to $A'(w)w = p$ in each country and the national factor market equilibrium conditions simplify to $A(w)y = v$ and $A(w)y^* = v^*$. In this case, the world market equilibrium condition for goods becomes

$$\left[I - \gamma(C(w))C(w)'\right]A(w)^{-1}(v + v^*) = 0, \tag{38}$$

where $C(w) = A'(w)w$ is the vector of unit cost functions.[19] This set of equations can be solved for the equilibrium factor price vector, w, recognizing that one equation is redundant (Walras's Law) and that the price vector can only be determined up to a factor of proportionality (homogeneity). Once w is determined, the product price vector, $p = C(w)$, and other endogenous variables such as y and y^* can be obtained. As with the general model above, the pattern of trade is determined by the production pattern, which now completely reflects the Rybczynski relationship between endowments and production. This is evident from (38), which can be rewritten as $\left[I - \gamma(C(w))C(w)'\right](y + y^*) = 0$, since $y = A(w)^{-1}v$.

I now move to the two-dimensional model, which can be expressed in terms of ratios of variables in view of the assumed constant returns to scale in production and homothetic preferences. If there is diversification in production, the profit maximization conditions (10) become $\pi = \pi(\omega)$ and express the product price ratio $\pi \equiv p_2/p_1$ as a function of the factor price ratio $\omega \equiv w_2/w_1$. The factor market equilibrium conditions (11) are linear equations in outputs, the solution for the output quantity ratio being

$$\eta \equiv y_2/y_1 = \alpha(\omega)(v - \kappa^1(\omega))/(\kappa^2(\omega) - v) \equiv \eta(\omega, v), \tag{39}$$

where $v \equiv v_2/v_1$ is the factor endowment ratio, $\kappa^j = \kappa^j(\omega) \equiv d_2^j(\omega)/d_1^j(\omega)$ is the factor intensity ratio in industry j and $\alpha(\omega) \equiv a_1^1(\omega)/a_1^2(\omega)$. Under factor price equalization, the world output ratio is obtained by replacing the world endowment ratio for v in (39) to get $\eta(\omega, \theta v + (1 - \theta)v^*)$, where $\theta \equiv v/(v + v^*)$ is the share of the home country in the world endowment of the first factor. Under the assumption of homothetic preferences, the ratio of demands, $\delta \equiv d_2/d_1$, is a function of the price ratio and independent of income. Since preferences are the same internationally, $\delta = \delta(\pi)$ is the consumption ratio in both countries.

International product market equilibrium requires the world demand ratio (common to both countries) to be equal to the world output ratio, whence

$$\delta(\pi(\omega)) = \eta(\omega, \theta v + (1 - \theta)v^*), \tag{40}$$

which may be solved for the common factor price ratio ω as a function of the factor endowment ratios and shares as $\omega = \omega(v, v^*, \theta)$.[20] If Home's endowment ratio, v, exceeds Foreign's endowment ratio, v^*, then $\eta(\omega, v) > \eta(\omega, v^*)$, since η is an increasing function of the endowment ratio when product 2 is relatively factor 2 intensive in production.[21] Thus, since $\eta(\omega, v) > \delta(\pi(\omega)) > \eta(\omega, v^*)$, Home has a greater production than consumption ratio and so will export good 2 while Foreign, having a smaller production ratio, will import it. This is the Heckscher–Ohlin–Samuelson trade pattern prediction; Home exports the good that uses relatively intensively its relatively abundant factor and imports the other good.

The logic of the Heckscher–Ohlin–Samuelson model can be explained verbally, making use of the above relationships. Assume that the two countries are identical initially. They have, under the assumptions, identical autarky equilibria. If free trade is now permitted, the solution would be unchanged since there is no incentive to trade. Both countries have the same free-trade equilibria with zero trade.

Now suppose that the home country's endowment of factor 2 rises by α percent so that the home country has a relative abundance of this factor. If world prices remain unchanged, then factor prices at home will also be unchanged and the home country will produce proportionately more of product 2, assuming that product 2 is, and remains, factor 2 intensive. This is due to the Rybczynski theorem, which is at the heart of the Heckscher–Ohlin–Samuelson theorem. Income at home will increase and the consumer will demand more of each good in equal proportions. Thus, the home country will increase its exports of good 2 and increase its imports of good 1 if product prices are unchanged. This situation cannot be an equilibrium for now there will be a world excess supply of good 2 and an excess demand for good 1. The relative market price for good 2 will have to fall to reestablish market equilibrium for goods. This fall in the relative price for good 2 will ameliorate the changes in the home country described above, and will encourage the foreign country to produce less of product 2 and more of product 1. The upshot is that, at the new equilibrium, the home country will export good 2, which will be willingly imported by the foreign country.

Similarly, the foreign country's increased production of good 1 will be willingly imported by the home country.

Figure 3.9 depicts equilibrium for the Heckscher–Ohlin–Samuelson model of trade in product space, which provides direct information about production, consumption and trade levels. The integrated world equilibrium for the model is given at point E at which the product price vector p is such that the production sector chooses output vector E and the income-constrained, utility-maximizing consumer chooses consumption vector E, thus establishing market equilibrium for goods. The figure also illustrates the competitive equilibrium for this world broken into two countries by dividing world factor endowments into two national vectors v and v^* with production sets $Y(v)$ and $Y(v^*)$. Home is relatively better endowed with the factor used relatively intensively in the production of product 2 and so allocates a relatively large amount of resources to its production via the Rybczynski theorem. Similarly, Foreign is relatively better endowed with the factor used relatively intensively in the production of product 1 and so allocates a relatively large amount of resources to its production. Under homotheticity of preferences, the consumption vectors lie along the same income-consumption ray. Thus, Home exports product 2 and imports product 1 from Foreign in equilibrium. This is the Heckscher–Ohlin–Samuelson outcome; countries export goods that are relatively intensive in their use of the relatively abundant factor of production and import goods that intensively use their relatively scarce factor of production. Households in both countries are better off under trade than autarky, of course.

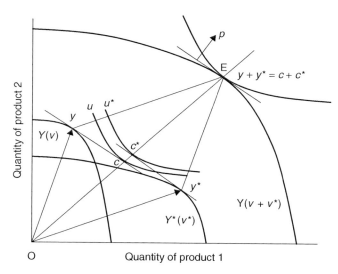

Figure 3.9 The Heckscher–Ohlin–Samuelson equilibrium in product space.

The Heckscher–Ohlin–Samuelson model has been used extensively in the international trade literature, since it provides a simple, effective expression of the idea that trade is due to factor endowment differences between countries. In its two-dimensional form, it provides clear predictions: the country (Home) with a relatively abundant supply of land, say, will export the good, food say, that uses land relatively intensively and will import the other good, cloth say, that intensively uses its relatively scarce endowment, labour say. In this way the pattern of trade is determined by the pattern of factor endowments, primarily through the Rybczynski theorem. Moreover, because of the assumption that technologies and preferences are the same in both countries, the opening up of trade will raise the price of food in Home and, by the Stolper–Samuelson theorem, raise the real income of landowners and reduce the real income of labour. In Foreign, this world price change analogously causes the real income of labour to increase and that of the relatively scarce factor, land, to decrease. Thus, trade has clear-cut income distributional consequences. Finally, factor price equalization ensues provided that the production changes brought about by trade do not lead to complete specialization on the part of either country.

Generalizations of the Heckscher–Ohlin–Samuelson model outcomes in higher dimensions include work by Deardorff (1982), Ethier (1982) and Dixit and Woodland (1982), all of whom focus on the correlation between endowments and the pattern of production and trade. Davis (1995) combines the Heckscher–Ohlin and Ricardian models to allow for both endowment and technology differences between countries to demonstrate the possibility of intra-industry trade. Ruffin (1988) provides a Ricardian approach to the factor endowments theory of trade.

5.5   Dornbusch–Fischer–Samuelson HOS model

Dornbusch, Fischer and Samuelson (1980) provided a variation of the above Heckscher–Ohlin–Samuelson model for the case with a continuum of goods that contributed an important additional dimension to the model.

As with the Dornbusch–Fischer–Samuelson continuous version on the Ricardian model, goods are defined by the index $z \in [0,1]$. The variables $p(z)$, $y(z)$ and $c(w,z)$ denote the price, output and unit cost function for a good with index z. The production sector equilibrium conditions (10)–(11) for the home country then become

$$c(w,z) - p(z) \geq 0 \leq y(z), \quad z \in [0,1], \tag{41}$$

$$\int_{z \in [0,1]} a(w,z)y(z) - v \leq 0 \leq w, \tag{42}$$

where v is the endowment vector, w is the factor price vector and $a(w,z) = \partial c(w,z)/\partial w$ is the vector of input–output coefficients for good z. A similar set of

conditions may be specified for the foreign country, obtained by replacing factor prices, endowments and outputs in (41) and (42) by w^*, v^* and $y^*(z)$, assuming common technologies as applicable to the Heckscher–Ohlin–Samuelson framework. Homothetic preferences, the same for both countries, imply that the budget shares depend only on relative prices and, assuming Cobb–Douglas preferences for further simplicity, may be expressed independently of prices as $s(z)$.

Using these simplifying assumptions, the world market equilibrium condition for goods may be expressed in value terms as

$$p(z)[y(z) + y^*(z)] = s(z)(w'v + w^{*\prime}v^*), \quad z \in [0,1].$$ (43)

Together, these national production sector and world market equilibrium conditions determine the world prices, national outputs and factor prices for the continuum of goods $z \in [0,1]$.

This formulation is rather general, so it is instructive to consider the case where there are just two factors, say labour and capital, as in Dornbusch, Fischer and Samuelson (1980). When there are just two factors of production, say labour and capital, and the wage rate is normalized to unity, the cost function and the input–output functions may be expressed as a function of the rental–wage ratio as $\omega \equiv w_2/w_1$. Additionally, Cobb–Douglas preferences ensure that consumption is positive for every good z and, hence, that prices are positive. Full employment is assumed.

Dornbusch, Fischer and Samuelson (1980) consider several different cases of free trade. In the first case, it is assumed that endowments are sufficiently similar for there to be factor price equalization. In this case, all goods are producible in both countries at zero profit, so $c(w,z) = p(z)$, $z \in [0,1]$. The world economy is just like a single economy except that there are two production sectors and two consumers. Accordingly, the equilibrium condition is similar to that for a closed economy in view of the factor price equalization assumption. Dornbusch, Fischer and Samuelson elegantly show that, in my notation, the free trade equilibrium may be obtained by solving the equation (reflecting factor market equilibrium)

$$\int_{z \in [0,1]} s(z) \frac{1 + \omega \widehat{k}}{1 + \omega k(\omega, z)} [k(\omega, z) - \widehat{k}] dz = 0$$ (44)

for the common rental–wage ratio, ω, where $k(\omega, z) = a_2(\omega, z)/a_1(\omega, z)$ is the capital–labour ratio for product z, $k \equiv v_2/v_1$ and $k^* \equiv v_2^*/v_1^*$ are the national capital–labour endowment ratios, $\widehat{k} \equiv \pi k + (1 - \pi)k^*$ is the world capital–labour ratio and $\pi \equiv v_1/(v_1 + v_1^*)$ is the home country's share of the world labour force. Once this equilibrium rental–wage ratio is obtained, the remaining endogenous variables are determined.[22]

In the free-trade equilibrium, the production pattern is indeterminate except that, if Home is relatively capital abundant, then Home will be a net exporter of capital services and a net importer of labour services. The production pattern is indeterminate since there is a continuum of goods that can be produced at zero profit and there are just two factors. It is well known in the trade literature that when there are more goods than (fully used) factors equilibrium in the production sector does not pin down the outputs; there are an infinity of solutions for the (many) production levels satisfying the two factor market equilibrium conditions. Here there are an infinity of goods, so the same outcome arises.

When there is no factor price equalization Dornbusch, Fischer and Samuelson show that specialization occurs, whereby the capital abundant country (Home, say) produces the most capital intensive goods, while Foreign produces the most labour intensive goods. The critical value $z = \bar{z}$ that defines the good that can be produced in both countries is determined by the equilibrium conditions, along with the rental–wage ratios, ω and ω^*, in the two countries. In this context, changes in exogenous variables (such as endowments) alter the pattern of production and specialization for goods; one country will produce a larger range of goods, while the other country will produce a smaller range.

The Dornbusch, Fischer and Samuelson extension of the Heckscher–Ohlin–Samuelson model to deal with a continuum of goods is valuable in that it provides a generalization in one dimension (number of goods) that focuses attention on the factor content of trade and allows trade to determine a ranges of goods that are imported, exported or not traded based upon their factor intensities. This Heckscher–Ohlin–Samuelson model with a continuum of goods and the Ricardian model with a continuum of goods have been generalized and extended into a general model of comparative advantage with a continuum of goods by Xu (1993), these two models becoming special cases. More recently, Costinot (2009) has developed a general approach, based upon the concept of log-supermodularity of functions, to comparative advantage in a model that incorporates both technological and endowment differences among nations. This follows the path established by Deardorff (1980) towards general results on comparative advantage and the sources of trade that are not dependant on the dimensionality of simpler models.

6 Conclusion

This chapter has reviewed and characterized the main literature on competitive general equilibrium methods and models in international trade. This may be classed as the traditional or classical/neoclassical approach to international trade, an approach that has a long and venerable intellectual history. While its previous dominance in international trade has necessarily given way to a more diversified intellectual tool kit that now incorporates dimensions such as imperfectly competitive behaviour on the part of firms, internal and external economies of scale, partial equilibrium and heterogeneous firms, the competitive general equilibrium approach remains an essential and important approach to analysis. This chapter has attempted to bring out the important aspects of that literature.

The primary value of competitive general equilibrium modeling in international trade is not so much that it relies on competitive behaviour (though it does), but that it treats the economy as a whole. Consumers and producers are assumed to choose their demands for, and supplies of, commodities by optimizing their objective functions given market prices and constraints, and these market prices are assumed to be endogenously and simultaneously determined by the requirement that markets are in equilibrium. In short, it is the 'general equilibrium' aspect that provides most value, not the 'competitive' aspect.

The consequence of this is that national or domestic markets are interconnected through trade in international markets. This inter-connectedness ensures that the analysis of positive and normative issues in international trade (such as examining the consequences of endowment changes or trade policy changes or welfare evaluations) cannot be confined to a sector of an economy, or to the country even, but must take into account the general equilibrium effects. It is perhaps this general equilibrium aspect of much of international trade theory that gives it its richness.

International trade theory does not stay still and changes through time as new problems, issues and applications arise. Whatever the future path of this evolution, the principles of the competitive general equilibrium approach outlined in this chapter are likely to constitute guiding lights for the analysis of many international trade issues.

Notes

* This chapter has benefited considerably from comments on earlier drafts by Daniel Bernhofen, Mauro Caselli, Xiao Chen, Christos Kotsogiannis and Mark Melatos. The research was financially supported by the Australian Research Council.
† School of Economics, University of New South Wales.
1. The assumption of constant returns to scale at the industry level can be justified approximately by assuming that a decreasing returns to scale firm's optimal production plan can be replicated by an arbitrary number of potential firms. That is, doubling an output plan can be achieved by doubling the number of firms.
2. System (5) is sometimes referred to as a system of complementary slackness conditions.
3. Since the two consumers face different prices in autarky, it is possible to take some of a good from one person, who values it lowly, and give it to the other consumer, who values it highly, and do the opposite transfer with the other good. In this way, both consumers can gain. More generally, Pareto improvements such as this can be obtained whenever agents face different prices (opportunity costs).

4. The duality approach to production was initiated by Shephard (1953) and developed further by Diewert (1971). An exposition for the production sector is in Woodland (1977).

5. This result shows a symmetry between the Stolper–Samuelson and Rybczynski theorems discussed later.

6. That is, the vector inequalities $x \geq 0 \leq y$ are taken as shorthand for the conditions $x \geq 0$, $y \geq 0$ and $x'y = 0$. In component form, these imply that $x_i \geq 0$, $y_i \geq 0$ and $x_i y_i = 0$ for all i.

7. Alternatively, one can use the expenditure function $E(p,u) = \min\{p'd : u(d) \geq u\}$ together with the budget constraint $E(p,u) = r$, where r is household income. In this case, $d(p,r) = \partial E(p,u)/\partial p$, where $E(p,u) = r$.

8. In this case, treating u as a vector of utilities for the H households and r as a vector of incomes, one can define $E(p,u)$ as a vector of household expenditure functions, $e^h(p,u)$, and the budget constraints are written in vector form as $E(p,u) = r$. The household incomes must then satisfy the aggregate budget condition $1'r = R(p,v)$.

9. As a matter of strategy, it is generally most efficient to specify a model in terms of the variables of direct interest.

10. See Woodland (2008) for a recent review of non-traded goods in international trade theory.

11. The economy-wide unit value isoquant can be interpreted as the set of factor endowments for which the revenue function takes a value of 1, that is, $\{v : R(p,v) = 1\}$. The linear segment BC shows endowments that are optimally allocated between the production of goods 1 and 2; on segment DE the allocation is between goods 2 and 3. The curved portions AB, CD and EF correspond to specializations in goods 1, 2 and 3 respectively. Thus, the whole curve provides endowments yielding a dollar's worth of output for the production sector.

12. As indicated earlier, the Rybczynski and Stolper–Samuelson results are intimately related and dual to one another. Hence the literatures on their generalization coincide and focus on the properties of $A(w)$.

13. See Woodland (1980) on the trade utility function and its properties, and Lloyd and Schweinberger (1988) on the trade expenditure function.

14. For example, in figure 3.7 suppose the national endowments are at point E. If factor prices were equal to those inside the parallelogram then Home would specialize in good 2 at E, while Foreign would specialize in good 1 at F. However, this is inconsistent with factor market equilibrium as there is an excess supply of factor 1 of EF in Foreign. Thus, our supposition of factor price equalization at endowment point E is incorrect.

15. While this is true within the context of competitive equilibrium, it may not be true in other contexts. For example, in models with monopolistically competitive firms producing different varieties of products two way trade in varieties might occur even though autarky prices are equal.

16. It is actually possible for the equilibrium price ratio to coincide with one of the autrarky price ratios, in which case one country does not benefit from international trade.

17. The continuum goods model may be interpreted as the limiting case of a discrete goods model, with goods ranked according to their input coefficients. The continuum specification has the advantage of analytical convenience.

18. If only homothetic preferences are assumed, rather than the very special Cobb–Douglas preferences, then the budget shares depend on the prices of all goods. This complicates the analysis somewhat.

19. The market equilibrium conditions can, alternatively, be expressed in terms of the product price vector as $[I - \gamma(p)p']A(w(p))^{-1}(v+v^*) = 0$, where $w(p) = C^{-1}(p) = [A'(w)]^{-1}p$ is the inverse of the vector of unit cost functions, $C(w)$. This is less straightforward, as it relies upon the inversion of the cost functions and these may have multiple solutions in general.

20. The world market equilibrium condition can, alternatively, be expressed in terms of the product price ratio, π, as $\delta(\pi) = \eta(\omega^{-1}(\pi), \theta v + (1-\theta)v^*)$. This expression is not as straightforward, as the inversion of the cost function ratio may involve multiple solutions.

21. It can be shown that $\partial\eta(\omega, v)/\partial v = \alpha(\kappa^2 - \kappa^1)/(\kappa^2 - v)^2$, which has the sign of $\kappa^2 - \kappa^1$.

22. The two autarky rental–wage ratios may be obtained from similar equations, obtained by replacing $\hat{k}$ by k and k^* respectively.

References

Abe, K. (1992) 'Tariff reform in a small open economy with public production', *International Economic Review*, 33(1), 209–22.

Bernhofen, D.M. (2010) 'The empirics of general equilibrium trade theory', this volume.

Bhagwati, J. (1958) 'Immiserizing growth: a geometric note', *Review of Economic Studies*, 25, 201–05.

Chang, W.W. (1979) 'Some theorems of trade and general equilibrium with many goods and factors', *Econometrica*, 47(3), 709–26.

Costinot A. (2009) 'An elementary theory of comparative advantage', *Econometrica*, 77(4), 1165–92.

Davis, D.R. (1995) 'Intra-industry trade: A Heckscher–Ohlin–Ricardo approach', *Journal of International Economics*, XXXIX, 201–26.

Debreu, G. (1959) *Theory of Value*. New York: John Wiley.

Deardorff, A.V. (1980) 'The general validity of the Law of Comparative Advantage', *Journal of Political Economy*, 88, 941–57.

—— (1982) 'The general validity of the Heckscher–Ohlin theorem', *American Economic Review*, 72(4), 683–94.

Diewert, W.E. (1971) 'An application of the Shephard duality theorem: A generalized Leontief production function', *Journal of Political Economy*, 79(3), 481–507.

Diewert, W.E., A.H. Turunen-Red and A.D. Woodland (1989) 'Productivity- and Pareto-improving changes in taxes and tariffs', *The Review of Economic Studies*, 56(2), 199–215.

Diewert, W.E., and A.D. Woodland (1977) 'Frank Knight's theorem in linear programming revisited', *Econometrica*, 45(2), 375–98.

Dixit, A.K., and V. Norman (1980) *Theory of international trade*: J. Nisbet/Cambridge University Press.

Dixit A.K., and A.D. Woodland (1982) 'The relationship between factor endowments and commodity trade', *Journal of International Economics*, 13, 201–14.

Dixit, A.K. (2010) 'The integrated world equilibrium diagram from international trade theory', in Blaug, Mark, and P.J. Lloyd (eds), *Famous Figures and Diagrams in Economics*, forthcoming.

Dornbusch, R., S. Fischer and P. Samuelson (1977) 'Comparative advantage, trade and payments in a Ricardian model with a continuum of goods', *American Economic Review*, LXVII, 823–39.

—— (1980) 'Heckscher–Ohlin trade theory with a continuum of goods', *Quarterly Journal of Economics*, XCV, 203–24.

Eaton, J. (1987) 'A dynamic specific-factors model of international trade', *Review of Economic Studies*, 54(2), 325–38.

Eaton, J., and S. Kortum (2002) 'Technology, geography, and trade,' *Econometrica*, 70, 1741–79.

Ethier, W. (1974) 'Some of the theorems of international trade with many goods and factors', *Journal of International Economics*, 4, 199–206.

——(1982) 'The general role of factor intensity in the theorems of international trade,' *Economics Letters*, 10(3–4), 337–42.

——(1984) 'Higher dimensional issues in trade theory,' in *Handbook of International Economics*, vol. 1, R.W. Jones and P.B. Kenen (eds). New York: Elsevier Science, 131–84.

Jones, R.W. (1965) 'The structure of simple general equilibrium models', *The Journal of Political Economy*, 73(6), 557–72.

Jones, R.W., and J. Scheinkman (1977) 'The relevance of the two-sector production model in trade theory', *Journal of Political Economy*, 85, 909–36.

Lloyd, P.J., and A.G. Schweinberger (1988) 'Trade expenditure functions and the gains from trade', *Journal of International Economics*, 24, 275–97.

Matsuyama, K. (2007) 'Beyond icebergs: Towards a theory of biased globalization', *Review of Economic Studies*, 74(1), 237–53.

——(2008) 'Ricardian trade theory', in L. Blume and S. Durlauf, (eds), *The New Palgrave Dictionary of Economics*, 2nd Ed. Macmillan.

McKenzie, L.W. (1954) 'Specialization and efficiency in world production', *Review of Economic Studies*, 21(3), 165–80.

Metzler, L. (1949) 'Tariffs, the terms of trade, and the distribution of the national income', *Journal of Political Economy*, 57, 1–29.

Neary, P. (1978) 'Short-run capital specificity and the pure theory of international trade', *Economic Journal*, 88(351), 488–510.

Romalis, J. (2004) 'Factor proportions and the structure of commodity trade,' *American Economic Review*, 14, 67–97.

Ruffin, R. (1988) 'The missing link: the Ricardian approach to the factor endowment Theory of Trade,' *American Economic Review*, 78, 759–72.

Rybczynski, T. (1955) 'Factor endowment and relative commodity prices', *Economica*, 22(84), 336–41.

Samuelson, P.A. (1953–54) 'Prices of Factors and Goods in General Equilibrium', *Review of Economic Studies*, 21, 1–20.

Shephard, R.W. (1953) *Cost and production functions* Princeton: Princeton University Press.

Stolper, W.F., and P.A. Samuelson (1941) 'Protection and real wages', *Review of Economic Studies*, 9, 58–73.

Uekawa, Y. (1971) 'Generalization of the Stolper–Samuelson theorem', *Econometrica*, 39(2), 197–217.

Uekawa Y., Kemp, M.C. and L.L. Wegge (1973) 'P- and PN-matrices, Minkowski- and Metzler- matrices, and generalizations of the Stolper–Samuelson and Samuelson-Rybczynski theorems', *Journal of International Economics*, 3(1), 53–76.

Wilson, C.A. (1980) 'On the general structure of Ricardian models with a continuum of goods: applications to growth, tariff theory, and technical change', *Econometrica*, 48(7), 1675–1702.

Woodland, A.D. (1977) 'A dual approach to equilibrium in the production sector in international trade theory', *Canadian Journal of Economics*, 10(1), 50–68.

—— (1980) 'Direct and indirect trade utility functions', *Review of Economic Studies*, 47(5), 907–26.

—— (1982) *International Trade and Resource Allocation*, Amsterdam: North-Holland Publishing Company.

—— (2008) 'Tradable and non-tradable commodities' in *The New Palgrave Dictionary of Economics*. 2nd Edition. S.N. Durlauf and L.E. Blume (eds) Palgrave Macmillan.

—— (2010) 'The factor price frontier', Chapter 35 in *Famous Figures and Diagrams in Economics*, M. Blaug and P. Lloyd (eds) Edward Elgar Publishing Company, Cheltenham, UK, 262–79.

Xu, Y. (1993) 'A general model of comparative advantage with two factors and a continuum of goods', *International Economic Review*, 34(2), 365–80.

4

The Empirics of General Equilibrium Trade Theory[1]

*Daniel M. Bernhofen**

1 Introduction

General equilibrium trade theory is one of the oldest subfields of economics. It has accumulated an impressive body of theoretical insights, many of which were discussed in the previous chapter of this handbook. This chapter surveys the empirical approaches that have been utilized linking the theory to the data. My emphasis will be on the development of the theoretical specifications that have been fruitfully applied to the empirical domain rather than on the empirical findings, per se.

The empirical literature on the neoclassical trade model has grown quite extensively during the past decades. Consequently, there have already been a number of excellent surveys published on the subject, such as Deardorff (1984), Leamer and Levinsohn (1995), Harrigan (2003), Davis and Weinstein (2003) and Feenstra (2004). The strategy of this chapter is to briefly discuss topics previously surveyed and examine in more depth subsequent empirical research.

A landmark goal of empirical work is either to refute or verify a theory.[2] Leontief's (1953) famous study, which concluded that the U.S. post–World War II trading pattern, was incompatible with the Heckscher–Ohlin prediction – the famous *Leontief paradox* – was for many years viewed as evidence against the competitive trade model. In fact, the Leontief paradox and Balassa's (1966) empirical documentation of substantial *intra-industry trade* among economies with similar factor endowments provided the key stimuli for the development of trade theories under imperfectly competitive markets, which are surveyed in several other chapters of this handbook.

During the 1980s tension between the simple formulations of the theories and the real world complexities launched an empirical research agenda aimed at refining and reformulating competitive trade theory to provide more convincing links between theoretical specification and the data. This empirical reorientation has led to a deeper understanding of competitive trade theory and of its position relative to the theories under imperfect competition. One of the key lessons we have learned is that the competitive and the new trade models are complementary, rather than competing, ways to look at many existing empirical regularities. The Leontief paradox has been long resolved (Leamer, 1980), and the existence of intra-industry trade (Davis, 1995), gravity (Eaton and Kortum, 2002) and firm heterogeneity (Bernard, Eaton, Jenson and Kortum, 2003) have all been shown to be compatible with different specifications of the competitive framework.

A distinguishing feature of the competitive model is that in a frictionless world, market prices convey important information about underlying fundamentals like technologies, endowments and preferences.[3] As a result, competitive goods and factor prices are able to yield predictions on the pattern, gains and distributional implications of international specialization without having to impose strong restrictions on the preferences of the underlying agents. Since prices are most informative about the economy's underlying fundamentals if they are observed in the absence of international trade, the most robust and general predictions are based on autarky goods or factor price data. Since prices do not play this role under imperfect competition, these predictions are a special feature of the competitive model.[4] Hence, empirical confirmations of these predictions, which will be reported later in the survey, provide strong scientific support for employing the competitive trade model in structural estimation exercises.

The competitive trade model is intrinsically linked to the concept of comparative advantage. Since there are different sources of comparative advantage, the competitive trade model comes in different formulations, each isolating specific determinants of comparative advantage. Topics are presented in the traditional way, beginning with the most general formulation of comparative advantage and then proceeding to the Ricardian and Heckscher–Ohlin submodels and the more recent hybrid specifications, which combine elements of both. Our focus will be on predictions regarding the pattern of international specializations, since predictions regarding the labour market effects of international trade are covered in chapter 14.

The natural starting point in Section 2 is the general price formulation of comparative advantage. Here, I highlight that the higher dimensional formulation of comparative advantage has the same underlying structure as the two-good textbook formulation. The setup of a natural experiment that allows for testing the comparative advantage prediction is discussed as is the estimation of the aggregate gains that arise from comparative advantage. This line of research has defied the conventional wisdom that comparative advantage is an untestable proposition.

Section 3 covers the Ricardian trade model which, until recently, was in the empirical shadow of the Heckscher–Ohlin framework. The recent seminal work by Eaton and Kortum (2002) has defied previous judgment of the Ricardian model to be empirically irrelevant. The key insight is that the randomization of technology provides a Ricardian explanation for the empirically highly relevant gravity equation. The multi-country dimension of the model has provided a new building block for structural estimation exercises pertaining to the pattern of world trade, and also refined Balassa's (1965) old insight that observed export shares reveal technological comparative advantage.

Section 4 discusses the Heckscher–Ohlin framework in its different formulations. Since a bulk of the empirical Heckscher–Ohlin–Vanek literature has been already surveyed in depth, only the seminal papers in the development of that literature have been included. The focus of this section will be on the recent tests of the multi-cone and price formulations of Heckscher–Ohlin.

Section 5 discusses some hybrid specifications which try to disentangle the different roles that technologies, endowments, or institutions play in determining the pattern of international specialization.

Section 6 concludes the survey.

2   Comparative advantage and the gains from trade

> Proofs of the static gains from trade fall into the unrefutable category yet these are some of the most important results in all of economics.
> (Leamer and Levinsohn, 1995, 1342)

We start out with the most general formulation of comparative advantage, but restrict ourselves initially to the case of only two commodities. Consider a small, open economy that considers trading with the rest of the world, called foreign. This implies that foreign prices p_1^f and p_2^f determine the country's terms of trade. The country's net import quantities are denoted by T_1 and T_2, with the balance of trade (BOT) being defined as:[5]

$$p_1^f T_1 + p_2^f T_2 = 0.$$

The BOT condition implies that there are only two feasible patterns of trade predictions: (i) export good 1 and import good 2 (i.e. $T_1 < 0$ and $T_2 > 0$) or (ii) import good 1 and export good 2 (i.e. $T_1 > 0$ and $T_2 < 0$). The law of comparative advantage predicts the pattern of trade by a comparison of relative prices under free trade with those prevailing if the economy had been operating in a state of no trade or autarky. Denoting the autarky prices with p_1^a and p_2^a, the predictions are: (i) if $p_1^a/p_2^a < p_1^f/p_2^f$, then $T_1 < 0$ and $T_2 > 0$ and (ii) if $p_1^a/p_2^a > p_1^f/p_2^f$, then $T_1 > 0$ and $T_2 < 0$. Using the balance of trade condition, it is easily verified that these conditional predictions can be expressed compactly in a single inequality:

$$p_1^a T_1 + p_2^a T_2 > 0. \tag{1}$$

Figure 4.1 depicts the economy's feasible trading patterns and how they are related to commodity prices. The balance of trade condition restricts the economy to trade along the BOT line. Relative prices are chosen such that $p_1^a/p_2^a < p_1^f/p_2^f$ which implies that the economy has a comparative advantage in good 1. Hence it will export good 1 and import good 2. An advantage of writing the two-good prediction as a single inequality is that it reveals that autarky goods prices impose a single refutable prediction on the commodity pattern of trade. For a given vector of data, denoted by T^*, to be compatible with the law of comparative advantage requires that $p_1^a T_1^* + p_2^a T_2^* > 0$. In addition, it highlights that the basic structure of the two-good prediction carries over to the n good formulation of comparative advantage, as formulated by Deardorff (1980) and Dixit and Norman (1980). Denoting p^a and T the economy's n-vectors of autarky prices and net import quantities, the general comparative advantage prediction is given by:

$$p^a T > 0. \qquad (2)$$

If $n > 2$, the prediction does not identify which particular good is exported or imported. The inequality is generally interpreted as a correlation version of comparative advantage which says that the economy will, on average, export goods with low autarky prices and import goods with high autarky prices. Figure 4.1 illustrates that the n-good formulation preserves the nature of the two good prediction. In particular, the hyperplane $p^a T = 0$ can be thought of cutting the set of feasible pattern of trading configurations (i.e. those that fulfil the balance

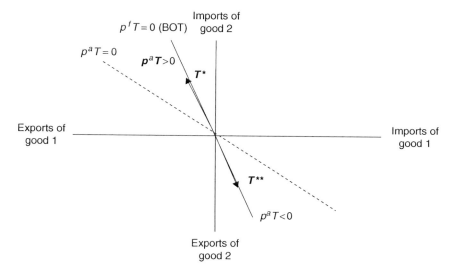

Figure 4.1 Comparative advantage prediction.

of trade condition $p^f T$) into half. The property that the economy's autarky price vector p^a yields a *single* refutable prediction on its net import vector T, with the rejection region given by $p^a T < 0$, is invariant to dimensionality. Finally, the prediction holds, as demonstrated by Deardorff (1980), under a minimum of critical assumptions on technologies, consumer preferences and government intervention. In particular, the only thing that needs to be assumed is that exports are, on average, not subsidized.

Bernhofen and Brown (2004) have identified Japan's opening up to international trade in the nineteenth century after two hundred years of self-imposed isolation as a natural experiment to test the general comparative advantage prediction (2). The unique feature of the case of Japan, and why it deserves to be called a natural experiment, is that it fulfils all the key assumptions of the neoclassical trade model. In particular, since Japan was a market-based economy producing fairly homogeneous products under autarky, Japan's autarky prices are good measures of the economy's opportunity costs. Furthermore, since Japan's move from autarky to free trade was rapid, Bernhofen and Brown were able to identify a 'free trade window' 1868–1875 in which the traded goods were compatible with the goods the economy was able to produce during its 'late autarky window' of 1851–1853. Matching detailed commodity market price data during the late autarky period with the observed trade data during 1868–1875, they find that the comparative advantage prediction holds in each single year.

The pattern of trade prediction is also tightly linked to the economy's aggregate gains from trade. In fact, the *sign* of the inner product $p^a T$ provides information about whether an observed net import vector T yields gains (or losses) to the economy and the *magnitude* of $p^a T$ provides information about the size of these gains. This can be illustrated in figure 4.1. The net import vector T^{**} yields a loss (i.e. $p^a T^{**} < 0$) since the international exchange of good 2 for good 1 occurs at the rate p_2^f/p_1^f which is less favourable than the domestic rate of exchange p_2^a/p_1^a under autarky. By the same reasoning, the net import vector T^* yields a welfare gain since $p_1^f/p_2^f > p_1^a/p_2^a$. This illustrates that the existence of gains from trade can, in principle, be refuted by the data.

The magnitude of $p^a T^*$ captures the size of the gains from trade. This can be seen as follows: fixing p_1^a/p_2^a, an increase in p_1^f/p_2^f leads to a more favourable terms of trade, which results in larger gains from trade. This will cause T^* to move further away from the hyperplane $p^a T = 0$; hence, a more favourable terms of trade is associated with an increase in $p^a T^*$.

A more rigorous treatment of the gains from trade relates the inner product to the Slutsky compensation measure of welfare, which is defined as the increase in income which would allow the economy to move from autarky to free-trade consumption when both are valued at autarky prices. However, as stressed in

Bernhofen and Brown (2005), since autarky and free trade are observed at different points in time, the comparison involves a counterfactual. In the case of Japan it involves a comparison between Japan's actual consumption point C_{1850}^a under autarky with the counterfactual consumption bundle C_{1850}^f that the economy could have obtained if trade had taken place during the 1850s. Denoting the counterfactual trading vector during the 1850s as T_{1850s}, the inner product $p^a T_{1850s}$ can be shown to provide an upper bound to the Slutsky welfare measure[6]:

$$\Delta W_{\text{Slutsky}} = p^a C_{1850s}^f - p^a C_{1850s}^a \leq p^a T_{1850s}. \tag{3}$$

The welfare question suggested by $\Delta W_{\text{Slutsky}}$ is then the following: 'By how much would real income have had to increase in Japan during its final autarky years 1851–1853 to afford the consumption bundle the economy could have obtained if it had been engaged in international trade during the period?'

Using different historical estimates on Japan's GDP levels at the time around its opening, Bernhofen and Brown obtain upper bounds on the gains from trade of about 8 to 9 percent of Japan's GDP.[7]

3 The Ricardian framework

In the Ricardian framework comparative advantage arises from technological differences. The multi-good formulation of the Ricardian model, which goes back to Haberler (1930), assumes a single factor (labour), two countries (home and foreign) and n goods. The technology of producing good i in home and foreign is given by the per unit labour requirements a_i and a_i^* which can be arranged into a productivity ordering or *a chain of comparative advantage*:

$$a_1^*/a_1 > a_2^*/a_2 > \cdots > a_n^*/a_n. \tag{4}$$

The productivity ordering (4) postulates that home has the highest productivity advantage in good 1 and the least productivity advantage in good n. Haberler postulated that demand factors will determine some breakpoint in the chain predicting that the home economy completely specializes in and exports the low indexed goods (i.e. to the left of the break) and the foreign economy will specialize and export the high indexed goods. Comparative advantage and trade are determined by relative productivity advantages in a bilateral comparison.

The first empirical studies which used the formulation (4) as the basis of an empirical analysis of the Ricardian model were conducted by Mac-Dougall (1951, 1952), who calculated relative labour productivity differences for U.S. and British manufacturing industries and linked them to the countries' relative export volumes. MacDougall found that in those industries in which the United States had a higher productivity advantage it had also a higher share of the export market relative to the UK. Subsequently, Stern (1962) and Balassa (1963) built upon MacDougall by using different data and methodology and also found a consistently positive and significant correlation between US and UK relative export shares and the corresponding productivity ratios.

These robust empirical regularities have been difficult to interpret on theoretical grounds since they consider export shares to third countries, whereas the chain logic (4) is tied to a two-country framework. Furthermore, there is nothing in the theoretical specification (4) suggesting a positive relationship between export shares and productivity ratios. An unsettling feature of this formulation is that it implies a sharp edge prediction of complete international specialization which are not expected to be found in aggregate data. For that reason, the Ricardian framework has for many years been judged to be of 'little empirical relevance' (Leamer and Levinsohn, 1995) compared to its Heckscher–Ohlin sibling.

This view has been challenged by Eaton and Kortum (2002), who opened a line of inquiry which has demonstrated that the Ricardian framework *is* empirically relevant. Since Eaton and Kortum is a multi-country extension of Dornbusch, Fischer and Samuelson (DFS) (1977), we sketch the main features of DFS.[8]

DFS generalizes Haberler's chain formulation (4) to a continuum of goods, which are indexed by $z \in [0,1]$. The comparative advantage ranking is then given by a relative productivity curve $A(z) = a^*(z)/a(z)$ which is assumed to be decreasing in z. Home has its highest productivity advantage in good 0 and it diminishes as one moves towards good 1. A key innovation of DFS is that they derive the breakpoint in an analytical model from underlying demand and cost fundamentals. In particular, free trade relative labour costs of home w/w^*, which can be thought of as the *factoral terms of trade*, yield the breakpoint by defining a marginal good m such that home will specialize and export $[0, m]$ and foreign will export $[m, 1]$.[9]

A second key innovation of DFS is the incorporation of trade frictions, modelled as iceberg trade costs τ ($\tau > 1$), into the Ricardian framework.[10] In the presence of trade costs, the equilibrium is characterized by two marginal goods m_1 and m_2 which partition the unit interval into three segments. Home and foreign will then specialize in and export those sectors where they have the highest relative productivity advantages, that is home in $[0, m_1]$ and foreign in $[m_2, 1]$ whereas $[m_1, m_2]$ is the endogenously determined non-traded sector. In many ways, DFS is the foundation article of modelling trade costs in a fully articulated general equilibrium model which allows for comparative statics.[11] For a given trade cost level τ, countries will export only in sectors (or activities) in which they have a high relative productivity advantage. A reduction in trade costs, that is, a fall in τ, will affect the volume of bilateral trade through both the intensive and extensive margin. Resource savings from less waste in international shipping will increase the volume of goods which have been traded before–the so-called *intensive margin*–via an income effect. Increased foreign competition will result in a shrinking of the non-traded sector and new trade in goods which were previously sheltered by trade costs, the so-called *extensive margin*.

Since the size of the non-traded sector is increasing in the trade costs, trade costs reduce the volume of trade. Furthermore, assuming identical and homothetic preferences it can be shown that the volume of two-way trade is increasing in the size of the economies' labour forces. As a result, DFS already yields a gravity prediction, where the volume of bilateral trade is increasing in the countries' relative country size and decreasing in trade costs, but only in the two-country case.

The key innovation of Eaton and Kortum (2002) is to extend DFS to a multi-country framework by modelling technological heterogeneity as a random process rather than assuming it to be deterministic. Country i's labour productivity $a^i(z)$ in producing good z is assumed to be a random variable with a Fréchet distribution, with the distribution function given by:

$$\Pr[a^i(z) \leq A] = F^i(A) = e^{-T^i A^{-\theta}}.$$

Furthermore, it is assumed that the productivity drawings are independent across goods and countries.

Since all goods fall in $[0, 1]$, $F^i(A)$ is also the fraction of goods for which country i's labour productivity is lower than or equal to A. This fraction is affected by the technology parameters T^i and θ. The country-specific parameter T^i captures the country's state of technology, reflecting its absolute advantage across the continuum and corresponds to the absolute size of the input coefficients in (4). The parameter θ corresponds to the steepness of $A(z)$ in the DFS formulation. A higher θ is equivalent to a flatter $A(z)$ schedule. In the limiting case where $A(z)$ is horizontal, the absence of relative productivity advantages would reduce the incentive for trade.

On the demand side, buyers–who could be final consumers or firms buying intermediate goods–purchase goods to maximize a CES objective. Buyers in country j compare prices from all source countries and are only willing to pay the minimum price for a good z. As in DFS, country-pair specific iceberg trade costs, τ^{ij}, impose frictions to trade as they affect prices at the point of delivery. A country i with a lower state of technology T^i which is more remote from its trading partners (i.e. τ^{ij} is high), will sell a narrower range of goods to the destination country j. A key feature of this model set up is that the probability that country i provides the good at the lowest price to country j is equal to the fraction of the goods that j purchases from i. As a result, the share of country j's expenditure on the goods from country i, x^{ij}, in its total expenditure e^j can be written in its gravity type form:

$$x^{ij}/e^j = Q^i/\Phi(\cdot), \tag{5}$$

where Q^i denotes the exporter's total sales. The function $\Phi(\cdot)$ in the denominator captures how the interaction of technological heterogeneity and geographical distance affects the volume of bilateral trade.

The gravity equation can also be derived from models that are based on product differentiation, as in the Armington model or the model of monopolistic competition (see chapter 17).[12] Consequently, the uniform empirical success of gravity regressions cannot be interpreted as empirical evidence for the Ricardian framework. Instead it suggests that the forces of gravity might work through the Ricardian mechanism where a decrease in trade costs increases the volume of trade as it induces countries to specialize in and export goods in which they have a productivity advantage. This is in contrast to models of product differentiation where a decrease in trade costs does not affect the set of traded goods, but rather induces consumers to spend more on each imported variety.[13]

An attractive feature of Eaton and Kortum (2002) is that it provides a structural multi-sector, multi-country model whose parameters can be estimated to explore comparative statics effects in general equilibrium. In their original paper, they apply their framework to 19 OECD countries and conduct a variety of counterfactual exercises regarding the gains from trade, the role of geographic barriers on international specialization, the welfare effects of tariff reductions and the benefits of new technology. Donaldson (2010) applies the Eaton and Kortum framework creatively to colonial India and estimates the general equilibrium effects of the colonial railroad expansion from 1853 to 1930. An attractive aspect of this application is that the empirical domain is compatible with the key features of the model where the production of homogenous products is dispersed geographically among Indian regions subject to productivity (or weather) shocks. He finds that this massive transportation infrastructure project improved overall welfare by regions exploiting their comparative advantage.[14]

An essential feature of the multi-sector Ricardian model is its emphasis on technological heterogeneity. Introducing Bertrand competition into the Eaton Kortum set up, Bernard, Eaton, Jenson and Kortum (2003) are able to generate empirical predictions that have been found in many plant level data sets around the world.[15] Regarding predictability, the Eaton Kortum framework is isomorphic to Melitz (2003). Both models imply new gains from trade in the form of overall productivity gains that stem from trade inducing the exit of low productivity and the expansion of high productivity activities.[16] Bernard, Eaton, Jenson and Kortum (2003) calibrate their model to bilateral trade between the U.S. and its trading partners and examine counterfactual exercises on the impacts of globalization on aggregate and plant level variables.

Building on Eaton and Kortum, Costinot, Donaldson and Komunjer (2010) develop a Ricardian structural model in which technological differences across countries yield predictions on the pattern of trade. They accomplish this by introducing exogenous productivity differences in the Eaton Kortum setup.

Consider a slight modification of the above setup by assuming that each good k comes in N^k varieties and N^k is assumed to be large. Technology is modelled such that labour productivity of variety v of good k in country i is given by:

$$\ln a_k^i(v) = \ln a_k^i + u_k^i(v),$$

where a_k^i is a deterministic labour unit requirement that is common to all varieties, and $u_k^i(v)$ is stochastic and variety-specific. The deterministic component a_k^i can be thought of capturing the fundamental productivity of country i in industry k. The stochastic component $u_k^i(v)$, which is assumed to be drawn independently from the same distribution, captures random productivity shocks which give rise to intra-industry heterogeneity. The degree of intra-industry heterogeneity is captured by the productivity parameter θ, which is similar to the specification discussed above.

A key feature of this specification is that cross-country and cross-industry variations in the distribution of productivity levels stem from variations in the fundamental productivity parameters a_k^i. The existence of exogenous productivity differences across industries shifts the indeterminacy in trade in individual industries to indeterminacy in trade in varieties.

Given a pair of countries i_1 and i_2, we can order the industries according to their relative fundamental productivities:

$$\frac{a_1^{i_1}}{a_1^{i_2}} \succ \frac{a_2^{i_1}}{a_2^{i_2}} \succ \cdots \succ \frac{a_n^{i_1}}{a_n^{i_2}},$$

which coincides with (4) for the two-country case with no random productivity shocks. However, in the presence of productivity shocks, the ranking of fundamental productivities implies a stochastic ranking of total labour requirements:

$$\frac{a_1^{i_1}(v)}{a_1^{i_2}(v)} \succ \frac{a_2^{i_1}(v)}{a_2^{i_2}(v)} \succ \cdots \succ \frac{a_n^{i_1}(v)}{a_n^{i_2}(v)}, \tag{6}$$

where $\succ$ denotes the first-order stochastic dominance operator. Since (6) is a stochastic ordering, there is some indeterminacy in the trading pattern of individual varieties. As a result, there is no sharp edge prediction of country i_1 producing and exporting all varieties in the high indexed industries. Rather that it is more likely to export relatively more of these varieties. However, the ranking of fundamental productivities determines the ranking of relative export shares to any third trading partner:

$$\left\{ \frac{a_1^{i_1}}{a_1^{i_2}} \succ \frac{a_2^{i_1}}{a_2^{i_2}} \succ \cdots \succ \frac{a_n^{i_1}}{a_n^{i_2}} \right\} \Leftrightarrow \left\{ \frac{x_1^{i_1j}}{x_1^{i_2j}} \prec \frac{x_2^{i_1j}}{x_2^{i_2j}} \prec \cdots \prec \frac{x_n^{i_1j}}{x_n^{i_2j}} \right\}, \tag{7}$$

where x_k^{ij} denotes the exports of country i to j in good k.[17] The one-to-one relationship in (7) is quite a remarkable result since it predicts an ordering of export shares to *any* trading partner from an ordering of relative labour productivities. Alternatively, (7) implies that the ranking of relative export shares reveals the ranking of relative fundamental productivity differences.

The idea that observed export shares reveal productivity differences resembles Balassa's (1965) concept of revealed comparative advantage, which has been widely used in the empirical trade literature. However, the literature on revealed comparative advantage has been criticized as having no trade-theoretical foundations. Balassa's approach used data on relative exports to infer the revealed pattern of comparative advantage across countries and industries. He aggregated exports across countries and industries to obtain a measure of revealed comparative advantage of country i in industry k against an ad-hoc benchmark, which is not rooted in economic theory. In contrast, (7) *is* derived from economic theory. It suggests that a pair-wise comparison of countries' productivities are linked to the corresponding export shares to a specific third country rather than a benchmark of countries.

Costinot, Donaldson and Komunjer (2010) use the ordering (7) to derive a structural equation that predicts how variations in observed productivity levels across countries and industries affect the variation in bilateral exports. Their empirical findings are consistent with the theoretical predictions and their estimated parameter of intra-industry heterogeneity θ is compatible with values found in previous studies.

The Eaton-Kortum model provides a useful general equilibrium framework conducive for deriving predictions on how trade costs affect the pattern of international specialization. Harrigan (2010) considers a variation of Eaton and Kortum by considering differences in trade costs across goods. He indexes goods $z \in [0,1]$ by increasing weight where good 0 is the lightest (computer chips) and good 1 is the heaviest (oil). Goods can be shipped by two modes of transportation: surface (i.e. ship, train or truck) or airfreight. Surface shipping costs are the same for all goods, but airfreight costs depend on weight and are therefore increasing in z. Since air transport is more costly, consumers must value speed. So Harrigan assumes that a good yields a higher utility if it is shipped by air.

Harrigan derives a prediction about the relationship between unit values of imported goods and distance for a specific country: imports from nearby trading partners have lower unit values than imports from more distant partners. The intuition for this finding is that nearby countries will specialize in low value/weight products which will be sent by surface; whereas, more distant countries specialize in high value/weight products shipped by air. Applying the model to U.S. imports data from 1990 to 2003, Harrigan finds empirical support for these predictions.

4 The Heckscher–Ohlin framework

In the Heckscher–Ohlin model comparative advantage arises from endowment differences. This requires a second factor of production, capital. The second factor of production can be mobile or specific to an industry; the latter gives rise to the specific factor model. Because the free-trade equilibrium is in the normal case characterized by incomplete specialization, the Heckscher–Ohlin model has long been viewed as empirically more relevant than the Ricardian model and inspired a considerable amount of empirical work.

The seminal study by Leontief (1953) was the first attempt to confront the Heckscher–Ohlin theory with data. Leontief developed input–output accounts for the U.S. economy in 1947 and used them to calculate the capital and labour content of aggregate U.S. export and import flows with the rest of the world. Leontief's analytical framework was the textbook two-good, two-factor version of the Heckscher–Ohlin model which predicts that a capital abundant country should export the capital-intensive good and import the labour-intensive good. Applying this prediction to the U.S. data, Leontief compared the capital-labour ratios of U.S. exports with that of its imports. Surprisingly, Leontief found that the capital-labour ratio of U.S. imports was larger than the capital-labour ratio of U.S. exports. Since the U.S. was clearly the most capital abundant country in the world at that time, his findings seemed at odds with the Heckscher–Ohlin prediction and the outcome of his test was famously labelled the *Leontief Paradox*.

Leontief's finding stimulated a large empirical literature aimed at providing explanations for this paradox and also provided a stimulus for extending the Heckscher–Ohlin model to higher dimensions.[18] Among the many explanations, Leamer (1980) provided the most convincing resolution of the paradox. Building on the theoretical work by Vanek (1968), Leamer argued that the Leontief Paradox is based on a conceptual misunderstanding of the Heckscher–Ohlin Theorem.

Leamer showed that Vanek's theoretically correct Heckscher–Ohlin prediction involves a comparison between the capital-labour ratios of a country's production and consumption rather than the capital-labour ratios of the country's exports and imports. When applying the correct comparison to Leontief's 1947 U.S. data, the paradox disappeared. Leamer's paper triggered a large research agenda aimed at investigating the empirical validity of the Heckscher–Ohlin Theorem in its Heckscher–Ohlin–Vanek (HOV) formulation.[19]

Since in the HOV model relative factor abundance is captured by differences in the countries' factor endowment, this is called the quantity formulation of Heckscher–Ohlin. Alternatively, relative factor abundance can be captured by differences in countries' factor prices giving rise to the price formulation of Heckscher–Ohlin. We start out by introducing the HOV model and discuss the key developments in this literature.[20] Then we review recent empirical work which is based on the price formulation of Heckscher–Ohlin.

4.1   Quantity formulation of Heckscher–Ohlin: HOV

Consider an integrated world economy with m countries, l factors and n goods and no impediments to international trade.[21] The Heckscher–Ohlin–Vanek model is based on three critical assumptions that characterize the integrated equilibrium. First, it assumes that countries have the same technology matrix, $A(\cdot) = < a_{vg}(\cdot) >$, where a_{vg} denotes the units of factor v necessary to produce one unit of good g. Second, it assumes that endowment differences are such that all countries produce the goods with the same production techniques. An implication of these two assumptions is that the free-trade equilibrium is characterized by factor price equalization (FPE).[22] A common factor price vector w implies that the input coefficients $a_{vg}(w)$ are the same everywhere. The third critical assumption is that all consumers in the world have the same homothetic preferences, which means that they consume all goods in the same proportions.

Figure 4.2 illustrates an integrated equilibrium with three countries, six goods and two factors (labour and capital). Countries are characterized by their endowment vectors V^1, V^2, V^3 which add up to the world endowment vector V^w and are capable of producing the six goods $g_1, \ldots g_6$ with the capital-labour ratios given in the diagram.[23] In a world with more than two goods, it is not possible to identify which particular good a country is either exporting or importing. However, the assumption of identical and homothetic preferences allows one to identify which particular factors are traded. Specifically, the homotheticity assumption implies that a country's equilibrium consumption vector is given by $C^i = s^i V^w$, where s^i denotes country i's share of world GDP. Figure 4.2 illustrates

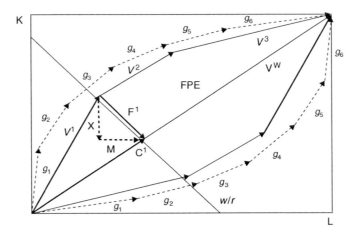

Figure 4.2   Heckscher–Ohlin–Vanek model.

Leamer's (1980) point that the Heckscher–Ohlin prediction involves a comparison of an economy's capital-labour ratio of production and consumption. For example, since country 1's endowment vector V^1 lies to the left of the diagonal, it is capital abundant relative to the world. But since the preference symmetry assumption implies that the country's equilibrium consumption vector C^1 also lies on the diagonal, it follows immediately that the capital-labour ratio of its production, which is its endowment, exceeds the capital-labour ratio of its consumption. In a free-trade equilibrium, country 1 will implicitly export X units of capital and import M units of labour.[24]

As a commodity trading vector is the difference between domestic production and domestic consumption, the factor content of trade is the difference between the factor content of consumption and the factor content of production. Country i's factor content of net imports F^i is constructed by multiplying the common technology matrix A with the country's net import vector T^i, that is, $F^i = AT^i$. Since the country's production vector is V^i and its consumption vector is $s^i V^w$, the Heckscher–Ohlin–Vanek (HOV) relationship for country i in factor k is given by:

$$F_k^i = AT_k^i = V_k^i - s^i V_k^w = V_k^i - s^i \sum_j V_k^j. \tag{8}$$

The HOV equation implies a sign prediction on the individual factors of production:

$$(V_k^i - s^i V_k^w)F_k^i > 0. \tag{9}$$

The restrictions (9) are derived from the factor-balance-of-trade equilibrium conditions given in (8). A pair-wise comparison of factor specific endowment differences between country i and the world in factor k predicts the sign of the factor content of trade in that factor. The number of restrictions increases with the number of factors and countries in the trading equilibrium. This is quite different to the comparative advantage formulation (2) which yields a single restriction that is invariant to the number of countries or factors in the trading equilibrium. The reason for this is that (2) is based on the gains from trade argument which does not depend on dimensionality and where the predictor stems from the autarky equilibrium.

In (9) the direction of trade of an individual factor is predicted by the country's endowment of this factor minus the world endowment scaled by the country size. Alternatively, we can rank the factors according to their factor scarcities relative to the world.

$$\frac{V_1}{V_1^w} < \frac{V_2}{V_2^w} < \cdots \frac{V_k}{V_k^w} < s < \frac{V_{k+1}}{V_{k+1}^w} < \cdots \frac{V_l}{V_l^w}. \tag{10}$$

The Heckscher–Ohlin–Vanek relationship implies then a chain prediction where the economy is a net importer of its scarce factors $(1,...,k)$ and a net exporter of its abundant factors $(k+1,...,l)$.

Bowen, Leamer and Sveikauskas (BLS) (1987) were the first to test the full implications of (8) on a broad data set comprising of 27 countries and 12 factors.[25] A key feature of BWL is their use of a single U.S. technology matrix to measure each country's factor content of trade. They tested both the sign predictions (9) and a rank comparison, that is, whether $F_k^i > F_l^i <=> (V_k^i - s^i V_k^w) > (V_l^i - s^i V_l^w)$, and found that both performed quite poorly. Their findings that the predictions of the model were no more successful than the toss of a coin dampened further inquiry of HOV.

Motivated by the observation that a common U.S. technology matrix is clearly an implausible assumption, Trefler (1993) reinvigorated interest in HOV by relaxing the assumption of identical technologies. Inspired by Leontief's (1953) claim that the United States is abundant in labour when labour is measured in 'productivity equivalents', Trefler asks whether one can find plausible factor productivity parameters π_k^i such that the data fit a productivity-adjusted HOV equation:

$$F_k^i = \pi_k^i V_k^i - s^i \sum_j \pi_k^j V_k^j. \tag{11}$$

The specification (11) allows factors in all countries to differ in their productivities. Taking the United States as a benchmark, π_k^i measures the productivity of factor k in country i relative to its productivity in the United States, assuming $\pi_k^{US} = 1$. From a measurement point of view, the factor content of trade in country i is still evaluated with a common U.S. technology matrix, that is, $F^i = A^{US} T^i$. However, a country's factor content of trade is now explained by productivity-adjusted endowment vectors $\pi^i V^i$ and factor price equalization is assumed to hold in a world of *effective endowments*. Trefler views (11) as a system of equations which can be solved for the unknown productivity parameters. From a methodological viewpoint this is quite a different approach from BLS as it shifts the emphasis from testing to 'reasonability of fit'. Trefler solves for the productivity parameters in (11) and argues that they are reasonable since the labour productivity parameters are highly correlated with wages and the capital productivity parameters correlate with the price of capital.[26] Trefler's finding can be interpreted as support of HOV as long as productivity differences are taken into account.

In a follow-up piece, Trefler (1995) goes back to (9), revisits BLS using an extended data set, confirms their negative finding for an unadjusted HOV equation and identifies an empirical regularity in the relative magnitudes of the left- and right-hand sides of (8). Trefler finds that the measured factor content of trade F_k^i is much smaller relative to its factor endowment prediction,

that is, $V_k^i - s^i V_k^w$, which he calls the *mystery of the missing trade*.[27] Trefler suggests then an alternative way of modeling productivity differences which does not lead to a perfect fit in the HOV equation. Assuming uniform productivity differences, a country's technology matrix A^i is given by $A^i = A^{US}/\delta^i$, where the single parameter δ^i captures the productivity difference of country i relative to the United States. If $\delta^i < 1$, country i is less productive than the United States in all factors. The modified HOV equation then becomes:

$$F_k^i = \delta^i V_k^i - s^i \sum_j \delta^j V_k^j, \tag{12}$$

where a country's factor content of trade is still evaluated using the U.S. technology matrix, that is, $F^i = A^{US} T^i$. The productivity parameters δ^i are then chosen to minimize the sum of squared residuals in (12). A comparison of the variance of the left-hand side with the estimated right-hand side of (8) or (12) can then be used as a measure of the R^2 of the model under the different specifications. Trefler finds that the incorporation of uniform productivity differences explains about one half of the missing trade and improves the success of the sign tests (9) from 50 percent to 62 percent.[28]

Davis and Weinstein (2001) depart from Trefler (1993, 1995) in empirical methodology and data approach. Rather than focusing on the technology matrix of a single country (that is the United States), they rely on OECD input–output data that allows them to construct technology matrices for ten OECD countries and for a composite rest of the world. Davis and Weinstein's approach is to spell out different hypotheses of why prior tests of HOV fail. In particular, they ask how relaxing one of the critical assumptions improves the fit of the model. They specify and estimate seven different specifications and judge submodel performance by the highest R^2. Their preferred model does not only allow for technical differences and non-homothetic preferences, but also for non-traded goods and costly trade.

Fisher and Marshall (2008) provide an alternative approach to incorporate technological differences into the HOV model. Rather than estimating productivity parameters relative to the United States, as done by Trefler (1993, 1995), or constructing technology matrices, as done by Davis and Weinstein (2001), they tackle the issue from the endowment side. Instead of using data on actual endowments as predictors for the factor content of trade, they suggest using *virtual endowments*.[29] A country's virtual endowment vector V^{vi} is defined as the factor services needed to produce a country's production output y^i using a reference country's technology matrix A°, that is, $V^{vi} = A^\circ y^i$. Since this approach imposes full employment at the reference country's factor prices and technology, it assumes that every country has the same technology and factor prices as the reference country. Accordingly, the virtual world endowment vector is then the sum of the individual country's virtual endowments. A country's factor content of trade is defined using the country's domestic technology matrix, that is, $F_k^i = A^i \, T^i$, which leads then to the following modified Heckscher–Ohlin prediction:

$$\left(V_k^{vi} - s^i \sum_j V_k^{vj} \right) F_k^i > 0. \tag{13}$$

Fisher and Marshall implement (13) on a sample of 33 countries and conduct the test using every country as a possible reference. Their results are quite striking. The success rate of the predictions ranges between 73 percent (Poland as a reference) and 93 percent (Taiwan as a reference). The hypothesis that the model does not predict the direction of trade better than the flip of a coin can be rejected with 99 percent for each reference country. In addition, since the magnitudes of the virtual endowment predictors come close to the magnitudes of the factor content of trade there is hardly any missing trade.

So, what accounts for this apparent improvement over the previous literature? Fisher and Marshall argue that the answer lies in the quality of the data. Previous studies gathered data on endowments and factor uses from sources other than input–output accounts and that are known to be plagued by measurement errors. Fisher and Marshall's approach picks up countries' endowment differences from differences in local output levels which are 'accurately' matched with local technology matrices.[30] A virtue of this approach is that they do not have to estimate anything and let the data speak for itself.

Since the Heckscher–Ohlin framework emphasizes country differences as a determinant of trade, we would expect that the theory would fare better explaining North–South trade than trade between similar economies. Motivated by Wood (1994), who has stressed that North–South trade has not been directly studied within the HOV framework, Debaere (2003) derives factor content expressions that relate bilateral differences in factor endowments to bilateral differences in factor contents. Since his relationships compare multilateral factor contents for two countries only, he is able to compare the predictions on the entire sample relative to North–South trade. Using Trefler's (1995) data set, Debaere finds that the bilateral factor content predictions show a success rate of 70 percent if one considers the entire sample, which improves up to 90 percent if one explicitly includes the factor content of North–South trade. In the case of North–South trade, the incorporation of Hicks-neutral differences do not significantly improve the results. Debaere's finding is important since it suggests a significant improvement if HOV is tested in a data domain where countries' endowments differ significantly.

In concluding our discussion of the HOV framework, it is worthwhile to point out that in the quest for improving the empirical fit of the HOV model, it has become apparent that the empirical literature has been suffering from what I previously called 'the tyranny of non-refutability'.[31] This stems from the fact that the HOV formulation is based on an identity. More precise measurement of this identity is expected to lead to a better fit. Now we turn to a factor content formulation which can overcome this identity problem.

4.2 Autarky price formulation

The Heckscher–Ohlin theory explains comparative advantage by relative factor scarcity. But factor scarcity can be measured in two different ways. The Heckscher–Ohlin–Vanek formulation follows the Leontief tradition which measures factor scarcity by differences in factor endowments. Alternatively, in Ohlin's (1933) original formulation factor scarcity is measured by differences in relative factor prices under autarky. Deardorff (1982) has provided a general formulation of the Hecksche-Ohlin Theorem which uses Ohlin's autarky price measure as a predictor for the factor content of trade. Denoting w^a and F the l-vectors of autarky factor prices and net factor content of imports respectively, the country's autarky factor prices impose a single restriction on a country's factor content of trade with the rest of the world:

$$w^a F > 0. \tag{14}$$

The prediction (14) is similar to the comparative advantage prediction in (2).

A country is predicted, on average, to import its scarce factors and export its abundant factors. Deardorff (1982) derives (14) using three different methods of measuring the factor content of trade but under the assumption of identical technologies.[32] Building on Deardorff (1982), Neary and Schweinberger (1986) have shown that as long as the factor content of trade is measured using the domestic technology matrix, the gains from trade is the only sufficient condition for deriving (14).

The link between the gains from trade and the prediction on the factor content of trade can be illustrated in a factor content diagram given in figure 4.3. The autarky price vector w^a defines a hyperplane $w^a F$ which identifies the rejection region. A factor content vector F^{**} which falls in that region (i.e. $w^a F^{**} < 0$) yields a loss (measured in units of factor 1) since the international exchange of factor 1 for factor 2 occurs at a less favourable rate than the domestic factor exchange rate given by the autarky factor prices. On the other hand, the factor content vector F^* yields positive gains from trade (measured in units of factor 2) and $w^a F^* > 0$.

An attractive feature of (14) is that it can be tested using data for a single economy without having to assume anything about the technologies of the trading partners. However, it requires compatible data of an economy observed under autarky and free trade. Bernhofen and Brown (2010) revisit the natural experiment of Japan to test (14). Since Bernhofen and Brown (2005) have

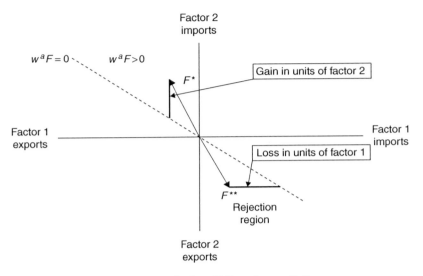

Figure 4.3   Heckscher–Ohlin price prediction.

already provided evidence that Japan experienced gains from trade, as discussed in Section 2, we already know that the data environment fulfils the critical assumption of the theory. As a result, there is something at stake in testing (14) since a rejection could not be explained by unmet assumptions. Bernhofen and Brown (2010) employ a self-constructed input–output matrix from around 1870 to obtain Japan's factor content of trade during its early trading period $F^i = A^{1870}T^i$ $(i = 1865, \ldots, 1876)$. When evaluating F^i at the factor prices w^{1850s} in the late autarky period, they are unable to reject (14) for each single trading year. Hence, the case of Japan provides further empirical support for the general Heckscher–Ohlin prediction in its autarky price formulation.

4.3   Multiple cones

In its core formulation, the Heckscher–Ohlin–Vanek model assumes that countries' endowments are not too dissimilar so that the free-trade equilibrium is characterized by factor price equalization and countries are said to be in a single cone of diversification. If endowments are sufficiently different, countries will specialize in different sets of goods and factor prices can differ in a free-trade equilibrium.

The empirical multi-cone literature focuses on two different, but related issues. The first approach attempts to derive hypotheses aimed at testing Heckscher–Ohlin specialization in the absence of factor price equalization. Lack of factor price equalization stems from multiple cones, rather than trade costs. The second approach asks whether countries occupy different cones. We first look at the testing literature and then survey the papers that aim to match countries to cones.

The theoretical framework for the multi-cone approach goes back to Deardorff (1979), who identified a Heckscher–Ohlin chain of comparative advantage ranking in the case of two factors. Ordering countries in terms of relative factor prices implies a ranking of relative factor abundance:

$$w^1/r^1 > w^2/r^2 > \cdots > w^m/r^m. \tag{15}$$

In (15) country 1 is most capital abundant and has therefore the highest wage rental ratio, whereas country m is least capital abundant and has the lowest wage rental ratio.

The implication for the pattern of specialization can be illustrated with the Lerner–Pearce diagram in figure 4.4 which depicts a free trade equilibrium with three countries, six goods and three cones C^1, C^2 and C^3.

Goods are ranked by their relative factor intensities, and the equilibrium production level is characterized by the tangency between the country-specific factor price line and the corresponding unit value isoquant.[33] The model predicts that the most capital abundant country 1 specializes in the most capital-intensive goods 1 and 2; country 2 specializes in goods 3 and 4 and country 3, which is most labour abundant, specializes in the most labour-intensive goods 5 and 6.

Deardorff's (1979) chain of comparative advantage goods prediction cannot be easily adapted to the data. Building on the cost efficiency logic of the free-trade equilibrium, Helpman (1984) derives restrictions on the factor content of bilateral trade which generalizes Deardorff (1979) to the case of an arbitrary number

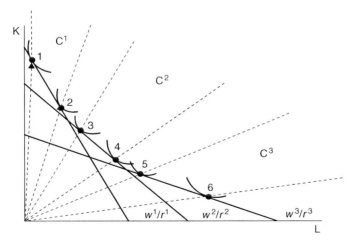

Figure 4.4 Multi-cone specification.

of factors. Consider a free trade equilibrium characterized by m l-vectors of factor prices $w^1, \ldots, w^m$, where w^i denotes the factor price vector of country i and a common technology matrix, $A(\cdot)$. If T^{ij} denotes the vector of gross exports from country i to country j, the corresponding factor content of exports F^{ij} is defined as $F^{ij} = A(w^i)T^{ij}$. Helpman (1984) shows then that the factor price difference $(w^i - w^j)$ imposes a restriction on F^{ij}:

$$(w^j - w^i)'F^{ij} > 0. \tag{16}$$

The restriction (16) has some similarity to (14) in the sense that factor prices impose a restriction on the factor content of trade. But whereas (14) constitutes a single refutable Heckscher–Ohlin prediction, (16) yields as many restrictions as there are country pairs. The intuition behind (16) is that since F^{ij} originates in country i, it is more expensive to evaluate F^{ij} at the foreign factor price vector w^j than at w^i. By symmetry, we obtain $(w^i - w^j)'F^{ji} > 0$ and adding the two restrictions implies a joint restriction on the net factor content of exports:

$$(w^j - w^i)'(F^{ij} - F^{ji}) > 0. \tag{17}$$

An attractive feature of (16) and (17) compared to the Heckscher–Ohlin–Vanek specification (9) is that they can be tested on a subset of countries. Choi and Krishna (2004) investigate (17) with a data set of eight OECD countries for which the identical technology assumption appears to be justified. An innovative feature of their study is their construction of economy-wide factor price data from cost components of GDP where GDP is decomposed into compensation of employees, operating surplus and an aggregate of other components such as indirect taxes and subsidies. They consider various factor classifications, where wage rates are disaggregated either into two or four subcategories. Their approach treats capital as a residual when employee compensation is taken out of GDP. They then propose two different rates of capital, depending on the treatment of taxes. Applying the different factor price measures to (17), Choi and Krishna find strong empirical support since the restrictions hold for over 80 percent of the bilateral factor flows between the 28 country-pairs. In a follow-up piece, Lai and Zhu (2007) test the restrictions on a broader data set of 41 countries. Since the assumption of identical technologies is now no longer justified, Lai and Zhu consider a modification of (17), which incorporates various forms of technological differences.

Bernhofen (2009b) extends Helpman (1984) by pointing out that Helpman obtains these restrictions by applying the cost efficiency logic to a bilateral factor cost comparison between two trading partners. However, since a free trade equilibrium is globally cost efficient, one obtains an extended set of restrictions:

$$(w^k - w^i)'F^{ij} > 0. \tag{18}$$

The inequality (18) can be thought of capturing global cost efficiency since it requires that F^{ij} is not only restricted by the factor price difference between countries i and j as in (16), but also by the factor price difference between country i and *any* other third country k. An important implication of this is that the multi-cone specification implies restrictions involving third country factor price comparisons. In addition, we are back to a Heckscher–Ohlin–Vanek world where a complete test requires data on *all* countries in the world economy. Bernhofen (2009b) applies (18) to Choi and Krishna's data set and finds limited empirical support for the extended set of restrictions and considerable variation in the success rate across the country sample. This is not too surprising given that a prior inspection of the country sample would have suggested endowment differences that are not too dissimilar.

Helpman's bilateral restrictions and their extensions rely on equilibrium factor price differences to generate restrictions on factor service flows. Alternatively, since the multi-cone framework depicted in figure 4.4 focuses just on production, it lends itself to a cross-country investigation of international production, without looking at trade. Building on Leamer (1987), Schott (2003) provides a dynamic interpretation of the multi-cone model, where capital accumulation moves a country into a more capital abundant cone (for example C^3 to C^1) and a higher wage-rental ratio. He develops an estimation technique that allows him to distinguish between the single and multi-cone specification. Employing his method to three-digit ISIC manufacturing industries, he rejects the single cone-specification. However, since he finds significant variation in input intensities within the three-digit classes, he clusters the industries into three Heckscher–Ohlin (HO) aggregates (labour-intensive, middle and capital-intensive). When applying his empirical model to HO aggregates he finds support for Deardorff's (1979) multi-cone notion that more capital abundant countries specialize in more capital-intensive industry clusters, whereas more labour-abundant countries specialize in more labour-abundant clusters.

4.4   Identification of cones

If countries are within a cone of diversification, the Heckscher–Ohlin–Vanek framework yields sharp predictions of how endowment differences affect a country's factor content of trade with the rest of the world. If countries are in different cones, equilibrium factor prices will be different and factor price differences will yield predictions on the bilateral factor content of trade as in (16)–(18). Besides yielding different types of predictions on the pattern of trade, the identification of countries to cones is important for predictions on how shocks in the form of factor inflows (that is immigration, capital inflows) affect domestic factor prices. For example, Hanson and Slaughter (2002) investigate how U.S. states absorb differential changes in relative labour supplies. Their finding that states absorb changes in employment through changes in their production techniques and changes in the output of traded goods rather than changes in factor prices provides evidence that U.S. states are within a cone.

Debaere and Demiroglu (2003) focus on a cross-section of developed and developing countries and investigate whether they are in a single cone. Their analytical framework is based on figure 4.2, which provides a condition for factor price equalization. The factor price equalization set FPE, which is spanned by the endowment vectors V^1, V^2 and V^3, can be viewed as an endowment lens. The sectoral employment vectors $g_1, \ldots, g_6$ define a goods lens. Following Deardorff (1994), countries will produce the same set of goods if the endowment lens lies within the goods lens. Applying this logic to their data set, Debaere and Demiroglu find that only the rich OECD countries are sufficiently similar to constitute a cone.

A distinctive feature of the aforementioned empirical studies of diversification cones is that they assume identical technologies and employ cross-country panels of industry data where the industry codes might represent different goods for different industries. Xiang (2007) suggests overcoming these difficulties by looking at distribution functions of factor usage intensities. Since Xiang's approach is based on a two-factor formulation it can be illustrated in figure 4.4. If countries are in different cones, there should be distinct differences in the capital-labour ratios and the between-cone differences should be statistically larger than the within-cone differences. Applying this logic to a set of ten OECD countries, Xiang identifies a country clustering around three different groups which, under the assumption of zero-trade costs, is compatible with figure 4.4, where each group is associated with a cone. This finding is an important departure from Debaere and Demiroglu (2003) as it suggests multiple cones even within the OECD. However, the model compatibility is not unique. Alternatively, the results are also consistent with Romalis' (2004) hybrid Heckcher Ohlin monopolistic competition model with non-zero trade costs, which we discuss in the next section.

5   Hybrids

In this section, I briefly survey empirical approaches that combine elements from Ricardian, Heckscher–Ohlin, monopolistic competition and, more recently, contract theory models. Since the literature has not yet produced a coherent framework for organizing the individual determinants of international specialization, empirical researchers have taken different approaches to estimating the individual sources of comparative advantage.[34]

Harrigan (1997) focuses only on the production side of the Heckscher–Ohlin model and estimates the joint effects of technology and factor supply differences on industry output. He considers a specification in which the output share of an industry in a country's GDP depends on productivities and factor endowments, and he finds that his estimated Rybczynski effects are in line with theoretical conjecture and previous empirical work.[35] A key lesson of Harrigan's paper is that technological differences are an important determinant of international specialization even within the OECD.

Romalis (2004) considers a hybrid specification that incorporates Krugman's (1980) monopolistic competition model with trade costs into Dornbusch, Fischer and Samuelson's (1980) continuum of goods Heckscher–Ohlin model. Transportation costs make the commodity structure of trade determinate, and monopolistic competition generates predictions about the volume of trade. Combined, Romalis' hybrid model predicts that countries that use their abundant factors intensively will have larger shares of world production and trade in goods. Since the theory is based on a two-factor framework, there is a bit of a leap of faith between the theory and his empirical specification which allows for multiple factors. Applying his predictions to the data, Romalis finds strong empirical support for his predictions.

Morrow (2010) builds a structural model that augments Romalis (2004) by incorporating productivity differences. He derives expressions that allow him to test for the contributions of Ricardian and Heckscher–Ohlin forces in production data. He emphasizes that Rybczynski regressions *à la* Harrigan (1995, 1997) provide valid comparative statics exercises as long as total factor productivity is uncorrelated with factor intensity. He confirms previous findings of a joint role of factor productivity and factor abundance in affecting the pattern of international specialization. But since he is working with a two-factor model, his specification suffers from potential omitted factor biases.

Finally, recent theoretical work on trade and contracts has suggested a role of contract enforcement on international specialization and comparative advantage. Nunn (2007) considers an empirical specification that aims to focus on one specific channel through which contract enforcement affects the pattern of trade: underinvestment in relation-specific investments.[36] His hypothesis is that, ceteris paribus, countries with better contract enforcement should specialize in industries where relation-specific investments are more important. Nunn's major innovation is to construct an industry-level measure of contract intensity and interact it with a country-level measure of the quality of a country's contract enforcement institutions. He examines his hypothesis empirically by using this interaction variable as an explanatory variable in a cross-industry, cross-country export regression equation. Nunn claims that his contract intensity variable explains more of the export variation than 'the traditional' capital and labour measures (which are his controls) combined. Although a creative exercise, it suffers–like some of the other hybrid approaches–from a lack of a general theoretical framework from which the predictions are derived.

6   Conclusion

Over half a century of research on refining the theoretical formulations of the general equilibrium trade model and confronting it with data have revealed the resilience and usefulness of this model. Apparent paradoxes and empirical regularities, which at the time appeared to threaten–the *Leontief Paradox*, the occurrence of *intra-industry trade*, the *mystery of the missing trade*–have left the framework unharmed. In fact, theses empirical challenges have resulted in a deeper understanding of the model and an appreciation for what it is able to explain empirically.

In this chapter, I focused only on empirical approaches which examined patterns of international specialization. The general price formulations of the model have yielded refutable predictions about the pattern and gains from trade that could not be refuted by the data. Patterns of international specialization are driven both by endowment differences (Heckscher–Ohlin forces) and technological differences (Ricardian forces). Heckscher–Ohlin specifications that either do not rely on the identical technology assumption and depart from it in creative ways find broad empirical support. The recent multi-country extension of the Ricardian model has provided a framework for structural estimation involving many useful policy experiments.

Regarding future research, more work is needed on empirical examination of the influence that sector-specific trade costs have on international specialization. This will call for general equilibrium modelling that goes beyond the uniform iceberg assumption, as in Matsuyama (2007). Second, although the empirical general equilibrium literature has taught us quite a bit about the pattern of international trade, we still have very scarce theory-based evidence on the aggregate gains from international trade. The key theoretical challenge here will be the inference of the magnitude and sources of these gains from data in a trading equilibrium in the absence of strong parametric assumptions about the underlying fundamentals.

Notes

* University of Nottingham and GEP.
1. The core of this chapter was written during a CES-ifo research visit at the University of Munich in the spring of 2009. I benefitted from comments by Laura Bernhofen, Dave Donaldson, Rod Falvey and Udo Kreickemeier on an earlier draft.
2. Some philosophers of science argue that we are never in the position to verify a theory, but we can either refute or not refute.
3. The insight that in a market economy prices convey information about underlying fundamentals goes back to the seminal work by Hayek (1945).
4. As Krugman (2009, p. 566) has pointed out in his Nobel Prize lecture, specialization based on economies of scale is arbitrary at the product level. The standard

model of monopolistic competition invokes "some notion of randomness, but without any explicit random mechanism in mind". In contrast, the competitive trade model is based on the notion of the 'invisible hand' which works through the price mechanism.

5. If $T_i > 0$ (<0), good i is imported (exported).

6. In the case of constant opportunity costs, as in the Ricardian 1-factor case, $p^a T_{1850s}$ gives an exact measure of the gains from trade.

7. Irwin (2005) identifies the U.S. 1807–09 trade embargo as another opportunity to estimate the welfare costs of autarky. However, since the trade embargo lasted only for about 14 months Irwin is not able to cast his analysis in terms of a counterfactual, and the welfare comparison needs to be treated with some caution. Using fairly aggregated trade and price indices, Irwin provides welfare costs of about 5 percent of GDP. This seems quite high given that the economy had little time to reallocate its resources along the new prices under the embargo. One might expect that U.S. producers anticipated that the embargo might not be lasting.

8. See the preceding chapter by Woodland (2011) for a thorough discussion of DFS.

9. On the demand side, DFS assume identical and homothetic preferences. But the framework also accommodates non-homothetic preferences.

10. Samuelson's iceberg assumption implies that delivering one unit of a good to a foreign destination requires the shipment of τ units, where $\tau > 1$.

11. Matsuyama (2007) exploits the DFS setup for a creative general equilibrium approach of modelling trade costs not using the iceberg framework. I am not aware of any empirical work which is guided by Matsuyama's approach.

12. In the Armington model, goods are imperfect substitutes because they come from different locations. Under monopolistic competition consumers have a taste for product variety and scale economies induce countries to specialize in distinct varieties.

13. Deardorff (1998) derives a gravity equation in a Heckscher–Ohlin model with complete specialization. However, by assuming that each country produces a different good, the underlying mechanism generating gravity is complete specialization and product differentiation rather than comparative advantage. By contrast, in Eaton and Kortum (2002) the same homogeneous good is produced by multiple producers.

14. Donaldson (2010) argues that by employing a general equilibrium approach he does not assume that policy treatments by one unit of observation do not affect outcomes of any other unit, as it is usually done in the policy evaluation literature. He suggests that ignoring general equilibrium effects would bias his estimates by almost 20 percent.

15. For example: exporters are larger and appear to be more productive than non-exporters. However, in most empirical studies measured productivity is only correlated with export status and might be driven by other factors, like firm investment, etc.

16. The key difference is that Bernard, Eaton, Jenson and Kortum (2003) consider competition within a variety while Melitz (2003) focuses on competition between varieties. I am not aware of any empirical work that exploits this distinction between the two models.

17. It should be noted that (7) is derived from (6) under the assumption that the productivity of the varieties are drawn independently from a Fréchet distribution.

18. The prominent early empirical papers are Baldwin (1971), Harkness (1978), Stern and Maskus (1981), Brecher and Choudhri (1982) and Maskus (1985), which are reviewed

in Deardorff (1984). See Ethier (1984) for a review of the theoretical Heckscher–Ohlin formulations in higher dimensions.

19. This research agenda was launched by Leamer's (1984) influential monograph.
20. See Davis and Weinstein (2003) and chapters 2 and 3 in Feenstra (2004) for a more in-depth coverage of the HOV literature.
21. For expositional reasons we assume a discrete number of goods. In some instances it is more convenient to use the Heckscher–Ohlin continuous goods formulation, introduced by Dornbusch, Fischer and Samuelson (1980), as in Romalis (2004) which I discuss later.
22. It is common to talk about the factor price equalization assumption. From a theory perspective, factor price equalization is a prediction of the model rather than an assumption (see Woodland, 2011). It is the implication of assuming that countries have identical technologies and that factor endowments are 'not too dissimilar'. 'Not too dissimilar' is made rigorous by requiring that factor endowments lie in the FPE set given in figure 4.2. See Helpman and Krugman (1985) for a formal definition of the FPE set in higher dimensions.
23. Each country is capable of producing the six goods with the given techniques since each country's capital-labour ratio is below the capital-labour ratio of the most capital intensive good g_1 and above the capital-labour ratio of the least capital intensive good g_6.
24. Geometrically, the consumption point C^1 is linked to the endowment point V^1 by a line with slope w/r, where w and r are the free-trade factor prices. This line can be interpreted as the factoral terms of trade line.
25. Maskus (1985) provided an earlier test of (8), but only for a single country across factors. In contrast, BLS were able to test HOV across factors and countries.
26. Gabaix (1999) points out that, if the labour content of trade is small, the correlation just reflects correlation between wages and per capita GDP which has nothing to do with the Heckscher–Ohlin model.
27. The mystery of the missing trade has been also identified in other data sets and inspired quite a lot of followup work aimed at providing explanations for it. Estevadeorale and Taylor (2002) identify the missing trade when applying the HOV model to a 1913 data set. Conway (2002) explains the missing trade by noticing an anti-trade bias which is rooted in factor specific differences in domestic factor mobility. Feenstra and Hanson (2000) stress the role of aggregation bias. Reimer (2006) investigates how accounting for traded intermediate inputs in the measured factor content of trade affects the missing trade.
28. Trefler also considers modifications of HOV that account for home bias in consumption but finds that this accounts only for a small fraction of the missing trade.
29. Their methodology echoes Davis, Weinstein, Bradford and Shimpo (1997), who construct imputed world endowments to investigate the HOV relationship using Japanese regional trade data. There is also some similarity to Hakura (2001), who uses actual technology matrices to investigate the role of technological differences on bilateral trade in the HOV framework.
30. However, as a tradeoff, Fisher and Marshall's analysis is restricted to three factors of production: capital. labour and social capital.
31. See Bernhofen (2005, 2009a) for general discussions of refutability in competitive trade theory.

32. The factor content of trade can be measured using either the domestic technologies, technologies at the location of production or based on the actual content of consumption.
33. This specification assumes that countries have identical technologies.
34. Applying the concept of log-super modularity, Costinot (2009) has taken an important step towards a unifying theory of comparative advantage. His approach is a bit more restrictive than Deardorff's (1980) autarky price formulation but has the advantage of focusing just on the trading equilibrium.
35. Harrigan's approach builds on Kohli (1991) and Harrigan (1995). See Harrigan (2003) for an in-depth discussion of empirical approaches to the neoclassical trade model that build on the Rybczynski relationships.
36. See also Levchenko (2007) and Levchenko and Do (2007) for alternative approaches that examine the role of institutions on trade patterns.

References

Balassa, B. (1963) 'An empirical demonstration of classical comparative cost theory', *Review of Economics and Statistics*, XLV, 231–38.
——(1965) 'Trade liberalization and comparative advantage', *The Manchester School of Economics and Social Studies*, XXXIII, 99–123.
——(1966) 'Tariff reductions and trade in manufactures among the industrial countries'. *American Economic Review*, LVI, 466–73.
Baldwin, R. (1971) 'Determinants of the commodity structure of US trade', *American Economic Review*, LXI, 126–46.
Bernard, A.B., J. Eaton, J.B. Jensen and S. Kortum (2003) 'Plants and productivity in international trade', *American Economic Review*, XCIII, 1268–90.
Bernhofen, D.M. (2005) 'The empirics of comparative advantage: overcoming the tyranny of nonrefutability', *Review of International Economics* XIII, 1017–1023.
Bernhofen, D.M., and J.C. Brown (2004) 'A direct test of the theory of comparative advantage: the case of Japan', *Journal of Political Economy*, CXII, 48–67.
——(2005) 'An empirical assessment of the comparative advantage gains from trade: evidence from Japan', *American Economic Review*, XCV, 208–25.
Bernhofen, D.M. (2009a) 'On predictability in the neoclassical trade model: a synthesis', *Economic Theory*, XLI, 5–21.
——(2009b) 'Multiple cones, factor price differences and the factor content of trade', *Journal of International Economics*, LXXIX (2), 266–71.
Bernhofen, D.M., and J.C. Brown (2010) 'Testing the price formulation of the Heckscher–Ohlin Theorem: the natural experiment of Japan', University of Nottingham, mimeo.
Bowen, H., E. Leamer and L. Sveikauskas (1987) 'Multi-country, multi-factor tests of factor abundance theory', *American Economic Review*, LXXVII, 791–809.
Brecher, R., and E. Choudhri (1982) 'The Leontief paradox, continued', *Journal of Political Economy*, XC, 820–23.
——(1993) 'Some empirical support for the Heckscher–Ohlin model of production', *Canadian Journal of Economics*, XXVI, 272–85.
Choi, Y., and P. Krishna (2004) 'The factor content of bilateral trade: An empirical test', *Journal of Political Economy*, CXII, 887–913.
Conway, P.J., (2002) 'The case of missing trade and other mysteries: comment', *American Economic Review*, XCII, 394–404.

Costinot, A. (2009) 'An elementary theory of comparative advantage', *Econometrica*, LXXVII, 1165–92.

Costinot, A., D. Donaldson and I. Komunjer (2010) 'What goods do countries trade? A quantitative exploration of Ricardo's ideas', MIT mimeo.

Davis, D.R. (1995) 'Intra-industry trade: A Heckscher–Ohlin Ricardo approach', *Journal of International Economics*, XXXIX, 201–26.

Davis, D.R., D. Weinstein, S.C. Bradford and K. Shimpo (1997) 'Using international and Japanese regional data to determine when factor abundance theory of trade works,' *American Economic Review*, LXXXVII, 421–46.

Davis, D.R., and D. Weinstein (2001) 'An account of global factor trade,' *American Economic Review*, XCI, 1423–53.

—— (2003) 'The factor content of trade', in E. Kwan Choi and J. Harrigan (eds.) *Handbook of International Trade*. Blackwell.

Deardorff, A.V. (1979) 'Weak links in the chain of comparative advantage', *Journal of International Economics*, IX, 197–209.

—— (1980) 'The general validity of the law of comparative advantage', *Journal of Political Economy*, LXXXVIII, 941–57.

—— (1982) 'The general validity of the Heckscher–Ohlin Theorem', *American Economic Review*, LXXII, 683–94.

—— (1984) 'Test trade theories and predicting trade flows' in R.W. Kenen and P.B Jones (eds) *Handbook of International Economics*, vol. 1. Amsterdam: North-Holland.

—— (1994) 'The possibility of factor price equalization revisited', *Journal of International Economics*, XXXVI, 167–75.

—— (1998) 'Determinants of bilateral trade: Does gravity work in a neoclassical work?' in J.A. Frenkel (ed.) *The Regionalization of the World Economy*. Chicago: University of Chicago Press.

Debaere, P. (2003) 'Relative factor abundance and trade', *Journal of Political Economy*, CXI, 589–612.

Debaere, P., and U. Demiroglu (2003) 'On the similarity of country endowments', *Journal of International Economics*, LIX, 101–36.

Dixit, A.K., and V. Norman (1980) *Theory of International Trade*. Cambridge University Press.

Donaldson, D. (2010) 'Railroads of the Raj: Estimating the impact of transportation infrastructure', MIT mimeo.

Dornbusch, R., S. Fischer and P. Samuelson (1977) 'Comparative advantage, trade and payments in a Ricardian model with a continuum of goods', *American Economic Review*, LXVII, 823–39.

—— (1980) 'Heckscher–Ohlin trade theory with a continuum of goods', *Quarterly Journal of Economics*, XCV, 203–24.

Eaton, J., and S. Kortum (2002) 'Technology, geography and trade', *Econometrica*, LXX, 1741–79.

Estevadeorale, A., and A.M. Taylor (2002) 'A century of missing trade?', *American Economic Review*, XCII, 383–93.

Ethier, W. (1984) 'Higher dimensional issues in trade theory' in R.W. Kenen and P.B. Jones (eds) *Handbook of International Economics*, vol. 1. Amsterdam: North-Holland.

Feenstra, R., and G. Hanson (2000) 'Aggregation bias in the factor content of trade: evidence from US manufacturing', *American Economic Review Papers and Proceedings*, XC, 155–60.

Feenstra, R. (2004) *Advanced International Trade: Theory and Evidence*. Princeton: Princeton University Press.

Fisher, E., and K. Marshall (2008) 'The factor content of trade when countries have different technologies', California Polytechnic State University, mimeo.

Gabaix, X. (1999) 'The factor content of trade: a rejection of the Heckscher–Ohlin Leontief hypothesis', MIT, mimeo.

Haberler, G. (1930) 'Die Theorie der komparativen Kosten und ihre Auswertung fuer die Begruendung des Freihandels', *Weltwirtschaftliches Archiv*, XXXII, 350–70, translated as 'The Theory of comparative costs and its use in the defense of free trade', in A.Y.C. Koo (ed.) (1985) *Selected Essays of Gottfried Haberler*. Cambridge, MA: MIT Press.

Hakura, D. (2001) 'Why does HOV fail? The role of technological differences within the EC', *Journal of International Economics*, LII, 361–82.

Hanson, G.H., and M. Slaughter (2002) 'Labor-market adjustments in open economies: evidence from US states', *Journal of International Economics*, LVII, 3–29.

Harkness, J. (1978) 'Factor abundance and comparative advantage', *American Economic Review*, LXVIII, 784–800.

Harrigan, J. (1995) 'Factor endowments and the international location of production: econometric evidence from the OECD, 1970–1985', *Journal of International Economics*, XXXIX, 123–41.

——(1997) 'Technology, factor supplies, and international specialization: estimating the neoclassical model', *American Economic Review*, LXXXVII, 475–94.

——(2003) 'Do the data obey the laws?' in E. Kwan Choi and J. Harrigan (eds) *Handbook of International Trade*. Oxford: Blackwell.

——(2010) 'Airplanes and comparative advantage', *Journal of International Economics*, LXXXII, 181–94.

Hayek, F.A. (1945) 'The use of knowledge in society', *American Economic Review*, XXXV, 519–30.

Helpman, E. (1984) 'The factor content of foreign trade', *Economic Journal*, XCIV, 84–94.

Helpman, E., and P. Krugman (1985) *Market Structure and Foreign Trade*. Cambridge, MA: MIT Press.

Irwin, D. (2005) 'The welfare cost of autarky: evidence from the Jeffersonian trade embargo, 1807–1809', *Review of International Economics*, XIII, 631–45.

Kohli, U. (1991) *Technology, Duality and Trade*. Ann Arbor, MI: University of Michigan Press.

Krugman, P. (1980) 'Scale economies, product differentiation and the pattern of trade', *American Economic Review* LXX, 950–59.

——(2009) 'The increasing returns revolution in trade and geography', *American Economic Review*, XCIX, 561–571.

Lai, H., and S. Zhu (2007) 'Technology, endowments, and the factor content of bilateral trade', *Journal of International Economics*, LXXI, 389–409.

Leamer, E. (1980) 'The Leontief Paradox , Reconsidered', *Journal of Political Economy*, LXXXVIII, 495–503.

——(1984) *Sources of Comparative Advantage: Theory and Evidence*. Cambridge, MA: MIT Press.

——(1987) 'Paths of development in the three-factor, n-good general equilibrium model', *Journal of Political Economy*, XCV, 961–99.

Leamer, E., and J. Levinsohn (1995) 'International trade theory: the evidence' in Gene M. Grossman and Kenneth S. Rogoff (eds), *Handbook of International Economics*, vol. III. New York: Elsevier Science.

Leontief, W. (1953) 'Domestic production and foreign trade: the American capital position re-examined', *Proceedings of the American Philosophical Society*, XCVII, 332–49.

Levchenko, A. (2007) 'Institutional quality and international trade', *Review of Economic Studies*, LXXIII, 791–819.

Levchenko, A., and Q. Do (2007) 'Comparative advantage, demand for external finance, and financial development', *Journal of Financial Economics*, LXXXVI, 796–834.

MacDougall, G. (1951) 'British and American exports: A suggested study by the theory of comparative costs, Part I', *Economic Journal*, LXI, 697–724.

—— (1952) 'British and American exports: A suggested study by the theory of comparative costs, Part II', *Economic Journal*, LXII, 487–521.

Maskus, K. (1985) 'A test of the Heckscher–Ohlin–Vanek Theorem: The Leontief Commonplace', *Journal of International Economics*, XIX, 3–4.

Matsuyama, K. (2007) 'Beyond icebergs: towards a theory of biased globalization', *Review of Economic Studies*, LXXIV, 237–53.

Melitz, M. (2003) 'The impact of trade on aggregate intra industry reallocations and aggregate industry productivity', *Econometrica*, LXXI, 1695–1725.

Morrow, P. (2010) 'Ricardian-Heckscher–Ohlin comparative advantage: theory and evidence', *Journal of International Economics* 82(2), 137–51.

Neary, P., and A. Schweinberger (1986) 'Factor content functions and the theory of international trade', *Review of Economic Studies*, LIII, 421–32.

Nunn, N. (2007) 'Relation specificity, incomplete contracts and the pattern of trade', *Quarterly Journal of Economics*, CXXII, 569–600.

Ohlin, B. (1933) *Interregional and international trade*. Cambridge, MA: Harvard University Press.

Reimer, J. (2006) 'Global production sharing and trade in the services of factors', *Journal of International Economics*, LXVIII, 384–408.

Romalis, J. (2004) 'Factor proportions and the structure of commodity trade', *American Economic Review*, XCIV, 67–97.

Schott, P. (2003) 'One size fits all? Heckscher–Ohlin specification in global production', *American Economic Review*, XCIII, 686–708.

Stern, R.M. (1962) 'British and American productivity and comparative costs in international trade', *Oxford Economic Papers*, XIV, 275–303.

Stern, R., and K. Maskus (1981) 'Determinants of the structure of US foreign trade, 1958–76', *Journal of International Economics*, XI, 207–24.

Trefler, D. (1993) 'International factor price differences: Leontief Was Right!', *Journal of Political Economy*, CI, 961–87.

—— (1995) 'The case of the missing trade and other HOV mysteries', *American Economic Review*, LXXXV, 1029–46.

Vanek, J. (1968) 'The Factor Proportions Theory: The N factor case', *Kyklos*, XXI, 749–56.

Wood, A. (1994) 'Give Heckscher–Ohlin a chance!', *Weltwirtschaftliches Archiv*, CXXX, 20–49.

Woodland, A. (2011) 'General Equilibrium trade theory', chapter 3, this volume.

Xiang, C. (2007) 'Diversification cones, trade costs and factor market linkages', *Journal of International Economics*, LXXI, 448–66.

5

General Equilibrium Trade Theory and Firm Behaviour

Kristian Behrens* and Gianmarco I.P. Ottaviano†

1 Introduction

What determines countries' specialization patterns and the structure of world trade? What are the effects of international trade liberalization on national economies? While these have always been the driving questions of international trade theory, the answers have varied through time depending on historical contingencies (Irwin, 1996).

The recent history of international relations can be divided into 'two waves of globalization' (Baldwin and Martin, 1999). The first wave went from the mid-nineteenth century to the eve of World War I. It roughly coincided with the second Industrial Revolution, during which new manufacturing, transportation and communications technologies diffused from Great Britain to continental Europe and a small set of other countries worldwide. The result was the emergence of an industrialized 'North' exporting manufactures to a less developed, and often colonized 'South', in exchange for raw materials and primary products. Hence, during this first wave of globalization, international trade was characterized by the exchange of *different goods* between structurally *different countries*. Such an intersectoral pattern of international trade soon found two accomplished theoretical explanations. Both highlighted the role of relative cost differences between countries, predicting that a country would export the goods that it is able to produce at relatively lower costs. The two explanations differed, however, in terms of the sources of cost differences that were to be found in either the uneven international distribution of technologies (Ricardian model) or in relative factor endowments (Heckscher–Ohlin model).

The second wave of globalization started to mount up just after World War II and is still going on. In this period, further technological improvements in production, transportation and communication technologies, and their steady diffusion to a growing number of countries, brought a substantial change in international trade patterns. These started to be dominated by the exchange of *similar goods* between structurally *similar northern countries sharing more or less identical technologies and relative factor endowments.* The rise of intra-industry trade between rich countries created a conundrum for the Ricardian and Heckscher–Ohlin theories explaining bilateral trade flows in terms of differences between trading partners (Linder, 1961; Grubel and Lloyd, 1975; Greenaway and Milner, 1986). How to explain that similar countries actually traded more than dissimilar countries?

The counterfactual predictions of the Ricardian and Heckscher–Ohlin models derived from two specific simplifying assumptions: constant returns to scale at the firm level and perfect competition in all markets. These assumptions anchored those models to the standard Arrow–Debreu paradigm of general equilibrium theory, in which incentives to trade arise only when traders have different individual assessments of the relative values of the transacted goods. The larger the difference in those assessments, the higher their incentives to transact and, thus, the volumes of trade. Vice versa, individuals sharing the same assessments have no incentive to trade. This is indeed the case of countries sharing the same technologies and relative factor endowments, as their autarky relative prices are identical.[1] While it was clear that the Arrow–Debreu assumptions were putting a straitjacket on the ability to explain the structure of world trade, for a long time the lack of tractable general equilibrium models with increasing returns to scale and imperfect competition hampered progress in international trade theory (and economic theory at large). This state of affairs started to change in the late 1970s when new partial equilibrium models of oligopoly and monopolistic competition were borrowed from industrial organization and transplanted to the general equilibrium setup of international trade theory (Helpman, 1984a). By the end of the 1970s and the beginning of the 1980s the so-called 'new trade theory', which would deeply transform the field, had been born (see, e.g., Krugman, 1979 and 1980; Dixit and Norman, 1980; Markusen, 1981; Brander and Krugman, 1983; Helpman, 1984b).[2]

With the benefit of hindsight, it is now transparent that what had held international trade theory back had been its 'obsession' with general equilibrium. This obsession is easily explained and justified by the fact that the assessment of the effects of international trade liberalization on the national economy necessarily requires an understanding of what happens to factor incomes and prices. In other words, 'you want a *general-equilibrium* story, in which it is clear where the money comes from and where it goes' (Fujita and Krugman, 2004, 141). At the same time, even armchair evidence makes it clear that a theoretical account of the structure of world trade cannot fly without a model of firm behaviour. By assumption, however, in the perfectly competitive Arrow–Debreu paradigm, the boundaries of the firm are undetermined. A firm, whatever that may be in an Arrow–Debreu world, is indeed just a production function and, as such, has no 'behaviour' whatsoever. Yet, firm behaviour is important in many respects: firms decide whether to launch new products and dispense with old ones, where to produce and where to sell their goods, whether to compete in prices or quantities, how to organize their operations.

This chapter provides a selective overview of how firm behaviour has been introduced into the general equilibrium approach of international trade theory. In terms of market structure, it focuses on monopolistic competition. General oligopolistic equilibrium models are presented in the complementary chapter 7 by Dermot Leahy and Peter Neary. In particular, Section 2 starts with a general review of the role of monopolistic competition in general equilibrium trade models with imperfect market structure. In so doing, it distills the main insights and properties that make monopolistic competition well suited to international trade analysis. It also discusses some of the limitations of the workhorse model as proposed by Krugman (1980) in the wake of Dixit and Stiglitz (1977). Section 3 highlights the new insights that monopolistic competition adds to the analysis of specialization and trade, tracing out the impacts of market size and endowment differences, as well as their interactions, on industry structure and trade. Section 4 then shows how firm-level heterogeneity can be incorporated into monopolistic competition models to highlight the impact of trade liberalization on intra-industry reallocations. Section 5 extends the analysis to situations in which heterogeneous firms choose the organizational structure of their foreign operations. The specific aim of this section is to bring back more forcefully the concept of 'firm' into general equilibrium trade theory. A more general assessment of the ways in which location and internalization decisions frame the organization of multinational firms is to be found in Chapter 8 by James Markusen. Section 6 concludes the chapter by presenting some final remarks.

2 Monopolistic competition

The idea of monopolistic competition is a rather old one, dating at least back to the early 1930s. Chamberlin (1933) introduced the idea of 'large group competition', where firms retain some monopoly power thanks to product differentiation yet are small in the aggregate economy. The idea that firms are small in the economy can be made precise by assuming that there is a *continuum of firms*. In such a setting, firms are aware that they are price makers as they face finitely elastic demands for their products, yet their behaviour has no impact on market aggregates like GDP, the number of firms, consumer incomes, and aggregate profits and price indices. Such 'non-strategic' behaviour allows one to sidestep a myriad of thorny technical problems that arise once we seriously think about oligopoly in general equilibrium (see chapter 7 by Dermot Leahy and Peter Neary for further details).[3] It further makes redundant the recurrent discussion on price versus quantity competition, since both are equivalent in monopolistic competition with a continuum of firms (Vives, 1999); and as there is free entry, we also do not need to tackle the question of how oligopoly results change depending on whether entry is fixed or free. Though one may argue that these properties are rather special and may limit the generality of the analysis, they offer the advantage of laying out a clear framework within which macroeconomic issues can be parsimoniously analyzed.

We begin by developing a slightly more 'general' monopolistic competition framework than the canonical Dixit–Stiglitz–Krugman (DSK) model used in international trade theory.[4] Our aim is to distill the key insights and properties of the DSK model and to highlight some of its shortcomings for international trade analysis by contrasting its predictions with those derived from alternative specifications. The framework we develop is flexible enough to nest the canonical DSK model, to embed it into a Heckscher–Ohlin world, and to incorporate various more recent extensions like heterogeneity and firms' organizational choices.

2.1   Preferences and demands

Since there is to date no general theory of monopolistic competition, all models must rely on special representations of preferences and must be viewed as being 'examples' only. Following Spence (1976) and Dixit and Stiglitz (1977), most of the literature builds upon demand systems with a representative consumer who values product diversity and consumes a large set of horizontally differentiated varieties of the same good.[5] This so-called 'love-of-variety' formulation has become the backbone model of international trade theory under monopolistic competition. Following the basic formulation by Helpman and Krugman (1985), we rely on a particular and relatively simple specification that allows us to cut through the analytical complexities and isolate the key features useful to international trade theory.

To simplify the exposition, consider a world with 2 sectors and 2 countries. In what follows, subscripts $i = 1, 2$ denote countries and superscripts $s = 1, 2$ denote sectors. Each country i is endowed with a given number L_i of workers and a given amount K_i of capital. All workers are identical and are also the consumers and factor owners of the economy.[6] The preferences of each consumer located in country i are represented by $U_i \equiv U_i(U_i^1(\cdot), U_i^2(\cdot))$, where U_i is a homothetic upper-tier utility that is strictly increasing in all its arguments and which aggregates the different lower-tier utilities U_i^s derived from the consumption of good s in country i. If good s is a *homogeneous good*, we assume that $U_i^s = d_i^s \equiv d_{1i}^s + d_{2i}^s$, where d_{ji}^s denotes the quantity of good s produced in country j and consumed in country i. Observe that since s is homogeneous, only the total quantity consumed matters for welfare. If s is a *differentiated good*, we assume that the sub-utility in country i can be represented by

$$U_i^s \equiv g_i \left(\int_{\Omega_{1i}^s} u_i^s(d_{1i}^s(v)) \mathrm{d}v + \int_{\Omega_{2i}^s} u_i^s(d_{2i}^s(v)) \mathrm{d}v \right), \tag{1}$$

where $d_{ji}^s(v)$ denotes the consumption of variety v produced in j; where g_i is a strictly increasing and concave function; where Ω_{ji}^s denotes the set of country j firms in sector s selling to country i; and where u_i^s is a strictly increasing and strictly concave sub-utility function, with $u_i^s(0) = 0$. Note that the strict concavity of u_i^s implies that the indifference curves are strictly convex so that consumers want to distribute their expenditure across all varieties of a differentiated good. Put differently, they have a 'love-of-variety'.

Let e_i denote the representative consumer's income (i.e., expenditure) in country i. By definition, a homogeneous good s has a unique price p_i^s in market i. Letting $\mathcal{H}$ and $\mathcal{D}$ denote the sets of homogeneous and of differentiated goods, respectively, the budget constraint can be expressed as follows: $\sum_{s\in\mathcal{H}} p_i^s d_i^s + \sum_{s\in\mathcal{D}} \left[\int_{\Omega_{1i}^s} p_{1i}^s(v) d_{1i}^s(v) dv + \int_{\Omega_{2i}^s} p_{2i}^s(v) d_{2i}^s(v) dv \right] = e_i$. The first-order conditions for utility maximization are given by

$$\frac{\partial U_i}{\partial U_i^s}(\cdot) - \lambda p_i^s = 0 \tag{2}$$

for a homogeneous good s; and by

$$\frac{\partial U_i}{\partial U_i^s}\left(g_i(\cdot)\right)g_i'(\cdot)u_i^{s\prime}\left(d_{ji}^s(v)\right) - \lambda p_{ji}^s(v) = 0 \tag{3}$$

for each variety v of a differentiated good s. Since u_i^s is strictly increasing and strictly concave, equation (3) can be inverted and rewritten in implicit form to yield

$$d_{ji}^s(v) = \left(u_i^{s\prime}\right)^{-1}\left(p_{ji}^s(v)\frac{\lambda}{\frac{\partial U_i}{\partial U_i^s}\left(g_i(\cdot)\right)g_i'(\cdot)}\right). \tag{4}$$

In the remainder of this section, we focus on a differentiated good sector. To alleviate the notational burden, we hence suppress the sectoral superscript whenever possible in what follows. It is clear that we cannot, in general, solve (4) explicitly for the demand functions. Yet, they can be theoretically expressed as $d_{ji}(v) = \left(u_i'\right)^{-1}\left(p_{ji}(v)f_i(\mathbb{P}_i, e_i)\right)$, where $\mathbb{P}_i$ is a vector of *price aggregates* in market i and where f_i is some real-valued positive function.[7] The important point to note here is that $\mathbb{P}_i$ *and e_i cannot be affected by any individual firm since each firm is of measure zero*. The firm, hence, faces a finitely elastic and decreasing demand in its own price, which is parametrized by market aggregates and preferences on which the firm has no influence.

A few special cases yield simple solutions, and those 'examples' are useful for modelling international trade. They also allow us to highlight some common properties of monopolistic competition models. To begin with, note that the problem is greatly simplified in the special case where preferences are quasi-linear, that is, linear in a homogeneous good (the 'outside good') since $\lambda = 1$ in that case. Such an approach allows for a relatively simple analysis, yet rules out income effects in the other sector as all fall on the outside good (the demands $d_{ij}(v)$ are independent of e_j). Though analytically convenient, quasi-linear preferences have a strong partial equilibrium flavor.[8]

When preferences are not quasi-linear, Behrens and Murata (2007) have shown that explicit solutions for the demands can be obtained when $(u_i')^{-1}$ satisfies some separability assumptions. Intuitively, the price $p_{ji}(v)$ and the Lagrange multiplier λ need to be separated in the first-order condition (3), which can be achieved if, for example, $(u_i')^{-1}$ can be split either additively or multiplicatively. In both cases, we can then get rid of the Lagrange multiplier which allows one to obtain explicit solutions. The most commonly used model, namely the CES model pioneered by Dixit and Stiglitz (1977) and introduced into trade theory by Krugman (1980), is one that displays *multiplicative separability*. In that model, the sub-utility u_i is given by

$$u_i(\cdot) = (\cdot)^{\frac{\sigma_i-1}{\sigma_i}}, \quad \text{with } \sigma_i > 1. \tag{5}$$

Since $(u_i')^{-1}(\cdot) = \left[\frac{\sigma_i}{\sigma_i-1}(\cdot)\right]^{-\sigma_i}$, the demand functions are then given by

$$d_{ji}(v) = \left[\frac{\sigma_i}{\sigma_i-1}f_i(\mathbb{P}_i, e_i)\right]^{-\sigma_i} p_{ji}(v)^{-\sigma_i}. \tag{6}$$

A less commonly used model is one that displays additive separability, namely the negative exponential model pioneered by Behrens and Murata (2007). This model also provides explicit solutions which offer a simple illustration of the VES framework introduced into trade theory by Krugman (1979). In that model, the sub-utility u_i is given by

$$u_i(\cdot) = 1 - e^{-\alpha_i(\cdot)}, \quad \text{with } \alpha_i > 0. \tag{7}$$

Since $(u_i')^{-1}(\cdot) = \frac{1}{\alpha_i}\ln\left[\frac{\alpha_i}{(\cdot)}\right]$, the demand functions are then given by

$$d_{ji}(v) = \frac{1}{\alpha_i}\ln\left[\frac{\alpha_i}{f_i(\mathbb{P}_i, e_i)}\right] - \frac{1}{\alpha_i}\ln(p_{ji}(v)). \tag{8}$$

Note that the ratio of two demands in (6) is independent of f_i, while the difference of two demands in (8) is independent of f_i (and thus of λ), which is very convenient for solving the demands explicitly. Note further that in both (6) and (8) we have $\partial f_i(\mathbb{P}_i, e_i)/\partial p_{ji}(v) = 0$ since each firm is negligible to the market. This is the essence of monopolistic competition that makes this approach so useful to general equilibrium analysis with imperfect competition as it allows for 'simple' profit maximization.

A quick comparison of the CES and the VES demands allows us to highlight a few of the features that may make the CES approach restrictive for analyzing trade. First, the CES demands are positive regardless of the (finite) price a firm quotes for its variety. Since international trade flows are dominated by zeros, the CES model requires trade barriers of the fixed-cost type to cut off trade flows (more on this in Section 4). On the contrary, in the VES case there exists a finite reservation price above which demands are no longer positive. Thus, as in Melitz and Ottaviano (2008) or Behrens and others (2009b), variable trade and transport costs will choke off trade beyond some threshold. Second, demands in the CES case are by definition iso-elastic with constant demand elasticity $\varepsilon_{ji}(v) = \sigma_i$. Note that although σ_i may be country (and sector) specific, *it remains an exogenous parameter which is not tied to underlying country characteristics like income or the mass of firms selling in the market.* On the contrary, in the VES case the elasticity of demand is $\varepsilon_{ji}(v) = 1/|\alpha_i d_{ji}(v)|$, which is decreasing with the quantity sold in the market. This property seems desirable in an international trade context since empirical evidence suggests that prices and markups are higher in high-income countries where demands are less elastic and firms can, ceteris paribus, charge higher markups by pricing in the less elastic portion of their demand (see Alessandria and Kaboski, 2007; Simonovska, 2008). Last, note that the sub-utilities in the CES case are unbounded, whereas they are bounded by unity in the VES case. This unboundedness in the CES case has two implications. Firstly, for any given set of varieties, consumers can reach infinite utility by consuming an infinite quantity of any of these varieties. Secondly, as we will see later on, the product space does not become more crowded as the number of varieties increases in the CES case, whereas it does in the VES case. The effects of competition and the existence of a competitive limit are hence very different in both models.

2.2 Technology and profit maximization

To keep the analysis simple and to derive a few clear results, let us focus here on the frequently used scenario in which a good is homogeneous while the other is differentiated. The homogeneous good is produced using a constant returns to scale technology. Let $c_i(w_i, r_i)$ denote the unit cost of producing one unit of such a good, where w_i denotes the wage rate and r_i the rental rate of capital in country $i = 1, 2$. Assuming perfect competition for each homogeneous good, its price is such that $p_i \leq c_i(w_i, r_i)$, with production taking place in i if and only if the equality holds.

Each firm in the differentiated sector has a monopoly for its own variety, and varieties are imperfect substitutes in consumption.[9] Production of differentiated varieties involves a firm-specific unit input requirement $1/\varphi_i(v)$. Hence, firm v in country i has 'productivity' $\varphi_i(v)$. Furthermore, each firm incurrs either a recurrent fixed cost (paid in each period), or a sunk setup cost (paid only once) for entering the market. We denote both by F_i and focus on the fixed cost interpretation for now (more on sunk costs in Section 4). Following Markusen and Venables (2000) and Bernard et al. (2007a), we assume that the cost function is homothetic, and that the ratio of marginal cost to average cost depends solely on the firm's output $X_i(v)$:[10]

$$C_i(v) \equiv \left[F_i + \frac{X_i(v)}{\varphi_i(v)} \right] c_i, \tag{9}$$

where $c_i \equiv c_i(w_i, r_i)$ for simplicity. Note that all firms have the same cost function, but may differ in terms of productivity via $\varphi_i(v)$. In the foregoing expression, marginal cost $c_i/\varphi_i(v)$ has all the standard properties of a cost function and we assume that it *does not depend on the level of output.*

As in Krugman (1980), we assume that trade is costly. More precisely, there are iceberg trade costs $\tau_{ij}^s \geq 1$ between countries i and j in industry s. It is well known that iceberg trade costs, though analytically convenient, have a few undesirable properties that invite us to be careful when using them. Firstly, in the CES model where consumers in all countries have the same preferences, they imply that mill- and discriminatory-pricing are equivalent. Put differently, firms' choices of pricing strategies are irrelevant, which is due to the constant elasticity of demand across all countries that is preserved by the iceberg trade cost (Fujita et al., 1999). Yet, as recently argued by Fujita and Thisse (2002, 306 and 347), the constant demand elasticity 'conflicts with research in spatial pricing theory in which demand elasticity varies with distance [...] although the iceberg cost is able to capture the fact that shipping is resource-consuming, such a modelling strategy implies that any increase in the mill price is accompanied with a proportional increase in transport costs, which often seems unrealistic [...] this is enough to cast doubt on the generality of the results derived under the iceberg assumption'. Furthermore, since iceberg trade costs are proportional to marginal input requirement, more productive firms also have de facto lower variable trade costs. Whether this is a reasonable property is an empirical question, but the available evidence suggests it is unlikely to be so (Hummels and Skiba, 2004).[11]

Given the iceberg assumption, output of a differentiated goods firm v in country i is given by

$$X_i(v) = L_1 \tau_{i1} d_{i1}(v) + L_2 \tau_{i2} d_{i2}(v).$$

Hence, its profit can be expressed as follows:

$$\Pi_i(v) = p_{i1}(v) L_1 d_{i1}(v) + p_{i2}(v) L_2 d_{i2}(v) - \frac{c_i}{\varphi_i(v)} X_i(v) - F_i c_i. \tag{10}$$

In what follows, we assume that firms maximize profits with respect to prices and that markets are segmented. There is indeed ample empirical evidence that pricing-to-market is a prevalent feature of the international landscape (e.g. Haskel and Wolf, 2001). Constant marginal cost then implies that each firm maximizes operating profits on each market separately. Because of the continuum assumption, we have the following first-order conditions:

$$\frac{1}{\varepsilon_{ij}(v)} = 1 - \frac{\tau_{ij}c_i}{\varphi_i(v)p_{ij}(v)} \tag{11}$$

for both markets $j = 1, 2$ the firm sells to. Note that these first-order conditions depend in general on consumer expenditure e_j and on the price aggregates $\mathbb{P}_j$, which depend themselves on the prices set by all firms selling in market j.

It is convenient to separate the analysis into two steps. First, factor prices w_i and r_i, consumer expenditure e_i, the firm mass N_i for the differentiated good sector, and prices for the homogeneous good sector are considered as given when determining a *price equilibrium*. Formally, each firm operating in the differentiated good industry sets its optimal price, expecting all other firms to do the same. Second, given a price equilibrium, we determine a *trade equilibrium* where entry and exit occurs until profits are zero, and where factor prices adjust in each country such that factor markets clear and trade is balanced.

2.3 Price and trade equilibrium

A defining characteristic of monopolistic competition models is that although there are no strategic interactions among firms (as would be the case in oligopoly), these must correctly anticipate the aggregate pricing decisions of their competitors. In other words, there is some 'indirect interaction' via the price aggregates. The equilibrium concept that is used is similar to that of a Nash equilibrium with a continuum of players. Indeed, condition (11) may be viewed as firm v's 'reaction function' when the market 'plays' $\mathbb{P}_j$. Let

$$p_{ij}(v) = \frac{\varepsilon_{ij}(\mathbb{P}_j)}{\varepsilon_{ij}(\mathbb{P}_j) - 1} \frac{\tau_{ij}c_i}{\varphi_i(v)}$$

be firm v's 'reaction function'.[12] A price equilibrium is a fixed point such that

$$p_{ij}^*(v) = p_{ij}^*(v, \mathbb{P}_j^*), \quad \forall i, j, v.$$

We do not discuss the issues of existence and of uniqueness here, which are generally problematic. However, all tractable monopolistic competition models that we will rely on in this chapter are such that a unique price equilibrium exists. Note that stability is not an issue. Indeed, no single firm can affect the first-order conditions of its competitors via a unilateral price deviation, so that quasi-concavity of the profit function is sufficient for stability.[13]

To see how equilibrium prices are determined, consider two simple special cases. Focusing first on the CES case, we have:

$$\frac{1}{\sigma_j} = 1 - \frac{\tau_{ij}c_i}{\varphi_i(v)p_{ij}(v)} \Rightarrow p_{ij}^*(v) = \frac{\sigma_j}{\sigma_j - 1} \frac{\tau_{ij}c_i}{\varphi_i(v)},$$

which shows the familiar constant markup pricing result. Note that the equilibrium prices in the CES case can be determined *without any reference to the price aggregates in the destination market.* In other words, firm v always 'plays' the same strategy irrespective of what the market 'plays', that is, the price equilibrium is a dominant strategy Nash equilibrium. This is obviously a very special case that does not carry over to alternative monopolistic competition specifications with positively sloped reaction functions.

To see how a non-CES case works, consider next the negative exponential VES specification. Using the expression for the demand elasticity, the first-order conditions are given by

$$\alpha_j d_{ij}(v) = 1 - \frac{\tau_{ij}c_i}{\varphi_i(v)p_{ij}(v)} \Rightarrow p_{ij}(v) = \frac{\tau_{ij}c_i}{\varphi_i(v)[1 - \alpha_j d_{ij}(v)]} \equiv p_{ij}(v, \mathbb{P}_j).$$

Clearly, the price depends on the market aggregates, which depend themselves on the prices set by all firms. Although the general case is not easy to deal with, we can consider a special case for illustrative purposes, namely the one where all firms are identical and in which there is a single market without trade costs (Behrens et al., 2009b, deal with heterogeneous firms and trade costs). Assume that $\varphi_i(v) = \varphi$ for all i and v. From the budget constraint $Npd = e$ we then have $\alpha d = \alpha(e/Np)$, which yields

$$\alpha \frac{e}{Np} = 1 - \frac{c}{\varphi p} \Rightarrow p^*_{VES} = \frac{c}{\varphi} + \frac{\alpha e}{N},$$

and which we can compare to the corresponding symmetric CES price given by $p^*_{CES} = [\sigma/(\sigma - 1)](c/\varphi)$. Note that the CES price displays: (i) no wealth effects (since it does not depend on consumers' expenditure); (ii) no pro-competitive effects since the markup is independent of the mass of firms N competing in the economy; (iii) and no competitive limit since the price does not converge to marginal cost as the mass of firms gets arbitrarily large. On the contrary, the VES price equilibrium displays wealth effects, pro-competitive effects and has a competitive limit.

To close the model, we impose the following three standard conditions: (i) free entry and exit, such that imperfectly competitive firms in the differentiated sector earn zero profits; (ii) national factor market clearing at the equilibrium prices and demands; and (iii) balanced trade for each of the two countries. These three conditions generally allow us to pin down factor prices and the mass of differentiated firms.

3   Intra- and inter-industry trade

Endowment differences are usually viewed as driving specialization at the industry level, whereas product differentiation and economies of scale drive specialization at the product level. This section deals with these issues. We first start by showing that *idiosyncratic market size differences* may also serve to drive specialization at the sectoral level in increasing returns industries. Put differently, a larger local demand for a good may well serve as an 'export basis' and make a country a net exporter of that good (Krugman, 1980; Helpman and Krugman, 1985). We can thus have a 'scale economy view' for both intra- and inter-industry trade even in the absence of any endowment differences. Second, we revisit the inter- vs intra-industry trade issue in a world where endowment differences matter (Helpman and Krugman, 1985; Markusen and Venables, 2000). We present a few 'simple' examples that allow us to analyze the distribution of production, of demand, and the volume and pattern of trade.

3.1 The 'pure' role of market size

Consider a world where countries differ neither in technologies nor in relative factor endowments, yet *do differ in terms of size and accessibility to demand*. Given this setup, we show that a larger size can be either an absolute advantage, which maps into higher factor prices; or a relative ('comparative') advantage, which maps into specialization and trade patterns. The key question we ask is: How does market size affect factor prices, the location of industry, and the structure and volume of trade?

Common framework. In what follows, we rely on a special instance of the more general model proposed in the foregoing section. We impose strong assumptions on preferences and technologies, which allow us to obtain particularly sharp results.[14] Assume that there is only a single production factor, call it labour. There are L_i workers in each country $i = 1, 2$, each of whom supplies inelastically one unit of labour. We denote by w_i the (unique) wage rate in country i. Assume that the upper-tier utility function is Cobb–Douglas over the two goods: $U_i \equiv (U_i^1)^{\mu_i^1} (U_i^2)^{\mu_i^2}$, with $\mu_i^1 + \mu_i^2 = 1$ and $\mu_i^s > 0$ for $s = 1, 2$. Assume furthermore that both lower-tier utilities are CES with $\sigma_i^1 = \sigma_i^2 = \sigma$ for both countries. We further impose that firms are perfectly symmetric (i.e. $\varphi_i^1(v) = \varphi_i^2(v) = \varphi$ and $F_i^1 = F_i^2 = F$). Hence, firms differ only by the variety they produce and by the country they are located in. Given these assumptions, and imposing symmetry across firms, the aggregate demands (6) for firms in country $i = 1, 2$ are given by

$$L_j d_{ij}^1 = \frac{(p_{ij}^1)^{-\sigma}}{(\mathbb{P}_j^1)^{1-\sigma}} \mu_j^1 L_j e_j, \quad \text{with } \left(\mathbb{P}_j^1\right)^{1-\sigma} = \sum_k N_k^1 (p_{kj}^1)^{1-\sigma}.$$

Mirror expressions hold for sector 2. Note that in the absence of fixed costs for exporting, all firms sell to all markets so that the mass of producers N_k^s from all countries in sector s appears in the price index. Consider a sector 1 firm located in country 1. Using the constant markup pricing result from the foregoing section, and equating (10) to zero yields

$$X_i^1 = \tau_{i1}^1 L_1 d_{i1}^1 + \tau_{i2}^1 L_2 d_{i2}^1 = F(\sigma - 1)\varphi. \tag{12}$$

In words, at any zero profit equilibrium each firm's output X_i^1 must be equal to $F(\sigma - 1)\varphi$ for the firm to break even. Observe that this output level is a constant bundle of parameters that is independent from supply and demand conditions. Substituting $L_j d_{ij}^1$ and p_{ij}^1, and letting $\phi_{ij}^1 \equiv (\tau_{ij}^1)^{1-\sigma} \in [0,1]$ denote the freeness of trade in sector 1, we finally obtain the *wage equations* (Fujita et al., 1999):

$$\frac{w_i^{-\sigma} \phi_{i1}^1 \mu_1^1 L_1 w_1}{w_1^{1-\sigma} \phi_{11}^1 N_1^1 + w_2^{1-\sigma} \phi_{21}^1 N_2^1} + \frac{w_i^{-\sigma} \phi_{i2}^1 \mu_2^1 L_2 w_2}{w_1^{1-\sigma} \phi_{12}^1 N_1^1 + w_2^{1-\sigma} \phi_{22}^1 N_2^1} = \sigma F, \quad i = 1, 2. \qquad (13)$$

Symmetric expressions hold for sector 2 firms. The wage equations define a system of 2×2 equations in 3×2 unknows (the 2 wages w_i and the 2×2 industry allocations N_i^s). Across regions they identify the masses of firms that drive profits to zero for any given vector of factor prices.

The wage equations can be analyzed under two alternative sets of assumptions. First, we can pin down wages by assuming that one of the goods can be traded at no costs, which then implies that wages will be equalized across countries as long as each country produces at least some of that good. Alternatively, we can consider that trading all goods is costly and impose either the trade balance conditions or, equivalently, the factor market clearing conditions for all countries. The former can be expressed as

$$L_i \sum_{j,s} \mu_i^s \frac{N_j^s \phi_{ji}^s w_j^{1-\sigma}}{\sum_k N_k^s \phi_{ki}^s w_k^{1-\sigma}} = w_i^{-\sigma} \sum_{j,s} N_i^s \frac{w_j L_j \mu_j^s \phi_{ij}^s}{\sum_k N_k^s \phi_{kj} w_k^{1-\sigma}}, \quad i = 1, 2. \qquad (14)$$

Our key objective is to now show that: (i) a large domestic demand in a country leads to either higher wages there, with no country specializing in a particular industry; or (ii) leads to a more than proportionate share of imperfectly competitive firms of one industry locating in each country, with each country being a net exporter of the differentiated good for which it has a relatively larger domestic demand. Using the classical terminology, the former case has a strong 'absolute advantage' flavor, whereas the second case has a strong 'comparative advantage' flavor.

'Absolute advantage'. Following Krugman (1980), assume that there are two countries that are identical in all respects except for their sizes. Without loss of generality, we assume that $L_1 > L_2$.[15] Trade costs are symmetric between countries and goods ($\tau_{12}^s = \tau_{21}^s = \tau$ for $s = 1, 2$) and there are no trade costs within countries ($\tau_{11}^s = \tau_{22}^s = 1$ for $s = 1, 2$). Preferences are identical across countries, which have the same spending patterns for the two goods: $\mu_1^1 = \mu_2^1 = \mu$ and $\mu_1^2 =$

$\mu_2^2 = 1 - \mu$, with $\mu > 1/2$. When combined with $L_1 > L_2$, we see that country 1 has the larger market for both goods. In that sense, this country has an 'absolute advantage' since given positive trade costs, all firms face ceteris paribus a larger demand there.

Letting $w_1 \equiv 1$ by choice of *numéraire*, we can show the following result (see the Appendix):

Proposition 1 Assume that preferences are identical across countries and that country 1 has the larger market ($L_1 > L_2$). Then the equilibrium is such that

$$N_i^{1*} = \frac{\mu L_i}{\sigma F} \quad \text{and} \quad N_i^{2*} = \frac{(1 - \mu)L_i}{\sigma F} \tag{15}$$

for $i = 1, 2$. The equilibrium relative wage satisfies $0 < w_2^* < 1$.

Proposition 1 reveals three results. First, the equilibrium is *proportional* in the sense that each country's share of firms in a sector is proportional to that country's size (countries are simply 'scaled replicas' of each other). Since preferences are identical and homothetic, this implies that intra-industry trade within each sector is balanced. Put differently, *no country is a net exporter of any good*, that is, there is no sectoral specialization. Trade does, of course, occur since goods are differentiated, but the aggregate pattern of trade is balanced and all trade is of the intra-industry type. Second, country 1 offers an *absolute locational advantage* since it is the larger market for all goods. Everything works as if firms in the larger country face a better technology, since they require less factor inputs (inclusive of transportation) to serve their demand. Hence, in equilibrium, firms have to pay a higher wage there to offset this locational advantage. Third, the wage gap across countries is increasing in the level of trade costs, that is, decreasing in ϕ. Freer trade thus favors the convergence of factor prices, even in the presence of trade costs, scale economies and imperfect competition.[16]

'Comparative advantage'. Assume now that the two countries are of the same size ($L_1 = L_2 = L$), whereas preferences are antisymmetric across countries: $\mu_1^1 = \mu_2^2 = \mu$ and $\mu_1^2 = \mu_2^1 = 1 - \mu$, with $\mu > 1/2$. In words, country 1 has now ceteris paribus the larger market for good 1, whereas country 2 has the larger market for good 2. Letting $w_1 \equiv 1$ by choice of *numéraire*, we can show the following result (see the appendix):

Proposition 2 Assume that preferences are antisymmetric across countries and that both countries are of the same size ($L_1 = L_2$). Then the equilibrium is such that

$$N_1^{1*} = N_2^{2*} = \frac{L}{\sigma F} \frac{\mu(1+\phi) - \phi}{1 - \phi}$$

and

$$N_1^{2*} = N_2^{1*} = \frac{L}{\sigma F} \frac{1 - \mu(1+\phi)}{1 - \phi}$$

The equilibrium relative wage satisfies $w_2^* = 1$.

Observe that positive output of good 1 in country 1 and of good 2 in country 2 is assured since $\mu > 1/2 \geq \phi/(1+\phi)$. Furthermore, an equilibrium without full specialization requires that $\mu < 1/(1+\phi)$. In case this latter condition does not hold, country 1 is fully specialized in the production of good 1 and country 2 in the production of good 2, and the foregoing results may not apply. Proposition 2 reveals a few interesting insights. First, note that we have

$$\frac{N_1^{1*}}{N_1^{2*}} = \frac{\mu(1+\phi) - \phi}{1 - \mu(1+\phi)}$$

which is increasing in μ and greater than 1 for $\mu > 1/2$. Hence, countries progressively specialize in the production of the good for which they have the relatively larger local demand as that demand increases. We also have

$$\frac{N_1^{1*}}{N_1^{1*} + N_2^{1*}} = \frac{\mu(1+\phi) - \phi}{1 - \phi} > \mu$$

for all $\mu > 1/2$ since $0 < \phi < 1$. This reveals that the share of sector 1 firms exceeds country 1's share of demand for that good. This effect has come to be known as the *home market effect*, which states that idiosyncratic local demand translates into more than proportional production of goods featuring increasing returns to scale and transport costs.[17] Because of homothetic preferences and factor price equalization, country 1 is then a net exporter of good 1 and country 2 is a net exporter of good 2. Note also from the foregoing expression that the 'industry gap' increases as trade gets freer (i.e. decreases in ϕ): lower trade costs increase specialization. This latter result has a direct consequence for the pattern of trade. Indeed, specialization increases inter-industry trade flows at the expense of intra-industry trade flows. One can check that the volume of inter-industry trade $|N_1^{1*}p_{12}^1 L_2 d_{12}^1 - N_2^{1*}p_{21}^1 L_1 d_{21}^1|$ is increasing in μ as long as there is no full specialization, whereas it is zero when $\mu = 1/2$ so that there is only intra-industry trade.[18] Hence, the more dissimilar the countries are in terms of preferences (relative market sizes), the larger the volume of inter-industry trade and the smaller the volume of intra-industry trade. In a certain sense, differences in relative market sizes work like *comparative advantage* and lead to specialization. Finally, note that since trade in all goods is subject to trade costs, higher trade costs reduce the volume of both intra- and inter-industry trade.

3.2 Factor endowments and market size

Until now, we have abstracted from endowment differences to focus on the 'pure' role of market size. We now embed the monopolistic competition model in a Heckscher–Ohlin framework to take into account endowment effects. In so doing, we basically follow the work of Helpman and Krugman (1985). However, unlike Helpman and Krugman (1985), we will make some more specific assumptions that will allow us to deal with positive trade costs as in Markusen and Venables (2000). Positive trade costs will be important in Section 4 where we will allow for firm-level heterogeneity.

Assume that sector 1 produces a homogeneous good, whereas sector 2 produces a differentiated good under monopolistic competition as in the Sections 2.2 and 2.3. Both labour (L) and capital (K) are internationally immobile and used in the production of both goods. To keep the analysis simple, we assume that the homogeneous good can be traded costlessly. Hence, for that good, production patterns are only driven by resource constraints and equality of world demand and supply. The exact sourcing of the different units of the homogeneous good that satisfy demands in each country is immaterial. We assume that good 1 (say 'food') is relatively labour-intensive, whereas good 2 (say 'manufactures') is relatively capital intensive. Finally, country 1 is relatively capital abundant (with endowments ratios $\overline{K}_1/\overline{L}_1 > \overline{K}_2/\overline{L}_2$) and both countries have access to the same technology in both sectors. Preferences are identical and homothetic and of the Cobb–Douglas and CES forms as before so that: $D_j^1 = (1 - \mu)(L_j w_j + K_j r_j)/p^1$ and $L_j d_{ij}^2 = (p_{ij})^{-\sigma} \mu (L_j w_j + K_j r_j)/\mathbb{P}_j^{1-\sigma}$. In what follows, we restrict the analysis to the case where factor endowments are in the diversification set (i.e., each country produces both goods).[19]

Letting $p^1 \equiv 1$ by choice of *numéraire*, the equilibrium is characterized by the following set of conditions. First of all, we have two zero profit conditions for the differentiated sector in the two countries:

$$\frac{(p_{11})^{-\sigma} E_1^2}{\mathbb{P}_1^{1-\sigma}} + \tau \frac{(p_{12})^{-\sigma} E_2^2}{\mathbb{P}_2^{1-\sigma}} = F(\sigma - 1)\varphi,$$

$$\tau \frac{(p_{21})^{-\sigma} E_1^2}{\mathbb{P}_1^{1-\sigma}} + \frac{(p_{22})^{-\sigma} E_2^2}{\mathbb{P}_2^{1-\sigma}} = F(\sigma - 1)\varphi,$$

(16)

where $E_i^2 = \mu(L_i w_i + K_i r_i)$ denotes country i's aggregate expenditure allocated to the differentiated good. Then, we have four factor market clearing conditions in the two countries:

$$a_L^{11} X_1^1 + a_L^{21} N_1 \sigma F = L_1 \qquad a_K^{11} X_1^1 + a_K^{21} N_1 \sigma F = K_1,$$

$$a_L^{12} X_2^1 + a_L^{22} N_2 \sigma F = L_2 \qquad a_K^{12} X_2^1 + a_K^{22} N_2 \sigma F = K_2,$$

(17)

where $a_L^{ij} \equiv \partial c^i(r_j, w_j)/\partial w$ and $a_K^{ij} \equiv \partial c^i(r_j, w_j)/\partial r$ are the unit input coefficients in both countries. Finally, we have two zero profit conditions for the homogeneous sector in the two countries:

$$c^1(r_1, w_1) = c^1(r_2, w_2) = 1.$$

This gives a system of eight equations in the eight unknowns: w_1, w_2, r_1, r_2, N_1, N_2, X_1^1 and X_2^2.

Inter-industry trade (single factor).   Before developing the two-factor model, it is useful to briefly review a special case (Helpman and Krugman, 1985). Assume that $K_1 = K_2 = a_K^{ij} = 0$, and that $c^1(w) = w$ so that $a_L^{1i} = 1$ for $i = 1, 2$. In words, there is a single factor of production (labour) and the homogeneous good requires one unit of labour per unit of output in both countries.

Since the homogeneous good can be traded at no cost, provided this good is produced in both countries (which we assume to be the case) product prices will be equalized. This in turn also equalizes factor prices. Assume that countries differ in size ($L_1 > L_2$, with $L_1 = \theta L$ and $L_2 = L$ and $\theta \geq 1$). Given that $w_1 = w_2 = 1$ by choice of *numéraire*, the zero profit conditions reduce to,

$$\frac{L_1}{N_1 + \phi N_2} + \frac{\phi L_2}{\phi N_1 + N_2} = \frac{\sigma F}{\mu} \quad \text{and} \quad \frac{\phi L_1}{N_1 + \phi N_2} + \frac{L_2}{\phi N_1 + N_2} = \frac{\sigma F}{\mu}$$

and they can be uniquely solved to yield

$$N_1^* = \frac{\mu L}{\sigma F} \frac{\theta - \phi}{1 - \phi} \quad \text{and} \quad N_2^* = \frac{\mu L}{\sigma F} \frac{1 - \phi \theta}{1 - \phi}.$$

Note that $N_2^* > 0$ if and only if $\theta < 1/\phi$. Note further that the homogeneous good is produced in both countries if and only if $\theta < \mu/(1 - \mu)$, that is, the expenditure share of the differentiated good must be large enough. We see that this equilibrium is similar to the one derived in Proposition 2. Clearly, when $\theta > 1$ we have that $N_1^* > N_2^*$, which under identical and homothetic preferences implies that country 1 is a net exporter of the differentiated good (and thus a net importer of the homogeneous good). Since $N^* = N_1^* + N_2^* = [L(1 + \theta)\mu]/(\sigma F)$, we see that

$$\frac{N_1^*}{N^*} - \frac{N_2^*}{N^*} = \frac{1 + \phi}{1 - \phi} \left(\frac{\theta}{1 + \theta} - \frac{1}{1 + \theta} \right).$$

In words, the difference in industry and production shares across the two countries is proportional to the countries' difference in income shares, magnified by a coefficient of $(1 + \phi)/(1 - \phi) > 1$. Hence, the larger country produces a more than proportionate share of the differentiated good and is a net exporter of that good, and the more so the lower the trade costs (the larger is ϕ).

Finally, the volume of intra-industry trade is measured by the index of trade overlap, which takes a particularly simple form in this case:

$$\text{Intra} = 1 - \frac{|X_{12}^1 - X_{21}^1| + |X_{12}^2 - X_{21}^2|}{X_{12}^1 + X_{21}^1 + X_{12}^2 + X_{21}^2} = 1 - \frac{(\theta - 1)(1 + \phi)}{\theta - \phi}.$$

This index is decreasing in the size asymmetry θ, and decreasing as trade gets freer (larger ϕ). Hence, the freer trade and the more asymmetric the countries' sizes, the larger the share of inter-industry trade. On the contrary, when $\theta = 1$, there is only intra-industry trade.

Inter-industry trade (two factors). Following Markusen and Venables (2000), we now analyze the more general case with two factors and with trade costs for the differentiated good.[20] We assume that the differentiated good 2 is relatively more capital intensive than the homogeneous good 1, and that there are no factor intensity reversals. Using $p_{11} = p_1 = |\sigma/(\sigma-1)||c^2(r_1,w_1)/\varphi|$, $p_{22} = p_2 = |\sigma/(\sigma-1)||c^2(r_2,w_2)/\varphi|$, $p_{12} = \tau p_1$ and $p_{21} = \tau p_2$, the zero profit conditions (16) can be solved to yield

$$E_1^2 \mathbb{P}_1^{\sigma-1} = \frac{\varphi F(\sigma-1)|p_1^\sigma - \phi p_2^\sigma|}{1-\phi^2} \quad \text{and} \quad E_2^2 \mathbb{P}_2^{\sigma-1} = \frac{\varphi F(\sigma-1)|p_2^\sigma - \phi p_1^\sigma|}{1-\phi^2}.$$

We simplify notation by letting $c_j^i \equiv c^j(w_i, r_i)$ denote the unit cost for good j in country i (at that country's factor prices). Using the expressions of the price aggregates, the foregoing expressions can be written as

$$\frac{E_1^2}{N_1(c_1^2)^{1-\sigma} + N_2\phi(c_2^2)^{1-\sigma}} = \frac{F\sigma|(c_1^2)^\sigma - \phi(c_2^2)^\sigma|}{1-\phi^2}$$

$$\frac{E_2^2}{N_1\phi(c_1^2)^{1-\sigma} + N_2(c_2^2)^{1-\sigma}} = \frac{F\sigma|(c_2^2)^\sigma - \phi(c_1^2)^\sigma|}{1-\phi^2}$$

which can be solved for N_i and $i = 1, 2$ to yield:

$$N_i = \frac{(c_i^2)^{\sigma-1}|(c_i^2)^\sigma (E_i^2 + E_j^2)\phi - (c_j^2)^\sigma (E_i^2 + \phi^2 E_j^2)|}{F(\sigma-1)\varphi|\phi(c_i^2)^\sigma - (c_j^2)^\sigma ||(c_i^2)^\sigma - \phi(c_j^2)^\sigma|}, \quad i \neq j.$$

Assume, without loss of generality, that country 1 is the high-cost country for the differentiated good (i.e. $c_1^2 \geq c_2^2$). In that case, the following two conditions on trade costs and expenditures (market size) have to hold for production of the differentiated good to take place in both countries (in which case we remain in the diversification set):

$$\phi < \left(\frac{c_2^2}{c_1^2}\right)^\sigma < \left(\frac{c_1^2}{c_2^2}\right)^\sigma \quad \text{and} \quad \frac{E_1^2}{E_2^2} > \frac{1}{\phi}\frac{(c_1^2)^\sigma - \phi(c_2^2)^\sigma}{(c_2^2)^\sigma - \phi(c_1^2)^\sigma} > 1.$$

These conditions obviously hold when trade is either impossible ($\phi = 0$) or when costs (or factor prices) are equalized. When trade is either too free as compared to cost differences or when country 1 is small, there will be no production of differentiated goods there. Low trade costs make it worthwhile to import the differentiated goods from the low-cost country, whereas a small expenditure share makes country 1 unattractive as a production site. Since country 1 has higher costs, a necessary condition for production to occur there is that country 1 has a larger market (as measured by expenditure on the differentiated good). It is readily verified that $\partial N_1/\partial E_1^2 > \partial N_1/\partial E_2^2 > 0$, that is, an increasing expenditure gap widens the industry gap $N_1 - N_2$.

The factor market clearing conditions (17) can be uniquely solved for outputs of the homogeneous good X_1^1 and X_2^1 and the firm masses N_1 and N_2 to yield:

$$N_1 = L_1 \frac{a_L^{11} k_1 - a_K^{11}}{\Delta_1 \sigma F} \quad \text{and} \quad N_2 = L_2 \frac{a_L^{12} k_2 - a_K^{12}}{\Delta_2 \sigma F},$$

where $k_i \equiv K_i / L_i$; and where $\Delta_1 = a_K^{21} a_L^{11} - a_K^{11} a_L^{21} > 0$ and $\Delta_2 = a_K^{22} a_L^{12} - a_K^{12} a_L^{22} > 0$ since the differentiated good is relatively more capital intensive and since we assume that there are no factor intensity reversals.

For the sake of simplicity, we examine three special cases of the model (see Markusen and Venables, 2000, for a more detailed discussion and for numerical representations of the complete set of cases): (i) the case with factor price equalization; (ii) the impact of size, holding relative endowments constant; and (iii) the impact of endowment differences.

FPE and market size. Consider first the case where factor price equalization holds. As shown by Markusen and Venables (2000) this is a rather 'unlikely' case since the FPE set has no longer full dimensionality but is a one-dimensional subset of the endowment space. If there is FPE, $r_1 = r_2 = r$ and $w_1 = w_2 = w$ so that costs are the same in both countries. Consequently, $p_1 = p_2 = p = [\sigma/(\sigma-1)](c/\varphi)$, $\mathbb{P}_1^{1-\sigma} = p^{1-\sigma}(N_1 + N_2\phi)$ and $\mathbb{P}_2^{1-\sigma} = p^{1-\sigma}(N_1\phi + N_2)$. The solutions of N_1 and N_2 then yield:[21]

$$N_1 = \frac{E_1^2 - \phi E_2^2}{F\varphi(\sigma-1)(1-\phi)p} = \frac{E_1^2 - \phi E_2^2}{F(1-\phi)\sigma c(r,w)} \quad \text{and}$$

$$N_2 = \frac{E_2^2 - \phi E_1^2}{F\varphi(\sigma-1)(1-\phi)p} = \frac{E_2^2 - \phi E_1^2}{F(1-\phi)\sigma c(r,w)}.$$

Note that output of the differentiated good will be positive in both countries if and only if their difference in world income shares is not too large: $\phi < \min\{E_1/E_2, E_2/E_1\}$. When trade costs are prohibitive, each country produces the differentiated good in proportion to its own market size, whereas freer trade gradually shifts differentiated goods production towards the larger market. Summing N_1 and N_2, the total mass of firms is $N = (E_1 + E_2)/[F\varphi(\sigma-1)p] = (E_1 + E_2)/(F\sigma c)$. We furthermore have

$$\frac{N_1}{N_1 + N_2} = \frac{1+\phi}{1-\phi} \frac{E_1^2}{E_1^2 + E_2^2} - \frac{\phi}{1-\phi} \quad \text{and} \quad \frac{N_2}{N_1 + N_2} = \frac{1+\phi}{1-\phi} \frac{E_2^2}{E_1^2 + E_2^2} - \frac{\phi}{1-\phi}.$$

If country 1 is the larger country (as measured by its share of world income), it will host a larger (more than proportional) industry share and will be a net exporter of the differentiated good. To see this, note that

$$\frac{N_1}{N_1 + N_2} - \frac{E_1^2}{E_1^2 + E_2^2} = \frac{2\phi}{1-\phi} \left(\frac{E_1^2}{E_1^2 + E_2^2} - \frac{1}{2} \right)$$

which reveals the presence of the home market effect: country 1's industry and output shares exceed its share in world expenditure of the differentiated good. Furthermore, since $(1 + \phi)/(1 - \phi) > 1$, any increase in its world income share will increase disproportionally its share in world output of the differentiated good (referred to as the 'HME magnification'). The value of inter-industry trade is readily computed and it is proportional to $N_1 - N_2$ in the FPE set:

$$\frac{\phi F \sigma c}{1 - \phi}(N_1 - N_2) = \frac{\phi(1 + \phi)}{(1 - \phi)^2}(E_1^2 - E_2^2).$$

Hence, inter-industry trade will be large when: (i) countries have different market sizes; and (ii) trade costs are low (larger ϕ). These two effects stem as before from firms' entry decisions, which favor the larger market. Hence, the bigger country specializes in the production of the differentiated good, the more so the less costly this good is to trade.

Factor endowments and market size. Consider first the case where we start at the equal endowment point (point A in figure 5.1): $L_1 = L_2 = L$ and $K_1 = K_2 = K$. Clearly, by construction, this point satisfies factor price equalization.

Now consider a move in endowment space such that $L_1 w + K_1 r$ increases, but such that FPE still holds (e.g. point B in figure 5.1).[22] As expenditure increases in country 1 relative to expenditure in country 2, whereas factor prices remain unchanged, the production of differentiated goods becomes relatively more profitable in country 1. Hence, restoring equilibrium when production costs are identical across countries requires entry of differentiated firms in country 1.

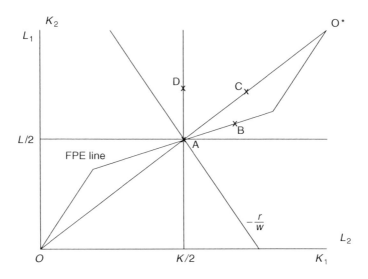

Figure 5.1   Specialization and trade with increasing returns and endowment differences.

Such entry restores equilibrium by reducing profitability. Note that at any point in the FPE set such that country 1 is relatively capital abundant (i.e. below the diagonal), country 1 is a net exporter of the differentiated good and there is inter-industry trade. This inter-industry trade is purely driven by the larger local market size in country 1.

Consider next the case where we start from the equal endowment point, and move upwards along the diagonal (e.g. to point C in figure 5.1). In this case, country 1 increases both its capital and its labour endowment, but the capital–labour ratios remain identical across countries. To see that FPE cannot hold, observe that with FPE, country 1's share of world expenditure rises whereas that of country 2 falls, while production costs remain unchanged. From the zero-profit condition, we then know that country 1's differentiated goods production share (i.e. N_1) must increase. Yet, since relative factor prices in both countries are the same under FPE, and since good 1 is labour intensive whereas good 2 is capital-intensive, there is no way that both countries can fully employ their factors at equal relative factor prices. As can be seen from figure 5.1, moving up along the diagonal increases country 1's share of world expenditure, which makes it the larger market and attracts production of the increasing returns sector. Consequently, for both countries to fully employ their factors, country 1 must switch to more labour-intensive techniques, and country 2 to more capital-intensive ones. In words, $r_1 > r_2$ and $w_1 < w_2$, which raises costs and prices of differentiated goods firms in country 1 ($c^2(w_1, r_1) > c^2(w_2, r_2)$ and $p_1 > p_2$). However, despite higher production costs for differentiated goods and country 1's rising rental rate of capital, it still becomes the net exporter of this good. The reason is that it has to expand its production of good 2 to maintain its capital stock in full employment (recall that good 2 is relatively more intensive in capital). As can be seen from figure 5.2, country 1's share of good 2 production exceeds its share in world income, that is, there is a home market effect. Furthermore, there is inter-industry trade despite the countries' relative factor endowments being identical, and the more so the more different the countries' shares in world expenditure. Last, note that each country is a net exporter of the good for which it has relatively high production costs. This is an interesting result that runs against the standard wisdom that countries export, on average, the goods that are relatively intensive in their relatively cheap factors (Helpman, 1984b). Country size interacts with increasing returns and endowment differences to yield an export pattern in which the country exports the good that uses intensively its relatively expensive factor.

Consider finally the case where starting from the equal endowment point A in the FPE set we decrease country 1's capital–labour ratio (e.g. move to point D in figure 5.1). Again, FPE must break down, else country 1 would see its expenditure share rise, which would require it to increase its share of capital-intensive good 2 production whereas its capital–labour ratio falls. As can be seen from figure 5.3,

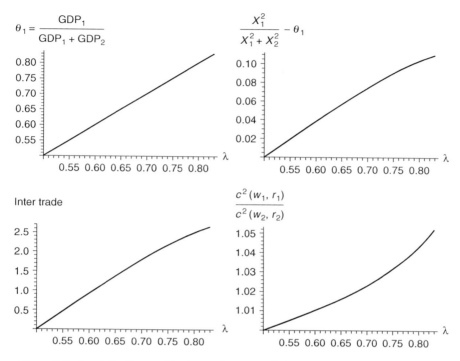

Figure 5.2 Specialization and trade as a function of absolute endowment differences.
Notes: All simulations assume that cost functions are Cobb–Douglas, with $c^1(w,r) = w^\beta r^{1-\beta}$ and $c^2(w,r) = w^\gamma r^{1-\gamma}$. We assume that $\beta > \gamma$, i.e., good 1 is relatively labour intensive. The parameter values are set as follows: $\beta = 0.6$, $\gamma = 0.4$, $\sigma = 4$, $\mu = 0.4$, $\varphi = 1$, $F = 2$, $\tau = 1.7$, $K_1 = \lambda K$, $L_1 = \lambda L$, $K_2 = (1-\lambda)K$, $L_2 = (1-\lambda)L$. We fix world endowments at $K = 20$ and $L = 40$

increasing country 1's labour share, holding capital endowments fixed, raises country 1's share in world income. Hence, ceteris paribus, country 1 should become a more profitable production location for differentiated goods. Yet, the expansion of production of the capital-intensive good is limited by the fall in its capital–labour ratio. For a fixed capital stock, this requires moving capital out of the increasing returns sector. Thus, country 1 must switch to more labour-intensive techniques to absorb its labour supply ($w_1 < w_2$ and $r_1 > r_2$). This further implies that production costs in the differentiated goods sector increase and fall in the homogeneous goods sector, and country 1's production of the differentiated good falls and it becomes a net exporter of the homogeneous good. Moving up vertically from the FPE set thus reduces country 1's output of differentiated good (which is a Rybczynski effect) and increases p_1 relative to p_2. Put differently, the standard Heckscher–Ohlin endowment effect dominates the

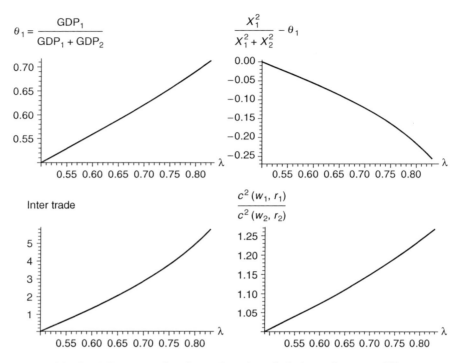

Figure 5.3   Specialization and trade as a function of relative endowment differences .
Notes: All simulations assume that cost functions are Cobb–Douglas, with $c^1(w,r) = w^\beta r^{1-\beta}$ and $c^2(w,r) = w^\gamma r^{1-\gamma}$. We assume that $\beta > \gamma$, i.e., good 1 is relatively labor intensive. The parameter values are set as follows: $\beta = 0.6$, $\gamma = 0.4$, $\sigma = 4$, $\mu = 0.4$, $\varphi = 1$, $F = 2$, $\tau = 1.7$, $K_1 = K/2$, $L_1 = \lambda L$, $K_2 = K/2$, $L_2 = (1-\lambda)L$. We fix world endowments at $K = 20$ and $L = 40$.

market size effect and the trade pattern reflects comparative advantage as each country exports the good that uses intensively its relatively cheap factor.

4   Firm heterogeneity

The theories surveyed so far highlight several sources of gains from trade: enhanced specialization according to comparative advantage; richer product variety; less market power for firms; and better exploitation of scale economies. Among them, only the latter suggests a channel through which trade liberalization can directly interact with an individual firm's efficiency.

In recent models with heterogeneous firms, trade liberalization has an additional positive impact on aggregate productivity through the selection of the most efficient firms (e.g. Bernard et al., 2003; Melitz, 2003; Melitz and Ottaviano, 2008; Behrens et al., 2009b). The reason for this is a combination of import competition and export market access. On the one hand, as lower trade costs allow foreign producers to target the domestic markets, the operating profits of domestic firms in those markets shrink whatever their productivities. On the other hand, some domestic firms gain access to foreign markets and earn additional profits from their foreign ventures. These are the firms that are productive enough to cope with the additional costs of foreign activity (such as those due to transportation and various administrative duties, or institutional and cultural barriers). The result is a productivity-based partition of the initially active domestic firms in three groups. In the first one, the least productive firms are forced to exit as they start making losses in their home markets without gaining access to foreign markets. On the contrary, in the third one, the most productive firms survive and expand their market shares as they are able to compensate lost profits on home sales with new profits on foreign sales. Finally, firms with intermediate productivity also survive but, not being productive enough to access foreign markets, are relegated to home sales only so that their market shares shrink. Since international trade integration eliminates the least productive firms, aggregate productivity grows through the reallocation of resources from less to more efficient producers.

This mechanism has found empirical support in firm-level analyses that try to identify the direction of causation hidden in the positive correlation between a firm's export status and its productivity (called 'exceptional exporter performance' by Bernard and Jensen, 1999). This is a crucial issue for trade policy. Causation going from export status to firm performance would reveal the existence of 'learning by exporting' and, therefore, call for export promotion. However, apart from peculiar cases concerning developing countries, most of the evidence supports reverse causation in the form of 'selection into export status': firms that already perform better have a stronger propensity to export than other firms do (Tybout, 2003). Selection comes with two additional effects that are consistent with the theoretical arguments discussed above. First, exposure to trade forces the least productive firms to shut down (Clerides et al., 1998; Bernard and Jensen, 1999; Aw et al., 2000). Second, trade liberalization leads to market share reallocations towards the most productive firms (Pavcnik, 2002; Bernard et al., 2006). On both counts, aggregate productivity improves in the liberalizing countries. In the last few years a burgeoning empirical literature has confirmed those early results (see chapter 6 by David Greenaway, Danny McGowan and Richard Kneller).

4.1   Modelling firm heterogeneity

The simplest way to model firm heterogeneity is to follow Melitz (2003) by introducing it as the outcome of an R&D effort with uncertain outcome. In what follows, we focus on a single differentiated goods sector and therefore drop the superscript s, as already done in section 2.

Let us assume that, in order to enter the market, each firm has to make an irreversible ('sunk') investment in terms of labour to 'invent' its own variety. In country $i = 1, 2$ the sunk investment is equal to $I_i c_i$. A prospective entrant knows for certain that it will invent a new variety and use a technology implying the cost function (9). It does not know, however, its individual efficiency, as this is randomly assigned only after the sunk cost has been paid. In particular, upon entry each firm v draws its productivity level $\varphi_i(v)$ from a common and known cumulative density function G_i with support $[0, \infty)$. Since the entry cost $I_i c_i$ is sunk, only entrants that can cover their production and trade costs to a certain market will serve that market in equilibrium. Entrants that are not able to serve any market will, instead, exit without even starting production.

Trade costs have both a variable component of the iceberg type, embedded in ϕ_{ij}, as well as a fixed component. Specifically, each firm located in country i has to pay a fixed trade cost $F_{ij} c_i$ whatever its volume of sales to country j. A natural assumption to make is not only $\phi_{ii} > \phi_{ij}$ but also $F_{ii} < F_{ij}$, thus implying that the fixed trade cost is lower for shipments to the local market than to any distant market.[23] Accordingly, under standard CES preferences, the profit from sales from country i to country j is given by

$$\pi_{ij}(\varphi_i(v)) = \frac{1}{\sigma} \left[\frac{\varphi_i(v)}{c_i \widetilde{\varphi}_j} \right]^{\sigma-1} E_j \phi_{ij} - F_{ij} c_i, \tag{18}$$

with

$$\widetilde{\varphi}_j \equiv \left[\phi_{1j} c_1^{1-\sigma} \int_{\Omega_{1j}} \varphi_1(\omega)^{\sigma-1} d\omega + \phi_{2j} c_2^{1-\sigma} \int_{\Omega_{2j}} \varphi_2(\omega)^{\sigma-1} d\omega \right]^{\frac{1}{\sigma-1}}. \tag{19}$$

Observe that $\widetilde{\varphi}_j$ is the weighted (geometric) average productivity of all firms selling in market j (which is a common and given constant for each firm because of the continuum assumption); and where Ω_{kj} is the set of varieties exported from country k to country j. Since π_{ij} is an increasing function of $\varphi_i(v)$ over the productivity support $[0, \infty)$ and, due to the fixed trade cost, is negative for zero productivity ($\varphi_i(v) = 0$), we can determine a unique productivity cutoff $\overline{\varphi}_{ij}$ satisfying $\pi_{ij}(\overline{\varphi}_{ij}) = F_{ij} c_i$ such that only more productive firms with productivity $\varphi_i(v) > \overline{\varphi}_{ij}$ actually sell from i to j. As stated before, selection into sales would not arise in the absence of the fixed trade cost as all firms would be able to cover their production and trade costs to any destination irrespective of their productivity levels.

Given the definition of the productivity cutoff, $1 - G_i(\overline{\varphi}_{ij})$ is (ex ante) the probability that an entrant in country i is able to serve country j. Due to the Law of Large Numbers, it is also (ex post) the share of entrants in country i that actually serve country j. We call $\overline{\varphi}_i = \min_j \overline{\varphi}_{ij}$ the minimum cutoff productivity an entrant in country i has to achieve in order to be able to sell in at least one market. This implies that $1 - G_i(\overline{\varphi}_i)$ is (ex ante) the probability that an entrant in country i is able to produce at all and (ex post) the share of producers located in country i. Accordingly, $\rho_{ij} \equiv \left[1 - G(\overline{\varphi}_{ij})\right]/[1 - G(\overline{\varphi}_i)]$ is the share of producers located in country i that, at equilibrium, serve country j.

Due to the CES assumption, all firms drawing the same productivity level φ_i in country $i = 1, 2$ face not only the same cost function but also the same demand conditions. This allows us to rewrite the average productivity in terms of productivity levels φ_i rather than in variety v as

$$(\widetilde{\varphi}_j)^{\sigma-1} \equiv \sum_{k=1}^{2} \left\{ \frac{\rho_{kj} N_k}{\sum_k \rho_{kj} N_k} \left[\frac{\phi_{kj} c_k^{1-\sigma}}{1 - G_k(\overline{\varphi}_{kj})} \int_{\overline{\varphi}_{kj}}^{\infty} (\varphi_i)^{\sigma-1} dG_i(\varphi_i) \right]^{\frac{1}{1-\sigma}} \right\},$$

where N_k is the number of producers in country k (the number of entrants times the probability to be able to produce at all). A key property of this geometric definition of average productivity is that all average performance variables for firms selling from i to j can be written as functions of $\widetilde{\varphi}_j$. In particular, the average profit made by firms located in country i from sales to country j equals the profit of the average seller from i to j: $\widetilde{\pi}_{ij} = \pi_{ij}(\widetilde{\varphi}_j)$. Hence, we can use (18) and $\pi_{ij}(\overline{\varphi}_{ij}) = 0$ to write

$$\widetilde{\pi}_{ij} = F_{ij} c_i \left[\left(\frac{\widetilde{\varphi}_j}{\overline{\varphi}_{ij}} \right)^{\sigma-1} - 1 \right]. \tag{20}$$

The foregoing expression links the average profit $\widetilde{\pi}_{ij}$ from sales from i to j to the cutoff productivity level $\overline{\varphi}_{ij}$ both directly through the denominator of the ratio between parentheses, and indirectly through the average productivity $\widetilde{\varphi}_j$ at the ratio's numerator. As the direct effect of changing $\overline{\varphi}_{ij}$ is stronger than the indirect effect, expression (20) reveals that the average profit from sales from i to j is a decreasing function of the cutoff in country j: a larger cutoff makes it harder to sell from i to j as firms are on average more productive there.

Let us call $\widetilde{\pi}_i$ the average profit made in country i from sales to both countries. This is equal to the sum of average profits $\widetilde{\pi}_{ij}$ from sales to both countries weighted by the share of producers serving each destination: $\widetilde{\pi}_i = \rho_{i1} \widetilde{\pi}_{i1} + \rho_{i2} \widetilde{\pi}_{i2}$. Then, expression (20) can be used to write

$$\frac{\widetilde{\pi}_i}{c_i} = \rho_{i1} F_{i1} \kappa(\overline{\varphi}_{i1}) + \rho_{i2} F_{i2} \kappa(\overline{\varphi}_{i2}), \tag{21}$$

where $\kappa(\overline{\varphi}_{ij}) \equiv (\widetilde{\varphi}_j/\overline{\varphi}_{ij})^{\sigma-1} - 1$ is a decreasing function of $\overline{\varphi}_{ij}$. We call (21) the "zero cutoff profit" (ZCP) condition.

Free entry implies that the net value of entry is zero in equilibrium. This happens in country i when the sunk entry cost $I_i c_i$ exactly matches the expected profit from entry, which is equal to the average profit $\widetilde{\pi}_i$ of a producer times the probability $1 - G_i(\overline{\varphi}_i)$ that an entrant becomes a producer. Hence, we can write the 'free entry' (FE) condition as

$$\frac{\widetilde{\pi}_i}{c_i} = \frac{I_i}{1 - G_i(\overline{\varphi}_i)}. \tag{22}$$

The number of unknown cutoffs $\overline{\varphi}_{ij}$ can be reduced by noting that, together with (18), $\pi_{ij}(\overline{\varphi}_{ij}) = F_{ij}c_i$ and $\pi_{jj}(\overline{\varphi}_{jj}) = F_{jj}c_j$ imply that all cutoffs for distant sales to country j can be expressed as functions of its local cutoff only:

$$\left(\overline{\varphi}_{ij}\right)^{\sigma-1} = \frac{\phi_{jj}}{\phi_{ij}} \frac{F_{ij}}{F_{jj}} \left(\frac{c_i}{c_j}\right)^{\sigma} \left(\overline{\varphi}_{jj}\right)^{\sigma-1}. \tag{23}$$

Finally, the equilibrium of the model is fully characterized by imposing factor market clearing conditions analogous to (17).

4.2   Trade liberalization and selection

To derive some fundamental insights from the model, it is useful to follow Melitz (2003) in assuming a perfectly symmetric setup ($E_i = E$, $c_i = c$, $F_{ii} = F$, $G_i(\cdot) = G(\cdot)$ for $i = 1, 2$) facing no iceberg costs for local sales ($\phi_{ii} = 1$) and the same bilateral trade costs for distant sales ($\phi_{ij} = \phi_{ji} = \tau^{1-\sigma}$ and $F_{ij} = F_x$). In this symmetric setup, the cutoff productivity levels are the same in both countries. Then, (23) generates a simple linear relationship between the common cutoff for distant sales $\overline{\varphi}_x$ and the common cutoff for local sales $\overline{\varphi}$. In particular, we have

$$\overline{\varphi}_x = \overline{\varphi}\tau \left(\frac{F_x}{F}\right)^{\frac{1}{\sigma-1}} \tag{24}$$

which implies $\overline{\varphi}_x > \overline{\varphi}$ as, by assumption, $\tau > 1$ and $F_x > F$. Since the cutoff is higher for distant sales, exporters are more productive than purely domestic producers. The model therefore predicts 'selection into export status' as only the more productive firms are able to overcome trade barriers.[24] Under symmetry, the ZCP condition (21) becomes

$$\frac{\widetilde{\pi}}{c} = F\kappa(\overline{\varphi}) + \rho_x F_x \kappa(\overline{\varphi}_x) \tag{25}$$

where $\rho_x \equiv [1 - G(\overline{\varphi}_x)] / [1 - G(\overline{\varphi})]$ measures the probability that a producer is an exporter.

By (24), $\overline{\varphi}_x$ is increasing in $\overline{\varphi}$, so $\kappa(\overline{\varphi})$, $\kappa(\overline{\varphi}_x)$ and ρ_x are all decreasing functions of $\overline{\varphi}$. Thus, the ZCP condition establishes a negative relation between average profit $\widetilde{\pi}$ and cutoff productivity $\overline{\varphi}$. Turning to the FE condition, with symmetry (22) simplifies to

$$\frac{\widetilde{\pi}}{c} = \frac{I}{1 - G(\overline{\varphi})}. \tag{26}$$

Therefore, since $1 - G(\overline{\varphi})$ is decreasing in $\overline{\varphi}$ and Ic is constant, the FE condition (22) establishes a positive relation between average profit $\tilde{\pi}$ and cutoff productivity $\overline{\varphi}$. The ZCP and FE conditions are depicted in the top panel of figure 5.4. Their crossing determines the equilibrium cutoff productivity for local sales $\overline{\varphi}_e$ and the corresponding equilibrium average profit $\tilde{\pi}$ (recall that c is constant). Uniqueness of the equilibrium is guaranteed by the opposite slopes of the two curves. The bottom panel of figure 5.4 depicts, instead, the linear relationship between $\overline{\varphi}_x$ and $\overline{\varphi}$ as given by (24). The figure shows two rounds of selection. Specifically, the top panel shows that only entrants that are productive enough ($\varphi > \overline{\varphi}_e$) survive and produce. Among them, only those who are very productive ($\varphi > \overline{\varphi}_{xe} > \overline{\varphi}_e$) also export while all other entrants are confined to their local markets.

Figure 5.4 can be used to establish how trade liberalization affects the industry equilibrium. Consider, in particular, the impact of a reduction in the iceberg trade cost τ. Most naturally, the bottom panel shows that a lower τ rotates the cutoff relation (24) counterclockwise bringing $\overline{\varphi}_x$ closer to the 45-degree line due the fact that it becomes easier to export. The top panel shows, instead, that the ZCP condition (25) shifts upwards due to the fact that expected profits

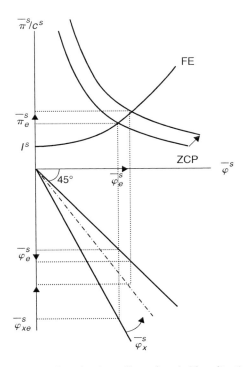

Figure 5.4   The selection effect of trade liberalization.

from exports increase. The result is that fewer entrants are now able to survive and produce as $\overline{\varphi}_e$ increases, which increases average aggregate productivity in the industry. This selection effect of trade liberalization represents a new gain from trade impossible to get in models without firm heterogeneity.[25] At the same time, shipments to distant markets also increase due to two concurrent adjustments: because of lower trade barriers not only firms that already served distant markets increase their shipments, but also new firms are now able to export as $\overline{\varphi}_x^s$ falls. The former phenomenon is called the adjustment along the 'intensive margin' and does not depend on firms being heterogeneous. The latter is called the adjustment along the 'extensive margin' and comes from firm heterogeneity.

4.3 Factor endowments and selection

As it relies on the same demand system and the same technological constraints, the model of Melitz (2003) is a natural extension of the model of Krugman (1980). The extension is achieved through the introduction of uncertainty at the entry stage leading to heterogeneity at the production stage. In Krugman (1980), all entrants are ex ante and ex post identical so that the free entry and free exit conditions coincide. In Melitz (2003), entrants are ex ante identical as they face the same uncertainty on their productivity levels, but become different ex post as these productivity levels are randomly assigned. Entry decisions are then made by ex ante homogeneous firms whereas exit decisions are made by ex post heterogeneous firms. As a firm makes its entry and exit decisions based on different information sets, the free entry condition and the free exit condition do not coincide, the latter giving rise to the cutoff rule captured by the ZCP condition.

Bernard et al. (2007a) exploit the formal similarities between Krugman (1980) and Melitz (2003) to introduce firm heterogeneity in the two-country general equilibrium models of Helpman and Krugman (1985) and Markusen and Venables (2000) we discussed in Section 3.2. By so doing they shed light on the interactions between trade liberalization, firm heterogeneity and comparative advantage of the Heckscher–Ohlin type. Assume that there are two differentiated goods sectors $s = 1, 2$, that country 1 is relatively abundant of capital, and that good 1 is relatively intensive in capital. Hence, country 1 has a comparative advantage in the production of good 1. In our notation, that implies $c_1^2/c_1^1 > c_2^2/c_2^1$. Relative factor endowments are the only difference between the two countries and factor intensities are the only differences between goods ($F_{ii}^s = F$, $I_i^s = I$ and $G_i^s(\cdot) = G(\cdot)$). There are no iceberg costs for local sales ($\phi_{ii}^s = 1$) and the same bilateral trade costs for distant sales ($\phi_{ij}^s = \phi_{ji}^s = \tau^{1-\sigma}$ and $F_{ij}^s = F_x$).

By (21) and (22), the ZCP and FE conditions for country 1 and sector s are respectively

$$\frac{\tilde{\pi}_1^s}{c_1^s} = F\kappa(\overline{\varphi}_{11}^s) + \rho_{12}^s F_x \kappa(\overline{\varphi}_{12}^s) \tag{27}$$

and

$$\frac{\tilde{\pi}_1^s}{c_1^s} = \frac{I}{1 - G(\overline{\varphi}_{11}^s)}, \tag{28}$$

while the cutoff relation (23) can be restated as

$$\overline{\varphi}_{12}^s = \tau \left(\frac{F_x}{F}\right)^{\frac{1}{\sigma-1}} \left(\frac{c_1^s}{c_2^s}\right)^{\frac{\sigma}{\sigma-1}} \overline{\varphi}_{22}^s. \tag{29}$$

The ZCP condition (27) and the FE condition (28) are portrayed in the top panel of figure 5.5. Consider first the autarkic situation corresponding to the solid curves. In this case the share of exporters is zero ($\rho_{12}^s = 0$), which implies that the cutoff productivity level is the same in both sectors: $\overline{\varphi}_{11}^1 = \overline{\varphi}_{11}^2$. Hence, as in a model without firm heterogeneity, factor prices and, therefore, relative costs are determined only by relative factor endowments: $(c_1^1/\overline{\varphi}_{11}^1)/(c_1^2/\overline{\varphi}_{11}^2) = c_1^1/c_1^2$. Accordingly, when trade is liberalized, country 1 will be a net exported of good 1.

In figure 5.5 the dashed and the dash-dotted curves correspond to sectors 2 and 1 respectively. Their positions with respect to the autarkic configuration are based on three pieces of information. First, a producer is more likely to be an exporter in the country's sector of comparative advantage ($\rho_{12}^1 > \rho_{12}^2$). Second, the export profit is higher for an exporter in the sector of comparative advantage ($\kappa(\overline{\varphi}_{12}^1) > \kappa(\overline{\varphi}_{12}^2)$). Third, $\overline{\varphi}_{22}^2$ is closer to $\widetilde{\varphi}_2^2$ than $\overline{\varphi}_{22}^1$ is to $\widetilde{\varphi}_2^1$. To see this, note that expression (29) implies

$$\left[\left(\frac{\overline{\varphi}_{12}^1}{\overline{\varphi}_{22}^1}\right) \Big/ \left(\frac{\overline{\varphi}_{12}^2}{\overline{\varphi}_{22}^2}\right)\right]^{\sigma-1} = \left[\left(\frac{c_1^1}{c_1^2}\right) \Big/ \left(\frac{c_2^1}{c_2^2}\right)\right]^{\sigma} < 1,$$

where the inequality is granted by $c_1^2/c_1^1 > c_2^2/c_2^1$, so that $\overline{\varphi}_{12}^1$ is closer to $\widetilde{\varphi}_2^1$ than $\overline{\varphi}_{12}^2$ is to $\widetilde{\varphi}_2^2$. Then, by definition of $\kappa(\overline{\varphi}_{ij}^s)$ and the above result, we can write

$$\frac{\kappa(\overline{\varphi}_{12}^1) + 1}{\kappa(\overline{\varphi}_{12}^2) + 1} = \left[\left(\frac{\widetilde{\varphi}_2^1}{\overline{\varphi}_{22}^1}\right) \Big/ \left(\frac{\widetilde{\varphi}_2^2}{\overline{\varphi}_{22}^2}\right)\right]^{\sigma-1} \left[\left(\frac{c_2^1}{c_2^2}\right) \Big/ \left(\frac{c_1^1}{c_1^2}\right)\right]^{\sigma} > 1$$

since $\widetilde{\varphi}_2^s$ is more distant from $\overline{\varphi}_{22}^s$ in the sector of comparative disadvantage of country 2. Hence, $\kappa(\overline{\varphi}_{12}^1) > \kappa(\overline{\varphi}_{12}^2)$. As a result, in sector 1 the ZCP curve shifts outwards more than in sector 2, which implies that $\overline{\varphi}_{11}^1$ rises more than $\overline{\varphi}_{11}^2$. As the selection effect in country 1 is stronger in sector 1, the productivity gain from selection reinforces the country's cost advantage in the sector that more

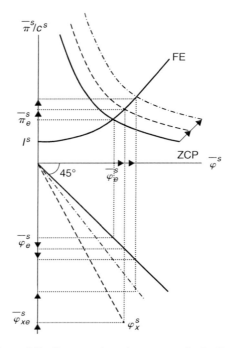

Figure 5.5   Comparative advantage and selection.

intensively uses its relatively abundant factor. In other words, selection amplifies the Heckscher–Ohlin comparative advantage through an endogenous Ricardian comparative advantage.[26]

5   Organizational choice

Until now, we have assumed that firms always serve foreign markets through exports. Yet, exports are not the only way to serve distant markets as firms vastly differ in their internationalization modes. While these are discussed in chapter 8 by James Markusen, here we simply want to show how models with heterogeneous firms have been used to link a firm's efficiency to its specific internationalization mode.[27]

5.1   FDI and selection

As reported by Helpman and others (2004), Bernard et al. (2007b), Mayer and Ottaviano (2007), and Tomiura (2007), just as exporters are more productive than purely domestic firms, multinationals tend to be more productive than pure exporters.

This fact is explained by Helpman and others (2004), who extend the model of Melitz (2003) by allowing firms to serve distant markets not only by exports, as discussed so far, but also by foreign direct investment (FDI). To highlight the key insights of their model, it is useful to go back to a perfectly symmetric situation with two identical countries ($E_i = E$, $c_i = c$, $F_{ii} = F$ and $G_i(\cdot) = G(\cdot)$) facing no iceberg costs for local sales ($\phi_{ii} = 1$) and the same bilateral trade costs for export sales ($\phi_{ij} = \phi_{ji} = \tau^{1-\sigma}$ and $F_{ij} = F_x$). We can then characterize FDI as an organizational mode that makes it possible for a firm to serve distant markets by avoiding trade costs ($\tau = 1$, $F_x = 0$) at the price of incurring higher fixed costs associated with local production in those markets ($F_f > F_x = 0$).

These assumptions generate a linear relation between the FDI productivity cutoff $\overline{\varphi}_f$ and the domestic productivity cutoff $\overline{\varphi}$ analogous to (24). In particular, we have

$$\overline{\varphi}_f = \left(\frac{F_f}{F}\right)^{\frac{1}{\sigma-1}} \overline{\varphi} \tag{30}$$

which implies $\overline{\varphi}_f > \overline{\varphi}$ as, by assumption, $F_f > F$. If we further assume that

$$F_f > \tau^{\sigma-1} F_x, \tag{31}$$

then we also have $\overline{\varphi}_f > \overline{\varphi}_x$ so that the FDI cutoff is higher than the export one. This implies that producers are partitioned in three groups depending on their productivity levels: those with low productivity ($\overline{\varphi} < \varphi < \overline{\varphi}_x$) serve only their local market; those with intermediate productivity serve also the distant market through exports ($\overline{\varphi}_x < \varphi < \overline{\varphi}_f$); whereas those with high productivity ($\varphi > \overline{\varphi}_f$) also serve the distant market but through FDI. As stated in the foregoing, this ranking is the one observed in the data. Based on that partition, the ZCP condition (21) becomes

$$\frac{\widetilde{\pi}}{c} = F\kappa(\overline{\varphi}) + \rho_x F_x \kappa(\overline{\varphi}_x) + \rho_f F_f \kappa(\overline{\varphi}_f), \tag{32}$$

where the third additional term on the right-hand side comes from the average profit of multinationals with $\rho_f \equiv \left[1 - G(\overline{\varphi}_f)\right] / [1 - G(\overline{\varphi})]$ measuring the probability that a producer is a multinational. Since $\overline{\varphi}_f$ is increasing in $\overline{\varphi}$, the functions $\kappa(\overline{\varphi}_f)$ and ρ_f are both decreasing in $\overline{\varphi}$ so that the ZCP condition establishes a negative relation between average profit $\widetilde{\pi}$ and domestic cutoff productivity $\overline{\varphi}$.

Nothing changes, instead, concerning the FE condition which is still given by (26), thus establishing a positive relation between between average profit $\widetilde{\pi}$ and cutoff productivity $\overline{\varphi}$. The ZCP and FE conditions with FDI are depicted in the top panel of figure 5.6. Their crossing determines the equilibrium cutoff productivity for local sales $\overline{\varphi}_e$ and the equilibrium average profit $\widetilde{\pi}_e$. Uniqueness is still guaranteed by the opposite slopes of the two curves. The bottom panel depicts the linear relation (24) between $\overline{\varphi}_x$ and $\overline{\varphi}$ as well as the linear relation

(30) between $\overline{\varphi}_f$ and $\overline{\varphi}$. The latter relation is steeper than the former due to (30) and (31).

Figure 5.6 reveals three rounds of selection. Specifically, the top panel shows that only entrants that are productive enough ($\varphi > \overline{\varphi}_e$) survive and produce. Among them, the bottom panel shows that those with low productivity ($\overline{\varphi}_e < \varphi < \overline{\varphi}_{xe}$) serve only their local market, those with intermediate productivity serve the distant market through exports ($\overline{\varphi}_{xe} < \varphi < \overline{\varphi}_{fe}$), and those with high productivity ($\varphi > \overline{\varphi}_{fe}$) also serve the distant market but through FDI. As for trade liberalization, a lower FDI cost F_f shifts the ZCP curve upwards, thus raising $\overline{\varphi}$ and reducing $\overline{\varphi}_f$. This implies that fewer entrants make it to the production stage but, among the survivors, the relative number of multinationals increases. As before, lower τ and lower F_x also shift the ZCP curve upwards, thus raising $\overline{\varphi}$ and reducing $\overline{\varphi}_x$. This implies that fewer entrants become producers but, among them, the relative number of exporters increases. Hence, no matter whether favoring exports or FDI, trade liberalization has a productivity enhancing effect on industry performance.[28]

If we allowed for different relative factor endowments, we would find analogous results to those in Section 4.3: in each country lower barriers to trade or FDI

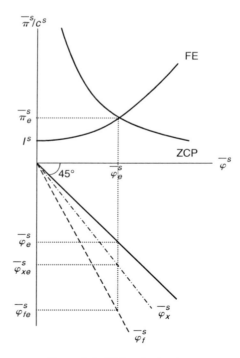

Figure 5.6   FDI and selection.

shift the ZCP curve upwards more in its sector of comparative advantage. Such a stronger selection effect would reinforce the Heckscher–Ohlin comparative advantage through an endogenous Ricardian comparative advantage.

5.2 Outsourcing and selection

Following Grossman and Helpman (2002) and Antràs (2003), a recent class of models tries to explain the observed internationalization modes in terms of the decisions that firms make regarding their boundaries in the presence of contractual incompleteness. Getting into the details of the contract theory underpinning these models is beyond the scope of the present chapter. Nonetheless, we can use our theoretical framework to provide some intuition on their insights. To do so, let us reinterpret our final goods as intermediates and our fixed costs as the cost of assembling those intermediates. In particular, let F represent the cost of assembly for final sales in the country where intermediates are produced; let F_x represent the cost of assembly for final sales in a foreign country to which intermediates are shipped *outside a firm's boundaries*; and let F_f represent the cost of assembly for final sales in a foreign country to which intermediates are shipped *inside a firm's boundaries*. While all international shipments face the same trade cost τ, shipments outside a firm's boundaries ('outsourcing') face an additional 'contractual cost' $h > 1$. On the other hand, shipments inside a firm's boundaries ('vertical integration') save on contractual costs but require higher fixed costs due to the more complex governance structure of a multinational organization (i.e. $F_f > F_x$).

These assumptions generate two linear relations between the productivity cut-offs similar to those in (24). In particular, the relation between the cutoff for arm's length exports $\bar{\varphi}_x$ and the local cutoff $\bar{\varphi}$ in the destination market is

$$\bar{\varphi}_x = \tau h \left(\frac{F_x}{F} \right)^{\frac{1}{\sigma-1}} \bar{\varphi}. \tag{33}$$

Analogously, the relation between the cutoff for intra-firm export $\bar{\varphi}_f$ and the local cutoff $\bar{\varphi}$ in the destination market is

$$\bar{\varphi}_f = \tau \left(\frac{F_f}{F} \right)^{\frac{1}{\sigma-1}} \bar{\varphi}.$$

Whether higher firm productivity is associated with arm's length or intra-firm transaction depends on the relative costs of the two internationalization modes. For example, if we assume

$$F_f > h^{\sigma-1} F_x$$

we obtain $\bar{\varphi} < \bar{\varphi}_x < \bar{\varphi}_f$ so that producers with low productivity ($\bar{\varphi} < \varphi < \bar{\varphi}_x$) serve only their local market, those with intermediate productivity serve the distant market through arm's length exports ($\overline{\varphi}_x < \varphi < \overline{\varphi}_f$), and those with high productivity ($\varphi > \overline{\varphi}_f$) also serve the distant market but through intra-firm exports.

Based on this partition, the ZCP condition is just like (32) while the FE condition is still equal to (26). Hence, we can reinterpret figure 5.6 to discuss the implications of changing contractual costs. Specifically, in the bottom panel of figure 5.6 the dashed line now corresponds to intra-firm export whereas the dot-dashed line corresponds to arm's length export. A reduction in the contractual cost (lower h^s) has the same impact as the reduction in the fixed export cost F^s_x. In the top panel, by shifting the ZCP curve upwards, it excludes low productivity firms from the market so that aggregate industry productivity increases. In the bottom panel, by rotating the cutoff relation (33) counterclockwise, it raises the share of arm's length exporters.

In the case where relative factor endowments differ between the two countries and relative factor intensities differ between sectors, a lower contractual cost h^s shifts the ZCP curve upwards more in the sector of comparative advantage. This stronger selection effect reinforces the Heckscher–Ohlin comparative advantage through an additional endogenous Ricardian comparative advantage.

This simple framework can be used to understand the answer given by Antràs (2003) to the following question: Why are capital-intensive goods transacted within the boundaries of multinational firms, while labour-intensive goods are traded at arm's length? A possible answer is that in capital-intensive sectors the contractual cost h^s is higher.[29] This then reduces the relative number of firms that transact at arm's length as in those sectors the dash-dotted curve of figure 5.6 is steeper.

6   Conclusion

In the perfectly competitive Arrow–Debreu paradigm, on which the Ricardian and Heckscher–Ohlin models are based, firms' boundaries are undetermined. The reason is that 'firms' are just production functions and, as such, have no individual 'behaviour' proper. This chapter has provided an overview of how monopolistic competition has been used to model firm behaviour in general equilibrium. In so doing, the chapter has covered several dimensions of firm behaviour, including the choices on whether to launch new products or dispense with old ones, where to produce and where to sell these products, and how to organize international operations.

To conclude, we want to highlight three promising directions for future research. The first concerns the study of the general equilibrium effects of trade liberalization channeled through changes in firms' product mix (in terms of product range and quality) in a world in which the bulk of aggregate trade flows is driven by firms exporting several products to several destinations (see, e.g.,

Bernard et al., 2007b; Mayer and Ottaviano, 2007). In a second direction, more effort should be put into teasing out the general equilibrium effects of trade in multi-country models, possibly adding an internal geographical dimension to traditionally featureless countries (Behrens et al., 2009a; Behrens et al., 2009b). Finally, in their investigation of organizational choices, current models with firm heterogeneity still rely too much on somehow ad hoc assumptions on the cost ranking across different organizational modes. This is particularly troubling in the case of fixed costs, which have been so far treated as 'black boxes'. We believe that replacing old 'black boxes' with new ones might not be the most promising road to travel.

Notes

* Department of Economics, Université du Québec à Montréal (UQAM), Canada; CIRPÉE, Canada; and CEPR, UK.
† Department of Economics and KITeS, Bocconi University, Italy; FEEM, Italy; and CEPR, UK.
1. See chapter 3 by Alan Woodland.
2. See, e.g., Hummels and Levinsohn (1995) and Debaere (2005) for empirical support to the fact that 'new trade theory' explains international trade patterns between more developed countries.
3. As shown by Roberts and Sonnenschein (1977), the existence of (price) equilibria is usually problematic in monopolistic competition models with a discrete number of firms since firms' reaction functions may be discontinuous. That is why this chapter focuses on monopolistic competition models with a continuum of firms that are individually negligible as these models usually do not display such problems. The same holds usually true for oligopoly models with a continuum of sectors. Neary (2003) uses such a general equilibrium model of oligopolistic competition, where firms are 'large' in their own markets but 'negligible' in the whole economy, which allows to reestablish equilibrium. Furthermore, as under monopolistic competition with a continuum of firms profits vanish in a free-entry equilibrium, one does not have to care about whether firms maximize profits or the welfare of their shareholders, which is a cause of concern in oligopoly models (Gabszewicz and Vial, 1972).
4. The basic DSK model considers final goods only. However, it is homomorphic to a model in which the differentiated final good is replaced by a homogenous one that is produced by assembling the varieties of a horizontally differentiated intermediate (see Ethier, 1982).
5. We focus only on non-address models of monopolistic competition. See Spence (1976), Helpman and Krugman (1985) and Anderson et al. (1992) for further developments on ideal variety and discrete choice models of product differentiation, respectively.
6. The assumption of a representative consumer can be relaxed provided that the income distribution does not matter for the aggregate market outcome. Yet, the normative implications of trade for each agent may, as always, depend on his position in the income distribution and on his ownership claims to production factors.
7. By definition, the demand $d_{ij}(\nu)$ is a function of all the prices $p_{ij}(\omega)$ in all sectors and of consumer expenditure e_i only. The term $\lambda \big/ [\frac{\partial U_i}{\partial U_i^s}(g_i(\cdot))g_i'(\cdot)]$ in expression (4) depends

hence on different functions ('aggregates') of all prices and on expenditure. Note that the vector of price aggregates $\mathbb{P}_i$ can include the average price (or the geometric average, as in Dixit and Stiglitz, 1977) and some measure of dispersion, e.g., the variance (Ottaviano et al., 2002; Melitz and Ottaviano, 2008) or the entropy (Behrens and Murata, 2007) of the sectoral price distributions.

8. Dixit and Norman (1980) heavily draw on quasi-linear preferences when discussing trade under imperfect competition. Recently, Ottaviano et al. (2002), Asplund and Nocke (2006), and Melitz and Ottaviano (2008) use quadratic quasi-linear preferences, as initially pioneered by Vives (1999), for the analysis of trade, location, and industry dynamics. We do not further discuss the quasi-linear approach in this chapter.

9. We assume that there is a one-to-one correspondence between firms and varieties. This is the case if firms can costlessly differentiate their varieties and if there are no scope economies in producing different varieties simultaneously. In that case, firms will never produce the same varieties as this would make them compete *à la* Bertrand on common varieties and thus end up with lower profits.

10. As argued by Helpman and Krugman (1985, p. 143), this may be too strong an assumption since factor intensities are the same for fixed and for variable costs.

11. If transportation is mostly provided in-house, more productive firms might indeed also be more productive in shipping goods. However, according to 1992 U.S. Bureau of Transport Statistic figures, 61.4 percent of the value of transportation services ($192 billion out of $313 billion) were generated by for-hire transportation. Furthermore, the manufacturing sector uses the largest share of for-hire transportation (about 80 percent).

12. Profits may be positive at this stage since the mass of firms is taken as given. Hence, $e_i = w_i L_i + r_i K_i + \Pi(\cdot)$ where the third term denotes the distribution of profits. Contrary to oligopoly, the price of an individual firm does not feed back into profits (there is no 'Ford effect' as in d'Aspremont et al., 1996).

13. We do not consider stability in the sense of a simultaneous deviation of a measurable subset of firms. Indeed, such a deviation requires collusion, a case which we do not consider in our non-cooperative setup.

14. As with almost all trade models, multi-country and multi-sector extensions are quite involved to deal with. See Behrens et al. (2009a) for the multi-country version of the model with factor price equalization, and Hanson and Xiang (2006) for the multi-industry two-country version of the model without factor price equalization.

15. Strictly speaking, we present a modified version of Krugman (1980). Indeed, Krugman assumes that consumers have only preferences over one type of each good; that is, he considers the limit case where $\mu_1^1 = \mu_2^2 = 0$. However, in his model there are two types of consumers which are asymmetrically distributed across the two countries. Both approaches are isomorphic and yield qualitatively identical results.

16. Note, however, that this result crucially hinges upon the assumption that expenditures are internationally immobile. In a world of 'new economic geography', where consumers and expenditures are mobile across locations, falling trade costs may trigger a process of factor price divergence (Krugman, 1991; Krugman and Venables, 1995). See chapter 16 by Stephen Redding for more details.

17. Note that the home market effect is one the building blocks of the economic geography models presented by Stephen Redding in chapter 16.

18. The algebra is straightforward but somewhat tedious, so we omit the proof.

19. As is well known, the diversification set and the FPE set are no longer identical in the presence of trade costs (Markusen and Venables, 2000).

20. We do not discuss the benchmark case in which there are no costs for trading any good (i.e. $\phi \equiv 1$). See Helpman and Krugman (1985) for a detailed analysis of this case.

21. Given identical Cobb–Douglas preferences, we have $E_1 = \mu(L_1 w + K_1 r)$ and $E_2 = \mu(L_2 w + K_2 r)$. Hence, N_1 and N_2 are linear functions of the factor endowments in the FPE space. Note also that differentiated goods output is then a linear function of expenditure in the FPE set since $N_1 pF\varphi(\sigma - 1) = (E_1 - \phi E_2)/(1 - \phi)$ and $N_2 pF\varphi(\sigma - 1) = (E_2 - \phi E_1)/(1 - \phi)$.

22. As shown by Markusen and Venables (2000), the FPE set is piecewise linear and it cuts the diagonal of the Edgeworth endowment box (in K–L space) from above. Its slope is constrained by $|-r/w, 1|$, with a smaller slope the freer is trade. The reason is that industry location becomes more sensitive to size asymmetries when trade is free (HME magnification), which requires that country sizes (as measured by expenditure shares) do not get too different. Note also that, given equal factor prices, any move to the right along the FPE set unambiguously raises country 1's share of world income.

23. When $F_{ij} = 0$ the heterogeneous firm model boils down to the homogeneous firm model of the previous section provided that one assumes that all firms of the latter are identical to the average firm of the former.

24. Recall that the productivity draws occur prior to the export decision. Note that one could allow for technological upgrading (which increases productivity) after the initial draw is observed, and this decision would then depend on productivity and would thus be correlated with export status. Allowing for such a possibility amounts to introduce some 'learning by exporting' into the model (see, e.g., Bustos, 2011).

25. Using (24) and the definition $\kappa(\overline{\varphi}_x)$, it is readily verified that a lower F_x^y has a similar impact.

26. Melitz and Ottaviano (2008) consider instead comparative advantage originating from technological differences by assuming that, with respect to entrants in country 2, entrants in country 1 are more likely to get higher productivity draws in sector 1 than in sector 2. This introduces a notion of stochastic Ricardian advantage in the spirit of Eaton and Kortum (2002) except that the advantage is tied to firms and not to countries. Also in this case trade liberalization induces tougher selection in the comparative advantage sector: selection amplifies the exogenous Ricardian comparative advantage through an additional endogenous Ricardian comparative advantage.

27. An overview of theoretical and empirical work on internationalization modes can be found, for example, in Markusen (2002) as well as in Barba Navaretti and Venables (2004).

28. Behrens et al. (2009c) provide an empirical application to the EU countries, quantifying the respective industry-level gains from trade vs FDI liberalization in the model by Melitz and Ottaviano (2008).

29. An alternative explanation could be that capital-intensive goods contain more information that could 'leak' to competitors in the case of outsourcing, and that internalization can provide insurance against such 'leakage'.

References

Alessandria, G., and J. Kaboski (2007) 'Pricing-to-market and the failure of absolute PPP'. Federal Reserve Bank of Philadelphia, Working Paper No. 07–29.

Anderson, S.P., A. de Palma and J.-F. Thisse (1992) *Discrete Choice Theory of Product Differentiation*. Cambridge, MA: MIT Press.

Antràs, P. (2003) 'Firms, contracts, and trade structure', *Quarterly Journal of Economics* 118, 1375–1418.

Asplund, M., and V. Nocke (2006) 'Firm turnover in imperfectly competitive markets', *Review of Economic Studies* 73, 295–327.

Aw B., S. Chung and M. Roberts (2000) 'Productivity and turnover in the export market: Micro-level evidence from the Republic of Korea and Taiwan (China)', *World Bank Economic Review* 14, 65–90.

Baldwin, R.E., and Ph. Martin (1999) 'Two waves of globalisation: superficial similarities, fundamental differences', NBER Working Paper No. 6904.

Barba, Navaretti G., and A.J. Venables (2004) *Multinationals Firms in the World Economy*. Princeton: Princeton University Press.

Behrens, K., A.R. Lamorgese, G.I.P. Ottaviano and T. Tabuchi (2009a) 'Beyond the home market effect: Market size and specialization in a multi-country world', *Journal of International Economics*, 79(2), 259–265.

Behrens, K., G. Mion, Y. Murata and J. Südekum (2009b) 'Trade, wages and productivity'. CEPR Discussion Paper No. 7369.

Behrens, K., G. Mion and G.I.P. Ottaviano (2009c) 'Economic integration and industry reallocations: Some theory with numbers'. In Jovanovic, M. (ed.), *International Handbook of Economic Integration*, Cheltenham: Edward Elgar Publishers, pp. 169–206.

Behrens, K., and Y. Murata (2007) 'General equilibrium models of monopolistic competition: a new approach', *Journal of Economic Theory* 136, 776–87.

Bernard, A.B., and B. Jensen (1999) 'Exceptional exporter performance: Cause, effect, or both?', *Journal of International Economics* 47, 1–25.

Bernard, A.B., B. Jensen and P.K. Schott (2006) 'Trade costs, firms and productivity', *Journal of Monetary Economics* 53, 917–37.

Bernard, A.B., S.J. Redding and P.K. Schott (2007a) 'Comparative advantage and heterogeneous firms', *Review of Economic Studies* 74, 31–66.

——— (2007b) 'Firms in international trade', *Journal of Economic Perspectives* 21, 105–30.

Bernard A.B., J. Eaton, J. Jensen and S. Kortum (2003) 'Plants and productivity in international trade', *American Economic Review* 93, 1268–90.

Brander, J.A., and P.R. Krugman (1983) 'A "reciprocal dumping" model of international trade', *Journal of International Economics* 15, 313–23.

Bustos, P. (2011) 'Trade liberalization, exports and technology upgrading: Evidence on the impact of MERCOSUR on Argentinian firms', *American Economic Review* 101(1), 2011, 304–340.

Chamberlin, E.H. (1933) *The Theory of Monopolistic Competition*. Cambridge, MA: Harvard University Press.

Clerides, S., S. Lach and J. Tybout (1998) 'Is learning by exporting important? Microdynamic evidence from Colombia, Mexico, and Morocco', *Quarterly Journal of Economics* 113, 903–47.

d'Aspremont, C., R. Dos Santos Ferreira and L.-A. Gérard-Varet (1996) 'On the Dixit–Stiglitz model of monopolistic competition', *American Economic Review* 86, 623–29.

Debaere, P. (2005) 'Monopolistic competition and trade, revisited: testing the model without testing for gravity', *Journal of International Economics* 66, 249–66.

Dixit, A.K., and V. Norman (1980) *Theory of International Trade: A Dual General Equilibrium Approach*. Cambridge: Cambridge University Press.

Dixit, A.K., and J.E. Stiglitz (1977) 'Monopolistic competition and optimum product diversity', *American Economic Review* 67, 297–308.

Ethier, W. (1982) 'National and international returns to scale in the modern theory of international trade', *American Economic Review* 72, 389–405.

Fujita M., and P.R. Krugman (2004), 'The new economic geography: Past, present and future', *Papers in Regional Science* 83, 139–64.

Fujita, M., and J.-F. Thisse (2002) *Economics of Agglomeration: Cities, Industrial Location, and Regional Growth*. Cambridge: Cambridge University Press.

Fujita, M., P.R. Krugman and A.J. Venables (1999) *The Spatial Economy: Cities, Regions and International Trade*. Cambridge: MIT Press

Gabszewicz, J.-J. and J.-Ph. Vial (1972) 'Oligopoly *à la* Cournot in general equilibrium analysis', *Journal of Economic Theory* 4, 381–400.

Greenaway, D., and C. Milner (1986) *The Economics of Intra-Industry Trade*. London: Basil Blackwell.

Grossman, G., and E. Helpman (2002) 'Integration vs. outsourcing in industry equilibrium', *Quarterly Journal of Economics* 117, 85–120.

Grubel, H.G., and P.J. Lloyd (1975) *Intra-Industry Trade: The Theory of Measurement of International Trade in Differentiated Products*. New York: John Wiley.

Hanson, G.H., and C. Xiang (2004) 'The home market effect and bilateral trade patterns', *American Economic Review* 94, 1108–92.

Haskel, J., and H. Wolf (2001) 'The law of one price – a case study', *Scandinavian Journal of Economics* 103, 545–58.

Helpman, E. (1984a) 'Increasing returns, imperfect markets, and trade theory', in R.W. Jones and P.B. Kenen (eds) *Handbook of International Economics*, vol. 1. Amsterdam: North-Holland.

——(1984b) 'The factor content of foreign trade', *Economic Journal* 94, 84–94.

Helpman, E., and P.R. Krugman (1985) *Market Structure and Foreign Trade*. Cambridge, MA: MIT Press.

Helpman E., M. Melitz and S. Yeaple (2004) 'Export versus FDI with heterogeneous firms', *American Economic Review* 94, 300–16.

Hummels, D., and J. Levinsohn (1995) 'Monopolistic competition and international trade: Reconsidering the evidence', *Quarterly Journal of Economics* 110, 799–836.

Hummels, D., and A. Skiba (2004) 'Shipping the good apples out? An empirical confirmation of the Alchian-Allen conjecture', *Journal of Political Economy* 112, 1384–1402.

Irwin, D. (1996) *Against the Tide*. Princeton: Princeton University Press.

Krugman, P.R. (1979) 'Increasing returns, monopolistic competition, and international trade', *Journal of International Economics* 9, 469–79.

——(1980) 'Scale economies, product differentiation and the pattern of trade', *American Economic Review* 70, 950–59.

Krugman, P.R. (1991) 'Increasing returns and economic geography', *Journal of Political Economy* 99, 483–99.

Krugman, P.R., and A.J. Venables (1995) 'Globalization and the inequality of nations', *Quarterly Journal of Economics* 110, 857–80.

Laguerre, E.N. (1883) 'Mémoire sur la théorie des équations numériques', *Journal de Mathématiques Pures et Appliquées* 3, 99–146. Trans. by S.A. Levin (2002), 'On the theory of numeric equations', Stanford, CA: Stanford University.

Linder, S.B. (1961) *An Essay on Trade and Transformation*. New York: John Wiley.

Markusen, J.R. (1981) 'Trade and gains from trade with imperfect competition', *Journal of International Economics* 11, 531–51.

——(2002) *Multinational Firms and the Theory of International Trade*. Cambridge, MA: MIT Press.

Markusen, J.R., and A.J. Venables (2000) 'The theory of endowment, intra-industry and multi-national trade', *Journal of International Economics* 52, 209–34.

Mayer, T., and G.I.P. Ottaviano (2007) 'The happy few: The internationalisation of European firms', Brussels: Bruegel, Blueprint 3.
Melitz, M.J. (2003) 'The impact of trade on intra-industry reallocations and aggregate industry productivity', *Econometrica* 71, 1695–1725.
Melitz, M.J., and G.I.P. Ottaviano (2008) 'Market size, trade, and productivity', *Review of Economic Studies* 75, 295–316.
Neary, P.J. (2003) 'International trade in general oligopolistic equilibrium'. Mimeo, University College: Dublin.
Ottaviano, G.I.P., T. Tabuchi and J.-F. Thisse (2002) 'Agglomeration and trade revisited', *International Economic Review* 43, 409–36.
Pavcnik, N. (2002) Trade liberalization, exit, and productivity improvements: Evidence from Chilean plants, *Review of Economic Studies* 69, 245–76.
Roberts, J., and H. Sonnenschein (1977) 'On the foundations of monopolistic competition', *Econometrica* 45, 101–13.
Simonovska, I. (2008) 'Income differences and prices of tradables'. Mimeo, University of Minnesota.
Spence, M. (1976) 'Product selection, fixed costs, and monopolistic competition', *Review of Economic Studies* 43, 217–35.
Tomiura, E. (2007) Foreign outsourcing, exporting, and FDI: A productivity comparison at the firm level, *Journal of International Economics* 72, 113–27.
Tybout, J. (2003) 'Plant and firm-level evidence on new trade theories', in Harrigan, J. (ed) *Handbook of International Economics*, vol. 38, Oxford: Basil-Blackwell.
Vives, X. (1999) *Oligopoly Pricing: Old Ideas and New Tools*. Cambridge, MA: MIT Press.

Appendix

Proof of Proposition 1

Proof. Evaluate (13) and (14) at the equilibrium candidate (15), using $w_1 \equiv 1$, $\phi_{11}^s = \phi_{22}^s = 1$ and $\phi_{12}^s = \phi_{21}^s = \phi$, to obtain the unique condition

$$\frac{L_1}{L_2} w_2^{\sigma-1} \left(w_2^\sigma - \phi \right) = 1 - w_2^\sigma \phi. \tag{34}$$

By Laguerre's (1883) generalization of Descartes's rule of signs, we know that there are at most as many positive roots as there are sign changes between the successive powers of w_2. Since condition (34) can be rewritten as $\frac{L_1}{L_2} w_2^\sigma + \phi w_2 - w_2^{1-\sigma} - \frac{L_1}{L_2}\phi = 0$, there is only one such change which establishes that the solution is unique. Clearly, when $L_1 = L_2$, this solution is such that $w_2^* = 1$. Starting from this point, assume that $L_1/L_2 > 1$. Since the LHS of (34) is increasing in w_2 in the neighborhood of $w_2 = 1$, whereas the RHS is decreasing, $0 < w_2^* < 1$ must hold. ∎

Proof of Proposition 2

Proof. By symmetry of the setup across the two sectors, we can just focus on the wage equations for sector 1 in the two countries (mirror expressions hold for sector 2). Using $L_1 = L_2 = L$, $w_1 = w_2 = 1$, $\mu_1^1 = \mu_2^2 = \mu$ and $\mu_1^2 = \mu_2^1 = 1 - \mu$, as well as $\tau_{ii}^s = 1$ and $\tau_{ij}^s = \tau$, we obtain two linear equations in the masses N_1^1 and N_2^1 of firms:

$$\frac{\mu L}{N_1^1 + \phi N_2^1} + \frac{(1-\mu)L\phi}{\phi N_1^1 + N_2^1} = F\sigma \quad \text{and} \quad \frac{\mu L\phi}{N_1^1 + \phi N_2^1} + \frac{(1-\mu)L}{\phi N_1^1 + N_2^1} = F\sigma,$$

which uniquely solve to yield N_1^{1*} and N_2^{1*}. The results for sector 2 follow by symmetry. It is readily verified that labour markets clear and that trade is balanced at N_1^{1*}, N_2^{1*}, N_1^{2*} and N_2^{2*}. ∎

6
Firms' Internationalisation Strategies: The Evidence

*David Greenaway, Richard Kneller and Danny McGowan**

1 Introduction

It is widely recognised that the pioneering papers of Krugman (1979) and Lancaster (1979) triggered a revolution in the way in which we think about and model international trade. These theoretical insights were in fact motivated by empirical observation, namely intra-industry trade, which appeared to sit oddly with what we would expect in a world where trade patterns are fashioned by differences in factor endowments. The huge literature which these papers triggered yielded new insights into the role of imperfect competition, scale economies and preference diversity in driving trade.

Rich as these theoretical models were in terms of insight, their representation of firms' internationalisation strategies was basic and failed to account for a number of features that we now know to be important. Most obviously, following the early work of Bernard and Jensen (1995) it is clear that not all firms export. Subsequent work building on that paper has revealed other important characteristics of firms which export and, indeed, firms which choose to follow alternative internationalisation strategies, such as foreign direct investment or offshoring. This work has made apparent the differences in the internationalisation strategy within a firm across its product range and its production process.

As Ottaviano and Beherens have shown in Chapter 5 and Markusen in Chapter 8, a rich theoretical literature has developed to underpin and explain these empirical findings, which means we now have a much more complete basis for understanding the drivers of trade at the firm level.

This chapter complements those of Ottaviano and Beherens and Markusen, in reviewing and appraising the empirical literature on firms' internationalisation strategies. It is structured as follows: we begin in Section 2 by setting out some stylised facts on exporting and importing; in Section 3 we focus on the drivers of exporting behaviour; Sections 4 and 5 focus on multiproduct and multinational firms respectively; Section 6 concludes and offers some observations on future directions for this literature.

2   Stylised facts of exports and imports

The empirical observations made by Bernard and Jensen (1995) and in subsequent papers stimulated interest in developing models of international trade consistent with the set of stylised facts of firm export behaviour they uncovered. Contrary to the representative firm assumption of the monopolistic competition strand of new trade theory models by Krugman (1979) and others, these papers drew attention to the fact that exporting and non-exporting firms coexisted in the same industry but were marked by clear defining characteristics. These empirical observations called into question the representative firm assumption used in this type of 'new trade theory' models. Firms do not all follow the same path but rather, as shown in figure 6.1, make different choices about whether to export or not. This regularity has since been shown to hold across virtually all countries studied thus far (see Greenaway and Kneller, 2007a, for a review of evidence).

A defining characteristic of exporters is their productivity advantage over firms that just operate domestically. As shown in figure 6.2 for the United States, exporters feature more commonly than non-exporters at the upper end of the labour productivity distribution. Similar evidence has been found for Germany (Bernard and Wagner, 1997), Sweden (Hansson and Lundin, 2004), Taiwan (Aw and Hwang, 1995) and the United Kingdom (Greenaway and Kneller, 2004,

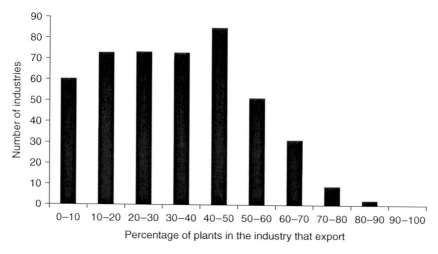

Figure 6.1   The incidence of exporting.
Source: Bernard, Eaton, Jensen and Kortum (2003).

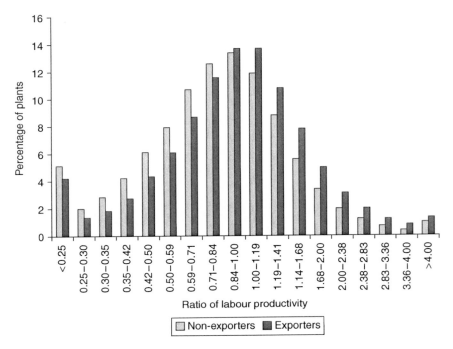

Figure 6.2   Ratio of plant productivity to four-digit industry mean.
Source: Bernard, Eaton, Jensen and Kortum (2003).

2008). To date, these studies have been largely limited to the manufacturing sector due to data constraints.

Exporters have also been shown to possess superior characteristics in a wide range of other dimensions. In particular they tend to be older, larger, have higher capital intensities, are more human capital intensive and more likely to conduct research and development (R&D). As shown in table 6.1 these characteristics are again consistently reported across countries. The extent of differences between exporters and non-exporters does vary substantially across countries however. For example, UK exporters are approximately 13 percent larger than non-exporters (Greenaway and Kneller, 2004) but in Taiwan they are seven times as big (Aw and Hwang, 1995). In part these differences reflect policy factors, the industries included in the sample as well as the sunk costs of market entry.

Typically these differences in firm performance have been found to increase with the value of exports of the firm. As we discuss in further detail below, for future exporters they are also found to pre-exist compared to firms that never export.

Given the widespread use of intermediate inputs and offshoring, importing firms have recently begun to attract attention, though the evidence base is

Table 6.1   Characteristics of exporters relative to non-exporters.

Authors	Country	Sample	Difference
Aw and Hwang (1995)	Taiwan	Firms	717% larger, 31% more capital intensive, 60% older, 56% LP
Bernard and Jensen (1995)	United States, 1976–87	193,463 plants	400% larger, 19% higher wages, 37% LP, 48% more capital intensive, 61% multiplant owned
Bernard and Wagner (1997)	Germany, 1978–92	7,624 plants	30–50% larger, 7% higher wages, 0% LP
Greenaway and Kneller (2008)	United Kingdom	Firms	12.6% larger, 0.5% higher wages, 2.2% LP, 9.7% TFP
Hansson and Lundin (2004)	Sweden, 1990–99	3,275 firms	110% larger, 34% TFP, 0% wages, 20% more capital intensive

Notes: TFP = total factor productivity, LP = labour productivity
Comparisons are made between exporters and non-exporters.

thinner than for exporting. It should be noted here that this refers to direct imports. A comparison between the extent of direct imports and those which the firm makes indirectly through wholesalers, retailers or other agents has not yet been made. Nonetheless, firms that import have been found to share some common traits with exporters. Relative to domestic producers, importers are found to be larger, more productive and more capital intensive. This has been reported for Belgium (Muuls and Pisu, 2007) and Italy (Castellani, Serti and Tomasi, 2008) and suggests a fixed cost element to importing in the same way as has been suggested is important for exporting. It should be noted however, there is no theoretical basis for that inference, and what those sunk costs might include has not been investigated empirically. Comparing importers and exporters, Castellani and others (2008) find that importing firms are marginally more productive than exporters, although smaller and with lower sales. Both Muuls and Pisu (2007) and Castellani, Serti and Tomasi (2008) also yield insights on two-way traders. The results suggest that importing and exporting firms are generally the 'best' firms in the industry. In the Italian context they are, on average, 74, 39 and 36 percent more productive than domestic producers, exporters and importers respectively.

Superstar exporters: The early literature revealed substantial differences in the characteristics of exporters and non-exporting firms. These results have proven to be robust and consistent across myriad countries regardless of level of economic development. As new, richer data has become available a second set of stylised facts about firms and their internationalisation choices has begun to emerge. Indeed these findings have proved to be almost as robust across different countries as those found from the first wave of studies. The added value of these new data was the inclusion of information on the destination of exports (and imports), often by product, for each firm.

The core insight from this new wave of studies was that aggregate exports were determined by a few superstar exporters. A few large firms supplied many foreign markets with many differentiated products. This points to the existence of a process through which only firms that are large enough and have a sufficiently rich portfolio of products can withstand the rigours of international competition. These exceptional exporters were much more likely to be multinationals (Baldwin and Gu, 2004; Kneller and Pisu, 2004) and accounted for a similarly disproportionate share of total imports (Mayer and Ottaviano, 2008).

Using data from seven European countries, Mayer and Ottaviano (2008) find remarkably similar patterns across countries: the top 1, 5 and 10 percent of exporters account for in excess of 40, 70 and 80 percent of aggregate exports. In the case of Germany, Hungary and the United Kingdom the results are less extreme (though this is probably attributable to sample selection bias in favour of large firms). The distribution of exports in French firms is plotted in figure 6.3 with exporters ranked in descending size from the left. For comparison the distribution of employment is also provided in the figure. It is immediately obvious that the concentration of exports is even higher than the concentration of employment.

The narrow concentration of exports among a small band of firms is mirrored by similar skewedness in firms' export intensities. Eliasson, Hansson and Lindvert (2009) report the aggregate export intensity among Swedish manufacturers to be 64 percent. This is partly attributable to Sweden's large export sector and integration into world markets (see Greenaway, Gullstrand and Kneller 2005). However, there are variations according to firm size. Micro firms with less than ten employees have export intensities of 1.4 percent while firms with more than 50 workers export 32.5 percent of their output. Mayer and Ottaviano (2008) report that between 1 and 3 percent of firms in Germany, France, Italy, Norway and the UK export 90 percent or more of their turnover. However, these firms have a disproportionate representation in total exports accounting for between 6 percent (Germany) and 29 percent (Norway) of aggregate exports. When the threshold is set at 50 percent of turnover the figures are even more striking, with such firms accounting for between half and 75 percent of total exports. A similar pattern emerges for the United States. Although 21 percent of

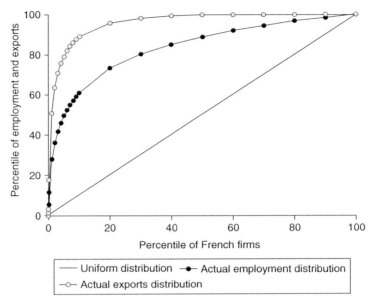

Figure 6.3   The superstar exporters phenomenon.
Source: Mayer and Ottaviano (2008).

plants there export, 66 percent export less than 10 percent of their output, while only 0.7 percent export in excess of 90 percent of their output (Bernard, Eaton et al., 2003) suggesting a high degree of dispersion in productivity within the exporting class. However, top exporters do not necessarily exhibit top export intensity, which implies these firms must be large.

The increasing availability of detailed micro datasets has prompted deeper investigation within firms. The number of products a firm exports (the firm product extensive margin) and number of foreign markets served (the firm market extensive margin) appears to be bimodal: 30 percent of firms export one product to one country while firms exporting ten or more products to more than ten destinations account for 11 percent of exporters (Mayer and Ottaviano, 2008). However, the share of total exports these groups account for is dramatically different with the former contributing 0.70 percent and the latter 76 percent of aggregate exports. Eliasson, Hansson and Lindvert (2009) also find a high degree of heterogeneity in the number of destinations served, and number of products exported according to firm size. Micro enterprises (fewer than ten employees) serve, on average, 0.2 foreign markets and export 0.1 products. At the other extreme the largest firms (with in excess of 50 workers) sell to approximately 19 destinations and export ten products.

For some countries this information is available at a remarkable level of detail. Bernard, Redding and Schott (2010) report that firms exporting five or more products, where products are defined at the ten-digit (HS) level, account for 98 percent of aggregate U.S. exports. Moreover, exports by firms to five or more destinations represent 93 percent of total exports. Indeed there is a high correlation between these activities given that 92 percent of exports are due to firms that export five or more varieties to five or more destinations. This highlights the importance of the extensive margins in describing trade patterns at the firm product level.

For developing countries the distinction between exporting firms appears to be less significant. In contrast to the bimodal evidence from developed countries, Iacovone and Javorcik (2008) find that 80 percent of Mexican exporters sell either one or two products abroad and account for over a third of total exports. Only 10 percent export more than five varieties. Although such firms still account for a disproportionate share of total exports (50 percent) the value is substantially lower than in the United States.[1]

These patterns are again similar for importing. Indeed, a characteristic of U.S. importers is that they import a wider range of products than exporters sell abroad (Bernard, Jensen and Schott, 2007). On average they import ten or more products in the period 1993 to 2000, while exporters sell between 6.1 and 8.9 products abroad. They also find that importing intensity is essentially unchanged over the period.

3   Drivers of export market behaviour

Heterogeneous firm models of international trade point to differing performance characteristics of exporters and non-exporters. But were these differences apparent before the firm started to export or do they appear as a direct result of that decision? This causality question, sparked in part by the ongoing debate over the relationship between openness and growth at the aggregate level has, by some margin, received most attention within the micro literature. Thus, we first consider determinants of export market entry as well as evidence on potential feedback from export market participation to firm performance. To provide some structure we begin with evidence relating to participation in export markets more generally.

Exchange rates: Macroeconomic evidence on the effect of exchange rates on trade levels and volatility suggests effects that are either significant but small in magnitude, or insignificant (Pozo, 1992; Chowdhury, 1993; Parley and Wei, 1993). This suggests exchange rate movements play little or no role as a factor that affects the short run competitiveness of firms and therefore export volumes, or at least that they can successfully manage this risk. The micro evidence suggests, however, that these results are a product of aggregation, and exchange rates are important. In the presence of sunk costs to export market entry, export responsiveness is likely to be higher amongst current exporters compared to non-exporters. That is, changes in exchange rates are more likely to lead to changes in the intensive rather than extensive margin. Bernard and Jensen (2004b), for example, study the export response of U.S. manufacturing plants to dollar depreciation in the 1980s, and report that 87 percent of the expansion was from increased export intensity and 13 percent from entry of new firms. A similarly strong correlation is reported by Bugamelli and Infante (2002) and Bernard and Jensen (2004a).

While useful for future comparative work, this literature is unlikely to provide a complete explanation of the effect of exchange rates on exports for three reasons. First, Das and others (2004) find significant cross-industry variation in the effects of exchange rate movements. Simulating a 20 percent devaluation for three Colombian industries they report that the industry response depends on previous export exposure, homogeneity of expected profit flows between firms and their proximity to the export market entry threshold. Ten years after devaluation the industry level effect varies between 14 and 107 percent (although unfortunately they do not break this into that generated by new entrants and that from existing exporters).

Secondly, there is evidence that some firms appear to be harmed, not helped, by favourable exchange rate movements. According to Blalock and Roy (2007) the two-to-one devaluation of the Indonesian rupiah against the U.S. dollar between 1996 and 1998 did not lead to an aggregate export boom. Deeper analysis showed that although there was an expansion of activity by established exporters and new entry by non-exporters, this new activity was offset by cessation of exporting by previous exporters. Bernard and Jensen (2004b) also find evidence of exit for the U.S. Anecdotal evidence from the peso devaluation in the mid-1990s suggests a temporary increase in the incidence of exporting among Mexican firms (Iacovone and Javorcik, 2008). In the aftermath of the devaluation the percentage of firms exporting rose to one third but by 2003 the figure had returned to its initial level. Blalock and Roy (2007) offer an explanation: firms that ceased exporting were no more likely to report liquidity constraints, or infrastructure problems, compared to firms that continued and were no less productive; but were less likely to be foreign and less likely to have made R&D or training investments. These same variables predicted which firms would become new exporters. An alternative explanation can be found in Maloney and Azevado (1995), where in a model in which firms export to diversify revenue streams fitted to Mexican data, exchange rate volatility and the comovement of domestic and foreign demand shocks can lead to counterintuitive movements in export volumes following changes in exchange rates.

Finally, all of the detailed micro level analysis of exchange rate movements has been of episodes during which the domestic currency depreciated. It is not known whether the effect of an appreciation of the domestic currency is symmetric, or whether there is hysteresis in the export market behaviour of firms. An exception is Greenaway, Kneller and Zhang (2010) who account for the role of imported intermediates in their analysis. They find that although a negative effect of appreciation on exports in the UK can be identified, there tend to be offsetting effects via imported intermediates. Moreover, there is a degree of heterogeneity across firms, with the largest exporters being least responsive to exchange rate changes.

Trade policy: Export decisions are likely to be influenced by the environment in which the firm operates, where policy changes can impact on both intensive and extensive margins. For example, were policy to lead to within firm improvement in productivity perhaps because of increased competition or reduced costs of intermediate imports, it may be more likely that non-exporters enter export markets, but also easier for current exporters to increase export sales to existing or new markets. Unfortunately however we have little evidence on what aspects of policy are important for export volumes. In fact the evidence is concentrated in just five studies across two types of policy, trade liberalisation and export promotion, the results for which are summarised in table 6.2.

Evidence on trade liberalisation suggests an effect on both margins. Blalock and Gertler (2004) find that liberalisation in Indonesia between 1990 and 1996 doubled the number of exporters, while in their study of the effects of NAFTA on Canadian firms, Baldwin and Gu (2004) report increases in both the number of exporters (the share of plants that export increased from 37 to 53 percent between 1984 and 1990) and export intensity (in 48 percent of exporters). Using more sophisticated econometric techniques they find the effect of policy on the export entry decision to be substantial. The 4.5 percent reduction in Canadian/U.S. tariffs that occurred increased the probability of exporting by 63 percent.

Export promotion is pervasive, and most governments intervene in one way or another, ranging from infrastructure support to offering direct export subsidies. Empirical evidence is again mixed, although this may be a result of both the question asked and level of detail available. Both Bernard and Jensen (2004a) and Alvarez (2004) find an insignificant effect from export promotion, the former for exporters versus non-exporters; the latter for permanent versus infrequent exporters. Alvarez (2004) does however find differences in detail. Trade missions and trade shows do not increase the probability that a firm will become a permanent exporter, whereas market studies and arranged meetings with clients, authorities and experts do, even when controlling for other firm and industry determinants. Finally, it is worth noting the evidence of self-selection when evaluating export promotion schemes, a problem thus far not dealt with. Alvarez (2004) finds that established exporters are much more likely than sporadic exporters to have used public instruments for export promotion.

Table 6.2 Evidence on policy intervention and firm export responses.

Authors	Sample	Policy intervention	Outcome
Alvarez (2004)	Chile, 1990–96	Trade shows Trade missions Exporter committees	No effect on export market success No effect on export market success Positive effect on export market success
Baldwin and Gu (2004)	Canada, 1984–96	Canadian–U.S. commodity tariff rates	4.5% reduction in Canadian tariffs increased the probability of exporting by 24% and export intensity by 46%
Bernard and Jensen (2004a)	U.S., 1984–92	State expenditures on export promotion	Insignificant effect on export market participation
Blalock and Gertler (2004)	Indonesia, 1990–96	Trade regime liberalisation: reduced import tariffs, reformed customs administration and more reduced duties levied on inputs used in producing exports.	Productivity increase between 2% and 5% when the firm starts exporting. Productivity gain mainly attributable to initiation of exports
Görg, Henry and Strobl (2008)	Ireland, 1983–98	Capital grants, training grants, rent subsidies, employment grants, feasibility study grants, technology acquisition grants, loan guarantees, research and development grants	In a matched sample large grants lead to additional exports. No evidence of additional entry. Withdrawal of grants does not lead to exit

More detailed information on the payment of grants to firms is available for Ireland, as discussed by Görg and others (2007). Using matching to control for selection problems, the authors find only limited success from intervention; large grants can induce existing exporters to expand overseas sales further but fail to encourage additional entry from those that did not previously export.

Learning versus self-selection into export markets: Entry can have a number of different impacts on the firm and aggregate economy. Some have provoked less discussion than others. For example there is widespread evidence of an aggregate productivity effect through resource reallocation (Bernard and Jensen, 2004a; Hansson and Lundin, 2004; Falvey et al., 2004). The area given greatest attention, however, is the direction of causality between exporting and within firm changes in productivity. We focus on that, although other important effects might relate to survival probability of exporters (Bernard and Wagner, 1997; Bernard and Jensen, 1999).

In its infancy this literature was seen as a straight test between the hypothesis of self-selection and learning, even though the umbrella label 'learning' in fact contains three separate channels. First, interaction with foreign competitors and customers may provide information about the production processes they use or product quality and design issues, reducing costs and raising quality, which can be interpreted as learning by exporting. Second, exporting allows firms to increase scale.[2] Third, increased competition in foreign markets forces firms to be more efficient and stimulates innovation. Over time, however, the hypothesis under test evolved, to one of a bicausal relationship. Self-selection is important, but leads also to endogenous changes in productivity either as a result of learning by exporting or learning to export.

The arguments in favour of self-selection are most powerfully put by Bernard and Jensen (1999, 2004). They found productivity growth of exporters was not significantly different from non-exporters, independent of whether productivity was measured as labour productivity or TFP. This implies that the productivity distribution in any given industry does not widen continuously over time or, put differently, the growth effects from learning are not permanent. They also provided evidence that out of the pool of non-exporters, new exporters were already among the best and differed significantly from the average non-exporter. This evidence, summarised in the first part of table 6.3, has been replicated almost without fail across numerous countries.[3] Export market entry is associated with significant changes in performance around the point at which export sales begin.

This argument for self-selection is therefore based on a comparison between established exporters and non-exporters and a difference in the performance of new export firms around the point of entry, which is not permanent. Future entrants have many of the right characteristics that make them likely to export and faster productivity growth than non-exporters when they do. But, after a short period they become indistinguishable from other exporters. Recognising that new exporters appeared to already have many of the right characteristics to become exporters one can test whether the surge in productivity associated with entry was explained by the decision to become an exporter, or whether the productivity surge led to the export decision. As a consequence of the change in focus, methodology also evolved, with attempts to control for self-selection using either instrumental variable or matching (alone or in combination with difference in differences). As argued in Van Biesebroeck (2005) not controlling for self-selection will overstate evidence of learning for new exporters in the data.

Table 6.3   Evidence on export market entry effects and firms.

Authors	Sample	Methodology	Pre-entry difference	Post-entry difference
Self-selection Versus Learning				
Aw, Chung and Roberts (2000)	Korea, 1983–93 and Taiwan (China), 1981–91	New Exporters vs. non-exporters	5+% TFP Taiwan? TFP Korea	6+% ΔTFP Taiwan? ΔTFP Korea
Baldwin and Gu (2004)	Canada, 1974–96	New Exporters vs. non-exporters	3% ΔLP, 0% ΔTFP	6% ΔLP, 2% ΔTFP
Bernard and Jensen (1999)	U.S., 1984–92	New Exporters vs. non-exporters	6% TFP, 7–8% LP	3% ΔTFP, 3% ΔLP – short run 1% ΔTFP, 1–2% ΔLP – medium run 1% ΔTFP, 1–2% ΔLP – long run
Bernard and Jensen, (2004b)	U.S., 1983–92	New Exporters vs. non-exporters	3% TFP	6% TFP, 2% ΔTFP
Bernard and Wagner (1998)	Germany, 1978–92	New Exporters vs. non-exporters	5% LP, 0% ΔLP	5% ΔLP
Castellani (2002)	Italy, 1989–94	Exporters vs. non-exporters	+ TFP, 0 ΔTFP	
Damijan, Polanec and Prašnikar (2006)	Slovenia, 1994–2002	Exporters vs. non-exporters	0% TFP	0% TFP t_0 0% TFP when export to non-OECD countries t_1 11+% TFP when export to OECD countries t_1
Delgado, Farinas and Ruano, (2002)	Spain, 1991–96	New Exporters vs. non-exporters Stochastic dominance	+ TFP	0 ΔTFP
Greenaway and Yu (2004)	UK chemicals industry, 1990–2000	Dynamic panel		10% increase in exports = 1% TFP, 6% LP

continued

Table 6.3   (continued)

Authors	Sample	Methodology	Pre-entry difference	Post-entry difference
Hahn (2004)	Korea, 1990–98	New Exporters vs. non-exporters	4% TFP	7% TFP
Hansson and Lundin (2004)	Sweden, 1990–99	New Exporters vs. non-exporters	0% ΔTFP, 0% ΔLP	0% ΔTFP, 5% ΔLP
Isgut (2001)	Colombia, 1981–91	New Exporters vs. non-exporters	20% LP, 4% ΔLP	5% ΔLP[1]
Kraay (1999)	China, 1988–92	Dynamic panel		1s.d. increase in exports = 2% TFP, 13% LP
Liu, Tsou and Hammitt (1999)	Taiwan, 1989–93	New Exporters vs. non-exporters	0% ΔLP, 6% ΔTFP	7% ΔLP, 0% ΔTFP

Self-selection with Endogenous Productivity Change Post-entry effects

Authors	Sample	Methodology	Pre-entry difference	Post-entry difference
Arnold and Hussinger (2005)	Germany, 1992–00	Matched D-i-D	+ ΔTFP non-matched sample	0% ΔTFP matched sample
Baldwin and Gu (2004)	Canada, 1974–96	GMM	3.4% LP, 0% TFP non-matched sample	5.5% LP, 1.7% TFP non-matched sample 11% LP, 1% TFP GMM results
Bigsten et al. (2000)	4 African countries 1992–95	Dynamic system		+ ΔTechnical efficiency
Blalock and Gertler (2004)	Indonesian firms, 1990–96	1. Fixed effects 2. IV – OP & LP 3. timing	3. 0% ΔTFP	1. 5% TFP 2. 2–5% TFP 3. 4% ΔTFP
Cleides, Lach and Tybout (1998)	Colombia 1981–91, Mexico, 1986–90 and Morocco 1984–91	GMM	Colombia + LP Mexico 0 LP Morocco + LP	Colombia + LP Mexico 0 LP Morocco + LP
De Loecker (2007a)	Slovenia, 1994–2000	Matched D-i-D		22% TFP t_0

Table 6.3   (continued)

Authors	Sample	Methodology	Pre-entry difference	Post-entry difference
Girma, Greenaway and Kneller (2004)	UK, 1988–98	Matched D-i-D	0% ΔTFP, 0% ΔLP in matched sample 1% ΔTFP, 0% ΔLP in unmatched sample	ΔTFP:2% ΔLP:2% in matched sample ΔTFP:2% ΔLP:1% in unmatched sample
Greenaway & Kneller (2008)	UK, 1989–2002	Matched D-i-D	0% ΔTFP, 0% ΔLP in matched sample	ΔTFP:3% ΔLP:5.5% Effect stronger when interacted with export share
Greenaway, Gullstrand and Kneller (2005)	Sweden, 1980–97	Matched D-i-D	0% ΔLP 0% ΔTFP	0% ΔLP 0% ΔTFP
Van Biesebroeck (2005)	9 African countries, 1992–96	GMM		35% TFP
Wagner (2002)	Germany, 1978–89	matching	0% LP	0% ΔLP
Self-selection with Endogenous Productivity Change Pre-entry effects				
Alvarez and Lopez (2005)	Chile, 1990–96	Matched D-i-D	+ ΔINV, + ΔSKILL + TFP, + LP non-matched results	0% ΔTFP, ?% ΔLP matched sample
Lopez (2004)	Chile, 1990–96	New Exporters vs. non-exporters	+ ΔINV, 0% ΔDOMSALE + ΔTFP	

Notes:
Where possible the results refer to a comparison of new exporters versus non-exporters.
TFP = total factor productivity, LP = labour productivity, □ = growth.
+ the difference relative to the control group is positive and significant, − the difference relative to the control group is negative and significant, 0 the difference relative to the control group is insignificant, ? the difference relative to the control group changes sign and/or significance through the paper.
These results refer to firms that survive in export markets, as reported in table 10 and for value added per worker.
Castellani (2002) compares exporters versus non-exporters.

Instrumental variable approaches have usually been estimated using generalised method of moments (GMM). See Van Bieserbroeck (2005) Baldwin and Gu (2004) as examples. While they have the advantage of being relatively easy to estimate, one faces the perennial issue of instrument validity. By contrast, matching reduces heterogeneity between new and non-exporters by using observable characteristics. It has the disadvantage of removing observations from a data set and requiring specific assumptions about non-observable factors (such as managerial ability). Establishing causality remains the most challenging issue facing researchers in this area.

The impact of applying these alternative techniques has been largely to confirm self-selection is more important than learning. For example, comparisons of new exporters and non-exporters without controlling for selection in Germany (Bernard and Wagner, 1997) and the United Kingdom (Girma et al., 2004) shows significant pre-entry differences in performance, whereas differences are not evident with methods controlling for selection. Yet while evidence of post-entry productivity changes are reported for the United Kingdom (Girma et al., 2004) they are not for Germany (Wagner, 2002). Indeed while both GMM and matching advance on simply comparing new exporters with all non-export firms, they do not guarantee post-entry productivity changes will be observed. As table 6.3 shows, more studies report evidence for learning than fail to find such effects (and these tend to be studies that use matching).

So what explains this divergence? Two issues have been explored, heterogeneity and timing. Some have argued that learning is likely to be specific to some firms, such as those that are young (Delgado et al., 2002; Fernandes and Isgut, 2005), or highly exposed to export markets (Kraay, 1999; Castellani, 2002; Girma et al., 2003; Damijan et al., 2006). Others have found post-entry changes depend on existing industry wide scope for learning; productivity changes are lower in industries in which current exposure to foreign firms (through arms length trade and FDI) is high (Greenaway and Kneller, 2007b). A final sub set of studies argued that if firms really learnt new things from their exposure to foreign markets then there ought to be no decline in productivity for those that quit export markets. On balance the evidence would tend to support learning. As with entry, self-selection appears to be important. Export quitters tend to have lower productivity compared to firms that continue (Aw et al., 2000; Baldwin and Gu, 2004; Girma et al., 2003) and no significant difference from, or in some cases, lower productivity (growth) than non-exporters (Bernard and Jensen, 1999, Hansson and Lundin, 2003; Hahn, 2004). Of those not conditioning for self-selection Hansson and Lundin (2003) and Hahn (2004) find no obvious post-exit productivity changes, whereas Girma and others (2003) and Blalock and Gertler (2004) report similar results conditioning on self-selection. By contrast, for the U.S., Bernard and Jensen (1999, 2004) report post-exit changes, not controlling for self-selection.

More recently Lopez (2004) and Alvarez and Lopez (2005) have questioned the timing issue, arguing that productivity changes occur after the decision to export, that is they may predate the point at which sales begin.[4] Firms invest in new technologies leading to pre-entry changes in productivity: they learn to export rather than learn by exporting. This has existed as an idea within the case study literature for some time (see the review by Pack, 2000) and a number of studies report anecdotal evidence (Lopez 2004; Alvarez and Lopez, 2005; Van Biesebroeck, 2005; and Blalock and Gertler, 2004). It takes the view that learning effects are neither inevitable nor automatic but require investments in domestic technology (Keller, 2004). Similarly, Yeaple (2005) demonstrates that where a decrease in trade costs induces firms to adopt new technology, productivity is endogenous with the export decision. Empirical testing of the learning to export hypothesis using micro data sets becomes more difficult owing to the unobservable nature of the time at which the decision to export is made, and the likelihood that preparation time varies across firms. As Lopez (2004) notes however, without information on timing of the decision, the time path of an endogenous change in productivity is likely to look similar to that of an exogenous change and it becomes harder to conclude that observed productivity changes are orthogonal to the export entry decision.

Among the pioneers in this field were Alvarez and Lopez (2005).[5] Using data on approximately five thousand Chilean manufacturing plants they find that a 1 percent increase in investment raises the probability of a plant becoming an exporter by 0.2 percent. Investment two periods prior to export market entry also increased the probability of exporting, though the magnitude of the effect is lower at 0.1 percent. This suggests that cumulative investments may be necessary to upgrade a plant's TFP.

Perhaps the most comprehensive testing of this new hypothesis can however be found in a study using Mexican product level data by Iacovone and Javorcik (2008). They observe that future export products carry no domestic price premium until two years prior to the commencement of export sales. They interpret this as being indicative of firms consciously readying themselves for export market entry. In subsequent probit regressions they find that the introduction of a product into the export market is preceded by a 1.7 percent increase in physical asset investment. The probability of exporting a new variety is also found to increase with the number of products the firm sold in the previous period but is decreasing in plant skill intensity, size and age.

A related branch of this literature has begun to exploit detailed information on the investments that firms make in order to start to export. Aw and others (2006) study the evolution of productivity and R&D for exporters in Taiwanese electronics. They find that those that do not invest in R&D have lower productivity growth than those that just export, which in turn is lower than those firms that invest in both.[6] They argue these findings are consistent with an interpretation that R&D investments are necessary to benefit from exposure to international markets.

Others have investigated whether the process by which firms create new ideas differs according to the nature of their exposure to international markets. Criscuolo and others (2005), for example, report on the use of information internal or external to the firm in the innovation process. They report that on average UK multinationals use information from a greater number of sources than exporters who in turn make more use of information external to the firm than non-exporters. Similar evidence can be found for Belgium in Veuglers and Cassiman (2004). They find that subsidiaries of foreign multinationals located in Belgium are more likely to acquire technology internationally.

Ultimately perhaps issues surrounding timing of the decision and investment in new plant, equipment or personnel are difficult to answer with available data. While case studies offer one solution, a potentially more interesting approach is that used by Baldwin and Gu (2004) who combine micro data with questionnaires about export behaviour. They find evidence consistent with changes in scale, increased efficiency through competition and learning. Canadian exporters used more foreign technologies, were more likely to have R&D collaboration with foreign firms and improved the flow of information about foreign technologies to Canadian firms. That also led to increased innovation and investments in absorptive capacity.

4   Multiproduct firms

The modern economic landscape is heavily influenced by multiproduct firms. Despite the significant attention they have attracted in the industrial organisation arena, they have until recently been neglected in international trade circles. In contrast to earlier innovations in trade, theoretical research on the topic preceded empirical studies. However, advancements in the degree of sophistication of micro data sets have facilitated deeper firm level analysis. Several open economy models of multiproduct firms have appeared in the trade literature; each with a distinctive twist. For example, Eckel and Neary (2006) focus on an oligopolistic framework with strategic interaction between a fixed number of symmetric multiproduct firms. Agur (2006) and Feenstra and Ma (2008) examine the relationship between trade liberalisation and the proliferation of product variety with multiproduct firms. Nocke and Yeaple (2006) consider a model in which firms with higher organisational capability allows them to produce a larger number of products, but as the range of goods expands the common cost of producing every product also rises. Bernard, Redding and Schott (2010) develop a model of multiproduct firms which extends Melitz (2003). In this setting, trade liberalisation leads to reallocations within firms as well as across industries.

The multiproduct firm literature has to a certain extent provided more detailed analysis of phenomena found at the firm level and sheds light on superstar exporters. The case of developed European countries outlined in Mayer and Ottaviano (2008) demonstrated the importance of the extensive margin in driving a country's total exports. Similar evidence is found by Bernard, Redding and Schott (2010) for the United States, where firms exporting more than five products account for 98 percent of total exports. However, although limited, the evidence from developing countries is that the reverse holds. In the case of Mexico, Iacovone and Javorcik (2008) find that although the extensive margin is non-negligible, it is the intensive margin that accounts for the majority of the increase in exports following a devaluation of the domestic currency. This brings into question the importance of differences in trade regimes across countries since developed countries have been integrated in global markets for considerably longer than developing countries.

Within this literature, firm productivity is again found to be strongly correlated with the production range chosen by firms. Using a matched panel of Belgian multiproduct firms De Loecker (2007b) shows that abolishing quota protection over a three year period increases firm level productivity by 4.6 percent. This hints at within firm productivity being a consequence of the goods they specialise in producing. Productivity is also found to drive the intensive and extensive margins: a 1 percent increase in labour productivity increases a firm's extensive margin by 0.47 percent and the number of countries it serves by 0.43 percent (Bernard, Redding and Schott, 2009). There is also a positive correlation between the volume of exports and number of products exported and destinations served (0.38 percent and 0.35 percent). They also find strong compositional effects: the distribution of exports across products within a firm are far from uniform with the largest accounting for approximately 50 percent of firm exports. A similar skewedness in the distribution of exports across destinations is observed.

At the firm level, trade liberalisation is found to generate substantial churning of the population of enterprises through entry and exit. This process also appears to be important within multiproduct firms as they drop their weakest products and reallocate resources towards their strongest. Evidence of this is found for the United States (Bernard, Redding and Schott, 2009) and Mexico (Iacovone and Javorcik, 2008) where, in any given year, between 10 and 20 percent of exporters introduce new export products while a marginally smaller number drop export varieties. Despite cross sector variation in churning it is most prevalent in the textiles, garments and leather and wood products sectors.

The net effect of this creative destruction appears to be a reduction in the number of varieties the firm sells (Baldwin and Gu, 2009; Bernard, Redding and Schott, 2010; Iacovone and Javorcik, 2008). Baldwin and Gu (2009) use the Canada–United States free trade agreement as a proxy for trade liberalisation. Following the signing of the NAFTA agreement there appears to have been considerable changes in the product variety of multiproduct firms, regardless of whether they export or not. The average decline in the number of products was 16 percent, though among exporters the decline was more rapid. By 1997 the level of diversification between exporting and non-exporting firms was slight compared to a higher degree of diversification at the start of the period in 1973.

Trade liberalization was found to produce further asymmetric results according to firm size, with larger plants taking advantage of the reforms to add products to their catalogue. Despite having initially lower product diversity relative to non-exporting firms, post trade liberalization exporters increase the diversity of their portfolio, a possible indication of learning about new opportunities from foreign operations. Bernard, Redding and Schott (2010) produce similar results. The number of exporting firms and number of exported products decline by 1.17 and 1.10 percent in response to a 1 percent increase in distance between the partner country and the United States. They find a strongly negative impact of distance on the extensive margin but a positive and insignificant effect on the intensive margin.

Following the release of firm product data, patterns in firms' pre-export entry strategies have come under renewed scrutiny. For example, Iacovone and Javorcik (2008) find that on average new exporters in Mexico begin their sales in foreign markets with 1.7 export varieties before increasing this towards two over time. Initial export volumes mirror this with first year exports accounting for a small fraction of the firm's total sales. While the value increases over time it does not rise in tandem with the firm's output. However, more nuanced results have also been found. For example, in 68–89 percent of cases, Mexican firms enter the export market with a product that was previously sold domestically, but existing exporters are more likely than export market entrants to introduce an export variety not previously sold in the domestic arena. This hints at possible learning by exporting, whereby the firm establishes new business opportunities they have identified while active abroad. When firms decide to introduce a new variety in foreign markets they appear to do so aggressively. The absolute value of sales of new export products that have not been sold domestically are on average 12 million pesos relative to 6.5 million for products that were sold in the domestic market prior to export entry. Equivalently, 43 percent of total production of a product is exported when a product is sold abroad for the first time and the product has not been sold domestically, compared with 13 percent when the good was sold in the domestic market.

A positive correlation between the extensive and intensive margins is also found among Mexican firms: the average export sales per product increases with the number of products exported. However, this expansion tends to be focused on the firm's core products while fringe products are most likely to be dropped.

Regardless of whether a product's importance to the exporter is measured as the log of export value, its share in the firm's total exports or the log of the number of years the product has been exported, regressions return consistently negative coefficients when these variables are regressed on a binary variable equal to one if the product is dropped.

5 Multinational firms

To go abroad or stay at home?: At the simplest level, exports and FDI are substitute strategies for internationalisation.[7] The conditions for foreign production become more favourable relative to exporting as the size of the foreign market increases and costs of exporting increase; and less favourable as costs of setting up foreign production grow. This is the proximity concentration trade-off explained by Brainard (1993). The contribution of Helpman, Melitz and Yeaple (2004) to this is analogous to Melitz's (2003) contribution to the basic model of trade. Adding heterogeneity allows this choice to differ across firms within the same industry and determines which firms export and which become multinationals. The interesting properties of the model in this regard are generated through the assumptions of different costs (largely fixed) associated with serving domestic and foreign markets (through FDI or exports), along with heterogeneity in productivity across firms.

The sunk costs of exporting are typically thought to include fixed costs of research into product compliance, distribution networks, advertising and so on. Goods exported are also subject to transportation costs. The fixed costs of FDI are the duplication of costs in establishing domestic production facilities. They are assumed to be greater than those for exporting, FDI eliminates variable transport costs, but involves higher fixed costs. Heterogeneous productivity then ensures self-selection. Only the most productive firms become multinationals; firms whose productivity falls in an intermediate range export, and the least productive only sell domestically.

Empirical tests of the heterogeneous firm model have generally followed one of two lines. First, testing within industries for substitution between exports and FDI related to productivity differences. Second, testing the cross industry/country predictions – the volume of exports relative to FDI we might expect. While there is a large literature comparing productivity levels of multinationals against non-multinationals and exporters against non exporters, there are only a small number of studies that compare exporters and multinationals. In part this is because it is a relatively new question, and in part because for many countries information on which domestic firms export and which are multinational is not available. Empirical tests on productivity differences have either followed Head and Ries (2003) in comparing mean values (see, for example, Castellani and Zanfei, 2004, and Kimura and Kioyata, 2004) or Girma, Kneller and Pisu (2005a) in using Kolmogrov-Smirnov tests of stochastic dominance (see Girma, Görg and Strobl, 2004, Arnold and Hussinger, 2005, and Wagner, 2005). This approach compares the cumulative distribution of productivity for different types of firms and not just the mean. Despite the difference in methodology, the prediction with regard to exports versus FDI would appear to have strong support (Head and Ries, 2003 being the exception), while ironically that between exporters and non-exporters less so. While explaining differences across a small number of studies is never easy, several report a bias towards large firms, and therefore a bias against finding significant productivity differences, and there is a suggestion that this is most severe in Head and Ries (2003), who use information on publicly listed firms.

The second strand concerns itself with proximity concentration predictions, the relative level of exports to FDI. Helpman, Melitz and Yeaple (2004) predict FDI will be more common relative to exports, the greater is the dispersion of productivity levels within an industry. The data requirements of such a test are demanding, however, particularly with regard to foreign sales by domestic multinationals and measures of dispersion within an industry. They use U.S. data and consistently find that dispersion has the expected effect on relative sales: industries in which firm size is highly dispersed are associated with relatively more FDI than exports.

Export platforms: While in a single product world exports and FDI are substitutes, in practice multinationals also export. Indeed several studies report that foreign multinationals contribute disproportionately to exports compared to employment or output shares (Baldwin and Gu, 2004; Kneller and Pisu, 2004). To some extent this should be expected, a well established result is the superior performance of foreign owned firms with respect to employment, wages and productivity, all of which are important determinants of exports. Should the export decision of multinational firms be modelled as identical to that of domestic firms however? Kneller and Pisu (2004) find that even controlling for characteristics, foreign firms are more likely to export than indigenous ones, and export more intensively.

So what explains the export decisions of multinationals? Initial modelling developed at first along two lines: export platform FDI and complementarity. The former is typically defined as the establishment of foreign production facilities and allocation of part or all of the output to serve a third country. It therefore refers to exports of a single product line, where these are not to the home country. Complementarity refers instead to multiproduct firms, to multiple stages of production and to export and FDI flows from the home to foreign countries: exports and FDI become positively correlated if there are horizontal or vertical complementarities across product lines.

Theories of export platform FDI have developed by adding more countries and stages of production to traditional theories of FDI and in more recent developments in cross firm heterogeneity, FDI becomes complex. Vertical FDI occurs when the stages of production are located in more than one country, and horizontal when the same stage is located in more than one country. Vertical FDI is factor seeking; horizontal, market seeking. When there are more than two countries and more than two stages of production, multinationals are likely to undertake more complex FDI choices which involve intra-firm trade and export platform FDI. The effect of adding more countries is to allow for the possibility of a horizontal motive for export platform FDI, adding more stages allows for a vertical motive.

Motta and Norman (1996) consider three identical countries and a single stage of production. Production costs do not differ between countries but trade costs do (because two either enter a free trade agreement or raise external barriers against the third). If we start with each firm exporting to the other two countries from its home base, raising external barriers or creating a free trade area encourages the outside firm to set up production facilities inside the free trade area and export to the other country in the bloc. Where the outside country chooses to locate production in and to export from is left undetermined. Again, because of identical costs neither of the inside countries choose export platform FDI as a strategy.

The conditions under which export platform FDI is likely have been analysed by Ekholm et al. (2003), where there are two identical countries in the North (A and B), one in the South, and multiple stages of production. Each firm produces intermediates and a final good. Firms must provide headquarters services from their home northern country but can choose where to produce intermediates as well as assemble the final product. Two of the countries, one northern (A) and one southern, are members of a free trade area. The drivers of the model include assumptions about the size of the cost advantage of southern firms and trading costs between different sets of countries. The free trade area between A and the Southern country means it is always optimal for the northern country to locate production in the South and export home. Therefore, unlike Motta and Norman (1996), when there are no vertical motives, the country inside the free trade area always has a motive to undertake export platform FDI.

For the other northern country (B) the model predicts three outcomes. First, no FDI: firm B produces at home and exports to the free trade area; second, export platform FDI: firm B produces to sell domestically, whereas the final product sold in the other northern country is produced in the South and exported; third, vertical FDI: firm B locates all production in the South and exports to both markets in the North. The last is hybrid because toward the home country, the firm undertakes vertical FDI, whereas, toward the other northern country, it undertakes export platform FDI. Which strategy is adopted depends on the size of the cost advantage to southern firms, and trade costs.

The predictions of these models are driven primarily on cross country differences in costs. Grossman, Helpman and Szeidl (2003) and Yeaple (2003) show that firm characteristics may also be important. If firms in the same industry are heterogeneous in productivity they may make different choices, even though costs of exporting and FDI are the same. They assume three countries (two North and one South); firms must provide headquarters services, produce intermediates and assemble the final product. Their analysis allows for coexistence in the same sector of a rich array of profitable FDI strategies. The general lesson is that least productive firms will not undertake FDI. More productive firms choose complex strategies that involve a mix of FDI and exports. In most situations these can be classified as neither purely horizontal nor purely vertical, and involve the export of intermediates and/or final products.

Models of export platform FDI simplify the analysis to a single product firm. An alternative set of models consistent with the idea that multinationals may also export comes from the literature on complementarity (for example Head and Ries, 2004). Again there are horizontal and vertical elements. In a multiproduct firm, exports and FDI become positively correlated if there are horizontal or vertical complementarities. For example, in the former, increased demand for the good supplied by foreign production may lead to increased demand for all goods produced by that firm, some of which may be supplied through arms length trade. For vertical complementarities, establishment of a plant in a foreign country to produce or assemble final goods displaces exports of this product, but at the same time increase exports of intermediates from the home country. Net complementarity may arise if displaced exports of the final good more than compensate increased exports of intermediates.

Empirical evidence on the export decision of multinationals has concentrated largely on sign of correlation rather than explanation. In all cases, at the firm level this has been found to be positive, for example Lipsey and Weiss (1984) for the United States, Swedenborg (1985) for Sweden, and Lipsey and others (2000) and Kiyota and Urata (2005) for Japan. Attempts at explaining any correlation are limited to Head and Ries (2003), Kiyota and Urata (2005) and Girma and others (2005b). This probably reflects the limitations of most data sets. Information can be found for the range of products that are exported by a firm, and the location and industry of its overseas affiliates, but often not together.

Head and Ries (2003), Kiyota and Urata (2005) test for the effect of vertical FDI on exports using export demand equations for the firm (for Japan) and find similar results. Head and Ries (2001) find complementarity between exports and FDI for the most vertically integrated firms and substitution can be found for the least integrated, whereas Kiyota and Utata (2005) find that intra-firm exports grow faster than total exports – with increased FDI some of the inter-firm exports shift to intra-firm exports. By contrast Girma and others (2005b) test for export platform FDI for the UK. They find multinationals tend to acquire domestic firms that export. However there are differences in the post acquisition export trajectories of acquired firms according to whether they are inside or outside the EU. For firms outside, export intensity rises, whereas it falls for firms inside.

Outsourcing: More recent explanations for the exports and imports of multinationals have tended to focus on the roles played by outsourcing and offshoring. Extensions to the models of firm boundaries to include the costs of offshoring by Antras (2003), Antras and Helpman (2004) and others, have greatly enriched economists' understanding of the complex patterns that appear in the trade of intermediate inputs between firms in different countries. Firms source inputs from abroad; they offshore, to take advantage of lower production costs, but can then choose procurement either through a vertically integrated affiliate or by outsourcing their production. Tying model predictions on the method of procurement together with data on offshoring versus outsourcing at the firm level has proved difficult. Instead, the literature on offshoring and outsourcing has focussed primarily on the individual effects these have on productivity, plant survival and labour outcomes.

As we have seen, sunk costs play a major role in determining entry into foreign markets through exporting and FDI. Foreign outsourcing also appears to be affected in a similar manner. A significantly negative correlation between a firm's human skills and foreign business experience is found by Tomiura (2005, 2007) for Japanese outsourcing firms. The incidence of outsourcing in Japan appears to be high, but relatively little is international in nature. While half of all firms outsource, only 3 percent of all firms outsource abroad (Tomiura, 2007).[8] Evidence from Girma and Görg (2004) and Tomiura (2007) suggest that the cost-saving motive is an important determinant of outsourcing but that outsourcing is positively related to the labour intensity of the task (Tomiura, 2007) and average wages (Girma and Görg, 2004). High productivity firms are also more likely to outsource.

Despite considerable evidence on outsourcing domestically, the evidence base on outsourcing across borders has predominantly been conducted through analyses at the industry level. However, Head and Ries (2002) show that international fragmentation of production causes firms to move lower-skill activities abroad and to raise productivity. Another motive behind outsourcing is that it allows a firm to concentrate on its core competences. Outsourcing would then be expected to lead to productivity gains. An increase in international outsourcing is found by Görg and Hanley (2005) to lead to firm level productivity gains, with a 1 percent increase causing a 1.1 percent rise in productivity. When they investigate whether this arises due to the offshoring of materials or services, only materials outsourcing is found to be significant. Further regressions show these results only hold for firms with low export intensities, suggesting that these firms gain benefit from international procurement of inputs. Görg, Hanley and Strobl (2004) find broadly similar results for plants that are already linked into

Table 6.4   The impact of offshoring and outsourcing on firm productivity.

Author(s)	Country	Sample	Findings
Effect of Outsourcing on Firm Outcomes			
Görzig and Stephan (2002)	Germany, 1992–2000	43,000 manu-facturing firms	+ firm profitability
Girma and Görg (2004)	United Kingdom, 1982–1992	? plants with more than 100 employees	+ productivity (especially in foreign owned plants) 0% LP, + TFP in chemicals and engineering sectors
Görg and Hanley (2005)	Republic of Ireland,		+ TFP
Görg, Hanley and Stobl (2004)	Republic of Ireland, 1990–98		No productivity effect of outsourcing services, + 1.2% LP from material outsourcing
Criscuolo and Leaver (2005)	United Kingdom, 2000–03	37,000 estab-lishments	+ plant productivity from offshoring of services in manufacturing sectors
Lui and Tung (2004)	Taiwan, 2000–01	1,336 manu-facturing exporters	+ LP from export outsourcing

international production networks, such as foreign owned plants and domestic exporters. No such productivity effects are found for non-exporting firms. In their study of Taiwanese firms over the period 2000–01 Lui and Tung (2005) show that foreign direct investment does not lead to improvements in labour productivity unless it is linked with export outsourcing. A 1 percent increase in outsourcing raises labour productivity by 0.22 percent. Interestingly, small firms are found to perform better when they outsource their export orders.

Offshoring: Whereas outsourcing leads firms to contract activities to outside firms, offshoring entails the establishment of production facilities abroad. The attractiveness of this depends on trade costs and fixed costs of foreign invest-ment. The ability to fragment production, coupled with economies of scale and low trade costs, can give rise to vertical FDI (as in Antras and Helpman, 2004).

They relocate low-skill intensive activities for example, in countries that are low-skill abundant (Head and Ries, 2002; Simpson, 2008).[9]

A small number of papers have focussed on the consequences of outward FDI decisions for aspects of the firm. Head and Ries (2002), Brainard and Riker (1997) and Braconier and Ekholm (2000) all find that firms undertaking outward FDI is associated with changes in employment levels and the skill mix of workers at home. Using data for the UK, Simpson (2008) finds that overseas investment in low wage economies changes the structure of the firm through plant closure. These effects are found to be strongest for multinationals operating in low-skilled industries with affiliates in low skill abundant countries compared to firms in the same industry not investing in low wage economies.

Desai, Foley and Hines (2009) find that investment by U.S. multinationals in foreign operations triggers more investment in domestic operations. This suggests offshoring allows firms to reallocate resources more efficiently within the firm. A 10 percent increase in foreign capital investment causes 2.6 percent additional capital investment. Anecdotal evidence on the motives for offshoring by multiplant firms is found by Inui, Kneller, Matsuura and McGowan (2010) for Japan. They show that a one-standard deviation increase in the ratio of a plant's average wage relative to its parent raises the likelihood that it will close by six percentage points even when controlling for a host of plant, firm and industry characteristics.

Location, location, location: The choice of where to locate an affiliate depends on local factor costs, tariffs and fixed costs of investment. Accessibility or proximity of factors, such as skilled labour, also matter. Models of economic geography posit the importance of agglomeration in determining location. Empirical applications have studied agglomeration at the national level (Devereux and Griffith, 1998), choice of U.S. state (Head, Ries and Swenson, 1995; 1999) and at finer regional areas within countries such as *concelhos* in Portugal (Guimares, Figuiredo and Woodward, 2000), Irish counties (Barrios, Görg and Strobl, 2006) and French *departements* (Crozet, Mayer and Mucchielli, 2004). Widespread evidence in support of the role of agglomeration in determining multinational location has been found. Nor has the concentration of domestic producers been found to be the only factor behind these results. Where firms from the multinational's home country are already clustered, raises the probability that it will also locate there (Head, Ries and Swenson, 1995; Head, Ries and Swenson, 1999; Crozet, Mayer and Mucchielli, 2004).

Policy makers have often sought to use incentives to attract multinationals to try and influence the location of economic activity in lagging regions. Multinationals are often particularly coveted for the new employment they create and for perceived productivity spillovers. Theories of agglomeration may also lead policy makers to believe that attracting a first critical wave of firms will generate virtuous self-reinforcing agglomeration (Crozet, Mayer and Mucchielli, 2004).

The efficacy of regional policies has often been found to be mixed. For example, Crozet, Mayer and Mucchielli (2004) find that grants by the French government to encourage locating in certain areas has a positive effect, but is dwarfed by agglomeration variables. Even when they study EU grants to firms locating in poorer French *departements*, only Belgian, German and Italian firms respond positively. Barrios, Görg and Strobl (2006) find that regional subsidies directed at poorer regions in the West of Ireland succeeded in increasing by 24 percent the probability that a low tech multinational will locate there. For high tech multinationals no effect is found. Free trade zones within U.S. states are found by Head, Ries and Swenson (1999) to raise the likelihood that a Japanese firm will locate there. However, states with a state promotion office in Japan do not attract significantly more MNEs.

Other papers have investigated the role of taxation. Devereux and Griffith (1998) find that conditional on producing in Europe a 1 percent increase in the effective average tax rate in the UK would lead to a reduction by 1.3 percentage points in the probability of a U.S. firm choosing to produce there. For France and Germany they estimate the marginal effect to be 0.5 and 1 percentage point respectively. However, the effective average tax rate is not significant when a U.S. multinational decides between producing in Europe as opposed to exporting to Europe or not serving the European market at all. High corporate taxes and the presence of unitary taxes are found to deter Japanese investment in U.S. states (Head, Ries and Swenson, 1999), while labour and capital subsidies are positively related to location, though the latter is insignificant.

Evidence on the role of wages in determining location is also mixed. For example, Guimares, Figueiredo and Woodward (2000) do not find relatively low wage regions of Portugal attract significantly more multinationals. They argue that wages are more likely to alter the European country a firm decides to produce in. However, this view is challenged by Crozet, Mayer and Mucchielli (2004), who find a 1 percent increase in a French *departement's* wage rate lowers the probability of locating there by 0.43 percent. When they group regions according to the EU's NUTS three classification system this result disappears.

Offshore outsourcing: The literature that combines offshoring and outsourcing together within a single empirical model might be broadly categorised into three types. In the first group can be placed those studies that model how input and country characteristics affect the share of intra-firm trade in total imports of a particular product. That is, they rely on trade flows aggregated across firms. A second group compares the characteristics of those firms that offshore, outsource or are multinationals, while a final group focuses primarily on firm, final good and country variables.

Thus far the bulk of the empirical work on FDI versus offshore outsourcing has centred on a set of predictions taken from the Antras (2003) and Antras and Helpman (2004) models. These include whether capital intensive (measured by the capital intensity of the export industry) imports are more likely to be produced inside the firm and sourced from capital abundant countries. Antras (2003), Yeaple (2006) and Nunn and Trefler (2008) using six-digt HS level data and Bernard and others (2010) using ten-digit HS level data find support for both of these. Other measures of the characteristics of the input have however proved less robust. Yeaple (2006) finds that the share of intra-firm imports is increasing in the R&D intensity of the industry, but like Antras (2003) finds no role for human capital intensity. In contrast Nunn and Trefler (2008) and Bernard and others (2010) find a positive correlation with human capital. Bernard and others (2010) also find that product contractibility, measured by the level of intermediation, leads to lower levels of imports from vertically integrated suppliers.

Drawing on the extensions of the model to allow for firm heterogeneity (Antras and Helpman, 2004), the empirical literature has also consistently found that firms that have affiliates abroad, or import goods and services, are different from those firms that do not. Tomiura (2007, 2009), Criscuolo and Leaver (2005), Kurz (2006) and Görg and others (2007) model a firm's decision to outsource and find a positive correlation between firm productivity and outsourcing. In a more complete test Tomiura (2007) compares the characteristics of those firms engaged in FDI and international outsourcing for Japan, finding that those firms which undertake FDI are more productive than those that offshore by outsourcing.

Most recently a number of studies have begun to include firm, industry and country level variables as determinants of the type of offshoring (Jabbour, 2008; Defever and Toubal, 2007; and Corcos et al., 2009). Using data for French firms these papers model whether a firm imports an intermediate input from a given country through outsourcing or FDI, and in the case of Jabbour (2008) also through partnerships. Defever and Toubal (2007) focus on a small number of explanatory variables, suggested from a theoretical model of offshoring they develop. Their main explanatory variables are a measure of productivity of the firm, the quality of the contracting environment in the exporting country and what they label as the supplier's input intensity of production.[10] Jabbour (2008), in contrast, focuses on testing a larger number of predictions from the recent theoretical models of offshoring, in particular the relative productivity of those firms choosing international outsourcing versus FDI, as well as country characteristics such as capital intensity, the quality of the legal system and market thickness and input characteristics such as capital and R&D intensity. Corcos and others (2009) are interested in the robustness of a similar set of variables, in particular those on firm characteristics, to a broader sample of firms.

6   Conclusions and direction of future research

In comparison to just a decade ago, firms' internationalisation strategies are now unquestionably at the heart of research into international trade. Indeed, the very recent research on this topic has begun to disaggregate information on the firm still further, to consider how it chooses its product range and what determines the scope and location of the production process.

The starting point for this development was the inability of the then-standard trade models to explain why firms that export could coexist with others in the same industry that did not. This changed with the development of heterogeneous firm models. These models explained how firms that exported are more productive and this, together with the reallocation of output which occurs as less productive firms contract or go out of business, points to a direct link between exports and productivity at the macro level. The framework was then extended to allow for the fact that some firms choose to produce abroad rather than export.

Empirical testing of these models grew fast and now extends across a large number of industrialised, transitional and developing countries. The main questions of interest were the effects of different globalisation strategies on firm performance and why firms chose those strategies. The bulk of research effort was focused on the former, with considerable efforts spent trying to disentangle the direction of causation between productivity and exporting at the firm level. The generally agreed conclusion from these efforts is that self-selection effects dominate, although the decision to start to export does often provide a motivation for changes within a firm that have real effects on its performance. Despite this, in the broad sense, the simplifying assumption of the heterogeneous firm model of no feed back from global markets to firm productivity would seem a reasonable approximation.

Over time more detailed data on firms' internationalisation strategies generated a new set of stylised facts. Two developments have been particularly popular here. First, they questioned the simplifying assumption of the original heterogeneous firm models that firms produced only a single output. It became clear very quickly that such an assumption was difficult to support. Firms were instead multiproduct and some products were much more successful on global markets than others. A theoretical, and, somewhat more belatedly, an empirical literature, has sprung up to attempt to explain what determines the product range chosen by the firm and how exposure to international markets affects those choices.

A second data development has been the increased availability of information on the activities of overseas affiliates and firm level import data. This encouraged the disaggregation of the production process to consider which intermediate inputs are produced inside the firm and which outside, and where those inputs are procured. Often these studies have focused on single aspects of this relationship, the effects of outsourcing or offshoring say, although there has been some recent analysis of this combined choice.

What then is the likely direction of future research in the area of firms' internationalisation strategies? No doubt this will be fashioned to a large extent by theoretical developments on this topic. However, given the importance of the release of new types of data in explaining where we are currently, it is difficult to imagine that this will not be also be a significant factor that drives where we get to in the future. Traditionally, trade economists worked with export and import data that varied across industries countries and time. Adding firms to this increased the dimensions of variation (to firm industries, countries and time), opening up new research questions by allowing a link between the import, exports and FDI activities of a single firm. Different globalisation strategies, whether as exports versus FDI or outsourcing versus vertical integration, could now be compared within a single theoretical model. Those dimensions of variation (and the number of observations) have been further increased as data has been released on each product exported to each destination by each firm, with similar information on the import side. Now which products the firm produced and how it produced them became endogenous choices. There are many questions regarding multiproduct firms, export dynamics and offshoring and outsourcing that are still to be tested using data of this type.

In the future it is feasible to imagine that other dimensions of variation will be added. For example, where trade data between countries can be linked together this would allow the consideration of how what is being sold, and the characteristics of both the buyer and the seller, affect the type of international trade relationships that are observed. This might then offer the possibility to test models that include strategic interactions between firms as one example.

The ability to link trade data with other types of information has over time also encouraged economists to reconsider older research questions at a more disaggregated level. Linked employer–employee data is becoming increasingly common, for example, as have been links with surveys on investments in R&D and human capital. That has allowed consideration of the employment and wage effects of internationalisation on narrow groups of workers, and how the skills and experience of those workers shape the type of global engagement chosen by the firm. Again, it is difficult to imagine that this process will not continue, and that the effects of exports, imports and FDI on other aspects of the firm will not be encouraged by this process.

It therefore seems likely that firms' internationalisation strategies will remain a rich source of research questions to applied researchers into the future. The limits to this process are likely to be the unevenness of data quality across countries; the existing access restrictions to using many of these data sets; limits of computer power to deal with the potentially large number of observations available; and identifying which dimensions of variation within the data are of most interest.

Notes

* University of Nottingham.
1. It could be that the more disaggregated dataset used by Iacovone and Javorcik (2008) gives rise to these differences. Compared to Bernard, Redding and Schott (2010) they have almost twice the number of unique products: 3,396 in Iacovone and Javorcik (2008) versus approximately 1,800 in Bernard, Redding and Schott (2010).
2. Evidence from Tybout and Westbrook (1995) suggests that this may be an unimportant source of efficiency change.
3. The evidence for Sweden (Hansson and Lundin, 2003; Greenaway et al., 2005) and Slovenia (Damijan et al., 2006) are exceptions.
4. Alvarez and Lopez (2005) label pre-entry effects as 'learning to export' compared to 'learning by exporting' for post-entry effects. The common element between these is the effect of the decision to export on the firm's productivity.
5. The concept is also proposed in Lopez (2004) as 'conscious self selection' though no empirical tests are conducted.
6. A number of papers have found that exporters have higher levels of R&D but do not establish the direction of causality; see for example Bleaney and Wakelin (2002) and Roper and Love (2002) for the UK, Bernard and Jensen (2004a) for the United States, Aw et al. (2005) for Taiwan and Baldwin and Gu (2004) for Canada.
7. We concentrate here on the evidence at the level of the firm. The issue of complementarity and substitution between exports and FDI has been studied at many other levels of aggregation for which a summary of the evidence can be found in Head and Ries (2004).
8. The high degree of domestic outsourcing is partly attributable to the *keiretsu* industrial structure.
9. In practice FDI decisions often contain elements of both horizontal and vertical motives. For theoretical models consistent with this view see Helpman (1984) Venables (1999) and Yeaple (2003).
10. This later variable is measured at the firm level and is calculated as the share in total output of all externally supplied inputs, where the numerator is defined by the total amount of inputs supplied to the firm by independent and affiliated suppliers irrespective of their location. They predict that outsourcing is more likely the greater is the share of output that a firm produces externally (the greater is the supplier's input intensity).

References

Agur, I. (2006) 'Firm heterogeneity and the two sources of gains from trade', EUI Working Papers ECO No. 2006/38.

Alvarez, R., and R.A. López (2005) 'Exporting and firm performance: evidence from Chilean plants', *Canadian Journal of Economics*, vol. 38, 1384–1400.

Alvarez, R. (2004) 'Sources of export success in small and medium-sized enterprises: the impact of public programs', *International Business Review*, vol. 13, 383–400.

Antras, P. (2003) 'Firms, contracts and trade structure', *Quarterly Journal of Economics*, vol. 118, 1375–1418.

Antras, P., and E. Helpman (2004) 'Global sourcing', *Journal of Political Economy*, vol. 112, 552–80.

Arnold, J., and K. Hussinger (2005) 'Exports versus FDI in German manufacturing: firm performance and participation in international markets', mimeo, World Bank.

Aw, B.Y., X. Chen and M.J. Roberts (2000) 'Plant level evidence on productivity differentials, turnover and exports in Taiwanese manufacturing', mimeo, Pennsylvania State University.

Aw, B.Y., S. Chung and M.J. Roberts (2000) 'Productivity and turnover in the export market: micro-level evidence from the Republic of Korea and Taiwan (China)', *World Bank Economic Review*, vol. 14, 65–90.

Aw, B.Y., M.J. Roberts and T. Winston (2006) 'The complementary role of exports and R&D investments as sources of productivity growth', *The World Economy*, 30, 83–104.

Aw, B.Y., and A.R. Hwang (1995) 'Productivity and the export market: a firm-level analysis', *Journal of Development Economics*, vol. 47, 313–32.

Baldwin, J.R., and W. Gu (2003) 'Export market participation and productivity performance in Canadian manufacturing', *Canadian Journal of Economics*, vol. 36, 634–57.

—— (2004) 'Trade liberalisation: export-market participation, productivity growth and innovation', *Oxford Review of Economic Policy*, vol. 20, 372–92.

—— (2009) 'The impact of trade on plant scale, production-run length and diversification', in T. Dunne, J.B. Jensen and M.J. Roberts (eds) *Producer Dynamics: New Evidence from Micro Data*. University of Chicago Press.

Barrios, S., H. Görg and E. Strobl (2006) 'Multinationals' location choice, agglomeration economies, and public incentives', *International Regional Science Review*, vol. 29, 81–107.

Bernard, A., and J.B. Jensen (1995) 'Exporters, jobs and wages in US manufacturing: 1976–87', Brookings Papers on Economic Activity, Microeconomics, 67–119.

—— (1999) 'Exceptional exporters performance: cause, effect or both?', *Journal of International Economics*, vol. 47, 1–25.

—— (2004a) 'Why some firms export', *Review of Economics and Statistics*, vol. 86, 561–69.

—— (2004b) 'Entry, expansion and intensity in the U.S. export boom, 1987-92', *Review of International Economics*, vol. 12, 662–75.

Bernard, A., and J. Wagner (1997) 'Exports and success in German manufacturing', *Review of World Economics/Weltwirtschaftliches* Archiv, vol. 133, 134–57.

—— (1998) 'Export entry and exit by German firms', *Review of World Economics/Weltwirtschaftliches* Archiv, 2001, vol. 137, 134–57.

Bernard, A.B., J.B. Jensen, S.J. Redding and P.K. Schott (2010) 'Intra-firm trade and product contractibility' (long version). NBER Working Papers No. 15881, National Bureau of Economic Research, Inc.

Bernard, A., J. Eaton, J.B. Jensen and S. Kortum (2003) 'Plants and productivity in international trade', *American Economic Review*, vol. 93, 1268–90.

Bernard, A., J.B. Jensen and P. Schott (2007) 'Importers, exporters and multinationals: a portrait of firms in the U.S. that trade goods', NBER Working Paper No. 11404.

Bernard, A., S. Redding and P. Schott (2010) 'Multiple-product firms and product switching', *American Economic Review*, vol. 100(1), 70–97.

Bigsten, A., P. Collier, S. Decron, M. Fafchamps, B. Gauthier, J.W. Gunning, J. Habarurema, A. Oduro, R. Oostendrop, C. Pattilito, M. Soderbom, F. Teal and A. Zeufack (2000) 'Exports and firm efficiency in African manufacturing', Centre for the Study of African Economies, WPS/2000-16, Oxford University.

Blalock, G., and P.J. Gertler (2004) 'Learning from exporting revisited in less developed setting', *Journal of Development Economics*, vol. 75, 397–416.

Blalock, G., and S. Roy (2007) 'A firm-level examination of the exports puzzle: why East Asian exports didn't increase after the 1997–1998 financial crisis', *The World Economy*, vol. 30(1), 39–59.

Bleaney, M.F., and K. Wakelin (2002) 'Efficiency, innovation and exports', *Oxford Bulletin of Economics and Statistics*, vol. 64, 3–15.

Blundell, R., and M. Costa Dias (2000) 'Evaluation methods for non-experimental data', *Fiscal Studies*, vol. 21, 427–68.

Braconier, H., and K. Ekholm (2000) 'Swedish multinationals and competition from high- and low-wage locations', *Review of International Economics*, vol. 8(3), 448–61.

Brainard, S. L., and D. Riker (1997) 'Are U.S. multinationals exporting U.S. Jobs,' NBER Working Paper No. 5958.

Brainard, S.L. (1993) 'A simple theory of multinational corporations and trade with a trade-off between proximity and concentration', NBER Working Paper No. 4269.

Castellani, D. (2002). 'Export behaviour and productivity growth: evidence from Italian manufacturing firms', *Review of World Economics/Weltwirtschaftliches* Archiv, vol. 138, 605–28.

Castellani, D., and A. Zanfei (2004) 'Internationalisation, innovation and productivity: how do firms differ in Italy?' mimeo, University of Urbino.

Castellani, D., F. Serti and C. Tomasi (2008) 'Firms in international trade: importers and exporters heterogeneity in the Italian manufacturing industry', LEM Papers Series 2008/04.

Chowdhury, A.R. (1993) 'Does exchange rate volatility depress trade flows? Evidence from error correction models', *Review of Economics and Statistics*, vol. 75, 700–06.

Clerides, S., S. Lach and J. Tybout (1998) 'Is learning by exporting important? Micro-dynamic evidence from Colombia, Mexico and Morocco', *Quarterly Journal of Economics*, vol. 113, 903–48.

Corcos, G., D.M. Irac, G. Mion and T. Verdier (2008) 'The determinants of intra-firm trade', development working papers, Centro Studi Luca dÁgliano, University of Milano.

Criscuolo, C., and M. Leaver (2006) 'Offshore outsourcing and productivity', mimeo, Office for National Statistics, London.

Criscuolo, C., J. Haskel and M. Slaughter (2005) 'Global engagement and the innovation activities of firms' NBER Working Paper No. 11479.

Crozet, M., T. Mayer and J. Mucchielli (2004) 'How do firms agglomerate? A study of FDI in France', Regional Science and Urban Economics, vol. 34, 27–54.

Damijan, J., S. Polanec and J. Prašnikar (2006) 'Self-selection, export market heterogeneity and productivity improvements: Firm level evidence from Slovenia', *The World Economy*, vol. 29, (forthcoming).

Das, S., M.J. Roberts and J. Tybout (2004) 'Market entry costs, producer heterogeneity, and export dynamics' NBER Working Paper No. 8629.

—— (2004) 'Micro-foundations of export dynamics', mimeo. Pennsylvania State University.

De Loecker, J. (2007a) 'Do exports generate higher productivity? Evidence from Slovenia', *Journal of International Economics*, vol. 73(1), 69–98.

—— (2007b) 'Product differentiation, multi-product firms and estimating the impact of trade liberalization on productivity', NBER Working Paper No. 13155.

Defever, F., and F. Toubal (2007) 'Productivity and the sourcing modes of multinational firms: Evidence from French firm-level data'. Cep discussion papers, Centre for Economic Performance, LSE.

Delgado, M., J. Fariñas and S. Ruano (2002) 'Firm productivity and export markets: A non-parametric approach', *Journal of International Economics*, vol. 57, 397–422.

Desai, M.A., C.F. Foley and J. Hines (2009) 'Domestic effects of the foreign activities of U.S. Multinationals', *American Economic Journal: Economic Policy*, vol. 1, 181–203.

Devereux, M., and R. Griffith (1998) 'Taxes and the location of production: evidence from a panel of U.S. multinationals', *Journal of Public Economics*, 68, 335–67.

Eckel, C., and J.P. Neary (2006) 'Multi-product firms and flexible manufacturing in the global economy', University of Oxford Department of Economics Discussion Paper Series No. 292.

Ekholm, K., R. Forslid and J.R. Markusen (2003) 'Export-platform foreign direct investment', NBER Working Paper No. 9517.

Eliasson, K., P. Hansson and M. Lindvert (2009) 'Do firms learn by exporting or learn to export? evidence from small and medium-sized (SMEs) in Swedish manufacturing', Orebro University Working Paper No. 15/2009.

Falvey, R., D. Greenaway, J. Gullstrand and Z. Yu (2004) 'Exports, restructuring and industry productivity growth', GEP Research Paper 04/40, Leverhulme Centre for Research on Globalisation and Economic Policy, University of Nottingham.

Feenstra, R., and A. Ma (2008) 'Optimal choice of product scope for multinational firms under monopolistic competition', NBER Working Paper No. 13703.

Fernandes, A.M., and A. Isgut (2005) 'Learning-by-doing, learning-by-exporting, and productivity: evidence from Colombia', World Bank Policy Research Working Paper No. 3544.

Girma, S., and H. Görg (2004) 'Outsourcing, foreign ownership, and productivity: evidence from UK establishment-level data', *Review of International Economics*, vol. 12(5), 817–32.

Girma, S., H. Görg and E. Strobl (2004) 'Exports, international investment, and plant performance: evidence from a non-parametric test', *Economics Letters* vol. 83, 317–24.

Girma, S., D. Greenaway and R. Kneller (2003) 'Export market exit and performance dynamics: a causality analysis of matched firms', *Economics Letters*, vol. 80, 181–87.

——(2004) 'Does exporting increase productivity? A microeconometric analysis of matched firms', *Review of International Economics*, vol. 12, 855–66.

Girma, S., R. Kneller and M. Pisu (2005a) 'Exports versus FDI: an empirical test', *Review of World Economics/Weltwirtschaftliches* Archiv, vol 12, 855–66.

——(2005b) 'Trade creation, destruction and replacement in regional trade agreements: micro level evidence for the UK', mimeo, GEP University of Nottingham.

Görg, H., and A. Hanley (2005) 'International outsourcing and productivity: evidence from the Irish electronics industry', *The North America Journal of Economics and Finance*, vol. 16, 255–69.

Görg, H., A. Hanley and E. Strobl (2004) 'Outsourcing, foreign ownership, exporting and productivity: an empirical investigation with plant level data', University of Nottingham GEP Research Paper 2004/08.

——(2007) 'Productivity effects of international outsourcing: evidence from plant level data', CEPR Discussion Papers 6361.

Görg, H., M. Henry and E. Strobl (2008) 'Grant support and exporting activity' *Review of Economics and Statistics*, vol. 90, 168–74.

Görzig, B., and A. Stephan (2002) 'Outsourcing and firm-level performance', DIW Discussion Paper 309.

Greenaway, D., and R. Kneller (2007b) 'Industry differences in the effect of export market entry: learning by exporting?' *Review of World Economics*, vol. 143, 416–32.

—— (2004) 'Exporting and productivity in the United Kingdom', *Oxford Review of Economic Policy*, vol. 20, 358–71.

—— (2008) 'Exporting, productivity and agglomeration', *European Economic Review*, vol. 51, 919–39.

—— (2007a) 'Firm heterogeneity, exporting and foreign direct investment', *Economic Journal*, vol. 117, F134–61.

Greenaway, D., and Z. Yu (2004) 'Firm level interactions between exporting and productivity: industry-specific evidence', *Review of World Economics/Weltwirtschaftliches Archiv*, vol. 140, 376–92.

Greenaway, D., J. Gullstrand and R. Kneller (2005) 'Exporting may not always boost firm productivity', *Review of World Economics*, vol. 142, 561–82.

Greenaway, D., R. Kneller and X. Zhang (2010) 'The effect of exchange rates on firm exports : the role of intermediate inputs' *The World Economy*, vol. 33, 961–86.

Grossman, G.M., E. Helpman and A. Szeidl (2003) 'Optimal integration strategies for the multinational firm', NBER Working Paper No. 10189.

Guimares, P., O. Figueiredo and D. Woodward (2000) 'Agglomeration and the location of foreign direct investment in Portugal', *Journal of Urban Economics*, vol. 47, 115–35.

Hahn, C.H. (2004) 'Exporting and performance of plants: evidence from Korean manufacturing', NBER Working Paper No. 10208.

Hansson, P., and N. Lundin (2004) 'Exports as indicator on or a promoter of successful Swedish manufacturing firms in the 1990s', *Review of World Economics/Weltwirtschaftliches Archiv*, vol. 140, 415–45.

Head, K., and J. Ries (2001) 'Overseas investment and firm exports', *Review of International Economics*, vol. 9, 108–22.

—— (2002) 'Offshore production and skill upgrading by Japanese manufacturing firms', *Journal of International Economics*, vol. 58, 81–105.

—— (2004) 'Exporting and FDI as alternative strategies', *Oxford Review of Economic Policy*, vol. 20, 409–23.

—— (2003) 'Heterogeneity and the foreign direct investment versus exports decision of Japanese manufacturers.' *Journal of the Japanese and International Economies*, vol. 17, 448–67.

Head, K., J. Ries and D. Swenson (1995) 'Agglomeration benefits and location choice: evidence from Japanese manufacturing investments in the United States', *Journal of International Economics*, vol. 38, 223–47.

—— (1999) 'Attracting foreign manufacturing: investment promotion and agglomeration', *Regional Science and Urban Economics*, vol. 29, 197–218.

Helpman, E., M. Melitz and S. Yeaple (2004) 'Export versus FDI', *American Economic Review*, vol. 94, 300–16.

Helpman, E. (1984) 'A simple theory of international trade with multinational corporations', *Journal of Political Economy*, vol. 92, 451–71.

Iacovone, L., and B. Javorcik (2008) 'Multi-product exporters: diversification and micro-level dynamics', World Bank Policy Research Working Paper 4723.

Inui, T., R. Kneller, T. Matsuura and D. McGowan (2010) 'Globalisation, multinationals and productivity in Japan's lost decade', GEP Working Paper No. 2010/04.

Isgut, A. (2001) 'What's different about exporters? Evidence from Colombian manufacturing', *Journal of Development Studies*, vol. 37, 57–82.

Jabbour, L. (2008) 'Slicing the value chain internationally: Empirical evidence on the offshoring strategy by French firms', GEP Working Papers No. 2008/02.

Keller, W. (2004) 'International technology diffusion', *Journal of Economic Literature*, vol. 42, 752–82.

Kimura, F., and K. Kiyota (2004) 'Exports, FDI and productivity of firm: cause and effect,' Faculty of Business Administration, Yokohama National University, Working Paper No. 216.

Kiyota, K., and S. Urata (2005) 'The role of multinational firms in international trade: the case of Japan', RIETI Discussion Paper Series 05-E-012, Yokohama National University.

Kneller, R., and M. Pisu (2004) 'Export-oriented FDI in the UK', *Oxford Review of Economic Policy*, vol. 20, 424–39.

Kraay, A. (1999) 'Exports and economic performance: evidence from a panel of Chinese enterprises', *Revue d'Economie du Development*, 2, 183–207.

Krugman, P.R. (1979) 'Increasing returns, monopolistic competition, and international trade', *Journal of International Economics*, vol. 9, 469–79.

Kurz, C.J. (2006) 'Outstanding outsourcers: a firm and plant level analysis of production sharing', Working Paper, Federal Reserve Board, Washington, D.C.

Lancaster, K. (1979) *Variety, Equity and Efficiency*, Oxford: Blackwell.

Lipsey, R.E., and Weiss, M.Y. (1984) 'Foreign production and exports of individual firms', *Review of Economics and Statistics*, vol. 66, 304–08.

Lipsey, R.E., E. Ramstetter and M. Blomström (2000) 'Outward FDI and parent exports and employment: Japan, the United States, and Sweden', *Global Economy Quarterly*, vol. 1, 285–302.

Liu, B.J, and A.C. Tung (2004) 'Export outsourcing and foreign direct investment: evidence from Taiwanese exporting firms', *Dynamics, Economic Growth, and International Trade*, conference paper.

Liu, J-T., M-W. Tsou and J.K. Hammitt (1999) 'Export activity and productivity: evidence from the Taiwan electronics industry', *Review of World Economics*, vol. 135, 675–91.

López, R.A. (2004) 'Self-selection into the export markets: a conscious decision?', mimeo, Department of Economics, Indiana University.

Maloney, W.F., and R. Azevado (1995) 'Trade reform, uncertainty, and export promotion: Mexico 1982–88', *Journal of Development Economics*, vol. 48(1), 67–89.

Mayer, T., and G. Ottaviano (2008) 'The happy few: the internationalisation of European firms', *Review of European Economic Policy*, vol. 43(3), 135–48.

Melitz, M. (2003) 'The impact of trade on intra-industry reallocations and aggregate industry productivity', *Econometrica*, vol. 71, 1695–725.

Motta, M., and G. Norman (1996) 'Does economic integration cause foreign direct investment?', *International Economic Review*, vol. 37(4), 757–83.

Muuls, M., and M. Pisu (2007) 'Imports and exports at the level of the firm: evidence from Belgium', CEP Discussion Paper No. 801.

Nocke, V., and S. Yeaple (2006) 'Globalization and endogenous firm scope', PIER Working Paper Archive 06-015, Penn Institute for Economics Research, Department of Economics, University of Pennsylvania.

Nunn, N., and D. Trefler (2008) 'The boundaries of the multinational firm: an empirical analysis,' in E. Helpman and D. Marin (eds), *Globalization and the Organization of Firms and Markets*. Cambridge, MA: Harvard University Press.

Pack, H. (2000) 'Modes of technology transfer at the firm level', mimeo, University of Pennsylvania.

Parley, D., and S. Wei (1993) 'In significant and inconsequential hypothesis: the case of US, bilateral trade,' *Review of Economics and Statistics*, 74, 606–15.

Pozo, S. (1992) 'Are flexible exchange rates really more volatile? evidence from the early 1990s', *Applied Economics*, vol. 3, 87–105.

Roper, S. and J.H. Love (2002) 'Innovation and export performance: evidence from the UK and German manufacturing plants', *Research Policy*, vol. 31, 1087–102.

Simpson, H. (2008) 'Investment abroad and adjustment at home: evidence from UK multinational firms', CMPO Working Paper No. 08/207.

Swedenborg, B. (1985) 'Sweden', in J. Dunning (ed.), *Multinational Enterprises, Economic Structure, and International Competitiveness, Wiley/IRM Series on Multinationals*. Chichester, UK: Wiley/IRM.

Tomiura, E. (2005) 'Foreign outsourcing and firm-level characteristics: evidence from Japanese manufacturers', *Journal of the Japanese and International Economies*, vol. 19(2), 255–71.

—— (2007) 'Foreign outsourcing, exporting, and FDI: a productivity comparison at the firm level', *Journal of International Economics*, vol. 72(1), 113–27.

Tybout, J., and M.D. Westbrook (1995) 'Trade liberalization and dimensions of efficiency change in Mexican manufacturing industries', *Journal of International Economics*, vol. 31, 53–78.

Van Biesebroeck, J. (2005) 'Exporting raises productivity in Sub-Saharan manufacturing plants', *Journal of International Economics*, vol. 67(2), 373–91.

Venables, A.J. (1999) 'Fragmentation and multinational production', *European Economic Review*, vol. 43(4–6), 935–45.

Veugelars, R., and B. Cassiman (2004) 'Foreign subsidiaries as a channel of international technology diffusion: Some direct firm level evidence from Belgium', *European Economic Review*, vol. 48, 455–76.

Wagner, J. (2002) 'The causal effects of exports on firm size and labor productivity: first evidence from a matching approach', *Economics Letters*, vol. 77, 287–92.

—— (2005) 'Exports, foreign direct investment and productivity: evidence from German firm level data', mimeo, University of Lueneberg.

Yeaple, S. (2006) 'Offshoring, foreign direct investment and the structure of U.S. trade,' *Journal of the European Economic Association, Papers and Proceedings*, vol. 4(2–3), 602–11.

Yeaple, S.R. (2003) 'The complex integration strategies of multinationals and cross country dependencies in the structure of foreign direct investment', *Journal of International Economics*, vol. 60, 293–314.

7
Oligopoly and Trade*

Dermot Leahy[†] and J. Peter Neary[‡]

1 Introduction

Oligopoly means competition among the few, and the study of markets with a relatively small number of large firms is an important branch of industrial organisation and microeconomics more generally. However, it plays a smaller role in the theory of international trade. From its inception in the work of Ricardo in 1817 until the 1980s, trade theory was dominated by perfectly competitive models. What is sometimes called the 'new trade theory' revolution from 1979 onwards led to a surge of interest in the implications for trade of imperfectly competitive models.[1] Since then, two different routes to incorporating imperfect competition into trade theory have been explored, so different that the process could be described as two revolutions rather than one. On the one hand, monopolistically competitive models of large-group competition have been applied to the study of intra-industry trade and a host of other topics; on the other hand, oligopolistic models have been applied to both positive and normative questions. Of these two, monopolistic competition quickly became the preferred approach, so much so that, in the words of Paul Krugman, it could be said that there are now 'Two and a Half Theories of Trade', with the theory of oligopoly a poor relation of the two dominant paradigms, perfect and monopolistic competition.[2]

However, despite their dominance, there are many issues in trade which the theories of perfect and monopolistic competition are inherently ill-fitted to address. The assumptions which they share, of an infinitely elastic supply of atomistic firms, that are *ex ante* identical and do not engage in strategic interaction, are not obviously appropriate to many global markets. Casual empiricism suggests that many industries are dominated by a small number of firms, and an increasing body of applied work shows that large firms account for a dominant share of exports as well as foreign direct investment and spending on research and development.[3] By contrast, the theory of oligopoly is suited to study the distinctive features of concentrated industries, and in particular, the persistence of profits, as well as strategic behaviour by firms and governments to preserve and enhance these profits.

In this survey, we present an analytic overview of some of the main theoretical results of trade under oligopoly. Following Brander (1995), we concentrate on two canonical models. Section 2 considers the 'reciprocal-markets' model, which has been used to analyse a variety of positive and normative questions in cases where both domestic and foreign firms compete both at home and away. Most notable among these was the demonstration by Brander (1981) that oligopolistic competition is an independent source of trade, and in particular of intra-industry trade, distinct from either comparative advantage or product differentiation. Section 3 turns to consider issues of 'strategic' trade and industrial policy in models of multi-stage competition, which are most easily studied in the 'third-market' model first developed by Spencer and Brander (1983). Finally, Section 4 turns to consider the objection that oligopoly models have not been embedded in general equilibrium, and reviews some recent work which tries to overcome this.

2 Trade under Oligopoly

2.1 The 'reciprocal-markets' model

The reciprocal-markets model is a simple framework for studying trade under oligopoly, which has the convenient property that it is possible to study each country's market in isolation. An essential assumption which makes this possible is that national markets are segmented. On the one hand, this implies that third-party arbitrage is not possible, so a firm's output can command different equilibrium prices in different countries. On the other hand, it implies that firms make distinct output or price decisions for each market. The latter is not a primitive assumption, and Venables (1990) and Ben-Zvi and Helpman (1992) have explored the conditions under which it will emerge as an equilibrium outcome of a multi-stage game where firms first invest in their worldwide capacity and then decide on prices and/or sales volumes for each market. Such models have the attractive feature that firms decide endogenously how to supply different markets, but their greater complexity has limited their appeal. As a result, most of the literature has continued to adopt the segmented markets assumption and we follow that approach here.[4]

In addition to market segmentation, the ability to consider one market in isolation requires that firms produce under constant marginal costs. Otherwise, output or price decisions in one market have implications for the costs at which other markets can be served. A rare example of a model with such cost linkages between markets is provided by Krugman (1984). He assumes falling marginal costs and shows that an import protection policy that raises a firm's home sales also increases that firm's market share in its export market. Here, by contrast, we will follow most of the literature and assume that marginal costs are independent of scale. The combination of this and the assumption of segmented markets implies that changes in policy or other exogenous variables in one market have no effect on the other market.

Armed with these assumptions, we can now explore the properties of a canonical reciprocal-markets model, first presented by Brander (1981). Consider a single oligopolistic industry, the output of which is consumed in two countries, labelled home and foreign. The firms competing in this industry are also from the home and foreign country, with just one firm in each.[5] We confine attention to the symmetric case, where the home and foreign firms have the same marginal cost of production c and face the same trade cost t. For most of the discussion the trade costs are assumed to reflect natural barriers to trade, though we note on occasions where tariffs have different implications. Without loss of generality we will restrict attention to the home market, where the sales of the home and foreign firms are denoted x and y respectively. Because of symmetry, foreign market sales of the home and foreign firms are also equal to y and x respectively.

Brander (1981) and Brander and Krugman (1983) used the reciprocal-markets model to consider multilateral trade liberalisation between two identical countries under Cournot competition with identical goods. They demonstrated that under Cournot competition intra-industry trade can occur in equilibrium even when goods are identical, and they showed that welfare is U-shaped in transport costs. In the next subsection we will illustrate their results in a more general setup that allows for product differentiation.[6] Then, in Section 2.3 we will illustrate the corresponding results under Bertrand competition that were first derived by Clarke and Collie (2003). Finally, in Section 2.4 we extend the analysis to repeated interaction between firms, and explore how trade liberalisation affects the incentives for firms to collude.

Throughout this section, we use a simple common specification of preferences and technology to obtain explicit solutions and to allow us to compare the results under Cournot and Bertrand competition. On the demand side we assume that preferences are quadratic; the qualitative results continue to hold for more general specifications. Thus the domestic utility from consumption of the oligopolistic goods is represented by the following:[7]

$$u = a(x+y) - \frac{1}{2}b(x^2 + 2exy + y^2),\tag{1}$$

where e is an inverse measure of the degree of product differentiation, ranging from the case of perfect substitutes ($e = 1$) to that of independent demands ($e = 0$). This yields linear inverse demand functions:

$$p = a - b(x + ey),\tag{2}$$

$$p^* = a - b(ex + y), \tag{3}$$

where p and p^* are the prices of the home and foreign varieties respectively. On the cost side, we assume that marginal costs are constant and we ignore fixed costs. Hence the home and foreign firms' operating profits in the home market are:

$$\pi = (p - c)x, \tag{4}$$

$$\pi^* = (p - c^* - t)y, \tag{5}$$

where c and c^* are the marginal production costs of the home and foreign firms, assumed to be independent of output, and t is the per-unit cost of international transportation.

2.2   Quantity competition

We will first consider the output effects of symmetric multilateral trade liberalisation between two identical countries under quantity competition. As the countries are mirror images of each other we need only consider the effect of a transport cost reduction on equilibrium in the home market. Using the linear inverse demand functions (2) and (3), the firms' first-order conditions for output are $bx = p - c$ and $by = p^* - c - t$. These can then be solved for the Cournot-Nash equilibrium outputs:

$$x = \frac{1}{b(2+e)} \left[a - c + \frac{e}{2-e} t \right], \tag{6}$$

$$y = \frac{1}{b(2+e)} \left[a - c - \frac{2}{2-e} t \right]. \tag{7}$$

At free trade ($t = 0$), imports y equal the home firm's sales x, giving the first result of the model: oligopolistic competition is an independent determinant of trade. Most remarkably, this is true even when products are identical ($e = 1$), the case of 'cross-hauling' or 'two-way trade in identical products' in the words of Brander (1981). As goods become more differentiated, e falls below one and the volume of trade rises further: consumers' love of variety is a second source of intra-industry trade, though in this model it is a less important one than oligopolistic competition.[8]

As trade costs increase, cross-hauling persists, though at a diminishing level: home sales rise and imports fall. They finally reach zero at the prohibitive level of trade costs $\widehat{t}^C$, which from (7) equals:

$$\widehat{t}^C = \frac{2-e}{2}(a - c). \tag{8}$$

For any level of trade costs between zero and $\widehat{t}^C$, and any degree of product differentiation e, each firm is selling more in its home market than abroad, because it faces a cost penalty on its foreign sales. As a result, the prices it obtains in equilibrium yield a lower markup over cost on its exports than on its home sales. This is the second key result of the model, which Brander and Krugman (1983) called 'reciprocal dumping'. Because the two markets are symmetric, the dumping margin, the difference between the prices obtained by each firm in its home and foreign markets (where the latter equals the f.o.b. – free on board – price, that is, the price net of trade costs), equals:

$$p - (p^* - t) = \frac{1}{2 - e}t. \tag{9}$$

This is increasing in both t and e: dumping is more pronounced the higher are trade costs and the greater the substitutability between goods.[9]

It is natural to consider the implications of this kind of trade for welfare, but a useful preliminary step, which is also of independent interest, is its implications for profits. Focusing on the home firm, its total profits equal the sum of its profits on home sales and on exports. The first are given by (4) while the second equal the foreign firm's profits in the home market (5), because of the symmetry of the model. Substituting in turn from the first-order conditions, these are proportional to home and export sales respectively: $\pi = bx^2$ and $\pi^* = by^2$. Differentiating (6) and (7), the effect of a multilateral change in trade costs on total profits can be shown to equal:

$$\frac{d(\pi + \pi^*)}{dt} = 2bx\frac{dx}{dt} + 2by\frac{dy}{dt} = \frac{2e}{4 - e^2}x - \frac{4}{4 - e^2}y \begin{cases} < 0 & \text{when } t = 0 \text{ (so } x = y) \\ > 0 & \text{when } t = \widehat{t}^C \text{ (so } y = 0) \end{cases} \tag{10}$$

The key finding is that profits are *decreasing* in trade costs at free trade, but *increasing* in them in the neighbourhood of autarky. With linear demands, it follows that profits must be a U-shaped function of trade costs, reaching their maximum in autarky and their minimum above free trade. The intuition for this is straightforward. First, starting from free trade, exports are harmed more by an increase in the firm's own costs than home sales are helped by an equal rise in its rival's costs; hence total sales and profits fall for a small increase in t at free trade. Second, starting from autarky, exports are initially zero, so a small fall in trade costs has a negligible effect on profits in the export market. By contrast, home sales are initially at the monopoly level, so a small fall in the foreign firm's trade costs has a first-order effect on home-market profits. Hence, overall profits fall for a small reduction in t at autarky.

Finally, we can consider the effect of changes in trade costs on welfare. Home welfare equals:

$$W = \chi + \Pi, \tag{11}$$

where χ is home consumer surplus and $\Pi = \pi + \pi^*$ are the profits of the home firm in both markets. Once again, since we are assuming symmetric trade liberalisation between identical countries, we can make use of the fact that the profits of the home firm in the foreign market are equal to the profits of the foreign firm in the home market.

Consider in turn the components of welfare in (11). Consumer surplus must rise monotonically as trade costs fall. This is because a reduction in trade costs lowers the prices of both goods to home consumers.[10] To this must be added the U-shaped relationship between profits and trade costs already derived. In the neighbourhood of free trade, welfare is clearly falling in trade costs. All that is left is to consider the sum of consumer surplus and profits for a small fall in t starting in autarky (where $t = \hat{t}^C$). Consumer surplus rises because the price falls, but profits on home sales fall both because the price falls and because sales are reduced. The price effects cancel, so the total fall in profits outweighs the rise in consumer surplus.[11] Thus home welfare (the sum of profits and consumer surplus) is also a U-shaped function of t, reaching its maximum at free trade but its minimum below the prohibitive level of trade costs, as shown by the curve labelled W^C in figure 7.1. An alternative intuitive explanation for this is that a fall in trade costs from the prohibitive level leads to a pro-competitive increase in sales, helping to undo the monopoly distortion; however, it also brings about trade at very high transport costs, which is wasteful. In the neighbourhood of the prohibitive trade cost the latter effect dominates, but at lower trade costs the pro-competitive effect is dominant. Note, finally, that this argument does not apply to tariffs, at least when tariff revenue is fully reimbursed to consumers. In that

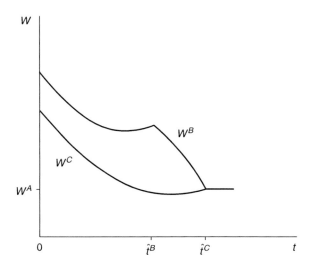

Figure 7.1   Welfare and trade costs under Cournot and Bertrand competition.

case, the trade costs are merely a transfer payment, and so the pro-competitive effect dominates at all levels of tariffs, and welfare falls monotonically as tariffs rise.[12]

2.3 Price competition

How are the effects of trade liberalisation on trade and welfare affected if firms compete in price rather than quantity? A first issue to be addressed is that the outcome of price competition is fundamentally different from that of quantity competition when home and foreign goods are perfect substitutes ($e = 1$). This feature is not peculiar to a trading economy, but rather a reflection of the highly competitive nature of price competition in this case. In a closed-economy duopoly, the lowest-cost firm captures the whole market. In an open economy, even an infinitesimal trade cost ensures that no trade occurs. Hence, the key prediction of the Cournot model, cross-hauling of identical goods, does not apply when firms compete on price and goods are identical.[13] However, the other prediction, that trade liberalisation has a competition effect, applies even more strongly. Even though no actual trade may take place in equilibrium, the head-to-head competition between rival firms prevents either of them charging a price greater than their rival's marginal cost inclusive of the trade cost.

The case of price competition with perfect substitutes is an extreme one. By contrast, there is much greater similarity between price and quantity competition in the more plausible case where goods are imperfect substitutes. To solve for the Bertrand equilibrium in this case, we need to use the direct demand functions, which can be obtained by inverting the system in (2) and (3):

$$x = \frac{1}{b(1-e^2)} \left[(1-e)a - (p - ep^*) \right],$$ (12)

$$y = \frac{1}{b(1-e^2)} \left[(1-e)a - (p^* - ep) \right].$$ (13)

For the moment consider only interior equilibria in which both firms export positive quantities. We will return to corner solutions later. The first-order conditions for the optimal choice of prices are $p - c = b(1-e^2)x$ for the home firm and $p - c - t = b(1-e^2)y$ for the foreign firm. These can be solved for the Bertrand-Nash equilibrium prices:

$$p = \frac{(1-e)a+c}{2-e} + \frac{e}{4-e^2}t,$$ (14)

$$p^* = \frac{(1-e)a+c}{2-e} + \frac{2}{4-e^2}t.$$ (15)

These in turn can be combined with the direct demand functions to obtain the equilibrium quantities under Bertrand competition:

$$x = \frac{1}{b(1+e)(2-e)}\left[a-c+\frac{e}{(1-e)(2+e)}t\right], \tag{16}$$

$$y = \frac{1}{b(1+e)(2-e)}\left[a-c-\frac{2-e^2}{(1-e)(2+e)}t\right]. \tag{17}$$

As in the Cournot case, imports equal the home firm's sales at free trade and are decreasing in trade costs, falling to zero when trade costs reach the threshold level which sets (17) equal to zero:

$$\widehat{t}^B = \frac{(1-e)(2+e)}{2-e^2}(a-c). \tag{18}$$

For trade costs strictly between zero and $\widehat{t}^B$, and any value of e less than one, there is reciprocal dumping just as in Cournot competition. In this case the dumping margin equals:

$$p-(p^*-t) = \frac{1+e}{2+e}t. \tag{19}$$

This is lower than in the Cournot case, provided e is strictly positive, reflecting the more competitive nature of price competition; and, as in the Cournot case, it is increasing in both e and t.

Profits and welfare also behave quite similarly to quantity competition for trade costs between zero and $\widehat{t}^B$. Using the first-order conditions for prices, maximised profits are equal to $b(1-e^2)x^2$ and $b(1-e^2)y^2$. Total profits for the home firm are then equal to the sum of these, and their behaviour as trade costs change can be shown to equal:

$$\frac{d(\pi+\pi^*)}{dt} = 2b(1-e^2)\left[x\frac{dx}{dt}+y\frac{dy}{dt}\right]$$

$$\propto ex-\left(2-e^2\right)y\begin{cases} <0 \text{ when } t=0 \text{ (so } x=y) \\ >0 \text{ when } t=\widehat{t}^B \text{ (so } y=0) \end{cases} \tag{20}$$

Once again, therefore, profits are a U-shaped function of trade costs. This in turn, combined with the fact that consumer surplus is monotonically decreasing in trade costs, implies that welfare is U-shaped in t, for the same reasons as in the Cournot case.

However, unlike under Cournot competition this is not the end of the story. Even when trade costs are too high for exports to take place, they may not be too high to prevent the threat of exports from affecting domestic firms' behaviour. Recall from (18) that $\widehat{t}^B$ is the prohibitive level of trade costs under Bertrand competition. Substituting this into (16) shows that the home firm's output is

$x = (a-c)/b(2-e^2)$ at this level of trade costs, which is above the unconstrained monopoly output level, $x^M = (a-c)/2b$. However, the home firm does not have an incentive to raise its price, since its rival would then make positive sales, so lowering the home firm's profits.[14] In this sense, we can describe the equilibrium as one where the home firm is constrained by the threat of potential competition. As the trade costs rise further the home firm has greater scope to raise its price. Only when trade costs reach the prohibitive level under Cournot competition, as given by (8) in Section 2.2, can the home firm behave as an unconstrained monopolist. At intermediate levels of trade costs, $\widehat{t}^B \leq t \leq \widehat{t}^C$, the home firm chooses a price at which the foreign firm is just unable to produce. In this region the home firm's output is:[15]

$$x = \frac{a-c-t}{be} \tag{21}$$

which is clearly falling in t. Combining this with (16), which applies in the region $0 \leq t \leq \widehat{t}^B$, home sales are an inverted-V function of trade costs.

Finally, consider the level of welfare in this region of potential though not actual competition from imports. Welfare in the absence of trade is consumer surplus plus home profits. This can be written as $W = (a-c)x - \frac{1}{2}bx^2$. Totally differentiate this to get:

$$dW = (a-c-bx)dx. \tag{22}$$

It is then clear from (21) and (22) that welfare is falling in trade costs in the region $\widehat{t}^B \leq t \leq \widehat{t}^C$. Hence, unlike the Cournot case, under Bertrand competition trade liberalisation starting from autarky initially raises welfare: the home firm is disciplined by the threat of trade, without any trade taking place, and hence without any socially wasteful transport costs being incurred.[16]

The locus labelled W^B in figure 7.1 summarises the relationship between welfare and the level of trade costs under Bertrand competition. (The figure is drawn for an intermediate value of the substitution parameter e; 0.8 in this case.) Welfare in autarky is at the monopoly level, where the mode of competition with the foreign firm is irrelevant, so W^B and W^C coincide. As t falls (moving to the left away from $\widehat{t}^C$), the home firm's profit-maximising strategy is to lower its price thereby raising output and welfare even though no imports actually occur. Below the threshold level $\widehat{t}^B$, imports become profitable, and have the same effect as in Cournot competition, generating a U-shaped relationship between welfare and t. However, as shown by Clarke and Collie (2003), the level of welfare never falls below the autarky level. So, while trade liberalisation may lower welfare in a local sense, opening up to trade can never induce net losses from trade as in the Cournot case.

To summarise the Bertrand case, it differs from Cournot in that the key prediction of cross-hauling of identical goods no longer applies. On the other hand, the other main finding, that trade imposes a competition effect, is enhanced rather than weakened. Even if no trade actually occurs, it may still induce more competitive behaviour by the domestic firm, so raising welfare. As trade costs fall further, actual imports occur, and welfare is a U-shaped function of trade costs as in the Cournot case. However, the level of welfare never falls below the autarky level: in this respect too, the competition effect of trade is stronger under Bertrand competition than under Cournot.

2.4   Repeated interaction and collusion

So far we have shown that once trade costs fall below some critical level firms will invade each others markets. However, the increased competition between the firms will reduce their profits. Could firms decide to collude by refraining from exporting to each others market? Clearly such a collusive arrangement will not be possible to sustain in a one-shot noncooperative game setting. However, it has been shown by several authors that if the game is repeated infinitely then whether or not such a collusive arrangement can be sustained will depend on the degree of impatience of the firms.[17]

Both the quantity setting and the price setting games we have examined above have a prisoner's dilemma character, in the sense that the firms would collectively do better if they could collude and share the markets, but they have a unilateral incentive to deviate from such an agreement. Assume that the game is repeated infinitely and that the firms have an identical discount factor δ. If a firm deviates from collusion (cheats) it will be punished in the future. We will follow most of this literature and assume that if a firm cheats its rival will never again cooperate with it. This is a so-called 'grim trigger strategy' and it implies that a period of cheating is followed by reversion to the Nash equilibrium in each period forever after.

Given that its rival chooses the collusive action, a firm must weigh the one-period gain from cheating against the lower profits in all subsequent periods in the future. The less impatient are firms, the less valuable will be the short-term gains from cheating and the more they will be concerned with the loss of profits in the infinite punishment phase. There is a critical threshold discount factor $\widehat{\delta}$, above which collusion can be sustained. This critical discount factor depends (among other things) on the level of trade costs. Tacit collusion supported by grim trigger strategies is possible for any discount rate δ above the threshold level, which is defined by:

$$\widehat{\delta} \equiv \frac{\pi^D - \pi^J}{\pi^D - \pi^N},\tag{23}$$

where π^J is per-period profit for a firm when both firms collude (i.e., engage in joint profit maximization), π^N is per-period profit for a firm under noncooperation, and π^D is the one-period profit of defecting from the collu-sive agreement when the rival keeps to the tacit agreement. The ranking of these per-period profits is: $\pi^D > \pi^J > \pi^N$.

The simplest special case is that of Cournot competition with identical prod-ucts. In this case, first studied by Pinto (1986), collusion implies that the firms do not export and behave as monopolists in their own markets. If collusion breaks down, the firms play Cournot in both markets, just as in section 2.2. A reduction in t increases π^D, the short-run profitability of defecting from the collusive agreement. This is because the gains from invading the rival's market are larger the lower are trade costs. A fall in t also influences a firm's profits in the punishment phase π^N. However the effect is small relative to the effect on π^D and it is non-monotonic. As we saw in section 2.2 (see equation (20)), this non-monotonicity arises from the fact that a reduction in trade costs raises profits on export sales but increases competition from the rival in the home mar-ket. With homogeneous-product quantity-setting firms, the increased short-run profitability of the cheating dominates. Hence, trade liberalisation increases $\hat{\delta}$ and thus reduces the range of δ over which collusion can occur and so has an unambiguously pro-competitive effect.

The unambiguously beneficial effect of trade liberalisation on competition has recently been challenged by Ashournia, Hansen and Hansen (2008) who show that this result is sensitive to the assumption of identical products.[18] Following earlier work by Fung (1991) they show that colluding firms will not in general refrain from entering each others' home markets. Given a taste for variety on the part of consumers and provided that transport costs are not too high, the profits of the cartel can be increased by selling both of the different varieties in the two markets. The collusive outputs in the home market are:

$$bx = \frac{(1-e)(a-c)+et}{2(1-e^2)}, \quad \text{and} \quad by = \frac{(1-e)(a-c)-t}{2(1-e^2)}. \tag{24}$$

Hence there is intra-industry trade in a collusive equilibrium provided that $t < \hat{t}^T \equiv (1-e)(a-c)$. This threshold is below the prohibitive trade cost under Cournot given in (8). When trade costs are below $\hat{t}^T$ so that trade occurs under collusion, then a lowering of trade costs will lower the critical threshold level of the discount factor thus making collusion easier. The intuition for this surpris-ing result is that trade liberalisation raises firms' profitability in the presence of collusive trade while it leaves profits unchanged when firms do not trade under collusion. Thus when there is trade under collusion there is an additional reason why trade liberalisation strengthens the incentive to cooperate. This is suffi-cient to make trade liberalisation anti-competitive in the presence of collusive trade.[19]

3   Strategic trade and industrial policy

3.1   A general strategic trade model

In their seminal paper on strategic trade policy Brander and Spencer (1985) developed a model in which it is optimal to subsidize exports. They consider an oligopolistic setting in which pure profits are earned in equilibrium, and an export subsidy can be used to shift these rents from foreigners to home residents.

In their model Brander and Spencer assume that the firms play Cournot and that quantities are strategic substitutes, so that the firms' reaction functions are negatively sloped. However, it was soon demonstrated that the strategic trade argument for an export subsidy is very sensitive to changes in these key assumptions. Eaton and Grossman (1986) showed that when firms compete in a Bertrand manner and prices are strategic complements then an export tax is optimal.[20] We will now present these contrasting results using the unifying framework of a general strategic trade model that allows for both quantity and price competition. This is a slightly modified version of a model first presented by Brander (1995).

Assume that a home and foreign firm export to a third market. Only the home government is policy-active.[21] The 'third market' assumption implies that the interests of consumers do not enter the home country's welfare function and this allows us to focus on the strategic interaction between the firms in its purest form. The home and foreign firms play a Nash game in actions A and B respectively. These actions may be either outputs or prices. The advantage of setting up the model in this more general way is that we do not need to specify whether firms compete on quantities or prices. Firms' profits depend on their own and their rival's actions and on the home government's export subsidy. Thus the home firm's profit function is:

$$\Pi(A, B, s) = \pi(A, B) + sx(A, B), \tag{25}$$

where π represents operating profits (sales revenue net of production costs) and sx is subsidy income. The foreign firm is not subsidized and its profits are given by

$$\pi^*(A, B). \tag{26}$$

The home government and the two firms play a two-stage game. In the first stage the government sets the per-unit subsidy s (which could be negative). In the second stage the firms simultaneously choose their market actions. Solving for the sub-game perfect Nash equilibrium we begin by looking at stage 2.

Taking the per-unit subsidy as given, the first-order conditions for the firms' market actions are:

$$\Pi_A(A, B, s) = \pi_A(A, B) + sx_A(A, B) = 0, \tag{27}$$

and

$$\pi_B^*(A, B) = 0, \tag{28}$$

where subscripts denote partial derivatives. The partial derivative x_A of home output x with respect to the home action A is positive and equal to unity if the market action is output, while it is negative and equal to the slope of the home firm's demand curve x_p if the action is price. Equation (28) implicitly defines the foreign firm's reaction function, giving B as a function of A. This function will play an important role below.

We now consider the first stage in which the home government sets the subsidy anticipating how this will affect second-stage actions. We will assume that the subsidies are financed by non-distortionary lump-sum taxes. Since all output is exported, home welfare is just the home firm's profits net of subsidy payments:

$$W(A, B) = \Pi(A, B, s) - sx(A, B) = \pi(A, B). \tag{29}$$

Totally differentiate this and make use of the home firm's first-order condition to get:

$$dW = -sx_A dA + \pi_B dB. \tag{30}$$

The optimal subsidy is then:

$$s^o = (x_A)^{-1} \pi_B \frac{dB}{dA}, \tag{31}$$

where dB/dA is the slope of the foreign firm's reaction function. The sign of the optimal subsidy depends on the signs of π_B, x_A and dB/dA. The term π_B is the cross-effect of the foreign firm's market action on the home firm's profits, and we follow Brander in saying that the actions are 'friendly' if this term is positive. When actions are unfriendly the foreign action reduces home profits. Outputs under Cournot competition are unfriendly ($\pi_B < 0$), while prices under Bertrand competition are friendly ($\pi_B > 0$). However, the derivative x_A is negative when prices are the strategic variable while it is positive (equal to unity) when firms are choosing quantities. Hence, regardless of whether firms play Cournot or Bertrand the combined term $(x_A)^{-1}\pi_B$ is negative. Thus the sign of the optimal subsidy turns on the slope of the foreign reaction function dB/dA. Outputs are typically strategic substitutes under Cournot competition, giving rise to an incentive to subsidize. However, prices are typically strategic complements under Bertrand competition, giving rise to an incentive to tax exports.

Clearly the Cournot and Bertrand cases differ in detail. In Cournot (assuming outputs are strategic substitutes), the optimal policy is a subsidy, which shifts profits from the foreign to the home firm and lowers price so consumers in the third country gain. By contrast, in Bertrand (assuming prices are strategic complements), the optimal policy is a tax, which shifts profits from the home to the foreign firm and raises prices of both goods so consumers in the third country lose. Nevertheless, there is an important sense in which the two cases are formally identical. In both, the home government uses its superior commitment power to bring about an equilibrium which the home firm cannot attain on its own. That equilibrium is identical to the Stackelberg equilibrium which would prevail if the home firm were (arbitrarily) assumed to be able to choose its action before the foreign firm. It is as if the home government transfers its first-mover advantage to the home firm.

3.2   The robustness of export subsidies

While, as we have seen, the optimal policy towards an exporting firm is sensitive to the nature of competition, it can also be affected by other factors. For instance, even under Cournot competition with strategic substitutes, the presence of more home firms can change the optimal policy from a subsidy to a tax.[22] This is because the presence of more home firms introduces a terms-of-trade argument for intervention that must be balanced against the strategic trade motive. Another issue is the social cost of raising government revenue. The argument for a subsidy is weakened when we allow for the possibility that the cost of raising the necessary revenue to finance the subsidy is increased by the distortionary effects of taxation (see for instance Neary, 1994, and Neary and Leahy, 2004). A final qualification to the case for export subsidies is that an expansion of one home firm may draw resources away from oligopolistic firms in other sectors. As Dixit and Grossman (1986) show, the case for subsidisation must then be qualified to rest on the desirability of subsidising one sector relative to all others. In an extreme case, if a symmetric group of oligopolistic sectors draw on a common fixed factor, say skilled labour, then subsidy rents would be fully captured by that factor, and laissez-faire is the optimal policy. For all these reasons, the fact that the policy recommendations are so sensitive to the assumptions implies that governments need to know quite a lot about a particular industry in order to design the optimal intervention.

So far we have assumed that only the home government intervenes. An obvious extension is to allow for both governments to be policy active. The most natural way to model this is to assume that the home and the foreign governments choose their subsidies simultaneously in the first stage and then the firms choose their market actions A and B in the second stage. What difference does this make? In one important sense multilateral intervention makes no difference. If the firms' reaction functions are negatively sloped, then each country still has a unilateral incentive to subsidize, and if they are positively sloped, then each has an incentive to tax. However, a unilateral incentive to subsidize runs counter to the collective interest of countries to reduce exports and thus improve the terms of trade: as Brander and Spencer (1985) showed, the game between countries is a prisoner's dilemma, at least when the countries are symmetric, in that intervention by both countries lowers their welfare. By contrast, if the firms' reaction functions are upward-sloping, the policy game with symmetric countries yields an outcome closer to the joint optimum.[23]

3.3 The robustness of investment subsidies

While the strategic trade argument for an export subsidy is highly sensitive to whether firms engage in quantity or price competition, the strategic investment policy argument for a subsidy is much more robust. We will now demonstrate that, although ambiguous in principle, the case for strategic investment subsidies is reasonably robust in practice.[24]

Consider a setup like that in Section 3.1 in which a home and a foreign firm export to a third market. As before, the firms choose actions A and B. However, now assume the home and foreign firms also choose investment levels k and k^* respectively before the market actions are set. We do not need to be very specific regarding the form of the investment carried out by the firms. The investment could be in capital or in process R&D, in which case it leads to a reduction in the firm's production costs. It could also be in marketing or product quality, which shifts the demand function it faces. In addition the investment spending of each firm may affect the profits of its rival because of R&D or other spillovers. The government of the home country is policy active and sets an investment subsidy σ (but no export subsidy) before the firms decide on their investment levels. The profits of the home firm are:

$$\Pi(k,k^*,A,B,\sigma) = \pi(k,k^*,A,B) - \sigma k, \tag{32}$$

where σk represents the firm's subsidy income. The foreign firm does not receive a subsidy and its profit function is represented by:

$$\pi^*(k,k^*,A,B). \tag{33}$$

In the final stage of the game the firms choose their market actions taking the investments and the subsidies as given. The resulting first-order conditions do not depend directly on the investment subsidy:

$$\pi_A(k,k^*,A,B) = 0 \quad \text{and} \quad \pi_B^*(k,k^*,A,B) = 0. \tag{34}$$

From these we can obtain the Nash equilibrium actions $A(k,k^*)$ and $B(k,k^*)$ which depend on the levels of investment. We can use the equilibrium level of the actions to eliminate A and B in the profit functions. The resulting 'reduced-form' operating profit functions are distinguished by hats:

$$\widehat{\pi}(k,k^*) = \pi[k,k^*,A(k,k^*),B(k,k^*)] \quad \text{and} \quad \widehat{\pi}^*(k,k^*) = \pi^*[k,k^*,A(k,k^*),B(k,k^*)],$$
(35)

for the home and foreign firms respectively.

We turn now to the second stage of the game in which the firms simultaneously choose their investment levels given the subsidy and anticipating how the investments will affect the subsequent equilibrium in actions. The home firm maximizes the following reduced-form total profit function, equal to operating profit plus subsidy revenue:

$$\widehat{\Pi}(k,k^*,\sigma) = \widehat{\pi}(k,k^*) + \sigma k.$$
(36)

As for the government in the home country, it wishes to maximise:

$$\widehat{W}(k,k^*) = \widehat{\Pi}(k,k^*,\sigma) - \sigma k = \widehat{\pi}(k,k^*).$$
(37)

It is clear by inspection that the reduced-form profit and welfare functions in (36) and (37) have the same form as the corresponding functions (25) and (29) in section 3.1. Hence we can immediately determine the optimal subsidy:

$$\sigma^0 = \widehat{\pi}_{k^*} \frac{dk^*}{dk}.$$
(38)

As before, the sign of the optimal subsidy depends on the signs of the friendliness term $\widehat{\pi}_{k^*}$ and on the slope of the foreign reaction function dk^*/dk. The slope of the reaction function can be written as:

$$\frac{dk^*}{dk} = -\frac{\widehat{\pi}^*_{k^*k}}{\widehat{\pi}^*_{k^*k^*}}.$$
(39)

The denominator is negative from the foreign firm's second-order condition for profit maximisation. Therefore the slope of the reaction function depends on the sign of $\widehat{\pi}_{k^*k}$, which indicates whether foreign investment is a strategic substitute ($\widehat{\pi}^*_{k^*k} < 0$) or strategic complement ($\widehat{\pi}^*_{k^*k} > 0$) for home investment. Hence, we can say that the optimal strategic industrial policy is an investment subsidy if and only if an increase in investment by one firm has the same qualitative effect on its rival's profits in total and at the margin: that is, if and only if $\widehat{\pi}_{k^*}$ and $\widehat{\pi}^*_{k^*k}$ have the same sign. With simple functional forms these two concepts tend to have the same sign. As we show in Leahy and Neary (2001), we can expect that the optimal policy will be a subsidy because there is a presumption that unfriendliness ($\widehat{\pi}_{k^*} < 0$) and strategic substitutability ($\widehat{\pi}^*_{k^*k} < 0$) will be found together, as will friendliness ($\widehat{\pi}_{k^*} > 0$) and strategic complementarity ($\widehat{\pi}^*_{k^*k} > 0$). So, although the general expression for the subsidy in (38) seems to indicate that not much can be said about the likelihood that subsidization will be the optimal policy, this turns out to be the case for most functional forms.

3.4 Multilateral investment subsidy games

As we have just seen, governments have a unilateral incentive to use rent-shifting investment subsidies. This remains the case when we extend the model to allow for the governments of an arbitrary number of countries to choose their investment subsidies simultaneously. However, such subsidy wars among exporters can give rise to a prisoner's dilemma. In that case, all the exporting countries would be better off if they agreed to ban investment subsidies altogether. However, if investment is in R&D and this generates international spillovers then investment subsidies may be friendly to other countries. We will compare welfare when governments choose investment subsidies with welfare in the non-intervention regime.

We extend the model of the previous subsection to a symmetric oligopolistic industry with n identical firms, each of which is located in one of n countries, and sells on a single outside market with no tariffs or transport costs. Once again, the game consists of three stages. In the first stage, subsidies are set either by national governments or by a supra-national authority. Then, as in earlier subsections, the firms choose in turn their investments and market actions. The model used is a version of the multi-country multi-firm model in Leahy and Neary (2009). Collie (2005) and Haaland and Kind (2006, 2008) consider similar issues in the context of R&D subsidies, though in relatively special models.[25]

Modify equation (36) slightly to extend the notation to cover many firms. A typical firm maximizes the following reduced-form total profit function:

$$\widehat{\Pi}^i(k^i, \mathbf{k}^{-i}, \sigma^i) = \widehat{\pi}^i(k^i, \mathbf{k}^{-i}) + \sigma^i k^i. \tag{40}$$

where variables in bold denote vectors, so $\mathbf{k}^{-i}$ is the vector of investments by firms other than firm i. We continue to assume that the firms export to a third country so that consumer surplus does not enter the welfare function. (The consequences of relaxing this assumption are discussed in detail in Leahy and Neary, 2009.) The government in country i wishes to maximise:

$$\widehat{W}^i(k^i, \mathbf{k}^{-i}) = \widehat{\Pi}^i(k^i, \mathbf{k}^{-i}, \sigma^i) - \sigma^i k^i = \widehat{\pi}^i(k^i, \mathbf{k}^{-i}). \tag{41}$$

Aggregate welfare of the n countries is:

$$\widehat{W}(\mathbf{k}) = \sum \widehat{\pi}^i(k^i, \mathbf{k}^{-i}). \tag{42}$$

We consider three different regimes which we will refer to as laissez-faire (L), non-cooperative intervention (N) and cooperative intervention (C) respectively. The laissez-faire equilibrium arises when all subsidies σ^i are zero, and can be thought of as arising from a commitment to non-intervention on the part of the n countries' governments. In the non-cooperative intervention case, countries play a Nash game in subsidies, each seeking to maximise national welfare. Finally, the cooperative equilibrium occurs when a supra-national authority chooses a uniform subsidy to maximise the countries' aggregate welfare, which is simply the sum of their individual welfare levels. This regime yields the highest level of welfare and we use it as a benchmark with which to compare the other two regimes.

In the laissez-faire regime the typical firm maximises (40) with σ^i set at zero. The first-order condition is $\hat{\pi}_i^i = 0$. It proves useful to introduce a function $m^L(\kappa)$ which is the marginal return to investment net of marginal investment costs under laissez-faire evaluated at a symmetric level of investment, κ. Thus the first-order condition under laissez-faire can be rewritten as $m^L(\kappa^L) = \hat{\pi}_i^i = 0$.

In the non-cooperative regime the typical government chooses its subsidy to maximise national welfare (41). The typical government has one instrument (its investment subsidy) with which it can target the investment level of its firm. It is very convenient to see the government as using its subsidy to control its own firm's investment with the other firms' investments adjusting according to their reaction functions. This yields the first-order condition:

$$m^N(\kappa^N) = \hat{\pi}_i^i + (n-1)\hat{\pi}_j^i \frac{dk^j}{dk^i} = 0, \tag{43}$$

where m^N is the net marginal return to investment in the non-cooperative case. Likewise, in the cooperative regime the supra-national authority can be seen as choosing all the investment levels to maximise aggregate welfare (42). The first-order condition is:

$$m^C(\kappa^C) = \hat{\pi}_i^i + (n-1)\hat{\pi}_i^j = 0, \tag{44}$$

where m^C is the net marginal return to investment in the cooperative case.

We now wish to compare the levels of investment in the different regimes. To do this we must compare the net marginal returns to investment in the different regimes. Naturally we need to be cautious as $m^L(\kappa^L)$, $m^N(\kappa^N)$ and $m^C(\kappa^C)$ are evaluated at different symmetric investment levels. However, we can compare the different net marginal returns to investment at any common point. We show in Leahy and Neary (2009) that provided the rankings of marginal returns to investment are the same in all three regimes and some other stability assumptions are made then the ranking of symmetric equilibrium investment levels (κ) across the three regimes is the same as the ranking of the marginal returns to investment. A comparison of m^L and m^N at any common point yields:

$$m^N(\kappa) - m^L(\kappa) = (n-1)\hat{\pi}_j^i \frac{dk^j}{dk^i}. \tag{45}$$

This is a generalization of the two-firm case considered in the earlier section. It shows that the investment levels will be higher when governments intervene than when they do not provided that $\hat{\pi}_j^i$ (the friendliness term) and dk^j/dk^i (which is positive if and only if investments are strategic complements) have the same sign. This is also the same condition as the one that determines the sign of the non-cooperative investment subsidy. So, as explained earlier, there is a presumption that $m^N - m^L$ is positive and thus that the governments will give positive subsidies and that $\kappa^N > \kappa^L$.

Is it in the countries' collective interest to subsidize investment? To answer this question we must compare m^C and m^L. This yields:

$$m^C(\kappa) - m^L(\kappa) = (n-1)\widehat{\pi}_i^j \tag{46}$$

which is positive if and only if investments are friendly. If there are no positive spillovers then this is negative and so it is in the interests of the group of countries to use a tax to reduce the level of investment. However if there are sufficiently strong spillovers that investments raise rivals' profits then the cooperative subsidy is positive and κ^C is bigger than κ^L. The sign of the friendliness term also determines whether or not the non-cooperative investment level is too high from the point of view of the collective:

$$m^C(\kappa) - m^N(\kappa) = (n-1)\widehat{\pi}_j^i \left(1 - \frac{dk^j}{dk^i}\right). \tag{47}$$

The right-hand side depends only on the sign of $\widehat{\pi}_j^i$ as $1 - dk^j/dk^i$ is always positive due to stability considerations as we show in Leahy and Neary (2009).

The investment rankings in the different equilibria are reported in table 7.1. As noted in Section 3.3, there is a presumption that unfriendliness and strategic substitutability are found together, as are friendliness and strategic complementarity. Hence we can focus on the diagonal entries in the table. In the top left-hand entry, where investments are unfriendly and strategic substitutes, the level of investment is highest under non-cooperation and lowest under cooperation. The cooperative investment level is always the one that maximises the welfare of the group of countries. If we assume that welfare is concave in κ then, since κ^L is closer to κ^C than is κ^N, governments acting alone over-subsidise: welfare is higher under laissez-faire than under non-cooperative subsidy setting. This case is more likely to prevail if positive spillovers are low and the firms compete very intensely (goods are close substitutes). By contrast, in the bottom

Table 7.1 Rankings of investment levels in different equilibria.

		$\widehat{\pi}_i^j$	
		− Unfriendly	+ Friendly
$\widehat{\pi}_{ij}^i$	− Strategic substitutes	$\kappa^N > \kappa^L > \kappa^C$	$\kappa^C > \kappa^L > \kappa^N$
	+ Strategic complements	$\kappa^L > \kappa^N > \kappa^C$	$\kappa^C > \kappa^N > \kappa^L$

right-hand entry, where investments are friendly and strategic complements, the level of investment is highest under cooperation and lowest under laissez-faire. In this case the individual governments do not subsidise enough from the perspective of the collective. This case is more likely to hold if beneficial spillovers are high and/or firms do not compete too intensely.

3.5   Trade and industrial policy towards dynamic oligopoly

In this subsection we consider an extension of the strategic trade and investment model to an indefinite (though finite) number T of time periods. However, we return to the setup with one home and one foreign firm and one policy active government. In each period t, each firm takes an action, choosing the value of some variable, A_t for the home firm and B_t for the foreign firm. This specification encompasses all those cases considered so far: in each period the decision variables might be output, price, R&D or marketing. In a further departure from previous subsections, we allow for the possibility that the policy active government can set subsidies in more than one time period.

The firms' profits depend on a vector of their own actions and a vector of their rival's actions and on all the home government's subsidies. The home firm's profit function is:

$$\Pi(\mathbf{A}, \mathbf{B}, \mathbf{s}) = \pi(\mathbf{A}, \mathbf{B}) + S(\mathbf{A}, \mathbf{B}, \mathbf{s}), \tag{48}$$

where $\mathbf{A}$ and $\mathbf{B}$ are the vectors of the home and foreign firm's actions respectively and $\mathbf{s}$ is the vector of subsidies. As before, the firm's gross profits Π are made up of profits net of subsidy income π and its subsidy income S. In many applications, the subsidy income is linear in the firm's decision variables, so that $S^t = s_t a_t$ where S^t is subsidy income in period t. Examples of this include an R&D subsidy or an output subsidy under Cournot competition. By contrast, as we have seen in section 3.1, subsidy income depends in a more complicated way on the subsidy rate in the case of an output subsidy under Bertrand competition. It is clear that equation (48) is a T-period generalisation of equation (25). The foreign firm's profits are now given by

$$\pi^*(\mathbf{A}, \mathbf{B}), \tag{49}$$

which is similarly a T-period generalisation of equation (26).

Each firm now has T first-order conditions, one for each period. These can be written in vector notation as:

$$\left(\frac{d\Pi}{d\mathbf{A}}\right)' = \Pi'_A + \Pi'_B \frac{d\mathbf{B}}{d\mathbf{A}} + \Pi'_s \frac{d\mathbf{s}}{d\mathbf{A}} = 0, \tag{50}$$

and

$$\left(\frac{d\pi^*}{d\mathbf{B}}\right)' = \pi'^*_B + \pi'^*_A \frac{d\mathbf{A}}{d\mathbf{B}} = 0, \tag{51}$$

where a prime denotes the transpose of a vector. It is instructive to compare these with the corresponding first-order conditions when the firms choose an action in one period only (see section 3.1). Apart from the obvious difference that these are now vectors rather than scalars the key difference is the presence of strategic terms. An action chosen by a firm before the other firm or the government chooses its action may affect the value of that action. (These effects are captured by the matrices $d\mathbf{B}/d\mathbf{A}$, $d\mathbf{s}/d\mathbf{A}$ and $d\mathbf{A}/d\mathbf{B}$.) This in turn affects the profits of the firm in a manner that depends on whether the affected action is friendly or unfriendly.

The home welfare function:

$$W(\mathbf{A}, \mathbf{B}) = \Pi(\mathbf{A}, \mathbf{B}, \mathbf{s}) - S(\mathbf{A}, \mathbf{B}, \mathbf{s}) = \pi(\mathbf{A}, \mathbf{B}) \tag{52}$$

is a T-period generalisation of (29). When does the government set its subsidies in this T-period game? One possibility is that all the subsidies are set at the very start of the game before any of the actions of the firms are chosen. In that case we can say that the government has superior *intertemporal* commitment power to the home firm. (Note then that a subsidy labelled s_t is chosen in period 1 but the subsidized action A_t occurs in period t.) Another possibility is that the subsidies are actually set in the period in which they become effective. Our setup allows for both possibilities and for any of the cases in between. However, we do impose the following minimum structure on the T-period game. We assume that within time periods the firms play a Nash game, setting A_t and B_t simultaneously, but that if the government subsidizes the period t activities of its firm then the corresponding subsidy s_t is always chosen before A_t and B_t. (However, it is not necessarily chosen before *every* action by the firms.) Thus we say that the government always has superior *intratemporal* commitment power to the home firm.

To obtain the optimal subsidies, totally differentiate (52) to get a necessary condition for welfare maximisation:

$$dW = \pi'_{\mathbf{A}} d\mathbf{A} + \pi'_{\mathbf{B}} d\mathbf{B} = 0. \tag{53}$$

As we show in Neary and Leahy (2000) it is possible to solve the foreign first-order condition equations for generalised reaction functions, which express the foreign firm's actions as functions of all of the home firm's: $\mathbf{B} = \widetilde{\mathbf{B}}(\mathbf{A})$. In differential form this is $d\mathbf{B} = \widetilde{\mathbf{B}}_{\mathbf{A}} d\mathbf{A}$. Use this to eliminate $d\mathbf{B}$ in (53). We can also use the home firm's first-order conditions and the fact that $\Pi_{\mathbf{A}} = \pi_{\mathbf{A}} + S_{\mathbf{A}}$ to eliminate $\pi_{\mathbf{A}}$ in (53). This yields the following expression for the optimal subsidies:

$$S'_{\mathbf{A}} = \pi'_{\mathbf{B}} \widetilde{\mathbf{B}}_{\mathbf{A}} - \Pi'_{\mathbf{B}} \frac{d\mathbf{B}}{d\mathbf{A}} - \Pi'_{\mathbf{s}} \frac{d\mathbf{s}}{d\mathbf{A}}. \tag{54}$$

When we compare this expression to (31), which gives the optimal subsidy in the one-period strategic trade model, we see that the first term is simply a dynamic generalisation of the rent-shifting effect in the static strategic trade model. Algebraically this term is obtained by multiplying the friendliness term π_B by the slope of the foreign reaction function $\tilde{B}_A$. The remaining terms on the right-hand side are new in a dynamic setting and reflect the fact that the government must correct for the home firm's strategic behaviour.[26]

To obtain more concrete results consider a two-period example in which the government cannot commit to its subsidies in advance of the time period in which they become effective. Thus s_t is chosen in period t before A_t and B_t, and the game now consists of four stages. From equation (54) the optimal first-period subsidy in this case is:

$$S_{A_1}^1 + \rho S_{A_1}^2 = (\pi_{B_1}^1 + \rho \pi_{B_1}^2)\tilde{B}_{11} + \rho \pi_{B_2}^2 \tilde{B}_{21} - \left(\Pi_{B_2} \frac{dB_2}{dA_1} + \Pi_{s_2} \frac{ds_2}{dA_1} \right), \tag{55}$$

where π^t refers to period t operating profit, ρ denotes the discount factor, and the rent-shifting and strategic correction terms are written in full. In period 2 the government's problem is now particularly simple. With A_1 and B_1 already determined, it faces a standard static problem and the optimal subsidy is given by the static rent-shifting formula $S_{A_2}^2 = \pi_{B_2}^2 \tilde{B}_{22}$ which can be rewritten as (31) above. Note that neither firm can play strategically against its rival in the final stage of the game, and so the government only needs to correct firm strategic behaviour in period 1 with adjustments to the first-period subsidy.

To take a specific example, suppose that the firms play Cournot for two periods and that a firm's marginal cost in period 2 is a decreasing function of period-1 output due to learning by doing (see Leahy and Neary, 1999). Then the term $\Pi_{B_2} dB_2/dA_1$ will be positive as firm 1 strategically overproduces in period 1 to reduce its rival's output in period 2. As seen in (55) this will require the government to reduce the first-period subsidy to correct for this. Furthermore if the period-2 subsidy s_2 is chosen after the period-1 action A_1, then the firm will overproduce to gain a higher period-2 subsidy. (The term $\Pi_{s_2} ds_2/dA_1$ will be positive.) Anticipating this, the government will further reduce the first-period subsidy.

In this example, the home firm's overproduction in period 1 illustrates what Fudenberg and Tirole (1984) call 'Top Dog' behaviour: because a higher action by the home firm in period 1 reduces the rival firm's period-2 profits, and period-2 actions are strategic substitutes, the home firm has an incentive to behave more aggressively in period 1. Fudenberg and Tirole extend this insight to present a full 'animal spirits' taxonomy of behaviour in games of this kind. Such behaviour in turn justifies a policy intervention, since the home firm's aggressive action consumes real resources. In this example, a lower subsidy is warranted to deter the overproduction. In the terminology of Neary and Leahy (2000), the government should intervene to 'restrain' the 'Top Dog'. The same paper extends this idea to show that Fudenberg and Tirole's 'animal spirits' taxonomy of strategies by firms implies a corresponding 'animal training' taxonomy of optimal policy responses by governments.

4 Trade in general oligopolistic equilibrium

4.1 From partial to general equilibrium[27]

So far, all the models considered have focused on a single industry only. They can be given a general-equilibrium foundation, though only under special assumptions. It is instructive to begin by spelling these out, and then considering how they may be relaxed.

As already noted in Section 2.1, utility functions such as (1) defined over consumption levels of a single industry can be rationalised if the upper-tier utility function is quasi-linear:

$$U = x_0 + u(x). \tag{56}$$

Here x_0 is the consumption of the 'outside good', which is really a composite commodity defined over all the other goods in the economy, which are assumed to be produced under perfect competition. As before, x is the consumption of the output of the oligopolistic sector. (For simplicity we assume in this section that goods within each sector are homogeneous.) Maximising (56) subject to a budget constraint, it can be seen that the marginal propensity to consume x is zero: all income effects fall on the outside good, so the demand function for x can be considered independently of the level of income. In practice the price of the outside good is often normalised to equal one, and it is then called the '*numéraire* good', though this is just a convenient choice of measuring rod rather than a primitive property.

To move from the quasi-linear utility function (56) to the partial-equilibrium welfare function (11), we first make use of the identity between national expenditure and national income:

$$x_0 + px = wl_0 + (wl + \Pi). \tag{57}$$

Here l_0 and l denote employment levels in the two sectors. (This is fully consistent with any number of factors of production, provided their relative prices are given.) Assuming that the same wages are paid in all sectors, we can invoke the full-employment condition $l_0 + l = L$ to rewrite (57) as an equality between national expenditure and national product at factor cost wL plus profits Π:

$$x_0 + px = wL + \Pi. \tag{58}$$

Finally, use this to eliminate consumption of the *numéraire* good x_0 from (56):

$$U = wL + \chi + \Pi \quad \text{where:} \quad \chi \equiv u(x) - px \tag{59}$$

Equation (59) shows that the quasi-linear utility function (56) can be reexpressed as the sum of three components: wL is national product valued at factor cost; $\chi \equiv u(x) - px$ is consumer surplus in the non-numéraire sector; and Π is profits in that sector. Hence, provided w can be taken as given (i.e., provided the non-*numéraire* sector is small in factor markets relative to the *numéraire* one), utility and welfare equal simply the sum of consumer surplus and profits, just as in (11).

A similar derivation was used by Brander and Spencer (1984, pp. 198–9) to justify their claim that models of strategic trade policy have valid general-equilibrium underpinnings.[28] Their conclusion is worth quoting in full: 'The essential question is not whether a model is partial or general equilibrium but whether the industry in question is large enough to give rise to income effects, cross-substitution effects in demand and factor price effects'. While we fully agree on the substance, we also believe that it is convenient to have a single shorthand term to refer to the very special case of general equilibrium in which we can ignore income effects and inter-sectoral substitution effects on the demand side, and cost changes on the factor-market side. Rather than inventing a new term, it seems natural to use the label 'partial equilibrium' for the case in which the industry is not large enough to give rise to the latter effects.

The substantive question remains: is it justifiable to make these 'partial equilibrium' assumptions? There are clearly many contexts where it is. In industrial organisation, for example, it is natural to have a partial-equilibrium focus: to understand the workings of a single market, it makes sense to ignore the wider context. And as previous sections have shown, there are a great many issues in international trade which can be illuminated by partial-equilibrium models. Nevertheless, many of the central questions in international trade involve comparisons between sectors, and links between goods and factor markets. This is true, for example, of the determinants of trade patterns, the economy-wide gains from trade, and the effects of trade on income distribution. A full understanding of such questions requires a framework which allows for multiple sectors and which explicitly models the links between goods and factor markets, in other words, a general-equilibrium framework which does not rely on the special assumptions listed above.

However, embedding oligopoly models in general equilibrium has generally been viewed as posing severe technical problems. This arises from the perception that a general-equilibrium model of oligopoly should require firms to solve general-equilibrium problems while still playing strategically against each other, a combination which implies extremely complex modelling. For example, Roberts and Sonnenschein (1977) showed that if oligopolists rationally anticipate the effects of their choices on national income, the resulting reaction functions are extremely badly behaved, and even in simple models an equilibrium may not exist. A different problem, highlighted by Gabszewicz and Vial (1972), is that if oligopolists anticipate their impact on the aggregate price level, then the consequences of their actions are sensitive to the deflator used to evaluate the real value of profits.[29] It is true that considerable progress can be made by ignoring these problems (examples include Markusen, 1984, and Ruffin, 2003), but this has not met with universal approval.

A consistent approach to modelling oligopoly in general equilibrium requires that firms are 'large in the small but small in the large': playing strategically against a small number of competitors in their own sectors, just like the firms in earlier sections; while at the same time too small in the economy as a whole to influence aggregate variables such as national income or the price level. A natural framework in which to formalise this idea is the continuum-of-sectors model of Dornbusch, Fischer and Samuelson (1977). Originally presented in a competitive framework, with a continuum of firms in each sector, this model can be modified to allow for only a small number of firms producing a homogeneous good in each sector, so allowing for a consistent model of oligopoly in general equilibrium.

A key step in operationalising the 'large in the small but small in the large' approach is to specify a tractable specification of preferences. From this perspective, a very desirable feature of preferences is that they are additively separable. This implies that the inverse demand for each good depends only on its own consumption $q(z)$ and on the marginal utility of income in the economy, λ: $p(z) = f[q(z), \lambda]$. (Here $z \in [0, 1]$ denotes sectors.) Hence λ is a 'sufficient statistic' for all the determinants of demand coming from outside the sector. Rationally, firms take λ as given when competing strategically against their rivals in sector z, whereas it is endogenous in the economy as a whole. The distinction between the demand function with λ parametric and with λ endogenously determined parallels the distinction between 'perceived' and 'actual' demand functions in the literature on monopolistic competition. Finally, to get closed-form solutions, it is convenient to focus on the special case of additive preferences where the demand function is linear in prices, so it takes the form: $p(z) = a' - b'q(z)$, with $a' \equiv a/\lambda$ and $b' \equiv b/\lambda$. In the remainder of this section we sketch this approach, following Neary (2002b, 2003a), and discuss some applications and extensions.

4.2 Specialisation patterns in international oligopoly

To understand the model, it is useful to begin by taking a firms'-eye view, focusing on equilibrium in individual sectors with wages and the marginal utility of income taken as parametric. We assume that firms engage in Cournot competition on an integrated world market. Following Neary (2003a), we assume that firms differ between countries but not within. So in the home country there are n firms, each with unit cost c, producing a level of output x. Similarly in the foreign country, there are n^* firms, each with unit cost c^*, producing a level of output y. (For convenience, we suppress the sector index z in this subsection.) The possible equilibrium patterns of international specialisation are then as illustrated in figure 7.2, in the space of home and foreign costs.[30] First, if all firms have costs above the maximum price that consumers are willing to pay, a', then the good will not be produced in either country, as illustrated by region O. Next, we can ask what is the equilibrium output of a home firm. Standard calculations show that this equals:

$$x = \frac{a' - (n^* + 1)c + n^* c^*}{b(n + n^* + 1)}. \tag{60}$$

Hence, ignoring fixed costs for simplicity, home firms will produce positive output ($x > 0$) if and only if their costs are sufficiently low, such that $c < a' + n^* c^* / n^* + 1$. The threshold value of c defines the locus which separates the F and HF regions in figure 7.2, where F has active foreign firms only, while HF has active firms in both countries. A corresponding argument defines the locus which represents zero output by foreign firms ($y = 0$), separating the HF and H regions.

The most interesting of these regions is HF. We can call it a 'cone of diversification', and it is special to oligopoly. Under perfectly competitive assumptions, the model would be identical to that of Dornbusch, Fischer and Samuelson (1977), complete specialisation would take place, and so the HF region would collapse to the 45° line. By contrast, in oligopoly, high- and low-cost firms coexist in the HF region. For example, at any point above the 45° line in this cone, home

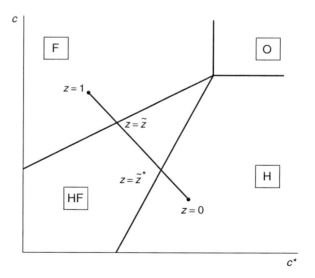

Figure 7.2   Equilibrium production patterns for a given cost distribution.

firms have higher costs than foreign firms and therefore (in a free-trade equilibrium) they have lower output.[31] However, they are not driven out of business, because of the barriers to entry which underpin the oligopoly equilibrium. Foreign firms with lower costs are making greater profits, and if entry were free, the number of foreign firms would grow until all home firms had been driven out of business. Thus, entry barriers in the low-cost country serve to cushion high-cost firms from foreign competition under free trade, just as tariff barriers in a perfectly competitive model allow for the coexistence of high and low-cost firms (see Dornbusch, Fischer and Samuelson (1977), Section III.C).

So far, figure 7.2 illustrates all the possible equilibria conditional on production costs and the marginal utility of income λ taken as given. To embed this in general equilibrium, we first invoke the standard Ricardian assumptions about technology and labour markets, relating unit costs in all sectors to local wages and technology. Assume therefore that labour is the only factor of production and that the unit labour requirements for home and foreign firms are fixed, denoted by $\alpha(z)$ and $\alpha^*(z)$ respectively. We assume in addition that labour is perfectly mobile within countries, but immobile internationally, and that labour markets are perfectly competitive. Hence, the production cost in each sector equals the product of its exogenously determined unit labour requirement and the national wage rate:

$$c(z) = w\alpha(z) \quad \text{and} \quad c^*(z) = w^*\alpha^*(z) \tag{61}$$

in the home and foreign countries, respectively. Next we need to assume that the sectors can be ranked such that home and foreign costs can be directly compared. A sufficient condition for this is that home labour requirements are increasing in z and foreign labour requirements are decreasing in z: $\alpha'(z) > 0$ and $\alpha^{*\prime}(z) < 0$.[32] For given wages in both countries, we can then express the cost of production in each sector at home as a decreasing function of the corresponding cost abroad.[33] This is illustrated by the downward-sloping locus in figure 7.2. In the case shown, this implies that there are three kinds of sectors, with the boundaries between them denoted $\tilde{z}^*$ and $\tilde{z}$. In all sectors for which z is less than $\tilde{z}^*$, only home firms make non-negative profits; while in all sectors for which z is greater than $\tilde{z}$, only foreign firms make non-negative profits. The third kind of sectors are those in the cone of diversification, with values of z lying between $\tilde{z}^*$ and $\tilde{z}$, in which both home and foreign firms are active. These threshold sectors, $\tilde{z}$ and $\tilde{z}^*$, which are endogenously determined in general equilibrium, demarcate the extensive margins of production in the home and foreign countries respectively. Note that the configuration illustrated in figure 7.2 is only one possible outcome. For example, the equilibrium value of $\tilde{z}$ could equal one, in which case home firms would be active in all sectors; similarly, the equilibrium value of $\tilde{z}^*$ could equal zero, in which case foreign firms would be active in all sectors.

So far the wage rates have been taken as exogenous. Their equilibrium values are implied by assumptions already made, with the additional assumption (natural in a trade model) that total labour supplies are fixed in each country. Thus, in the home country, the equilibrium wage rate adjusts to equate supply of and demand for labour:

$$
L = \int_0^{\tilde{z}} n\alpha(z)x(z)\,dz \quad \text{where: } x(z) = \begin{cases} \frac{a'-c}{b(n+1)} & \text{for } z \in [0, \tilde{z}^*] \\ \frac{a'-(n^*+1)c+n^*c^*}{b(n+n^*+1)} & \text{for } z \in [\tilde{z}^*, \tilde{z}] \end{cases} \tag{62}
$$

The aggregate demand for labour is simply the integral of the demands from all sectors with active home firms: in other words, firm output $x(z)$ times its unit labour requirement $\alpha(z)$ times the number of firms n. The only complication is that the expression for firm output differs between sectors. In sectors with $z \in [0, \tilde{z}^*]$, foreign firms cannot compete, so home firms face only domestic competition; while sectors with $z \in [\tilde{z}^*, \tilde{z}]$ lie in the cone of diversification, so both home and foreign firms are active and the output of a typical home firm is given by (60). An exactly analogous equation equates demand and supply of labour in the foreign country. Hence we have four equations in total, two labour-market equilibrium equations plus two equations specifying zero output for each of the threshold sectors, which combine to determine simultaneously the four endogenous variables: the home and foreign wage rates and the values of the threshold sectors.

4.3   Autarky versus free trade: welfare, income distribution and trade patterns

A natural question which arises in this model is the comparison between autarky and free trade. To facilitate this, it is convenient to assume that countries are symmetric and always produce all goods (so the $\{c, c^*\}$ locus lies strictly inside the *HF* region).[34] The assumption of full diversification precludes the complete specialisation in production which drives the gains from trade in a competitive model. However, there are other sources of gain from trade in oligopoly. First, domestic firms face more competition in free trade than in autarky, which reduces their markups, lowering prices to consumers in all sectors. Second, comparative advantage still operates, even though complete specialisation does not occur. In sectors where home firms are more efficient, they expand their scale of operations, while foreign firms contract; and conversely in sectors where foreign firms are more efficient. As a result, labour is reallocated from low- to high-productivity sectors, generating a further gain from trade.

Thus, comparative advantage and pro-competitive effects combine to raise welfare. However, where income distribution is concerned, they work in opposite directions. Note that, although there is only one primary factor of production in this Ricardian model, the persistence of pure profits allows the consideration of income distribution. Moving from autarky to free trade, the competition effect tends to squeeze profits, as increased demand for labour bids up wages. By contrast, specialisation according to comparative advantage implies that resources are reallocated towards the more productive sectors. With a fixed number of firms, this process tends to benefit profit recipients, as workers are laid off more in less-productive sectors than they are absorbed in more-productive ones. As a result, the gains from comparative advantage accrue to profit recipients, and it is even possible that they can outweigh the positive effects of greater competition, leading to a fall in the share of wages in free trade relative to autarky.

Of course, because of oligopoly, there are 'missing gains from trade': if barriers to entry were removed, the two countries would specialise completely and welfare would be higher. In the same way, oligopoly provides a potential explanation for 'missing trade'.[35] The volume of trade is reduced relative to a perfectly competitive trading equilibrium on both the supply and demand sides. Because welfare is lower, the demand for all goods including imports is reduced. And because of oligopolistic barriers to entry, output of each sector is also lower than it would be in the competitive case. It follows that trade volumes are less than they would be if the barriers to entry were removed.

4.4 Extensions and applications

Models of oligopoly in general equilibrium have been applied to a range of issues. Grossman and Rossi-Hansberg (2010) develop a model similar to that described above, but assuming that firms compete on price rather than on quantity, and apply the model to consider the role of external economies. The assumption of a continuum of sectors allows for a clean analysis of the properties of the model, without the discontinuities found in classic treatments of external economies such as Ethier (1982b), where firms are large in the economy as a whole as well as in their own market. A different approach to modelling the mode of competition between firms is adopted by Neary and Tharakan (2006). Building on Kreps and Scheinkman (1983) and Maggi (1996), they assume that firms first invest in capacity and then compete on price. If the cost advantage of investing in capacity is sufficiently large, then the outcome of this two-stage game resembles that of a one-stage Cournot game where firms compete only in quantities. Maggi considered only a single industry in partial equilibrium, where the advantage of investing in capacity was exogenous and determined by technology alone. By contrast, in the general-equilibrium model of Neary and Tharakan, sectors differ in the cost advantage of investing in capacity, and capacity requires a different mix of factors from production. As a result, relative factor prices play a role in determining the extent of competition in the economy, and factor prices are themselves determined endogenously in general equilibrium. As a result, the model allows for the endogenous determination of the mix of sectors between those exhibiting more and less competitive, or Bertrand and Cournot, behaviour.

Intersectoral differences in factor mix can also provide insights into the impact of international trade on relative wages, as shown by Neary (2002a). In both perfectly and monopolistically competitive models, increased foreign competition impacts on domestic firms only via changes in the prices they face, but empirical studies have failed to find a sufficiently large effect of import prices. This has led many researchers to conclude that rises in the skill premium, the higher wage enjoyed by skilled relative to unskilled workers, are due to skill-biased technological progress rather than increased competition and trade from low-wage countries. However, models of oligopoly introduce the possibility of non-price interaction between firms. An extreme example of this in Neary (2002a) is where domestic firms are induced to engage in what Wood (1994) calls 'defensive innovation', even though no imports actually occur. The source of this is the threat of trade (as imports become potentially more competitive) which encourages home firms to engage in strategic investment to deter entry. Provided investment is relatively skill-intensive, this in turn leads to an increase in the skill premium.

In the same vein, models of oligopoly in general equilibrium have been shown to shed light on particular issues which cannot be considered in either competitive general-equilibrium models or oligopolistic partial-equilibrium models. Neary (2003b) considers a unilateral increase in the number of firms in each sector as an improvement in the economy's competitive advantage, and shows how this interacts with comparative advantage: the economy gains as it specialises in those sectors in which it is relatively more efficient, though the higher wage induced by greater competition between firms causes marginal sectors to cease production. Bastos and Kreickemeier (2009) explore the implications of unionisation in a subset of sectors, and show that it can reverse the conclusions of partial-equilibrium models. Because the outside option of unionised workers is endogenous in general equilibrium, they show that union wages may increase with firm entry and may be higher in free trade than in autarky. Finally, models of oligopoly make it possible to explore the implications of endogenous changes in market structure. Neary (2007) shows that trade liberalisation in the model of the last subsection creates incentives for cross-border mergers. Moreover, the model predicts that such mergers will generate flows of foreign direct investment that take place in the same direction as trade flows: home firms in sectors which enjoy a comparative advantage will also have a greater incentive to take over smaller less productive foreign firms. This is in contrast with standard models of greenfield foreign direct investment which predict counterfactually that trade and foreign direct investment are always substitutes.

5   Conclusion

In this chapter, we have given a selective survey of the theory of international trade under oligopoly, concentrating on three topics: oligopoly as an independent determinant of trade, as illustrated by the reciprocal-markets model of Brander (1981); oligopoly as an independent rationale for government intervention, as illustrated by strategic trade and industrial policy in the third-market model of Spencer and Brander (1983) and Brander and Spencer (1985); and the challenges and potential of embedding trade under oligopoly in general equilibrium.

Naturally, space constraints have forced us to omit many important topics which have also been considered in the literature. For example, our discussion of strategic trade policy concentrated on the third-market model and ignored policies towards imports, both tariffs and quantitative restrictions. These were first considered by Brander and Spencer (1984) and Krishna (1989) respectively, and the general issues of strategic trade policy in the reciprocal-markets model are surveyed by Brander (1995). We have paid no attention to strategic trade policy under uncertainty, which has been addressed by Cooper and Riezman (1989) and Dewit and Leahy (2004); nor under asymmetric information, which has been explored by Collie and Hviid (1993) and Brainard and Martimort (1997). We have also ignored the important topic of competition policy, which arises naturally in an oligopoly context and can be analysed in the same way as strategic trade policy. The possibility of affecting national welfare by controlling the number of domestic firms was first explored by Dixit (1984), and related aspects of competition policy in open-economy oligopoly models have been considered by Horn and Levinsohn (2001) and Francois and Horn (2007). In addition, we have ignored foreign direct investment, at least of the greenfield kind, and given only a brief discussion of one approach to strategic aspects of cross-border mergers in Section 4. These topics are covered in more detail in chapter 8 of this volume. Finally, we have not considered the implications of oligopoly for preferential trade agreements and international trade negotiations, topics which are attracting increasing attention (see, for example, Yi, 1996, and Mrázová, 2010).

Turning from theory to empirics, oligopoly in trade does not lend itself easily to empirical work, at least using large firm-level data sets of the kind that have become available in the 1990s and 2000s, which have made applied trade theory such an exciting field of research. Most empirical applications of oligopolistic trade models so far have been in the normative area. See for example the papers in Krugman and Smith (1994), as well as Baldwin and Flam (1989), which use calibration methods to quantify the gains and losses from strategic trade policy.[36] The real-world example most often cited in this context is international competition between Airbus and Boeing in the commercial aircraft industry (see Dixit and Kyle, 1985). Irwin (1991) applies the strategic trade policy framework to a much earlier industry. He uses a duopoly model calibrated with data from the East India spice trade in the early seventeenth century to illustrate the effects of trade policies and institutional arrangements on the rivalry between the English and the Dutch East India companies. As for the positive theory of trade under oligopoly, empirical studies of intra-industry trade patterns arising from oligopolistic competition have been carried out by Bernhofen (1999) and Friberg and Ganslandt (2006). A related paper by Feenstra, Markusen and Rose (2001) shows that a wide range of theories are consistent with a gravity-type equation, and finds empirical results that fit the predictions of the reciprocal dumping model with homogeneous goods and restricted entry.

A frequently heard criticism of oligopolistic trade models is that their predictions are highly sensitive to the mode of competition. Arguably this perception has been overstated. To a large extent, it arose from the early demonstration by Eaton and Grossman (1986) that one of the first and highest-profile results on strategic trade policy, the Brander-Spencer (1985) finding that export subsidies are optimal, is reversed when we move from Cournot to Bertrand competition. Nonetheless, the general case for intervention is the same in both cases: governments can improve national welfare by exercising their superior commitment power relative to domestic and foreign firms. Moreover, as we have seen, the argument for activist investment policies is more robust than that for export policies. Similarly, in the reciprocal markets model, the prediction of cross-hauling of identical goods is sensitive to the mode of competition, at least in the sense that the extreme case of identical products with Bertrand competition and no trade costs leads to an indeterminate pattern of production and trade. However, the pro-competition effect is not at all sensitive; indeed, it is stronger with Bertrand competition than with Cournot, because even potential trade encourages the home firm to behave in a more competitive manner.

Another frequently-heard objection to oligopolistic trade models is the assumption of an exogenous number of firms. This can be overcome by allowing entry. Indeed trade models with Cournot competition and free entry have been developed (see for instance Venables, 1985), but these treat the number of firms as a continuous variable. As a result, free entry ensures that there are zero profits in equilibrium. Because these models ignore the so-called integer problem (the technical difficulties arising from the requirement that the number of firms must be an integer), their predictions are similar to those from models of monopolistic competition (or even perfect competition, if goods are homogeneous). If the integer problem is not ignored, then profits continue to be earned in most equilibria, and so the key features of oligopoly survive. However, models incorporating these features have yet to be developed.[37] For the present, a defence of the relevance of oligopolistic models with fixed numbers of firms can fall back on their realism in many real-world applications. Ignoring entry at least of large firms is very plausible for the short run in most markets, and even over longer time horizons in many markets, where the major players have shown great persistence over time, notwithstanding the spread of globalisation.

In conclusion, a key contribution of oligopoly in trade theory is its focus on central features of the real world: the persistence of pure profits and the strategies adopted by firms to raise them. Indeed the importance of profits can hardly be underestimated. They are key to the results of the reciprocal-markets model, starting with the pathbreaking finding by Brander (1981) that intra-industry trade can arise from firms' incentives to capture foreign monopoly rents. Profits are also the essential focus of strategic trade policy, not in the sense that optimal policy necessarily implies profit-shifting towards domestic firms (for example, if firms compete on price, then the optimal policy implies taxing a home firm, which in effect shifts profits from it towards its foreign competitor), but rather that the motivation for policy arises from the desire to raise profits net of taxes and subsidies, which in the third-market model is identical to social welfare. Finally, in general equilibrium, the persistence of profits adds a new dimension to discussions of income distribution: aggregate gains from trade can coexist with redistribution away from productive factors (labour in our example) towards profit recipients.

Notes

* We are grateful to Daniel Bernhofen, Monika Mrázová and Tony Venables for helpful discussions. Dermot Leahy acknowledges the support of the Science Foundation Ireland Research Frontiers Programme (Grant MAT 017).

† Department of Economics, National University of Ireland, Maynooth.

‡ Department of Economics, University of Oxford, and CEPR.

1. See Krugman (1979) for an early contribution, and Neary (2009) for an overview and further references.
2. See Neary (2010) for further discussion.
3. See Bernard, Jensen, Redding and Schott (2007) and Mayer and Ottaviano (2007).
4. Empirical studies by Goldberg and Verboven (2001) and others document an apparently high degree of market segmentation in oligopolistic industries.
5. Bernhofen (1999) extends the basic duopoly model to allow for more home and foreign firms.
6. Bernhofen (2001) introduced product differentiation into Cournot and Bertrand oligopoly models of intra-industry trade, focusing on the effect of trade on profits and consumer surplus.
7. This ignores the utility derived from other goods. One justification for this specification is that u is a sub-utility function where the upper-tier utility function is quasi-linear. See Section 4 for further discussion.
8. We can attribute to oligopolistic competition alone the amount of trade which would occur in the absence of trade barriers if goods were identical: when $e = 1$, $y = (a - c)/3b$. The remainder of trade, $\frac{a-c}{b(2+e)} - \frac{a-c}{3b}$, is due to product differentiation, so the share of trade attributable to product differentiation rather than

to oligopolistic competition is $(1-e)/3$. This rises from zero (when $e=1$) to one third (when $e=0$) as products become more differentiated. This contrasts with models of monopolistic competition under CES preferences, in which the share of intra-industry trade in total trade is independent of the degree of product differentiation. This empirically implausible prediction was first pointed out by Ethier (1982a, Proposition 12). See Bernhofen (2001) for further discussion.

9. Article VI of the GATT permits the imposition of an anti-dumping duty not greater in amount than the margin given in (9).

10. This is intuitively obvious, and easily proved using the first-order conditions and the expressions for output (6) and (7). These yield:
$$\frac{dp}{dt} = \frac{d(bx)}{dt} = \frac{e}{4-e^2} > 0 \text{ and } \frac{dp^*}{dt} = 1 + \frac{d(by)}{dt} = \frac{2-e^2}{4-e^2} > 0.$$

11. With consumer surplus denoted by $\chi = u(x,y) - px - p^*y$, the change in consumer surplus is $d\chi = -xdp - ydp^*$, which equals $-xdp$ in the neighbourhood of autarky where imports y are zero. Profits on exports are also zero in the neighbourhood of autarky. As for profits on home sales, $\pi = (p-c)x$, the change in this is $d\pi = (p-c)dx + xdp$. In the neighbourhood of autarky, $d\chi + d\Pi = (p-c)dx$ which is negative as the tariff falls.

12. This qualifies the statement made in Neary (2009), p. 242, footnote 25.

13. Strictly speaking, this is only true for positive trade costs. Cross-hauling can occur when goods are identical $(e=1)$ and trade is unrestricted $(t=0)$, although the volume of trade is indeterminate without additional assumptions. One natural case is where consumers buy first from their home firm, so trade is zero even with no trade costs. An alternative case is where consumers are indifferent and purchase half and half from each firm, so cross-hauling constitutes a high proportion of trade.

14. For further details see Clarke and Collie (2003).

15. To see this, find the level of p that sets imports equal to zero for any given p^*. From (13) with $y=0$, this is: $p = \frac{p^*-(1-e)a}{e}$. In this region, with $\widehat{t}^B \le t \le \widehat{t}^C$, the foreign firm is just kept out of the market so the incipient price of imports is simply their unit cost: $p^* = c+t$. Eliminating prices p and p^* from these two equations and the demand function $p = a - bx$ yields (21).

16. This equilibrium resembles those with explicit entry-deterrence behaviour, as in Dixit (1980) or Fudenberg and Tirole (1984). However, unlike those cases, here the firms move simultaneously in a one-shot game.

17. See for instance Pinto (1986), Fung (1991, 1992), Lommerud and Sørgard (2001) and Ashournia, Hansen and Hansen (2008).

18. Lommerud and Sørgard (2001) demonstrate that this result is also reversed under Bertrand competition with homogeneous products.

19. Fung (1991) also examines cartel stability under collusive trade. However, he does not discuss the role of trade liberalisation.

20. Throughout this section, our discussion of Cournot competition holds whether products are homogeneous or differentiated. By contrast, in the Bertrand case, we need to assume that products are sufficiently differentiated such that an interior equilibrium exists.

21. Multilateral subsidy games will be discussed later.

22. This was first pointed out by Dixit (1984).

23. See Helpman and Krugman (1989), 111. Further applications of such policy games under both Cournot and Bertrand competition are considered by Collie (2000, 2002).

24. Our presentation here follows Leahy and Neary (2001). Spencer and Brander (1983), Bagwell and Staiger (1994), Maggi (1996) and Neary and Leahy (2000) among others

have also shown in different contexts that an investment subsidy is typically optimal when a domestic oligopolist faces foreign rivals and an export subsidy is unavailable.

25. Besley and Seabright (1999) present a related but different approach to international competition which takes the form of state aids to industry.

26. The first two terms on the right-hand side of (54) may appear to be very similar except in sign. Both consist of a friendliness term multiplied by the slope of a foreign reaction function. Moreover, $\Pi_B - \pi_B = S_B = 0$ in the many applications in which the subsidy income is linear in the firm's decision variables. However, the matrices $\widetilde{B}_A$ and dB/dA differ in an important respect which reflects the government's superior commitment power. The matrix $\widetilde{B}_A$ gives the derivatives of foreign actions with respect to home actions from the perspective of the home government. This differs in general from the matrix dB/dA in which the derivatives are from the perspective of the home firm. The difference between the two reflects the fact that within any time period the home and foreign firm choose their actions simultaneously, so all elements on and above the principal diagonal of the matrix dB/dA are zero; whereas the home government always has superior commitment power (at least intratemporally), so some or all of the corresponding elements in the matrix $\widetilde{B}_A$ are non-zero.

27. This subsection draws on Neary (2003a).

28. As Feenstra and Rose (2000, p. 11) point out: 'Brander and Spencer (1985) ... arose out of an attempt to convince Ron Jones that their earlier paper on international R&D rivalry [Spencer and Brander (1983)] worked in a general equilibrium setting'.

29. Gabszewicz and Vial (1972) call this outcome a sensitivity to the choice of *numéraire*.

30. For an independent development of this figure, see Collie (1991).

31. Note that, even with different numbers of firms at home and abroad, the locus along which outputs are the same is the 45° line. To see this, equate equation (60) to the corresponding equation for the foreign firm.

32. This condition is much stronger than necessary, but very convenient. For further discussion, see Neary (2002b).

33. Formally, this involves combining the two equations in (61) to eliminate z: $c = w\alpha\left[\alpha^{*-1}\left(c^*/w^*\right)\right]$.

34. The fact that countries are symmetric does not mean that they are identical. In particular, while the average labour productivity over all sectors is the same in both countries, there is scope for comparative advantage differences: $\alpha(z) = \alpha^*(1-z)$ and $\int_0^1 \alpha(z)\,dz = \int_0^1 \alpha^*(z)\,dz$, but in general $\alpha(z) \neq \alpha^*(z)$.

35. See also Ruffin (2003). The 'mystery of the missing trade', the fact that world trade is less than we would expect from international differences in factor endowments, was first highlighted by Trefler (1995). Other possible explanations are explored by Davis and Weinstein (2001).

36. Norman (1990) and Francois and Roland-Holst (1997) provide overviews of this literature.

37. Some possible approaches to this problem are sketched in Neary (2010).

References

Ashournia, Damoun, Per Svejstrup Hansen and Jonas Worm Hansen (2008) 'Trade liberalization and the degree of competition in international duopoly', presented at the European Trade Study Group Conference, Warsaw.

Bagwell, Kyle, and Robert W. Staiger (1994) 'The sensitivity of strategic and corrective R&D policy in oligopolistic industries', *Journal of International Economics*, 36, 133–50.

Baldwin, Richard, and Harry Flam (1989) 'Strategic trade policies in the market for 30–40 seat commuter aircraft', *Review of World Economics*, 125, 484–500.

Baldwin, Richard, and Paul Krugman (1988) 'Market access and international competition: A simulation study of 16K random access memories', in R.C. Feenstra (ed.), *Empirical Methods in International Trade*, Cambridge, MA: MIT Press, 171–97.

Bastos, Paulo, and Udo Kreickemeier (2009) 'Unions, competition and international trade in general equilibrium', *Journal of International Economics*, 79, 238–47.

Ben-Zvi, Shmuel, and Elhanan Helpman (1992) 'Oligopoly in segmented markets', in G. Grossman (ed.), *Imperfect Competition and International Trade*. Cambridge, MA: MIT Press, 31–53.

Bernard, Andrew B., J. Bradford Jensen, Stephen J. Redding and Peter K. Schott (2007) 'Firms in International Trade', *Journal of Economic Perspectives*, 21, 105–30.

Bernhofen, Daniel M. (1999) 'Intra-industry trade and strategic interaction: Theory and evidence', *Journal of International Economics*, 47, 225–44.

—— (2001) 'Product differentiation, competition, and international trade', *Canadian Journal of Economics*, 34, 1010–23.

Besley, Tim, and Paul Seabright (1999) 'The effects and policy implications of state aids to industry: An economic analysis', *Economic Policy*, 28, 14–53.

Brander, James A. (1981) 'Intra-industry trade in identical commodities', *Journal of International Economics*, 11, 1–14.

—— (1995) 'Strategic trade policy', in G. Grossman and K. Rogoff (eds), *Handbook of International Economics*, vol. 3. Amsterdam: North-Holland, 1395–1455.

Brander, James A., and Paul Krugman (1983) 'A "reciprocal dumping" model of international trade', *Journal of International Economics*, 15, 313–21.

Brander, James A., and Barbara J. Spencer (1984) 'Tariff protection and imperfect competition', in H. Kierzkowski (ed.), *Monopolistic Competition and International Trade*. Oxford: Clarendon Press.

—— (1985) 'Export subsidies and international market share rivalry', *Journal of International Economics*, 18, 83–100.

Brainard, S. Lael, and David Martimort (1997) 'Strategic trade policy with incompletely informed policymakers', *Journal of International Economics*, 42, 33–65.

Clarke, Roger, and David R. Collie (2003) 'Product differentiation and the gains from trade under Bertrand duopoly', *Canadian Journal of Economics*, 36, 658–73.

Collie, David R. (1991) 'Optimum welfare and maximum revenue tariffs under oligopoly', *Scottish Journal of Political Economy*, 38, 398–401.

—— (2000) 'State aid in the European union: The prohibition of subsidies in an integrated market', *International Journal of Industrial Organisation*, 18, 867–84.

—— (2002) 'Prohibiting state aid in an integrated market: Cournot and Bertrand oligopolies with differentiated products', *Journal of Industry, Competition and Trade*, 2, 215–31.

—— (2005) 'State aid to investment and R&D', *European Economy Economic Papers*, No. 231, European Commission, Brussels.

Collie, David R., and Morten Hviid (1993) 'Export subsidies as signals of competitiveness', *Scandinavian Journal of Economics*, 95, 327–39.

Commission of the European Communities (2005) *State Aid Action Plan: Less and Better Targeted State Aid: A Roadmap for State Aid Reform 2005–2009*. Brussels.

Cooper, Russell, and Raymond Riezman (1989) 'Uncertainty and the choice of trade policy in oligopolistic industries', *Review of Economic Studies*, 56, 129–40.

Davis, D.R., and D. Weinstein (2001) 'An account of global factor trade', *American Economic Review*, 91, 1423–53.

Dewit, Gerda, and Dermot Leahy (2004) 'Rivalry in uncertain export markets: Commitment versus flexibility', *Journal of International Economics*, 64, 195–209.

Dixit, Avinash (1980) 'The role of investment in entry deterrence', *Economic Journal*, 90, 95–106.

—— (1984) 'International trade policies for oligopolistic industries', *Economic Journal* (Supplement), 94, 1–16.

Dixit, Avinash K., and Gene M. Grossman (1986) 'Targeted export promotion with several oligopolistic industries', *Journal of International Economics*, 21, 233–49.

Dixit, Avinash K., and Albert S. Kyle (1985) 'The use of protection and subsidies for entry promotion and deterrence', *American Economic Review*, 75, 139–52.

Dornbusch, Rudiger, Stanley Fischer and Paul A. Samuelson (1977) 'Comparative advantage, trade and payments in a Ricardian model with a continuum of goods', *American Economic Review*, 67, 823–39.

Eaton, Jonathan, and Gene M. Grossman (1986) 'Optimal trade and industrial policy under oligopoly', *Quarterly Journal of Economics*, 101, 383–406.

Ethier, Wilfred J. (1982a) 'National and international returns to scale in the modern theory of international trade', *American Economic Review*, 72, 389–405.

—— (1982b) 'Decreasing costs in international trade and Frank Graham's argument for protection', *Econometrica*, 50, 1243–68.

Feenstra, Robert C. (2003) *Advanced International Trade: Theory and Evidence*. Princeton: Princeton University Press.

Feenstra, Robert C., James R. Markusen and Andrew K. Rose (2001) 'Using the gravity equation to differentiate among alternative theories of trade', *Canadian Journal of Economics*, 34, 430–47.

Feenstra, Robert C., and Andrew K. Rose (2000) 'The *Journal of International Economics* at Fifty: A Retrospective', *Journal of International Economics*, 50, 3–15.

Francois, Joseph, and Henrik Horn (2007) 'Antitrust in open economies', in V. Ghosal and J. Stennek (eds), *The Political Economy of Antitrust*, Amsterdam: Elsevier Science.

Francois, Joseph F., and D. Roland-Holst (1997) 'Scale economies and imperfect competition', in J. Francois and K. Reinert (eds), *Applied Methods for Trade Policy Analysis: A Handbook*. Cambridge: Cambridge University Press.

Friberg, R., and M. Ganslandt (2006) 'An empirical assessment of the welfare effects of reciprocal dumping', *Journal of International Economics*, 70, 1–24.

Fudenberg, Drew, and Jean Tirole (1984) 'The fat-cat effect, the puppy-dog ploy, and the lean and hungry look', *American Economic Review, Papers and Proceedings*, 74, 361–66.

Fung, K.C. (1991) 'Collusive intra-industry trade', *Canadian Journal of Economics*, 24, 391–404.

—— (1992) 'Economic integration as competitive discipline', *International Economic Review*, 33, 837–47.

Gabszewicz, Jean Jaskold, and Jean-Philippe Vial (1972) 'Oligopoly à la Cournot in a general equilibrium analysis', *Journal of Economic Theory*, 4, 381–400.

Goldberg, Pinelopi Koujianou, and Frank Verboven (2001) 'The evolution of price dispersion in the European car market', *Review of Economic Studies*, 68, 811–48.

Grossman, Gene, and Kenneth Rogoff (eds), (1995) *Handbook of International Economics*, vol. 3, Amsterdam: North-Holland.

Grossman, Gene, and Esteban Rossi-Hansberg (2010) 'External economies and international trade redux', forthcoming in the *Quarterly Journal of Economics*.

Haaland, Jan I., and Hans Jarle Kind (2006) 'Cooperative and non-cooperative R&D policy in an economic union', *Review of World Economics*, 142, 720–45.

—— (2008) 'R&D policies, trade and process innovation', *Journal of International Economics*, 74, 170–87.

Helpman, Elhanan, and Paul Krugman (1989) *Trade Policy and Market Structure*. Cambridge, MA: MIT Press.

Horn, Henrik, and James Levinsohn (2001) 'Merger policies and trade liberalisation', *Economic Journal*, 111, 244–76.

Irwin, Douglas A. (1991) 'Mercantilism as strategic trade policy: The Anglo-Dutch rivalry for the East India trade' *Journal of Political Economy*, 99, 1296–1314.

Kreps, David M., and José A. Scheinkman (1983) 'Quantity precommitment and Bertrand competition yield Cournot outcomes', *Bell Journal of Economics*, 14, 326–37.

Krishna, Kala (1989) 'Trade restrictions as facilitating practices', *Journal of International Economics*, 26, 251–70.

Krugman, Paul (1979) 'Increasing returns, monopolistic competition, and international trade', *Journal of International Economics*, 9, 469–79.

—— (1984) 'Import protection as export promotion: International competition in the presence of oligopoly and economies of scale', in H. Kierzkowski (ed.), *Monopolistic Competition in International Trade*. Oxford: Oxford University Press, 180–93.

—— (1987) 'Is free trade passé?', *Journal of Economic Perspectives*, 1, 131–44.

Krugman, Paul, and Alasdair Smith (eds), (1994) *Empirical Studies of Strategic Trade Policy*, Chicago: University of Chicago Press.

Leahy, Dermot, and J. Peter Neary (1999) 'Learning by doing, precommitment and infant industry promotion', *Review of Economic Studies*, 66, 447–74.

—— (2001) 'Robust rules for industrial policy in open economies', *Journal of International Trade and Economic Development*, 10, 393–409.

—— (2009) 'Multilateral subsidy games', *Economic Theory*, 41, 41–66.

Lommerud, Kjell Erik, and Lars Sørgard (2001) 'Trade liberalization and cartel stability', *Review of International Economics*, 9, 343–55.

Maggi, Giovanni (1996) 'Strategic trade policies with endogenous mode of competition', *American Economic Review*, 86, 237–58.

Markusen, James R. (1984) 'Multinationals, multi-plant economies, and the gains from trade', *Journal of International Economics*, 16, 205–26.

Mayer, Thierry, and Gianmarco I.P. Ottaviano (2007) *The Happy Few: The Internationalisation of European Firms. New Facts Based on Firm-Level Evidence*, Brussels: Bruegel.

Mrázová, Monika (2010) 'Trade negotiations when market access matters: Insights from oligopoly', mimeo, London School of Economics.

Neary, J. Peter (1994) 'Cost asymmetries in international subsidy games: Should governments help winners or losers?', *Journal of International Economics*, 37, 197–218.

—— (2002a) 'Foreign competition and wage inequality', *Review of International Economics*, 10, 680–93.

—— (2002b) 'International trade in general oligopolistic equilibrium', mimeo, University College Dublin; revised 2009.

—— (2003a) 'Globalization and market structure', *Journal of the European Economic Association*, 1, 245–71.

—— (2003b) 'Competitive versus comparative advantage', *The World Economy*, 26, 457–70.

—— (2007) 'Cross-border mergers as instruments of comparative advantage', *Review of Economic Studies*, 74, 1229–57.

—— (2009) 'Putting the "new" into new trade theory: Paul Krugman's Nobel Memorial Prize in Economics', *Scandinavian Journal of Economics*, 111, 217–50.

—— (2010) 'Two and a half theories of trade', *The World Economy*, 33, 1–19.

Neary, J. Peter, and Dermot Leahy (2000) 'Strategic trade and industrial policy towards dynamic oligopolies', *Economic Journal*, 110, 484–508.

Neary, J. Peter, and Dermot Leahy (2004) 'Revenue-constrained strategic trade and industrial policy', *Economics Letters*, 82, 409–14.

Neary, J. Peter, and Joe Tharakan (2006) 'Endogenous mode of competition in general equilibrium', Discussion Paper 5943, London: CEPR.

Norman, Victor D. (1990) 'Assessing trade and welfare effects of trade liberalization : A comparison of alternative approaches to CGE modelling with imperfect competition', *European Economic Review*, 34, 725–45.

Pinto, Brian (1986) 'Repeated games and the "reciprocal dumping" model of trade', *Journal of International Economics*, 20, 357–66.

Roberts, John, and Hugo Sonnenschein (1977) 'On the foundations of the theory of monopolistic competition', *Econometrica*, 45, 101–13.

Ruffin, Roy J. (2003) 'Oligopoly and trade: What, how much, and for whom?', *Journal of International Economics*, 60, 313–35.

Spencer, Barbara J., and James A. Brander (1983) 'International R&D rivalry and industrial strategy', *Review of Economic Studies*, 50, 707–22.

Trefler, D. (1995) 'The case of the missing trade and other mysteries', *American Economic Review*, 85, 1029–46.

Venables, Anthony J. (1985) 'Trade and trade policy with imperfect competition: The case of identical products and free entry', *Journal of International Economics*, 19, 1–19.

—— (1990) 'International capacity choice and national market games', *Journal of International Economics*, 29, 23–42.

Wood, Adrian (1994) *North–South Trade, Employment and Inequality: Changing Fortunes in a Skill-Driven World*. Oxford: Clarendon Press.

Yi, Sang-Seung (1996) 'Endogenous formation of customs unions under imperfect competition: Open regionalism is good', *Journal of International Economics*, 41, 153–77.

8
Multinational Firms
*James R. Markusen**

1 Introduction

Traditionally, foreign direct investment (FDI) was viewed as part of the capital account and the macroeconomics side of international economics. However, while FDI remains an important topic in international macroeconomics, we now understand that multinational firms play a major role in the modern world and must be considered as a vital part of the real production side of international economics. The standard figure one hears is that the sales of foreign affiliates of multinational corporations is now about five times to the total value of world trade.

This chapter reviews some of the new theoretical thinking about multinational firms as players in the world allocation of real economic activity that has developed in the last two decades or so. While the capital market side of multinationals and FDI remains of considerable interest and importance, I cannot consider it here and instead focus on the types of questions that are of interest to international trade economists. It is probably reasonable to imagine that the revolution that has resulted in the integration of the multinational firm into international trade theory began by confronting nagging facts that were fundamentally at odds with traditional views. These stylized facts are the starting point of my story.

2 Empirical Evidence as a Guide to Theory

Several decades ago, FDI was viewed as simply a capital movement. Consistent with the dominant theory of the day, Heckscher/Ohlin theory, capital should flow from capital rich, high income countries to poor capital scarce countries. That sums up what I was taught in graduate school and it seems that no one was paying any attention to data. During the 1980s, it became very obvious that the old view was at best inadequate and, at worst, simply wrong. Here is a list of

Table 8.1   Developed countries as source but also as destination for FDI.

Panel A: Developed countries' share of total world flows and stocks of FDI

	FDI inflows	FDI outflows
2007	0.66	0.85
	FDI inward stock	FDI outward stock
1990	0.73	0.92
2000	0.69	0.86
2007	0.69	0.84

Panel B: FDI flows and stocks as a share of gross fixed capital formation: developed and developing country totals

	FDI inflows	FDI outflows
2007		
Developed	0.16	0.21
Developing	0.13	0.06
	FDI inward stock	FDI outward stock
1990		
Developed	0.08	0.10
Developing	0.14	0.04
2000		
Developed	0.16	0.21
Developing	0.25	0.13
2007		
Developed	0.27	0.34
Developing	0.30	0.17

what are now well established facts that forced a rethinking and a search for a new approach.

(A) FDI flows primarily from high income developed countries to other high income countries, not from capital rich to capital poor countries.

Table 8.1 gives some evidence on this. The top panel gives flows of new FDI for 2007, expressed as the developed countries' share of total flows, in both inward and outward directions. These figures are followed by the corresponding shares for the stock of FDI in 1990, 2000, and 2007. Clearly, the developed countries are the major source of FDI, but what is less appreciated is that they are also the major recipients of FDI. The shares of stocks and investment flows which go to developed countries has trended down a bit over the last two decades, but it remains the major portion, at least two-thirds, of all FDI.

It can be argued that the developed countries also account for the overwhelming portion of world investment and income, so it is not surprising that we see these figures. The lower panel of table 8.1 thus expresses the stocks and flows for developed countries as a share of their gross fixed capital formation and does so for the developing countries as well. Here we see clearly that the developed countries are net outward investors and developing countries net recipients. Yet it is also clear that (a) outward and inward stocks and flows are fairly balanced in the developed countries and that (a) the stock inward shares for the developed countries have increased significantly and are not much different from those for the developing countries by 2007.

A related point is that there is often a geographical disconnect between real investments and the source of financing. Financing of a foreign plant or acquisition can come from home funds (e.g. retained earnings, debt issue, new equity), from host country sources and, indeed, often comes from third countries. The value of real FDI is not highly correlated with financial capital flows.

The conclusion that I and others have drawn from these numbers is that we must abandon the notion that FDI is easily characterized as simply a capital flow from capital rich to capital poor countries. That archaic view is at best misleading and likely to move us toward entirely wrong policy recommendations.

(B) Affiliate production is primarily for local sale and not for export back to the parent country.

Another myth that persists in the popular press, though I hope not in the economics literature, is that multinationals move production to poor countries to pay low wages and export the output back home. Table 8.2 breaks down sales of foreign manufacturing affiliates of U.S. parents data into local sales, export sales back to the United States and export sales to third countries for the 39

Table 8.2   Sales by U.S. manufacturing affiliates: exports to the United States and exports to third countries as shares in total sales and total exports, 2003..

	Local sales	Export sales to the US	Export sales to 3rd countries	Share of total export sales to 3rd countries
All countries in sample (39)	0.60	0.13	0.26	0.66
Ireland		NA	0.69	NA
Belgium	0.39	0.05	0.56	0.92
Greece	0.92	0.01	0.08	0.91
Netherlands	0.42	0.05	0.53	0.92
Portugal	0.59	0.02	0.38	0.94
Spain	0.59	0.02	0.39	0.96
Hong Kong	0.57	0.15	0.28	0.65
Indonesia	0.85	0.02	0.13	0.86
Malaysia	0.33	0.39	0.28	0.42
Philippines	0.28	0.35	0.38	0.52
Singapore	0.41	0.15	0.43	0.74
China	0.69	0.08	0.23	0.75
Canada	0.61	0.34	0.05	0.12
Mexico	0.54	0.31	0.15	0.32

countries for which publicly available data exist. In 2003, local sales account for 60 percent of all sales, but that still leaves a large portion for export. But columns 2 and 3 reveal that most of the exports do not go back to the United States, they go, instead, to third countries.

It is not obvious how to explain exports to third countries, often referred to as 'export-platform' sales or production. Table 8.2 thus adds some specific examples in order to give some clues. The first group is smaller EU countries, and here we see that United States manufacturing affiliates export a lot, but that virtually none of it goes back to the United States. Almost all of it is going to other EU countries. The last two countries, the NAFTA partner countries Canada and Mexico, show the opposite pattern. While they have large shares sold locally, exports go to the United States and not much to third countries. I believe that the European and NAFTA data are saying the same thing: most export platform sales are going to close by countries inside a regional trade block. They are in this sense, very similar to local sales.

Where we do see some significant export sales back to the United States is in the middle group of countries, developing Southeast Asia. These countries, which most business journalists probably think of as the low wage countries receiving investments to serve the United States market, nevertheless still display the pattern that a very significant part of sales is local sales. Note in particular the surprisingly high local sales figures for Indonesia and China. The highest figures in the group for the shares of total sales that go back to the United States are Malaysia at 39 percent and the Philippines at 35 percent.

(C) FDI is attracted to large markets and high income markets

The point about Indonesia and China having high numbers for local sales is reinforced in table 8.3, which shows that per capita investments are higher in large markets. This again fits well with the idea that production is largely for local or regional sale and, if there are fixed costs of setting up or acquiring new plants, then such investments are more likely to be observed in large and high income markets. If multinationals were simply in search of low wages to produce for export back home, then we should not observe firms choosing high income markets and there should be little relationship to host country size.

(D) There are high levels of intra-industry cross investment, particularly among the high income countries

Much has been written about intra-industry trade, or 'cross-hauling' over the last several decades. It seems to be less well known that exactly the same phenomenon is observed for affiliate sales. Table 8.4 shows data derived from the sales of affiliates of U.S. firms abroad and sales of foreign affiliates within the United States. These are expressed as Grubel/Lloyd intra-industry trade statistics.

Table 8.3   Country size as a determinant of inward FDI, 1993.

GDA per capita (U.S.$)	Country size	FDI per capita (U.S.$)
>5000	Large	242
	Small	54
2500–5000	Large	46
	Small	32
1200–2500	Large	33
	Small	31
600–1200	Large	11
	Small	3

Table 8.4   Grubel–Lloyd indices, all countries in sample.

	Affiliate sales 1997	Total trade 1997
Total manufacturing	82.9	84.4
Food products	73.5	86.1
Chemical products	86.8	86.5
Primary metals	71.5	68.5
Machinery	52.3	93.2
Electrical machinery	98.4	90.9
Transportation equip.	52.6	86.9
Other manufacturing	81.6	63.0
	Affiliate Sales 1997 (Total Manufacturing)	
All countries in sample	82.9	
Canada	52.0	
France	88.0	
Germany	80.7	
Netherlands	82.2	
Switzerland	30.7	
United Kingdom	98.9	
Australia	71.8	
Japan	46.0	
Other Asia-Pacific	23.6	
Latin America	16.6	

The Grubel/Lloyd statistics on affiliate sales are compared to figures on U.S. trade in the upper part of the table. The data is quite aggregated due to limitations on the affiliate sales data, but it is clear that intra-industry cross penetration by multinational firms is as high as that for trade.

The lower section of table 8.4 reports the numbers for some U.S. trading partners. The intra-industry affiliate sales indices are very high for European partners except Switzerland, which is a very heavy net outward investor given its small domestic market size. The figure for Japan is somewhat lower. Other Asia Pacific and Latin America have much lower numbers: the United States is a large net investor in these countries, which have little outward FDI.

Combined with earlier statistics, these numbers emphasize that a satisfactory theory of multinational firms must be consistent with large volumes of cross investment (intra-industry affiliate production) among similar large, high income countries. However it must also, of course, be able to explain the fact that firms from the high income countries are net investors in developing countries.

The weight of these statistics also suggests that much, if not most, FDI is 'horizontal' or 'market seeking'; that is, foreign affiliates of multinational firms are doing much the same things in foreign countries as they are at home. The same products and services are produced, generally for local and regional sale. 'Vertical' or 'resource seeking' (e.g., low cost labour) investments involve the fragmentation of the production process into stages, with stages located where the factors of production they use intensively are relatively cheap. While not the dominant motivation for FDI, vertical investments may nevertheless be quite important in developing countries.

3 Basic Conceptual Framework

Modern theory often begins with the premise that firms incur significant costs of doing business abroad relative to domestic firms. Therefore, for a firm to become a multinational, it must have offsetting advantages. A limited but very useful organizing framework for inquiring into the nature of these advantages was proposed by John Dunning (1977). Dunning proposed that there are three conditions needed for firms to have a strong incentive to undertake direct foreign investments.

(1) Ownership advantage: the firm must have a product or a production process such that the firm enjoys some market power advantage in foreign markets.
(2) Location advantage: the firm must have a reason to want to locate production abroad rather than concentrate it in the home country, especially if there are scale economies at the plant level.
(3) Internalization advantage: the firm must have a reason to want to exploit its ownership advantage internally, rather than license or sell its product/process to a foreign firm.

Internalization is often nowadays referred to as 'vertical integration', and the choice between an owned subsidiary versus licensing is often now referred to as the 'outsourcing decision', which is the same thing put the other way around.

The basic idea is shown in figure 8.1. A firm wanting to produce in a foreign country for local sale has a location decision between producing there and

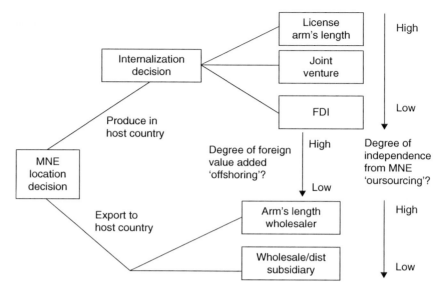

Figure 8.1   Decision tree for FDI.
Motive: serve host-country market (aka, horizontal, market-seeking).

exporting. We can refer to this as the 'offshoring' decision. If the multinational chooses foreign production it has a further choice between an owned subsidiary, perhaps some sort of joint venture, and an arm's length licensing contract. We can refer to this as the internalization or outsourcing decision, whether or not to produce outside the ownership boundaries of the firm.

Consider first ownership advantages. Evidence indicates that multinationals are related to R&D, marketing, scientific and technical workers, product newness and complexity and product differentiation (Caves, 2007, Markusen, 2002). This suggests that multinationals are firms which are intensive in the use of knowledge capital. This is a broad term which includes the human capital of the employees, patents, blueprints, procedures, and other proprietary knowledge, and finally marketing assets such as trademarks, reputations and brand names.

There are several reasons why the association of multinationals with knowledge-based assets, rather than physical capital, is appealing. First, the services of these assets may be easily used in distant plants, such as managers and engineers visiting those plants. Second and more subtly, knowledge capital often has a joint-input or non-rivalled property within the firm. Blueprints, chemical formulae, or even reputation capital may be very costly to produce, but once they are created, they can be supplied at relatively low cost to foreign production facilities without reducing the value or productivity of those assets in existing facilities.

The sources of location advantages are varied, primarily because they can differ between horizontal and vertical firms. Consider horizontal firms that produce the same goods and services in each of the several locations. Given the existence of plant-level scale economies, there are two principal sources of location advantages in a particular market. The first is the existence of trade costs between that market and the multinational enterprises' (MNEs) home country, in the form of transport costs (both distance and time), tariffs and quotas, and more intangible proximity advantages. The second source of location advantage, again following from the existence of plant level scale economies, is a large market in the potential host country. If that market is very small, it will not pay for a firm to establish a local production facility and the firm will instead service that market by exports.

The sources of location advantage for vertical multinationals are somewhat different. This type of investment is likely to be encouraged by low trade costs rather than by high trade costs and by factor price differences across countries. Low trade costs facilitate the intra-firm trade of intermediate and final goods and thus facilitate the geographic breaking up of the production chain.

Internalization advantages (or outsourcing disadvantages) are the most abstract of the three. The topic quickly gets into fundamental issues such as what is a firm, and why and how agency problems might be better solved within a firm rather than through an arm's length arrangement with a licensee or contractor. Basically, it is my view that internalization advantages often arise from the same joint-input, non-rivalled property of knowledge that create ownership advantages.

4 A Simple Monopoly Model of Location Choice

In this section, we explore the most basic model imaginable in order to get the crucial intuition as to the optimal international organization of a firm. Questions of outsourcing versus vertical integration (internalization) are left to a later section. There are two countries, home and foreign, and one monopoly firm in country h. There is a linear inverse demand for the product where the intercept is α and slope is $(1/L)$, L = market size. The price (p_i), quantity (X_i) and market size (L_i) in market $i = h, f$ are related as follows, where the second equation is firm revenues (R_i) in market i.

$$p_i = \alpha - X_i/L_i \quad R_i = p_i X_i = (\alpha - X_i/L_i)X_i. \tag{8.1}$$

There is a constant marginal cost c_i in market i and a specific trade cost t between markets. Profits before fixed costs for a plant producing in market i and selling in i and a plant producing in i and selling in j are given by

$$\pi_{ii} = (\alpha - X_{ii}/L_i)X_{ii} - c_i X_{ii} \quad \pi_{ij} = (\alpha - X_{ij}/L_j)X_{ij} - (c_i + t)X_{ij}. \tag{8.2}$$

Taking the first-order conditions for profit maximization given the optimal levels of domestic and export supply.

$$X_{ii} = \left(\frac{\alpha - c_i}{2}\right) L_i \quad X_{ij} = \left(\frac{\alpha - c_i - t}{2}\right) L_j. \tag{8.3}$$

The firm is headquartered in country h but may choose between three (discrete) alternatives. It can choose a single plant at home in country h, exporting to country f. We refer to this as a national or domestic firm (d). It can also have a single plant in country f, exporting back to h; a vertical (v) structure. Or it can be a horizontal multinational with plants in both countries (m). There is a firm specific fixed cost F, and a plant specific fixed cost G, where the latter must be incurred for each plant. If you substitute (8.3) into the two equations of (8.2) and add in fixed costs, you will find that the profits for each of the multinational firm's three choice are given as follows.

Profits of a national firm: one plant at home i exporting to j

$$\Pi^d = \Pi_{hh} + \Pi_{hf} = \left[\frac{\alpha - c_h}{2}\right]^2 L_h + \left[\frac{\alpha - c_h - t}{2}\right]^2 L_f - G - F. \tag{8.4}$$

Profits of a vertical firm: one plant in j exporting back to i

$$\Pi^v = \Pi_{fh} + \Pi_{ff} = \left[\frac{\alpha - c_f - t}{2}\right]^2 L_h + \left[\frac{\alpha - c_f}{2}\right]^2 L_f - G - F. \tag{8.5}$$

Profits of a horizontal firm: plants in both countries.

$$\Pi^m = \Pi_{hh} + \Pi_{ff} = \left[\frac{\alpha - c_h}{2}\right]^2 L_h + \left[\frac{\alpha - c_f}{2}\right]^2 L_f - 2G - F. \tag{8.6}$$

This is really a surprisingly rich little model. If you stare at these three equations long enough you will conclude that a two-plant horizontal structure is more likely as:

Both markets are large	characteristic of markets
Markets of similar size	characteristic of markets
Marginal costs are similar	characteristic of markets
Firm fixed costs > plant fixed costs	characteristic of industry
Transport/tariff costs are large	geography/policy

Large markets mean that the added fixed costs of a second plant outweigh the higher variable costs of exporting. The intuition behind the second and third results is that if one market is much larger and/or production costs much smaller, then it pays to put a single plant there and export to the smaller/costlier market. For the third result, note that if we raise F and lower G in the same amounts, this increases the profits of a type-m firm while leaving the profits of a type-d or type-v firm unchanged. Trade costs reduce the profits of a type-d or type-v firm but leave the profits of a type-m firm unchanged.

Despite its simplicity, this model fits the data well: horizontal firms will be important between similar, large (rich) markets in industries where knowledge capital is important (F is large relative to G).

A vertical structure is preferred to a national structure as:

Foreign market is larger
Foreign marginal cost is low
Low trade costs: vertical structure if $c_f < c_h$ even if country f is very small

As noted above, if you are going to have a single plant, put it in the large and/or low-cost market. Note however that the importance of the local market size disappears as trade costs go to zero. As t converges to zero, the relationship between (8.4) an (8.5) is determined entirely by which is the low-cost location, and note that the horizontal structure will never be chosen at $t = 0$ ($G > 0$). As t goes to zero, we can say that the vertical structure is chosen if and only if country f is the low-cost location.

An extension of this model to one firm headquartered in each country is straightforward (Horstmann and Markusen 1992). Duopoly in exports will occur if markets are small, trade costs are low, or if G is large relative to F (could proxy physical capital intensity). A duopoly in foreign production with both firms of type-h will occur under the opposite conditions. Asymmetries such as one country being significantly larger can lead to asymmetric outcomes: the firm headquartered in the large country is type-d, exporting to the small country, whereas the firm in the small country is type-m, with plants in both countries.

5 General Equilibrium Approaches: Horizontal Versus Vertical

The simple model above, and its extension to a duopoly situation with firms in both countries, is an excellent start and vehicle for developing intuition. However, it is lacking in the realism needed to form the basis for empirical work in several regards. First, it is a partial equilibrium with a single factor of production and no endogenous costs. Yet many theories of the multinational, casual and formal, involve different factor prices for different stages of production and different factor prices across countries. Second, there is no entry and exit of firms permitted, whereas this is surely a fundamental part of any satisfactory story. The headquarters countries of multinational firms are surely not randomly and exogenously distributed over countries.

Several early formal models moved the theory towards a more satisfactory approach, though in limited sorts of ways. An early formal model of vertical multinationals was Helpman (1984) and an early formal model of horizontal multinationals was Markusen (1984). Helpman's paper was a straightforward extension of the Heckscher/Ohlin model, with monopolistically competitive firms in one industry able to geographically fragment production into a skilled labour or capital intensive headquarters activity and a labour intensive production activity. Extensions are found in Helpman and Krugman (1985). Helpman and Helpman/Krugman's papers concentrated on the case of costless trade and showed that multinationals would arise outside of the factor price equalization set (defined for free trade in goods). Firms would essentially arbitrage factor price differences, locating headquarters in the capital abundant country and plants in the labour abundant country. Given the strong limiting assumptions, multinational firms would of course never arise between similar countries, a crucial and prominent feature of real world data.

Markusen's paper was also restrictive and took a very different approach. He assumed firm level fixed costs that were joint (non-rivalled) inputs across plants, and focused precisely on the case of two identical economies. Horizontal multinational firms with plants in both countries would arise due to the incentive to spread the fixed costs over multiple plants. Markusen showed the gains that arose from the introduction of multinationals and, of course, showed why FDI can arise between even identical countries. This was extended to a more satisfactory explicit treatment of duopoly competition in Horstmann and Markusen (1992) as mentioned in the previous section, though the latter remained a partial equilibrium treatment.

These developments left us with two disjointed approaches: firstly the horizontal approach, with multinationals as multi-plant firms motivated by firm level scale economies, and secondly the vertical approach, with multinationals as single-plant firms motivated by the incentive to geographically separate activities by factor intensities.

The literature was then given a push by the important empirical paper of Brainard (1995), who revived interest by explicitly considering whether or not foreign affiliates of U.S. multinationals are 'market seeking' (essentially horizontal firms) or 'resource seeking', essentially vertical firms. She provided strong evidence that the market seeking motive was dominant, consistent with our more casual discussion of the data in section 8.2.

Several formal theoretical papers endogenizing horizontal multinationals followed, particularly Markusen and Venables (1998, 2000). These papers used the world Edgeworth box as a tool following Helpman (1984) and Helpman and Krugman (1985), but Markusen and Venables arrive at conclusions essentially opposite to the latter two papers. In the horizontal approach, multinationals arise when countries are similar in both size and in relative factor endowments, whereas in the vertical approach they arise when countries are sufficiently dissimilar in relative factor endowments.

6 The Knowledge–Capital Model

While it somewhat awkward for the author of this chapter to say so, exten-sive citations and significant empirical research suggest that the next important development was Markusen's knowledge–capital model. The full definition of the model is found in Markusen (2002) – (several working papers in the mid-1990s were left unpublished).

The knowledge–capital model is a general equilibrium approach that incorpo-rates both horizontal and vertical motives for multinationals. The configuration of firms that arises in equilibrium depends on country characteristics (size, rel-ative size, and relative endowments), industry characteristics (firm versus plant level fixed costs or scale economies) and trade costs.

There are two goods, X and Y and two factors of production, skilled and unskilled labour, S and L. There are two countries i and j. Y is produced with constant returns by a competitive industry and unskilled labour intensive. X is produced with increasing returns by imperfectly competitive firms. There are both firm level and plant-level fixed costs and trade costs and firm level fixed costs result in the creation of 'knowledge-based assets'.

There are three defining assumptions for the knowledge–capital model.

(1) Fragmentation: the location of knowledge-based assets may be fragmented from production. Any incremental cost of supplying services of the asset to a single foreign plant versus the cost to a single domestic plant is small.
(2) Skilled labour intensity: knowledge-based assets are skilled labour intensive relative to final production.
(3) Jointness: the services of knowledge-based assets are (at least partially) joint (non-rivalled) inputs into multiple production facilities. The added cost of a second plant is small compared to the cost of establishing a firm with a single plant.

There are three possible firm 'types' that can exist in equilibrium in either country (so six firm types in all), and there is free entry and exist into and out of firm types.

Type m – horizontal multinationals which maintain plants in both countries, with headquarters located in country i or j.

Type d – national firms that maintain a single plant and headquarters in country i or j. Type d_i firms may or may not export to the other country.

Type v – vertical multinationals that maintain a single plant in one country, and headquarters in the other country. Type v_i firms may or may not export back to their headquarters country.

Various assumptions can be made about factor intensities and they do make some quantitative difference to the results. The ones used to generate the diagrams attached below assume that the skilled labour intensity of activities are:

[headquarters only] > [integrated X] > [plant only] > [Y]

When countries are similar in size and relative endowments, and trade costs are moderate to high, horizontal firms will have the advantage over type d or type v. When countries differ substantially in relative endowments, vertical firms will have an advantage over type n firms, because they can locate the headquarters and plant independently on the basis of factor prices.

As most readers know from the monopolistic competition literature, there is typically a 'fudge' in free entry and exit models via the assumption that the number of firms is a continuous variable. This allows the zero profit condition, which is associated with the variable for the number of firms active in equilibrium, to be expressed as a weak inequality as discussed below. To put it another way, the assumption that the number of firms is a continuous variable turns an awkward integer programming problem into a continuous problem which can be easily attacked by analytical and numerical methods.

A second feature of free entry and exit approach is that it is modelled as a non-linear complementarity problem rather than as a game. The full model is thus a set of non-linear weak inequalities with associated non-negative complementary variables. If a weak inequality holds as a strict equality in equilibrium, the associated complementary variable is positive. If a weak inequality holds as a strict inequality in equilibrium, the complementary variable is zero.

Two factors make this type of model resist attack by traditional analytical techniques. First, even a basic model has lots of dimensions (inequalities and unknowns), typically more than 30, with the one shown later having 47. Second, which weak inequalities hold as strict equalities and which as strict inequalities are determined in the solution to the model. As a consequence, numerical simulation techniques are used to solve the models (e.g., Berstrand and Egger (2007), Markusen and Venables (1998, 2000)). In general, the models have subsets of inequalities something like the following:

Pricing inequalities	Complementary variable
Price ≤ marginal cost	Competitive good outputs
Marginal revenue ≤ marginal cost	Outputs of X producers
Markup revenues ≤ fixed costs	Number of firms of a given type

Market clearing inequalities	Complementary variables
Demand ≤ Supply (goods)	Goods prices
Demand ≤ Supply (factors)	Factor prices
Demand ≤ Supply (fixed costs)	Price of fixed costs (e.g. a factory)

Auxiliary equations	Complementary variables
Markup equations	Markups
Income balance equations	Incomes

In order to understand the logic of complementarity, just consider the first line, price and marginal cost in the competitive industry Y. If the inequality is strict in equilibrium, then the good is unprofitable and is not produced in equilibrium ($Y = 0$). For a supply/demand inequality, if supply strictly exceeds demand in equilibrium, then the good is free and its equilibrium price is zero ($p = 0$).

Let's look at a simple example to help understand this approach to general equilibrium problems. Take a simple economy producing a homogeneous good Y with constant returns and perfect competition and a differentiated good X produced with increasing returns to scale. There is a single factor of production L with a wage rate w that we will use as numeraire giving it a price of 1 ($w = 1$). Thus L gives total income. p_x and p_y are the prices of X and Y. Let the utility function be Cobb–Douglas between Y and X and let there be a Dixit/Stiglitz 'love of variety' approach to the differentiated X goods; α is strictly between 0 and 1 and σ denotes the elasticity of substitution between X varieties.

With symmetric demand for the X varieties and also identical cost functions for producing them, the model is characterized by symmetry: any X good that is produced will be produced in the same amount and sell for the same price. Let n, which is endogenous, denote the number of X goods produced in equilibrium. The utility function and the budget constraint are then given by

$$U = \left[\sum_i X_i^\alpha \right]^{\frac{0.5}{\alpha}} Y^{0.5} \quad \sigma = \frac{1}{1-\alpha} \quad L = np_x X + p_y Y. \tag{8.7}$$

If you solve the optimization problem, the consumer's demands for X varieties and Y are

$$Y = \frac{L}{2p_y} \quad X_i = p_i^{-\sigma} \left[\sum_i p_i^{1-\sigma} \right]^{-1} \frac{L}{2} \quad nX = \frac{L}{2p_x}. \tag{8.8}$$

The so-called 'large group' assumption in monopolistic competition is that there are many varieties and so each individual X firm takes the term in square brackets in (8.8) as a constant. Thus the elasticity of demand (defined as positive) for an individual good is just σ and the optimal markup for a producer is then $1/\sigma$. You can show that marginal revenue is given by $p_x(1 - 1/\sigma)$.

Marginal costs in units of labour for producing X and Y are mc_x and mc_y and fc_x denotes the fixed cost of a new X variety. Free entry implies zero profits and this in turn implies that revenues minus marginal costs are equal to fixed costs. But the former must equal mark up revenues, and so the free entry condition can be written compactly as mark up revenues equal fixed costs. We can think of this as a pricing equation for firm entry and it is associated with the variable n, the number of firms in equilibrium. This is the general equilibrium model.

Inequality	Definition	Complementary	Variable
$p_y \leq mc_y$	Pricing for Y	Y	(8.9)
$p_x(1 - 1/\sigma) \leq mc_x$	Pricing for X	X	(8.10)
$(p_x/\sigma)X \leq fc_x$	Pricing for n (free entry)	n	(8.11)
$L/(2p_y) \leq Y$	Demand/supply Y	p_y	(8.12)
$L/(2p_x) \leq nX$	Demand/supply X varieties	p_x	(8.13)
$(mc_y)Y + n(mc_x)X + n(fc_x) = L$	Demand/supply L	w	(8.14)

where w is the wage rate. We have chosen this as numeraire, so $w = 1$ and the last equation can be dropped. This is a consequence of Walras's law: if the first five equations hold, then the last one must hold as well.

This model is easily solved analytically, assuming that all weak inequalities hold as strict equalities, which they will in this very simple case. (8.9) solves for p_y and then (8.12) solves for Y. Multiply (8.10) through by X, and then (8.10) and (8.11) together solve for X and then p_x. n can then be solved for from (8.13). The solution values are given by

$$X = (\sigma - 1)\frac{fc_x}{mc_x} \quad n = \frac{L}{2\sigma fc_x} \quad Y = \frac{L}{2mc_y}. \tag{8.15}$$

If we expand L, making the economy bigger, note that the X sector expands only through adding new varieties of X, not through any changes in the output of any good that is produced.

Consider now a simple experiment in which we have two absolutely identical countries like this. Trade in X is prohibitively costly, but horizontal multinationals can enter, establishing plants in both countries for a fixed cost βfc_x, where $2 > \beta > 1$; that is, there are firm level scale economies, with the costs of a two-plant firm being less than double the fixed costs of a one-plant-firm. We can exploit symmetry in the solution (p_x and p_y will be the same in each country): with multinationals allowed for the identical countries, all you have to do to inequalities (8.2)–(8.9) is replace fc_x with βfc_x and replace L with $2L$ (X and Y are now the total two-country output of an X variety and total Y output respectively). If you work through it, you will get the equilibrium values:

$$X = (\sigma - 1)\beta \frac{fc_x}{mc_x} \quad n = \frac{L}{\beta \sigma fc_x} \quad Y = \frac{L}{mc_y}. \tag{8.16}$$

Given $2 > \beta > 1$, note that output per firm increases (increased technical effi-cient) and that the number of varieties available to consumers from domestic and foreign firms increases in the ratio $(2/\beta) > 1$. If $\beta = 1.5$, for example, then n increases in the proportion $(4/3)$. If you then take these results back to the utility function, consumers in each country are strictly better off with the multi-national firms. Two-country utility (half to each) can be written as follows using (8.9):

$$U = (nX^{\alpha})^{\frac{0.5}{\alpha}} Y^{0.5} = (n^{1-\alpha} n^{\alpha} X^{\alpha})^{\frac{0.5}{\alpha}} Y^{0.5} = n^{\frac{1-\alpha}{\alpha} 0.5} \left[(nX)^{0.5} Y^{0.5} \right]. \tag{8.17}$$

Note in comparing (8.15) and (8.16) that the values nX and Y exactly double, so each country individually gets the same values of nX and Y (half the totals) they had before multinationals were introduced. The term in square bracket on the right-hand side of (8.17) is unchanged for a single country with multinationals. Denoting the autarky value of n as n_a and then, since the new value is $n_m = (2/\beta)n_a$, the ratio of utility in the multinational regime to autarky is given by

$$\frac{U_m}{U_n} = (n_m/n_a)^{\frac{1-\alpha}{\alpha} 0.5} = (2/\beta)^{\frac{1-\alpha}{\alpha} 0.5} > 1. \tag{8.18}$$

If $\beta = 1.5$ and $\alpha = 0.75$ (an elasticity of substitution of 4 between X varieties), then this ratio is 1.05: there is a 5 percent gain in per capita welfare (10 percent gain in utility from X) from introducing horizontal multinationals. Horizontal multinationals improve welfare by exploiting firm level scale economies; that is, the non-rivalled property of knowledge based assets.

While there are other approaches to solving a simple model analytically, the methods outlined here are very robust to the addition of more countries, more factors of production and more firm types (national, horizontal multinationals, vertical multinationals). Thus this has been the approach taken (e.g., devel-oped by Markusen and Venables 1998, 2000, Markusen 2002, and Egger and Bergstrand 2007) in numerical modelling of much more complex models.

Figures 8.2–8.4 attached are drawn from Markusen (2002) and shown the value of foreign affiliate sales over the world Edgeworth box (see Bergstrand and Egger (2007) for a three-factor three-country version). The three figures are for a case with moderate trade costs. Foreign affiliate production is defined as the sales of a firm's foreign plant and does not count its home plant if it has one (a vertical firm has only a foreign plant). In the centre of the box in figure 8.2 when countries are identical, all firms are horizontal multinationals with identical home and foreign plants and so half of all world production is affiliate production. But the highest levels of affiliate sales occur when one country is small and skilled labour abundant. In that case, in the extreme all world production of X can be affiliate sales: all firms are vertical with their headquarters in the small, skilled labour abundant country and their single plant in another country. The latter

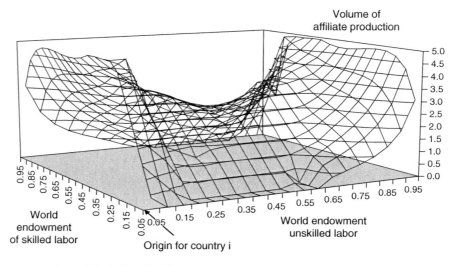

Figure 8.2   Value of affiliate production over the world Edgeworth box.

occurs both because production is unskilled labour intensive and because it is advantageous to locate the single plant in the large market due to trade costs.

Figure 8.3 shows the effect of restricting the model to no vertical firms (a firm must have a single plant together with its headquarters) and assuming that fixed and variable costs have the same factor intensity (skilled labour intensive relative to Y). Multinationals, when they exist, are horizontal, and are most important when countries are similar in both size and in relative endowments. When countries are very different in size or in endowments, the advantage goes to single-plant national firms located in the large and/or skilled labour abundant country, exporting to the other country.

Figure 8.4 shows the effect of eliminating firm level scale economies: that is, the fixed costs of a two-plant firm are equal to the total fixed costs of two single-plant firms. The assumption that fixed costs are skilled labour intensive relative to production costs is reintroduced. The effect of this is to eliminate horizontal multinationals in equilibrium. When countries are relatively similar in size and/or relative endowments there is no multinational production. If we also lowered trade costs to zero we would essentially have Helpman's model (1984).

Trade costs have an ambiguous role in this model. Lower trade costs would discourage horizontal production as firms choose cheaper exporting, so the mountain in figure 8.3 diminishes. Lower trade costs encourage vertical production, however, so liberalization or technical improvements in transport raise the cliffs in figure 8.4. This prediction is exploited in empirical specifications.

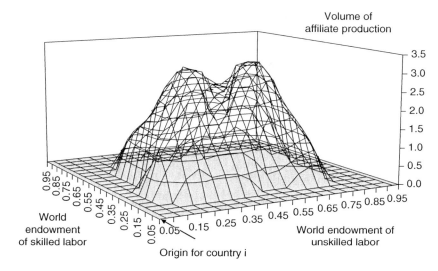

Figure 8.3   Affiliate production over the world Edgeworth box: the horizontal model.

There are, of course, many variations on and extensions to these ideas, but space precludes a more thorough treatment here. One thing that is badly needed is more work on multi-country models. Articles by Bergstrand and Egger (2007), Blonigen et al. (2007), Ekholm, Forslid and Markusen (2007), and Yeaple (2003) are a start.

7   Recent Empirical Evidence

Again, I cannot hope to review an extensive and relatively young empirical literature here. More will be done in the following chapter and I will confine my remarks largely to evidence relating to the ideas discussed above. A good deal of empirical evidence is found in Caves (2007) and Markusen (2002). Caves gives a broad ranging study while Markusen is more narrowly focused on formal models that tie multinationals into the theory of international trade.

Brainard (1997) is an important paper as noted above. It gave convincing evidence for the first time that FDI is not closely related to factor endowments (further discrediting the simple cost-of-capital approach), but much more closely related to country similarity. The ratio of foreign affiliate production to home exports for the host market is increasing in trade costs, increasing in corporate scales economies, and decreasing in plant scale economies. Only the proportion of affiliate production which is destined for export is related to factor endowments, but that of course makes sense from the vertical motive for foreign production.

Since Brainard's paper, the introduction of newer theory has proved a good starting place for empirical analysis. Figures 8.1–8.4 provide, if you like, a 'reduced form' for thinking about the implications of the theory for econometric analysis. They suggest how the pattern of bilateral affiliate activity between two countries should be related to countries' sizes, differences in country sizes, differences in relative factor endowments, and trade and investment costs. It gives a guide to interrelationships among these factors, such as that between relative endowment differences and trade costs shown in figure 8.4.

Carr, Markusen and Maskus (2001) found good support for the knowledge–capital model, although there is no 'horse race' against alternative models. In subsequent work, Markusen and Maskus (see Markusen 2002) found strong support for the horizontal model, virtually no support for a pure vertical model, and could not reject the pure horizontal model in favour of the more complex knowledge–capital model. Combined with the Brainard paper, these results give strong confirmation to simple summary statistics that the vertical model, the most natural incorporation of the multinational firm into international trade theory, is a very poor fit.

However, more recent and more sophisticated work by Braconier, Norbäck and Urban (2006) and Davies (2007) have discovered more evidence in favour of vertical production, and have found it where Markusen's knowledge capital model suggests it should be found. The addition of physical capital and a third country in Bergstrand and Egger (2007) clears up a number of issues, as does

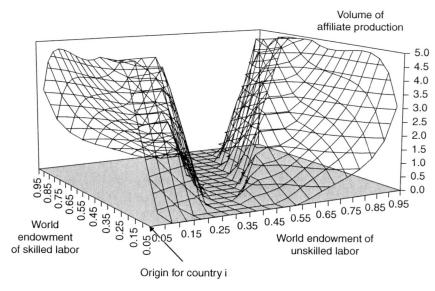

Figure 8.4   Affiliate production over the world Edgeworth box: the vertical model.

Blonigen (2001). Readers can find an empirical analysis of the horizontal model extended to heterogeneous firms in Helpman, Melitz, and Yeaple (2005). A start on multi-country models and the phenomenon of export platform FDI discussed in connection with table 8.2 are found in Bergstrand and Egger (2007), Blonigen et al. (2007), Ekholm, Forslid and Markusen (2007).

8 Outsourcing Versus Internalization (Vertical Integration)

The final node in the decision tree shown in figure 8.1 concerns the choice to maintain ownership of a foreign production facility or to outsource/license a foreign firm to produce for the multinational. While this is an old question in the international business literature, it has been only in the last two decades that it has attracted interests from international trade economists. There are two principal approaches and I will try to present simple versions here.

Some of the first formal models of the internalization decision were published in the late 1980s and the 1990s, and draw their empirical motivation from the strong association of multinationality with knowledge-based assets such as those described in the previous paragraph (again, see Caves (2007) and Markusen (2002)). On the one hand, these assets (or the services thereof) are easily transferred overseas, such as providing a blueprint, chemical formula, or procedure to a foreign plant. On the other hand, the same characteristics that make it easy to transfer these assets makes them easily learned by foreign managers, agents, or licensees. Once the agent sees the blueprint or license, he or she could defect to produce the product in a new firm. Knowledge is non-excludable, at least after some period of time. Relevant papers include Horstmann and Markusen (1987, 1996), Ethier and Markusen (1996), Glass and Saggi (2001), Forsfuri, Motta and Rønde (2001) and Markusen (2001). A related but rather different approach is taken in Ethier's early paper (Ethier 1986).

About the same time as this last set of papers appeared, an important advancement to the internalization question was being developed by several authors, including Antrás (2003, 2005), Grossman and Helpman (2004), and Feenstra and Hanson (2004). All of these authors substitute the term outsourcing for the term internalization. Their approach is sometimes termed the 'property rights' approach to the firm after contributions by Grossman and Hart (1986) and Hart and Moore (1990), following earlier contributions of Williamson (1985) and others in the international business literature.

The new literature combines a number of separate elements that together produce a coherent model that offers clear empirical predictions. The first element (in no particular order) is the assumption that production requires 'relation specific investments', meaning that a multinational and a foreign individual or firm must prior to production, incur sunk investments, that have no outside value if the relationship breaks down. The second element is the assumption of incomplete contracting: certain things are simply not contractible, or alternatively, any contract on these items is not enforceable. The assumptions of sunk investments and non-contractibility lead to a third problem, which is ex post 'hold up'. What happens after production occurs cannot be contracted ex ante, and so each party has some ability to negotiate ex post and to prevent the other party from fully utilizing the output. The final element of this approach is the notion of ownership, necessary in order to distinguish an owned subsidiary from an arm's length supplier. The property rights approach defines the owner of the foreign production facility as the party which has residual rights of control; that is, the party which owns any output or other assets of the firm in the event that bargaining breaks down.

The first set of papers, focusing on the non-excludability of knowledge which is learned by a local agent or manager, can be explained by a simple version of Markusen (2002). To economize on things, we will deal only on the issue of foreign production versus exports in order to focus clearly on the role of non-excludability of knowledge.

(1) The MNE introduces (or attempts to introduce) a new product every second time period. Two periods are referred to as a 'product cycle'. A product is economically obsolete at the end of the second period (end of the product cycle).

(2) The probability of the MNE successfully developing a new product in the next cycle is $1/(1+r)$ if there is a product in the current cycle, zero otherwise (i.e., once the firm fails to develop a new product, it is out of the game). The probability of having a product in the third cycle is $1/(1+r)^2$, etc. Ignore discounting.

(3) The MNE can serve a foreign market by exporting, or by creating a subsidiary to produce in the foreign market. Because of the costs of exporting, producing in the foreign country generates the most potential rents.

(4) But any local manager learns the technology in the first period of a cycle and can quit (defect) to start a rival firm in the second period. Similarly, the MNE can defect, dismissing the manager and hiring a new one in the second period. The (defecting) manager can only imitate, not innovate and compete in the next product cycle.

(5) No binding contracts can be written to prevent either partner from undertaking such a defection. I will assume that the MNE either offers a self-enforcing contract or exports.

R – Total per-period licensing rents from the foreign country.
E – Total per-period exporting rents ($E < R$).
F – Fixed cost of transferring the technology to a foreign partner. These include physical capital costs, training of the local manager, and so forth.

T – Training costs of a new manager that the MNE incurs if it dismisses the first one (i.e., if the MNE defects).

G – Fixed cost that the manager must incur if he/she defects. This could include costs of physical capital, etc.

L_i – Licensing or royalty fee charged to the subsidiary in period i ($i = 1,2$).

V – Rents earned by the manager in one product cycle: $V = (R - L_1) + (R - L_2)$.

V/r – Present value of rents to the manager of maintaining the relationship.

The manager ('a' for agent) has an individual rationality constraint (IR): the manager must earn non-negative rents. The manager also has an incentive-compatibility constraint (IC): the manager must not want to defect in the second period: second-period earnings plus the present value of earning from future products (if any) must exceed the single-period one-shot return from defecting.

$$(R - L_1) + (R - L_2) \geq 0 \quad IR_a, \tag{8.19}$$

$$(R - L_2) + V/r \geq (R - G) \quad IC_a, \tag{8.20}$$

where $V = (R - L_1) + (R - L_2)$ is the present value to the manager of the future rents, if there are any. $(R - G)$ is the payoff to unilaterally defecting.

The MNE similarly has an individual rationality constraint (IR): the MNE must earn non-negative rents. The MNE also has an incentive-compatibility constraint: the MNE must not want to defect (fire the manager) in the second period.

$$L_1 + L_2 - F \geq 2E \quad IR_m, \tag{8.21}$$

$$L_2 \geq R - T \quad IC_m. \tag{8.22}$$

Combine the IC constraints.

$$R - T \leq L_2 \leq G + V/r. \tag{8.23}$$

Firm's objective is to minimize V subject to this incentive compatibility. Making V as small as possible subject to (8.20) holding gives us:

$$2R - L_1 - L_2 = V = r(R - T - G) \geq 0 \quad \text{(rent share to the manager).} \tag{8.24}$$

Our first result is then that, if $R \leq G + T$, the MNE captures all rents in a product cycle, henceforth referred to as a rent–capture (RC) contract, and the agent's IR^a constraint holds with equality. This occurs when

(1) The market is relatively small.
(2) Defection costs for the MNE (T) are high.
(3) Defection costs for the manager (G) are high.

If $R > T + G$, there is no single-product fee schedule that will not cause one party to defect. In this case, the manager's IR^a constraint does not hold as a strict equality: that is, the MNE shares rents with the manager and the amount of rent sharing is given in (8.24). This is a credible commitment to a long-term relationship that we could think of as a subsidiary. However, it is costly for the multinational and if it gets too costly then the multinational will choose exporting instead: dissipating some rent is preferable to sharing a larger total. This is the inefficiency caused by the lack of contractibility of knowledge.

As noted above, the 'property-right' approach works rather differently. Here, I present a much simplified version on Antrás (2003). The idea is that the firm and the local agent must make ex-ante investments that are not contractible. The multinational invests capital K and the agent invests labour L. Ex post, they divide the surplus via the Nash bargaining solution, with the firm getting share *s* and the agent the share $(1 - s)$. As many or most readers know, the equilibrium share is a function of each party's 'bargaining power' and its outside option. Antrás assumes the firm has a bargaining power parameter of at least 1/2. Ownership is defined as a property right to anything left (e.g., an intermediate input) in the event of bargaining breakdown.

Under outsourcing, denoted with the subscript '*o*', any intermediate output produced is worthless to both in the event of a breakdown. Thus the outside option of both the firm and the agent is zero even though the agent owns what is left. Under FDI, denoted with the subscript '*v*' for vertical integration, the multinational has some use for what is left and so has an outside option. If $\varphi > 1/2$ denotes the multinational's bargaining power and δ denotes the share of the total potential rent (under a successful contract) remaining after breakdown the Nash solution gives the multinational the following shares:

$$s_o = \phi \quad s_v = \delta + \phi(1 - \delta) \quad sv > so > 1/2. \tag{8.25}$$

The second equation is a common result in the bargaining literature: the firm gets its outside option, plus its bargaining share of the total minus the sum of the outside options (the agent's outside option is zero).

Let revenues from the project be given by:

$$R = \left(\frac{K}{\beta}\right)^{\beta} \left(\frac{L}{\gamma}\right)^{\gamma} \quad \beta + \gamma < 1. \tag{8.26}$$

Knowing that there will be holdup and ex-post bargaining with equilibrium share *s*, the firm and the agent respectively maximize the following when choosing the input they control:

$$\max_{K} s \left(\frac{K}{\beta}\right)^{\beta} \left(\frac{L}{\gamma}\right)^{\gamma} - K \qquad \text{Firm chooses } K, \tag{8.27}$$

$$\max_{L} (1 - s) \left(\frac{K}{\beta}\right)^{\beta} \left(\frac{L}{\gamma}\right)^{\gamma} - L \quad \text{Agent chooses } L. \tag{8.28}$$

The first-order conditions for capital (chosen by the firm) and labour (chosen by the agent) are respectively given by:

$$\left(\frac{K}{\beta}\right)^{\beta-1}\left(\frac{L}{\gamma}\right)^{\gamma} = \frac{1}{s} = (1+t_k) \quad t_k \equiv \frac{(1-s)}{s}, \tag{8.29}$$

$$\left(\frac{K}{\beta}\right)^{\beta}\left(\frac{L}{\gamma}\right)^{\gamma-1} = \frac{1}{1-s} = (1+t_l) \quad t_l \equiv \frac{s}{(1-s)}. \tag{8.30}$$

The last equality in each line is just to emphasize that the agent problem here is much like having a tax on capital of $t_k = (1-s)/s$ and a tax on labour of $t_l = s/(1-s)$. Indeed, the first-order conditions are exactly those of a single integrated firm maximizing profits subject to these input taxes. Given (8.25), vertical integration is effectively a lower tax on capital than outsourcing, and vertical integration is effectively a higher tax on labour. The two first-order conditions can be solved to yield:

$$\frac{K}{L} = \frac{s}{1-s}\frac{\beta}{\gamma} \quad \frac{L}{\gamma} = \frac{1-s}{s}\frac{K}{\beta}. \tag{8.31}$$

These can be substituted back into the first-order conditions to give the equilibrium inputs:

$$K = \beta\left[s^{1-\gamma}(1-s)^{\gamma}\right]^{\frac{1}{1-\beta-\gamma}}, \tag{8.32}$$

$$L = \gamma\left[s^{1-\beta}(1-s)^{\beta}\right]^{\frac{1}{1-\beta-\gamma}}. \tag{8.33}$$

The profit level for the firm in (8.27) is then given by:

$$\Pi = (1-\beta)\left[s^{1-\gamma}(1-s)^{\gamma}\right]^{\frac{1}{1-\beta-\gamma}}. \tag{8.34}$$

The choice between vertical integration or outsourcing then reduces to evaluating the ratio

$$\frac{\Pi_V}{\Pi_o} = \left[\frac{s_V^{1-\gamma}(1-s_V)^{\gamma}}{s_o^{1-\gamma}(1-s_o)^{\gamma}}\right]^{\frac{1}{1-\beta-\gamma}}. \tag{8.35}$$

Given the assumption that $sv > so \geq 1/2$, it is true that $s_V(1-s_V) < s_o(1-s_o)$: the function reaches a maximum value of $1/4$ at $s = 1/2$ and falls off as s grows larger (or shrinks for that matter). As the share on labour becomes small (the industry is very labour intensive), (8.35) reduces to

$$\gamma \Rightarrow 0 \quad \frac{\Pi_V}{\Pi_o} \quad \Rightarrow \quad \frac{s_V}{s_o} > 1. \tag{8.36}$$

and so vertical integration is chosen by a capital intensive firm. At a value of $\gamma = 1/2$, implying a value of $\beta < 1/2$, we have:

$$\gamma = \frac{1}{2} \quad \frac{\Pi_V}{\Pi_O} = \left[\frac{s_V(1 - s_V)}{s_O(1 - s_O)} \right]^{\frac{0.5}{1 - \beta - \gamma}} < 1. \tag{8.37}$$

Thus outsourcing is chosen by a labour intensive firm. Antrás then presents empirical evidence, using intra-firm versus arm's length trade, that gives good support to his model. A nice extension of this idea to the concept of a product cycle is Antrás (2005).

This subfield is sufficiently young that there is not much work trying to compare the two approaches. In a new working paper, Chen, Horstmann and Markusen (2010) try to do this. They have two types of capital: knowledge capital, which is only partially excludable after one time period, and physical capital, which is fully excludable in the property-rights tradition. Multinational ownership of the subsidiary, meaning ownership of the physical capital, protects the knowledge capital by making it impossible for the agent to defect. But ownership by the multinational creates a moral hazard problem for the agent, resulting in the agent failing to properly use and maintain the physical capital. This model thus has the non-excludability property of the somewhat older literature wedded to the fundamental tension of the newer literature: vertical integration avoids holdup but suffers from weak incentives for the manager/ agent.

9 Summary

This chapter has provided an overview of the microeconomic approach to the multinational firm and how it has been integrated with trade theory over the last decade (or at most two). Much needs to be done. Work on multi-country models is in its infancy and clearly multinational firms are making multi-country decisions.

Much needs to be done integrating the theory of the multinational with so called new economic geography models. The latter spend a lot of time on multiple equilibria and in particular the tendency for symmetric equilibria to be unstable. Yet this instability often disappears if horizontal multinationals are allowed, or rather added, to the models. It is rather astonishing that multinationals are essentially completely ignored in the new economic geography even though the industries that they are focussing on are often dominated by multinationals.

A lot can be done interfacing the outsourcing decision with the location decision for firms. Both are often interrelated due to the non-excludability property of knowledge capital: the same characteristic that leads firms to exploit knowledge-based assets abroad creates problems of agent opportunism and asset dissipation. Much more empirical work on this relationship would be most welcome indeed.

Note

* University of Colorado, Boulder, and University College Dublin.

References

Antrás, Pol (2003) 'Firms, contracts, and trade structure', *Quarterly Journal of Economics* 118(4), 1375–1418.

—— (2005) 'Incomplete contracts and the product cycle', *American Economic Review* 95(3), 1054–71.

Bergstrand, Jeffrey H., and Peter Egger (2007) 'A knowledge-and-physical-capital model of international trade flows, foreign direct investment, and multinational enterprises'. *Journal of International Economics* 73(2), 278–308.

Blonigen Bruce A., Ronald B. Davies, Glenn R. Waddell and Helen T. Naughton (2007) 'FDI in space: Spatial autoregressive relationships in foreign direct investment', *European Economic Review* 51, 1303–25.

Blonigen, Bruce A. (2001) 'In search of substitution between foreign production and exports', *Journal of International Economics* 53, 81–104.

Braconier, Henrik, Pehr-Johan Norbäck and Dieter Urban (2005) 'Reconciling the evidence on the knowledge–capital model', *Review of International Economics* 13(4), 770–86.

Brainard, S. Lael (1997) 'An empirical assessment of the proximity–concentration tradeoff between multinational sales and trade', *American Economic Review* 87(4), 520–44.

Carr, David L., James R. Markusen and Keith E. Maskus (2001), 'Estimating the knowledge–capital model of the multinational enterprise', *American Economic Review* 91(3): 693–708.

Caves, Richard E. (2007) *Multinational Enterprise and Economic Analysis*. 3rd edition. Cambridge: Cambridge University Press.

Chen, Yongmin, Ignatius J. Horstmann and James R. Markusen (2011) 'Physical capital, knowledge capital, and the choice between FDI and Outsourcing', forthcoming in *Canadian Journal of Economics*.

Davies, Ronald B. (2008) 'Hunting high and low for vertical FDI'. *Review of International Economics* 16(2), 250–67.

Dunning, John H. (1977) 'The determinants of international production', *Oxford Economic Papers*, 25(3), 289–336.

Ekholm, Karolina, James R. Markusen and Rikard Forslid (2007) 'Export-platform foreign direct investment', *Journal of the European Economic Association* 5, 776–95.

Ethier, Wilfred, J. (1986) 'The multinational firm', *Quarterly Journal of Economics* 101, 805–33.

Ethier, Wilfred J., and James R. Markusen (1996) 'Multinational firms, technology diffusion and trade', *Journal of International Economics* 41, 1–28.

Feenstra, Robert C., and Gordon H. Hanson (2005) 'Ownership and control in outsourcing to China: estimating the property-rights theory of the firm', *Quarterly Journal of Economics* 120, 729–61.

Fosfuri, Andrea, Massimo Motta and Thomas Rønde (2001) 'Foreign direct investments and spillovers through workers' mobility', *Journal of International Economics* 53, 205–22.

Glass, Amy J., and Kamal Saggi (2002) 'Multinational firms and technology transfer', *Scandinavian Journal of Economics* 104, 495–513.

Grossman, Sanford J., and Oliver D. Hart (1986) 'The costs and benefits of ownership: a theory of vertical and lateral integration', *Journal of Political Economy* 94, 691–719.

Grossman Gene M., and Elhanan Helpman (2004) 'Managerial incentives and the international organization of production', *Journal of International Economics* 63, 237–62.

Hanson, Gordon H., Raymond J. Mataloni and Matthew J. Slaughter (2005) 'Vertical production networks in multinational firms', *Review of Economics and Statistics* 87, 664–78.

Hart, Oliver D., and John Moore (1990) 'Property rights and the nature of the firm', *Journal of Political Economy* 98, 1119–58.

Helpman, Elhanan (1984) 'A simple theory of trade with multinational corporations', *Journal of Political Economy* 92(3), 451–71.

Helpman, Elhanan, and Paul Krugman (1985) *Market Structure and Foreign Trade.* Cambridge, MA: MIT Press.

Helpman, Elhanan, Marc Melitz and Stephen Yeaple (2004) 'Exports versus FDI with heterogeneous firms'. *American Economic Review* 94(1), 300–16.

Horstmann, Ignatius J., and James R. Markusen (1987) 'Licensing versus direct investment: a model of internalization by the multinational enterprise', *Canadian Journal of Economics* 20, 464–81.

Horstmann, Ignatius, and James R. Markusen (1992), 'Endogenous market structures in international trade'. *Journal of International Economics* 32(1–2), 109–29.

Horstmann, Ignatius J., and James R. Markusen (1996) 'Exploring new markets: direct investment, contractual relations, and the multinational enterprise', *International Economic Review* 37, 1–20.

Markusen, James R. (1984) 'Multinationals, multi-plant economies, and the gains from trade', *Journal of International Economics* 16(3–4), 205–26.

—— (2002) *Multinational Firms and the Theory of International Trade.* Cambridge, MA: MIT Press.

Markusen, James R. (2001) 'Contracts, intellectual property rights, and multinational investment in developing countries', *Journal of International Economics* 53, 189–204.

Markusen, James R., and Anthony J. Venables (1998) 'Multinational firms and the new trade theory', *Journal of International Economics* 46(2), 183–203.

Markusen, James R., and Anthony J. Venables (2000) 'The theory of endowment, intra-industry, and multinational trade', *Journal of International Economics* 52(2): 209–34.

Williamson, Oliver E. (1985) *The Economic Institutions of Capitalism*, New York: Free Press.

Yeaple, Stephen R. (2003) 'The complex integration strategies of multinationals and cross country dependencies in the structure of foreign direct investment', *Journal of International Economics* 60, 293–314.

Part B
Policy

9

The Theory of Trade Policy and Reform*

Rod Falvey† and Udo Kreickemeier‡

1 Introduction

Historically, trade taxes have been an important source of government revenue in subsistence-oriented economies with large informal sectors. As countries developed and economic activity became more market-oriented, governments sourced revenue from broader, more efficient tax bases. But trade taxes remained, with protection of domestic import-competing activity, rather than revenue, becoming their primary motivation. This shift of motivation also facilitated the substitution of alternative policies, quantitative restrictions for example, which would limit import competition without necessarily generating revenue.

Our aim in this chapter is to review the theory of the economic effects of trade policies, to briefly consider the arguments put forward for their use and to discuss the issues that arise in constructing programmes of trade policy reform. In considering the effects of trade policies, we take the decision to impose the policy as given. Policy formation itself is examined in chapter 10, and the reader should note that the lobbying and other activities aimed at soliciting protection also have economic effects not considered here. As one might expect, ours is not the first survey of this area.[1] The early literature tended to concentrate on a competitive market structure, reflecting a focus on general equilibrium and the absence at the time of tractable general equilibrium models with imperfect competition. But the importance of other market structures, particularly monopoly, was recognised even if the analysis was confined to partial equilibrium. Later developments extended to imperfectly competitive market structures, starting with monopolistic competition in the new trade theory (discussed in chapter 5) and continuing in the growing literature on trade policy in oligopolistic markets (discussed in chapter 7)

Our approach is to use the simplest context in which an issue can sensibly be examined. Thus our consideration of individual trade policies in section 2 employs partial equilibrium analysis. Even for a small country the effects of trade policies will depend on the domestic market structure, and while the precise details will depend on a range of features, such as the nature of competition, the number of firms, and the presence or absence of barriers to entry and so forth, one can illustrate the essential differences by considering two polar cases – a competitive domestic industry and a single domestic firm. While the basic diagrammatic representations are familiar from undergraduate textbooks, we extend them to allow a systematic analysis and comparison of tariffs and quotas under both market structures.

The analysis provides the basis for our review of the major arguments for trade interventions in individual markets in Section 3. We illustrate the very limited range of arguments for which trade interventions are likely to be the best policy. But economies are not made up of markets in isolation, and trade interventions in one market will have ramifications in others. These interactions can only be analysed in general equilibrium and this we do in sections 4 and 5 in the context of formulating a programme of piecemeal trade policy reform.

2 Effects of trade policy

The main forms of direct trade interventions are *tariffs*, which are taxes on imports (expressed as either a *specific tariff* – a fixed charge per unit; or an *ad valorem tariff* – a proportion of the foreign price), and quotas, which are limits (expressed in physical or value terms) on the permitted volume of imports or exports. To identify, derive and compare the welfare effects of these policies in two different market structures, we must take care in specifying our production structure. We take the standard case of an industry producing a single homogeneous product at increasing marginal cost. To interpret the welfare effects of price and output changes then requires knowledge of the micro-foundations underlying these costs.

To this end, suppose that production of this output requires two types of inputs, both used in fixed proportions (one unit of each per unit of output), and both non-traded internationally. For one input this industry is a minor user and can purchase this input on the domestic market at a given price. We refer to this as the 'fixed-price' input, and suppose its price is w. But for the other input this industry is a major user and consequently the price it pays per unit depends on how much it purchases. We refer to this as the 'scarce' input and suppose its price is $r(K)$, where K is the quantity employed by this industry. This captures the notion that to obtain more and more units of one input this industry has to attract them from other activities with a rising opportunity cost. Because the industry cannot discriminate between these units, all of the latter are paid $r(K)$ – that is, the opportunity cost of the marginal unit employed. Then the total cost (TC) of producing y units of output is $[w + r(y)]y$, and the average cost (AC) is $w + r(y)$. Both are increasing in output. Since w and $r(y)$ represent the opportunity costs of the two inputs to this industry, AC represents the marginal social cost (MSC) of output in this industry. That is $w + r(y)$ is the value of the output sacrificed elsewhere in the economy to produce the yth unit of this output.

2.1 A competitive industry in a small country

A competitive industry is made up of a large number of firms, each of which takes the prices of both inputs and output as given. It therefore treats AC as its marginal cost (MC), and produces where price p equals MC. The autarky and trade equilibria are illustrated in figure 9.1. Absent international trading opportunities, the domestic price is p_A^c, with the quantity y_A^c consumed and produced. If this small country can trade this product on world markets at a given price p^*, then domestic consumption rises to x_F, output falls to y_F^c, and $x_F - y_F^c$ is imported.[2] Interpreting the demand curve as showing maximum willingness-to-pay for each unit, we find that the fall in price has increased consumer surplus (the difference between the price actually paid and the maximum willingness-to-pay for each unit sold) by area $p_A^c ABp^*$, and reduced producer surplus (the difference between the return received by each unit of the scarce factor and the minimum return necessary for that unit to be supplied to this industry) by area $p_A^c ACp^*$, leaving a net gain of ABC. While there are net gains from trade, there is also redistribution from producers to consumers.

2.1.1 Tariff

Now suppose this country levies a specific tax of t per unit on imports of this product. The cost of imports to consumers then rises to $p_T = p^* + t$. Since

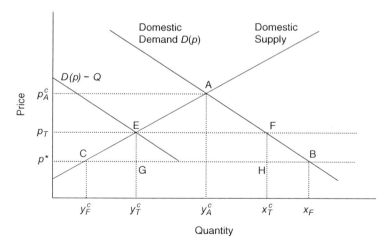

Figure 9.1 The competitive equilibrium.

the imported good and the domestically produced good are homogeneous, the domestic price for both imports and domestic output will rise by t.[3] As a result the quantity consumed domestically falls (from x_F to x_T^c), the quantity produced domestically rises (from y_F^c to y_T^c), and imports fall (to $x_T^c - y_T^c$), as illustrated in figure 9.1. The tariff is equivalent in its effects to a consumption tax and a production subsidy of equal size. The welfare implications are equally straightforward. Consumer surplus falls (by $p_T FBp^*$) and producer surplus rises (by $p_T ECp^*$). The gains from trade fall to AEF, but part of the loss is collected by the government as tariff revenue (EFHG). The net result is a welfare loss, shown by the two triangles CEG and BFH, each of which has a clear interpretation. Since the small country can buy or sell as much of this product as it wishes on the world market at the world price, this price represents the opportunity cost of this product for this economy. In the free trade equilibrium the domestic price was equal to the world price, and domestic consumers purchased units up to the point where their marginal benefit (MB) was equal to the domestic price which in turn equaled the opportunity cost and the domestic industry produced output up to the point where the perceived MC of production, which equaled the MSC of production, also equaled the domestic price and thus the opportunity cost. But under the tariff the domestic price, which guides the actions of private agents, exceeds the world price which continues to reflect the opportunity cost of this product to the small country. The result is a production distortion as domestic production takes place at a MSC above the world price (with an excess cost shown by CGE), and a consumption distortion as domestic consumers forego consumption of imports for which their MB exceeds the world price (with lost consumer surplus as shown by HBF). The tariff results in a deadweight loss reflecting these consumption and production distortions.

2.1.2 Quota

How would the outcome differ if a quantitative restriction had been employed in place of the tariff? It is straightforward to show that for a competitive industry a quota set at the same volume of imports as is generated in the tariff equilibrium (the 'import-equivalent' quota) will have identical effects on domestic output, consumption and imports. Suppose that the volume of imports was restricted to being no greater than $Q = x_T^c - y_T^c$. In equilibrium all of the quota will be filled and we can obtain the residual demand for domestic output by subtracting Q from the quantity demanded at each domestic price (above p^*), obtaining $D(p) - Q$. This residual demand curve intersects the domestic industry supply curve at p_T, thereby leading to the same domestic price as under the tariff. Domestic output, demand and imports are consequently the same in both cases. The major difference between the two policies lies in the disposition of the 'quota rents' – the profit made from purchasing products on the world market at a price of p^* and then reselling them on the domestic market at the higher price (the equivalent of the tariff revenue). Who obtains these rents depends on the manner in which the entitlements to import are distributed. These may be collected by the government if import licenses are 'auctioned' (rare), or by importers if licenses are distributed in accordance with historical import shares, or by exporters if they receive the licenses, as under VERs ('Voluntary' Export Restraints) where the system is administered in the exporting country.[4]

2.2 A single domestic firm in a small country

Outcomes can be rather different for imperfectly competitive market structures as we now illustrate using the case of a single domestic firm.[5] In autarky this firm would act as a *monopolist* in the product market (i.e. taking into account that to increase its sales it has to accept a lower price for all units sold) and as a *monopsonist* in the market for the scarce input (taking into account that the purchase of more of the scarce input raises the cost of all units purchased).[6] For this firm the marginal cost of a unit of the scarce input is $d[r(K)K]/dK = r(K)(1 + \varepsilon_K)$, where $\varepsilon_K \equiv r'(K)K/r(K) > 0$ is the supply elasticity of the scarce input. This implies that the marginal private cost of production (MPC) is $w + r(K)(1 + \varepsilon_K)$, which exceeds the marginal social cost $w + r(K)$.

In the autarky equilibrium, in which the firm acts as both monopolist and monopsonist in the domestic market, it equates MPC with MR. The result is shown in figure 9.2. The firm's sales are y_A^m, which sell at price p_A^m. The corresponding average cost is C_A^m. The autarky profits of the domestic firm are then given by area $C_A^m J I p_A^m$, but relative to the outcome with a competitive industry, consumer surplus is lower by area $p_A^c A I p_A^m$ and producer surplus by $C_A^m J A p_A^c$. The net welfare cost of the combined monopoly and monopsony distortions is then

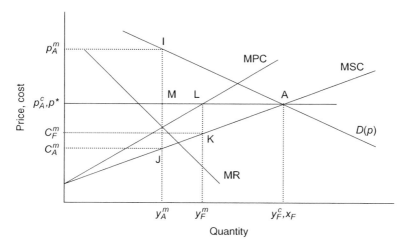

Figure 9.2   Autarky and trade with monopoly.

given by area JAI. Consumers equate MB to the domestic price which exceeds the MR of the firm. The firm equates MR with MPC which in turn exceeds the MSC of output. Thus in the autarky equilibrium MB exceeds MSC implying that production of additional units would cost society less than the value placed on them by consumers.

Given that this is a small country, a major impact of opening the domestic market to international trade is that the firm loses its monopoly power over domestic demand. Since consumers can purchase all they wish at the world price p^*, this is the highest price at which the domestic firm is able to sell its output. Its marginal revenue is therefore constant at p^*, which is also the domestic price in free trade. Compared with the competitive industry we have an additional source of gain from trade through the removal of the monopoly distortion. The monopsony distortion remains however. The trading equilibrium is shown in figure 9.2, where we have drawn the special case in which the world market price p^* is equal to p_A^c.[7] Consumption rises to x_F. Domestic output shifts to where MPC is equal to p^*, which is the maximum price the domestic firm can charge under free trade. In the case illustrated this involves a rise in domestic output relative to autarky, i.e. $y_F^m > y_A^m$.[8] The welfare consequences of opening to trade are slightly more complicated in this case. Consumer surplus increases by area $p^*AIp_A^m$; producer surplus rises by area $C_F^mKJC_A^m$; and firm profits are now $p^*LKC_F^m$, which are less than in autarky. The net result is a gain of area AMI plus area JKLM.

While free trade eliminates the monopoly distortion, the monopsony distortion is still present. Because the firm makes its production decision on the basis of private marginal costs which exceed social marginal costs, there is a range of imports (between y_F^m and y_F^c in figure 9.2) which could be produced domestically at marginal social costs lower than the marginal cost of imports. The underproduction due to this domestic distortion results in a welfare loss of KAL. Appropriate policies to deal with this type of distortion will be discussed below.

2.2.1   Tariff

If opening to trade removes the domestic firm's monopoly power, does restricting trade restore it? In order to answer this question we consider the effects of imposing ever more restrictive import tariffs, starting from the free trade equilibrium. There are four cases as considered in figure 9.3:

(1) Imposing a small tariff raises the cost of imports to $p^* + t$. This is now the highest price at which the domestic firm can sell its output domestically, and therefore its MR on domestic sales is now $p^* + t$. The domestic firm expands its output as the tariff rises, keeping MPC $= p^* + t$. Eventually $p^* + t$

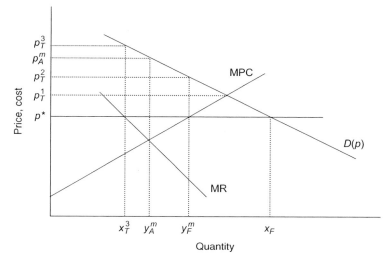

Figure 9.3 Tariff with a single domestic firm.

reaches p_T^1 where the domestic firm's MPC curve intersects $D(p)$. Domestic sales equal domestic output, and imports cease.

(2) Further increases in the tariff allow the domestic firm to charge higher prices on the domestic market, but only at the expense of lower sales. It will do this as long as the foregone marginal revenue (as indicated by the corresponding point on the MR curve) is less than MPC. Thus sales fall and output shifts back down the MPC curve. Although the country is not importing, the threat of imports keeps the domestic price down to $p^* + t$.

(3) Once $p^* + t$ reaches p_T^2 output falls back to the free trade level y_F^m. Further increases in the tariff result in a reduction in domestic sales (as MR is still less than MPC), but if production was cut to match the reduction in domestic sales the firm would then have a range of outputs for which MPC $< p^*$ which implies that exports become profitable. Thus for tariffs above $p_T^2 - p^*$ production remains constant (where MPC $= p^*$), and increases in the tariff result in higher domestic prices, reduced domestic sales and increased exports. Note that: (a) this range includes the autarky monopoly equilibrium, but this is no longer profit maximising for the domestic firm since it now has the option of exporting at a price greater than the autarky MPC; (b) the tariff is higher than is necessary to eliminate imports – referred to as 'water in the tariff' – but the tariff still constrains the domestic price; (c) the import tariff has induced exports and that the domestic firm uses the tariff to price discriminate between markets, selling at a lower price on the world market (where it has no price making power and hence faces a perfectly elastic demand curve). This is an instance of dumping.[9]

(4) When the tariff drives up the domestic price to p_T^3 we have $MR = p* = MPC$. While further increases in the tariff would permit the firm to charge a higher price domestically, the lost marginal revenue on the reduced domestic sales exceeds the return on the additional exports (p^*). Profits would therefore fall. Further increases in the tariff will have no effect on the domestic price, domestic sales or exports.

It is worth noting that case (3) only exists in our setup because we have assumed a world market price that is sufficiently high. One can easily check that it disappears if a world market price is assumed that is lower than the price at which the domestic MR curve intersects the MPC curve.

2.2.2   Quota

In a competitive market an import quota has the same effects on domestic price and output as a tariff. But the quota limits the potential competition from imports in a way quite different from the tariff, and where there is a single domestic firm (or as long as domestic firms are not price takers) this leads to different outcomes under the two policies. By restricting the allowed volume of imports, the quota presents the domestic firm with a 'residual' downward sloping demand curve, equal to the quantity demanded domestically minus the quota at each price above p^*.

Clearly any tariff that eliminated imports (i.e. leading to a domestic price of p_T^1 or higher in figure 9.3) would have an import-equivalent quota of zero. This would immediately restore the domestic firm's full monopoly power over domestic demand. In all these cases the result would be domestic production of y_F^m, domestic sales of x_T^3 at a price of p_T^3, and exports of $y_F^m - x_T^3$ at a price of p^*. Domestic sales are lower and the domestic price is higher under the quota (except for tariffs greater than $p_T^3 - p^*$ when they are the same). For tariffs that do not eliminate imports, the corresponding equivalent quota is positive. But even here it is straightforward to show that the import-equivalent quota results in reduced domestic sales and a higher domestic price. It is simplest to show this in the extreme case of a zero tariff and its equivalent quota set at the free trade volume of imports. In a competitive industry these policies would each result in the free trade equilibrium. But the single domestic firm will recognise that if it reduces domestic sales in the quota regime, domestic consumers will be unable to increase the volume of imports. Hence, the firm can charge a price above the world price and it will be profitable to do so as long as long as domestic MR is less than the marginal revenue obtainable on exports (p^*).

The corresponding equilibria are shown in figure 9.4. Under the zero tariff, the domestic price, sales and output are at their free trade values (p^*, y_F^m, x_F). Under a quota set at $x_F - y_F^m$, domestic output remains at y_F^m, but domestic sales are reduced to x_Q^m and sold at a price of p_Q^m (where the $MR_{(D-Q)} = p^*$), with $y_F^m - x_Q^m$

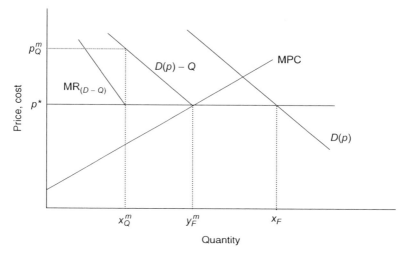

Figure 9.4   Quota with a single domestic firm.

exported. Domestic consumption is $x_Q^m + x_F - y_F^m$. Imports occur up to the quota level at the same time as some domestic production is exported.

While we have not compared the welfare effects of these trade policies, it is straightforward to show that a quota results in a greater welfare loss than the 'import-volume equivalent tariff' (except where they produce identical outcomes). The firm could always choose the tariff outcome under the quota if it wished, but it can usually find a more profitable (and more distortive) option. This reflects the way in which the quota removes the threat of imports at the margin, returning some monopoly power to the domestic firm. Hence, if protection must be offered, a tariff is preferred to the import-equivalent quota on welfare grounds.

3   Economic arguments for trade intervention

A wide range of arguments have been put forward in support of trade interventions. In the following, we focus on the correction of distortions, both international and domestic.

3.1   Extracting real income from foreigners

In the analysis so far we restricted our attention to situations where trade policy had no effect on the world market price. In this section, we look at two cases where the home country can use trade policy to reduce the price at which it buys imports, its terms of trade. By doing so, the country can extract real income from foreigners.

3.1.1   Rent extraction from a foreign monopolist

Suppose the domestic market for some product is supplied by a foreign monopolist. In figure 9.5, MC denotes the foreign monopolist's marginal cost (including any transportation costs), which we assume to be constant for simplicity.[10] In the absence of intervention, the monopolist would supply an amount m_F (determined where MR = MC) to the domestic market, selling at price p_F and receiving profits of $p_F - $ MC per unit.

If the home government wishes to intervene in such a way as to raise home welfare, the first-best intervention is to impose a price ceiling equal to the foreign monopolist's marginal cost (plus a small margin to keep the foreign supplier interested). This would remove the monopoly distortion. But this marginal cost is unlikely to be public information, making the location of the ceiling problematic, and in any case price ceilings on imports are quite unusual in practice. It is therefore worth examining the role of trade policies (i.e. tariffs and quotas) as second best policies. If the home government imposes a tariff t this raises the monopolist's unit cost of importing to MC $+ t$. The new equilibrium imports m_T are sold at price p_T. The net effect on domestic welfare depends on the relative magnitudes of the tariff revenue gain ([MC+t]FG[MC]) and the consumer surplus loss (p_TABp_F). Provided the demand curve is flatter than the marginal revenue curve, welfare gains will result for sufficiently small tariffs: If t is small, triangle ABE can be ignored and the total welfare effect is given by the comparison of rectangles p_TAEp_F and [MC+t]FG[MC]. Essentially the country gains from the tariff revenue collected per unit and loses from the reduction in consumer surplus induced by the rise in price.[11] As the tariff gets larger triangle ABE in the

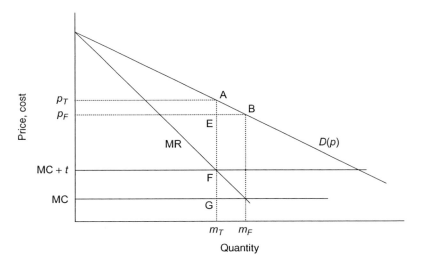

Figure 9.5   A foreign monopolist.

consumer surplus loss grows in importance, and eventually will offset the net gain from the fact that the domestic price has risen by less than the tariff. If the demand curve is steeper than the MR curve (as it can be if demand is non-linear) then a small import subsidy would be welfare improving (as then the domestic price would fall by more than the subsidy).

When considering quantitative restrictions we note than an import quota will be unable to duplicate the optimal tax intervention where this is, in fact, an import subsidy (this would require a minimum rather than a maximum import quota). On the other hand, the effect of an import tariff on the level of imports and the domestic price can be duplicated by an import quota set at the tariff-restricted import value.[12]

3.1.2   The optimum tariff

We now look at the case where the import good in question is supplied by perfectly competitive firms, but the importing country is large. A large importer has monopsony power on the world market, and its actions therefore influence the price at which it buys imports. This means that the opportunity cost of the (imported) product is not the (current) world price, but is higher than this since importing the marginal unit requires not only that a higher price be paid for that unit but for all other units. The marginal cost of imports (MCM) then exceeds the world price p^*. The implication is that free trade will result in excessive imports, an outcome illustrated for a competitive industry in figure 9.6.

The import demand schedule is derived as the difference between domestic demand and supply for each potential domestic price. It intersects the price axis

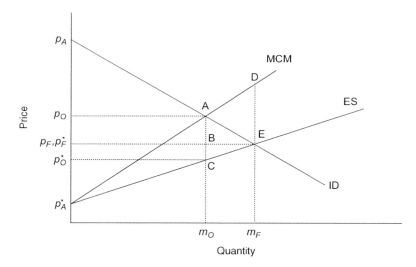

Figure 9.6   The optimum tariff.

at p_A, the domestic autarky price. The corresponding export supply schedule of the rest of the world can be constructed in an equivalent fashion using the difference between their (aggregated) supply and demand schedules. Our large country assumption implies that the export supply schedule (ES) is upward sloping, giving the MCM schedule shown.[13] It intersects the price axis at p_A^*, the rest of the world's autarky price.

The free trade equilibrium has m_F traded at a world price p_F^*, which equalises import demand ID and export supply ES. Free trade leads to gains from trade for both countries – area $p_A E p_F^*$ for the importer and area $p_A^* E p_F^*$ for the exporter. Still, imports are excessive from the importing country's perspective, in the sense that a small reduction in imports would generate an increase in welfare because at m_F the marginal cost of importing is higher than the marginal benefit, as given by the import demand curve ID.

The condition for welfare maximization of the importing country is that the marginal benefit of importing is equal to MCM. An appropriately chosen tariff (the optimal tariff) can achieve this outcome. A tariff on imports creates a wedge between the world price and the importer's domestic price, reducing the demand for imports at each world price. The optimal tariff is shown by $p_O - p_O^*$. At the implied domestic price p_O we have MB = MCM. The marginal costs of this product from the two sources (domestic production and imports) are equal both to each other and to the marginal benefit from consumption. The net result of this policy is a reduction in trade in this product from m_F to m_O. There are two equivalent ways of illustrating the welfare gains resulting from the optimum tariff. First, the gains are measured by the triangle ADE: This gives the excess marginal cost of imports over and above the marginal benefits, summed over all units of the good which are no longer imported due to the tariff. Second, the gains are the net effect of the dead weight loss of the tariff in the domestic market, which is given by the triangle ABE, and the terms of trade gain on the units imported after the tariff is imposed, which is given by $p_F^* B C p_O^*$. Clearly, we have $p_F^* B C p_O^* - ABE = ADE$. There is a loss to the exporter of $p_F^* E C p_O^*$. The optimum tariff is therefore a beggar-thy-neighbour policy. There is a global welfare loss, since the exporter's losses exceed the importer's gains. The same outcome can be achieved with an import quota set at m_O as long as the quota rents are retained in the importing country.

While logically consistent, the weakness in this optimum tariff argument is its symmetry. An identical argument can be made from the exporting country's perspective. That country has monopoly power on the world market, and hence can improve its terms of trade and welfare by restricting its export supply through an export tax (or, alternatively, an export quota). The ability of one country to capture these monopsony/monopoly gains depends on the other country passively accepting a deterioration in its own terms of trade. Retaliation by the trading partner may make both countries worse off than they were in free trade.

This problem is then likely to have the structure of a prisoner's dilemma. Each country has an incentive to restrict trade in this product if the other country adopts a free trade policy. But if both countries restrict trade, they are both likely to end up worse off than if they both adopted free trade policies![14] Constraining policy choice by means of international agreements (the GATT or a Preferential Trading Arrangement) or membership of international organisations (the WTO) can be seen as a means of escaping from this dilemma.

3.2   Production externality

Trade policy can be used to correct for domestic 'market failures'.[15] Throughout the history of trade, policy arguments have been put forward for government intervention to correct for supposed market failures that work to the detriment of domestic industries. These arguments for protection range from the naïve to the sophisticated, and take the general form that 'the domestic X industry should be protected from foreign competition because of (market failure) Y'. In analyzing these arguments it is important to separate their two aspects: (a) the economic validity of the argument as a case for intervention at all (i.e. is there a market failure?); and (b) if (a) is met, the optimal form of intervention (if any). Many of the historically popular arguments for protection fail to establish a case at step (a), and of those that survive almost all fail step (b), falling foul of the general principle that optimal intervention is directed at the market where the market failure occurs.

We can illustrate this general principle quite simply using a competitive industry in a small country where, for some reason, there is a market failure in that the marginal private cost of production exceeds its marginal social costs.[16] As noted above, the free trade equilibrium then involves a range of imports for which the domestic marginal social cost is less than the world price. We illustrate this case in figure 9.7, where domestic production in the free trade equilibrium is y_F^p instead of the social optimum y_F^s, and the resulting welfare loss equals CDG. To achieve the optimal output, producers need to receive a price of $\bar{p}$. Since this product is imported, one policy that can achieve this target is an import tariff of $\bar{p} - p^*$. But while the tariff induces the desired production change, it also introduces a byproduct consumption distortion. Domestic consumers now face a higher domestic price and reduce their consumption from x_F to x_T, incurring a welfare loss of BEF corresponding to the difference between their willingness to pay and the opportunity cost of those units no longer consumed. The tariff is effective in meeting the production target, but imposes an unnecessary welfare cost through the byproduct consumption distortion. A preferred policy is suggested once one recalls that a tariff is equivalent to a production subsidy and a consumption tax at the same rate. It is the production subsidy element that achieves the target, and the consumption tax element that generates the byproduct distortion cost. A production subsidy of $\bar{p} - p^*$ achieves the former and

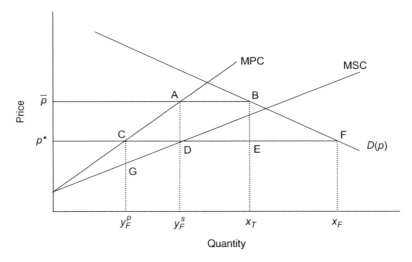

Figure 9.7   Correcting a production distortion.

avoids the latter. This illustrates that the optimal intervention for a *production target* is a *production* policy.[17]

Similarly a tariff can achieve a consumption-reduction target, but involves a by-product production distortion. A superior policy is a consumption tax that applies to both domestic output and imports. However, a tariff will be the optimal intervention if the target is to reduce the volume of imports – as in the optimal tariff case. By considering the potential policies to correct any given distortion, one can create a policy ranking – that is, an ordering of interventions in terms of their relative welfare costs of correcting a particular market failure.

3.3   Imperfect competition

Trade in imperfectly competitive markets is covered in chapters 5 and 7, and we will not duplicate that discussion here. Our concern is simply to identify the potential welfare gains from policy intervention by considering the distortions that imperfect competition implies.[18] We illustrate this by considering the case of monopolistic competition, which occurs in a differentiated product industry with a large number of firms, each possessing some market power with regard to its own product, but not perceiving any strategic interaction between itself and its competitors. There is free entry and exit, and hence zero economic profits in the long run. Economies of scale at the firm level ensure each variety is produced by a single firm, which generates intra-industry trade. In equilibrium each firm equates MR with MC, implying a price markup which depends on the price elasticity of demand. The effects of a tariff then depend on whether this demand elasticity is fixed. If it is then firm output and producer prices are unchanged by the tariff which just switches demand from imports to domestic output.

Tariffs can have a positive welfare effect in such an environment. Monopolistic competition gives rise to at least one distortion, since, although consumer prices reflect the opportunity cost of imported products in free trade, they exceed the resource cost of domestic products by the monopolistic markup. A welfare gain is then available from diverting expenditure to domestic varieties – an outcome generated by an import tariff, or, preferably, a subsidy on the consumption of domestic output. Monopolistic competition can also give rise to a second distortion, depending on whether the number of foreign varieties available to domestic consumers is fixed or not. In a love-of-variety context, welfare depends on the number of varieties consumed in addition to the total number of units consumed. If, as seems likely, domestic consumers do not take into account the effects of their spending on the number of foreign varieties available for domestic consumption, then there is a market failure. The precise intervention called for depends on how the number of varieties imported is related to total expenditure on these imports.[19]

A wide variety of arguments have been put forward to justify trade interventions, and policy-makers unsympathetic to a laissez-faire approach were not backward in taking advantage of them. The overall outcome was often a trade policy structure without coherence. High and variable tariffs and frequent recourse to quantitative restrictions left domestic relative prices far removed from opportunity costs (i.e. world relative prices for a small country). While it was clear that domestic resource allocations were distorted, how distorted they were and in whose favour was often difficult to say. How best to deal with this situation then became the challenge for trade policy reformers. Analysis of these issues can only be done in general equilibrium.

4   Trade policy in general equilibrium

We now take explicit account of the constraint that the use of trade policy to support production of one product, reduces output elsewhere.[20] This was implicit in the upward-sloping marginal cost curves above, where additional production required that some inputs be drawn away from alternative uses where they have an increasing opportunity cost. General equilibrium makes this more explicit. It also allows us to use the conditions for an optimal allocation in an undistorted competitive economy (see chapter 3).

In this case, demand can be thought of as resulting from utility maximisation by a single representative consumer, who treats the vector of domestic prices parametrically and chooses a consumption vector where the marginal rate of substitution in consumption is equated to domestic relative prices. Similarly domestic supply can be thought of as coming from profit maximisation by a single competitive multi-product firm, which also treats the vector of domestic prices parametrically. It chooses an output vector where relative marginal costs, which determine the marginal rate of transformation in production, are equated to domestic relative prices. In this context we can think of 'trade' as an alternative technology that allows us to transform units of some goods (exports) into units of others (imports). The rate at which this transformation can take place is the foreign rate of transformation. In free trade, domestic prices equal world prices, and, for a small country, world prices represent the rate at which exports can be transformed into imports on the world market. We then have $\text{MRS}^{\text{con}} = \text{MRT}^{\text{prod}} = \text{MRT}^{\text{trade}}$, and an optimal allocation of resources.[21]

The standard two good representation of the effects of an import tariff for a small country is shown in figure 9.8. There AB represents the domestic production possibility frontier (PPF). At the given world relative prices (shown by the slope of $Y_F^2 Y_F^1$), this country produces at y_F. Aggregate income is $0Y_F^2$ measured in units of good 2 ($0Y_F^1$ in units of good 1). $Y_F^2 Y_F^1$ represents the budget constraint at world (and domestic) prices, and if we assume a representative consumer, then consumption takes place at x_F where a community indifference curve is tangent to this budget constraint. In free trade this country exports $y_F 0_F$ of good 2 in exchange for $0_F x_F$ imports of good 1.

Now suppose this country imposes an import tariff that raises the domestic relative price of good 1 to that shown by the slope of the line tangent to the PPF at the new production point y_T. Output of the importable has increased and, since resources are fully employed, output of the exportable has contracted. Because this country is small on world markets, world (relative) prices are unaffected, so that the country's budget constraint at world prices is now given by $Y_T^2 Y_T^1$ (i.e. the value of domestic output has fallen at world prices, by $Y_T^2 Y_F^2$ in terms of good 2, or equivalently by $Y_T^1 Y_F^1$ in terms of good 1). Since trade must balance at world prices, the tariff distorted consumption point must lie along this budget constraint. But the tariff has also distorted the relative prices facing domestic consumers, so the consumption point will *not* occur at the tangency of a community indifference curve with this budget constraint (i.e. at x'), but where the marginal rate of substitution in consumption is equal to the domestic price ratio – a point such as x_T.[22] Trade has fallen, with $y_T 0_T$ now exported in exchange for $0_T x_T$. The total welfare cost of the tariff is represented by the shift from U_F to U_T, which can be decomposed into the cost associated with the implicit production distortion (U_F to U') and the cost associated with the implicit consumption distortion (U' to U_T).

What figure 9.8 reveals, and our partial equilibrium analysis could not, is that the same distorted equilibrium would occur if exports were taxed rather than imports. If p^* is the world relative price of good 2 in terms of good 1, then an ad valorem import tariff at rate τ_M will reduce the domestic relative price of

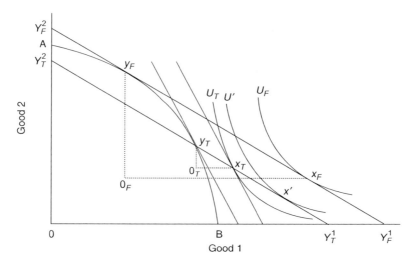

Figure 9.8   General equilibrium.

the exportable to $p^M = p^*/(1+\tau_M)$. Similarly, a tax on exports of good 2 at rate τ_X will mean that domestic producers receive a lower price from exports (given an unchanged world price) and hence will be willing to sell on the domestic market for the same reduced price. This also implies a lower domestic relative price of $p^X = p^*(1-\tau_X)$.[23] This result, known as the *Lerner Symmetry Theorem* (Lerner, 1936), emphasises that where trade is balanced, a tax on imports and a tax on exports have equivalent effects. The same logic implies that a subsidy on exports, which will increase the domestic relative price of the exportable, will have the same effects as a subsidy on imports. Trade will increase but welfare will again fall.

Another insight that is only forthcoming in general equilibrium is that the effect of a distortion in one sector depends on what is happening in the other sector(s). The famous case, used by Lerner (1933–34) to illustrate this point, is the case of two sector-specific monopoly firms. If the sector-specific distortion imposed by a monopoly is the same in both sectors of a two-sector economy, the allocation of resources between sectors is undistorted, and hence welfare is the same as in the first-best equilibrium. A final 'general equilibrium insight' concerns the difference between goods market distortions and factor market distortions. Consider a goods market distortion, such as a production externality in one sector. In figure 9.8 this would lead to a production point on the PPF, at which the marginal rate of transformation does not equal the relative goods price. This outcome illustrates two points: (i) Production occurs on the wrong point on the PPF since resources are not optimally allocated across sectors. (ii) Production occurs on the PPF (rather than inside the PPF) since resources within firms are allocated optimally, and resources are fully employed. Now consider a factor market distortion, for example an economy-wide binding minimum wage for one of the factors, as considered by Brecher (1974) for the case of a Heckscher–Ohlin economy.[24] This leads to unemployment of the factor in question, and to production inside the PPF.

5   Trade policy reform

The final section of this survey looks at the welfare effects of *piecemeal trade policy reform*, that is the incremental change in tariff rates. In the standard general equilibrium setup of a competitive small open economy with one import and one export sector, this question is straightforward to answer, and therefore not of great interest: moving towards the first best optimum of free trade by lowering the level of protection is unambiguously welfare increasing. This is no longer true – and things become therefore more interesting – if more than one sector is subject to import restrictions (quotas or tariffs). In this case, which is of obvious practical relevance, both the level of protection and the structure of protection across sectors are welfare relevant. It is possible, for example, that lowering one of two existing import tariffs lowers welfare, even though this change in tariffs arguably brings the economy 'closer' to free trade. The aim of the literature on piecemeal trade policy reform has been to identify reform strategies that increase welfare for every single reform step, thereby generating monotonically increasing welfare as the first-best optimum of free trade is approached.

5.1   The classical results

We consider a competitive open economy, consuming and producing $n+1$ tradable goods. There is a single export good, labelled 0, which is traded freely with the rest of the world.[25] Its domestic output and price are denoted by y_0 and p_0, respectively. The export good serves as *numéraire*, i.e. $p_0 \equiv 1$ throughout. The equilibrium is given by

$$e(p,u) = g(p,v) + t'm, \tag{1}$$

where p is the $n \times 1$ vector of domestic prices of non-*numéraire* goods, v is the vector of factor endowments, u is utility, t is the vector of (implicit or explicit) import tariffs, and m is the vector of import quantities. All vectors are column vectors, and their transposes are denoted by a prime. We normalise world market prices of all goods to one, which makes t the vector of *ad valorem* tariff rates. Expenditure at domestic prices, given by expenditure function $e(\cdot)$, equals the value of production at domestic prices, given by revenue function $g(\cdot)$, plus tariff or quota revenue $t'm$.

The welfare effects of changes in trade policy are derived by totally differentiating (1), holding factor endowments v fixed. We get:

$$e'_p dp + e_u du = g'_p dp + t' dm + m' dt. \tag{2}$$

We now can use the standard derivative properties of expenditure and revenue functions: The vector of partial derivatives of $e(\cdot)$ with respect to p, denoted by e_p, equals the demand vector $x(p,u)$, while g_p equals the supply vector $y(p,v)$. Their difference $e_p - g_p$ therefore gives the vector of net import demands $m(p,u,v)$. Using this result, as well as $dt = dp$ (since we have assumed a small open economy), we finally get

$$e_u du = t' dm. \tag{3}$$

Since e_u is the inverse of the marginal utility of income and therefore strictly positive, trade reforms are welfare increasing ($du > 0$) if a weighted average of imports in all sectors increases, where the weights are given by the differences between the domestic price and the world market price for the respective goods. For the case where *all* import restrictions take the form of import quotas, where the import quantities m are the policy instruments, this leads to a straightforward result, originally due to Corden and Falvey (1985): Relaxing any binding import quota m_i is welfare increasing, since $t' dm = t_i dm_i > 0$ for $dm_i > 0$ and $dm_j = 0 \ \forall j \neq i.$[26]

If protection takes the form of import tariffs, changes in import quantities are endogenous. In order to relate welfare changes to changes in the policy instruments dt, one has to substitute for dm in (3). Differentiating $m = e_p - g_p$ gives

$$dm = e_{pp} dp + e_{pu} du - g_{pp} dp = S dp + e_{pu} du,$$

where the elements of matrix $S \equiv e_{pp} - g_{pp}$ are the own-price and cross-price derivatives of the compensated net import demand functions for the non-*numéraire* goods. From standard properties of the expenditure and revenue functions, the matrix is negative semi-definite. We follow standard practice and assume that some substitutablity exists between the *numéraire* and the other goods, in which case S becomes negative definite.[27] Substituting back into (3), we get the key equation for tariff reforms in a small open economy:

$$\mu^{-1} e_u du = t' S dt \tag{4}$$

with $\mu \equiv (1 - t' e_{pu} e_u^{-1})^{-1}$.

All results on the welfare effects of piecemeal tariff reforms are derived using variants of (4). The term μ on the left hand side is the *shadow price of foreign exchange*. It measures the marginal welfare effect of an exogenous transfer to the country of one unit of the *numéraire*. One can see directly that it equals 1 in an undistorted economy, i.e. with $t = 0$. With some non-zero tariffs it is different from 1 in general since the transfer of the *numéraire* good potentially affects demand for all other goods via the income effect, which becomes welfare relevant if the economy is not in the first-best optimum. It is easy to find a condition for μ to be positive: Due to the linear homogeneity of $e(p, u)$ in all prices – including the price of the *numéraire* – we have $e = e_0 + p'e_p$, where e_0 is short for e_{p_0}. This implies $e_u = e_{0u} + p'e_{pu}$, and substituting for e_u in (4) we get:

$$\mu^{-1}e_u = e_{0u} + p^{*\prime}e_{pu}$$

Hence, the shadow price of foreign exchange is positive if and only if an increase in utility increases aggregate demand, measured at world market prices. This is clearly a very weak condition, and hence the assumption $\mu > 0$ is made throughout the literature on piecemeal trade reform.[28]

Going back to (4), $\mu > 0$ implies that changes in the tariff vector are welfare increasing if and only if they lead to $t'Sdt > 0$. It is now immediately clear that finding welfare increasing tariff reforms is a more complex task than finding welfare increasing quota reforms, since via the substitution matrix S changing any tariff has an effect of the net imports of *all* goods. Still there is one classic result that is straightforward to show: lowering all tariffs proportionally increases welfare. In order to see why this *radial reduction result*, originally due to Bruno (1972), holds, set $dt = -td\alpha$, $d\alpha > 0$. The right-hand side of (4) then becomes $-(t'St)d\alpha$, which is positive due to the fact that S is negative definite. Note that this reform does *not* change all prices in proportion to each other (which would, of course, leave welfare unchanged since import demand is homogenous of degree zero in prices): the tariff on the export good is zero by assumption, and therefore a radial reduction of tariffs reduces the prices of import goods relative to the price of the export good.

Now, suppose there are some tariffs that cannot be altered, and therefore the radial reduction strategy cannot be applied. There is a second classic result in the theory of trade policy reform, due to Hatta (1977), which is relevant to this case: a *concertina reform*, that is, a compression in the tariff structure resulting from either lowering the highest tariff, or increasing a tariff on a freely traded import, increases welfare. For concreteness, we look at the case of a change in a single tariff, t_1, holding all other tariffs constant. The change in welfare in this case is given by

$$\mu^{-1}e_u du = \sum_{i \neq 0} t_i S_{i1} dt_1. \tag{5}$$

It is easy to see that welfare can rise or fall in general following a change in t_1: S_{11} is negative, while S_{i1}, $i \neq 1$, is negative if good i is a complement for good 1 in import demand, and positive if good i is a substitute for good 1 in import demand. Hence, the summation term in (5) contains both negative and positive terms, and it is not clear *a priori* whether the sum is positive or negative. There are two alternative ways to rewrite (5) that allow us to elicit more information. First, we can make use of the fact that net import demand for any good is homogeneous of degree zero in all goods prices, and therefore $\sum_{j=0}^{n} S_{1j} p_j = 0$. Note that the summation includes the *numéraire*, and that S_{i0} is defined in analogy to the substitution terms in matrix S (which excludes good 0). Since the substitution matrix S is symmetric, we have $S_{ij} = S_{ji}$ and can therefore write $S_{11} = -(1/p_1) \sum_{i \neq 1} p_i S_{i1}$. Substituting for S_{11} in (5), and using $p_i = 1 + t_i$, yields

$$\mu^{-1} e_u du = -\frac{1}{p_1} \left[\sum_{i \neq 1} (t_1 - t_i) S_{i1} \right] dt_1. \tag{6}$$

Having eliminated S_{11}, the sum in brackets now only contains cross-price effects, and assuming all goods are substitutes for good 1 in import demand, all S_{i1} are positive. Under this condition, two results follow from (6). First, lowering the highest tariff increases welfare. With t_1 the highest tariff the coefficients $(t_1 - t_i)$ are all positive, and the result is immediate. Second, introducing a tariff on a previously freely traded good also increases welfare: With $t_1 = 0$ the coefficients are all equal to $-t_i$, and therefore non-positive, and the result is again immediate. Taken together, both results show that a compression of the tariff structure is welfare increasing.

Alternatively, (5) can be re-written as

$$\mu^{-1} e_u du = \left(\tau_1 - \sum_{i \neq 1} \omega_{i1} \tau_i \right) p_1 S_{11} dt_1, \tag{7}$$

where $\omega_{i1} \equiv -p_i S_{i1}/(p_1 S_{11})$, and $\tau_i \equiv t_i/p_i$ is the *ad valorem* tariff on good i, defined as a proportion of the *domestic* price. Using the same homogeneity restriction as above we have $\sum_{i \neq 1} \omega_{i1} = 1$, and if all goods are substitutes for good 1 in import demand, as assumed, all ω_{i1} are positive. Both versions of the concertina result are again immediate: With τ_1 the highest tariff, it exceeds the weighted average of all the other tariffs (where the average includes the zero tariff on the *numéraire*). The term in brackets is positive in this case, and $dt_1 < 0$ increases welfare. On the other hand, with $\tau_1 = 0$ the term in brackets is negative, and $dt_1 > 0$ increases welfare.

The intuition for the concertina result is as follows. Lowering the tariff on good 1 increases imports of this good, and – with all goods net substitutes for good 1 – lowers the imports of all other importables, while the exports of the *numéraire* increase. The relative size of these effects is constrained by the homogeneity condition on compensated net import demand functions, $\sum_i p_i S_{i1} = 0$. From this condition, the rise in exports of good 0 implies that the increase in the import value of good 1 exceeds the decrease in aggregate import value of goods

2 to n, all measured at *domestic* prices. With t_1 (or τ_1) the highest tariff rate, $p_1|S_{11}| > \sum_{i=2}^{n} p_i S_{i1}$ in turn implies $t_1|S_{11}| > \sum_{i=2}^{n} t_i S_{i1}$, and hence it follows from (5) that lowering t_1 increases welfare.[29]

5.2   Generalising reform strategies

In some sense, the combination of the concertina rule and the proportional reduction rule is all that is needed in order to find a path to free trade in a small open economy along which welfare increases monotonically: Start with lowering the highest tariff to the level of the second highest, then jointly lower these two tariffs until the level of the third highest tariff is reached, and proceed in this way until all tariff rates are identical. Then reduce them proportionally until free trade is reached. Still, both from a theoretical and from a practical point of view it seemed desirable to have a broader set of reform strategies that could be identified as welfare increasing. Anderson and Neary (2007) show that this goal can indeed be achieved. In particular, they show that – subject to some conditions discussed below – reforms that are similar to the proportional reduction of all tariffs are welfare increasing as well. In order to derive their result, two key variables have to be defined, namely the generalised mean and the generalised variance of the tariff vector.

To this end, we start by normalising the substitution matrix S:

$$\widetilde{S} \equiv -\bar{s}^{-1} D(p) S D(p) \quad \text{with } \bar{s} \equiv -p'Sp > 0,$$

where $D(p)$ is a diagonal matrix with the elements of price vector p on the main diagonal. As a consequence of the normalisation, $\widetilde{S}$ is positive definite, and its elements sum to one.

We can now rewrite equation (4) as

$$(\mu\bar{s})^{-1} e_u du = \tau'\widetilde{S}d\tau, \tag{4'}$$

where, as in eq. (7), we express the welfare change as a function of the *ad valorem* tariffs expressed relative to domestic prices. The generalised average tariff rate $\bar{\tau}$ and the generalised variance V are now given by

$$\bar{\tau} \equiv \iota'\widetilde{S}\tau \quad \text{and} \quad V \equiv \tau'\widetilde{S}\tau - \bar{\tau}^2,$$

respectively, with ι denoting an $n \times 1$ vector of ones. By construction, the weights in the determination of $\bar{\tau}$ sum to one. We assume in the following that $\bar{\tau}$ exceeds the minimum tariff rate $\tau_{\min}$.[30]

The changes of the generalised moments are defined as $d\bar{\tau} = \iota'\widetilde{S}d\tau$ and $dV = 2\tau'\widetilde{S}(d\tau - \iota d\bar{\tau})$, respectively.[31] Substitution into (4') gives

$$(\mu\bar{s})^{-1} e_u du = -\bar{\tau}d\bar{\tau} - \tfrac{1}{2}dV. \tag{8}$$

Hence, welfare increases with a decreasing average tariff rate and a decreasing variance of tariffs. Anderson and Neary's generalised moments thereby quantify the notion that high average tariffs and wide tariff dispersion are welfare reducing.

Consider now the set of reforms given by

$$d\tau = -[(1-\gamma)\tau + \gamma\iota]\,d\alpha, \tag{9}$$

where $\gamma \in [0,1]$. With $\gamma = 0$, we have the special case of a proportional reduction in tariff rates – the radial reform described above. The opposite extreme, $\gamma = 1$, is the case where all tariff rates are reduced by the same absolute amount. Hence, all reforms described by γ strictly larger than 0 amount to a more than proportional reduction of low tariff rates. The effect on the moments of the tariff distribution is given by

$$d\bar{\tau} = -[(1-\gamma)\bar{\tau}+\gamma]\,d\alpha \quad \text{and} \quad dV = -2(1-\gamma)V\,d\alpha, \tag{10}$$

respectively. Hence, reform (9) strictly reduces the average tariff rate and weakly reduces the variance of tariff rates, and is therefore welfare increasing. The variance-reducing effect can be understood as the result of two partial effects working in opposite directions: Lowering all tariff rates reduces the variance, ceteris paribus, while increasing the dispersion of tariff rates (by reducing low tariffs more than proportionally) increases the variance, ceteris paribus. The first effect dominates for reforms given by (9) as long as γ is smaller than one. In the case where γ is equal to one, both effects exactly offset each other, leaving the variance of tariff rates constant.

An alternative set of reforms is given by

$$d\tau = -[(1-\delta)\tau + \delta(\tau - \tau_{\min}\iota)]\,d\alpha \tag{11}$$

with $\delta \in [0,1]$. With $\delta = 0$, this again gives the special case of the radial reform. The opposite case $\delta = 1$ denotes a reform which reduces all tariff rates in proportion to their difference with the lowest tariff rate $\tau_{\min}$. Hence, all reforms described by δ strictly larger than 0 amount to a more than propotional reduction of high tariff rates. While (11) shows the analogy to (9) quite clearly in that it is a convex combination of two reforms, one of which is the radial reduction reform, it can be written more compactly as

$$d\tau = -(\tau - \delta\tau_{\min}\iota)\,d\alpha \tag{11$'$}$$

The effects on the moments of the tariff distribution are given by

$$d\bar{\tau} = -(\bar{\tau} - \delta\tau_{\min})\,d\alpha \quad \text{and} \quad dV = -2V\,d\alpha, \tag{12}$$

respectively. Hence, reform (11) reduces both the average tariff rate and the variance of tariff rates, and is therefore welfare increasing as well.

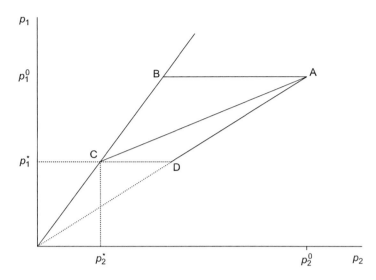

Figure 9.9   Restricted tariff reforms.

Together, (9) and (11) provide a set of welfare-increasing tariff reforms that generalise the traditional radial reduction result. For the case of only two import goods subject to tariffs, the reforms are illustrated in figure 9.9. The original tariff vector leads to domestic prices (p_1^0, p_2^0) for the non-*numéraire* goods. Starting at A, the radial reduction of tariff rates is given by movements along AC. The Anderson-Neary reforms (9) and (11) extend the set of tariff reductions known to be welfare increasing to the cone ABD. Moving along AB is the case $\delta = 1$. With only two importables subject to tariffs, this is the concertina reform, and in the general case of more than two importables, Anderson and Neary (2007) label this the 'super-concertina' reform. Moving along AD is the case $\gamma = 1$, that is, the uniform absolute reduction of tariff rates τ_i, which amounts to a uniform absolute reduction in domestic prices of importables.

5.3   Extending the standard model

There is a long list of papers that have looked at the applicability of the traditional tariff reform results – i.e. the concertina and radial reduction results – in cases where some deviations from the standard framework exist. In order to structure our (necessarily selective) discussion, it is useful to focus on four types of extensions, each of which abandons one key feature of the standard framework. These four features are: (a) there is a strict dichotomy between goods and factors, with the former traded at given world market prices, while the latter are internationally immobile; (b) government revenue is no concern, and any revenue that exists is distributed lump-sum to households; (c) the analysis focuses exclusively on welfare; (d) flexible factor returns lead to full employment.

Among the papers in the first group, Neary (1995) analyses trade reform in a large open economy and shows that the standard results survive in modified form if proper account is taken of the fact that the optimum tariff vector in this case is different from zero. Lopez and Panagariya (1992) analyse the case of imported intermediate inputs and argue that complementarities between goods in import demand become more important in this case. The (sufficient) condition for the concertina reform to lead to a welfare improvement would be violated in this case. Kreickemeier and Raimondos-Møller (2010) show that the standard concertina result may also cease to hold if some factors of production ('capital') are internationally mobile. In contrast, Neary and Ruane (1988) look at the radial reduction of all tariffs and find that the positive welfare effect of this reform is even enhanced by the presence of international capital mobility. They note that this result is an application of the Le Chatelier-Samuelson principle.[32]

Among the papers in the second group, Abe (1992) considers the case where the government provides a public good which is paid for exclusively by the tariff revenue. He assumes a small open economy with full employment where the representative consumer derives utility from consuming the public good. Therefore, it is not optimal in general in Abe's model to have a zero government budget and no tariffs. Diewert *et al.* (1989) assume that the public sector gives an exogenous lump-sum transfer to the representative consumer which can be financed alternatively by domestic commodity taxes or import tariffs. In a similar vein, Hatzipanayotou *et al.* (1994), Keen and Ligthart (2002), and Kreickemeier and Raimondos-Møller (2008) derive rules for coordinated tariff and commodity tax reforms that are both welfare and revenue increasing. Falvey (1994) looks at the same question when tariffs are the only instruments available.

As far as papers in the third group are concerned, Ju and Krishna (2000) show that welfare increasing tariff reductions do not necessarily increase market access, as measured by the value of imports at world market prices. This was a surprising result, since in the textbook model with a single import good lower tariffs necessarily lead to a higher value of imports. Anderson and Neary (2005, 2007) extend the analysis, using the generalised tariff moments described above. They show that with more than one import good subject to a tariff there is a fundamental tension between welfare increasing and market access increasing tariff reductions: While a lower average tariff promotes both welfare and market access, a lower variance increases welfare but reduces market access. Hence, the reduction of all tariff rates by the same absolute amount (reform AD in figure 9.9), which – as demonstrated earlier – leaves the generalised variance of tariffs constant, increases welfare and market access.

Finally, Kreickemeier (2005) and Falvey and Kreickemeier (2009) analyse the welfare effects of tariff reforms if the return for one of the factors ('labour') is downwardly rigid, resulting in involuntary unemployment of this factor. The effects of trade liberalisation are strengthened or weakened, depending on whether the import-competing sectors are labour intensive or not. If they are not labour intensive, trade liberalisation leads to an increase in aggregate employment, and the standard results hold. With labour intensive import-competing goods, trade liberalisation leads to lower aggregate employment, thereby weakening the case for lower tariffs (if they are the only instrument available). Notably though, welfare may go up despite falling aggregate employment.

6   Conclusion

This chapter has surveyed what may be labelled the traditional theory of trade policy, with no emphasis on models of monopolistic competition or oligopoly, which are covered in other chapters. As an organising principle, the aim was to present each issue in the simplest context possible, moving from partial equilibrium, via two-good general equilibrium to multi-good general equilibrium models. The latter class of models is needed if questions of trade policy reform are to be considered. This venerable part of the trade policy literature is given considerable room in the present survey, in part due to its importance for trade-policy practitioners, in part due to the fact that it has recently become an active area of research again.

Notes

*   We thank Hartmut Egger and Pascalis Raimondos-Møller for helpful comments. This work was substantially completed while the authors were at the University of Nottingham. We gratefully acknowledge financial support from the Leverhulme Trust under programme grant F/00 114/AM.
†   Bond University.
‡   University of Tübingen.
1. Early surveys include Meade (1955) and Bhagwati (1964). Corden (1971, 1974, 1997) provides an extensive analysis of the positive and normative aspects of trade policy, respectively. This work is updated and extended to cover a wider range of policies and market structures in Vousden (1990).
2. For simplicity we assume the country can import and export at world prices – that is, there are no transport costs. Unit transport costs of say τ could easily be allowed for by considering an import price of $p^* + \tau$ and an export price of $p^* - \tau$ where p^* is the price at the world market.
3. Imperfect substitutes can be dealt with straightforwardly. See Helpman and Krugman (1989).

4. This distinction between policies is not trivial given the possibility of lobbying in search of these rents and the scope for corruption in the allocations of import entitlements. When one adds the practical difficulties of determining the 'restrictiveness' of quantitative restrictions (through their tariff equivalents), one is left with a general preference for tariffs over quotas even before considering their respective outcomes in imperfect competition.

5. Since this firm will make profits in equilibrium, its privileged position must reflect the existence of some barriers to the entry of domestic competitors. One possibility is that production involves increasing returns to scale, a case discussed in detail in Vousden (1990), chapter 5. Here we continue with the assumption of increasing marginal costs, thus maintaining comparability with the competitive industry case.

6. Our assumptions have the advantage of providing a clear distinction between profits and producer surplus. An alternative assumption that yields similar outcomes is that production requires the services of two inputs, one available at a fixed price and the other in fixed supply to this industry. As long as the inputs are substitutable, the output of this industry is not fixed. However, if the underlying technology is constant returns to scale, an x percent increase in output requires a more than x percent increase in the fixed price factor and hence a rising marginal and average cost. Producer surplus is then the rents to the factor in fixed supply. Our analysis below follows analogously, provided the single firm pays the factor in fixed supply the value of its marginal product. Most textbook analyses of a single domestic firm with an upward sloping marginal cost curve simply ignore the implied monopsony power in input markets. For an analysis of monposony power in a general equilibrium trade model see chapter 24 in Bhagwati et al. (1998).

7. We have taken this special case just to simplify the diagram, but note that at this world price no trade would occur if the industry was competitive, and the trade generated here is solely due to the continuing monopsony distortion.

8. This need not be the case. If the world price is below the point where the domestic MR curve intersects the MPC curve, domestic output would be lower than in autarky, raising the potential for welfare losses due to the domestic production distortion being higher in the trading equilibrium than in autarky.

9. See Blonigen and Prusa (2003) for details of dumping and antidumping.

10. The analysis can readily be extended to include a 'competitive fringe' of import-competing producers and a rising marginal cost for the foreign exporter.

11. An alternative way to look at the welfare gain in this case is to note that the domestic price of imports increases by less than the tariff, and therefore the country experiences an improvement in its terms of trade.

12. It is not hard to imagine scenarios under which the foreign monopolist would be able to capture a substantial part of the quota rent. On welfare grounds, one would therefore be left with a preference of an import tariff over the 'equivalent' import quota.

13. With a linear export supply curve of the form $a + bm$ the total cost of imports is $m(a + bm)$, and therefore the marginal cost of importing equals $a + 2bm$.

14. It has long been noted that with asymmetric countries it is possible for one country to be better off with non-cooperative tariff setting than in free trade. The respective country is then said to be the 'winner of a tariff war'. Syropoulos (2002) shows that in the neoclassical trade model the larger country wins the tariff war if countries are sufficiently different in size.

15. Market failure occurs when markets do not bring about economic efficiency.

16. The single domestic firm considered above is one example of this. There the market failure arose because for the firm the marginal cost of the scarce input exceeded its current price, whereas the current price of the input equalled its actual opportunity cost. But more generally MPC and MSC can differ if production generates an externality, and the case we are considering is where production generates a positive externality.

17. The astute reader will have recognized that in the single domestic firm case, the problem is a failure in the market for the scarce input, rather than the output itself. The true best intervention is a subsidy on the use of the scarce input of $\varepsilon_K r(K)$. Because we assume that the two inputs are used in fixed proportions, a production subsidy of this amount will be equally as effective. But if there are substitution possibilities between the two inputs, then the firm will be under-employing the scarce input and over-employing the fixed-price input, relative to the social optimum, in addition to under-producing the final output. An appropriate scarce-input subsidy would then correct both distortions, while an output subsidy would leave the input-use distortion uncorrected.

18. The analysis in this section focuses on the effects of imperfect competition in a trading equilibrium. This is in contrast to our earlier analysis, in which the monopoly power resulting from imperfect competition in autarky was completely eroded in the transition to free trade.

19. See Demidova and Rodriguez-Clare (2009), Flam and Helpman (1987), and Helpman and Krugman (1989, chapter 7) for a fuller discussion. Flam and Helpman rule out the second distortion by assuming the number of foreign varieties available and their prices are fixed. Demidova and Rodriguez-Clare employ a heterogeneous firm trade model (see chapter 5), which leaves the number of foreign varieties exported variable, but holds the total number of foreign varieties produced fixed.

20. Except as noted below, this discussion assumes full employment of all resources. But even if some resources are not fully employed, it would indeed be unusual for the expansion of one industry not to draw other resources from employment elsewhere.

21. If the country has some market power on international markets, then the rates at which imports can be exchanged for exports depends on the volume of trade. Selling more of one product will drive down its international relative price, while buying more of another will drive up its international relative price. The marginal revenue from exports is less than their world prices and the marginal cost of imports is greater than theirs. This leads to a generalisation of the optimum tariff argument above to a multi-product context.

22. Tariff revenue is assumed to be redistributed as lump-sum transfers to domestic consumers.

23. Note that $p^M = p^X$ if $\tau_M = \tau_X/(1 - \tau_X)$.

24. For a systematic treatment of this and other factor market distortions see chapters 25 to 27 in Bhagwati et al. (1998).

25. Alternatively, the export good may be reinterpreted as a bundle of freely traded goods with constant relative world market prices.

26. Falvey (1988) analyses the case where some sectors are subject to quotas, while others are subject to tariffs. With tariffs present, relaxing an import quota is no longer unambiguously welfare improving. Anderson and Neary (1992) extends the analysis to the case where the domestic economy is able to capture a fraction of the quota revenue. For an excellent discussion of the difference between price and quantity distortions in international trade models, see Krishna and Panagariya (2000).

27. See Dixit and Norman (1980, 130). Formally, pre- and post-multiplying a negative definite matrix S with the same vector b of the appropriate dimension yields a negative scalar: $b'Sb < 0$.
28. See Neary (1995, 540) for an elaboration of this point.
29. The balance of trade condition must not be invoked here, since it does not hold for compensated net import demands. That is, changes in net import values at *world market* prices do not sum to zero for a given level of utility. Rather, a tariff reform that increases welfare must lead to a trade surplus at constant utility. Formally, this can be seen by rewriting (5) as $\mu^{-1}e_u du = -\sum_i p_i^* S_{i1} dt_1$. Allowing utility to adjust to the post-reform level increases domestic demand, thereby bringing the trade balance back to zero.
30. This is implied by the (clearly too strong) condition that all weights in the determination of $\bar{\tau}$ are positive, which will be the case if all importables are substitutes in net import demand for the *numéraire*.
31. As explained in Anderson and Neary (2007), the changes thus defined should be interpreted as Laspeyres-type approximations of the true changes (which would take account of changes in S and p).
32. A non-technical introduction to the Le Chatelier-Samuelson principle is given in Samuelson's Nobel Prize lecture, Samuelson (1972). For an overview of applications of the principle in international trade, see Kreickemeier (2006).

References

Abe, K. (1992) 'Tariff reform in a small open economy with public production', *International Economic Review* 33, 209–22.

Anderson, J.E. (1994) 'The theory of protection', in D. Greenaway and L.A. Winters (eds), *Surveys in International Trade*. Oxford: Wiley-Blackwell, 107–38.

Anderson, J.E., Neary, J.P. (1992) 'Trade reform with quotas, partial rent retention and tariffs', *Econometrica* 60, 57–76.

—— (2005) *Measuring the restrictiveness of international trade policy*. Cambridge, MA: MIT Press.

—— (2007) 'Welfare versus market access: the implications of tariff structure for tariff reform', *Journal of International Economics* 71, 187–205.

Bhagwati, J. (1964) 'The Pure Theory of International Trade: A Survey', *Economic Journal* 74, 1–81.

Bhagwati, J., Panagariya, A. and Srinivasan, T.N. (1998). *Lectures on International Trade*, 2nd ed. Cambridge, MA: MIT Press.

Blonigen, B., Prusa, T.J. (2003). 'Antidumping', in: Choi, E.K., Harrigan, J. (eds), *Handbook of International Trade*. Oxford: Blackwell.

Brecher, R. (1974) 'Minimum wage rates and the pure theory of international trade', *Quarterly Journal of Economics* 88, 98–116.

Bruno, M. (1972) 'Market Distortions and Reform', *Review of Economic Studies* 39, 373–83.

Corden, W.M. (1971) *The Theory of Protection*. Oxford: Clarendon Press.

—— (1974) Trade Policy and Economic Welfare. Oxford: Clarendon Press.

—— (1997) *Trade Policy and Economic Welfare*, 2nd ed. Oxford: Clarendon Press.

Corden, W.M., Falvey, R. (1985) 'Quotas and the second best', *Economics Letters* 18, 67–70.

Demidova, S., Rodriguez-Clare, A. (2009) 'Trade policy under firm-level heterogeneity in a small economy', *Journal of International Economics* 78, 100–12.

Diewert, E., Turunen-Red, A. and Woodland, A. (1989) 'Productivity- and Pareto-Improving Changes in Taxes and Tariffs', *Review of Economic Studies* 56, 199–216.

Falvey, R. (1988) 'Tariffs, quotas, and piecemeal policy reform', *Journal of International Economics* 25, 177–83.

—— (1994). 'Revenue enhancing tariff reform', *Weltwirtschaftliches* Archiv 130, 175–89.

Falvey, R., Kreickemeier, U. (2009) 'Tariff reforms with rigid wages', *Economic Theory* 41, 23–39.

Flam, H., Helpman, E. (1987) 'Industrial policy under monopolistic competition', *Journal of International Economics* 22, 79–102.

Hatta, T. (1977) 'A recommendation for a better tariff structure', *Econometrica* 45, 1859–69.

Hatzipanayotou, P., Michael, M., Miller, S. (1994) 'Win-win indirect tax reform', *Economics Letters* 44, 147–51.

Helpman, E., Krugman, P. (1989) *Trade Policy and Market Structure*. Cambridge, MA: MIT Press.

Ju, J., Krishna, K. (2000) 'Welfare and market access effects of piecemeal tariff reform', *Journal of International Economics* 51, 305–16.

Keen, M., Ligthart, J. (2002) 'Coordinating tariff reduction and domestic tax reform', *Journal of International Economics* 56, 489–507.

Kreickemeier, U. (2005) 'Unemployment and the welfare effects of trade policy', *Canadian Journal of Economics* 38, 194–210.

—— (2006) 'The Le Chatelier Principle in the theory of international trade', *Journal of Economics* 89, 245–66.

Kreickemeier, U., Raimondos-Møller, P. (2008) 'Tariff-tax reforms and market access', *Journal of Development Economics* 87, 85–91.

—— (2010) 'Market access, welfare, and international capital mobility', mimeo, Copenhagen Business School.

Krishna, P., Panagariya, A. (2000) 'A Unification of Second Best Results in International Trade', *Journal of International Economics* 52, 235–57.

Meade, J.E. (1955) *The Theory of International Economic Policy*, vol. 2, *Trade and Welfare*. Oxford: Oxford University Press.

Lerner, A. (1933) 'The concept of monopoly and the measurement of monopoly power', *Review of Economic Studies* 1, 157–75.

—— (1936) 'The Symmetry between Import and Export Taxes', *Economica* N.S. 3. 306–13.

Lopéz, R., Panagariya, A. (1992) 'On the theory of piecemeal tariff reform: the case of imported intermediate inputs', *American Economic Review* 82, 615–25.

Neary, J.P. (1995) 'Trade liberalization and shadow prices in the presence of tariffs and quotas', *International Economic Review* 36, 531–54.

Neary, J.P., Ruane, F. (1988) 'International capital mobility, shadow prices, and the cost of protection', *International Economic Review* 29, 571–85.

Samuelson, P. (1972) 'Maximum principles in analytical economics', *American Economic Review* 62, 249–62.

Syropoulos, C. (2002) 'Optimum tariffs and retaliation revisited: How country size matters', *Review of Economic Studies* 69, 707–27.

Vousden, N. (1990) *The Economics of Trade Protection*. Cambridge: Cambridge University Press.

10
The Political Economy of Protection
Wilfred J. Ethier[*]

1 Introduction

International trade theory has traditionally examined protection from a *normative* perspective: What are its consequences and when is it justified from the point of view of national welfare? Beginning in the 1980s increasing attention has been paid to analyzing protection from a *positive* perspective: What actually determines it? These two approaches are obviously complementary – both are necessary. This chapter addresses the latter. Other surveys are provided by Nelson (1988), Magee (1994) and Rodrik (1995).

I address the ability of our theory adequately to explain trade policy and trade agreements. My bottom line will be tentative: We have made much progress, but we have a good way to go. It is important that we make the effort.

2 An analytical framework

To facilitate comparison across contributions it helps enormously to have a common theoretical framework in which to view them. I shall use the following.

Assume two countries (*Home* and *Foreign*), two factors (*Kapital* and *Labor*), and $N + 1$ traded goods $(0, 1, \ldots, N)$. Good 0 is a *numéraire* good, produced by labour alone. Goods 1 to N are produced by capital and labour, with capital specific to each of these sectors. H imports goods 1 to n and exports goods $n + 1$ to N.

I follow the preponderant part of the political-economy literature in assuming a sector-specific factor. There are two reasons for this. *First*, much of the literature suggests that specific factors are much more likely to be able to organize and so exert political influence. See Olson (1965), Pincus (1975), and Caves (1976). *Second*, specific factors, together with the demand separability discussed below, allows the analysis to employ simple partial-equilibrium techniques.

Ownership of each specific factor i is distributed uniformly over a fraction α_i of the population (labour force), with each individual owning some of at most one of the specific factors. Let $\alpha = \alpha_1 + \cdots + \alpha_N$ denote the fraction of the population owning some of a specific factor. Choose units so that a unit of good 0 is produced by a unit of labour. Thus, assuming good 0 is actually produced, the wage $w = 1$.

In each country individual preferences are summarized by the utility function

$$U = c_0 + u_1(c_1) + \cdots + u_N(c_N),$$

where c_i denotes consumption of good i. This implies individual demand functions $d_i = d_i(Q_i)$, $i = 1, \ldots, N$, where Q_i denotes the domestic relative price of good i in terms of good 0. Residual income is all spent on the numéraire good 0. I assume that endowments in both countries are such that each both produces and consumes good 0. Then an individual's utility can be expressed in the indirect form

$$v(Q_1, \ldots, Q_N; y) = \sum S_i(Q_i) + y, \tag{1}$$

where $S_i(Q_i) = u_i(d_i(Q_i)) - Q_i d_i(Q_i)$, the consumer surplus derived from good i, and y denotes the individual's income.

3   Unilateral trade policy

I briefly describe the principal alternative explanations of tariff determination, before focusing in more detail on the one that has most been used.

3.1   Voting models

Wolfgang Mayer (1984) introduced voting models to endogenize tariff formation.

The median voter approach. To see how this might work in a simple framework, suppose that $n = N = 1$, so that good 1 is imported in exchange for the *numéraire* good, and that H is small, so that the world relative price $P_1 \equiv P$ is given. Thus $Q = P(1+t)$, where t denotes the tariff on good 1. If ϕ denotes some individual's share of national income Y.

$$y = \phi Y = \phi[L + \pi(Q) + tPM]. \tag{2}$$

The three terms in brackets respectively denote labour income, specific-factor income and tariff revenue. Substitute (2) into (1) and differentiate to see the effect of a change in t on the individual.

$$\frac{\partial v}{\partial t} = t\phi P \frac{\partial M}{\partial t} + LPd\left[\phi - \frac{1}{L}\right] + Y\frac{\partial \phi}{\partial t}. \tag{3}$$

(Use has been made of the facts that the derivative of consumer surplus is commodity demand and that that of specific-factor income is commodity supply.) Setting $\partial v / \partial t = 0$ yields the individual's most preferred tariff:

$$t' = \frac{Pd\left[\phi - \frac{1}{L}\right] + Y \frac{\partial \phi}{\partial t}}{-\phi P \frac{\partial M}{\partial t}}. \tag{4}$$

The denominator of the right-hand side of (4) is positive, since an increase in t lowers M. Assume that tariff revenue is distributed to the population in a manner neutral in the sense of Ethier (1984): proportional to each individual's share in factor income. Thus ϕ equals the individual's factor income share.

Individuals in the $1 - \alpha$ share of the population that owns no capital have a share of national income ϕ below their share of labour income $(1/L)$, and a tariff will lower their share of national income. Thus $t' < 0$ for such workers: They prefer a particular import subsidy. Since the ownership of capital is distributed uniformly over the share α of the population, this situation is the reverse for them: They all prefer a particular tariff.

Suppose trade policy is decided by a direct popular vote. A majority (and so the median voter) will support the tariff if and only if $\alpha > 1/2$; otherwise the subsidy wins (ignoring the minute possibility of a tie). Mayer investigates such voting in the Heckscher–Ohlin–Samuelson model and in a specific-factors model, but the above simple framework suffices to illustrate several key points.

3.1.1   Key points about the median-voter approach

First, the great advantage is that this approach grounds trade policy in a fully specified political-economy model. The political component is not reduced to a black box.

Second, a disadvantage is that trade policy is almost never voted on directly by the public: It is implemented by governments. Elections in which the parties or candidates compete solely on trade policy may proxy for direct voting. Perhaps that did occur sometimes in the nineteenth century, but it is very rare now.

Third, by focusing only on direct voting, this approach excludes lobbying and political campaigning. In particular, it gives no scope to the factors determining the potential for special interests to organize, as emphasized by Olson (1965).

Fourth, the interior solution for t' in (4) is critically due to the fact that individual voters care about their share of trade-tax revenue. If such revenue is ignored, capitalists, if they do want a tariff (which they must do if the import-competing sector is initially large enough), wish it to be prohibitive, and laborers want a very large import subsidy, that is, one large enough that the effect on trade-tax revenue cannot be ignored. But we observe neither this result nor, in the case of industrial countries, any real interest in trade tax revenue (Regan, 2006). Still, trade-tax revenue exists, so it should logically be included in our models, but the critical role it then assumes in the theory seems totally at odds with its apparent negligible practical importance. I refer to this as the Cognitive-Dissonance (CD) issue. I assign it a label because, as will become apparent, it is pervasive in the literature on the political economy of trade policy.

3.1.2 Partisan politics

Brock and Magee (1978) did focus explicitly on the roles of lobbies and parties in the electoral process. See also Magee, Brock and Young (1979) and Austen-Smith (1991). Suppose, in the above context, that capital and labour organize lobbies to influence the outcome of an election between two political parties. This outcome is inherently uncertain, with the probability of success of a particular party dependent on the contributions received by the two parties from the two lobbies plus the platforms announced by the parties. Those platforms consist of proposed tariffs. Each party, eyeing its rival and aware of how lobbies determine their contributions, sets its platform to maximize its chance of success. Each lobby, eyeing the other, reacts to the platforms by making the contribution that will maximize its expected welfare.

This approach accommodates partisan politics and lobbying at the expense of relegating the electoral process itself to a black box (the BB issue). The substitution is, on the whole, a step toward greater realism. But, because of its cumbersome analysis, the approach has been little used.

3.2 Political support

The portion of the literature discussed thus far has focused on the electoral process, but another, larger, portion has addressed the behaviour of an incumbent government in office.

3.2.1 The basic political-support approach

Hillman (1982) introduced the concept of a political-support function to analyze the behaviour of an incumbent government confronted by a special-interest group. See also Hillman (1989, 1990), Long and Vousden (1991) Hillman, Long and Moser (1995), and Hillman and Moser (1996).

Suppose, in the model of section 2, that the owners of capital specific to an import sector i constitute an interest group desiring tariff protection. The incumbent government wishes to set a tariff that will maximize its political support:

$$W^i = f^i(\psi(Q_i) - \psi(P_i), \ Q_i - P_i). \tag{5}$$

Here ψ measures the concerns of the interest group. The first argument of f^i accounts for the influence of the interest group on political support and the second argument that of the population at large. In both arguments, political support depends not only on the outcome (Q_i) but on how that outcome differs from what it would be were the government to take no action. The idea is that the government would be held politically accountable only for what it has done. This is an important distinction. But it is relevant only in cases where the economy is subject to an external shock that influences the free-trade equilibrium – Hillman (1982) for example. So subsume for now the free-trade situation into the functional form. Assuming that f^i is increasing in its first argument and decreasing in its second, the government will maximize its political support W^i in (5) by trading off the general welfare for that of the interest group.

To be more specific, assume that the measure of interest-group benefit is the income of the corresponding specific factor $\pi_i(Q_i)$ and that the measure of the effect of policy on the general welfare is the effect on the per-capita consumer surplus derived from the corresponding good: $S_i(Q_i)$. Then, suppressing for convenience the index i, (5) can be expressed as follows:

$$W = W(\pi(Q[t]), \ S(Q[t])), \tag{6}$$

where W is increasing in both arguments. Differentiating (6) with respect to t and rearranging terms yields

$$\frac{1}{PW_2}\frac{dW}{dt} = I(Q)x - M, \tag{7}$$

where x denotes the output of the sector, and $I(Q) \equiv (W_1 - W_2)/W_2$ can be interpreted as an index of the political influence of the special-interest group. Call the interest group *influential* if the right-hand side of (7) is positive when $t = 0$; that is, an influential interest group is able to obtain protection.

A tariff will increase x in (7) and lower M, so, *unless I also falls sufficiently rapidly*, the government will impose a prohibitive tariff whenever confronted by an influential interest group.

There are two ways to alter the model to avoid this extreme result. One is to add trade-tax revenue appropriately to the arguments of (6), as was done in the voting model discussed above. But of course this will also introduce the CD issue: The chosen tariff or subsidy will depend *crucially* upon its effect on trade-tax revenue.

The second way to alter the model is to suppose that the influence of an influential special-interest group is limited, that is, that I declines as t (and so Q) increases. If I declines rapidly enough, (7) will have an interior solution corresponding to a non-prohibitive tariff. Consider this possibility in more detail.

The influence of a special-interest group can be measured by the value of I when $t = 0$, that is, $I(P)$, and also by the rate of its decline: $I' < 0$. Assume for simplicity that these measures are in accord: $I(P)$ is larger when the absolute value of I' is smaller.

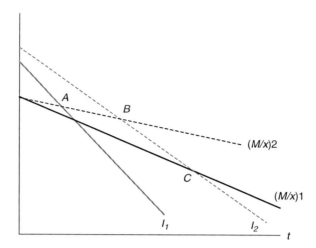

Figure 10.1   The tariff with an influential interest group.

Figure 10.1 shows the case of an influential interest group (the right-hand side of (7) is positive when $t = 0$) where I falls rapidly enough to give an interior solution (at point A). I_2 (where point B indicates the equilibrium) shows more influence than I_1. Other things equal, a greater influence implies a larger t and a lower import-penetration ratio M/x.

The elasticity e of import demand plays an important role in many tariff issues,[1] so it is of interest to examine its effect. This is more complex. In figure 10.1 $(M/x)_2$ reflects a lower elasticity than $(M/x)_1$. Along a given I_1 the reduction in e lowers t and raises M/x. But a lower e also implies a lower dead-weight loss to increasing t, so the lobby should become more influential, which is reflected in I_2 replacing I_1. This raises t and lowers M/x, so the net effect is ambiguous. For a given reduction in e, as reflected in given $(M/x)_1$ and $(M/x)_2$, this net effect depends upon the sensitivity of lobby influence to e. With low sensitivity, t falls and M/x increases; with intermediate sensitivity, t and M/x both increase; with high sensitivity, t increases and M/x falls. In other words, at a given level of import penetration, t is negatively related to e.

An influential interest group will of course be concerned that any protection it receives not be undone by the government of a trading partner subsidizing its exports. That the home government shares this concern is implied by (5), which says that the home government is rewarded on the basis of the net effects of its actions. Thus we should expect the government to implement a countervailing duty law, providing that any foreign subsidy be countervailed by an increase in the home tariff. To my knowledge, the political-support literature has not actually made this point, but it seems a clear inference from its approach.

The above discussion applies to an influential interest group. But what happens when it is not influential? There seem to be two alternatives.

(a) An interest group for which the right-hand side of (7) is negative when $t = 0$ will induce the government to subsidize imports without bound (or as much as the treasury will bear) unless I rises sufficiently rapidly as the subsidy is increased.

(b) This literature seems based on the observation that import-competing interests are individually much more affected by trade policy regarding their goods than are the more numerous but more diffused consumers. Then such interests, even if not politically organized at all, are much more likely than consumers to vote on the basis of such policy. This suggests assuming that the right-hand side of (7) is never negative when $t = 0$: It is positive for an influential group and zero for a non-influential group. Thus the latter will result in $t = 0$.

Of these alternatives, (b) seems to me more in accord with the spirit of the general support-function approach, so I shall take it as characterizing that approach. But, to my knowledge, that literature again has not addressed these alternatives at all, much less providing a formal framework to indicate when one or the other might be more appropriate.

Suppose, finally, that the interest group corresponds to an export sector. Analogously to the above, an influential group would be able to induce the government to provide an export subsidy. However, if, as discussed above, foreign governments have adopted countervailing-duty laws, such a subsidy would amount to a cost that conferred no benefit on the interest group and so would not be adopted. The government is powerless to aid such a group with trade policy. Non-influential groups can be treated analogously to such groups in import-competing sectors. That is, $t = 0$ in export sectors with non-influential interest groups. Again, this seems to be a reasonable inference from the nature of the political-support approach, though it is not discussed in that literature.

3.2.2   Key points about the political-support approach

First, political support depends upon the effect of the government's actions on agents' well-being, not just the latter itself.

Second, the approach exhibits the BB issue: the political-support function is not derived from microeconomic fundamentals.

Third, for influential import-competing sectors the degree of influence is positively correlated with the tariff rate.

Fourth, for influential import-competing sectors the tariff is negatively correlated with the import-penetration ratio.

Fifth, for influential import-competing sectors the tariff is negatively correlated with the elasticity of import demand, at a given import-penetration ratio.

Sixth*, if the country has at least one influential import-competing sector it will adopt a countervailing-duty law.

Seventh*, non-influential import-competing sectors are likely to be characterized by an absence of trade-policy intervention.

Eighth, the government is unable to do anything for, and therefore to extract political support from, influential export sectors.

Ninth*, non-influential export sectors are likely to be characterized by an absence of trade-policy intervention.

(An asterisk indicates a point that reasonably characterizes the political-support approach but that, to my knowledge, has not been discussed explicitly in its literature.)

3.2.3   The campaign-contributions variant of the political-support approach

This variant of the political-support approach, due to Grossman and Helpman (1994, 2002), identifies such support as financial contributions (or bribes). Following the authors, we can denote this approach as Protection For Sale, or PFS. This has become the most widely used political-economy model of protection, not because it is realistic – or even plausible – but because it delivers a tariff formula based squarely on a complete micro political-economy description of behavior.

The distinguishing assumptions of this version of the political-support approach are as follows: (a) The N specific factors are exogenously divided into N^1 that are politically organized and N^0 that are not (so $N = N^0 + N^1$). (b) Political support consists of campaign contributions (or bribes). (c) Each lobby, with an eye on the other lobbies, offers the government a *contribution schedule* detailing the contribution it will make as a function of the vector of all N trade policies. The lobby wishes to maximize the excess of its specific-factor income over its actual contribution. (d) The government wishes to maximize a weighted average of national income and total contributions,

$$W = \beta Y + (1 - \beta) \sum_{N^1} C^i, \tag{8}$$

where C^i denotes the actual contribution of lobby i and $\beta \leq 1$ the weight the government attaches to national income. (e) The outcome is modeled as a menu-auction equilibrium in the sense of B. Douglas Bernheim and Michael Whinston (1986).

The PFS model yields equilibrium contributions and tariffs. The former are of little interest, given the contrived nature of the model. But the latter, as pointed out by Goldberg and Maggi (1999), follow directly as necessary conditions for maximizing the joint surplus of the government and the lobbies, regardless otherwise of the actual bargaining model. The equilibrium tariffs are given by

$$\frac{t_i}{1+t_i} = \frac{\xi_i - \alpha}{\beta/(1-\beta)+\alpha} \cdot \frac{1}{(M_i/x_i) \cdot e_i} \tag{9}$$

where $\xi_i = 1$ if the industry is politically organized and 0 if it is not.

Note that if the government cares only about social welfare ($\beta = 1$) it adopts a policy of free trade. This is also the result if everyone belongs to some organized lobby ($\alpha = 1$), but this latter result is of little interest as it just reflects the extreme assumptions that all organized sectors are equally potent politically and that they all lobby equally about all trade policies.

Equation (9) implies the following. *Organized import-competing sectors* ($\xi_i = 1$) will receive positive protection that is positively related to the degree of influence ξ_i (though of course that is here constrained to be only zero or unity), and negatively related to the import-penetration ratio and to the elasticity of import demand. This is exactly what the general political-support function approach predicts, of which the PFS model is a special case.

Unorganized import-competing sectors ($\xi_i = 0$) will be confronted with subsidized imports. This contrasts with my interpretation of the spirit of the political-support approach ($t = 0$), though, as pointed out above, that literature has not been explicit about this.

Organized export sectors ($\xi_i = 1$) will find their exports subsidized. This also contrasts with the predictions of the general political-support approach.

Unorganized export sectors ($\xi_i = 0$) will find their exports taxed. This again contrasts with my interpretation of the spirit of the political-support approach ($t = 0$), though, again, that literature has not been explicit about this.

3.2.4 Empirical investigations of the PFS variant

The PFS model has received considerable empirical attention; see Goldberg and Maggi (1999), Gawande and Bandyopadhyay (2000), Mitra, Thomakos, and Ulubasoglu (2002), and McCallum (2004). These papers uniformly claim support for the PFS model, but in a highly selective way. They have confined themselves to import-competing sectors. An important claim in this literature is that they are estimating (9), an equation that comes directly from a detailed microeconomic model (i.e., no BB issue).

These papers do not employ actual tariffs[2] because they are constrained by international trade agreements, not part of the basic PFS model. So data on administered protection is used instead. It is not clear how much this helps, since administered protection very often involves a good deal of bilateral negotiation; for example, Goldberg and Maggi, 1999, 159). But there are more serious concerns.

Administered protection using tariffs involves primarily antidumping and countervailing duties. These are imposed as a result of a well-defined legal procedure that, in sharp contrast to the PFS model, gives no weight to either national welfare or tariff revenue. So if such data does fit (9), even though we *know* it was not generated by what the PFS approach models, one must wonder what such a fit means. (Political organization also plays no role in the administrative procedure, but one might conjecture that politically organized sectors are also better able to file petitions.)

Administered protection using non-tariff barriers involves, in data from the 1980s, primarily voluntary export restraints (VERs). A key property of VERs is that the rents from the barriers are captured by exporters, whereas the assumption in the PFS model that the importing country captures those rents is crucial to the derivation of (9). If the PFS model is altered to constrain the importing country from capturing the rents, necessary if VER data is used, the model predicts nothing like (9). So a good fit to (9) is not a confirmation of the PFS model: Indeed it is a rejection if (9) fits better than what the PFS model would imply for VER data.

The empirical studies have also not investigated the predictions of the PFS model that most closely reflect its central assumptions: import subsidies for all politically unorganized import-competing sectors and export taxes for all politically unorganized export sectors. These predictions involve instruments that are *not* constrained by international trade agreements and are therefore free of the issues that prevented the use of conventional tariffs. But it appears obvious that these predictions are not borne out by the facts.

Thus the empirical work has not provided support for the PFS model itself (apparently the CD issue dominates). But it has given powerful evidence that, in politically organized import-competing sectors, protection is negatively related to the import-penetration ratio, presumably reflecting the tug between sectoral special interests and consumer surplus central to most political-economy approaches to trade policy (see Ethier 2006). Also in such sectors, protection appears to be negatively related to the domestic elasticity of import demand. Furthermore, this literature argues persuasively that distinguishing between politically organized and unorganized sectors is crucial to understanding this dependence.

So we have support not for the PFS model in particular, but for 'something else'. What else? The general political-support approach makes just those predictions that have been verified and is free of the issues attending the PFS model, mentioned above. Thus the empirical literature can be interpreted as providing strong evidence for the general political-support approach, but not for its PFS variant.

This is a notable accomplishment. In my mind it is the most valuable contribution to date in the large empirical literature addressing the political economy of trade policy. And the PFS model, by supplying (9) in explicit form, was critical in stimulating this contribution. However, the more general approach does not derive the political-support function from microeconomic fundamentals, so the BB issue remains. Thus, the empirical literature, intriguing as it is, cannot be interpreted as successfully confirming a structural model derived directly from a theory based on microeconomic fundamentals. More work is called for.

The empirical literature on the PFS model uses its parameter estimates to infer the size of the structural parameter β, the weight the government attaches to social welfare. Typically this weight turns out to be quite high: The government is seen as valuing social welfare much more than contributions. But since that literature has not succeeded in confirming the structure specific to the PFS model, it is not clear what significance, if any, can be attached to this seemingly optimistic inference.

3.2.5 Key points about the PFS variant

First, political support is identified with contributions (bribes).

Second, the approach is free from the BB issue: both the contributions and the trade policies are derived from microeconomic fundamentals.

Third, the PFS variant is subject to the CD issue.

Fourth, for politically organized import-competing sectors the degree of influence is positively correlated with the tariff rate.

Fifth, for organized import-competing sectors the tariff is negatively correlated with the import-penetration ratio.

Sixth, for organized import-competing sectors the tariff is negatively correlated with the elasticity of import demand, at a given import-penetration ratio.

Seventh, unorganized import-competing sectors are characterized by import subsidies.

Eighth, unorganized export sectors are characterized by export taxes.

Ninth, the empirical literature supports those predictions of the PFS model that overlap with the general support-function approach, but fails to support those that distinguish the PFS model from the general approach.

4 An analytical framework for trade agreements

I next turn to the political economy of international trade agreements. For this it is convenient first to extend the analytical framework presented in section 2 to an international equilibrium with two countries.

Each country may tax or subsidize either imports or exports. For H, let Q_i and P_i denote, respectively, the domestic and international relative price (in terms of the *numéraire*) of good i, and τ_i one plus the *ad-valorem* trade tax t_i. Thus

$$Q_i = \tau_i P_i \quad \text{for } i = 1, \ldots, n,$$

and

$$Q_j = P_j/\tau_j \quad \text{for } j = n+1, \ldots, N.$$

Analogous F variables will be distinguished by asterisks.

Equilibrium in the world market for good i, $i = 1, \ldots, n$, is represented by

$$M_i(\tau_i P_i) = X_i^*(P_i/\tau_i^*), \tag{10}$$

where M_i and X_i^* respectively denote H import demand and F export supply. H's import tax and F's export tax thus determine P_i, independently of other sectors. This in turn implies the following:

$$\frac{\tau_i}{P_i} \frac{dP_i}{dt_i} = -\frac{e_i}{e_i + f_i^*} \tag{11}$$

and

$$\frac{\tau_i}{Q_i} \frac{dQ_i}{dt_i} = \frac{\tau_i}{P_i} \frac{dP_i}{dt_i} + 1 = \frac{f_i^*}{e_i + f_i^*},$$

where $e_i \equiv -\tau_i P_i M_i'/M_i > 0$ and $f_i^* \equiv P_i X_i^{*\prime}/\tau_i^* X_i^* > 0$.

Similarly, equilibrium in the world market for goods $n+1$ to N can be represented by $M_j^*(\tau_j^* P_j) = X_j(P_j/\tau_j)$.

Thus,

$$\frac{\tau_j}{P_j} \frac{dP_j}{dt_j} = \frac{f_j}{f_j + e_j^*}$$

and

$$\frac{\tau_j}{Q_j} \frac{dQ_j}{dt_j} = \frac{\tau_j}{P_j} \frac{dP_j}{dt_j} - 1 = -\frac{e_j^*}{f_j + e_j^*}.$$

H imports of goods $1, \ldots, n$ need not equal in value H exports of goods $n+1, \ldots, N$: Trade balance is reached with a net exchange of good 0.

5   International trade agreements

The political economy of trade agreements must be derivative from the political economy of protection. As there are variants of the latter, there are variants of the former.

There are two basic approaches to trade agreements. The *terms-of-trade externality approach* sees the sole basis for a trade agreement as the possibility that national governments, conducting national policies, ignore the effects of those policies on trading partners through the terms of trade. Thus, all can gain by expanding trade at unchanged terms of trade.

The *exchange-of-market-access approach* sees the attraction of a trade agreement for a national government as due to the fact that such an agreement enables the government to do something for export interests that it cannot do unilaterally. As this applies to all governments, it can serve as a basis for negotiation.

The terms-of-trade externality approach has by far received the most formal attention by trade theorists. But this has not at all been echoed by trade policy makers, who virtually without exception speak in terms of the exchange of market access. Furthermore, some of the formal papers claiming to espouse the exchange-of-market-access approach actually use an analytical framework equivalent to that of the terms-of-trade externality approach, so that, in essence, they offer only an alternative rhetoric.

5.1 The terms-of-trade externality approach

A prominent twentieth-century accomplishment of international trade theory was its theory of international trade policy and trade agreements. Building on Harry Johnson's classic paper (1953–54), scores of contributions developed and elaborated what is now often called the terms-of-trade externality approach. The deservedly influential work of Bagwell and Staiger (1999, 2002) may justly be seen as triumphantly completing the research agenda implied by Johnson nearly half a century earlier. See also Grossman and Helpman (1995).

Suppose initially that $N = 1$, so that H imports good 1 from F in exchange for the *numéraire* good. The H government wishes to maximize the objective function $W(Q, P)$; the subscript 1 is omitted for simplicity. W is assumed to have the following properties:

$$W_1(P,P) > 0, \qquad W_2(Q,P) < 0. \tag{12}$$

W can be thought of as an example of a political-support function. The first assumed property, that W can be increased by departing from trade to protect the import-competing sector, allows the political dimension; the second property simply says that a terms-of-trade deterioration lowers W, presumably because of its negative effect on social welfare. This formulation is consistent with many political-economy models, including much of the political-support approach literature such as the PFS campaign-contributions variant.

The F government analogously wishes to maximize the objective function $W^*(1/Q^*, 1/P)$, where $Q^* = P/\tau^*$, and τ^* denotes one plus the F tariff on the *numéraire* good. $W*$ is assumed to have the properties:

$$W_1^*(1/P, 1/P) > 0, \qquad W_2^*(1/Q^*, 1/P) < 0. \tag{13}$$

Here the political dimension reflects a benefit to the F government from aiding labour via protection, since the import-competing sector in F uses only labour.

5.1.1   *The role of trade agreements*

If neither government cares about the terms of trade ($W_2 \equiv 0 \equiv W_2^*$), each government's objective depends only upon the respective relative domestic price. This can be controlled unilaterally by each government with trade policy, so there is no scope for international cooperation about such policies. In this context concern for the terms of trade is necessary to motivate a trade agreement.

Suppose, by contrast, that both governments care only about social welfare. Then global efficiency requires that agents in both countries face the same prices, $Q = Q^*$, indicating that opportunities for gainful trade are being fully exploited. This will be true when $\tau \tau^* = 1$ (Mayer 1981). This *social efficiency locus* includes free trade plus cases where one country taxes imports and the other subsidizes exports, in effect using trade policy to add an international side payment to the free-trade outcome.

However, W and W^* include political influences, so there is no reason to believe that social efficiency will coincide with political efficiency. The set of politically efficient policy pairs can be determined by solving the problem:

maximize $W(Q,P)$ subject to $W^*(Q^*,P) = W_0^*$

for all feasible values of W_0^*. This problem has the following first-order conditions, for each feasible value of W_0^*:

$$\frac{\partial W}{\partial \tau} + \lambda \frac{\partial W^*}{\partial \tau} = 0,$$

$$\frac{\partial W}{\partial \tau^*} + \lambda \frac{\partial W^*}{\partial \tau^*} = 0,$$

where λ denotes the Lagrange multiplier. Solving to eliminate λ gives an implicit relation in τ and τ^*: the *political efficiency locus*.

The multiplier λ represents the shadow cost to each government in being constrained in its policy choice by the size of the negative externality it can impose on the other government. In the Nash equilibrium (where each government is implementing the tariff that maximizes its own objective function given the tariff chosen by the other government) λ is in effect set at zero, whereas it is positive along the political efficiency locus. Thus, there is something to be gained by cooperation. So, in the present framework: *A desire to deal with a terms-of-trade externality can motivate a trade agreement, and it is the ONLY thing that can motivate a trade agreement.*

5.1.2   *Reciprocity*

Such a trade agreement is necessarily reciprocal in the sense that each country is departing from its Nash tariff in exchange for its partner doing the same. But the central role of the terms of trade in the present framework suggests a natural precise definition of reciprocity. Let P_0 denote the value of P that obtains in the

Nash equilibrium. Then a *price-reciprocity schedule* can be defined as the set of all $\tau - \tau^*$ pairs that satisfy:

$$M(\tau P_0) = X^*(P_0/\tau^*).$$

Along this schedule,

$$\frac{\tau}{\tau^*} \frac{d\tau}{d\tau^*} = \frac{f^*}{e}.$$

A trade agreement implemented on the price-reciprocity schedule involves the two countries altering their trade policies in such a way as to keep the terms of trade unchanged.

Figure 10.2 illustrates the terms-of-trade externality approach. The SEL, PEL, and PRS curves respectively depict the social efficiency locus, the political efficiency locus and the price-reciprocity schedule. N and TA illustrate the Nash equilibrium and an efficient trade agreement. As the two governments move from N towards TA along PRS they are reciprocally reducing their tariffs so as to leave the terms of trade unchanged. The tariff reductions generate beneficial reductions in the consumption costs and production costs caused by the tariffs, but they also generate political costs. Initially the efficiency benefits outweigh the political costs because of the terms-of-trade externalities in place at N. Beyond TA further political costs begin to outweigh further efficiency benefits.

TA is an efficient reciprocal trade agreement in the sense that any other agreement on PRS could be renegotiated to the mutual benefit of both countries. If governments cared only about social welfare, *TA* would coincide with *S*; if governments were unconcerned with the terms of trade, N would be at TA.

5.1.3 *Key points about the terms-of-trade externality approach*

First, this approach takes the government objective functions W and W* as given. But this is *not* an example of the BB issue. Rather, it is a source of generality since many models featuring government behavior based on microeconomic fundamentals are special cases of these objective functions.

Second, the approach does display the CD issue. Indeed, it does so in an extreme form, as it posits that government concern for the terms of trade, and so for trade-tax revenue, is the *sole* reason for a trade agreement.

Third, the approach sits uncomfortably with actual trade agreements. While WTO members have bound their tariffs on literally thousands of imports, only a few have bound only a few taxes on exports. The WTO explicitly allows the taxation of unbound exports. Thus actual trade agreements do not prevent countries from manipulating their terms-of-trade. At a trade agreement such as TA in figure 10.2, each country has an incentive to use trade policy to turn the terms of trade in its favour. With the existing GATT/WTO framework of trade agreements, it is fully entitled to do so with export taxes.

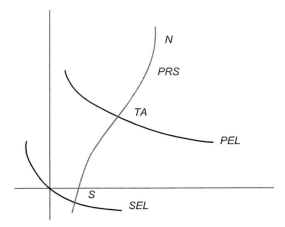

Figure 10.2   The terms-of-trade externality approach.

In the simple model described above, a trade agreement that bound each country's tariff but left export taxes unbound would be completely meaningless, regardless of its purpose. But that extreme result is an artifact of the two-good assumption. If a country binds tariffs on many imports it does constrain its ability to use trade policy to influence the relative prices of those imports in terms of each other. Thus actual trade agreements do have real effects, but constraining terms-of-trade manipulation is not one of them.

There is one exception to this. The U.S. Constitution prohibits the U.S. government from taxing exports. So, from the terms-of-trade externality perspective this raises the following question: Why does the United States sign on to trade agreements that prevent it from influencing the terms of trade in its favor while imposing no such constraint on its trading partners?

While the GATT/WTO allows countries to tax their exports, it significantly constrains their ability to subsidize exports. That is, it explicitly seeks to deny countries the option of conferring a positive terms-of-trade externality upon their trading partners.

Fourth, although this approach is consistent with much of the political-support literature, it does differ from it in a potentially significant way. That literature emphasizes that political support depends on the perceived *actions* of a government, not on *outcomes*. The approach just described, however, makes political support depend entirely on outcomes: Q and P. In some cases this distinction may not matter – if there is a transparent one-to-one relation between actions and outcomes, for example – but in other cases it may. To see this, consider the following simple example.[3] Suppose the H government cares nothing about the terms of trade. Now suppose there is an exogenous, from the H point of view, increase in τ^*. The H government then alters τ to keep Q unchanged.

The political support it receives will not change if that support depends only upon outcomes, which have not changed, but it will increase if that support depends upon H government actions, which have changed in response to an event beyond its control.[4] There is a real issue here, which the terms-of-trade externality approach assumes away.

5.2 The exchange-of-market-access approach

A large literature insists that trade agreements seek to *exchange market access*: I will grant your exporters increased access to my market in exchange for increased access to your market for my exporters. For an institutional approach, see Hauser (1986), Finger (1988, 1991), and Moser (1990); for a more formal approach, see Hillman, Long and Moser (1995), Hillman and Moser (1996) and Ethier (2008). Bagwell and Staiger use similar terminology to describe their approach. For example, they state (2002, 28–29), 'we may interpret "cost shifting", "terms-of-trade gain", and "market-access restriction" as three phrases that describe … [a] single economic experience'. The earlier literature, it seems clear, had 'something else' in mind. But drawing an analytical distinction has proved elusive, largely because the earlier literature, when it expressed its ideas in formal terms (e.g., Hillman and Moser, 1996), did so in models that, as Bagwell and Staiger (2002, 20) correctly observe, were very often special cases of their own. In such cases the distinction from the terms-of-trade externality argument is entirely one of rhetoric, not substance.

The description in Section 3 of the basic political-support approach can provide a formal basis to define trade agreements based on the exchange of market access and to distinguish them from those that are not. The essential idea behind the exchange of market access seems to be that each country, for whatever reason, agrees to allow increased imports of a particular good in exchange for increased exports of another particular good. That is, such trade agreements are necessarily *inter-sectoral*.

The analytical framework of Sections 2 and 4 features extensive separability: equilibrium policies in each sector are determined independently of those in the other sectors. With policies in each sector determined independently, there could be an incentive for independent sector-by-sector international negotiations not involving inter-sectoral trade-offs, such as the 1965 United States – Canada automobile agreement. In such an *intra-sectoral* negotiation the governments would bargain over t_1 and t_1^*, with any implied change in $M_1 = X_1^*$ settled by a change in the trade volume of the *numéraire* good.

Consider the following question. With policy determination in each sector independent of that in the other sector, is it *necessary*, for trade negotiations to serve a useful purpose, that they address inter-sectoral trade-offs? If so, we may regard the negotiations as motivated by a desire to exchange market access:

trade agreements can be said to be based on the exchange of market access if and only if there is no reason for sector-by-sector negotiations.

Note that this definition requires the necessity of inter-sectoral negotiations. Since in this analytical framework agents ignore cross-sectional effects, negotiations addressing those effects could well be useful, as would national policymaking addressing those effects. So defining the exchange of market access on the *sufficiency* of inter-sectoral negotiations would not be a useful discriminatory device.

Our analytical framework and discussion of the basic political-support approach in Section 2 offers no opportunity for an intra-sectoral trade agreement. In sector 1, for example, F is implementing no policy and so can offer H nothing in return for a lower tariff. Thus any trade agreement must be based on the exchange of market access.

To focus on such an exchange in the sharpest possible way, consider a simple trade agreement involving only goods 1 and $n+1$. Suppose for simplicity that the two implemented tariffs are both prohibitive.

The motive for a trade agreement based on the exchange of market access would be to enable each government to offer its export sector something while taking something less from its import-competing sector. It is true that, with a non-cooperative equilibrium featuring countervailing-duty laws, each government is powerless to offer its export sector something in any other way. But it is not clear that it will be tempted to use this way. The reason is that, since retreating from the imposed t_1 would impose a first-order cost on H, doing so would be tempting to H only if the implied negotiated benefit for good $n+1$ is large enough. It is not clear that a trade agreement can be found that would do this for both countries simultaneously.

Now consider a hypothetical trade agreement stipulating $dt_1 < 0$ and $dt^*_{n+1} = \gamma\, dt_1$ for some parameter γ. Such an agreement will raise the joint surplus in each country, and so be perceived as beneficial by each government, if and only if the following holds:

$$\frac{\partial W_1}{\partial t_1} + \gamma \frac{\partial W_2}{\partial t^*_{n+1}} > 0,$$

$$\frac{\partial W_1^*}{\partial t_1} + \gamma \frac{\partial W_2^*}{\partial t^*_{n+1}} > 0.$$

This will in turn be possible for some choice of $\gamma > 0$ if and only if the following condition is met:

$$\left(\frac{\partial W_1^*}{\partial t_1}\right)\left(\frac{\partial W_{n+1}}{\partial t^*_{n+1}}\right) > \left(\frac{\partial W_{n+1}^*}{\partial t^*_{n+1}}\right)\left(\frac{\partial W_1}{\partial t_1}\right) \tag{14}$$

Figure 10.3 illustrates how satisfaction of (14) is equivalent to the existence of a mutually beneficial trade agreement. The vectors labeled t_1 and t^*_{n+1} depict the

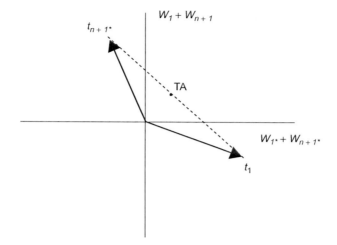

Figure 10.3 A mutually beneficial trade agreement.

effects of reductions in the respective tariffs on the two joint surpluses. When these vectors have the relative slopes illustrated, reflecting (14), an appropriate linear combination, such as at point TA, will be mutually beneficial.[5]

Condition (14) in effect requires that, at the margin, tariffs have relatively greater impact on export lobbies than on import lobbies. This is intuitively understandable, and, since in Nash equilibrium the tariffs were set with exclusive reliance on the effects on the latter lobbies, unlikely to be demanding. So we have the following result: *With (14) a mutually-beneficial trade agreement is feasible. This agreement is based on the exchange of market access, and it need not constrain export taxes.*

Condition (14) may appear problematical. But recall that we have chosen this pair of goods arbitrarily. The existence of a trade agreement based on the exchange of market access requires only that the analog of (14) hold for *some* set of goods from both countries. So, this argument can deliver trade agreements resembling those that actually exist.

5.2.1 Key points about the exchange-of-market-access approach

First, the terms of trade play no necessary role in this approach, so it is free of the CD issue.

Second, the exchange of market access is potentially attractive because it enables governments to confer on exporters benefits that they cannot deliver unilaterally. This is due to the countervailing duty laws suggested by the general support-function approach.

Third, the exchange of market access is inherently an exercise in reciprocity.

Fourth, because it is a consequence of the general support-function view, the exchange-of-market-access approach potentially suffers from the BB issue.

5.3   Does it matter?

The terms-of-trade externality and the exchange-of-market-access approach offer very different explanations of why trade agreements exist. But they both imply trade agreements with features broadly like what we see. So does it really matter which explanation is more relevant?

My answer is *yes*, because the actual explanation of the reason for a trade agreement can reveal its points of fragility. In a trade agreement as described by the terms-of-trade externality approach a country is tempted to deviate with measures that will improve its terms of trade; in a trade agreement as described by the exchange-of-market-access approach the temptation is to limit foreign access for the benefit of domestic import-competing firms.

These objectives need not be at odds. If a country were brazenly to violate a trade agreement by simply raising tariffs above their bound levels both objectives would be met. Where the difference matters is with the 'escape valves' that countries use to adjust how they fulfill their obligations without actually repudiating them. Basically, these exist because there is no international policeman to enforce trade agreements between sovereign states, so, in the end, such agreements must be self-enforcing. This involves providing escape valves and/or tolerating those not explicitly provided for. Understanding the true explanation for trade agreements is essential for understanding these escape valves and for recommending policy about them. There are several classes of such escape valves.

5.3.1   *Administered protection*

This involves measures that are both sanctioned by the GATT/WTO and embedded into national law: primarily antidumping law, countervailing-duty law, and safeguards, with antidumping the most important in practice. See Finger, Hall and Nelson (1982) and Ethier (2002). Antidumping and countervailing-duty laws do indeed provide for tariffs to be levied, but the basic purpose of such laws is simply to force foreign exporters to raise their prices: if they do so the duties are not levied. In other words, the intent is to limit home market access to foreign firms at the expense of a terms-of-trade deterioration. Safeguards are more complex because of the variety of ways in which they might be implemented, but it seems clear that in practice they are used to retreat from obligations to grant market access.

5.3.2   *Voluntary export restraints*

Before the Uruguay Round these were the most pervasive forms of escape valves. They were in violation of the GATT but tolerated because no one complained.

The Uruguay Round attacked them, partly because they had clearly become a major drag on trade and partly as a component of an implicit bargain between rich countries and poorer countries to eliminate the Multi-fiber Arrangement in exchange for adopting measures to protect intellectual property. But they are still indicative of how escape valves are used. Basically, a country pushing for a trading partner to adopt a VER was offering to accept a terms-of-trade deterioration in return for a denial of market access.

5.3.3   Unresolved trade disputes

If one country complains that another has violated its WTO obligations, if the WTO Dispute Settlement Mechanism rules against the defendant, and if the latter refuses to comply, the complainant is ultimately authorized to retaliate. This authorization is explicitly intended to maintain reciprocity in an exchange-of-market-access sense: the complainant may reduce imports from the defendant in the same amount that the defendant's actions have reduced the complainant's exports. It is possible that this test serves as a rough and ready attempt to maintain price reciprocity and that the agents involved just do not appreciate their own true motives. But actual retaliatory acts seem intended either to maximize the political damage to the defendant government or to limit market access to politically sensitive sectors.

5.3.4   Renegotiation

The GATT/WTO does provide a procedure for the renegotiation of concessions. The principle is the same as with unresolved trade disputes: the maintenance of reciprocity in an exchange-of-market-access sense. Similar comments apply.

5.3.5   So

The escape valves clearly involve a concern for the exchange-of-market-access with virtually no terms-of-trade concern. But this should not be interpreted as evidence against the terms-of-trade externality approach. That approach explicitly allows for political considerations. Countries may wish to deviate from trade agreements to get a step up on their partners. But they also may just be reacting to unexpected political developments. In the latter case, a reaction that addresses market access may well be consistent with a trade agreement that was negotiated to deal with a terms-of-trade externality.

Still, the basic fact is that the escape valves address exchange-of-market-access concerns. If the latter is the reason for trade agreements, this is appropriate. But if trade agreements exist to deal with terms-of-trade externalities the escape valves are likely to be seriously, perhaps fatally, deficient. So it matters.

5.4   Nondiscrimination

The GATT and the WTO impose nondiscrimination as a basic principle. The tariff that each WTO member imposes on a specific good must be the same for all other WTO members. Thus, there is a sharp distinction between liberalization and discrimination: Liberalization is an issue for negotiation; discrimination is not.

Of course 'discrimination' is a negatively loaded word, so that 'non-discrimination' sounds good. But imposing non-discrimination at the outset simply means that we are ruling out discriminatory trade agreements that might potentially dominate those allowed. Furthermore, we are introducing a free-rider issue: If non-discrimination is a basic rule, countries have an incentive to refrain from making concessions, knowing that they will benefit from concessions negotiated by other countries.

So why non-discrimination? The facile explanation is that, historically, countries who were serious about negotiating meaningful trade agreements with other countries did include Most Favored Nation clauses in those agreements. But, more substantively, what does such a requirement do? There are two explanations, and they are not mutually inconsistent. The answers are associated with the terms-of-trade externality approach and the exchange-of-market-access approach respectively, but the logic of each answer applies to the other approach as well.

5.4.1   *Relative-price externality*

This answer relates naturally to the terms-of-trade externality approach. Suppose some country has tariffs that discriminate between trading partners. Another country changes its policies in response to its own internal goals in ways that result in this country importing more from countries on which it levies low tariffs and less from countries for which high tariffs apply. This makes the country worse off. This could happen even if this country's terms of trade overall are unchanged. Thus this externality is distinct from the terms-of-trade externality.

Non-discrimination will prevent this relative-price externality. But it is not clear why non-discrimination should be imposed at the outset as a basic principle rather than being the object of negotiation, as is the case for amelioration of the effects of the terms-of-trade externality.

5.4.2   *Concession diversion*

This answer is more fundamental, as it involves whether trade agreements are possible at all. Suppose that H offers F^1 a reduction of 20 percent on its tariff on imports of good 1 from F^1 in exchange for a reciprocal reduction of 20 percent on its tariff on imports of good $n+1$ from H. (It does not matter whether this is part of a broader multilateral agreement or not.) Both governments view the implied exchange of market access as beneficial. But F^1 would reasonably fear that H might subsequently negotiate a reciprocal tariff reduction of 21 percent with another exporter of good $n+1$, say F^2. This would divert the market access in H that F^1 thought it had obtained to another country instead. Of course H would reasonably entertain a reciprocal suspicion about F^1. See Schwartz and Sykes (1996), Horn and Mavroidis (2001), and Ethier (2004). How serious such 'concession diversion' would be depends upon how substitutable exports from different countries are for each other. It could well render impossible the negotiation of any trade agreements.

To deal with this issue the trade agreement between H and F^1 could include a Most Favored Nation clause: Each country would guarantee the other that its goods will receive the lowest tariff applied to similar goods from other countries. Thus, in the above example, F^1 would have assurance that the 21 percent reduction that H might subsequently negotiate with F^2 would apply to its own exports as well. This would ameliorate the issue of concession diversion, but it would not eliminate it. F^1 would still fear that the access to H's market it had negotiated for might subsequently have to be shared with F^2.

The issue can be eliminated if non-discrimination is made a basic principle, rather than something to be negotiated on a deal-by-deal basis. In this case concession diversion becomes impossible, and the bargain between H and F^1 will reflect each country's desired trade policy with the rest of the world. The key feature from the point of view of F^1 is not that it has most favored nation status with H, but that all other countries are bound by non-discrimination as well.

With non-discrimination a general principle, the scope for bilateral deals will become exhausted since, to obtain market access from its partner, each country must grant it to all other countries. Such 'concession saturation' is akin to the free-rider issue. See Caplin and Krishna (1988), Ludema (1991) and Ethier (2004). Dealing with this requires that bargaining become more truly multilateral. This has indeed been the case: while the earlier GATT rounds consisted basically of collections of bilateral deals (or deals negotiated by a few countries), more recent rounds have involved more substantively multilateral issues, such as bargaining over general tariff-cutting formulas, GATT-wide standards on intellectual property, investment and so on.

6 Conclusion

In recent decades the political economy of trade policy has made significant progress. While before it was basically a footnote to the literature on international trade, it is now a major component.

I have argued that much of the literature is characterized either by the DC issue (a dramatic contrast between what policymakers say they are doing and what trade theorists model them as doing) or by the BB issue (a lack of microeconomic fundamentals). When one issue is absent, usually the other is there.

But this should not be viewed with dismay. It just means that, though we have come quite a way, we still have much more work to do.

Notes

I thank Arye Hillman, Donald Regan and Robert Staiger for useful discussions.

* Department of Economics University of Pennsylvania International School of Economics at TSU Tbilisi, Georgia.
1. For contrasting recent examples, see Broda, Limão and Weinstein (2008) and Magee and Magee (2008).
2. McCallum (2004) is an exception.
3. In this example, I have benefitted from discussions with Don Regan and Bob Staiger.
4. This conclusion is sensitive to what the H government's 'action' actually is. If that government had earlier acted by committing to allow no change in Q, come hell or high water, then its support will not increase as a result of abiding by that commitment. Such an action corresponds to a variable levy, which the WTO now prohibits.
5. The attentive reader will recognize this logic as that behind the familiar Hawkins-Simon (1949) condition for the feasibility of an input–output system.

References

Austen-Smith, D. (1991) 'Rational consumers and irrational voters', *Economics and Politics* 3: 73–93.

Bagwell, K., and R. Staiger (1999) 'An economic theory of GATT', *American Economic Review* 89: 215–48.

Bagwell, K., and R.W. Staiger (2002) *The Economics of the World Trading System*. (Cambridge, MA: The MIT Press).

Bernheim, B.D., and M. Whinston (1986) 'Menu auctions, resource allocation, and economic influence', *Quarterly Journal of Economics* 101(1): 1–31.

Broda, C., N. Limão and D.E. Weinstein (2008) 'Optimal tariffs and market power: the evidence', *American Economic Review* 98(5): 2032–65.

Brock, W.A., and S.P. Magee (1978) 'The economics of special interest politics', *American Economic Review* 68: 246–50.

Caplin, A., and K. Krishna (1988) 'Tariffs and the most favored-nation clause,' *Seoul Journal of Economics* 1: 267–89.

Caves, R.A. 1976, 'Economic models of political choice: Canada's tariff structure', *Canadian Journal of Economics* 9: 278–300.

Ethier, W.J. (1984) 'Protection and real incomes once again,' *Quarterly Journal of Economics* 99(1): 193–200.

——(2002) 'Unilateralism in a multilateral world', *Economic Journal* 112: 266–92.

——2004, 'Political Externalities, Nondiscrimination, and a Multilateral World,' Review of International Economics 12: 303–320.

——(2006) 'Selling "Protection for Sale"', *Asia-Pacific Journal of Accounting and Economics* 13: 153–62.

——(2007) 'The theory of trade policy and trade agreements: a critique', *European Journal of Political Economy* 23(3): 605–23.

——(2008) 'International trade agreements', in Margit, S. and E. Yu, *Contemporary and Emerging Issues in Trade Theory and Policy* Howard House, UK: Emerald: 381–95.

Finger, J.M. (1988) 'Protectionist rules and internationalist discretion in the making of national trade policy', in H.-J. Vosgerau (ed.), *New Institutional Arrangements for the World Economy*. Heidelberg: Springer-Verlag: 310–23.

——(1991) 'The GATT as an international discipline over trade restrictions', in Vaubel, R., and T.D. Willett (eds), *The Political Economy of International Organizations*. Boulder: Westview Press: 125–41.

Finger, J.M., Hall, H.K. and Nelson, D.R. (1982) 'The political economy of administered protection', *American Economic Review* 72: 452–66.

Gawande, K., and U. Bandyopadhyay (2000) 'Is protection for sale? Evidence on the Grossman-Helpman theory of endogenous protection', *Review of Economics and Statistics* 82: 139–52.

Goldberg, P.K., and G. Maggi (1999) 'Protection for sale: an empirical investigation,' *American Economic Review* 89: 1135–55.

Grossman, G., and E. Helpman (1994) 'Protection for sale', *American Economic Review* 84: 833–50.

Grossman G.M., and E. Helpman (1995) 'Trade wars and trade talks,' *Journal of Political Economy* 103: 675–708.

Grossman, G., and E. Helpman (2002) *Interest Groups and Trade Policy*. Princeton: Princeton University Press.

Hauser, H. (1986) 'Domestic policy foundation and domestic policy function of international trade rules', *Aussenwirtschaft* 41: 171–84.

Hawkins, D., and H. Simon (1949) 'Some conditions of macroeconomic stability', *Econometrica* 17: 245–48.

Hillman, A.L. (1982) 'Declining industries and political-support protectionist motives', *American Economic Review* 72: 1180–87.

——(1989) *The Political Economy of Protection*. Chur, London and New York: Harwood Academic Publishers; reprinted 2001: London: Routledge.

——(1990) 'Protectionist policies as the regulation of international industry', *Public Choice* 67: 101–10.

Hillman, A.L., Long, N.V. and Moser, P. (1995) 'Modeling reciprocal trade liberalization: the political-economy and national-welfare Perspectives', *Swiss Journal of Economics and Statistics* 131: 503–15.

Hillman, A.L., and P. Moser (1996) 'Trade liberalization as politically optimal exchange of market access', in Canzoneri, M., W.J. Ethier, and V. Grilli (eds), *The New Transatlantic Economy*. New York: Cambridge University Press: 295–312.

Horn, H., and P.C. Mavroidis (2001) 'Economic and legal aspects of the most-favored nation clause', *European Journal of Political Economy* 17: 233–79.

Johnson, H.G. (1953–54) 'Optimum tariffs and retaliation', *Review of Economic Studies* 21: 142–53.

Long, N.V., and N. Vousden (1991) 'Protectionist responses and declining industries', *Journal of International Economics* 30: 87–103.

Ludema, R. (1991) 'International trade bargaining and the most favored nation clause', *Economics and Politics* 3.

Magee, C., and S.P. Magee (2008) 'The United States is a small country in world trade', *Review of International Economics* 16(5): 990–1004.

Magee, S.P. (1994) 'Endogenous protection: a survey', in Mueller, D.C. (ed.), *Handbook of Public Choice*. Cambridge, MA: Basil Blackwell.

Magee, S., W.A. Brock and L. Young (1989) *Black Hole Tariffs and Endogenous Policy Theory: Political Economy in General Equilibrium*. Cambridge: Cambridge University Press.

Mayer, W. (1981) 'Theoretical considerations on negotiated tariff adjustments', *Oxford Economic Papers*, New Series 33: 135–53.

—— (1984) 'Endogenous tariff formation', *American Economic Review* 74: 970–85.

McCallum, P. (2004) 'Protection for sale and trade liberalization: an empirical investigation', *Review of International Economics* 12: 81–94.

Mitra, D., D.D. Thomakos and M.A. Ulubasoglu (2002) '"Protection for sale" in a developing country: democracy vs. dictatorship', *Review of Economics and Statistics* 84: 497–508.

Moser, P. (1990) *The Political Economy of the GATT*. Grüsch: Verlag Ruegger.

Nelson, D. (1988) 'Endogenous tariff theory: a critical survey', *American Journal of Political Science* 32: 796–837.

Olson, M. (1965) *The Logic of Collective Action*. Cambridge, MA: Harvard University Press.

Pincus, J.J. (1975) 'Pressure groups and the pattern of tariffs', *Journal of Political Economy* 83(4): 757–78.

Regan, D.H. (2006) 'What are trade agreements for? – two conflicting stories told by economists, with a lesson for lawyers', *Journal of International Economic Law* 9(4): 951–88.

Rodrik, D. (1995) 'Political economy of trade policy', in Grossman, G., and K. Rogoff (eds), *Handbook of International Economics*. Amsterdam: North Holland: 1457–95.

Schwartz, W., and A. Sykes 1996 'Towards a positive theory of the most-favored nation obligation and its exceptions in the WTO/GATT System', *International Review of Law and Economics* 16: 27–51.

11
Measurement of Protection

*James E. Anderson**

This chapter surveys the measurement of protection. *Protection* is defined here to cover governmental action (or inaction) that effectively discriminates in favor of home producers against foreign producers. Protection consists of transparent formal barriers such as tariffs and quotas, less transparent formal barriers such as licensing requirements and product standards, and informal barriers such as effectively discriminatory access to law enforcement, contract enforcement and market information. The broad definition of protection is adopted because there is good evidence that informal barriers are considerably higher than formal barriers, but not uniformly so across goods or countries. A disadvantage of the broad definition is that at the informal end of the spectrum, the barriers are less obviously connected to governmental action or inaction.

Two distinct aspects of *Measurement* are treated. The first is observing or inferring protection at the disaggregated product line. The second aspect is appropriately aggregating the product line protection so observed or inferred. Aggregation is a central concern because all empirical work requires reducing the very high dimensionality of product line trade barriers[1] to a manageable size. Aggregation should be consistent with the purpose of the analysis, and inconsistent aggregation leads to highly biased results.

Section 1 deals with product line measurement of protection. The main emphasis is on inference because that is where the difficulties lie. Only a small portion of protection is directly observable as an ad valorem tariff set down in national tariff schedules. The problem is to go from what is observable to an ad valorem tariff equivalent of protection inferred.

Quotas exemplify the problem in a simple form. When no price information is available the tariff equivalent of the quota can be inferred using an economic model, for example a model of import demand and supply limited by the quantity restriction. Turning to informal protection, anecdotes of discriminatory treatment against foreign producers abound. Informal protection can be inferred from trade flows that are 'too small' to be explained within the model by observable trade costs, geography and other natural features not subject to government policy. The shortfall can be related to measures of informal institutional performance such as contract enforcement and corruption, and a tariff equivalent extracted. The gravity model has been used with success following this strategy of inference. Evidently, inference is only as accurate as the model on which it is based.

Section 2 deals with the appropriate aggregation of product line measures of protection. Until very recently, atheoretic aggregation has been the standard practice. There are several appropriate aggregators in a recently developed literature, each one ideal for a particular purpose. The survey reviews the most significant ones. Applications thus far show that atheoretic aggregation results in significantly biased aggregate measures of protection.

Section 3 discusses the complications that arise for aggregation when world prices are affected by a country's trade policies. An operational measure is proposed for protection that discriminates across countries within a product class, motivated by the discriminatory non-tariff barriers that characterize much of world trade as well as the discrimination arising from free trade areas.

1   Primary measures of protection

Some instruments of protection are directly observable. Here the analyst still faces a few data problems outlined below, with deepening complexity as the instruments depart from simple tax rates. Protection can be inferred from international price differences where these are available. This is usually not possible, but it is possible to infer protection from trade flows in the context of a model. See Anderson and van Wincoop (2004) for more discussion of the points developed below.

1.1   Directly observable measures

When countries tax trade on an ad valorem basis, national tariff schedules with published rates at the product line level are published and some of this data is available in online databases. There is a primary classification issue to be resolved stemming from the fact that product line definitions used by national customs authorities are not common. Since the classification issues become less severe as data is aggregated (as an extreme example, everyone's definition of imports is the same), the primary measures are often taken as atheoretic trade-weighted averages at a higher level of aggregation than the finest available. The main source for this type of data is UNCTAD's TRAINS database. The World Bank's WITS software is a front end for TRAINS and the trade flow data of COMTRADE, allowing the user to construct tariff measures at the product line level for a substantial number of countries over the last 20 years.

More problematic are the many tariffs that are specific (e.g., dollars per unit). These require division by an appropriate price to convert to an ad valorem tariff equivalent. The difficulty is to find the appropriate price. The World Bank database has supplemented TRAINS with a significant number of conversions of specific to ad valorem equivalent tariffs.

1.2 Inference from prices

Quotas can be given an ad valorem tariff equivalent by finding both a foreign and a domestic price for conversion using the formula $\tau = (p - p^*)/p^*$ where τ is the tariff equivalent, p is the domestic price and p^* is the foreign price inclusive of transport costs. The difficulty is to find internationally comparable price data at the product line. This is only sometimes possible.[2]

Where quota licenses are tradable, license prices can also be used to form tariff equivalents, the license price being interpreted as τ. The complications of actual trade in licenses present some difficulties in using this method. See Anderson and Neary (2005, chapter 14; 1994) for example.

Other formal or informal protection measures can similarly be given an ad valorem equivalent when internationally comparable prices are available.

A key problem with inference from prices is that the price differential represents *all* sources of price difference, not just those due to formal or informal protection. The apparent advantage of a model free measure is vitiated by the likelihood that the measure is contaminated by the presence of factors other than protection, such as mismeasured transport costs, costs of information, monopoly rents or mismeasured prices.

1.3 Inference from trade flows

Models of trade flows predict volumes conditional on supply and demand side determinants and trade frictions. 'Missing trade' suggests the work of unobservable trade frictions, and these can be related to observable variables that indicate formal or informal protection. The model structure can be used to convert the missing volume into a tariff equivalent.

The most prominent and empirically successful example of this strategy of inference is the gravity model. Because the model always gives a good fit and exhibits stable coefficients over time and space, empirical economists have confidence that its main components capture the important determinants of the pattern of bilateral trade. Deviations from the fitted model can then be examined for indications of protection. Additionally attractive, the gravity model has a theoretical foundation.

Gravity will be given a fuller development below, but for present purposes the end result of its derivation gives the predicted value of shipments of some generic good between country or region i and country or region j as

$$X_{ij} = \frac{Y_i E_j}{Y} \left(\frac{t_{ij}}{\Pi_i P_j} \right)^{1-\sigma}, \tag{1}$$

where X_{ij} is the predicted value of shipments from i to j at destination prices, Y_i is the total value of shipments (at destination prices) from i to all destinations, E_j is the value of spending on goods in destination j from all origins i, Y is the world aggregate of shipments $Y = \sum_i Y_i$, $t_{ij} > 1$ is the bilateral trade cost factor marking up goods shipped from i to j; and Π_i and P_j are indexes of bilateral trade costs that are defined below. σ is the elasticity of substitution parameter for the generic goods class.

The first ratio on the right-hand side of (1) represents the predicted trade flow in a frictionless world. Rearranging the equation gives the frictionless prediction of trade flows as $X_{ij}/E_j = Y_i/Y$. In a frictionless world, country j's expenditure share on goods from i (on the left) is equal to the world's expenditure share on goods from i (on the right, understanding that market clearance implies $\sum_j X_{ij} = Y_i$). Behind the scenes, the assumption leading to this intuitively appealing result is that tastes are the same across the world. Trade costs act on trade through the second ratio on the right hand side of (1).[3] In effect, $t_{ij} - 1$ of the shipment melts away en route from origin to destination, so this form of trade cost is called 'iceberg-melting'.

Neither t_{ij} nor the price indexes Π_i or P_j are observable. They can be inferred econometrically by relating actual trade flow data to (1) altered on the right hand side to allow for random influences, usually represented by a multiplicative error term. A typical econometric practice is to control for the influence of Π_i or P_j with exporter and importer fixed effects. The fixed effects also encompass Y_i and E_j, which might alternatively be divided through into the dependent variable X_{ij}. The unobservable t_{ij} is related to observables such as direct measures of tariffs and transport costs, and proxies for trade costs such as distance, contiguity, common language and the like. Notice that t_{ij} enters (1) with the exponent $1 - \sigma$, so conversion of an estimated component of t to a tariff equivalent requires an estimate of σ. Fortunately, σ is identified with the coefficient $1 - \sigma$ that attaches to directly measured trade costs such as tariffs.

It is useful for several purposes to calculate the Π and P index terms given estimates of the t's and data on the E's and Y's. The procedure will be developed in section 3.

Consider the trade cost function that relates t_{ij} to observable proxies more carefully. t_{ij} denotes the variable trade cost factor on shipment of goods from i to j in some generic goods class. t_{ij} is usually modeled as a loglinear function of the proxies for trade costs. This is very convenient but may be false. One example is the treatment of bilateral distance. Eaton and Kortum (2002) show that allowing for shorter logs of distance to have a different effect on the log of trade than longer distances gives a significantly superior fit to the data. Another example is that insecure institutions are likely to affect some partners more than others – a common language or cultural heritage might help with contract default or extortion at the border. See Anderson and van Wincoop (2004) for more discussion.

A consequential usual practice is to ignore fixed costs of trade. Helpman, Melitz and Rubinstein (2008) set out a method to structurally identify fixed costs and their effect on volume, and report that it makes a big difference to the coefficients of the estimated t function. Their identification strategy is controversial, so many economists are skeptical of the results. (Common religion is assumed to affect the decision to enter a market, but not the volume of trade in a market already entered.) Moreover, Prusa and Besedes (2003) report that detailed product line bilateral trade flows disappear frequently, which tends to imply that fixed costs are not important.

An important limitation to gravity-based inferences about protection is that most of the literature has been highly aggregated. Typically each country produces one good (its GDP) and trades it for the GDP of all its trading partners. The theory behind the gravity model is more plausible at a disaggregated level (each country or region produces wine or clothing) and the buyers benefit from variety in their purchases of the product class. Moreover, what evidence there is from disaggregated gravity models confirms the intuition that trade costs are very different for different product classes. Differential costs over product lines would in particular be important for measurement of protection – institutional quality, membership in a FTA and nontariff barriers such as quotas would normally have different effects by product class.

1.3.1   Institutional insecurity

Bad institutions destroy domestic trade as well as inter-regional or international trade, but it is highly plausible that foreigners are more affected, all else equal. This hypothesis has been confirmed by Anderson and Marcouiller (2002). They supplement the gravity model with national measures of institutional quality based on survey responses of business people to questions about the quality of contract enforcement and corruption. The result is that institutional quality matters a lot. Moving the quality of the Latin American countries in their study of 1996 trade flows up to the average quality of the EU would increase their trade by as much as eliminating their tariffs.

Let the institutional quality variable be denoted by Q_j for importer j. Then the component of t_{ij} that is due to insecurity is given by Q_j^{γ} where γ is the estimated regression coefficient. Anderson and Marcouiller find that $(1 + \tau_{LA})^{1-\sigma} \approx (Q_{LA}/Q_{EU})^{\gamma}$, so that the tariff equivalent of the poor Latin American institutions destroys about as much trade as their tariffs on average.

It is possible that insecurity operates on the extensive margin in a way that does not lend itself so readily to a tariff equivalent measure. Crozet, Koenig and Rebeyrol (2008) model insecurity as affecting the fixed cost of exporting. Firms that are highly productive may nevertheless be excluded from exporting due the bad luck of facing big extortion demands. The resulting change in the selection can explain why, in French firm data on exports, some exporting firms serve small distant markets while not serving closer larger markets. The pure fixed cost of exports model cannot explain this pattern. On prior reasoning, however, it seems likely that extortion is quite plausibly a variable cost – either a particular shipment gets held up or not. The question of whether extortion falls mostly on variable or fixed costs is important, and in my opinion is unsettled at present.

The World Bank's *Doing Business* database has subsequently greatly enriched the set of institutional quality measures available. Unfortunately, these (and the earlier surveys) are available only as national aggregates. Presumably the quality of institutions differ in their effect on each sector.

A problem with inference about the effect of institutions on trade is that the opportunity to trade may affect the quality of institutions. Institutions change slowly, so the link to trade patterns may be weak. The reverse causality issue can be handled with good instruments for institutional quality drawn from a model of how institutions change with trade opportunities. The current state of modeling here is not yet mature enough to really help. See Dixit (2004) for some very interesting beginnings.

1.3.2   Free trade agreements

The best estimate of the effect of free trade agreements (FTA) on trade flows is due to Baier and Bergstrand (2007). They report that on average a common FTA doubles trade after 10 years. An extensive earlier literature used gravity models to assess the impact of free trade agreements on trade flows with much lower estimates, often finding no significant effect. Baier and Bergstrand argue convincingly that this is due to bias caused by FTA membership being endogenously chosen by countries that already trade a lot with each other. By controlling properly for the decision to join a FTA, they quintuple the estimated effect on trade volume.

Their estimation is done with aggregate trade flows, and the FTA effect is an average effect over all members of all FTA sets. Thus there is aggregation bias over product lines and over FTA memberships, probably acting to reduce the size of estimated effects. At the product line level, an FTA will matter far more for some products than for others. Across countries, FTA's matter far more for some than for others just reasoning from the differential tariff levels they have prior to the agreement. For example, Mexico has much higher tariffs than the United States or Canada, so its trade increase would be larger due to cutting a bigger bilateral barrier.

The doubling of average trade volume found by Baier and Bergstrand indicates a tariff equivalent effect of 19 percent if the elasticity is equal to 5, a tariff equivalent of 10 percent if the elasticity is equal to 8 and a tariff equivalent of 8 percent if the elasticity is equal to 10. The gravity literature places estimates of σ in the range of 5 to 10.

1.3.3 Nontariff barriers

Measures of the presence or absence of 'non-tariff barriers to trade' have a highly significant impact on trade volume in models that use the cross-product dimension of sectoral trade flow data to identify the effect. The underlying non-tariff barrier (NTB) data are constructed from lists of potential barriers. The main source used by analysts is TRAINS, produced by UNCTAD. Some barriers are obvious, such as quotas (although even here it is possible that a quota does not bind). Others are less obvious, such as licensing requirements (which can range in effect from non-binding drivers licensing to onerous building site licensing). Technical standards and health standards have public purposes that are non-discriminatory, but are often manipulated to discriminate against imports. Antidumping cases can result in a plethora of 'remedies' that in the past have included government imposed market sharing and price fixing arrangements, but are represented in the underlying data by the presence or absence of antidumping actions.

In the face of this plethora of possible barriers, analysts have constructed NTB coverage ratios (the percentage of disaggregated product lines comprising the sector that have a nontariff barrier to trade) for sectors at, for example, the two digit level of aggregation. Provided that the coverage ratio has the same relationship to the volume restricted in each sector, the tariff equivalent of the NTB in sector k, τ_k, can be inferred from $NTB_k^{\beta} = (1 + \tau_k)^{1-\sigma}$, where β is the estimated NTB coefficient from the cross section regression that controls for other determinants of trade flow magnitude.

Another tack is to attempt to identify elasticities econometrically from the cross country variation of prices, then use the elasticities to compute tariff equivalents of NTB's. The most notable work is by Kee, Nicita and Olarreaga (2009), drawing on their 2008 paper that estimates an import demand system yielding a set of price (own and cross) elasticities. They address the endogeneity of prices problem (due to the endogeneity of trade policy as well as violation of the small country assumption) with some success. They generate large and believable tariff equivalents.

NTB coverage data has not been used much in gravity models, reflecting the paucity of disaggregated gravity analyses. The cross country dimension of the data for a given sector identifies the volume-restricting effect of the NTB (measured by coverage ratios). As with the cross-sector regression, the identifying assumption is that the coverage ratio has a constant relationship to the volume restricted across observations, an assumption at least as dubious across countries as across commodities.

Another problem with using NTB coverage data to infer protection is posed by Trefler (1993). Political economy suggests that the presence of absence of NTB's is driven by the incentives of economic actors to lobby politicians. Trefler shows that controlling for the endogeneity of the NTB in U.S. data greatly increased the (absolute value of the) estimate of $\beta < 0$.[4] As noted above, institutional quality is also ultimately endogenous, but over long time horizons. Thus, while the endogeneity problem also affects inference about the importance of institutions, it is presumably less significant than with NTB's.

A promising avenue of investigation is to use surveys of business persons classified by sector to obtain their rankings of the importance of various nontariff barriers to trade within their sectors. So far, the survey method has been used only at the aggregate level to measure the cross-country difficulty of doing business that is due to such factors as extortion, unreliable contractual enforcement, costly delays from officialdom.

2   Aggregation of protection

The need for aggregation is ubiquitous in empirical work. For simple comprehensibility to the answers to such obvious questions as 'How high are protectionist barriers?', reporting lists with thousand of elements is useless. Econometric inference of demand or supply relationships is seldom feasible at the level of detail of the many thousands of protectionist barriers. Applied general equilibrium simulation modeling seldom attempts to compute equilibria of models with thousands of markets. Apart from computational burden, the complexity of relationships among so many variables defeats even sophisticated readers' comprehension.

Aggregation being necessary, the key question becomes 'Aggregation for what purpose?'. Anderson and Neary (2005) supply answers. Each particular purpose and each particular economic environment has an ideal aggregator that preserves the relationship between the object of interest and the tariff vector being aggregated. The list of potential ideal aggregators is as long as the list of purposes supplied by empirical imagination, but the main ones detailed below suffice to illustrate a method that can be applied to extend the list.

The main focus of the literature has been on aggregation across goods. Welfare equivalent aggregation is developed first and illustrated: the uniform tariff across goods that yields the same welfare as the actual tariff vector. Then volume equivalent aggregation is developed and applied: the uniform tariff that yields the same value of trade valued at world prices. Finally, sectoral income equivalent aggregation is developed. The setting is one where world prices are taken as given – the small country case. See Anderson and Neary (2005) for treatment of ideal aggregation when world prices are endogenous to the aggregation.

The initial setting is one where world prices are taken as given – the small country case. The complexities introduced when world prices are affected by a country's tariffs are discussed in section 3.

2.1 Conceptual base

Typical national tariff schedules contain thousands of lines. The rates are widely dispersed, by one to two orders of magnitude. A simple sense of how high are tariffs seems to require some sort of index number. Anderson and Neary (2005) describe an approach they developed which provides theoretically satisfactory yet practically implementable procedures for measuring the restrictiveness of trade policy.

The simplest context in which the aggregation problem arises is when tariffs are the only form of trade policy and the tariffs vary across products within a country. The issues are illustrated in a mainly diagrammatic analysis of an extended two-good example.

A tariff aggregator is a scalar index number that aggregates the vector of trade restrictions applying to a number of individual markets. Whether a particular index number formula is satisfactory depends on the uses to which the measure of restrictiveness is to be put. Some indices are fully satisfactory for one purpose but quite misleading for another. Other indices, lacking a clear theoretical foundation, are not satisfactory for any purpose. Three measures will be developed in some detail, each an ideal response to a different purpose.

The Trade Restrictiveness Index (TRI) is an index which aggregates trade restrictions while holding constant the level of real income. This is the natural aggregate to use in studies which attempt to link growth in income to measures of a country's trade policy stance. It would not make sense to 'explain' income growth in terms of a measure of trade policy which itself varies with income. The TRI is also the natural index to use in evaluating a country's progress towards trade liberalisation, for example, in the context of the World Banks Structural Adjustment Loans. Since loan conditionality is predicated on the assumption of a link between trade policy and income growth, it is desirable to measure the two concepts independently.

In a trade negotiations context, where foreign exporters are concerned with domestic market access, it makes sense to aggregate trade restrictions in a way which holds constant the volume of imports rather than real income. The 'volume' of imports is sensibly defined for this purpose as the value of restricted trade at external (world) prices. This leads to the Mercantilist Trade Restrictiveness Index (MTRI).

Political economy suggests strongly that protection is granted to factors of production that are specific to sectors. The pattern of earnings by job classification by sector suggests some proportion of earnings is sector specific rents. Thus it makes sense to construct an index that aggregates protection such that sector specific income is constant, sector by sector. The effective rate of protection was an early attempt to provide such an index, defined in an environment of partial equilibrium. The effective rate of protection focused exclusively on the cross-effect between sectors due to intermediate stages of production: tariffs on sector i's inputs harm sectoral incomes while sector i's own output tariff helps sectoral incomes. But general equilibrium suggests other powerful cross-effects: sector i's specific income is harmed by the flight of mobile factors of production to sector j induced by j's tariff even if i does not require the products of j for inputs. The sectoral income equivalent uniform tariff is defined in general equilibrium and is equal to to the effective rate of protection when general equilibrium forces become negligible.

In contrast to these theoretically based measures, it is useful to juxtapose measures which have been used in practice to aggregate across tariffs. (For simplicity the treatment here abstracts from consideration of quotas and other nontariff barriers.) These include different measures of average tariffs and alternative measures of tariff dispersion, such as the standard deviation and coefficient of variation of tariffs. The properties of these measures contrast with those of the alternative theory-based measures in a very simple context, a linear two-good partial-equilibrium model. Subsequently the treatment is extended to general equilibrium.

2.1.1   Trade-weighted average tariff issues

Intuitively, tariffs should be weighted by their relative importance in some sense. The simplest and most commonly used method of doing so is to use actual trade volumes as weights.[5] The trade-weighted average tariff is defined as:

$$\tau^a = \frac{\sum_i m_i \pi_i^* \tau_i}{\sum_i m_i \pi_i^*}, \tag{2}$$

where τ_i is the ad valorem tariff rate on good i, m_i is its import volume and π_i^* its world price. This index is very easy to calculate: it equals total tariff revenue divided by the value of imports at world prices. The average tariff can be rewritten as a weighted average of tariff rates:

$$\tau^a = \sum_i \omega_i^* \tau_i \tag{3}$$

where $\omega_i^* \equiv m_i \pi_i^* / \sum_i m_i \pi_i^*$. Note that the weights ω_i^* are valued at world prices π_i^* rather than at domestic prices π_i.

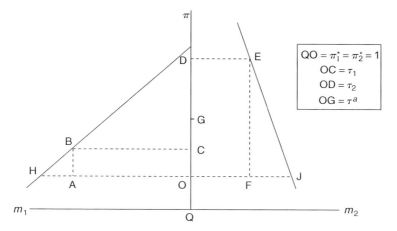

Figure 11.1   The trade-weighted average tariff: tariff rates and import demand elasticities negatively correlated.

Despite its convenience, the trade-weighted average tariff has well-known problems. As the tariff on any good rises, its imports fall, so the now higher tariff gets a lower weight in the index. For high tariffs this fall in the weight may be so large that the index is decreasing in the tariff rate. More subtly, tariffs have greater effects on both welfare and trade volume when they apply to imports in relatively elastic demand; but it is precisely these goods whose weights fall fastest.

Figures 11.1 and 11.2 (taken from Anderson and Neary, 2005) illustrate these considerations in a linear two-good example.

Each panel of figure 11.1 depicts the domestic market for one of the goods, whose home import demand curve is $m_i(\pi_i), i = 1, 2$. For ease of exposition, the world prices of the two goods, π_1^* and π_2^*, are normalized at unity. Domestic producers and consumers face the tariff-inclusive prices π_i^0 represented by QC for good 1 and QD for good 2. As drawn, the import demand curve for good 1 is more elastic[6] than that for good 2, whereas good 1 has a lower tariff than good 2. So, in this example, tariff rates and import demand elasticities are negatively correlated. The trade-weighted average tariff, obtained by weighting the two tariff rates by the imports (valued at world prices) of the two goods, AO and OF, is indicated by τ^a.

Next, consider a change in trade policy which leads to the situation illustrated in figure 11.2. The two import demand functions are the same but the configuration of tariff levels is reversed: now, the correlation between demand elasticities and tariff levels is positive rather than negative. In the left-hand panel, imports of the more elastic good 1 are almost eliminated, so its high tariff receives a very low weight in the average tariff. In the right-hand panel, the low tariff on the

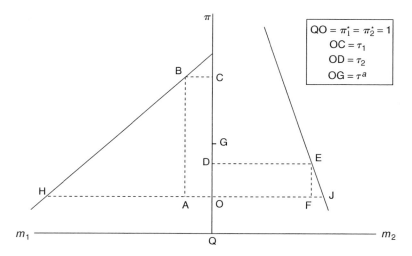

Figure 11.2   The trade-weighted average tariff: tariff rates and import demand elasticities positively correlated.

low-elasticity good 2 receives a high weight. As a result, the calculated average tariff (again denoted by τ^a) is low, considerably lower than that in figure 11.1. Yet, it seems intuitively obvious that trade is more restricted in figure 11.2 than in figure 11.1, since both welfare and the volume of trade have fallen. (Given the partial equilibrium perspective of this chapter, the deadweight loss or welfare cost of protection resulting from the two tariffs is measured by the sum of the Marshallian triangles BAH and EFJ. The volume of trade equals AF in both figures.) The index has thus moved in the wrong direction, since its value has fallen even though trade is now more restricted.

The difficulties caused by using current import volumes to construct trade-weighted average tariffs has led some authors to suggest using instead the import volumes which would prevail in free trade as weights. The choice between actual and free-trade import weights is identical in principle to that between Paasche (current-weighted) and Laspeyres (base-weighted) indices in any other branch of economics. In practice, some plausible compromise between the two (such as their geometric mean, the Fisher Ideal index) is often used.

But a central theme of the economic approach to index numbers (see, for example, Pollak, 1971, and Diewert, 1981) is that the choice between alternative index-number formulae should primarily be based not on informal issues of plausibility but on the extent to which they approximate some 'true' or benchmark index, which answers some well-defined economic question.

Many other weighting schemes have been proposed, but none has a superior theoretical foundation and all suffer from practical disadvantages. One possibility, discussed by Leamer (1974), is to use world exports. These have two advantages: like domestic imports, data on them are easily available; and, unlike imports, they are much less likely to be influenced by domestic tariffs. However, this virtue reflects a basic problem with using any external variables as weights: they take no account of the special features of the country being studied. Other possible sources of weights are domestic consumption or production levels. However, these also exhibit some odd features. Production shares give zero weight to tariffs on non-competing imports; while consumption shares, like import shares, may be low for high tariffs precisely because they restrict trade so much. Finally, note that the implications of either consumption or production shares cannot be illustrated in figures 11.1 and 11.2, since these figures as drawn are consistent with an infinite range of consumption and production levels. Thus the high tariff on good 1 in figure 11.2 (which causes a large drop in imports and a considerable welfare cost) might get a low weight if sector 1 is less important than sector 2 in domestic consumption or production.

One implication of the previous two figures is that the problem of constructing a satisfactory aggregate tariff measure increases with the dispersion of tariff rates. This has led many practitioners to supplement weighted averages of tariff rates by measures of tariff dispersion to try and get a full picture of the restrictiveness of a tariff system. Just as with average tariffs, a key issue in choosing between different measures of tariff dispersion is which weights should be used. More generally, there is no satisfactory rule for combining the measures of average and dispersion to yield a scalar measure which might, even in principle, be comparable across countries or across time.

2.2   Welfare equivalent uniform tariff

The discussion so far shows the problems with purely statistical measures such as the trade-weighted average tariff or the standard deviation of tariffs. All, in the memorable phrase of Afriat (1977), provide 'answers without questions'. Since they do not start from any explicit criterion of trade policy restrictiveness, their merits can be evaluated only on intuitive ad hoc grounds. And even on such grounds they do not correspond to measures of restrictiveness in any reasonable sense. A more formal approach, starting from an explicit concept of trade policy restrictiveness, is required.

The two central themes of Anderson and Neary (2005) are, first, that measures of trade policy restrictiveness should start from a formal criterion against which restrictiveness is measured; and second, that a natural criterion for an economist to adopt is the effect of the structure of trade policy on national welfare. This approach can easily be adapted to allow for other criteria, but the welfare-theoretic perspective is a natural starting point. It leads to an index number of tariffs which they call the 'TRI uniform tariff' or the 'welfare-equivalent uniform tariff'.

It is straightforward to see how this perspective leads to an alternative measure of trade policy restrictiveness in the example given earlier. Taking welfare as the standpoint, the appropriate way of answering the question 'How do we measure trade restrictiveness?' is to ask: what is the uniform tariff which, if applied to both goods, would be equivalent to the actual tariffs, in the sense of yielding the same welfare loss. Marginal deadweight loss is equal to $(\pi_i - \pi_i^*)dm_i$, the product of the change in trade volume and the difference between marginal willingness to pay π_i and marginal cost π_i^*. The change in the trade policy is responsible for the change in trade: $dm_i = m_i'd\pi_i$. The answer the question thus involves reducing dispersion in such a way that the welfare-equivalent uniform tariff is closer to the actual tariff on the high-elasticity good 1: this accords with the intuition that a high tariff on that good is more restrictive than a high tariff on good 2.[7]

The partial equilibrium approach here extends to any number of goods. To solve for the welfare-equivalent uniform tariff, write the linear import demand function for good i as:

$$m_i = \alpha_i - \beta_i \pi_i$$

where β_i is the price-responsiveness of imports of good i (i.e., the slope of the import demand curve for good i relative to the vertical axes in Figures 11.1 and 11.2). Now, recall that with linear demands the welfare loss L_i from a tariff at rate τ_i on good i equals $(\tau_i \pi_i^*)^2 \beta_i/2$. The total welfare loss on all goods is $L = \sum_i L_i$ and so the welfare-equivalent uniform tariff τ^Δ is defined implicitly by the equation:

$$\sum_i (\tau^\Delta \pi_i^*)^2 \beta_i = \sum_i (\tau_i \pi_i^*)^2 \beta_i. \tag{4}$$

The right-hand side is the actual welfare loss from an arbitrary set of tariffs $\{\tau_i\}$; while the left-hand side is the hypothetical welfare loss from a uniform tariff rate τ^Δ. Equating the two and solving for τ^Δ gives the welfare-equivalent uniform tariff:

$$\tau^\Delta = \left\{ \sum_i \omega_i \tau_i^2 \right\}^{1/2},$$

where $\omega_i \equiv (\pi_i^*)^2 \beta_i / \sum_i (\pi_i^*)^2 \beta_i$. Note the differences from the formula for the trade-weighted average tariff τ^a in (2): τ^a is a weighted arithmetic mean of the tariff rates whereas τ^Δ is a weighted quadratic mean of the tariff rates; and, crucially, the weights used in constructing τ^a depend on the levels of imports, m_i, whereas those used in constructing τ^Δ depend on the marginal import responses, the β_i's. Moreover, the marginal effect of a rise in an individual tariff is invariant to the tariff in the case of average tariffs while it is proportional to the tariff in the case of τ^Δ. Marginal dead weight loss is given by $\tau_i \pi_i^* \beta_i$, so changes in τ^Δ are marginal-dead weight-loss weighted averages of the changes in the $\{\tau_i\}$.

Now consider briefly the implications of general equilibrium for the welfare equivalent tariff. See Anderson and Neary (2005) for a thorough development; the present treatment aims to give the general idea only. (4) equates a welfare loss due to a uniform tariff with the welfare loss of the actual tariff vector in partial equilibrium. In general equilibrium, the device analogous to the welfare loss L is the balance of trade function $B(\pi, \pi^*, u)$, where u is the real income of the representative economic agent, π is the domestic price vector of goods subject to protection and π^* is the external price vector for those goods. The welfare equivalent uniform tariff is defined by

$$B[\pi^*(1+\tau^\Delta), \pi^*, u^0] = B(\pi^0, \pi^*, u^0). \tag{5}$$

The parallel of (5) with (4) is obvious. The same operation is being performed: a vector of differentiated tariffs is being replaced by a uniform tariff that maintains the same level of welfare. $B(\cdot)$ is an implicit function that describes the workings of an economy. Operationalizing the calculation of τ^Δ requires specifying a computable general equilibrium model of the economy. This can be demanding in terms of information, but Anderson and Neary (2005) report results for a simple and readily operational model.

B is the balance of trade deficit (the amount that must be borrowed from foreigners). The full equilibrium of the economy is expressed by the external budget constraint $B(\pi, \pi^*, u) = b$ where b is the amount borrowed. The budget constraint implies the equilibrium real income for a given domestic price vector and the assumed exogenous external price π^* and external borrowing b. The domestic price vector is driven by domestic tariff policy due to the arbitrage equation $\pi_i = \pi_i^*(1+\tau_i)$.

The balance of trade function captures all the complex workings of the economy in a simple fashion. Behind the scenes, consumers shift their expenditures in response to trade policy changes and income changes, resources move from sector to sector, government collects and disburses tariff revenue, factor incomes rise and fall, all captured by the response of B to π. Other traded goods have prices that are constant (due to the small country assumption) while nontraded goods and factors have their prices determined endogenously in the background as functions of the price vector π and real income u. See Anderson and Neary for the many important details that go into constructing the balance of trade function and the variety of economic structures that it represents.

For present purposes it is sufficient to drive forward using B as a black box, just as auto drivers go forth with scant understanding of how their autos operate. The essential points are these. First, τ^Δ is a welfare equivalent uniform tariff. Second changes in tariffs induce changes in τ^Δ that are driven by marginal welfare responsiveness. Consider for example a change in τ_j. Differentiating (5), the required change in τ^Δ satisfies:

$$\left(\sum_i B_{\pi_i^\Delta} \pi_i^\Delta\right) \frac{d\tau^\Delta}{1+\tau^\Delta} = B_{\pi_j} \pi_j \frac{d\tau_j}{1+\tau_j}, \qquad (6)$$

where $\pi_i^\Delta \equiv \pi_i^*(1+\tau^\Delta)$ and $B_{\pi_i} \equiv \partial B/\partial \pi_i$. The interpretation of B_{π_i} is the same as dL_i in partial equilibrium: the marginal cost of raising a tariff, now identified with the extra foreign borrowing that is needed to keep real income constant with the new higher tariff. B_{π_i} reduces to dL_i in the linear partial equilibrium case but is in general a more complex object that need not always be positive.

(6) shows that changes in the welfare equivalent uniform tariff are based on marginal welfare responses to changes in the actual tariffs. Just as with partial equilibrium, there is good reason to suppose that marginal welfare weights are quite different from trade weights. See Anderson and Neary (2005) for more details and evidence based on computational forms for B that τ^Δ does indeed behave significantly differently from τ^a. See Kee, Nicita and Olarreaga (2009) for recent much more detailed estimates of a partial equilibrium version of the TRI based on their estimated import demand elasticity system. See Irwin (2007) for a time series calculation of the TRI for U.S. tariffs from 1859 to 1961.

2.3 Import volume equivalent uniform tariff

Now consider an index of tariffs which equals the uniform tariff that yields a constant volume of imports. There are two alternative valuations of imports that may be used to define 'constant volume', valuation at domestic and at foreign prices, each one being useful for a different purpose.

Valuation at domestic prices is useful in forming aggregates to be used in econometric or simulation modeling. For example, a model of the demand for imported footwear might usefully abstract from the details of types of footwear and their associated differential tariffs, giving rise to a need for a footwear tariff aggregator. Under the assumption that preferences or technology are separable with respect to the partition between footwear types on the one hand and all other goods on the other hand, an exact tariff aggregator is readily defined. Let p denote the domestic price of all other goods and let $\phi(\pi)$ be the exact price index that aggregates the individual footwear prices in the vector π. The tariff aggregator is the uniform tariff that results in the same price index value (and hence the same volume of imports). It is implicitly defined by

$$\phi[\pi^*(1+\tau^\delta)] = \phi(\pi). \qquad (7)$$

Anderson and Neary call τ^δ the True Average Tariff because it is analogous to the true cost of living index. Because the price aggregator function ϕ is homogeneous of degree one in its arguments, (7) has an explicit solution $\tau^\delta = \phi(\pi)/\phi(\pi^*) - 1$. The marginal response of the True Average Tariff to changes in the individual tariff items is based on trade weights, but evaluated at *domestic* prices. Moreover,

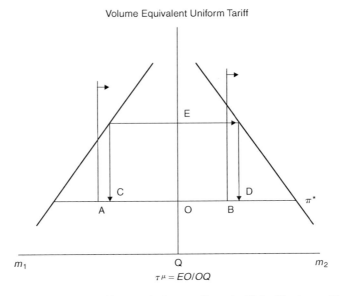

Figure 11.3   The TRI or welfare-equivalent uniform tariff: tariff rates and import demand elasticities negatively correlated.

the exact aggregation used in τ^{δ} makes appropriate allowance for substitution effects among the footwear types as opposed to using the actual trade weights. See Anderson and Neary for more discussion.

The 'import-volume-equivalent uniform tariff' or the 'Mercantilist TRI uniform tariff' ('MTRI' for short) maintains the value of trade at world prices. This is a natural reference point for trade negotiations because foreign governments care about the value of trade at *their* prices. The Mercantilist label is used because this concept recalls the concerns of Mercantilist writers with the balance of trade.

Its behavior in the two-good example is illustrated in figure 11.3. The initial volume AB = CD is maintained in moving to the uniform volume equivalent tariff $\tau^{\mu} = EO/OQ$.

The key analytic feature of figure 11.3 is that the MTRI uniform tariff is linear in both tariff rates but increases more rapidly in the tariff on the more elastically demanded good. Moreover, the Mercantilist index behaves somewhat similarly to the welfare-equivalent uniform tariff but very differently from the ad hoc indices such as trade weighted average tariffs.

The import-volume-equivalent uniform tariff is defined implicitly by the equation:

$$\sum_{i} \pi_i^*[\alpha_i - \beta_i(1 + \tau^{\mu})\pi_i^*] = \sum_{i} \pi_i^*[\alpha_i - \beta_i(1 + \tau_i)\pi_i^*]. \tag{8}$$

The right-hand side is the total value of imports given an arbitrary set of tariffs τ_i; while the left-hand side is the value of imports which would be generated by a uniform tariff rate τ^μ. Equating the two and solving for τ^μ gives the import-volume-equivalent uniform tariff:

$$\tau^\mu = \sum_i \omega_i \tau_i$$

This has the same linear form as the trade-weighted average tariff τ^a, but the same weights $\{\omega_i\}$ as the welfare-equivalent uniform tariff, τ^Δ, in its linear partial equilibrium version.

The general equilibrium version of the MTRI follows the same basic idea of construction, but allowing for general forms of substitution in demand, supply and the link of trade policy to income. See Anderson and Neary (2005) for details. The basic building block is the real-income-compensated import demand function $m_i(\pi,p,u)$ where p is the vector of non-distorted prices (for example the world price of exported goods) and u is the representative agent's real income. The volume of trade at world prices given the real income is the compensated trade volume

$$M^c \equiv \sum_i \pi_i^* m_i(\pi,p,u). \tag{9}$$

Real income is determined by the external budget constraint

$$B(\pi,p,u) = b$$

resulting in equilibrium real income

$$u = U(\pi,p,b). \tag{10}$$

Substituting (10) into (9) yields the trade volume function

$$M(\pi,p,b) \equiv M^c[\pi,p,U(\pi,p,b)]. \tag{11}$$

The volume equivalent uniform tariff is implicitly defined by

$$M(\pi^*(1+\tau^\mu),p,b) = M(\pi,p,b). \tag{12}$$

A sense of how the tariff aggregator τ^μ is related to its components is obtained by differentiating (12) with respect to π_j and solving for the resulting change in τ^μ:

$$\left(\sum_i M_{\pi_i}\pi_i^\mu\right)\frac{d\tau^\mu}{1+\tau^\mu} = M_{\pi_j}\pi_j\frac{d\tau_j}{1+\tau_j}. \tag{13}$$

Here, $\pi_i^\mu \equiv \pi_i^*(1+\tau_i)$ and $M_{\pi_i} = \partial M/\partial\pi_i$.

The responsiveness of the MTRI uniform tariff to changes in its component tariffs is given by marginal volume weights $M_{\pi_j}\pi_j$. These weights incorporate the substitution effects on the demand and supply sides of the economy but also the income effect of price changes acting through the factor markets and through the distribution of tariff revenue. Computation of simulation models is required to actually calculate τ^μ but its logic follows the partial equilibrium version. It is clear that the weights differ from those of the trade weighted average tariff.

Computations presented in Anderson and Neary (2005) suggest that in practice the MTRI uniform tariff has quite different implications than the trade weighted average tariff. Kee, Nicita and Olarreaga (2009) present much more detailed estimates of a partial equilibrium version of the MTRI. Effectively this is a compensated MTRI based on (9):

$$\tau^{c\mu}: M^c(\pi^*(1+\tau^{c\mu}),p,u) = M^c(\pi,p,u).$$

2.4 Sectoral income equivalent

Tariff structure is often important to specific factor owners. For example, the U.S. auto industry opposed the Bush administration steel tariffs in 2002 because the tariffs would raise the price of an important input into auto production. Of course, auto makers benefit from tariffs on imported motor vehicles at the same time (and from a differentiated tariff structure on different motor vehicle types) and lose from tariffs on other inputs such as textiles. These observations suggest the usefulness of an aggregate measure of the protection given by the U.S. tariff structure to its auto industry. The suggestion led to the development of the *effective rate of protection* (Anderson, 1998): the uniform tariff on inputs and outputs that yields the same sector specific factor income as the actual tariff structure. In the special case of partial equilibrium with fixed input coefficients and fixed output coefficients (or a single output), the effective rate of protection has a very simple form (Corden, 1965). The simple form is likely to be seriously misleading (Anderson, 1998, presents a computational example where this is so) but its failings have not prevented it from being widely used in applied trade policy analysis.

To sketch out the main idea, think for example of sector specific labor skills such as auto workers possess, earning them a premium over what they could obtain in their next best alternative job. Let the earnings to the sector specific factor in sector j be denoted as ρ_j. With competitive production and the assumption of cost minimizing behavior, ρ_j is the 'restricted profit function'. Let the price vector for nontraded inputs be denoted w while the domestic price vector for traded outputs and inputs is given by π. In partial equilibrium, for given w, the effective rate of protection τ^e is defined implicitly as

$$\rho_j[\pi^*(1+\tau^e),w^0] = \rho_j(\pi^0,w^0). \tag{14}$$

The properties of the restricted profit function can be used to derive the 'marginal profit weights' that arise from differentiating (14), following the lines of the preceding analysis of welfare equivalent and volume equivalent tariffs.

In the special case where there is only one output and where the input-output coefficients are fixed, (14) gives an explicit solution for τ_j^e as

$$\tau_j^e = \frac{\tau_j - \sum_i \alpha_{ij}\tau_i}{1 - \sum_i \alpha_{ij}}, \tag{15}$$

where the α's are the intermediate input cost shares at external prices. This is the formula usually used for the effective rate of protection. It is easy to verify that if all tariffs on the right-hand side are in fact equal to τ_j^e, then the equation is satisfied. Moreover, the formula implies the common sense implication that escalation in tariff structures affords extra protection to sectors:

$$\tau_j^e = \tau_j + \frac{\sum_i \alpha_{ij}(\tau_j - \tau_i)}{1 - \sum_i \alpha_{ij}} > \tau_j,$$

when $\tau_j > \sum_i \omega_{ij}\tau_i$ where $\omega_{ij} \equiv \alpha_{ij}/\sum_i \alpha_{ij}$. This condition says that the output tariff exceeds a weighted average of input tariffs where the weights are the traded input share weights.

The difficulties with the usual form of the effective rate of protection are two. First, the assumption of fixed input and output coefficients is not realistic; substitutability of input mixes and output mixes is significant even in the short run. In partial equilibrium it is possible to specify a form of the restricted profit function and use its properties to derive an exact effective rate of protection as in (14). This exact effective rate of protection has the same relation to (15) as the True Average Tariff τ^δ has to the trade weighted average tariff τ^a.

More importantly, both of the preceding definitions of the effective rate of protection are defined in partial equilibrium, holding constant w^0. Constant factor prices is never a plausible assumption because the operation in (14) involves changing the entire tariff structure of the economy. In general equilibrium the factor prices w are determined by factor market clearance as a reduced form function of the trade policy that drives the demand for factors of production. Formally, $\partial \rho_j/\partial w$ gives the vector of demands for intersectorally mobile factors due to the cost-minimizing property of the restricted profit function. Market clearance for the mobile factors is given by $\sum_j \partial \rho_j/\partial w = v$ where v is the vector of mobile factor endowments. The market clearance conditions solve for the equilibrium factor prices w as functions $W(\pi, v)$ of prices π and the factor endowments. The general equilibrium analog to ρ_j is $R_j(\pi, v) \equiv \rho_j[\pi, W(\pi, v)]$. Using the general equilibrium analog to ρ_j and the same form of definition of τ_j^e as in (14) leads to a general equilibrium version of effective rate of protection.[8] See Anderson (1998) for details. Computations reported there show that the proper general equilibrium effective rate of protection has low correlation with effective protection calculated by the usual method.

3   Multi-country issues

Measurement and aggregation of protection in a multi-country world presents two major issues. First, trade policies discriminate across countries. What is the appropriate protection aggregator across trading partners? Second, because the world market price is affected by tariffs, the incidence of the tariff, the proportion of the tax that falls on the seller's price or the buyer's price, becomes an key endogenous variable.

Discriminatory policy is discouraged under the World Trade Organization (WTO) rules (the Most Favored Nation principle), but with important exceptions. Free trade agreements are an explicit exception to the MFN principle. Their prominence means that discriminatory tariffs to affect substantial portions of world trade. There is also tacit acceptance by WTO members of many nontariff barriers (such as the 'voluntary export restraints' currently affecting U.S. and EU imports from China in textiles and apparel). Finally, there is explicit acceptance of restrictions (including market share arrangements, price fixing schemes and voluntary export restraints as well as tariffs) arising from antidumping policies so long as a country's antidumping regulations satisfy the WTO code.

In principle, the methods of section 2 using fixed world prices could apply to discriminatory policies, treating as separate goods the products imported from each country. For example, within a product class such as wine (or cabernet sauvignon), national varieties differ in their appeal to consumers. Despite EU and U.S. border policies that discriminates between French wine and California wine, EU and U.S. consumers purchase both. Given adequate detail on wine tastes, the welfare equivalent and volume equivalent TRIs can be constructed. Another dimension of differentiated protection takes the point of view of the exporter. The exporter's goods face different treatment across trading partners. For example, developing country exports (such as apparel) typically face high protection from developed countries whereas developed countries typically have low tariffs on each other's exports (such as high quality clothing or autos). Kee, Nicita and Olarreaga (2009) offer a partial equilibrium export volume equivalent index to capture 'average' restrictiveness from the exporter's viewpoint, the Market Access–Overall Trade Restrictiveness Index (MA–OTRI). The MA–OTRI gives an answer to the question, what uniform tariff levied by trade partners, across goods and partners, would yield the same volume of exports as the current tariff structure? Kee and others find that indeed poorer countries do face higher barriers to their exports on average.

Unfortunately, the price-taking assumption of section 2 and of Kee and others becomes dubious or even untenable when measuring policy aggregates that discriminate among finely differentiated goods. California wine sellers face downward-sloping demand schedules in France while French wine sellers face downward-sloping demand schedules in California. At a formal descriptive level, Anderson and Neary (2005) treat the calculation of the TRI and MTRI when world prices are endogenous to the aggregation, but operationalizing their method requires computational models of substantial detail and complexity. A common approach to computational models makes extensive use of separability to aggregate tariffs within product classes using the True Average Tariff (7). This method at least guarantees the correct relationship between aggregate trade volume and the True Average Tariff, but it fails to properly connect tariff revenue and the tariffs. Anderson (2009) proposes an operational solution that uses both the True Average Tariff and the trade-weighted average tariff to get both volume and revenue right in the multi-country setting with endogenous world prices. Unfortunately, all applied general equilibrium models are seen by most economists as suspect because they do a poor job of predicting trade outside the benchmark year.

A promising alternative is to focus on a single sector at a time and deal with appropriate aggregation of policy across countries in the context of the gravity model, drawing credibility from its generally good empirical fit. The analysis below sets out a readily operational uniform border policy index that consistently aggregates discriminatory policies across countries within a given product line. The idea is to replace the set of discriminatory import policies with a set of uniform tariff equivalents that preserve aggregate trade volumes in all the trading partners. This solution turns out to preserve world prices, even though world prices are generally endogenous in the model. (Thus the supporting general equilibrium between sectors of each country in the world economy is not disturbed.)

Section 3.1 sets out the structural gravity model to provide the base of analysis. Section 3.2 derives volume equivalent aggregators for discriminatory protection structures within a product class, one from the point of view of the importer and the other from the point of view of the exporter.

3.1 Structural gravity

Begin with definitions of variables for some generic class of goods. Let i denote a country of origin and let j denote a country of destination. Let X_{ij} denote the value of shipments at destination prices from i to j. Further, let E_j denote the expenditure at destination j on goods from all origins, while Y_i denotes the sales of goods at destination prices from i to all destinations. Expenditure levels, the E's, and sales levels, the Y's, are determined in an upper level general equilibrium allocation that is exogenous for present purposes. The budget constraints (one for each country's total expenditure on each goods class) and the market clearance equations (one for each goods class for goods from each country of origin) together with a CES demand specification combine to yield the gravity model.

The CES demand function (for either final or intermediate products) with competitive pricing[9] gives expenditure on goods shipped from origin i to destination j as:

$$X_{ij} = (\beta_i p_i^* t_{ij}/P_j)^{1-\sigma} E_j. \tag{16}$$

Here, the value of shipments includes the trade costs while p_i^* is the factory gate price and β_i is a CES share parameter. The price index is $P_j = [\sum_i (\beta_i p_i^* t_{ij})^{1-\sigma}]^{1/(1-\sigma)}$. To see this, sum (16) and use the budget constraint $\sum_i X_{ij} = E_j$ to simplify.

Next, impose market clearance:

$$Y_i = \sum_j (\beta_i p_i^*)^{1-\sigma} (t_{ij}/P_j)^{1-\sigma} E_j. \tag{17}$$

Define $Y \equiv \sum_i Y_i$. In a world with globally common CES preferences, the expenditure shares must effectively be generated by

$$(\beta_i p_i^* \Pi_i)^{1-\sigma} = Y_i/Y. \tag{18}$$

The left-hand side of (18) is recognized as a behavioural share equation for the globally common CES preferences when all countries face a common world price $p_i^* \Pi_i$. This follows from dividing through (16) by E_j to give the representative CES demand share and then understanding that the CES price index that usually appears in the denominator is equal to one in the case of (18) because summing (18) implies $\sum_i (\beta_i p_i^* \Pi_i)^{1-\sigma} = 1$.

To complete the derivation of the structural gravity model, use (18) to substitute for $\beta_i p_i^*$ in (16), (17) and the CES price index. Then:

$$X_{ij} = \frac{E_j Y_i}{Y} \left(\frac{t_{ij}}{P_j \Pi_i} \right)^{1-\sigma}, \tag{19}$$

$$(\Pi_i)^{1-\sigma} = \sum_j \left(\frac{t_{ij}}{P_j} \right)^{1-\sigma} \frac{E_j}{Y}, \tag{20}$$

$$(P_j)^{1-\sigma} = \sum_i \left(\frac{t_{ij}}{\Pi_i} \right)^{1-\sigma} \frac{Y_i}{Y}. \tag{21}$$

A key component of the structural gravity model is multilateral resistance, the indexes P_j and Π_i that aggregate *all* bilateral trade costs, policy and non-policy, cross-border and internal. Multilateral resistance is interpreted as the demand (P_j) and supply (Π_i) side incidence of trade costs. Outward multilateral resistance Π_i aggregates the set of bilateral trade costs as if in effect country i shipped its product to a single world market at markup Π_i. This is the intuitive meaning of (18). For any bilateral trade cost, taking out the supply side incidence means that t_{ij}/Π_i is the buyer's bilateral incidence of the trade cost. Then P_j, inward multilateral resistance, is the CES price index of the bilateral buyers incidences. It is as if the buyer in j goes to the world market and buys a bundle of goods, one from each seller, taking them home at the uniform markup P_j.

Since the system of equations (20)–(21) solves for $\{\Pi_i, P_j\}$ only up to a scalar,[10] an additional restriction from a normalization is needed. Relative multilateral resistances are what matters for resource allocation, so the normalization can be chosen for convenience in computation or interpretation – for example, $P_j = 1$ for some convenient reference country j.[11] See Anderson and Yotov (2008) for more details and an example of these methods applied to Canadian provincial trade.

The structural gravity model yields many other useful and intuitive indexes that decompose the incidence of trade costs. One is the uniform border policy index.

3.2   Uniform border policy

The uniform *policy* border barrier is defined by replacing the policy-related costs on all trade that crosses borders (i.e., excluding internal trade) with a border barrier for each country that is uniform across its trading partners subject to a constant value of the domestic value of international trade. The concept of uniform border barriers applied to *all* trade costs that act on borders, policy-related or not, was developed by Anderson and van Wincoop (2004) and discussed further in Anderson and Neary (2005, ch. 10).

The uniform border policy maintains the initial equilibrium demand and hence the initial world prices. It resembles the MTRI in being focused on international trade but it uses domestic as opposed to world prices to form the volume constraint. Like the compensated MTRI, it does not account for the effect on expenditure of changes in tariff revenue in going to the hypothetical uniform barrier. In the context of evaluating total trade costs, of which trade policy is a small part, abstraction from redistribution of tariff revenue and quota rent is a perhaps justifiable simplifying assumption.

The switch to a uniform border policy potentially implies that a new set of multilateral resistances are generated by (20)–(21). However, the preservation of domestic value of trade along with the equilibrium market clearance implies that the value of internal shipments is constant. This in turn implies that multilateral resistances (and factory gate prices for producers) do not change. Constant multilateral resistances greatly simplify the calculation of the uniform border barrier.

With constant P's and Π's, the requirement that the hypothetical uniform import policies yield equal domestic value of international trade implies that

$$\sum_{i\neq j}(1+\tau_j^M)^{1-\sigma}(\bar{t}_{ij}/\Pi_i)^{1-\sigma}Y_i/Y = \sum_{i\neq j}(t_{ij}/\Pi_i)^{1-\sigma}Y_i/Y, \quad \forall j\neq i, \tag{22}$$

where τ_j^M is the uniform border import policy (as an ad valorem tariff equivalent) and $\bar{t}_{ij}$ is the non-policy barrier that acts on the border. Solving (22) for $1+\tau_j^M$:

$$1+\tau_j^M = \left(\sum_{i\neq j}(t_{ij}/\bar{t}_{ij})^{1-\sigma}v_i^M\right)^{1/(1-\sigma)}, \quad \forall j\neq i;$$

where

$$v_i^M = \frac{(\bar{t}_{ij}/\Pi_i)^{1-\sigma}Y_i/Y}{\sum_{i\neq j}(\bar{t}_{ij}/\Pi_i)^{1-\sigma}Y_i/Y}.$$

The uniform border policy formula has an intuitive structure. It is a CES index of the bilateral policy border barriers $t_{ij}/\bar{t}_{ij}$. The weights v_i^M in the index are based on the demand side bilateral incidences on non-policy barriers $\bar{t}_{ij}/\Pi_i$, normalized by their sum.

Symmetric to the uniform import policy formula is the uniform export policy formula. For each exporting country, define the uniform-across-countries border policy that maintains the domestic value of international trade. Then paralleling (22), the uniform export policy is implicit in:

$$\sum_{j\neq i}(1+\tau_i^X)^{1-\sigma}(\bar{t}_{ij}/P_j)^{1-\sigma}E_j/Y = \sum_{j\neq i}(t_{ij}/P_j)^{1-\sigma}E_j/Y, \quad \forall i\neq j. \tag{23}$$

(23) yields a closed form solution for $1+\tau_i^X$:

$$1+\tau_i^X = \left(\sum_{j\neq i}(t_{ij}/\bar{t}_{ij})^{1-\sigma}v_j^X\right)^{1/(1-\sigma)}, \quad \forall i\neq j;$$

where

$$v_j^X = \frac{(\bar{t}_{ij}/P_j)^{1-\sigma}E_j/Y}{\sum_{j\neq i}(\bar{t}_{ij}/P_j)^{1-\sigma}E_j/Y}.$$

τ_i^X is a concept that resembles the Kee *et al.* MA–OTRI, but it controls for potentially endogenous world prices in a single goods class.

It is straightforward to rank the uniform import border policy relative to the trade-weighted average tariff: *the uniform border policy barrier exceeds the trade-weighted average policy trade cost.* For proof, see Anderson and Neary (2005, chapter 10). The reason is the substitution effect – the trade-weighted average under-weights high tariffs and over-weights low tariffs.

The ranking proposition implies that the amount by which the uniform border barrier exceeds the trade-weighted average rises with the dispersion of the discriminatory policy. Thus for example EU members that individually have trade-weighted average tariffs similar to the United States are likely to have bigger uniform border barriers because they discriminate on a larger portion of their cross border trade than does the United States.

3.3   Aggregating across sectors

It is natural to think of combining aggregation across trading partners with aggregation across sectors. The methods of the preceding section can be combined with the methods of this section. A survey is not the proper place for such a development, but the basic ingredients are here for an ambitious reader to combine. The essential trick is that the uniform border policy variable aggregates in such a way that world prices remain constant. Then it is possible to use the techniques of section 2 to aggregate across sectors to form volume equivalent uniform tariffs. The compensated MTRI formed in this way is fully consistent. The uncompensated MTRI and the TRI involve complications that are beyond the scope of the survey; interested readers should consult Anderson and Neary (2005) for more information.

4   Conclusion

Measurement of protection is an important problem. Progress toward better solutions has been made but more is possible on both empirical and theoretical fronts. As for empirics, the opaque and often arbitrary nature of many non-tariff barriers points to inferential methods, buttressed by opinion surveys of businessmen who experience the barriers first hand. As for theory, better models lead to more reliable inference and to more appropriate and believable aggregation. The existing evidence points to large remaining trade barriers of the kind that policy can reduce, despite the fact that many formal tariffs are quite low.

Notes

* Boston College and NBER.
1. For example, the tariff schedules of the U.S. contain some 10,000 lines.
2. For an illustrative example using internationally comparable cheese prices to infer US cheese quota protection at the product line, see Anderson (1985).
3. Taste differences, if admitted, would act just like trade costs on the gravity equation. Technically, gravity cannot distinguish between 'home bias' due to taste differences and home bias due to trade costs.
4. Tariffs, in contrast to NTB's, are constrained by WTO obligations, so they are arguably exogenous.

5. An alternative is the simple (i.e., unweighted) average of tariff rates across different commodities. However, this measure has obvious disadvantages: it treats all commodities identically, and it is sensitive to changes in the classification of commodities in the tariff code.

6. 'More elastic' is used loosely here. Strictly, good 1 has larger absolute slope: $-m'_1 > -m'_2$, and the statement of the text is strictly true if changed to 'import demand schedule for good 1 is more responsive than that for good 2...'. The elasticity ranking depends on where on the demand schedules the elasticity $-m'_i\pi_i/m_i$ is evaluated. Thus the 'more elastic' statement of the text is true only for a range of tariffs and of horizontal intercepts of the linear demand schedules.

7. The linear demand setup of the diagram implies elasticities that vary along the demand schedule, so equating larger absolute slope with higher elasticity is only valid in a range of tariff settings.

8. More complex economic structures are readily encompassed by essentially the same modeling strategy, encompassing complications such as nontraded goods, economies of scale or monopolistic competition.

9. The extension to monopolistic competition is an inessential complication because the markups in this setting are constant.

10. Notice that if $\{P_j^0, \Pi_i^0\}$ is a solution to (20)–(21) then so is $\{\lambda P_j^0, \Pi_i^0/\lambda\}$ for any $\lambda > 0$.

11. With information on the factory gate prices p_i^* and the distribution parameters β_i, the natural normalization is $\sum_i(\beta_i p_i^* \Pi_i)^{1-\sigma} = 1$. The natural normalization is required when applying the model in a larger general equilibrium computational setting which includes reallocations across product classes. For reallocations across trading partners within a product class, all normalizations are equivalent.

References

Anderson, James E., and J. Peter Neary (1994) 'The trade restrictiveness of the multi-fibre arrangement', *World Bank Economic Review*, May, 171–89.

—— (2005) *Measuring the Restrictiveness of International Trade Policy*. Cambridge MA: MIT Press.

Anderson, James E., and Eric van Wincoop (2004) 'Trade costs', *Journal of Economic Literature*, 42, 691–751.

Anderson, James E., and Yoto V. Yotov (2008) 'The changing incidence of geography', NBER Working Paper No. 14423.

Anderson, James E. (2009) 'Consistent trade policy aggregation', *International Economic Review*, 50(3), 903–27.

—— (1985) 'The relative inefficiency of quotas: the cheese case', *American Economic Review*, 75, 178–90.

Baier, Scott, and Jeffrey Bergstrand (2007) 'Do free trade agreements actually increase members international trade?', *Journal of International Economics*, 71, 72–95.

Besedes, Tibor, and Thomas J. Prusa (2003) 'On the Duration of Trade', NBER Working Paper No. 9936.

Crozet Matthieu, Pamina Koenig and Vincent Rebeyrol (2008) 'Exporting to Insecure Markets: a Firm-level Analysis' CEPII Working Paper No. 2008–13.

Dixit, Avinash K. (2004) *Lawlessness and Economics*. Princeton: Princeton University Press.

Eaton, Jonathan, and Samual Kortum (2002) 'Technology, geography and trade,' *Econometrica*, 70(5), 1741–79.

Helpman, Elhanan, Marc J. Melitz and Shona Rubinstein (2008) 'Trading volumes and trading patterns', *Quarterly Journal of Economics*, forthcoming.

Irwin, Douglas (2007) 'Trade Restrictiveness and Deadweight Losses from U.S. Tariffs, 1869–1961', NBER Working Paper No. 13450.

Kee, Hiau Looi, Alessandro Nicita and Marcelo Olarreaga (2008) 'Import Demand Elasticities and Trade Distortions', *Review of Economics and Statistics*, 90, 666–82.

——(2009) 'Estimating Trade Restrictiveness Indices', *Economic Journal*, 119, 172–99.

Trefler, Daniel (1993) 'Trade Liberalization and the Theory of Endogenous Protection', *Journal of Political Economy*, 101, 138–60.

12
Preferential Trade Agreements: Theory and Evidence

*Pravin Krishna**

1 Introduction

Strongly influenced by the perception that restricted commerce and preferences in trade relations had contributed to the economic depression of the 1930s and the subsequent outbreak of war, the discussions leading to the General Agreement on Tariffs and Trade (GATT) in 1947 were driven by the desire to create an international economic order based on a liberal and non-discriminatory multilateral trade system. Enshrined in Article I of the GATT, the principle of non-discrimination (commonly referred to as the most-favored-nation or MFN clause) precludes member countries from discriminating against imports based upon the country of origin. However, in an important exception this central prescript, the GATT, through its Article XXIV, permits its members to enter into preferential trade agreements (PTAs), provided these preferences are complete. In so doing, it sanctions the formation of Free Trade Areas (FTAs), whose members are obligated to eliminate internal import barriers, and Customs Unions (CUs), whose members additionally agree on a common external tariff against imports from non-members. Additional derogations to the principle of non-discrimination now include the *Enabling Clause,* which allows tariff preferences to be granted to developing countries (in accordance with the *Generalized System of Preferences*) and permits preferential trade agreements among developing countries in goods trade.

   Such preferential trade agreements are now in vogue. Even as multilateral approaches to trade liberalisation − through negotiations organized by the GATT/WTO − have made substantial progress in reducing international barriers to trade, GATT/WTO-sanctioned PTAs have rapidly increased in number in recent years. Among the more prominent existing PTAs are the North American Free Trade Agreement (NAFTA), the European Economic Community (EEC), both formed under Article XXIV, and the MERCOSUR (the CU between the Argentine Republic, Brazil, Paraguay, and Uruguay), formed under the Enabling

349

Clause. All in all, hundreds of PTAS are currently in existence, with nearly every member country of the WTO belonging to at least one PTA.

That a country liberalising its trade preferentially against select partners is doing something distinct from multilateral liberalisation (where it eliminates tariffs against all imports regardless of country of origin) should be easy to see. What this implies for the liberalising country is a little more difficult to understand. Even a good half century after the economic implications of trade preferences were first articulated by Viner (1950), the differences between preferential and multilateral liberalisation (or free trade areas versus free trade) remain a nuance that most policy analysts (and occasionally even distinguished economists) appear to miss.

It is with a discussion of these issues concerning the distinction between preferential and non-discriminatory trade liberalisation that we begin the analytical section of this chapter, which is intended as a brief and accessible primer on the economics of PTAs. Specifically, Section 2 develops the classic analysis of Viner (1950) and demonstrates the generally ambiguous welfare effects of preferential trade liberalisation. Section 3 discusses the role geographic proximity ('regionalism') may play in this discussion. The design of welfare-improving preferential trade agreements is discussed in Section 4. Section 5 discusses GATT/WTO regulations concerning PTA formation and asks how the existing provisions compare with the welfare improving designs for PTAs described in Section 4. Section 6 concludes.

2 Welfare analysis

2.1 Trade creation and trade diversion

Does preferential trade liberalisation in favor of particular trading partners have the same welfare consequences as non-discriminatory trade liberalisation in favor of all imports? Do a simple proportion of the welfare benefits of non-discriminatory free trade accrue with preferential liberalisation?

A thorough answer to these questions would require the reader to take a deep plunge into the abstruse world of the second-best (whose existence and complexities were indeed first discovered and developed by analysts working on the economics of PTAs). But the idea may be introduced in a rudimentary fashion using the following 'textbook' representation of Viner's analysis: Consider the case of two countries, A and B, and the rest of the world, W. A is our 'home' country. A produces a single specialized good and trades it for the exports of its trading partners B and W. Both B and W are assumed to export the same good and offer it to A at a fixed (but different) price. Initially, imports from B and W are subject to non-discriminatory trade restrictions: tariffs against B and W are equal. Imagine now that A eliminates its tariffs against B while maintaining its

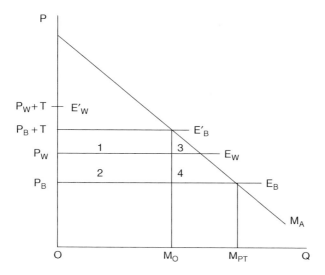

Figure 12.1   Trade creating tariff preferences

tariffs against W. This is a preferential tariff reduction as opposed to free trade, since the latter would require that tariffs against W be removed as well. It is very tempting to think that this reduction of tariffs against B is a step in the direction of free trade and therefore that this ought to deliver to country A a proportionate fraction of the benefits of complete free trade. But Viner (1950) showed that this need not (and generally would not) be the case. Indeed, while a complete move towards free trade would be welfare improving for country A, Viner demonstrated that the tariff preference granted to B through the FTA could in fact worsen A's welfare.

Figures 12.1 and 12.2 illustrate preferential tariff reform as respectively welfare enhancing and welfare worsening. The y-axes denote price and the x-axes denote quantities. M_A denotes the import demand curve of country A. E_B and E_W denote the price at which countries B and W are willing to supply A's demand; they represent the export supply curves of B and W respectively. In figure 12.1, B is assumed to be a more efficient supplier of A's import than is W: E_B is drawn below E_W, and its export price P_B is less than W's export price P_W. Let T denote the non-discriminatory per-unit tariff that is applied against B and W. This renders the tariff-inclusive price to importers in A as $P_B + T$ and $P_W + T$ respectively. With this non-discriminatory tariff in place, imports initially equal M_0 and the good is entirely imported from B. Tariff revenues in this initial situation equal the areas $(1+2)$. When tariffs against B are eliminated preferentially, imports rise to M_{PT}. Imports continue to come entirely from B (since the import price from B now, P_B, is lower than the tariff-inclusive price of imports from W, $P_W + T$).

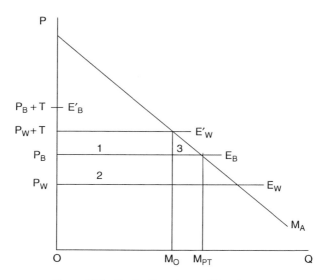

Figure 12.2   Trade diverting tariff preferences

The tariff preferences granted to B simply increase the volume of imports. This increase in the volume of trade with the country whose exports were initially being purchased by A anyway (i.e., with the more efficient producer) when tariffs against it are preferentially reduced is referred to as 'trade creation'. Trade creation here can be shown to be welfare improving. The increase in benefit to consumers (consumer surplus) in A following the reduction in consumption prices from $P_B + T$ to P_B equals the areas $(1 + 2 + 3 + 4)$. No tariff revenue is now earned and so the loss of tariff revenue equals areas $(1+2)$. The overall gain to A from this preferential tariff reduction equals areas $(1+2+3+4) - (1 + 2)$ = areas $(3 + 4)$, a positive number. The trade-creating tariff preference is thus welfare improving.

In demonstrating that the tariff preference we have considered is welfare improving for the home country, A, we have assumed that the partner which receives this tariff preference, B, is the more efficient supplier of the good. Figure 12.2 reverses this assumption, making W, the rest of the world, the more efficient supplier of the good. E_W is thus drawn below E_B. Initial imports are M_0. The tariff revenue collected is equal to the areas $(1 + 2)$. When tariffs are eliminated against B, the less efficient partner, the tariff-inclusive price of imports from W is higher than the tariff-exclusive price from B. This implies that all trade is now 'diverted' away from W to B. What is the welfare consequence of this trade diversion? The increase in consumer surplus is equal to the areas $(1+3)$ since consumers now pay a price equal to P_B for this good. The loss in tariff revenue is $(1+2)$. The overall gain to A equals the area $(3-2)$, which may or may not be positive. Thus, a trade diverting tariff preference may lead to a welfare reduction.

The preceding examples illustrate a central issue emphasized in the academic literature on the welfare consequences of preferential trade. Preferential trade liberalisation towards the country from whom the good was imported in the initial non-discriminatory situation creates more trade and increases welfare; preferential liberalisation that diverts trade instead may reduce welfare. Subsequent analysis also developed examples of both welfare improving trade-diversion and welfare decreasing trade creation in general equilibrium contexts broader than those considered by Viner. However, the intuitive appeal of the concepts of trade creation and trade diversion has ensured their continued use in the economic analysis of preferential trade agreements, especially in policy analysis. See Panagariya (2000) for a comprehensive survey.

Many recent empirical studies have quantified the adverse consequences of trade diversion and underscore the fact that trade diversion is not merely a theoretical concern. Yeats (1998) investigated the question of trade diversion within PTAs by performing an evaluation of trade patterns within MERCOSUR. To describe the orientation of MERCOSUR trade, goods were characterized using two measures. The first measure is a 'regional orientation' index which is the ratio of the share of that good in exports to the region to its share in exports to third countries. The second measure is the 'revealed comparative advantage' measure which is the ratio of the share of a good in MERCOSUR's exports to third countries to its share in world exports (exclusive of intra-MERCOSUR trade). Yeats then compares the change in goods' regional orientation index between 1988 and 1994 (before and after MERCOSUR) with their revealed comparative advantage ranking. The results of his study are striking. As he notes, the goods with the largest increase in regional orientation are goods with very low revealed comparative advantage rankings. Specifically, for the 30 groups of goods with the largest increases in regional orientation, only two had revealed comparative advantage indices above unity. That is, the largest increases in intra-MERCOSUR trade have been in goods in which MERCOSUR countries lack comparative advantage suggesting strong trade diversionary effects.

A more recent paper, Romalis (2007) investigates the effects of NAFTA and the previously formed Canada–United States Free Trade Agreement (CUSFTA) on trade flows. Romalis finds that NAFTA and CUSFTA had a substantial impact on international trade volumes, but a modest effect on prices and welfare. While he finds that, while NAFTA and CUSFTA increased North American output in many highly protected sectors, imports from nonmember countries were driven out, suggesting significant trade diversionary effects.

2.2   Internal terms of trade and revenue transfer effects

The Vinerian analysis illustrated in figures 12.1 and 12.2 has assumed that the home country is small relative to both the partner country and the rest of the world, with the exportable from the partner and the rest of the world being perfect substitutes. Specifically, when consumption is switched from the rest of the world to the partner country, the partner country is assumed to be able to satisfy all of the demand of the home country. What happens if B is so small that after receiving the tariff preference from A it is unable to satisfy all of A's demand for its importable. This implies that A continues to import some amount from the rest of the world W (which we assume for the moment is so large that it is able to handle all of the changes in A's demand without letting this affect its supply price) even after granting preferential access to B. Here, it can be shown that the home country loses unambiguously. The following example, provided by Panagariya (2000), illustrates. In figure 12.3, the export supply curve of country B is shown to be rising. The tariff inclusive supply curve faced by the home country is E_B^-. Total consumption of the importable initially is M_0 and imports from B are M_B^T. A tariff preference in favor of B simply shifts the effective export supply curve to E_B and the imports from B to M_B. Total imports stay at M_0. The domestic price of the importable in the home market in A is set by W (which continues to supply to A) and is the same as before (i.e., it stays at E_W^-). The outcomes in this case are quite stark. Since consumption of the importable continues to be at M_0, there is no change in consumer surplus in the home country. There is however a direct tariff revenue loss since no

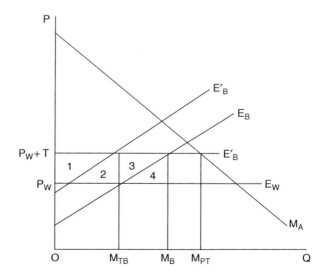

Figure 12.3   Partner country size and welfare

tariff revenue is now earned on imports from the partner. The loss in tariff revenue (which is equal to the overall loss to A) equals the areas $(1 + 2 + 3 + 4)$. In what can effectively be seen as a tariff revenue transfer to B, a gain of areas $(1 + 2 + 3)$ accrues to B in the form of an increase in producer surplus. Thus, preferential tariff liberalisation leads to a loss in welfare for the liberalising country, a (smaller) gain in welfare for its partner and a net loss of area (4) to the union as a whole.

In general, in the context of an exchange in tariff preferences negotiated under a preferential trade agreement, we may expect that tariff revenue losses to the home country in some sectors are made up for by gains in other sectors in which the home country gets preferential access to its partner's markets. Who gains more will depend upon the extent of tariff preferences exchanged and specific market circumstances (shapes of the supply and demand curves). The outcome is uncertain.

2.3 External terms of trade

Thus far, we have focused our discussion of the welfare consequences of preferential trade liberalisation on the countries undertaking the liberalisation. While we have not explicitly considered this so far, it should be easy to see that changes in demand by PTA members for the rest of the world's exports could lower the relative price of these exports (i.e., worsens the rest of the world's terms of trade). In general, the overall effect on the external terms of trade may be seen as a combination of income and substitution effects. The former represents the effect of real income changes due to the PTA on demand for imports from non-members and the latter reflects the substitution in trade towards partner countries (and away from non-member) due to the preferences in trade. In the case of a real-income reducing PTA, both effects would combine to lower demand from the rest of the world. This is also the case when substitution effects dominate the income effect.[1] The rest of the world experiences a deterioration in its terms of trade and is therefore adversely impacted. Some indication of how the terms of trade may change for non-member countries in practice is provided by the empirical analysis of Chang and Winters (2002), who examine the impact of MERCO-SUR (specifically, the exemption in tariffs that Brazil provided to is MERCOSUR partners) on the terms-of-trade (export prices) of countries excluded from the agreement. Theory would suggest that trade diversion would worsen the terms of trade of excluded countries and this indeed is what they find. Specifically, their analysis reports significant declines in the export prices of Brazil's major trading partners (the United States, Japan, Germany and Korea) following MERCOSUR. These associated welfare losses sustained by the excluded countries are significant as well – amounting to roughly 10 percent of the value of their exports to Brazil.[2]

In an earlier study, Grinols (1984) examined the effects of Britain joining the EEC in 1973. Measuring the prices for British exports and imports during the years after its membership in the EEC, Grinols found that British terms of trade had fallen and that the costs of this decline amounted to over 2 percent of British GDP. Furthermore, Grinols found that the efficiency gains from trade integration were quite small, leading to the overall conclusion that membership in the EEC in 1973 led to a welfare loss for Britain that averaged about 2 percent of GDP annually.

3 Geography and preferential trade agreements: is regionalism 'natural'?

The previous section has discussed some reasons why economists have been divided on the wisdom of preferential trade arrangements (PTAs). Following Viner's (1950) demonstration that the net welfare effects of PTAs are unpredictable and possibly negative, many attempts were made to refine the theory and identify member country characteristics that would ensure welfare improvement and thus eliminate the welfare ambiguities associated with preferential trade. However, these efforts yielded results that did not have any greater direct operational significance than did Viner (1950). This is to say that they did not yield any direct insights on what partner country characteristics would make trade creation rather than trade diversion a likely outcome.

More recently, however, increasing emphasis has been placed on geographic proximity as a criterion for membership in a PTA. Regionalism in preferential trade has been argued by some authors (see, for instance, Wonnacott and Lutz, 1987, Krugman, 1991, and Summers, 1991) as being key to generating better economic outcomes, with regional trading partners described as 'natural trading partners' in the context of preferential trade. The question of natural trading partners is immensely interesting for policy reasons. Many existing preferential trading arrangements are indeed regional. In addition, many extensions of existing arrangements along regional lines, such as the expansion of the North American Free Trade Area (NAFTA) to include Chile, Argentina and other South American countries, or that of the European Union (EU) to include other regional countries, are currently being debated and discussed in policy circles.

To evaluate the argument for geographic proximity as a membership criterion, we may start by noting that this argument itself rests on two economic hypotheses. First, that trade creation is greater and trade diversion lower when the initial volume of trade between the partners is higher (and trade with the rest of the world is lower) and second, that geographically proximate countries have larger volumes of trade with each other.

As Bhagwati (1993) and Bhagwati and Panagariya (1996) have pointed out, however, these are not robust principles. For instance, the contention that geographically proximate countries trade more with each other is generally only valid as a conditional statement. That is to say, it is only after we 'control' for a variety of other variables such as income levels of the partner country that we are able to say that trade is higher between countries which are closer to each other. Importantly, however, the choice of partners in a PTA need not be conditioned on these same variables – diluting the relevance of proximity in discussions over trade preferences. An example may serve to clarify this point. In a hypothetical world, where Japan's income and Mexico's income levels are equal (i.e., 'controlling' for income) U.S. trade with Mexico may well be higher than trade with Japan. As it stands however, Japan has a much higher income level than does Mexico. Its trade volume with the United States is also much higher. Thus, even if initial trade volumes were to be used as a criterion by the United States for choosing PTA members, the distant country (Japan) ought to be a preferred partner.

Furthermore, it is incorrect to suggest that preferences towards the more significant partner are more likely to result in trade creation. Panagariya (1996) offers a very clear argument on this point. Thus consider the economy discussed in section 2.2 and illustrated in figure 12.3. Recall that trade preferences towards country B result in a loss of welfare for the liberalising country A. Importantly, note that the losses (areas $1+2+3+4$) are greater the greater is the initial volume of trade. Thus, with changing internal terms of trade, the argument that greater initial volumes of trade result in larger increases in welfare is directly contradicted.

Finally, it should be noted that the argument concerning trade creation and larger initial volumes of trade is not robust – even when internal terms of trade do not change. To see this, note that welfare gains with trade policy changes generally depend upon substitutions at the margin (changes in trade volumes – with partners and the rest of the world) as well as the initial levels of trade. This raises two issues. First, the relevant substitution elasticities do not generally depend on the initial volumes of trade. Differences in trade elasticities may therefore offset any differences in initial trade volumes. Second and more importantly, significant trading partners generally also compete to a greater extent with the rest of the world than do less significant trading partners. For example, Japan is a more significant trading partner of the United States than is Ecuador, but it also competes in a wider range of markets and in larger volumes, say with EU suppliers, than Ecuador, which competes in a narrower and economically less significant set of markets. Importantly, while trade creation may be larger with significant partners, so may trade diversion. In the preceding example, this implies that trade preferences granted by the United States to Japan will divert larger volumes of trade – away from the EU – than trade preferences towards Ecuador.

The empirical analysis of Krishna (2003) finds evidence of just these effects in U.S. data. In an econometric investigation of U.S. trade, aimed at estimating trade creation and trade diversion effects under (hypothetical) trade preferences towards a variety of countries, trade creation and trade diversion are found to be correlated in their magnitudes. In his analysis, net welfare gains (i.e., gains from trade creation net of trade diversion losses) are found to be wholly uncorrelated with distance. All in all, arguments for regionalism in trade preferences do not appear to have a substantial basis in economic theory and are not supported by empirical analysis.

4   Necessarily welfare improving preferential trade areas

The generally ambiguous welfare results with trade preferences provoked an important question in the economic literature relating to the design of necessarily welfare improving PTAs. A classic result due to Kemp and Wan (1976) and Ohyama (1972) provides a welfare improving solution for the case of CUs. Starting from a situation with an arbitrary structure of trade barriers, if two or more countries freeze their net external trade vector with the rest of the world through a set of common external tariffs and eliminate the barriers to internal trade (implying the formation of a CU), the welfare of the union as a whole necessarily improves (weakly) and that of the rest of the world does not fall. The logic behind the Kemp–Wan theorem is as follows: by fixing the combined, net extra-union trade vector of member countries at its pre-union level, non-member countries are guaranteed their original level of welfare. Since there is no diversion of trade in this case, the welfare of the member countries is also not adversely affected. The PTA thus constructed has a common internal price vector, implying further a common external tariff for member countries. The Kemp–Wan–Ohyama design, by freezing the external trade vector and thus eliminating trade diversion, offers a way to sidestep the complexities and ambiguities inherent in the analysis of PTAs.

The Kemp–Wan–Ohyama analysis of welfare improving CUs does not extend easily to FTAs since member-specific tariff vectors in the case of FTAs imply that domestic-prices will differ across member countries. Panagariya and Krishna (2002) have, nevertheless, recently provided a corresponding construction of necessarily welfare improving FTAs. In complete analogy with the Kemp–Wan CU, Panagariya and Krishna (2002) require that the trade vector of each member country with the rest of the world be frozen at the pre-FTA level. Since, in FTAs different member countries impose different external tariffs, it is necessary to specify a set of rules-of-origin (ROO) to prevent a subversion of FTA tariffs by importing through the lower-tariff member country and directly trans-shipping goods to the higher-tariff country (which, if allowed, would bring the FTA arbitrarily close to a

CU). The Panagariya-Krishna solution requires that all goods with any value added within the FTA are to be traded freely. Goods which enter the FTA as final goods are to be wholly prevented from trans-shipment by suitable ROO.

Theory thus suggests that ensuring welfare improvement requires that along with elimination of internal barriers, external tariff vectors should eliminate trade diversion – member countries should continue to import the same amounts from the rest of the world as they did initially. In the next section, we examine how these theoretical prescriptions compare with WTO rules concerning the formation of PTAs.

5 PTA implementation and the WTO

The preceding discussion of necessarily welfare improving CUs and FTAs provided a precise description of the tariff vectors that ought to be implemented in these agreements. Specifically, internal barriers are to be completely eliminated and the external tariff vector in both cases (i.e., the CU or the FTA) should eliminate trade diversion – member countries should continue to import the same amounts from the rest of the world as they did initially. Can these tariffs be implemented in practice? And where do existing GATT/WTO provisions stand in relation to the theoretical specification?

Article XXIV of the GATT, which permits the formation of PTAs, also originally stipulated broadly that internal preferences needed to be complete (i.e., that internal barriers between the members were to be completely eliminated) and that external trade barriers were not to be more restrictive than initially. As we will discuss below, a number of questions arose in connection with GATT regulations regarding both internal and external tariffs – some having to do with their economic merit, others to do with implementation and possible abuse given the ambiguous and imprecise wording adopted in the original text of the GATT. As we will discuss further, while the more recent 'Understanding on the Interpretation' of Article XXIV issued by the GATT in 1994 clarified some of these issues, other questions still remain.

5.1 Internal barriers to trade

On internal barriers to trade, two questions arise. The first relates to coverage – do GATT regulations require a removal of all internal barriers? The second relates to timing – how much time do countries have to comply with the rules? On the former issue, it should be clarified that while the putative intent of the GATT was to require that internal barriers be eliminated completely, the actual text of the GATT only required that restrictions be eliminated on 'substantially all trade.' The ambiguous phrasing through the use of the qualifier 'substantially' opened up a number of possibilities for abuse. Whether 'substantial' should have been taken to imply a full 100 percent or something smaller was not clear and has not yet been clarified. In this context, it is worth noting that for a given level of external tariffs, member country welfare is not necessarily maximized with zero internal barriers.[3] From a purely economic standpoint, given the level of external tariffs, welfare may well be maximized by maintaining some particular level of internal restrictions. It may therefore be potentially argued that the ambiguous phrasing permitting non-elimination of internal barriers allowed member countries to aim at welfare maximizing outcomes. This is, however, quite unlikely. Any retention of internal barriers within PTAs is probably better explained by selective protectionist motivations on the part of country governments. Separately, it may be imagined that non-member countries would have an incentive to monitor and ensure the full dismantling of internal trade barriers within PTAs. However, it is also quite likely that the welfare of countries outside the union is higher when the discrimination against them is lower (i.e., when internal preferences are less than complete). Expost, the external monitoring incentive is therefore minimal. On the question of the timing and the phasing out of internal barriers to trade, GATT rules, rather than requiring an immediate removal of internal barriers in a PTA, allowed for this to take place within a 'reasonable length of time,' once again permitting substantial ambiguity in understanding and room for abuse.[4]

5.2 External barriers to trade

On external tariffs, the original GATT requirement was that external barriers not be more restrictive than initially. For FTAs, since countries retain individual tariff vectors, this could be taken to imply that no tariff was to rise. For CUs, since a common external tariff was to be chosen, and initial tariffs on the same good likely varied across countries, the tariff vector would necessarily change for each country. The expectation was then that the 'general incidence' of trade barriers would not be higher or more restrictive than before. Given the imprecise phrasing, there was once more substantial ambiguity as to what is implied – should the common external tariff equal the unweighted mean of initial tariffs in the member countries? Should it be the trade-weighted mean? Or something else? As Dam (1970), Bhagwati (1993) and several others have noted, it is clear that Article XXIV's ambiguity in this regard left plenty of room for opportunistic (i.e., protectionist) behaviour by member countries against non-members. The 1994 'Understanding on the Interpretation' of Article XXIV issued by the GATT provided substantial clarity on the issue of measurement and choice of the common external tariff – indicating that the GATT secretariat would compute weighted average tariff rates and duties collected in accordance with the methodology used in the assessment of tariff offers in the Uruguay round of trade negotiations and examine trade flow and other data to arrive at suitable measures of non-tariff barriers. While this relieves, at least partially, the issue of measurement of external barriers and the comparison with barriers in place initially, the economic concern regarding trade diversion is not addressed. Clearly, leaving external barriers at their initial level and removing internal barriers does not eliminate trade diversion (as theoretically required in the Kemp–Wan and Panagariya-Krishna constructions of welfare improving PTAs). Indeed, with this configuration, trade diversion is practically guaranteed.

Having pointed to the deficiencies in existing GATT regulations in relation to the elimination of trade diversion, it may be noted that picking or designing tariff vectors exante that would ensure zero trade diversion, good by good, is a rather difficult task; the necessary measures of the exact sensitivity of external trade flows to external barriers of the CU or the FTA would be hard if not impossible to estimate accurately. So there is little prospect of identifying the exact trade-diversion-eliminating Kemp–Wan tariff vector and implementing it in practice.[5] Nevertheless, designing other disciplines to minimize diversion is less difficult; one can certainly say that lowering external barriers simultaneously with the formation of a CU or an FTA is likely to lower the degree of trade diversion (by minimizing the substitution away from the goods supplied by the rest of the world to within-union goods). McMillan (1993) has suggested as a test of admissibility of any PTA the measurement (estimation) of whether that PTA will result in less trade with the rest of the world.[6] In a similar spirit, Bhagwati (1993) has suggested that the requirement of a simultaneous pro rata reduction of external trade barriers with the progressive elimination of internal barriers could replace the current requirements.

5.3 Rules of origin

In free trade areas, importers have a potential incentive to import goods into the bloc through the member country imposing the lowest tariff on that good and then to trans-ship that good into higher tariff member countries by availing themselves of the duty-free treatment within the bloc. To prevent this circumvention of the independent tariffs desired by member countries, however, FTAs need to be supported by rules of origin (ROO), which specify the circumstances under which a good may be given duty-free treatment within the union.[7]

The discussion in the previous section has provided a welfare-theoretic basis for very simple rules of origin – goods which undergo any genuine value-added transformation within the union must be allowed to move duty free within the union. For any good entirely produced outside the union, trade-deflection is to be prevented by imposing effectively on direct imports and also any trans-shipped units, the external tariff that is chosen by the member country where the good is eventually consumed. Rules of origin are more complex in practice, however. Rules of origin are differently concerned (depending on the good) with the fractional content of the good that is required to be produced within the union for the good to qualify for duty-free status.[8] More importantly, while putative intention of rules of origin is to simply to prevent deflection of trade, it has been argued that these rules have been used more flexibly as instruments of commercial policy (see, for instance, Krishna and Krueger (1995)).

That the opportunity to set rules of origin would be abused to achieve other ends should come as no surprise to anyone even moderately familiar with the political-economy of trade policy determination. While we may hope for FTA rules to be designed by welfare-maximizing governments concerned with the enhancement of internal efficiency and equity towards non-members, in practice, the rules of origin are determined in intensely political contexts in which a variety of additional factors influence policy. Governments are under great pressure to deviate from the high path of choosing rules of origin to simply prevent trade deflection towards fixing rules that favor politically active and aggressive constituencies in the economy. Because in an FTA there are no internal tariffs and because external tariffs themselves cannot be raised to further disadvantage non-member countries, it has been argued that in order to please their constituencies and protect them from the economic changes that come about due to the entry into the free trade area, governments manipulate rules of origin to protect both domestic suppliers of final and intermediate goods.[9] This may happen in the following ways:

(a) Protection for final good suppliers: Consider a final goods supplier in a member country facing greater competition from suppliers in other member countries due to the impending elimination of internal barriers of trade within the FTA. Consider further that this foreign competition uses, in its production, intermediates from outside of the FTA. Due to the political pressures brought to bear on the domestic government, whether it is from capitalists, affected voters, or displaced workers, that government will have reasons to negotiate intra-union content criteria severe enough to push those competing goods out of the duty-free category. In so doing they will insulate the home country supplier from that greater competition, but also undermine the intended competitive enhancement from joining an FTA.

(b) Protection for intermediate goods suppliers: governments can negotiate for rules of origin that specify a high degree of domestic (i.e., within-bloc) content, significantly diverting demand from goods produced with foreign intermediates to goods produced using intermediates from within the FTA.

However this use of rules of origin undermines the two key rules imposed by the WTO on its members for FTA formation. While complete internal liberalisation is sought by the WTO, this is negated by the selective use of rules of origin. Further, while the WTO requires that trade barriers against non-members not be raised by FTA members, the use of stringent rules of origin would divert imports of intermediates away from non-member exporters even if external tariffs are maintained at the same level as before.[10]

To what extent rules of origin are used to prevent trade deflection and to what extent they are politically motivated commercial policy instruments is ultimately an empirical question. While empirical research in this area is still in its infancy, Cadot, Estevadeordal and Suwa-Eisenmann (2003) have recently provided some interesting results. They examine directly the possible use of rules of origin to achieve protection for final goods producers and the creation of a captive market for intra-union suppliers of intermediate goods, as we have discussed above. Specifically, they measure the effects of rules of origin on Mexican imports to the U.S. market, to find that rules of origin are a large enough negative influence on intra-union trade flows so as to offset the tariff preferences granted by the trade agreement. Further, the creation of a protected market for intermediate goods producers also appears to be a key determinant of the rules of origin chosen.

5.4 Non-trade issues in preferential integration

Some proponents of preferential integration have argued (see, for instance, Lawrence, 1996) that PTAs achieve 'deep' integration. That is, rather than achieving simply trade liberalisation, as in multilateral liberalisation contexts, PTAs involve 'deep' integration through coordination, or harmonization, of other non-trade policies such as competition policies, environmental policies, labor standards, product standards and investment codes. It is further argued that such harmonization of policies will be efficiency enhancing and beneficial to member countries.

The proposition that harmonization of policies is uniformly beneficial to all of the member countries in a PTA has been met with skepticism by others (see, for instance, Panagariya, 1999) who note that there are good reasons for diversity in domestic policies and standards, and that harmonization is not an automatically welfare enhancing policy. Thus, for instance, the choice of optimal pollution levels and labor standards depend generally on the income level. While every country may prefer lower pollution, countries may reasonably disagree on what the optimal pollution levels are, what costs they should bear to lower pollution and where these efforts are best directed (for instance, developed countries may prefer to lower water pollution, while air pollution may be a greater concern for richer countries). Similarly, countries may disagree on minimum wage levels, worker-safety issues and the merits of permitting voluntary child labor. Thus, while harmonization may indeed bring some forms of efficiency enhancement, it is far from clear that such harmonization of policies will be beneficial overall, or that any benefits will accrue uniformly to all the member countries. A practical concern is that, under the guise of 'deep integration', the larger and more powerful countries in a PTA negotiation may be able to extract concessions not merely in trade but in other 'non-trade' matters as well.

6   Conclusion

PTAs, while conceived originally as minor exceptions to the GATT's central principle of non-discrimination, and only to be permitted under strict conditions, now number in the hundreds. A half-century of research has advanced significantly our understanding of the implications of trade discrimination even if the frequently equivocal theoretical and empirical results have established, among economists and policymakers, an ambivalent attitude towards preferential trade agreements. However, concerns regarding the fragmentation of the world trade system have grown with the rapid proliferation of preferential trade in recent years. Several hundred PTAs are currently in existence (with many countries belonging to multiple PTAs) and several more are in process. With this inexorable erosion of non-discriminatory disciplines within the trade system, research on preferential trade is certain to remain central to the field of international trade policy for many years to come.

Notes

*   Johns Hopkins University and NBER.
1. See Mundell (1964) for an analysis if how such extra-union terms of trade effects may complicate matters further for the tariff-reducing country, whose terms of trade with respect to the rest of the world may rise or fall following a preferential reduction in its tariffs against a particular partner. On this point see also the analysis by Panagariya (1997).
2. For instance, the United States is estimated to lose somewhere between $550–600 million on exports of about $5.5 billion, with Germany losing between $170–236 million on exports of about $2 billion.
3. It is important to keep in mind here that the elimination of internal tariffs maximizes the welfare of member countries for a given level of external trade (as in Kemp–Wan) and not for a given level of the external tariffs. With fixed tariffs, member country welfare may well be maximized with internal tariffs that are non-zero.
4. The more recent 'Understanding on the Interpretation' of Article XXIV issued in 1994 clarifies that the 'reasonable length of time' should exceed ten years in only 'exceptional cases.'
5. See, however, the paper by Srinivasan (1997) which attempts to identify and characterize the Kemp–Wan tariff vector in the context of a particular economic model.
6. Of course, the Kemp–Wan and Panagariya-Krishna schemes both require that the PTA trade exactly the same amount as before. A PTA that trades no less, as in the McMillan test, is not necessarily welfare improving, as in Winters (1997) has argued.
7. Since, in practice, at least some traded goods are not covered by the common external barriers of a CU, ROO are often used in CU as well.

8. See the papers by Estevadeordal and Suominen (2003) and Krishna (2003) for a detailed discussion of the different ways in which rules of origin are specified in practice.
9. Of course, it may be just such protection that enables a government to generate enough political support for the FTA in the first place, as Duttagupta and Panagariya (2001) have argued.
10. Ironically, however, highly severe rules of origin may result in greater imports from the rest of the world than before owing to the preference of importers to pay the external tariff rather than comply with demanding domestic-content standards.

References

Bhagwati, J. (1993) 'Regionalism and multilateralism: an overview', in Jaime deMelo and Arvind Panagariya (eds), *New Dimensions in Regional Integration*. Cambridge: Cambridge University Press.

Bhagwati, J., and A. Panagariya (1996) 'Free trade areas or free trade?' in *The Economics of Preferential Trade Areas*, American Enterprise Institute. Washington, D.C.: AEI Press.

Bhagwati, J., P. Krishna, and A. Panagariya (1999) *Trading Blocs: Alternative Approaches to Analyzing Preferential Trade Agreements*. Cambridge, MA: MIT Press.

Cadot, O., A. Estevadeordal, and A. Suwa-Eisenman (2003) 'Rules of origin as export subsidies', mimeo.

Chang, Won, and Alan Winters (2002) 'How regional trade blocs affect excluded countries: The Price Effects of MERCOSUR', *American Economic Review*, 92, 889–904.

Dam, K. (1970) *The GATT: Law and International Economic Organization*. University of Chicago Press, xvii, 480.

Duttagupta, Rupa, and Arvind Panagariya (2001) 'Free trade areas and rules of origin: economics and politics', mimeo, IMF Staff Papers.

Grossman, G., and E. Helpman (1995) 'The politics of free trade agreements', *American Economic Review*, 85(4): 667–90.

Grinols E. (1984) 'A thorn in the lion's paw: has Britain paid too much for common market membership?', *Journal of International Economics*, 16: 271–94.

Kemp, M., and H. Wan (1976) 'An elementary proposition concerning the formation of customs unions', *Journal of International Economics*, 6: 95–97, North-Holland Publishing Company.

Krishna, K., and A. Krueger (1995) 'Implementing free trade agreements: rules of origin and hidden protection', in Deardorff, Levinsohn and Stern (eds), *New Directions in Trade Theory*, Ann Arbor, MI: University of Michigan Press, 149–187.

Krishna, P. (2003) 'Are regional trading partners natural?', *Journal of Political Economy*, 111(1): 202–31.

Krishna, P. (2004) 'The economics of preferential trade agreements', in Hartigan and Choi (eds), *Handbook of International Trade*, vol. II. Oxford: Blackwell Publishing.

Krishna, P. (2005) *Trade Blocs: Economics and Politics*, Cambridge and New York: Cambridge University Press.

Krugman, P. (1991) 'The move to free trade zones', in Federal Reserve Bank of Kansas City, *Policy Implications of Trade and Currency Zones*. Kansas City: Federal Reserve Bank of Kansas City, 7–41.

Lawrence, Robert (1997) *Regionalism, Multilateralism and Deeper Integration*. Washington, D.C.: Brookings Institution.

McMillan, J. (1993) 'Does regional integration foster open trade? Economic theory and GATT's Article XXIV', in Anderson and Blackhurst eds., *Regional Integration and the Global Trading System*, New York: St. Martin's Press, 292–310.

McMillan, J., and E. McCann (1980) 'Welfare effects in customs unions', *Economic Journal*, 91, 697–703.

Mundell, R. (1964) 'Tariff preferences and the terms of trade', *Manchester School of Economic Studies*, 32: 1–13.

Ohyama, M. (1972) 'Trade and welfare in general equilibrium', *Keio Economic Studies*, 9, 37–73.

Panagariya, Arvind (1996) 'The free trade area of the Americas: good for Latin America?' *World Economy* 19, No. 5, September, 485–515.

Panagariya, A. (1997) 'Preferential trading and the myth of natural trading partners', *Japan and the World Economy*, 9: 471–89.

Panagariya, A. (1999) 'The regionalism debate: an overview', *World Economy*, 22(4): 477–511.

Panagariya, A. (2000) 'Preferential trade liberalisation: the traditional theory and new developments', *Journal of Economic Literature*, 38(2): 287–331.

Panagariya, A., and R. Findlay (1996) 'A political economy analysis of free trade areas and customs unions', in Feenstra, Irwin and Grossman (eds), *The Political Economy of Trade Reform: Essays in Honor of Jagdish Bhagwati*. Cambridge, MA: MIT Press.

Panagariya, A., and P. Krishna (2002) 'On the existence of necessarily welfare improving free trade areas', *Journal of International Economics*, 57(2): 353–67.

Romalis, J. (2007) 'NAFTA's and CUSFTA's Effects on international trade', *The Review of Economics and Statistics*, 89(3): 416–35.

Srinivasan, T.N. (1997) 'Common external tariffs of a customs union: the case of identical Cobb Douglas tastes', *Japan and the World Economy*, 9(4): 447–65.

Summers, L. (1991) 'Regionalism and the world trading system', in *Policy Implications of Trade and Currency Zones*. Kansas City: Federal Reserve Bank of Kansas City.

Vanek, J. (1965) *General Equilibrium of International Discrimination*, Cambridge, MA: Harvard University Press.

Viner, J. (1950) *The Customs Unions Issue*. New York: Carnegie Endowment for International Peace.

Winters, A. (1997) 'Regionalism and the rest of the world: the irrelevance of the Kemp–Wan Theorem', *Oxford Economic Papers*, 49, 228–34.

Wonnacott, P., and M. Lutz (1987) 'Is there a case for free trade areas?', in Jeffrey Schott, (ed.), *Free Trade Areas and US Trade Policy*. Washington, D.C.: Institute for International Economics.

Yi, S. (1996) 'Endogenous formation of customs unions under imperfect competition: open regionalism is good', *Journal of International Economics*, 41(1–2): 153–77.

Yeats, A. (1998) 'Does MERCOSUR's trade performance raise concerns about the effects of regional trade arrangements?' *The World Bank Economic Review*, 12, 1–28.

13
Trade Agreements

Carsten Kowalczyk* and Raymond Riezman†

1 Introduction

The topic of trade agreements is a broad one. We will define trade agreements as agreements concerning nations' treatment of goods, services, or factors of production as these cross borders or have the potential of affecting the economic welfare of foreign nationals. This means, of course, that trade agreements are ubiquitous. Parties to agreements may be national governments or non-government entities such as producers or consumers. Parties may also be international organizations or supra-national political or economic institutions.

Trade agreements may be explicit or implicit. They may be simple or complex. They may be long-term or be associated with an immediate and one-time transaction. Trade agreements may specify prices, quantities, or policies such as tariffs, subsidies, quotas, content, standards, or even detailed conditions on behaviour, such as competition.

Trade agreements may reflect an attempt by national governments to maximise some well-defined objective function. Such a function may be defined exclusively over national income, or it may have as arguments income of one or more special interest groups with the relative weighting of each group's income reflecting political influence through parliamentary processes, contributions or lobbying, or reflecting some social preference for income distribution. Indeed, parties to trade agreements may have any type of preferences that reflect the economic and political reality of each party's domestic conditions, including social norms. As is known from social choice theory, such 'aggregation' may well lead to criterion functions that are not consistent with standard axioms of rational conduct. This would suggest that at times it may be difficult to associate international trade strategies or agreements with any simple national criterion.

A positive theory of trade agreements would seek to develop a framework that would generate the trade agreements that we observe. A normative theory of trade agreements would help identify deals that would raise welfare, however defined, of the participants. Such deals may specify new policies or even institutions, and thus be *de novo*, or they may specify gradual changes in policies or institutions if there are economic, political or technological barriers to change.

We will confine our review in this chapter to a consideration of recent work that assumes that each national government seeks to maximise national income. We do so for two reasons: First, the assumption that national governments seek to maximize income has been, and remains, the standard assumption in trade theory. Secondly, the classical case for the attractiveness of free trade is that it maximises total world income. From the perspective of standard welfare economics, distributional concerns are best addressed with explicitly redistributive policies rather than with trade policies. In other words, free trade with appropriate redistribution policies welfare dominates policies that distort trade. Therefore, as long as higher income is desirable, that is as long as it raises utility, which surely is the case for the vast majority of the world's population, national income would serve as an important metric.[1]

In section 2, we present the welfare calculus for national income in a general equilibrium environment with perfect competition. We present two versions of the national economic welfare calculus: one for analysing changes in economic welfare when underlying changes are small, and one for changes in economic welfare when underlying changes are discrete. These approaches are mutually consistent, and we will refer to both as the *terms-of-trade* and *volume-of-trade* approach. We show in this chapter how each of the two welfare expressions can be used to answer key questions on trade agreements.

In section 3, we apply this welfare calculus to preferential trade agreements. Establishing new, or expanding already existing, preferential trade areas is a very active area of policy making with more than 300 new preferential agreements having been notified to the WTO since the mid-1990s.[2]

In section 4, we apply the welfare calculus to multilateral liberalization. We consider results on how various gradual reforms affect welfare along the resulting paths to global free trade. We also look at how discrete reform could be utilized to reach global free trade. In sections 3 and 4 we also discuss results from computable general equilibrium models on trade agreements. Some of these models have cast light on orders of magnitude of welfare effects; others have informed theoretical developments.

It is a long-standing and recognized challenge for trade agreements that traditionally there has not been an external enforcement mechanism, such as for example a court with the ability to order binding actions or sanctions, to ensure that nations put in practice that to which they have agreed. Thus, parties to agreements must rely on themselves to ensure that agreements are upheld which, in turn, implies that countries might not wish to enter into agreements that it will be difficult to enforce. This suggests that agreements should be self-enforcing. In section 5 we consider some results that emphasize this constraint and, hence, the types of agreements we would expect to observe nations establishing. We conclude, in section 6, that the welfare analyses in sections 3 and 4, and the analysis of self-enforcing agreements in section 5, are complementary. We also identify some questions for further research.

2   National economic welfare

Consider a world of n countries, each indexed by i $(i = 1,\ldots,n)$, where price-taking consumers and producers trade a finite number of goods k with price-taking producers and consumers in other countries. Let p^e be a vector of prices paid to foreign exporters or received by domestic exporters, and let p^i be the corresponding vector of domestic prices in country i. If trade taxes or subsidies are quoted as specific, they are given by the vector t^i, in which case $p^i = p^e + t^i$. If, instead, rates are ad valorem, they are given by the matrix τ^i, with elements τ_k^i, and $p^i = (1 + \tau^i)p^e$. Let u^i be the utility of the representative consumer in country i, and let v^i be an l-dimensional vector of factor endowments in country i. We denote the expenditure function for country i by $e^i(p^i, u^i)$, and the revenue function expressing the maximum value of production in country i by $r^i(p^i, v^i)$.[3] We assume for notational convenience, in the following derivations, that rates are specific. Then, if m^i denotes country i's vector of net imports, and if T^i denotes any net transfer of income to country i from abroad, we can write country i's budget constraint as

$$e^i(p^i, u^i) = r^i(p^i, v^i) + t^i m^i + T^i. \tag{1}$$

If factor supplies are fixed, $r_v^i = 0$, and if there are no net transfers from abroad, $T^i = 0$. Total differentiation yields, $e_p^i dp^i + e_u^i du^i = r_p^i dp^i + dt^i m^i + t^i dm^i$. Define $d\eta^i = e_u^i du^i$ to be the change in country i's welfare as expressed in terms of a *numéraire* good where we define higher welfare to mean $d\eta^i > 0$. Since the price derivative of the expenditure function is compensated demand and the price derivative of the revenue function is supply, $m^i = e_p^i - r_p^i$, and, since, $dp^i = dp^e + dt^i$, we have

$$d\eta^i = -m^i dp^e + (p^i - p^e) dm^i. \tag{2}$$

This expression states the change in real income as the sum of a terms-of-trade effect, $-m^i dp^e$, and a volume-of-trade effect, $(p^i - p^e) dm^i$, each of which evaluates changes with the initial values of trade flows and tariffs, respectively.[4] The terms-of-trade effect reflects that a country benefits from receiving higher world market prices for its exports or from paying lower world market prices for its imports. The volume-of-trade effect captures that a country benefits from purchasing more of a good that has a higher domestic valuation than the price at which the good is acquired in the world market place, the difference reflecting the wedge due to a tariff and being a source for further gains from trade.

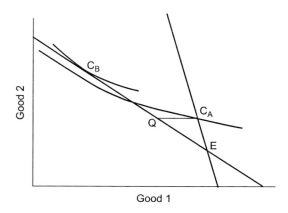

Figure 13.1   Terms-of-trade and volume-of-trade effects.

Consider figure 13.1 for illustration of the workings of the terms-of-trade and volume-of-trade approach. Point E indicates country i's endowment, and point c_A indicates its initial consumption bundle. We assume that country i initially has a tariff in place, implying that the slope of the indifference curve through point c_A, which will equal the domestic price p^i, is less than the slope of the country's budget line through points E and c_A, which equals the world market price p^e. Suppose the country eliminates its tariff. This raises world demand for good 2, its imported good, and, assuming country i is large, this raises the price country i pays to foreign exporters. This is reflected by a new flatter budget line for the country, as illustrated by the line through points E and c_B, where c_B indicates the post-change consumption bundle. As the price that country i pays to foreign exporters for its imports of good 2 has risen, country i experiences a welfare-reducing terms-of-trade worsening as indicated by the horizontal distance between c_A and Q. However, assuming no Metzler tariff paradox,[5] the lower tariff leads to a reduced domestic price of good 2, and to increased consumption, causing a welfare-improving volume-of-trade increase from Q to c_B. While figure 13.1, as drawn, presents a change that is welfare improving since the indifference curve through point c_B offers higher utility than the indifference curve through c_A, the more general point we wish to emphasize is that terms-of-trade and volume-of-trade effects may be of opposite signs, or of the same sign, depending on the characteristics of the economy and the underlying policy change.

There is a corresponding welfare expression if changes are discrete rather than infinitesimal.[6] Again, we will be comparing the effects on economic welfare in countries from changes in trade policies. We denote a pre-change situation by A and a post-change situation by B, and we will evaluate the change in economic welfare for country i by considering the compensating variation for country i as given by

$$\Delta \eta^i = e^i(p_B^i, u_B^i) - e^i(p_B^i, u_A^i). \tag{3}$$

We now define country i's economic welfare as having increased if $u_B^i > u_A^i$, or, equivalently, if $\Delta \eta^i > 0$.

Let y^i be the vector of production in country i, in which case we can write country i's net trade vector as $m^i = c^i - y^i$. Evaluated at domestic prices p^i, balanced trade for country i can be written as the requirement that spending equals all sources of income. For example, in post-change situation B, this budget constraint becomes

$$e^i(p_B^i, u_B^i) = p_B^i y_B^i + (p_B^i - p_B^e)m_B^i + T_B^i, \tag{4}$$

where $p_B^i y_B^i$ is income from domestic production, $(p_B^i - p_B^e)m_B^i$ is redistributed tariff revenue, and T_B^i is any other lump-sum income.[7]

Substituting (4) into (3), and subtracting and adding $p_B^i y_A^i$, and adding and subtracting $p_B^i c_A^i$ yields

$$\Delta \eta^i = p_B^i(y_B^i - y_A^i) + p_B^i y_A^i + (p_B^i - p_B^e)m_B^i + T_B^i + p_B^i c_A^i - e^i(p_B^i, u_A^i) - p_B^i c_A^i. \tag{5}$$

If the representative consumer in country i exhibits substitution as prices change from p_A^i to p_B^i, the initial utility level u_A^i can be obtained at lower total expenditure, than if the consumer continued to purchase the initial bundle c_A^i. We define the consumption gains S_γ^i to be the associated reduction in expenditure, evaluated at post-change prices, as given by

$$S_\gamma^i = p_B^i c_A^i - e^i(p_B^i, u_A^i) \geq 0. \tag{6}$$

Figure 13.2 illustrates the consumption gains. Suppose the initial domestic price faced by the consumers is p_A at which he or she chooses to consume bundle c_A yielding utility u_A. If the domestic price changes to p_B, an expenditure-minimizing consumer could obtain the same level of utility by switching to the bundle c_A^* as implied by the expenditure function $e^i(p_B^i, u_A^i)$. Evaluated in terms of good 1, and at the post-change price p_B, the horizontal distance between the projections of points c_A and c_A^*, then yields the consumption gains.

Suppose instead the economy is not one of fixed endowments, but one where profit maximizing producers are able to adjust their production in response to new prices. They will choose to do so if the value of the post-change plans exceeds the value of the pre-change plans when both plans are evaluated at the new prices. We define the production gains S_π^i to be the associated increase in the value of national production as given by

$$S_\pi^i = p_B^i(y_B^i - y_A^i) \geq 0. \tag{7}$$

Figure 13.3 illustrates the production gains. The country is assumed to have a bowed-out production possibilities frontier. If p_A denotes the initial domestic

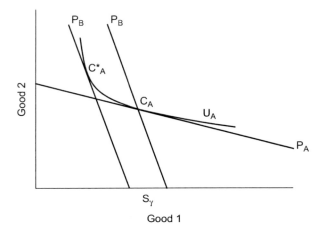

Figure 13.2   Consumption gains.

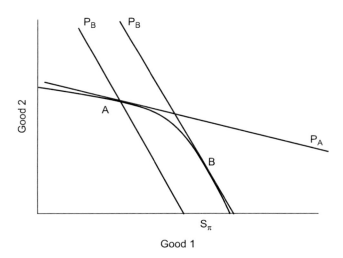

Figure 13.3   Production gains.

price faced by the country's producers, they will choose to produce the bundle corresponding to point A. If the domestic producer price changes to p_B, they will choose, instead, to produce the bundle indicated by point B of value $p_B y_B$. Had producers not changed production, but rather stuck with their initial output at point A, the value, at post-change prices would be $p_B y_A$. Evaluated at the post-change price p_B, the horizontal distance between the projections of production points A and B, thus yields the increase in national income due to production gains as measured in units of good 1.

It is convenient to define an efficiency effect S^i as the sum of the consumption and production gains

$$S^i = S^i_\gamma + S^i_\pi \geq 0. \tag{8}$$

Substitution into (5), and using that $-p^i_B(c^i_A - y^i_A) = -p^i_B m^i_A$, (5) simplifies to,

$$\Delta \eta^i = S^i + (p^i_B - p^e_B)m^i_B + T^i_B - p^i_B m^i_A. \tag{9}$$

Subtracting and adding $(p^i_B - p^e_B)m^i_A$, and subtracting T^i_A and adding $p^e_A m^i_A$, the steps in footnote 8 below[8] lead to an expression in the last line of the footnote that, when using that $\Delta m^i = m^i_B - m^i_A$, and $\Delta p^e = p^e_B - p^e_A$, becomes the following discrete change expression for welfare change

$$\Delta \eta^i = -m^i_A \Delta p^e + (p^i_B - p^e_B)\Delta m^i + S^i. \tag{10}$$

This states that the change in national welfare is given by the sum of a terms-of-trade effect, $-m^i_A \Delta p^e$; a tariff-revenue effect, $(p^i_B - p^e_B)\Delta m^i$; and a non-negative efficiency effect, S^i.

We refer to analyses drawing on either expression (2) or (10) as the terms-of-trade and volume-of-trade approach. In the general equilibrium theory of trade agreements, the small change expression (2) has proved useful for generating optimal tariff results, and for yielding the sign of change in welfare from inquiries into what are desirable directions of gradual policy reform. The discrete change expression (10) offers exact welfare estimates of policy changes and has been used to compare different liberalisation strategies, including customs unions and free trade. We assume that country i, if presented with different options, will seek the option that maximises its gains to welfare as given by (10) or, for questions of reform, will seek the reform that offers increased welfare as given by (2).

3   Preferential trade agreements

While GATT/WTO emphasises non-discrimination between its members, GATT Article XXIV allows WTO members to form free trade areas, which eliminate the barriers on mutual trade between the free trade area members while leaving each member's tariffs on its trade with non-members to that member country to decide, or customs unions, which eliminate the barriers to mutual trade on the union members while setting common external tariffs on trade with non-members.[9]

Traditional analysis of preferential arrangements has been cast in terms of the trade diversion and trade creation approach pioneered by Jacob Viner (1950). Kowalczyk (1990, 2000) emphasizes how Viner, by showing that a customs union has the potential to reduce, rather than raise, welfare in a world where free trade is first-best, provided a first demonstration of what was later to be recognized as the principle of the second-best, that a partial move towards Pareto optimality may or may not raise welfare everywhere along the path of reform. Kowalczyk also shows how the formation of trade agreements may imply effects in addition to Viner's trade diversion and trade creation effects even in a simple perfectly competitive world economy. For example, some countries forming a customs union may change world market prices on some of their trade with non-members. This would be neither trade diversion nor trade creation, and accounting for this would require that additional terms be introduced, both in theoretical and in empirical work. He concludes by proposing that the terms-of-trade and volume-of-trade approach from the theory of tariffs constitutes a potentially useful alternative since it is exhaustive, both in theoretical and in empirical work, and allows the researcher to focus on tariffs, trade flows, and prices, and their possible changes. Moreover, these are all variables that, in principle, can be observed or estimated. We follow this recommendation in this chapter as we present analyses and results in the language of the terms-of-trade and volume-of-trade effects.

3.1   Small country welfare

Consider first the question of a small country's trade policy strategy. Many of the world's free trade agreements or customs unions have one or more small countries as parties. Yet, conventional trade theory had that a small country's best trade policy is unilateral free trade. Paul Wonnacott and Ronald Wonnacott (1981) showed that a small country, in a world where preferential trade agreements are possible, would prefer a free trade agreement with a large country to unilateral free trade, since the large country's preferential tariff reduction benefits the small country. They also argued that the large country would lose from the arrangement.

Kowalczyk (2000) formalizes the analysis and shows that the extra benefit for the small country is due to a terms-of-trade improvement from the large country's tariff reduction. He shows also that a small country, under certain conditions, may prefer membership of many free trade agreements with various large countries, and that equi-proportionate gradual tariff reductions between the small country and its large partners would offer higher welfare at every step until internal free trade has been established. He shows, finally, that while indeed the large country would lose from the free trade agreement's implied terms-of-trade worsening on its trade with the small partner, the total net gains to the small and large partners are positive as the small country experiences a positive volume-of-trade effect due to its own tariff reduction. Since the between-member terms-of-trade effects cancel, this implies that there would exist a side payment from the small country to the large country equal to or larger than the large country's terms-of-trade loss that could make both countries gain from the free trade agreement.

3.2 Large country welfare, and the emergence of hubs and spokes

With this incentive for small countries to seek preferential agreements, and if appropriate side payments are applied, it is possible that a large country would be willing to sign free trade agreements with many small countries.[10] Kowalczyk and Wonnacott (1992) show how this could lead to a world trading system of overlapping hubs-and-spokes structures: a layer of agreements as each small country seeks an agreement with many large partner countries – and thus each small country becoming a hub – and a layer as each large country would become a hub with many small country spokes. They propose that each large hub country may prefer a large rather than a small number of small country spokes since liberalizing with a collection of small spokes could be like liberalizing with a larger country and hence imply a smaller terms-of-trade loss for the large hub country. They emphasize that the mode of integration may matter: if agreements are signed sequentially, an early small country spoke might seek to prevent the addition of new spokes since their entry may lead to worse terms of trade for the early spoke by the implied preference erosion. This could lead to a potential hold-up situation on further expansion due to a necessity to agree to a common external tariff in a customs union. To avoid this problem, even the large country might prefer free trade areas to customs unions as a vehicle for liberalisation.

In an exploration of the role of country size, Michael Michaely (1998) proposes that size be measured by the small country's potential exports as a share in the large country's total demand. Given this definition, he shows that the large country's welfare loss is bell-shaped as a function of the small country's size. A free trade agreement with a micro-state has virtually no effect on the large country's welfare, nor would a free trade agreement with a 'large' small country where the terms-of-trade loss for the large country would be only small. The largest loss would be from integrating with an intermediate size small country that is so large that it has the potential to be the sole exporter to the large country. Kowalczyk (2008), by use of equation (10) in this chapter, derives the upper limit on the welfare loss for the large country to be two times the tariff revenue it earns on its initial trade with the small country. If the small country is smaller than that critical size, both the large country's terms-of-trade loss on its initial trade with the small partner, and its loss of tariff revenue on imports from the non-member country, will be smaller since the trade flow from the smaller partner is less than the critical size. If the small country is larger than the critical size, the loss of tariff revenue would be the same for the large partner country, but its terms-of-trade loss would be smaller due to an assumption that a larger small country partner has a lower cost of production.

3.3   Comparing small country welfare from three different strategies

The WTO provides not only for free trade areas and customs unions, but also for higher income countries to extend preferential access without requesting developing country liberalisation in return. A question then becomes which of several different strategies would yield the higher developing country welfare? Would a free-trade agreement with the large partner? Or would one-sided preferential access by the large partner be better for the developing country? And how would unilateral liberalization by the developing country compare to each of these options? Assuming that the developing country is a small country, Kowalczyk (2006) shows that a free-trade agreement with a large country would yield the highest welfare for the small country, while the welfare ranking for the small country of one-sided preferential access to the large country market versus its own unilateral liberalization is ambiguous. From expressions (2) or (10) in this chapter, the ranking of the latter options would depend on whether the implied terms-of-trade gains without domestic liberalisation would offer a larger welfare improvement than the welfare-improving volume-of-trade increase from eliminating its own barriers. The size of the terms-of-trade effect depends on the size of the initial trade volume and the size of the large country's tariff. The size of the developing country's volume-of-trade effect is, in turn, a function of the size of its own initial tariff and its own trade elasticities.

Kowalczyk (2006) also shows that, if the small country has obtained preferential access to the large country market, the large country would lose even more if the small country subsequently were to liberalise unilaterally. This is because such liberalisation would expand the small country's trade with the large country. But, from equation (10), this increased trade would imply an even larger loss of tariff revenue on the large country's imports from its non-preferential partners. Thus a large country might not wish to see a small country with preferential access liberalise with others or even unilaterally. This result provides a new, an additional, reason for the concern that a process of preferential liberalisation may get stuck in some situation short of free trade. The existing concern, discussed above, is that a small partner would object to further large partner liberalisation with others due to a 'loss of preference.' If also a large country loses from a small partner country's liberalisation, then it could become difficult, if not contentious, to move away from a given preferential situation, since each nation might perceive the other's liberalization as detrimental to its own welfare.[11]

3.4   The effects on non-member countries

When some countries integrate in free trade areas or customs unions, what are the effects on non-member countries? In an attempt by the framers of GATT to restrict member nations' ability to use free trade areas or customs unions to extract better terms of trade from non-members, Article XXIV includes a stipulation that the average external tariff of members, upon integration, may not increase. However, this restriction is not sufficient to ensure that there are no spillovers onto non-members.

Jaroslev Vanek (1965) introduced the notion of the compensating common external tariff of a customs union as the rate that would leave the economic welfare of non-members unaffected. Michihiro Ohyama (1972) and Murray Kemp and Henry Wan (1976) demonstrated that not only do such tariffs, and hence customs unions, exist in a standard competitive world economy but so do within-union side payments such that no member country would be worse off from joining or expanding such a union. An important corollary is that global free trade could be reached through a gradual process of expanding Ohyama–Kemp–Wan customs unions without any country in the world ever losing.[12] Earl Grinols (1981) shows that a feasible intra-union compensation mechanism is to give each union member its pre-union trade vector, and that the sum of these transfers equals the union's tariff revenue. Kowalczyk and Sjöström (2000) show that Grinols's proposed transfers are equivalent to each country paying or receiving a transfer equal to its terms-of-trade gains or losses. When substituted into equation (10), together with the restrictions on the external tariffs such that there are no changes in trade volumes, this would imply that each country's welfare changes only by its non-negative efficiency effect. Hence the welfare-improvement from the Ohyama–Kemp–Wan customs union.

More generally, when external tariffs are not set at the compensating level, a free-trade agreement or a customs union may, if rates are set below, lead to more trade with non-members, or, if rates are set above, to less trade with non-members. Kowalczyk and Wonnacott (1991, 1992) refer to the former case as a *complement* trade agreement, to the latter as a *substitute* trade agreement, and to the case of no spillovers as a *neutral* trade agreement.[13] The case of substitute agreements is, of course, associated with the long-standing and important concern that trade agreements would tend to discriminate against exports from non-member countries. There may be complementarities, however, between goods produced or consumed within a preferential trading area and goods provided by non-member countries. For example, increased production within a customs union or a free-trade area could lead to increased import demand from non-members for inputs or for other goods or services that are complementary in production. And if a trade agreement is beneficial to its member countries, their real income would increase and, under reasonable assumptions on income propensities to import, so would desired imports from non-member countries, again leading to positive spillovers.

Ayhan Kose and Riezman (2000) show that while customs unions generally are more beneficial for the member countries than are free-trade areas, for non-members the reverse is true. The reason is that the members of a customs union set tariff policy jointly, that is, they coordinate, and hence internalize the benefits of own country tariffs for the other member countries who import the same goods as they do. In a free-trade area, external tariffs are set independently and members do not take full advantage of their potential to affect the terms-of-trade relative to non-members in their favor. Using numerical simulation methodology, Kose and Riezman (2002) show that a small country excluded from a customs union by large countries can experience large losses, whereas if the same large countries form a free-trade area the potential losses for the small country are much smaller.

Focusing on free-trade areas, Eric Bond, Riezman and Constantinos Syropoulos (2004) look at how the formation of a free-trade agreement between countries that set tariffs that are individually welfare-maximising affects equilibrium tariffs and the welfare of members and non-members when the latter also set their optimal tariffs. They also lend support to the notion of the complement trading bloc as they show that, at constant non-member tariffs, the liberalization of internal trade by symmetric members induces them to reduce their individually optimal external tariff below the compensating level, thereby causing the outside country's terms of trade to improve and its welfare to rise. If the non-member country behaves strategically, the formation of the free trade area leads the non-member country to behave more aggressively in its tariff policy. As a consequence, the non-member country benefits from integration even more. They show that, in this case, the member countries benefit only if the free-trade area is sufficiently large.

4   Multilateral trade agreements

In the world of policy making much economic reform is gradual. The over 50-year-old process of multilateral liberalization in GATT, and now in the WTO, seems to proceed at an almost glacial pace, and at times to be at an outright standstill. And when agreements are struck, whether multilateral or preferential, they usually specify many years for phasing out internal tariffs.

4.1   Trade policy reform – gradualism

Taking as a constraint that trade agreements should specify gradual changes in tariffs, scholars turned to investigating which formulae for tariff reductions nations could reasonably agree to in a multilateral negotiation. One type of agreement would specify that at each stage of reform the largest tariff be cut to the next highest level, and that this process be repeated until global free trade has been reached. Assuming the existence of only tariffs and the potential for international side payments, Tatsuo Hatta and Takashi Fukushima (1979) investigate the world welfare effects from this proposal for so-called *concertina* tariff reductions, by applying equation (2) of this chapter across all the world's countries and then to investigate whether the volume-of-trade effects implied by the proposed reform reveal whether goods are redirected towards where their domestic valuation is higher. They show that the *concertina* approach of reducing the highest tariff to the next highest rate, and so on, does raise world welfare at every stage. They consider also a proposal for all countries to cut their tariffs simultaneously by the same percentage at every stage. They are able to show that this so-called *radial* approach also raises world economic welfare at every stage of reform if all goods are substitutes.[14]

What if the initial situation has not only trade taxes but also trade subsidies, as is, for example, the case in agriculture? Kowalczyk (1989) shows that if rates are *ad valorem* then it is possible that a *radial* reduction of tariffs and subsidies may lower world welfare along a segment of the reform path. If, on the other hand, all rates are specific, then Fukushima and Namdoo Kim (1989) are able to show that such a welfare paradox is not possible: a *radial* reduction of all tariffs and subsidies will raise world welfare at every stage of reform. Kowalczyk (2002) shows how the *ad valorem* reform may expand the wedges between countries' domestic prices before reducing them, while the specific reform reduces the price wedges everywhere. He also shows that welfare is monotonic in price wedges. Hence, the difference between the welfare outcomes from these otherwise similar reforms of *ad valorem* and specific rates lies in their different implications for price wedges.

4.2 Is free trade in the core?

It is not only for theoretical convenience, but also for practical reasons that the world welfare or the potential Pareto criterion is important in the analysis of trade agreements: the long-standing criterion for agreement in multilateral negotiations is that any nation or group of nations can block a proposal and, hence, prevent an agreement. Put in the language of game theory, a proposal for a multilateral agreement must be in the core of the world trade game for that proposal to be implemented.[15]

4.2.1 The core without side payments

Assuming that countries cannot engage in international side payments, Riezman (1985), in a first application of the core to a multi-country trade policy game, shows that some countries might prefer to establish free trade agreements or customs unions rather than to agree to global free trade if countries cannot engage in international side payments. Later, Riezman (1999) uses the same model to argue that trade agreements might help or hinder the attainment of free trade, depending on the size distribution of countries. In the case of similar sized countries, he shows that if customs unions are not permitted, then free trade is in the core, but if countries can form customs unions then free trade is not in the core. If, instead, the size distribution is one large and two smaller countries then, if customs unions are not allowed, free trade is not in the core – the large country blocks free trade by charging an optimal tariff. If, however, customs unions are allowed, the large country cannot block free trade, and free trade is in the core. The intuition for this result is that if the two smaller countries can form a customs union then the large country cannot win a tariff war (because the two other countries will form a customs union) and, hence, cannot block free trade.

4.2.2   The core with side payments

Introducing international side payments into negotiations of multilateral agreements, Kowalczyk and Sjöström (1994) show that the core with such side payments is non-empty in a world where every country has a world-wide monopoly producer and nations can enter into trading blocs or strike a world-wide agreement on markup prices. They show that the Shapley Value, in particular, specifies a vector of payoffs, that is, of national incomes, that lies in the core of this trade policy game.[16] Assuming that the Shapley Value offers an agreeable standard for distributing the gains from cooperation, they then derive a formula for international side payments that, when put forward with a proposal to eliminate all distortions, would indeed be in the core of this world monopoly trade policy game.

In the standard competitive model, Konishi, Kowalczyk and Sjöström (2009) show that a proposal for immediate global free trade with a financial mechanism that compensates countries for any associated terms-of-trade losses with transfers from countries equal to their terms-of-trade improvements, is in the core of a world trade policy game where nations also can choose instead to remain at the initial, arbitrary, status quo or to form Ohyama–Kemp–Wan customs unions. In other words, since free trade with transfers cannot be blocked, Ohyama–Kemp–Wan customs unions (as well as the status quo) serve as an off-the-equilibrium option that no group of countries would choose. However, Konishi, Kowalczyk and Sjöström (2003) show that it is not possible to block any proposed Ohyama–Kemp–Wan customs union with a free-trade-with-transfers proposal. In other words, it matters for blocking what is put on the table. This has the important implication that it may be easier to reach free trade by proposing it outright than by seeking to approach it in a more gradual fashion such as via customs unions or free-trade agreements, or through multilateral agreements to cut all tariffs but by less than their full amount.

How large would the international side payments be in order to attain free trade? Thomas Hertel (2000) finds, from calculations derived from the GTAP model, that those regions of the world that would experience particularly large efficiency gains (more than 2 percent of GDP) also would tend to experience worse terms of trade, and he reports that such terms of trade losses may be large for some major emerging market economies – up to 60 percent of the efficiency gains as expressed by the S^i term in equation (10). Kowalczyk and Riezman (2009) present estimates of terms-of-trade effects from moving from a non-cooperative tariff equilibrium to global free trade in a CGE-model. For countries whose real income falls from free trade, the terms-of-trade losses are so large that they exceed any positive contribution from the efficiency effects. For countries whose terms-of-trade improve, such improvements may constitute more than half of the countries' total gains from free trade. They also find, in their examples, that terms-of-trade effects from free trade can be up to 9 percent of a nation's GDP, suggesting that the potential side payments that would lead to adoption of free trade could be large.

5   On self-enforcement in trade agreements

As we stated at the outset of this chapter, the purpose of our focus on the analytics of economic welfare is to provide a tool that can identify opportunities for trade agreements that have the potential to raise national income. The terms-of-trade and volume-of-trade approache allows for assessment of the welfare consequences from all types of reform, whether multilateral or preferential, gradual or discrete, and for all nations, whether they participate or are on the sidelines. From this type of analysis it is possible to characterize an opportunity set for possibly mutually beneficial agreements in the space of nations' tariffs. A natural question is then to ask which of these many possible tariff outcomes will actually emerge as an equilibrium? Which agreements will be struck?

The work and results reported in the previous sections of this chapter draw on the standard, static, competitive general equilibrium model. For any trade agreement, the usual strategy in that line of research has been to assume that national welfare maximizing governments set non-cooperative Nash tariffs on nations that are not parties to the agreement, and set tariffs on trade with partners according to some formula, whether it be zero, as required by Article XXIV for free trade areas and customs unions, or it be some percentage reduction of initial rates as in the work of gradual multilateral reform.

Each of these approaches to the determination of the non-cooperative and cooperative tariffs is subject to difficulties. Already, early contributors such as Harry Johnson (1953–54) and William Gorman (1958) showed that it is difficult to solve analytically for the welfare-maximizing non-cooperative tariff in theoretical work. Later, work by Bond (1990), who derives the unilateral optimal tariff vector with many goods, by Syropoulos (2002), who explores the determinants of trade elasticities in a two-country, non-cooperative tariff equilibrium, and by Bond and Syropoulos (1996), who consider the optimal tariff of a trading bloc as a function of its relative size, confirms that the challenges associated with such computations in theoretical work are considerable.

John Kennan and Riezman (1988, 1990) recognized these difficulties. They chose, instead, to develop a simple computable general equilibrium model with extensive separability in both supply and demand to find optimal tariffs and obtain equilibrium in early explorations of how preferential trade arrangements affect the possibility of attaining free trade. Later-generation computable general equilibrium models, such as the large-scale GTAP model, do not even seek to solve for optimal tariffs but, instead, derive numerical estimates of the welfare effects from specified, formulaic changes in tariffs.[17]

It is also a challenge to model, and hence to predict, the cooperative tariffs, that is, the rates nations would establish in trade agreements. Tibor Scitovsky (1942), Johnson (op cit.), Wolfgang Mayer (1981), and Avinash Dixit (1987) showed the difficulties of generating free trade or, more generally, a policy equilibrium on the contract curve, in standard static environments where nations use their non-cooperative optimal tariffs if no agreements are struck.

And formulaic approaches to the cooperative rates have shortcomings, too. For example, research on free trade areas and customs unions has usually assumed that partners to such agreements adhere to the letter of Article XXIV and agree to zero tariffs on internal trade. However, this may not be optimal: thus, John McMillan and Ewen McCann (1981) showed, in a three-good model, how two customs union partners, even if small, might jointly prefer an intra-union tariff (or subsidy) to internal free trade to obtain volume-of-trade gains through increased imports from the non-partner country.

Assuming that trading nations are in a repeated game and that a country can obtain short-term gains by deviating from an agreed tariff but at the expense of long-term losses as its trading partner retaliates in subsequent periods, Kyle Bagwell and Robert Staiger (2002) present findings on tariffs to which nations can credibly agree under conditions of discounting and assuming that countries are sufficiently similar that retaliation will eliminate any terms-of-trade gains from the initial deviation.[18] The framework can also generate paths of gradual tariff changes. For example, Bagwell and Staiger (1997a) show that if countries agree to form a free trade area in the future, which they assume is a *substitute* agreement once it is fully implemented, the 'most cooperative', most-favored-nation tariffs will temporarily increase as soon as the intention of establishing the free-trade agreement has been announced, but they will then begin to fall back to, and will ultimately reach, their initial value. If, on the other hand, the partner countries agree to form a customs union then, Bagwell and Staiger (1997b) show, the 'most cooperative', most-favored nation tariff path will be U-shaped instead: the tariffs fall on the announcement, but will then begin to rise as the customs union partners choose to renege on their most-favored-nation tariffs as they achieve increased market power once their tariffs have been fully harmonized in the customs union. Benjamin Zissimos (2007) shows that if the deviation from the initial agreed tariff is small, and if the punishment is limited, then trade liberalisation must be gradual, and free trade will never be reached, since, in the absence of severe punishment, only the promise of further liberalisation will prevent deviation in the present. But at free trade this promise cannot be made.

Another approach to generating the gradual phasing out of tariffs has been to introduce assumptions on production. For example, Michael Devereux (1997) considers learning-by-doing by export firms, Taiji Furusawa and Edwin Lai (1999) assume adjustment costs for labor when moving between sectors, and Bond and Jee-Hyeong Park (2002) and Richard Chisik (2003) consider the role of irreversible investment as proposed by John McLaren (1997).

6 Conclusions and further research

The area of trade agreements is obviously very large and one of much current research. We have focused, in this review, on research on the welfare economics of trade agreements and on research on self-enforcing trade agreements. Results from the former literature identify opportunities for cooperation and new combinations of policies that may yield outcomes that are welfare-superior to existing policies or institutions. The results on side payments are the most obvious example. This line of research usually assumes a many-good, many-agent general equilibrium setting, which may make it difficult to offer strong predictions on which equilibrium may emerge. The work on self-enforcing agreements, on the other hand, has offered results that help identify which policies and, hence, agreements might reasonably be observed. These results are often derived assuming two or three goods or countries, or by assuming explicit functional forms.

The two literatures are obviously complementary. Indeed, as is known from the theory of mechanism design, it is useful to apply cooperative approaches to identify outcomes that are 'desirable' according to some specified criterion and then to use non-cooperative approaches to explore whether it is possible to implement, at least approximately, these 'desirable' outcomes. Free trade is a 'desirable' outcome in the work on trade agreements for fundamental welfare economic reasons. We have reported how international side payments may be helpful to achieve this outcome. It is an interesting question how a financial mechanism would look if it had to be self-enforcing.

We have also reported on results on formulaic approaches to welfare-improving liberalization. It would be interesting to explore whether these formulae, in particular the ones specifying equi-proportionate and *concertina* approaches to rate reductions, can be generated as equilibrium paths in negotiations between optimizing governments.

It has been established in the literature that free trade can be attained if customs unions do not exert spillovers onto non-member countries. Could a proposal to revise Article XXIV to require that customs unions do not result in spillovers to non-member countries be agreed by the members of the WTO?

The work reported in this chapter also has implications for CGE modeling of trade policy. As our understanding of policy setting improves, it would be useful if such models incorporated elements of endogenous policy setting and reaction. The technical difficulties to do so may still be prohibitive but the return would be a 'realistic' model for world trade where policies adjust to underlying shocks. An important input into that project would be the work on political economy of trade policy, another area of active research that space limitations have prevented us from discussing here.

Finally, the terms-of-trade and volume-of-trade approach presented here can be implemented in empirical research on trade agreements by casting any ex ante analysis of proposed agreements, or any ex post analysis of realized agreements, in terms of standard economic variables that, in principle, can be estimated: the levels and changes in trade volumes, world market prices, and tariff rates.[19]

Notes

This chapter is part of the Globalization Project at the University of Aarhus. We are grateful for comments from the editors and from an anonymous referee. We also thank participants at the 2009 Fall Midwest Trade Meetings, and at seminars at Catholic University of Portugal, Lisbon, Copenhagen Business School, and University of Rochester, for comments.

* The Fletcher School, Tufts University, and School of Economics and Management, University of Aarhus.

† Department of Economics, University of Iowa.

1. For an example of work that assumes that policies are affected by lobbies, see Gene Grossman and Elhanan Helpman (1995).

2. See http://www.wto.org. We define the types of agreements provided by GATT, in particular, customs unions, free trade areas, and preferential agreements, in section 3 of this chapter.

3. We assume the expenditure function is non-decreasing, homogenous of degree one, concave and continuous in p^i, and increasing in u^i, and that the revenue function is non-decreasing and convex in p^i, and increasing in v^i. See Avinash Dixit and Victor Norman (1980) or Alan Woodland (2010) for further detail.

4. See Ronald Jones (1969) for derivation and discussion of this expression.

5. A Metzler tariff paradox would occur if a lower tariff raises the world market price by so much that the domestic price goes up in spite of the lower tariff.

6. This was originally shown by Michihiro Ohyama (1972). Our derivation in this chapter follows Earl Grinols and Kar-yiu Wong (1991).

7. Obviously, a similar expression holds for state A.

8. Subtracting and adding $(p^i_B - p^e_B)m^i_A$, and subtracting T^i_A and adding $p^e_A m^i_A$, (9) can be rewritten as $\Delta\eta^i = S^i + (p^i_B - p^e_B)(m^i_B - m^i_A) + (p^i_B - p^e_B)m^i_A + (T^i_B - T^i_A) - p^i_B m^i_A + p^e_A m^i_A = S^i + (p^i_B - p^e_B)(m^i_B - m^i_A) + t^i_B m^i_A + (T^i_B - T^i_A) - (t^i_B + p^e_B)m^i_A + p^e_A m^i_A = S^i + (p^i_B - p^e_B)(m^i_B - m^i_A) + (T^i_B - T^i_A) - (p^e_B - p^e_A)m^i_A.$

9. Additional requirements are that internal barriers must be eliminated on 'substantially all trade' and that the average rate of protection on trade with non-members must not increase. Unilateral, discriminatory liberalization is also provided for, if at least one of the parties is a developing country.

10. In more general environments, large countries might enter into free trade agreements with small countries in return for cooperation in other areas than trade such as, for example, taxation, antitrust, migration, health, the environment, labour standards, product standards, or in non-economic areas.

11. It does not follow, of course, that further liberalisation by either the large or the small country would not happen, or that it might not be possible for either country's external tariff reduction to be a potential Pareto improvement for both partner countries.

12. Pravin Krishna and Arvind Panagariya (2002) have derived a similar result for free-trade areas.

13. In an investigation of liberalization in Latin America in the 1990s, Antoni Estevadeordal, Caroline Freund, and Emanuel Ornelas (2008) find that preferential liberalization has to lower external tariffs for free trade areas but not for customs unions.

14. Ramón López and Arvind Panagariya (1992) consider reform when complementarities exist in production.

15. The core is the set of allocations that is blocked by no admissible coalition.

16. The Shapley Value, proposed by Lloyd Shapley (1953), is one of several alternative ways to distribute the gains from cooperation. It assigns to each player a payoff that reflects a weighted average of that player's marginal contributions to all possible coalitions where the weights reflect the probability of the various coalitions forming. See, for example, Dixit, David Reiley, Jr., and Susan Skeath (2004).

17. See, for example, Hertel (op. cit).

18. This notion of reciprocity, one that leaves the terms of trade constant, is obviously restrictive but is analytically tractable. It does not include, for example, the type of reciprocity between large and small countries discussed in Kowalczyk (2000) and in Kowalczyk and Donald Davis (1998). Robert Lawrence (1996) and J. Michael Finger (2005) offer further examples of broader notions of reciprocity. Daniel Kovenock and Marie Thursby (1992) propose that an additional cost to a country from deviation is that it loses credibility and hence reduced ability to enter into future agreements.

19. There has been considerable work on trade volumes. For example, Jeffrey Frankel (1997) offers an extensive discussion and results, with an emphasis on gravity equation approaches. For welfare analysis, estimates of terms-of-trade effects would be required in addition. Earl Grinols (1984) offers an example with his estimates of the effect on Britain's terms-of-trade from joining the European Common Market.

References

Bagwell, Kyle, and Robert Staiger (1997a) 'Multilateral tariff cooperation during the formation of free trade areas', *International Economic Review* 38, 291–319.

—— (1997b) 'Multilateral tariff cooperation during the formation of customs unions', *Journal of International Economics* 42, 91–123.

—— (2002) *The Economics of the World Trading System*. Cambridge, MA: MIT Press.

Bond, Eric (1990) 'The optimal tariff structure in higher dimensions', *International Economic Review* 31, 103–16.

Bond, Eric, and Jee-Hyeong Park (2002) 'Gradualism in trade agreements with asymmetric countries', *Review of Economic Studies* 69, 379–406.

Bond, Eric, and Constantinos Syropoulos (1996) 'The size of trading blocs: market power and world welfare effects', *Journal of International Economics* 40, 411–38.

Bond, Eric, Raymond Riezman and Constantinos Syropoulos (2004) 'A strategic and welfare theoretic theory of free trade areas', *Journal of International Economics* 64, 1–27.

Chisik, Richard (2003) 'Gradualism in free trade agreements: a theoretical justification', *Journal of International Economics* 59, 367–97.

Devereux, Michael (1997) 'Growth, specialization, and trade liberalization', *International Economic Review* 38, 565–85.

Dixit, Avinash (1987) 'Strategic aspects of trade policy', in Truman Bewley (ed.), *Advances in Economic Theory: Fifth World Congress*. New York: Cambridge University Press.

Dixit, Avinash, and Victor Norman (1980) *Theory of International Trade*. Cambridge: Cambridge University Press.

Dixit, Avinash, David H. Reiley, Jr. and Susan Skeath (2004) *Games of Strategy*, 3rd Edition. New York: W.W. Norton.

Estevadeordal, Antoni, Caroline Freund and Emanuel Ornelas (2008) 'Does regionalism affect trade liberalization toward nonmembers?' *Quarterly Journal of Economics* 124, 1531–75.

Finger, J. Michael (2005) 'A diplomat's economics: reciprocity in the Uruguay Round negotiations', *World Trade Review* 4, 27–40.

Frankel, Jeffrey (1997) *Regional Trading Blocs in the World Economic System*. Washington, D.C.: Institute for International Economics.

Fukushima, Takashi, and Namdoo Kim (1989) 'Welfare improving tariff changes', *Journal of International Economics* 26, 383–88.

Furusawa, Taiji, and Edwin Lai (1997) 'Adjustment costs and gradual trade liberalization', *Journal of International Economics* 49, 333–61.

Gorman, William M. (1958) 'Tariffs, retaliation, and the elasticity of demand for imports', *Review of Economic Studies* 25, 133–62.

Grinols, Earl L. (1981) 'An extension of the Kemp–Wan Theorem on the formation of customs unions', *Journal of International Economics* 6, 95–97.

—— (1984) 'The thorn in the lion's paw: has Britain paid too much for common Market membership?' *Journal of International Economics* 16, 271–93.

Grinols, Earl L., and Kar-yiu Wong (1991) 'An exact measure of welfare change', *Canadian Journal of Economics* 24, 61–64.

Grossman, Gene, and Elhanan Helpman (1995) 'The politics of free trade agreements', *American Economic Review* 85, 667–90.

Hatta, Tatsuo, and Takashi Fukushima (1979) 'The welfare effect of tariff rate reductions in a many country world', *Journal of International Economics* 9, 503–11.

Hertel, Thomas W. (2000) 'Potential gains from reducing trade barriers in manufacturing, services and agriculture', *Federal Reserve Bank of St. Louis Review* No. 4, 77–99.

Johnson, Harry G. (1953-54) 'Optimum tariffs and retaliation', *Review of Economic Studies* XXI, 142–53.

Jones, Ronald W. (1969) 'Tariffs and trade in general equilibrium: comment', *American Economic Review* 59, 418–24.

Kemp, Murray C., and Henry Y. Wan (1976) 'An elementary proposition concerning the formation of customs union', *Journal of International Economics* 6, 95–97.

Kennan, John, and Raymond Riezman (1988) 'Do big countries win tariff wars?' *International Economic Review* 29, 81–85.

—— (1990) 'Optimal tariff equilibria with customs unions', *Canadian Journal of Economics* 23, 70–83.

Konishi, Hideo, Carsten Kowalczyk and Tomas Sjöström (2003) 'Free trade, customs unions, and transfers', Social Science Research Network, July; http://ssrn.com/abstract=428346.

—— (2009) 'Global free trade is in the core of a customs union formation game', *Review of International Economics* 17, 304–09.

Kose, Ayhan, and Raymond Riezman (2000) 'Understanding the welfare implications of preferential trade agreements', *Review of International Economics* 8, 619–33.

—— (2002) 'Small countries and regional trade agreements: the innocent bystander problem', *The Pacific Economic Review* 7, 279–304.

Kovenock, Daniel, and Marie Thursby (1992) 'GATT, dispute settlement, and cooperation', *Economics and Politics* 4, 151–70.

Kowalczyk, Carsten (1989) 'Trade negotiations and world welfare', *American Economic Review* 79, 552–59.

Kowalczyk, Carsten (1990) 'Welfare and customs unions', NBER Working Paper No. 3476.

—— (2000) 'Welfare and integration', *International Economic Review* 41, 483–94. Reprinted in Rodney E. Falvey and Udo Kreickemeier (eds), *Recent Developments in International Trade Theory*. International Library of Critical Writings in Economics. Cheltenham, UK: Edward Elgar Publishing Ltd., 2005.

—— (2002) 'Reforming tariffs and subsidies in international trade', *Pacific Economic Review* 7, 305–18.

—— (2006) 'Liberalizing trade between large and small: the welfare from three different strategies', *The Asia-Pacific Journal of Accounting and Economics* 13, 2, 173–81.

—— (2008) 'Free trade between large and small: what's in it for the large country? what's in it for the small?', in Sugata Marjit and Eden Yu (eds), *Contemporary and Emerging Issues in Trade Theory and Policy. Frontiers of Economics and Globalization*, vol. 4. Bingley, UK: Emerald Group Publishing Ltd.

Kowalczyk, Carsten, and Donald Davis (1998) 'Tariff phase-outs: theory and evidence from GATT and NAFTA', in Jeffrey A. Frankel, (ed.), *The Regionalization of the World Economy*. Chicago: The University of Chicago Press.

Kowalczyk, Carsten, and Raymond Riezman (2009) 'Free trade: what are the terms-of-trade effects?' *Economic Theory* 41, 147–61.

Kowalczyk, Carsten, and Tomas Sjöström (1994) 'Bringing GATT into the Core', *Economica* 61, 301–17.

Kowalczyk, Carsten, and Tomas Sjöström (2000) 'Trade as transfers, GATT and the core', *Economics Letters* 66, 163–69.

Kowalczyk, Carsten, and Ronald Wonnacott (1991) 'Complement and substitute trading clubs', Dartmouth College, Department of Economics Working Paper No. 91–16, October.

—— (1992) 'Hubs and spokes and free trade in the Americas', NBER Working Paper No. 4198.

Krishna, Pravin, and Arvind Panagariya (2002) 'On necessarily welfare enhancing FTAs', *Journal of International Economics* 57, 353–67.

Lawrence, Robert Z. (1996) *Regionalism, Multilateralism, and Deeper Integration*. Washington, D.C.: The Brookings Institution.

López, Ramón, and Arvind Panagariya (1992) 'On the theory of piecemeal tariff reform: the case of pure imported intermediate inputs', *American Economic Review* 82, 615–25.

Mayer, Wolfgang (1981) 'Theoretical considerations on negotiated tariff adjustments', *Oxford Economic Papers* 33, 135–53.

McLaren, John (1997) 'Size, sunk costs and Judge Bowker's objections to free trade', *American Economic Review* 87, 400–20.

McMillan, John, and Ewen McCann (1981) 'Welfare effects in customs unions', *Economic Journal* 91, 697–703.

Michaely, Michael (1998) 'Partners to a preferential trade agreement: implications of varying size', *Journal of International Economics* 46, 73–85.

Ohyama, Michihiro (1972) 'Trade and welfare in general equilibrium', *Keio Economic Studies* 9, 73–73.

Riezman, Raymond (1985) 'Customs unions and the core', *Journal of International Economics* 19, 355–65.

—— (1999) 'Can bilateral trade agreements help to induce free trade?' *Canadian Journal of Economics* 32, 751–66.

Scitovsky, Tibor (1942) 'A reconsideration of the theory of tariffs', *Review of Economic Studies* 9, 89–110.

Shapley, Lloyd S. (1953) 'A value for n-person games', in H.W. Kuhn and A.W. Tucker (eds), *Contributions to the Theory of Games*, vol. 2 (*Annals of Mathematical Studies* 28, 307–17). Princeton: Princeton University Press.

Syropoulos, Constantinos (2002) 'Optimum tariffs and retaliation revisited: how country size matters', *Review of Economic Studies* 69, 707–27.

Vanek, Jaroslev (1965) *General Equilibrium of International Discrimination: The Case of Customs Unions*. Cambridge, MA: Harvard University Press.

Viner, Jacob (1950) *The Customs Union Issue*. New York: Carnegie Endowment for International Peace.

Wonnacott, Ronald, and Paul Wonnacott (1981) 'Is unilateral tariff reduction preferable to a customs union? The curious case of the missing foreign tariffs', *American Economic Review* 71, 704–14.

Woodland, Alan (2010) 'General equilibrium trade theory', Chapter 3 in this volume.

Zissimos, Benjamin (2007) 'The GATT and gradualism', *Journal of International Economics* 71, 410–33.

Part C
Special Topics

14
Trade and Labour Markets
*Carl Davidson and Steven J. Matusz**

1   One issue, many perspectives

What does increasing globalization mean for workers? This would appear to be a fairly straightforward question to which one might have a forthright answer. In fact, 'the answer' may just depend on one's perspective. To the auto worker in Detroit, increasing integration of the world economy means long-term unemployment, loss of human capital, and perhaps lost dreams. For the new university graduate in India, rapid globalization may mean the creation of exciting new opportunities for employment in well-paid jobs. Deeper integration with the world economy provides a campaign issue politicians of all stripes: some railing against the damage caused by a tsunami of cheap foreign imports with others extolling the vast benefits of greater access to foreign markets. For a trade economist, expanded trade might mean changes in relative price and the associated Stolper–Samuelson effects, reducing real wages in labour scarce countries while increasing real wages in labour abundant countries. In contrast a labour economist might suggest that the factor trade implicit in a country's net exports effectively augments (or diminishes) the country's available supply of labour, thereby reducing (or increasing) the wage.

There has clearly been a deep divide between the conventional economist's approach to understanding the implications that trade has for labour and the perspectives shared by non-economists. For that matter, economists do not agree among themselves on the proper perspective. Roughly speaking, the non-economist's perspective is all about jobs: does the shrinking globe create new opportunities or does it destroy existing jobs?[1] In contrast, the analytically beautiful general equilibrium models that dominate the trade economist's analysis of global integration preclude employment effects by assuming them away. In the frictionless world of perfect labour markets, the wage adjusts to always maintain full employment. While trade may have price effects, pushing the wage one way or the other, it never has employment effects. The neglect of employment

391

effects is typically shared with labour economists, though the commonality ends there, with labour economists tending to use partial-equilibrium reasoning in formulating their analyses. While the mechanism at work may be different than that identified in the general-equilibrium approach, the common refrain is that globalization can have wage effects but no implications for unemployment.

The divide between economist's and non-economist's perspectives has been gradually shrinking. The development of richer models of the labour market, allowing for a variety of imperfections resulting in equilibrium unemployment, has enabled economists to formally model the concerns that are passionately expressed by workers of all skills and those who shape policy. The inclusion of these labour market imperfections in our models has revealed new general-equilibrium relationships among trade, technology, wages, income distribution and the costs of adjustment that we are just now beginning to explore. Our intent in this chapter is to highlight this new line of research, point out the most prominent features in the landscape, and suggest areas which are ripe for further inquiry.

2   The trade wages debate

Arguably, labour economists first began thinking about international trade in the wake of the observation (first noted by labour economists) that despite the increase in the supply of skilled labour relative to that of unskilled labour, the return to skill increased rapidly in the United States during the 1980s.[2] Two 'obvious' explanations were the rapid growth of U.S. trade, particularly with respect to trade with low income countries, and the tidal wave of technological advancements that seemed to generate increased demands for skilled labour. Other significant changes during this time frame, including the decline of union power and a significant influx of low skilled immigrants, may have also contributed to the increase in income inequality.

The identification of trade and immigration as prime suspects attracted the interest of international trade specialists. The resulting intellectual debate uncovered a fundamental difference between the world view held by labour economists and that adopted by international trade economists. While both framed the analysis in terms of the supply and demand for skilled versus unskilled labour, the two groups diverged in their formulation of labour demand. This difference, well described in Johnson and Stafford (1999), Slaughter (1999) and Davidson and Matusz (2004a, chapter 2), centers on whether one models an economy as producing an aggregate output with a single (though changeable) technology, or maintains an assumption that the economy produces multiple (at least two) goods, each with a different technology. In a single good economy, changes that might differentially affect the demand or supply for skill types can only be equilibrated by changes in relative wage rates. Within a multiple good framework, the same kinds of changes can be accommodated by changing product mix, holding relative wages constant. This latter result, taken from trade theory, was first formulated by Samuelson (1948, 1949).[3]

Samuelson framed the result in terms of 'factor price equalization'. That is, two countries would have identical factor prices regardless of differences in factor endowments if the two countries shared identical technology, traded freely with each other, and produced a fully diversified bundle of goods. Leamer and Levinsohn (1995) insightfully shifted the focus of this result by renaming it the 'factor price insensitivity theorem', suggesting that changes in a country's factor endowments would have no effect on that country's factor prices as long as the country maintained diversified production and output prices were pinned down by the global economy.

Formally, consider an economy that produces one good (y) using skilled and unskilled labour (L_S, L_U) according to a constant returns to scale production function: $y = f(L_S, L_U)$. Cost minimizing firms hire each input up to the point where the value of its marginal product equals its wage. With constant returns to scale, the demand for skilled labour relative to unskilled (ℓ) is a decreasing function of the skilled wage relative to the unskilled wage (ω)

$$\ell = g(\omega), \qquad g'(\omega) < 0. \tag{1}$$

This relative demand curve is illustrated in figure 14.1, where we also show the relative supply of skilled versus unskilled labour ($\bar{\ell}$), which we take to be completely inelastic.[4]

Skill biased changes in technology are represented by a rightward shift of $g(\omega)$ as firms substitute skilled workers for unskilled workers at any given relative wage. Holding constant the skill mix of the labour force clearly increases ω: the skilled wage rises relative to the unskilled wage. Similarly, holding technology

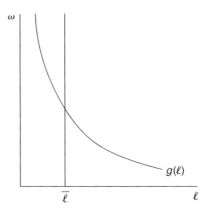

Figure 14.1 Relative demand curve.

constant, immigration of unskilled workers would shift $\bar{\ell}$ to the left, also increasing the skilled wage relative to the unskilled wage.[5] Likewise, goods trade can be viewed as an implicit way of importing and exporting the labour used in producing the traded goods. Adding net imports of skilled and unskilled labour to the economy's initial endowments could shift $\bar{\ell}$ leftward if the implied net imports of unskilled labour were sufficiently large relative to the implied net imports of skilled labour.

The empirical labour literature is then based on the world view contained in figure 14.1. While some studies have been more detailed and sophisticated than others, all boil down to figuring out if measured changes in technology, immigration or trade can shift the demand curve or the supply curve in figure 14.1 in the correct direction and by an amount sufficient to explain the observed change in income distribution.

Contrasting the above paradigm, a trade economist views a more disaggregate economy. While it is possible to consider any number of sectors, the main idea can be illustrated by considering just two sectors. To that end, consider an economy capable of producing two goods using skilled and unskilled labour according to the constant returns to scale production functions $y_i = f_i(L_{Si}, L_{Ui}), i = 1, 2$. Analogous with the one sector economy, we can derive the sector specific demands for skilled labour relative to unskilled labour. Because of the assumed constant returns to scale, each of these relative demands will be decreasing functions of ω:

$$\ell_i = g_i(\omega), \quad g_i'(\omega) < 0, \quad i = 1, 2. \tag{2}$$

The two functions represented in (2) are plotted in figure 14.2 where we have implicitly made the strong assumption that one sector is more skill intensive than the other regardless of the relative wage.[6] The economy wide demand for skilled labour relative to unskilled labour is a weighted average of the two sector specific relative demand curves. To see this, we begin by noting that the total demand for type-j labour is $L_{j1} + L_{j2}$, $j = S, U$ from which we derive the economy-wide relative demand:

$$\frac{L_{S1} + L_{S2}}{L_{U1} + L_{U2}} = \left(\frac{L_{U1}}{L_{U1} + L_{U2}} \right) g_1(\omega) + \left(\frac{L_{U2}}{L_{U1} + L_{U2}} \right) g_2(\omega). \tag{3}$$

A key insight from trade theory is that the weights on $g_i(\omega)$ are themselves functions of ω. In particular, one sector will almost always be able to outbid the other by paying proportionately higher wages for both types of labour. We show this in figure 14.3, where we draw the zero profit curves for both sectors and where w_i is the wage for type i workers. By Shephard's lemma, the demand for factor j is given by the partial derivative of the cost function with respect to the price of the j'th factor. Since cost is constant along the zero

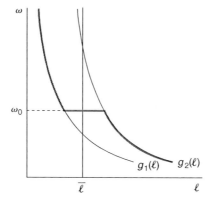

Figure 14.2   Demands for labour: skilled and unskilled

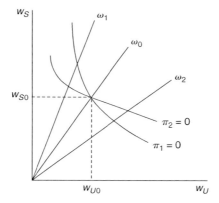

Figure 14.3   Zero profit curves.

profit curve, $\dfrac{dW_S}{dW_U}\Big|_{\pi_i=0} = -\dfrac{\partial\pi_i/W_U}{\partial\pi_i/W_S} = -g_i(\omega)^{-1}$. In figure 14.2, we have graphed

$g_2(\omega) > g_1(\omega)\forall\omega$. Therefore $\pi_i = 0$ is steeper than $\pi_2 = 0$ in figure 14.3.

When the skilled wage is high relative to the unskilled wage (e.g., $\omega = \omega_1$), the wages for both types of workers consistent with zero profit in sector one are higher than they are in the more skill intensive sector two. Conversely, when the skilled wage is low relative to the unskilled wage (e.g., $\omega = \omega_2$), it is the skill intensive sector two that can pay higher wages to both types of workers and still earn zero profit. If we assume (as is typical) that both types of workers can freely move between sectors, the sector that pays the higher wages will attract the entire labour force. In terms of (3), the weight on $g_1(\omega)$ is one for all $\omega > \omega_2$ and zero for all $\omega < \omega_2$, with corresponding weights of zero and one for the weight on $g_2(\omega)$.

The only relative wage at which neither sector can outbid the other is shown in figure 14.3 as ω_2. At this relative wage, the weight on $g_1(\omega)$ in (3) lies between zero and one, with the corresponding value for the weight on $g_2(\omega)$.

Putting all of the pieces together yields a step-shaped economy wide relative demand curve illustrated by the bold line in figure 14.2. The key here is that there exists an infinitely elastic portion of the curve. If the relative supply of skilled to unskilled labour intersects the relative demand curve along this perfectly elastic segment (as drawn in figure 14.2), then any change in relative supply has no effect on the relative wage as long as the change is not large enough to move the equilibrium off of the perfectly elastic portion of the relative demand curve.[7]

An upward shift of the perfectly elastic portion of the relative demand curve will increase the relative wage. From figure 14.3, it is evident that such an upward shift can occur if there are favourable changes biased in the direction of the skill intensive good. For example, either an increase in the price of the skill intensive good or any technological improvement that is concentrated in the skill intensive sector (skill biased or not) will shift the $\pi_2 = 0$ curve outward, leaving the $\pi_1 = 0$ curve in place. This shift implies that ω_0, the only relative wage for which both sectors can effectively compete for labour, increases.

The extreme version of the factor price insensitivity result (i.e., that the relative demand curve for labour has infinitely elastic portions) depends on the strong assumption that all inputs can easily and instantaneously move between sectors. As such, this is more of a long-run representation of an economy, but it does illustrate the main point that changing output mix can absorb various labour market shocks, removing some of the burden from wage adjustment. Moreover, this paradigm leads one to look for evidence that increased globalization was associated with changes in the relative price, or evidence that technological change had a sector bias rather than a factor bias. Unlike the labour economist view, changes in the skill mix of the workforce would have no impact on relative wage (if the trade model were to be taken literally), or a diminished impact (if one were to use the model as a basis for suggesting that openness greatly increases the elasticity of the economy-wide relative demand for labour).

Feenstra and Hanson (1996, 1999) provide yet another way of viewing the labour market effects of globalization. In their framework, y_1 and y_2 are interpreted as component parts of a final product (y). Initially, either cost conditions or technological necessity require both components to be produced in the same location. Since neither good can be traded, the relative price of components can be thought of as a shadow price, or the transfer price within the firm. As such, this relative price adjusts to accommodate changes in the relative factor price and the weighted average of g_1 and g_2 lies strictly between these two curves, eliminating the perfectly elastic segment. For example, if the relative wage is ω_1, the transfer price of y_2 increases relative to that of y_1 until the zero profit curves for both sectors intersect along the ray ω_1 in figure 14.3. If it then becomes economically feasible to offshore the least skill intensive component, the relative labour demand curve becomes g_2 since the weight on g_1 goes to zero. Offshoring is then another potential source of rising skill premia.[8]

3 Trade and steady state unemployment

Trade and labour economists may have different world views, but they operate in the same star system. In contrast, the questions that occupy mainstream economists seem to be a universe apart from those that reverberate in the larger society. As articulated in the introduction, many non-economists view trade as impacting the number and mix of jobs, whereas most economists dismiss this connection by assumption. All labour market consequences of trade work through wage effects, leaving aggregate employment unchanged. A fairly typical view is expressed by Slaughter (1999, 626).[9]

> Trade supporters, knowingly or not, are increasingly making specious arguments that are prone to fail and thereby lend support to opponents. Consider, for example, the argument that 'freer trade creates jobs'. No: on net, trade neither creates nor destroys jobs – it is about the kinds of jobs in the economy, not the number of jobs.

It is unclear what Slaughter means in this quote by the 'kinds of jobs' since in the world views of both trade and labour economists there are no 'good jobs' or 'bad jobs'. Workers care only about wages, and all similar workers earn similar wages. In contrast, many non-economists perceive the existence of well paid, long lasting jobs alongside poorly paid transitory jobs and fear that trade increases the number of the latter while reducing the number of the former.

Statements that dismiss any connection between trade and unemployment are tautologies, based on more than two centuries of economic thought that has implicitly or explicitly only considered perfectly competitive, frictionless labour markets in which the wage is permitted to instantaneously adjust to maintain full employment. In the end, it may indeed be the case that trade has little net effect on the number of jobs, but this is a matter to be investigated both theoretically and empirically. It is not sufficient to dismiss the question by assumption.

Swimming against the current, a number of researchers have explicitly considered the implications that trade might have for unemployment when labour markets are characterized by rigidities and imperfections. Brecher (1974a, b) was the pioneer, adding a downwardly rigid wage to an otherwise standard two sector, two factor model. Unemployment can be an equilibrium outcome in this context, and many standard trade theoretic results are turned upside down. The distortion created by the minimum wage creates the possibility that trade may increase unemployment beyond its autarky level and reduce welfare. If trade does reduce welfare, a prohibitive tariff is welfare superior to free trade. More generally, the optimal tariff for a small country need not be zero, while the optimal tariff for a large country need not be positive.

To get some flavor of Brecher's analysis, return to figure 14.3 and assume that there is a legally binding minimum wage for unskilled labour: $w_{min} = w_{U0}$. Defining y_1 as numeraire, the zero profit conditions are stated as

$$p = a_{S2}w_S + a_{U2}w_U,$$ (4a)

$$1 = a_{S1}w_S + a_{U1}w_U,$$ (4b)

where a_{ij} is the amount of type i labour used to produce one unit of j. Note that the a_{ij} are themselves functions of ω. Given p (and an assumption of no factor intensity reversals) this system of two equations in two unknowns can be solved for W_S and W_U. If, in contrast, we set $w_U = w_{min}$ and still maintain that p is exogenous, it would be a fluke if there were a value of W_S that would solve the system. Instead, we can think of p as being one of the two unknown variables in (4a) and (4b). Imposing a minimum wage then results in a unique pair (p, W_S) that permits zero profit in both sectors. If both goods are in positive demand regardless of relative price, this is the unique price that must emerge in autarky. Given $W_{min} = W_{U0}$, the equilibrium solution replicates figure 14.3 and places the economy on the completely elastic portion of the relative demand curve in figure 14.2.

In this equilibrium, it is possible for the economy to fully employ all of its labour (at the intersection of the relative labour demand curve with the relative labour supply curve), but it is just as possible that the economy shifts some resources to the production of the more skill intensive y_2, fully employing all skilled workers but leaving some unskilled workers unemployed. The market mechanism is short-circuited since the excess supply of unskilled labour cannot bid down the legally binding minimum wage.

The economy specializes to the production of the skill intensive y_2 for any p greater than its autarkic value. Successive increases in p drive up the wage for skilled workers while having no effect on the unskilled wage. This combination induces substitution toward unskilled labour, ultimately resulting in full employment for sufficiently high p. In contrast, a reduction in p raises the unskilled wage above the minimum and the economy jumps to full employment.

Davis (1998) pushes the minimum wage model further by combining a rigid labour market (Europe) with a flexible labour market (the United States) to show that the minimum wage imposed in one economy might prop up the wage in the other, with all unemployment occurring in the policy active economy. The introduction of trade between the two countries results in higher unemployment for the minimum wage economy. Furthermore, trade shocks emanating from some third country that might ordinarily result in a wage reduction (due to Stolper–Samuelson effects) instead have no impact on the flexible U.S. economy, but result in substantially increased unemployment in the sclerotic European economy.

To understand Davis's result, consider a single minimum wage economy in autarky. As in Brecher, equilibrium is characterized by some amount of unemployed unskilled labour. Now increase all inputs proportionately. With constant returns to scale, all outputs increase by the same proportion, as does the employment of all inputs. The unemployment rate is unchanged, but the level of unemployment increases proportionately. Now imagine that this larger economy is really the union of two distinct economies, and construct a factor price equalization set as in Dixit and Norman (1980). Continue to assume that the minimum wage binds in only one of the countries. As long as factor endowments in the two countries are not too different, the free-trade equilibrium mimics the autarky equilibrium of the integrated economy, with the same total employment and same total output. All unemployment, however, is concentrated in the minimum wage economy.

While instructive, models based on minimum wages leave many open questions pertaining to dynamics and general-equilibrium effects. These gaps began to be addressed as the microtheoretic foundations of equilibrium unemployment developed.

Matusz (1985, 1986) was the first to incorporate such models into the standard two sector general equilibrium frameworks that are commonly used in trade theory.[10] The assumed labour market in these early papers was characterized by implicit labour contracts, whereby risk averse workers were paid time invariant wages by risk neutral firms, trading off the possibility of temporary layoffs during periods of low product demand.[11] Subsequent research has explored trade related issues when labour markets are characterized by efficiency wages (Copeland, 1989; Brecher, 1992; Brecher and Choudhri, 1994; Matusz, 1994, 1996, 1998; Clemenz, 1995; Chin, 1998; Carter, 1999; Hoon, 2000, 2001a,b; Das, 2006; Davis and Harrigan, 2007; Altenberg and Brenken, 2008), the fair wage variant of efficiency wages (Agell and Lundborg, 1995; Kreickemeier and Nelson, 2006; Egger and Kreickemeier, 2008a,b, 2009), and search or matching frictions (Davidson, Martin and Matusz, 1987, 1988, 1991, 1999; Davidson and Matusz, 2000, 2004a, 2004c, 2006a, 2006b; Moore and Ranjan, 2005; Bradford, 2006; Davidson, Matusz and Shevchenko, 2008a,b; Felbermayr, Prat and Schmerer, 2008; Costinot, 2009a; Helpman and Itskhoki, 2009; Helpman, Itskhoki and Redding, 2009; Dutt, Mitra and Ranjan, 2009).

This growing body of work addresses many facets of international trade, with the specifics of each model largely tailored to the questions being asked. Despite the variety of approaches, most share certain common threads. Nearly all of the work in this area is dynamic, allowing for flows into and out of unemployment.

Moreover, diversified production requires that all jobs offer the same expected utility to prospective employees. And all of the research cited assumes easy entry and exit by firms, leading to some form of zero profit condition.

To get a sense of how the analysis proceeds, consider a two sector economy that operates in continuous time.[12] There can be any number of inputs, but we will assume that homogenous labour is the only input subject to unemployment. Let e_i and b_i (both strictly positive) represent the rates at which workers exit unemployment to become employed in sector i (i.e., the job acquisition rate) or become separated from their sector i job, becoming unemployed (the job destruction rate). Define w_i as the sector i wage. Finally, let V_{Ui} represent the expected lifetime income (properly discounted) for an unemployed worker searching for a sector i job. Expected lifetime utility is increasing in w_i and e_i, decreasing in b_i.

Three key conditions for this economy are

$$V_{U1}(w_1,e_1,b_1) = V_{U2}(w_2,e_2,b_2), \tag{5}$$

$$b_iL_{Ei} = e_iL_{Ui}, \tag{6}$$

$$\sum_{i=1,2}(L_{Ei}+L_{Ui}) = L, \tag{7}$$

where L_{Ei} and L_{Ui} represent total employment and unemployment in sector i, and L is the labour supply.

Equation (5) is the worker indifference condition, required for diversified production. Equation (6) is a steady state condition, ensuring that the flows into unemployment just balance the flows out. Finally, (7) is just an adding up condition.

The key issues revolve around how w_i, e_i, and b_i are determined. The job destruction rate is typically assumed to be exogenous; whereas the job acquisition rate is usually assumed to be a function of the number (or mass) of searching agents, although it is sometimes assumed to depend on search effort as well. If labour is the only input, the wage is easy to model as the value of the marginal product of labour. However, since trading frictions and search costs provide both firms and workers with some monopoly power, it is more common to assume that wages are determined through some other mechanism (e.g., bargaining).

Consider first the simplest case in which the job acquisition rates are exogenous. If we also assume that this is a small open economy, then the two wages must adjust to bring equality in (5).[13] An increase in sector one's job destruction rate (or a decrease in sector one's job acquisition rate) implies that workers must be 'compensated' by an increase in w_1. In turn, this increases the cost of producing good one, feeding through to relative output price and ultimately impacting the pattern of comparative advantage. Thus, the structure of a country's labour market, as reflected by its distribution of turnover rates across sectors, can influence the pattern of trade. All else equal, a country will be more likely to export goods produced in sectors with high job acquisition rates and stable jobs (i.e., low job destruction rates). Empirical support for this prediction is provided in Davidson and Matusz (2005).

Turning to the impact of trade on unemployment, we can define the sector specific unemployment rate as $\mu_i = L_{U_i}/(L_{E_i} + L_{U_i})$. From (7), this becomes

$$\mu_i = \frac{b_i}{b_i + e_i},\qquad(8)$$

so that the sector specific unemployment rate is increasing in the job destruction rate but decreasing in the job acquisition rate. In addition, it is useful to point out that an increase in the price of good one causes the wage for workers in sector one to increase (not explicitly shown in this reduced form analysis), drawing more workers to that sector. The economy-wide unemployment rate is a weighted average of the two sector specific rates. A change in the terms of trade increases or reduces overall unemployment as it causes labour to flow toward or away from the high unemployment sector. Thus, even in this simple setting with exogenous turnover rates, changes in the pattern of trade must influence the economy-wide unemployment rate.

The relationship between trade and unemployment becomes more complex when we expand the model to make job acquisition and job destruction rates endogenous. For example, one would expect the presence of congestion externalities in the search process – as more unemployed workers seek jobs in a particular sector, it should become harder for an individual worker to find a job in the sector. In addition, changes in the mix of factors attracted to an industry should affect that industry's unemployment rate. If more firms post vacancies, this should make it easier for searching workers to find new jobs in that sector. The implication is that as a sector grows or shrinks in size, its unemployment rate is likely to change. The overall impact of the change in the terms of trade (or any facet of globalization) is then the product of its impact on sector specific unemployment rates combined with the induced worker flows between sectors. A number of studies have investigated the link between trade and unemployment in such a setting and they all conclude that the relationship is ambiguous (see, e.g., Davidson, Martin and Matusz, 1987, 1988; Moore and Ranjan, 2005; or Helpman and Itskhoki, 2009).

Still more possibilities arise if search effort by workers or recruiting effort by firms is endogenous (as in Felbermayr, Prat and Schmerer, 2008) or if firms screen heterogeneous workers in an attempt to weed out and reject those with a low match value (as in Helpman, Itskhoki and Redding, 2009). Because of the plethora of possibilities, the theoretical literature has not yet reached a consensus on how trade impacts the overall unemployment rate. Moreover, the empirical evidence is extraordinarily limited and contradictory.[14] Perhaps the proper stance on the issue is to assert that there are channels by which trade can either increase or decrease the overall unemployment rate, but the current state of the literature is such that one cannot make a compelling argument that the direction is one way or the other. This is distinctly different than the stance shared by Slaughter, Krugman, Mussa and many others.

4   Trade, wages and inequality with unemployment

In section 2 we drew a contrast between the way that trade and labour economists approach the trade wages debate, highlighting the fact that trade economists tend to focus on general equilibrium models. However, we said very little about the actual predictions that come out of the general equilibrium models when full employment is assumed. In this section, we turn to those predictions, briefly review the logic behind them and then provide a heuristic description of how these predictions are altered by the presence of equilibrium unemployment.

In the canonical perfectly competitive general equilibrium models of trade, such as the Heckscher–Ohlin–Samuelson (HOS) and Ricardo–Viner (RV) model, the link between trade and factor returns is shaped by relative factor endowments, technology and factor mobility. We start with the two good, two factor HOS model in which factors are perfectly mobile across sectors. In such a setting, labour has no reason to prefer one sector over another, unless compensation varies across sectors. Similarly, capital flows to the sector that offers the highest return. The assumption that factors react instantly to changes in compensation has strong implications for the link between trade patterns and factor returns. For example, suppose that the world price of a good that is produced using a relatively labour intensive production process rises. This will cause domestic firms to increase production of that good, leading to an increase in the demand for *all* factors used in that sector. However, the aggregate demand for labour increases while that for capital falls since the factors that are released from the capital intensive sector are less labour intensive (more capital intensive) than those being absorbed by the labour intensive sector. When a new equilibrium is established, all labour benefits, regardless of where it is employed, while all capital is harmed.

We turn next to the RV model in which some factors are tied to a specific sector, while other factors (such as unskilled labour) are mobile. For example, machinery used to produce automobiles and computers cannot be substituted for each other all that easily. Thus, if the return to capital increases in Silicon Valley, we would not expect an immediate outflow of capital from the automobile industry to the computer industry. Likewise, when workers make an occupational choice they often acquire skills that are sector specific. If the average wage paid to engineers increases, we would not expect lawyers or economists to immediately quit their jobs and switch occupations. Rather, we might see a gradual increase in the number of students majoring in engineering and a decline in other areas. As a result, over time the number of engineers will grow and the number of economists may shrink. The RV model stresses that these short-run attachments bind the fortunes of each factor to the fortunes of the sector in which that factor is employed. If the world price for automobiles increases at the same time that the world price of computers falls, any factor that is specific to the automobile sector will gain while factors specific to the computer sector will lose.

Now, suppose that we take the standard two good, two factor HOS model and assume that search is required to find employment in either sector.[15] Thus, unemployed workers will have to choose a sector in which to seek employment and will be drawn to the sector offering the highest expected lifetime reward. It follows that in a diversified equilibrium, unemployed workers will distribute themselves across the two sectors so that the expected lifetime return to search is the same in both sectors that is, $V_{U1} = V_{U2}$, as in (5) above. In such a setting, it can be shown that under certain conditions the returns to *idle* factors vary according to the Stolper–Samuelson Theorem provided that factor intensities take into account the number of active searchers in each sector.[16] Thus, if a tariff is instituted in a relatively labour intensive industry, all *unemployed* labour will benefit while all *idle* capital will be harmed (in terms of expected lifetime returns). The reasoning is much like the logic behind the Stolper–Samuelson Theorem. An increase in the price of a good will draw idle factors toward that sector. If the growing sector is more labour intensive than the sector that is shrinking, the aggregate demand for labour will rise while the aggregate demand for capital falls. Consequently, the return to unemployed workers will increase while the return to idle capital falls. The key here is that in a setting with equilibrium unemployment it is the *idle* factors that are perfectly mobile across sectors and they are the factors that respond immediately to changes in product prices. These factors and their returns act exactly in the manner predicted by the HOS model and the Stolper–Samuelson Theorem.

This analysis does not address the issue of how changes in trade patterns or trade policy would affect the returns to *employed* factors. This issue was addressed in Davidson, Martin and Matusz (1999) where the authors show that search costs create an attachment to a sector that makes employed factors much like the specific factors in the RV model. Matched agents are reluctant to sever their match unless they are convinced that they can earn significantly more by searching for a different production opportunity elsewhere because it takes time for jobless workers and firms with vacancies to find each other. It follows that small changes in product prices will not cause employed factors to switch sectors. This implies that the reward earned by employed factors will be tied to the overall success of the sector. If an export sector is growing, this will tend to increase the reward to the labour and capital employed in that sector.

But, at some point, most jobs break up for one reason or another. When that happens, the firm must recruit a replacement for the lost employee and the worker must search for a new job. Thus, the expected lifetime income for employed factors includes what those factors expect to earn when they become unemployed (for labour) or idle (for capital). We have already argued that this component of expected lifetime income varies according to the Stolper–Samuelson Theorem. It follows that the overall return to each *employed* factor is driven both by Stolper–Samuelson *and* Ricardo–Viner forces. Moreover, the force that dominates depends upon the turnover rates in that sector. If jobs last for a long time or are difficult to find, then the attachment to a sector caused by search costs will be strong. This makes it more likely that the Ricardo–Viner force will dominate. On the other hand, if jobs are easy to find and/or do not last long, then employed factors will not feel a strong attachment to their sector. In this case, it is more likely that the Stolper–Samuelson forces will dominate.[17]

In summary, in the presence of equilibrium unemployment, factor returns are driven by two forces. The Stolper–Samuelson force, which dictates that an economy's abundant factor gains from trade while its scarce factor loses, and the Ricardo–Viner force, which dictates that a factor specific to an export sector gains from trade while a factor specific to an import sector loses from trade. While these are the two conventional channels that link factor rewards to trade patterns, they do not emerge simultaneously in full employment models. The Stolper–Samuelson force is present only when all factors are perfectly mobile across all sectors while the Specific Factors force emerges only in full employment models with imperfectly mobile factors. The key insight that is gained by allowing for unemployment is that market imperfections (like the transaction costs associated with search) generate an environment in which the returns to employed factors are determined by a weighted average of these two forces. In addition, it is the labour market turnover rates of each sector that determine which force is given more weight.

The new insights described above were derived in frameworks consistent with 'old trade theory', in which all firms within an industry are identical, technology is characterized by constant returns to scale, and perfect competition prevails. With identical firms competing in perfectly competitive output markets, 'inequality' refers to differences in factor rewards across industries and across factors of production. More recent modeling emphasizes markets characterized by imperfect competition and populated by heterogeneous firms operating under conditions of increasing returns to scale.

Heterogeneity among firm induces heterogeneity among workers even within the same industry. This line of research, awkwardly referenced as 'new new trade theory' (NNTT), was motivated by empirical work using firm level and plant level data showing that even in narrowly defined industries some firms are more productive than others, different firms use different skill mixes of workers and pay different wages and firms differ significantly in their participation in international markets.[18] In particular, we now know that the most productive firms within an industry tend to use a relatively more capital intensive production process, employ a more highly skilled workforce, pay higher wages and are more likely to export a fraction of their output than their less productive counterparts. The result that (all else equal) firms that are engaged in international commerce pay higher wages than their domestic competitors has led to new literature on the causes and extent of the 'exporter wage premium'.

Many NNTT models are designed to explain industry dynamics and focus on the impact of openness on the exporting behaviour of firms and the associated changes in productivity. One of the most important models, due to Melitz (2003), assumes that firms differ in productivity and that there are significant fixed costs associated with exporting. Since the most productive firms have an easier time covering these fixed costs, they are more likely to export than their less productive counterparts. Increases in openness then result in resource reallocation within the sector away from the weakest firms towards the strongest firms. This leads to an increase in the industry-wide measure of productivity. However, it is important to note that most Melitz based models assume that labour markets are perfectly competitive and therefore they do not provide an explanation of the exporter wage premium.

Two recent papers are exceptions in that they extend the Melitz framework to allow for the types of labour market imperfections that lead to equilibrium unemployment. In addition to generating unemployment, these imperfections create an environment in which workers with similar characteristics employed in the same industry may earn different wages. Egger and Kreickemeier (2008a) use a fair wage model in which each worker's notion of a 'fair wage' is tied to the profitability of its firm. Helpman, Itskhoki and Redding (2009) assume that there are frictions in the labour market so that equilibrium is characterized by search-generated unemployment. When workers and firms meet, they negotiate the wage rate and this leads them to split the surplus created by the job. In both models, ex ante identical workers will earn different wages if they are matched with firms that earn different profits. Thus, the wage earned by a worker is tied to the fortunes of its firm; and, since it is the most productive firms that have greater access to world markets, workers employed by exporting firms will earn higher wages. In addition, since increased openness benefit the strongest firms in the industry at the expense of the weakest, trade liberalization always leads to greater within-group inequality.

5   Trade and adjustment costs

Regardless of any disagreement with respect to globalization's long-run effects on unemployment and wages, there is near unanimity that workers may bear significant short-run costs of adjusting to trade shocks. Exploring the losses of workers displaced due to a variety of shocks, including those resulting from trade liberalization, Jacobson, LaLonde and Sullivan (1993a,b) find for the United States that the average dislocated worker suffers a loss in lifetime earnings of $80,000. Kletzer (2001) explicitly targets workers displaced because of exposure to international competition.[19] Focusing on wages that trade displaced workers eventually earn in their new jobs, she finds that the average dislocated worker accepts a 13 percent pay cut.[20]

While these short-run costs are certainly significant for those who bear the burden of adjustment, it is important to put them into perspective by comparing them to the long-run benefits of greater openness. The literature in this regard is quite thin and does not point to a consensus on the likely magnitude of adjustment costs.[21]

Magee (1972) and Baldwin, Richardson and Mutti (1980) represent the first attempts to quantify this cost-benefit ratio. In both instances, the authors estimated the number of jobs that would be lost due to liberalization, multiplying that number by an appropriate wage. The duration of unemployment was either arbitrarily specified as an exogenous parameter (Magee) or estimated based on demographic characteristics (Baldwin, Richardson and Mutti), making it possible to aggregate up the present discounted value of lost wages. Measuring the long-run gains from trade in the usual way, both studies reach the same conclusion, that adjustment costs are probably very small in relative terms. For example, with a 10 percent discount rate, they both estimate that the short-run costs of adjustment would eat away no more than 5 percent of the long-run gains from trade.

More recently, Trefler (2004) uses a differences-in-differences approach to quantify the employment and productivity effects that the Canada and U.S. free-trade agreement (CUSFTA) had on Canadian manufacturing. This agreement, which became effective on 1 January 1989, specified gradual removal of trade barriers, with the elimination of all tariffs to be completed by 1 January 1998. CUSFTA was supplanted on 1 January 1996 when the North American free-trade agreement came into force.

The key independent variables in Trefler's analysis are industry specific bilateral tariff rates relative to tariff rates imposed by each country on imports from the rest of the world. Specifically, define T_{it}^{kj} as the tariff rate levied by country k on imports of goods from industry i exported by country j at time t, where the countries are Canada (C), the United States (U), and the rest of the world (R). Trefler then defines the tariff cuts mandated by CUSFTA as

$$\tau_{it}^{C} = T_{it}^{CU} - T_{it}^{CR}, \tag{9a}$$

$$\tau_{it}^{U} = T_{it}^{UC} - T_{it}^{UR}, \tag{9b}$$

where (9a) is the reduction in Canadian tariffs on imports from the United States and (9b) is the reduction in U.S. tariffs on imports from Canada. Note that adherence to the Most Favored Nation clause of the GATT implies $\tau_{it}^C = 0 = \tau_{it}^U$ for all years prior to 1989. The only exception is the automotive sector, where tariff rates were set in the 1965 Canada and U.S. auto pact.

Next, define z_{it} as a the logarithm of some variable of interest. For example, this could be the log of Canadian employment in industry i at time t, or the log of worker productivity in industry i at time t.

Finally, Trefler selects 1980–86 as a pre-CUSFTA period (period 0) as a basis of comparison for the 1988–96 post-CUFSTA (period 1) results.[22] The key regression then becomes

$$(\Delta z_{i1} - \Delta z_{i0}) = \beta^C(\Delta \tau_{i1}^C - \Delta \tau_{i0}^C) + \beta^U(\Delta \tau_{i1}^U - \Delta \tau_{i0}^U) + \gamma X + \nu_1, \tag{10}$$

where X is a vector of (time, country and industry specific) controls, ν_i is an error term and[23]

$$\Delta z_{i0} = \frac{z_{i,1986} - z_{i,1980}}{1986 - 1980}, \tag{11a}$$

$$\Delta z_{i1} = \frac{z_{i,1996} - z_{i,1988}}{1996 - 1988}, \tag{11b}$$

$$\Delta \tau_{i0}^k = \frac{\tau_{i,1986}^k - \tau_{i,1980}^k}{1986 - 1980} \text{ for } i = \text{automotive sector, zero otherwise,} \tag{11c}$$

$$\Delta \tau_{i1}^k = \frac{\tau_{i,1996}^k - \tau_{i,1988}^k}{1996 - 1988}. \tag{11d}$$

Estimating this equation for employment and applying the results to the most impacted industries, Trefler concludes that Canadian tariff cuts resulted in a 12 percent loss of employment, whereas there was no statistically significant change in employment resulting from U.S. concessions. Considering the effect on all industries, Trefler's preferred estimate is that CUFSTA reduced Canadian manufacturing employment by 5 percent, equivalent to approximately a hundred thousand workers.

The gains generated by CUSFTA show up in very large estimates of increased labour productivity, on the order of a compound annual growth rate of 1.9 percent for industries most impacted by Canadian tariff cuts.[24]

It is difficult in this context to weigh the losses against the gains. First, Trefler is unable to determine the duration of unemployment suffered by the displaced workers, though his sense is that gains in other parts of Canadian manufacturing absorbed the initial losses within ten years. He bases his belief on the fact that there appeared to be no long-run effect on the Canadian employment rate (62 percent in April 1988 and in April 2002) and the fact that manufacturing employment increased in Canada between 1988 and 2002, while simultaneously falling in the United States and Japan. Second, the loss of employment is not correlated with lost output. One might surmise, however, that a 5 percent reduction in employment would result in a significant loss of manufacturing output. While that loss is surely less than 5 percent, it would not be unreasonable to imagine the loss to be on the order of 2 percent or 3 percent. Even if the displaced remain unemployed, with estimated productivity effects of 1.9 percent growth, manufacturing output could return to its initial level in between one and two years, thereafter rising above what it would have been in the absence of CUSFTA.

In an alternative approach, Davidson and Matusz (2004c) construct and calibrate a two sector model with a labour market characterized by search frictions. One sector is calibrated so that jobs require little training and are available on demand, but have relatively short duration. The other sector is the opposite, populated by jobs that require significant training (quantified in terms of both resource costs and time spent in training) and are difficult to find, but are quite durable. The structures of the two sectors, connected by a worker indifference condition as in (5), are illustrated in figure 14.4. In addition to the earlier defined variables, L_{Ti} is the number (mass) of workers training for a job in sector i, τ_i is the rate at which sector i workers exit training, and ϕ is the probability that a worker retains his skills in the event that he becomes separated from his job.[25]

The numbers (mass) of workers in each state (training, unemployed, or employed) changes over time and can be characterized by a system of differential

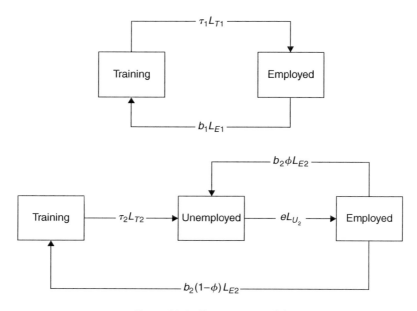

Figure 14.4   Two sector model

equations:

$$L_{E1}(t) = \tau_1 L_{T1}(t) - b_1 L_{E1}(t), \tag{12}$$

$$L_{T1}(t) = b_1 L_{E1}(t) - \tau_1 L_{T1}(t), \tag{13}$$

$$L_{E2}(t) = e L_{U2}(t) - b_2 L_{E2}(t), \tag{14}$$

$$L_{T2}(t) = b_2(1 - \phi)L_{E2}(t) - \tau_2 L_{T2}(t), \tag{15}$$

$$L_{U2}(t) = \tau_2 L_{T2}(t) + b_2\phi L_{E2}(t) - e L_{U2}(t), \tag{16}$$

where we have made explicit the functional dependence on time of L_{Ei}, L_{Ti}, and L_{Ui}. This system of equations is solvable, making it possible to trace out the entire time path of employment, training, and unemployment that is generated after a shock (such as trade liberalization) hits the economy. Davidson and Matusz (2004c) assume a simple Ricardian technology, allowing them to easily translate output to employment, tracing out the path taken by GDP subsequent to trade reform.

The thought experiment undertaken in Davidson and Matusz (2004c) is one in which sector one is initially protected by a 5 percent tariff. The tariff is then removed, setting the dynamics in motion. This results in some workers moving to sector two where they first undergo a spell of training, followed by a period during which they must search for employment. During this time, these workers are not producing output, so there is an immediate drop in GDP. As these workers gradually become employed, GDP begins to climb, eventually surpassing its initial steady-state value. The gains from trade are measured as the present discounted value of the increase in GDP if the economy were able to immediately jump to the new steady state. Adjustment costs are measured as the difference between the present discounted value of the new steady state GDP and actual GDP, measured along the adjustment path.

Davidson and Matusz (2004c) calibrate the model, drawing job turnover data from Davis, Haltiwanger and Schuh (1996) and assuming a range of values for the other key parameters. Their analysis suggests that adjustment costs can be significant, eating away as much as 80 percent of the gross gains from trade.

Cameron, Chaudhri and McLaren (2007) and Chaudhri and McLaren (2007) have taken a different route to modelling the adjustment process. In their discrete time framework, a worker who is in sector i at the end of time t receives an idiosyncratic shock ϵ_{it}, which can be either positive or negative.[26] The authors prefer to think of this as a non-pecuniary benefit or cost of being in the sector. For example, a worker who becomes bored with his job might have a negative shock, whereas one who has developed close friendships in the neighborhood might have a positive shock.

Each worker must decide whether to remain in his or her current sector or to switch sectors based upon his or her expectation of the value of ϵ_{it} versus

ϵ_{jt}, a time-invariant moving cost c, and expectations of future wages.[27] In a two sector model, there are gross flows of workers in both directions, even in a steady state where wages are equal and constant across sectors. In the context of trade, liberalization results in a net flow of workers into the export sector even as some workers move in the opposite direction because of their idiosyncratic shocks.

One advantage of modeling adjustment in this way is that it is possible to estimate the parameters of adjustment costs using standard techniques. This is done in Artuç, Chaudhri, and McLaren (2007). Using data from the United States Current Population Survey, they estimate that the mean value of the cost of switching sectors is between 8 and 13 times the wage, with a standard deviation falling between four and seven times the wage.[28] Even after adjusting for a variety of possible sources of upward biases, the authors conclude that adjustment costs are several times higher than wages.

While these individual costs are extraordinarily large, it is difficult to place them in perspective relative to the gains from trade. Recall that there are gross flows even in a steady state, so in some sense we need to know the magnitude of additional movement caused by liberalization, adding up the costs for this extra movement. Subject to that caveat, these results suggest the possibility that adjustment costs can be quite large relative to the gains from liberalization.

6   New frontiers: labour market sorting and trade

Most of the work that we have surveyed up to this point uses a framework that is largely consistent with what we referred to as 'old trade theory' in Section 4. That is, most of this work is based on the conventional Heckscher–Ohlin–Samuelson and Ricardian models of international trade in which the unit of analysis is the industry, with all firms within an industry assumed to be identical. These two models, once the primary workhorses for the field, have fallen out of favour in recent years.[29] This change began more than three decades ago as researchers began to borrow modelling techniques from industrial organization, macroeconomics and other areas to build richer models of product market interaction between firms in open economies. The once standard assumption of perfect competition in the product market has been abandoned in favor of more sophisticated models of monopolistic competition in which firms produce varieties of goods that are imperfect substitutes for each other. As a result, a rich body of predictions linking globalization to price cost markups, firm sizes, export behaviour and productivity (both at the firm and industry levels) has developed. Moreover, recent availability of new firm level and plant level data sets has allowed for tests of these predictions as well as the establishment of a wide variety of new stylized facts concerning the evolution of industrial structures in dynamic open economies (some of these were highlighted at the end of Section 4). Attempts to provide theoretical explanations for many of these stylized facts forced trade theorists to extend their models of monopolistic competition in new directions with the introduction of firm side heterogeneity (in terms of costs or productivity) now viewed as an essential component of many models. Thus, the unit of analysis has changed and we now have a large, well established literature that focuses on firm and plant level adjustment to globalization.

Perhaps inspired by the work on firm heterogeneity, a new literature has started to develop that underscores the role that worker heterogeneity plays for a variety of trade issues. New models that allow for non-trivial distributions of skills across the workforce have been developed, and they have raised a whole host of new and interesting questions. In this final section, we highlight a few of the more intriguing issues that have been addressed and suggest some avenues that we believe are ripe for investigation.

The questions that we find most interesting and promising are related to the manner in which the market sorts heterogeneous workers and the role that international trade plays in that sorting. There are two different ways to approach this question, based on whether the focus is on sorting workers across industries or across heterogeneous firms within a particular industry. The earliest papers in this literature took the former approach. Grossman and Maggi (2000) consider an economy in which workers differ in human capital and countries differ in the distribution of human capital across their populations. They also assume that the technologies used to produce different goods vary in the manner in which workers with different talents interact. For some goods, workers with different skill levels are complementary – they each perform different tasks, and since each task is vital for the production of the good, the production process 'is only as strong as its weakest link'. In this case, production is said to be *supermodular*, and the level of output is roughly tied to the average productivity of the workers engaged in the production process. In contrast, other goods are produced using a technology in which the talents of workers are substitutable for each other. This implies that production will be roughly tied to the productivity of the most talented worker engaged in the production process. In this latter case, production is said to be *submodular*.[30]

When both types of goods are produced, efficiency dictates that high productivity workers work together in the supermodular sector whereas workers should be cross matched in the submodular sector (so that no high productivity worker's talent will be wasted). Although they generate several interesting results, the one that we will highlight is that in a two good world the country with the *more diverse* talent base will have a comparative advantage in the good that is characterized by cross matching. The logic is based on the fact that the country with the more diverse talent base has more workers with extreme productivity measures, and their low productivity workers can be accommodated for by pairing them in the submodular sector with those workers with extremely high productivity measures. Moreover, since trade expands that sector, it is the workers with extreme productivity measures, those at the top and bottom of the wage distribution, that gain from trade while those with moderate productivity are harmed. These wage effects are unlike anything that arises in traditional trade models and are generated by the interaction of heterogeneity in worker ability and differences in the substitutability of worker talents across industries.[31]

Grossman and Maggi close their paper by considering what happens if talent is imperfectly observable, and they show that even though this leads to imperfect matching, their results with respect to comparative advantage are strengthened. Grossman (2004) picks up on this theme by considering a model in which worker ability is private information that can be observed to varying degrees based on the type of production process the worker is engaged in. Some production processes, such as large scale manufacturing, require work in teams, which makes it difficult to ascertain the skill level of each particular team member. In addition, in such sectors compensation will be tied to team production, which makes that type of employment unattractive to highly skilled workers. In contrast, there are other production processes in which individual contributions play a key role. Examples of this can be found in the service sector, where attorneys, financial advisors and doctors often work independently, or in high tech industries where the productivities of individual engineers and managers are often easy to observe. Such sectors will be attractive to highly skilled workers since they will not only be compensated for their talents, but they will be able to signal their productivity to outsiders and thereby increase their bargaining power. Grossman shows that when countries differ in their distributions of talents across workers, it is the country with the more heterogeneous workforce that will have a comparative advantage in the sector in which individual productivity is easier to discern. Moreover, since trade expands that sector, trade will tend to exacerbate inequality by pushing up the incomes of the country's most talented workers.

In Grossman and Maggi (2000) and Grossman (2004), workers differ in one attribute and, while countries have identical aggregate endowments of labour, they differ in their distribution of talent. Ohnsorge and Trefler (2007) develop a framework that is similar in that workers are heterogeneous in the talents that they offer, but they make an attempt to place the analysis firmly in a traditional trade setting by adopting many of the features of the HOS model. In particular, they assume that countries face identical technologies but differ in factor endowments and that all factors are perfectly mobile across sectors. With respect to workers, it is now assumed that each one has two attributes that are important for production: problem solving and communications skills. Industries differ in their skills requirements and workers sort across industries based on their comparative advantage – that is, they take the job that pays them the most for their particular bundle of skills. Ohnsorge and Trefler show that this model is much more powerful than either the HOS or Ricardo–Viner model, providing much sharper predictions about trade patterns, the demand for protection and the link between trade and the distribution of income. One key result is that the correlation between the workers' two attributes plays a critical role in shaping a country's comparative advantage and determining how trade affects income inequality within a country. Thus, just as in Grossman and Maggi (2000) and Grossman (2004), higher moments of the distribution of worker skills are critical for understanding the effects of trade.[32]

While these papers highlight the importance of labour market heterogeneity for understanding trade issues, they all continue to assume perfectly flexible wages and full employment. They are also consistent with 'old trade theory' in that they assume that firms within an industry are identical. In Section 4 we highlighted two papers that extend new trade models to allow for labour market imperfections, Egger and Kreickmeier (2008a) and Helpman, Itskhoki and Redding (2009), and discussed the new insights they offer in terms of trade and income inequality within industries. Yet, in both of these papers, workers are ex ante identical. Matters get far more complicated and interesting when heterogeneous firms within the same industry face a workforce with diversity in skills and/or ability. When there is heterogeneity on both sides of the labour market one must be concerned about the types of matches that are generated – should the most productive workers be matched with the most efficient firms? Or, would it be more efficient to pair together low productivity workers and high productivity firms? This is an issue that has been studied in labour economics (where it is known as an assignment problem), the literature on the economics of marriage (Becker, 1973) and search theory (Shimer and Smith, 2000; Legros and Newman, 2002). If production is supermodular, then positive assortative matching, in which good workers are paired with good firms, is optimal.

One paper that includes both worker and firm heterogeneity as well as imperfect labour markets is Davidson, Matusz and Shevchenko (2008a). In their model, workers manage the production process and differ in skill; firms that produce homogeneous goods differ in the technologies that they adopt; and labour markets are imperfect in that it takes time and effort for unemployed workers and firms with vacancies to find each other.[33] Firms can elect to use a modern production process, but this requires them to recruit a highly skilled manager and pay a high wage. Alternatively, they can use a basic production process which can be managed by any worker and pay a lower managerial wage. In equilibrium, firms of both types coexist and earn the same profits. Those firms that use the modern technology have a harder time filling their managerial vacancy and must pay a higher wage rate, but, once the vacancy is filled, they produce output at a higher rate.

Given the assumptions made about the production process, positive assortative matching would be efficient – that is, highly skilled managers *should* be paired with those firms that adopt the modern technology. However, with search required to find a job, some high skilled workers may wind up employed by low tech firms. This occurs if the gap in the revenues earned by the two types of firms is not too large. If this is the case, then the compensation that the two types of firms can offer high skilled workers will be sufficiently close and it will be optimal for high skilled workers to accept the first job that they are offered. Thus, some high skilled workers will be underemployed in equilibrium.

Davidson, Matusz and Shevchenko focus on how international trade affects the degree of underemployment. As in any model of trade with heterogeneous firms, it is those firms that adopt the modern technology (the most productive firms) that have the greatest access to international markets. If these firms compete in an export oriented market, then as trade costs fall the most productive firms will benefit relatively more with even greater access to foreign markets. This will widen the gap between the revenues earned by the two types of firms and make it *more difficult* for low tech firms to attract high skilled workers. As a result, globalization increases the degree of positive assortative matching in an export oriented market. This can be viewed as another source of gains from trade.

In contrast, if the good is sold in an import competing industry, globalization decreases the degree of positive assortative matching. In this case, as trade costs fall import penetration rises, pushing down the (common) domestic price for the good. Since this price is applied to a larger stock of output for high tech firms, they are harmed more by this change than their low tech counterparts. As a result, the gap in revenues earned by the two types of firms shrinks, making it *easier* for low tech firms to attract high skilled workers. The increase in underemployment that follows can be viewed as another cost of globalization.

The Davidson, Matusz and Shevchenko model yields sharp predictions about how openness should affect the types of worker firm matches that we observe. It also yields interesting predictions about the impact of openness on the wage distribution within an industry and on productivity at the firm and industry levels. In a similar vein, the Grossman and Maggi (2000), Grossman (2000) and Ohnsorge and Trefler (2007) papers all yield predictions about the implications of worker heterogeneity for trade patterns and inequality. Testing such theories requires matched worker firm data sets that include a rich source of information about the characteristics of the workers that firms employ. Fortunately, over the past decade a number of such data sets have become available and this opens up exciting new possibilities in terms of empirical research on labour market adjustment to globalization. This is all new ground, since most of the empirical work on labour market adjustment to date remains rooted in the standard competitive model. The availability of these new data sets should make it possible to derive a new set of stylized facts about the impact of openness on the labour market experiences of workers. For example, we should be able to gain a better understanding of how trade and commercial policy affect job turnover. In addition, we should be able to obtain new insights about the incidence of worker dislocation, the manner in which openness affects the job search process, the pattern of worker turnover across industries, and the manner in which the gains and losses from freer trade are distributed across firms and their workers within industries. In other words, it should be possible to do for the labour market what has already been done for the product market. Of course, the development of such a literature requires models that both emphasize the labour market imperfections that lead to non-trivial spells of unemployment and recognize that there is a great deal of heterogeneity in the workforce in terms of skills, education, and experience. The models that we have highlighted in this final section indicate that just such a literature is well on its way.

Notes

* Michigan State University and University of Nottingham, GEP.
1. As Mussa (1993) states 'from the broad support often seen for protectionist policies, it is clear that such support does not come only from those who have a vested interest in such policies. Rather, it is based on a widespread and deep-seated feeling that opportunities for employing domestic resources to meet domestic needs should somehow be protected from foreign competition. Simply put, the issue is "jobs, jobs, jobs".' The common-sense perception is that if foreigners are allowed to supplant domestic producers of some product, then the domestic resources used in such production will become unemployed; or, more succinctly, 'jobs will be lost'. He then goes on to assert that this perception is far from the reality of trade. See note 9.
2. Murphy and Welch (1989) report that in 1986, college-educated men earned 70 percent more per week than those with only a high-school degree, up from a 32 percent differential in 1979. Bound and Johnson (1992) peg the increased differential between 1979 and 1988 at a smaller, though still substantial, 15 percentage points.
3. Samuelson's result is that free international mobility of goods is a perfect substitute for free international mobility of factors, leading to complete factor price equalization. Samuelson's interest was motivated by Ohlin's (1933) statement that free international mobility of goods was a partial substitute for free international factor mobility, leading to partial factor price equalization.
4. The assumption of a completely inelastic relative labour supply curve is shared by all participants in the trade-wages debate.
5. While the change in ω is qualitatively similar in both circumstances, the implication for the real unskilled wage is different. In both instances, an increase in ω corresponds to an increase in the real wage for skilled workers. The impact on the real wage for unskilled workers is ambiguous if the change is due to improved technology since better technology could permit firms to pay higher wages to both types of workers. There is no ambiguity when the change is due to immigration. Holding technology constant, firms can only pay a higher wage to skilled workers if they simultaneously pay a lower wage to unskilled workers.

6. We could have allowed the sector ranking of skill intensity change along with the relative wage. For example, we could allow sector one to be skill intensive at high values of ω with sector two being skill intensive at low values of ω. We could even allow the ranking to switch multiple times. What matters for the analysis is that the ranking is unique in a local sense, to be made explicit below.

7. The perfectly elastic portion of the relative demand curve corresponds to the diversification cone in factor space, with the edges of the diversification cone corresponding to the factor intensities of the two sectors when the relative wage is ω_0.

8. To carry this story a bit further, the fragment of production that is subject to offshoring may be more skill intensive than existing production in the host country. If this is the case, moving production of this fragment from the source country to the host country has the effect of increasing the relative demand for skilled labour in the source country as well as in the host country, thereby increasing the return to skill in both countries. Indeed, the increase in the skill premium has been widespread, encompassing both industrialized and developing economies alike.

9. See also Krugman (1993) who writes that 'it should be possible to emphasize to students that the level of employment is a macroeconomic issue, depending in the short run on aggregate demand and depending in the long run on the natural rate of unemployment, with microeconomic policies like tariffs having little net effect. Trade policy should be debated in terms of its impact on efficiency, not in terms of phony numbers about jobs created or lost'. Mussa (1993) concurs with this sentiment when critiquing the popular notion that 'jobs will be lost' due to trade by stating that 'economists are trained to recognize this fallacy. We understand that the effect of protectionist policy is not on the overall employment of domestic resources, but rather on the allocation of these resources across productive activities

10. Matusz's work was inspired by Ethier's (1982) analysis of dumping. In that partial-equilibrium framework, the constancy of the wage implied that workers were paid in excess of their marginal product during periods of low demand and the firm dumped. Fernandez (1992) is the only other paper of which we are aware that explicitly uses the implicit contracts framework in international trade. Janeba (2009) implicitly uses implicit contracts.

11. See Baily (1974), Gordon (1974), and Azariadis (1975) for the foundation papers of implicit contract theory.

12. There are several one sector models of trade and unemployment. These models assume that firms produce differentiated goods in a monopolistically competitive market. Matusz (1996, 1998) and Hoon (2000, 2001a,b) assume that unemployment results from an efficiency-wage constraint. Opening to trade increases the real wage via the increased variety of available goods. The higher real wage relaxes the efficiency-wage constraint and reduces steady-state unemployment. Felbermayr, Prat and Schmerer (2008) merge a model of search-generated unemployment with a Melitz (2003) model of heterogeneous firms. They also find that openness reduces steady-state unemployment if productivity increases due to the shift toward higher-productivity firms.

13. Remember that there are other conditions (e.g., zero profit conditions) in the background, so this sketch is somewhat incomplete.

14. Dutt, Mitra and Ranjan (2009) use cross-country data on unemployment and trade policy to tease out the effect that openness has on steady-state unemployment.

Based on a panel study, they conclude that greater openness leads to more unemployment in the short run, but a reduction in steady-state unemployment. Similar results are offered by Felbermayr, Prat and Schmerer (2009) who use panel data on 20 OECD countries to provide evidence that increased openness leads to a reduction in an economy's unemployment rate. In contrast, Janiak (2007) sets up a theoretical model in the spirit of Melitz, whereby greater openness shifts resources away from the smallest, least productive firms (leading to job destruction) towards the largest, most productive firms (creating jobs). In the context of his model, Janiak shows that job destruction outweighs job creation, thereby increasing steady-state unemployment. He then takes the model to the data, investigating the employment effects of U.S. trade policy across 418 sectors from 1974 to 1978. He finds that the evidence supports the theoretical prediction that greater exposure to trade increases both job creation and job destruction, with the increase in job destruction dominating.

15. The analysis that follows in this paragraph is based on Davidson, Martin and Matusz (1988) and Hosios (1990).

16. It is worth noting that the two papers listed in footnote 15 differ in their emphasis. Davidson, Martin and Matusz (1988) emphasize that the Stolper–Samuelson Theorem holds only if bargaining between workers and employers leads to an efficient outcome. Hosios (1990) assumes that bargaining is efficient and then stresses that the Stolper–Samuelson Theorem holds for searching factors.

17. Magee, Davidson and Matusz (2005) find empirical support for these relationships.

18. The missing link between 'old trade theory' and NNTT is simply 'new trade theory' in which homogeneous firms operate under increasing returns to scale in imperfectly competitive markets. The added 'newness' of NNTT is therefore the element of firm heterogeneity.

19. She identifies these workers by industry affiliation, arguing that the displacement is more likely to be due to international competition if the industry is subject to a high degree of import penetration compared with industries that are not subject to the same degree of penetration.

20. Kletzer estimates that one quarter of those re-employed take a pay cut in excess of 30 percent, while more than one third earn at least as much as they did prior to being displaced.

21. There are a number of papers that explore the policy implications of adjustment costs without actually trying to quantify such costs. See Lapan (1976), Karp and Paul (1994, 1998) and Gaisford and Leger (2000).

22. Trefler argues the appropriateness of this comparison period on several counts, including similarity of the business cycles between the pre- and post-CUFSTA periods.

23. Trefler undertakes a parallel analysis in which the dependent variable is observed at the plant level.

24. Trefler found no statistically significant productivity effect of U.S. tariff concessions at the industry level, but there were significantly positive gains at the plant level. He argues that U.S. tariff concessions drew new plants in, and that productivity is low for young plants. The industry average incorporates this low productivity.

25. This methodology is similar to that used by Winters and Takacs (1991) in their study of the British footwear industry. The authors of that study collected data on job turnover in that industry in order to measure adjustment costs due to liberalization of that sector. They essentially assume that a pool of unemployment is generated at

the moment of liberalization, and that this pool is drawn down as additional workers leave the industry for retirement or to obtain jobs in other sectors. Davidson and Matusz (2004c) take the analysis further by considering equilibrium unemployment, training costs, and by incorporating a second sector, thereby capturing important general equilibrium effects.

26. See Artuç, Chaudhri and McLaren (2008a) for simulation results from this model.
27. Note that the total cost of moving from sector i to sector j is then $\epsilon_{it} - \epsilon_{jt} - c$.
28. The range of results is generated by assuming different parameter values for the discount rate.
29. However, there are signs that these models are making a comeback, with some arguing that new results, when interpreted properly, emerge naturally from these frameworks. See, for example, Feenstra (2010).
30. Grossman and Maggi point to any complicated manufacturing process, such as O-ring production, as a prime example of supermodularity, because failure at any stage of the production process destroys the value of the good. Their motivating example of submodularity is software programming, since it only takes a breakthrough by one of the engineers working on a project to achieve success.
31. The idea that production in teams is important and that trade can have an important impact on the types of teams that form (both domestically and across borders) can also be found in Antras, Garicano and Rossi-Hansberg (2006), Kremer and Maskin (2006) and Sly (2009).
32. See also Costinot (2009b) and Costinot and Vogel (2009), two important papers that highlight the role of heterogeneity for trade issues. Costinot's framework is quite general, including the Ohnsorge and Trefler (2007) model of worker heterogeneity and the Melitz (2003) model of firm heterogeneity as special cases, and provides a new theory of comparative advantage based on a form of complementarity 'log-supermodularity.' While the main goal of Costinot (2009b) is to derive a new theory of comparative advantage, Costinot and Vogel (2009) show how comparative statics can be carried out in such a setting and derive new predictions about the impact of trade on inequality when workers differ in skills. Both papers assume competitive labour markets.
33. The underlying structure of their labour market is based on Albrecht and Vroman (2002).

References

Agell, J. and P. Lundborg (1995). Fair wages in the open economy. *Economica*, 62: 325–51.
Albrecht, J. and S. Vroman (2002). A matching model with endogenous skill requirements. *International Economics Review*, 43(1): 282–305.
Altenberg, L. and A. Brenken (2008). Effort, trade and unemployment. *Canadian Journal of Economics*, 41(3): 864–93.
Antras, P., L. Garicano, and E. Rossi-Hansberg (2006). Offshoring in a knowledge economy. *Quarterly Journal of Economics*, 121: 31–77.
Artuç, E., S. Chaudhuri, and J. McLaren (2007). Trade shocks and labor adjustment: A structural empirical approach. NBER Working Paper # 13465.
—— (2008). Delay and dynamics in labor market adjustment: Simulation results. *Journal of International Economics*, 75(1): 1–13.
Azariadis, C. (1975). Implicit contracts and underemployment equilibria. *Journal of Political Economy*, 83(6): 1183–1202.

Baily, M. (1974). Wage and employment under uncertain demand. *Review of Economic Studies*, 41: 37–50.

Baldwin, R., J. Mutti, and D. Richardson (1980). Welfare effects on the United States of a significant multilateral tariff reduction. *Journal of International Economics*, 10(3): 405–23.

Becker, G. (1973). A theory of marriage: Part I. *Journal of Political Economy*, 81(4): 813–46.

Bound, J. and G. Johnson (1992). Changes in the structure of wages in the 1980s: An evaluation of alternative explanations. *The American Economic Review*, 82(3): 371–92.

Bradford, S. (2006). Protection and unemployment. *Journal of International Economics*, 69(2): 257–71.

Brecher, R. (1974a). Minimum wage rates and the pure theory of international trade. *Quarterly Journal of Economics*, 88(1): 98–116.

—— (1974b). Optimal commercial policy for a minimum-wage economy. *Journal of International Economics*, 4(2): 139–49.

—— (1992). An efficiency wage model with explicit monitoring: Unemployment and welfare in an open economy. *Journal of International Economics*, 32(1–2): 179–91.

Brecher, R. and E. Choudhri (1994). Pareto gains from trade, reconsidered: Compensating for jobs lost. *Journal of International Economics*, 36(3–4): 223–38.

Cameron, S., S. Chaudhuri, and J. McLaren (2007). Trade shocks and labor adjustment: Theory. NBER Working Paper # 13463.

Carter, T. (1999). Illegal immigration in an efficiency wage model. *Journal of International Economics*, 49(2): 385–401.

Chaudhuri, S. and J. McLaren (2007). Some simple analytics of trade and labor mobility. NBER Working Paper # 13464.

Chin, J. (1998). Rural-urban wage differentials, unemployment, and efficiency wages: An open economy policy analysis. *Southern Economic Journal*, 65(2): 294–307.

Clemenz, G. (1995). Adverse selection in labor markets and international trade. *Scandinavian Journal of Economics*, 97(1): 73–88.

Copeland, B. (1989). Efficiency wages in a Ricardian model of international trade. *Journal of International Economics*, 27(3–4): 221–44.

Costinot, A. (2009a). Jobs, jobs, jobs: A 'new' perspective on protectionism. *Journal of the European Economic Association*, 7(5): 1–31.

—— (2009b). An elementary theory of comparative advantage. *Econometrica*, 77(4): 1165–92.

Costinot, A. and J. Vogel (2009). Matching and inequality in the world economy. MIT working paper.

Das, S. (2006). Incentive pay, worker effort and trade protection. *Review of International Economics*, 4(2): 141–51.

Davidson, C., L. Martin, and S. Matusz (1987). Search, unemployment and the production of jobs. *Economic Journal*, 97(388): 857–76.

—— (1988). The structure of simple general equilibrium models with frictional unemployment. *Journal of Political Economy*, 96(6): 1267–93.

—— (1991). Multiple free trade equilibria in micro models of unemployment. *Journal of International Economics*, 31(1–2): 157–69.

—— (1999). Trade and search generated unemployment. *Journal of International Economics*, 48(2): 271–99.

Davidson, C. and S. Matusz (2000). Globalization and labour-market adjustment: How fast and at what cost? *Oxford Review of Economic Policy*, 16(3): 42–56.

—— (2004a). *International Trade and Labor Markets: Theory, Evidence and Policy Implications*. Kalamazoo, MI: W.E. Upjohn Institute.

——(2004b). An overlapping generations model of escape clause protection. *Review of International Economics*, 12(5): 749–68.

——(2004c). Should policy makers be concerned about adjustments costs? In *The Political Economy of Trade, Aid and Foreign Investment Policies* (D. Mitra and A. Panagariya, eds), Elsevier, Springer-Verlag and Edward Elgar: 31–68.

——(2005). Trade and turnover: Theory and evidence. *Review of International Economics*, 13(5): 861–80.

——(2006a). Trade liberalization and compensation. *International Economic Review*, 47(3): 723–47.

——(2006b). Long run lunacy, short run sanity: A simple model of trade with labor market turnover. *Review of International Economics*, 14(2): 261–76.

Davidson, C., S. Matusz, and A. Shevchenko (2008a). Globalization and firm level adjustment with imperfect labor markets. *Journal of International Economics*, 75(2): 295–309.

——(2008b). Outsourcing Peter to pay Paul: High-skill expectations and low-skill wages with imperfect labor markets. *Macroeconomic Dynamics*, 12(4): 463–79.

Davis, D. (1998). Does European unemployment prop up American wages? National labor markets and global trade. *American Economic Review*, 88(3): 478–94.

Davis, D. and J. Harrigan (2007). Good jobs, bad jobs and trade liberalization. Columbia University Working Paper.

Davis, S., J. Haltiwanger, and S. Schuh (1996). *Job Creation and Job Destruction*. Cambridge, MA: MIT Press.

Dixit, A. and V. Norman (1980). *Theory of International Trade*. London: Cambridge University Press.

Dutt, P., D. Mitra, and P. Ranjan (2009). International trade and unemployment: Theory and cross-national evidence. *Journal of International Economics*, 78(1): 32–44.

Egger, H. and U. Kreickemeier (2008a). Fairness, Trade, and Inequality. CESifo Working Paper 2344.

——(2008b). International fragmentation: Boon or bane for domestic employment. *European Economic Review*, 52(1): 116–32.

——(2009). Firm heterogeneity and the labor market effects of trade liberalization. *International Economic Review*, 50(1): 187–216.

Ethier, W. (1982). Dumping. *Journal of Political Economy*, 90(3): 487–506.

Feenstra, R. (2010). *Offshoring in the Global Economy: Microeconomic Structure and Macroeconomic Implications*. Cambridge: MIT Press.

Feenstra, R. and G. Hanson (1996). Globalization, outsourcing and wage inequality. *American Economic Review*, 86(2): 240–45.

——(1999). The impact of outsourcing and high-technology capital on wages: Estimates for the United States, 1979–1990. *Quarterly Journal of Economics*, 114(3): 907–40.

Felbermayr, G., J Prat, and H. Schmerer (2008). Globalization and labor market outcomes: Wage bargaining, search frictions and firm heterogeneity. IZA Discussion Paper 3363.

——(2009). Trade and unemployment: What do the data say? IZA Discussion Paper 4184.

Fernandez, R. (1992). Terms-of-trade uncertainty, incomplete markets and unemployment. *International Economic Review*, 33(4): 881–94.

Gaisford, J. and L. Leger (2000). Terms-of-trade shocks, labor-market adjustment and safeguard measures. *Review of International Economics*, 8: 100–12.

Gordon, D. (1974). A neo-classical theory of Keynesian unemployment. *Economic Inquiry*, 12: 431–59.

Grossman, G. (2004). The distribution of talent and the pattern and consequences of international Trade. *Journal of Political Economy,* 112(1): 209–39.

Grossman, G. and G. Maggi (2000). Diversity and trade. *American Economic Review,* 90(5): 1255–75.

Helpman, E. and O. Itskhoki (2009). Labor market rigidities, trade and unemployment. Harvard University Working Paper.

Helpman, E., O. Itskhoki and S. Redding (2009). Inequality and unemployment in a global economy. Harvard University working paper.

Hoon, H. (2000). *Trade, Jobs and Wages.* Northampton, MA: Edward Elgar Ltd.

—— (2001a). Adjustment of wages and equilibrium unemployment in a Ricardian global economy. *Journal of International Economics,* 54: 193–209.

—— (2001b). General-equilibrium implications of international product-market competition for jobs and wages. *Oxford Economic Papers,* 53: 138–56.

Hosios, A. (1990). Factor market search and the structure of simple general equilibrium models. *Journal of Political Economy,* 98(2): 325–5l.

Jacobson, L., R. LaLonde, and D. Sullivan (1993a). Earnings losses of displaced workers. *American Economic Review,* 83(4): 685–709.

—— (1993b). *The Costs of Worker Dislocation.* Kalamazoo, MI: W.E. Upjohn Institute for Employment Research.

Janeba, E. (1999). Exports, unemployment, and the welfare state. *Canadian Journal of Economics,* 42(3): 930–55.

Janiak, A. (2007). Does trade liberalization lead to unemployment: Theory and some evidence. ECARES, Universite Libre de Bruxelles Working Paper.

Johnson, G. and F. Stafford (1999). The labor market implications of international trade. In *Handbook of Labor Economics* (O. Ashenfelter and D. Card, eds.). Elsevier 1(3): 2215–88.

Karp, L. and T. Paul (1994). Phasing in and phasing out protectionism with costly adjustment of labour. *Economic Journal,* 104: 1379–92.

—— (1998). Labor adjustment and gradual reform: When is commitment important? *Journal of International Economics,* 46: 333–62.

Kletzer, L. (2001). *Job Loss from Imports: Measuring the Costs.* Washington D.C.: Peterson Institute for International Economics.

Kreickmeier, U. and D. Nelson (2006). Fair wages, unemployment and technological change in a global economy. *Journal of International Economics,* 70(2): 451–69.

Kremer, M. and E. Maskin (2006). Globalization and inequality. Harvard University Working Paper.

Krugman, P. (1993). What do undergraduates need to know about trade? *American Economic Review,* 83(2): 23–26.

Lapan, H. (1976). International trade, factor market distortions, and the optimal dynamic subsidy. *American Economic Review,* 66: 335–46.

Leamer, E. and J. Levinsohn (1995). International trade theory: The evidence. In *Handbook of International Economics,* Vol. 3 (G. Grossman and K. Rogoff, eds.). Amsterdam, Elsevier.

Legros, P. and A. Newman (2002). Monotone matching in perfect and imperfect worlds. *Review of Economic Studies,* 69(4): 925–42.

Magee, C., C. Davidson and S. Matusz (2005). Trade, turnover, and tithing. *Journal of International Economics,* 66(1): 157–76.

Magee, S. (1972). The welfare effects of restriction on US trade. *Brookings Papers on Economic Activity,* 3: 645–701.

Matusz, S. (1985). The Heckscher–Ohlin–Samuelson model with implicit contracts. *Quarterly Journal of Economics,* 100(4): 1313–29.

—— (1986). Implicit contracts, unemployment and international trade. *Economic Journal*, 96(382): 307–22.

—— (1994). International trade policy in a model of unemployment and wage differentials. *Canadian Journal of Economics*, 27(4): 939–49.

—— (1996). International trade, the division of labor, and unemployment. *International Economic Review*, 37(1): 71–84.

—— (1998). Calibrating the employment effects of trade. *Review of International Economics*, 6(4): 592–603.

Melitz, M. (2003). The impact of trade on intra-industry reallocations and aggregate industry productivity. *Econometrica*, 71: 1695–1725.

Moore, M. and P. Ranjan (2005). Globalisation and skill-biased technological change: Implications for unemployment and wage inequality. *Economic Journal*, 115(503): 391–422.

Murphy, K. and F. Welch (1989). Wage premiums for college graduates: recent growth and possible explanations. *Educational Researcher*, 18(4): 17–26.

Mussa, M. (1993). Making the practical case for freer trade. *American Economic Review*, 83(2): 372–76.

Ohlin, B. (1933). *Interregional and International Trade*. Cambridge, MA: Harvard University Press.

Ohnsorge, F. and D. Trefler (2007). Sorting it out: International trade with heterogeneous workers. *Journal of Political Economy*, 115(5): 868–92.

Samuelson, P. (1948). International trade and the equalization of factor prices. *Economic Journal*, 58(230): 163–84.

—— (1949). International factor-price equalization once again. *Economic Journal*, 59(234): 181–97.

Shimer, R. and L. Smith (2000). Assortative matching and search. *Econometrica*, 68: 343–70.

Sly, N. (2009). Labor matching behavior in open economies and trade adjustment. University of Oregon Working Paper.

Slaughter, M. (1999). Globalization and wages: A tale of two perspectives. *World Economy*, 22: 609–29.

Trefler, D. (2004). The long and short of the Canada–US Free Trade Agreement. *American Economic Review*, 94(4): 870–95.

Winters, A. and W. Tackas (1991). Labour adjustment costs and British footwear protection. *Oxford Economic Papers*, 43: 479–501.

15
Trade and the Environment
*Brian R. Copeland**

1 Introduction

During the last few decades there has been growing recognition and concern about the effects of the economy on the natural environment. There has also been a significant increase in the integration of the international economy. As the international trade regime has grown in complexity and visibility via the evolution of the General Agreement on Tariffs and Trade (GATT) into the World Trade Organization (WTO) and a wave of bilateral and regional free trade agreements, the interaction between globalization and the environment has become an important issue on the policy agenda.

Economic research on trade and the environment has its roots in some important work in the 1970s, such as Baumol (1971), Walter (1973), Markusen (1975), Pethig (1976), Siebert (1977), and others,[1] – and there has been a resurgence of work during the last two decades. This chapter is not a comprehensive overview of all that work,[2] but rather is meant to serve as an introduction to the literature by focusing on some of the key questions that have driven work in the area and the analytical frameworks that have been used to tackle these questions.

One question underlying much work in the area is whether or not globalization is bad for the environment. After setting up a simple general equilibrium trade model in section 2 of the chapter, section 3 considers both theoretical and empirical work on the overall effects of trade on the environment. Section 4 focuses on the pollution haven hypothesis. This is concerned with both the incidence and level of environmental degradation. The issue is whether trade liberalization causes polluting industry to shift systematically to developing countries with relatively weak environmental policy. Following Copeland and Taylor (2004), I distinguish between a pollution haven *effect*, which is the hypothesis that tightening up environmental policy reduces international competitiveness in the affected industry; and the stronger pollution haven

423

hypothesis, which is that the effects of pollution policy on competitiveness are strong enough to determine trade patterns. At this point it is important to distinguish between environmental problems generated by production from those generated by consumption, since the effects of policy on competitiveness can be very different depending on the type of pollution. Section 5 considers the interaction between trade liberalization and environmental capital. Much of the literature treats pollution as something that harms consumers but not producers. However it is clear from examples such as the effects of pollution on human health, renewable resource depletion, soil erosion, and climate change that the productivity effects of pollution and the stock of a country's 'environmental capital' are important for well-being.

Section 6 considers the effects of environmental problems on trade policy – covering issues such as whether standard results on trade policy are affected by the presence of environmental problems and the extent to which the absence of efficient environmental policy creates second-best arguments for trade protection. In section 7, I turn to the effects of trade liberalization on environmental policy. A major concern has been that trade liberalization might make governments reluctant to impose sufficiently stringent environmental policy in industries exposed to international competition, or that the elimination of trade barriers might create a 'race to the bottom' in environmental policy, with each jurisdiction trying, with weaker policy than their rivals, to attract polluting firms. After finding in section 7 that there is some theoretical support for the concern that trade liberalization may cause governments to manipulate policy for competitiveness purposes, in section 8, I review the implications for the design of trade agreements – focusing on issues such as whether environmental policy should be harmonized and whether the scope of trade agreements should be broadened to include environmental policy. Section 9 considers the interaction between trade, environmental policy and transboundary pollution. Section 10 concludes with a brief speculation concerning directions for future work.

2   Incorporating environmental constraints into a trade model

Much of the literature on trade and the environment uses generalizations of standard competitive trade models, such as the Heckscher–Ohlin, Specific Factors or Ricardian models. I will use such a model in much of what follows. Models with strategic interaction and firm level market power have also been used to investigate policy questions; and a relatively smaller branch of the literature has used a monopolistic competition and/or economic geography framework to investigate questions of both the pattern of trade and policy. These will be discussed later in the chapter.

2.1 Technology

The following model is drawn from Copeland and Taylor (2003).[3] For clarity and simplicity, I assume that pollution is generated during production but not consumption (consumption-generated pollution will be considered later). Pollution is assumed to harm consumers but not other producers, and it does not spill over international borders.

Let there be two goods, Y_1 and Y_2, and let $T(v, z)$ be a two-dimensional constant returns to scale convex production possibility set where v is a vector of primary factors and z is a given level of environmental services. That is, T is the set of all feasible combinations of Y_1 and Y_2 given the technology, resource, and environmental constraints. For many applications, we can think of z as a fixed level of pollution emissions. In some applications, z is a vector (see e.g., Copeland, 1994), but for simplicity I treat z as a scalar here (as does most of the literature). Although I am treating z as exogenous at this point, I will show how to treat it as endogenous below. Assume that good 1 pollutes during production and that good 2 does not pollute.[4] Good 2 is the numeraire; the price of good 1 is denoted by p.

As is standard in the trade literature, it is convenient to represent the production side of the economy with the national income function G, which is defined as:

$$G(p, v, z) = \max_{\{y_1, y_2\}} \{py_1 + y_2 : (y_1, y_2) \in T(v, z)\}.$$

One can show that the first-order conditions for the solution of this problem are the same as the conditions for competitive equilibrium in the economy if environmental policy is set efficiently such as via tradable permits or emission taxes.[5] Because it is an optimum value function, the national income function has a number of useful properties. Outputs can be obtained by differentiating with respect to goods prices:

$$y_i = \frac{\partial G}{\partial p_i}.$$

The assumption that good 1 pollutes means that output of sector 1 expands as access to environmental services is increased. That is, we have:

$$G_{pz} = \frac{\partial y_1}{\partial z} \geq 0. \tag{1}$$

Factor prices can be recovered by differentiating G with respect to the relevant endowment. For example if we let $v = (K, L)$ so that there are two primary factors [capital (K) and labour (L)] then we have

$$w = \frac{\partial G}{\partial L} \quad \text{and} \quad r = \frac{\partial G}{\partial K}$$

The shadow price of emissions (denoted by τ) is obtained by differentiating G with respect to z:

$$\tau = \frac{\partial G(p, v, z)}{\partial z}. \tag{2}$$

If a tradable permit system is used (and permits are freely tradable across all polluting sources in the domestic economy), then τ is the equilibrium permit price.

Equation (2) can be interpreted as a general-equilibrium marginal abatement cost curve. That is, if we think of reducing emissions by a unit, then the (monetary) cost to the economy is given by $\partial G/\partial z$. This takes into account the economy-wide adjustment to lower emission levels, including both increased use of abatement technology and adjustments in the relative production of clean and dirty goods.

The national income function also has a number of useful curvature properties: it is convex in goods prices; and (because we have assumed constant returns to scale) it is concave in factor endowments.[6]

The national income function as defined above treats emissions z as given, and so it is convenient for analyzing economy-wide emission quotas or cap and trade systems. To analyze pollution taxes, there are two possible approaches. One is to use the above framework and treat τ as the tax and assume it is fixed by the government. Then z is determined endogenously by (2). However, in many applications it is more convenient to use a different form of the national income function if the analysis focuses primarily on emission taxes. Define net revenue generated by the production sector for a given emission tax as $\tilde{G}$, where:

$$\tilde{G}(p, \tau, v) = \max_{\{y_1, y_2\}} \{py_1 + y_2 - \tau z : (y_1, y_2) \in T(v, z)\}. \tag{3}$$

This approach essentially treats emissions as a joint output with a negative price $(-\tau)$. $\tilde{G}$ has all the usual properties of a national income function discussed above; the difference is that it is a function of τ instead of z.[7] We can (as an application of Hotelling's Lemma) obtain the derived demand for emissions by differentiating $\tilde{G}$ with respect to τ:

$$z = -\frac{\partial \tilde{G}(p, \tau, v)}{\partial \tau}. \tag{4}$$

Because $\tilde{G}$ is convex in prices, the emission demand curve is downward-sloping.

Finally, note that G and $\tilde{G}$ are connected as follows. Let z_0 be the level of emissions that solves (3). Then we have:

$$G(p, v, z_0) = \tilde{G}(p, \tau, v) + \tau z_0.$$

That is, to obtain the full level of national income (including transfers to the government), we have to add emission tax revenue to $\tilde{G}$.

2.2 Consumers

Environmental quality is a public good – each unit of emissions is assumed to affect all consumers. I assume that consumers treat emissions from the rest of the economy as given when deciding on their consumption. For simplicity, I assume N identical consumers, and in most applications normalize N to 1. Consumers have a utility function of the following form:

$$U = u(y_1, y_2) - h(z), \tag{5}$$

where u is increasing, homothetic and concave; and h is increasing and convex. Homotheticity is a standard simplifying assumption in the trade literature. It allows us to write indirect utility as a function of real income; and it also allows us to focus on the role of regulation and relative production costs in determining trade patterns (because it implies that relative demands are independent of income). The strong separability between consumption and environmental damage is a simplifying assumption that ensures that relative demands are not influenced by environmental damage.

I will make use of the indirect utility and expenditure functions to represent preferences in much of what follows. Define *Real Income R* as

$$R = \frac{I}{\beta(p)},$$

where I is nominal income (GNP) and $\beta(p)$ is a price index implied by the utility function. Note that $\beta(p)$ is increasing in p. Then the indirect utility function implied by (5) can be written as

$$V(p, I, z) = v(R) - h(z), \tag{6}$$

where v is increasing and concave. The expenditure function implied by the utility function has the form

$$E(p, u, z) = \beta(p)\phi\left(u + h(z)\right),$$

where ϕ is increasing and convex.

2.3 Regulatory equilibrium

Equilibrium outcomes in this economy are critically dependent on environmental policy; hence, to proceed further we need to make some assumptions about the policy regime.

One approach is simply to assume that policy is set exogenously. This is useful in addressing issues such as the effects of environmental policy changes on welfare and trade flows, the effects of tighter environmental policy on competitiveness, and comparisons of different policy instruments. For many questions, however, it is essential to consider the endogenous response of environmental policy to other variables in the economy, such as the trade regime and real income. This because there is much evidence that environmental policy varies systematically across jurisdictions, especially in response to differences in real income and differences in the severity of environmental problems.[8]

A simple example illustrates the importance of the policy regime. Consider a trade liberalization that stimulates the polluting sector. If there is no environmental policy or an exogenous pollution tax, then the increase in polluting output will increase emissions. If instead there is an exogenous binding (and fully enforced) pollution quota then the increase in the output of the polluting sector will have no environmental effects (the shadow price of emissions will rise, but emission levels will not change). If there is a pollution tax or quota in place and the regulatory authorities increase the stringency of policy in response to increased pressure on the environment, then the effect of trade liberalization on the environment will depend on the strength of the policy response. That is, emissions could rise, fall or stay the same depending on the policy regime.

There have been three main approaches to modelling endogenous policy. One approach (more common in the context of renewable resources, and less common in dealing with emissions) is to focus on social norms or use a game-theoretic approach in which multiple polluters and victims interact and arrive at an outcome. Ostrom's (1990) work has influenced this approach and Coase (1960) bargaining could be thought of as another example. The other approaches assume that one or more levels of government set environmental policy. The benchmark case is where governments set optimal policy; the other modelling strategy is the political economy approach where governments respond to interest group pressures when setting policy.

Since it serves as a useful benchmark, I will focus mostly on the case where a government sets efficient policy. This is of interest for its own sake, but it is also important to understand before delving into the political economy literature because much of that literature builds on this – for example the Grossman-Helpman (1994) approach to lobbying has governments maximizing a weighted average of social welfare and campaign contributions.

A simple pollution demand and supply framework is a useful tool for thinking about most approaches to endogenous environmental policy.[9] The demand for emissions reflects demand by both producers and consumers for environmental services. This is a derived demand – if a producer wants to produce pulp and paper, then there is a flow of emissions and hence a derived demand for the right to pollute. Similarly, if we are modelling consumption-generated pollution, a consumer who drives a car has a derived demand for vehicle emissions. The demand for the right to pollute is essentially market-based just like any other demand curve – the demand shifts in and out as prices, incomes, technology and preferences change. The supply of environmental services, on the other hand, reflects the regulatory regime. It reflects the willingness of society or the regulator to allow emissions. The shape of this supply curve and its response to

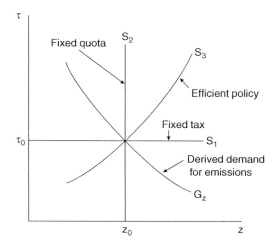

Figure 15.1 Pollution supply and demand: three scenarios.

exogenous changes (such as trade liberalization) is critically dependent on the regulatory regime.

Figure 15.1 illustrates this approach using the model of production-generated pollution developed above. The demand for emissions (labeled G_z) is given by equation (2) with goods prices and endowments given. The emission price is on the vertical axis and emissions are on the horizontal axis. The demand for emissions is downward-sloping: as the emission price falls, emissions rise, both because there is less abatement and because the polluting sector expands relative to the clean sector. Improvements in abatement technology would shift this demand curve in, increases in the price of polluting goods would shift it out, and increases in factors used intensively in the polluting sector would also shift it out.

Three different environmental service supply curves are illustrated in figure 15.1. S_1 is horizontal and represents a rigid emission tax. If the demand for emissions shifts out, then because the supply curve is flat, emissions rise. S_2 is vertical and represents a tradable emission permit scheme. In this case, an outward shift in the demand for emissions has no effect on pollution, but the permit price rises. S_3 is upward-sloping and represents the case of efficient policy (which will be developed below). If the demand for emissions shifts out, emission policy is tightened up. The supply curve slopes upward both because of increasing marginal damage from pollution and because of an income effect – increases in emissions generate increased income and because environmental quality is a normal good, the price needed to compensate for increased pollution rises as z rises. In the case of efficient policy represented by S_3, regulations could be implemented in various ways, including via emission taxes or tradable permits. The difference between S_3 and the other two supply curves illustrated here is that whatever regulatory instrument is used to implement policy, it is automatically adjusted in response to changes in the economy to ensure that policy remains efficient.

2.4   Efficient policy

Consider a small open economy with no distortions other than pollution externalities. The government chooses emissions to maximize indirect utility for a representative consumer subject to the economy's budget constraint:

$$\text{Max}_z\{V(p,I,z):I = G(p,v,z)/N\}.$$

The solution is

$$G_z(p,v,z) = -N\frac{V_z}{V_I}. \tag{7}$$

Note that $-V_z/V_I$ is the marginal rate of substitution between emissions and income for an individual consumer; in the environmental literature this is known as 'marginal damage'. Given the homotheticity assumption, it is a function of p, real income R, and pollution.[10] Thus we can define the marginal damage function, MD, as:

$$MD(p,R,z) \equiv -\frac{V_z}{V_I},$$

where

$$R = \frac{G(p,v,z)}{N\beta(p)}.$$

Then using (2) we can rewrite (7) as

$$\tau = N\cdot MD(p,R,z). \tag{8}$$

This is, of course, the Samuelson rule for optimal public goods provision: emissions are chosen so that the shadow price of emissions is equal to the sum of the marginal damages (or willingnesses to pay for emission reductions) across all affected individuals.

Equation (8) is the pollution supply curve for the case of efficient regulation. It is illustrated as S_3 in Figure 15.1. Equation (7) says that the derived demand for emissions should be set equal to the emission supply. It can also be interpreted more conventionally as the condition that the marginal abatement cost (G_z) be set equal to economy-wide marginal damage ($N\cdot MD$).

An alternative way to derive the efficient level of emissions is to use the expenditure function $E(p,u,z)$ implied by the utility function and choose z to maximize u subject to the budget constraint:

$$E(p,u,z) = \frac{G(p,v,z)}{N}. \tag{9}$$

The solution requires

$$N \cdot E_z(p,u,z) = G_z(p,v,z).\tag{10}$$

This is equivalent to (7). The term E_z is the compensated marginal damage curve; it measures the increase in income needed to keep utility constant when emissions rise by a unit.

I included 'N' in the above to highlight the role of the Samuelson rule here; however henceforth for simplicity, I will assume a representative consumer and set $N = 1$.

3 Effects of trade liberalization on pollution

One of the key questions in the trade and environmental literature is whether trade is bad for the environment. I will focus on effects of trade on the environment that are caused by induced changes in the environmental impact of production and consumption. There are also important direct effects of trade, notably due to emissions from transportation and the introduction of invasive species. On transportation, see OECD (2010) for an overview, and for recent contributions on trade and invasive species, see McAusland and Costello (2004) and Costello et al. (2007).

3.1 Effects of trade on the environment with optimal policy

How does trade affect pollution emissions when the government adjusts policy optimally in response to freer trade? Consider a small open economy with goods prices fixed in world markets.[11] We need to start by specifying the type of trade barriers initially in place. For expositional clarity, I assume that trade barriers take the form of binding quotas on trade.[12]

Let q be the domestic price of good 1 (recall that p is the world price) and assume for now that it is imported. Let M be a binding import quota. If emissions are initially determined optimally, they are determined by the following condition:

$$G_z(q,v,z) = \mathrm{MD}(q,R(q,v,z),z),\tag{11}$$

where MD is marginal damage and real income R consists of payments to factors of production plus quota rents, all deflated by the price index:

$$R = \frac{[G(q,v,z) + (q-p)M]}{\beta(q)}.\tag{12}$$

The domestic price of good 1 is determined by the condition that domestic demand equal domestic supply plus imports. To conserve space, I will simply assume that regularity conditions are imposed so that $dq/dM < 0$. That is, import

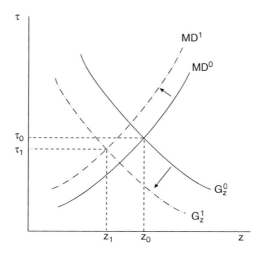

Figure 15.2   Effect of trade liberalization on pollution if the import-competing good pollutes.

quotas push the domestic price above the world price and relaxing the quota leads to a fall in the domestic price.

To determine the effects of trade liberalization on pollution totally differentiate (11) and solve for dz/dM:

$$\frac{dz}{dM} = \frac{\left[(G_{zq} - \mathrm{MD}_q)\dfrac{dq}{dM} - (q-p)\dfrac{\mathrm{MD}_R}{\beta(q)}\right]}{\Delta},$$

(13)

where $\Delta \equiv \mathrm{MD}_z + \mathrm{MD}_R R_z - G_{zz} > 0$. Referring to Figure 15.2, trade liberalization shifts both the demand for the right to pollute (the marginal benefit of polluting, G_z, changes), and the marginal damage curve. The shift in pollution demand is a pure substitution effect in production. Good 1 is pollution intensive ($G_{zq} > 0$), and since trade liberalization lowers its price, production declines. That is, the demand for the right to pollute shifts down and to the left. The marginal damage curve shifts via substitution and income effects. The income effect, the last term in (13), unambiguously reduces pollution. This is because trade liberalization raises real income and environmental quality is a normal good; hence MD shifts up and to the left via the income effect. To sign the substitution effect use (6) and Roy's identity to obtain:

$$\mathrm{MD}_q = \frac{\beta_q \mathrm{MD}}{\beta} > 0.$$

Hence the fall in the price of the polluting good tends to shift down the MD curve via the substitution effect. This is because consumer goods are getting cheaper relative to environmental quality and so consumers want to substitute away from environmental quality to consumption. This effect tends to increase pollution.

In summary, trade liberalization that lowers the price of the polluting good causes the marginal benefit of polluting to fall, and has an ambiguous effect on marginal damage. A sufficient condition for such a trade liberalization to reduce pollution is that the substitution effect in marginal damage be smaller than the income effect.[13] This is the case illustrated in Figure 15.2.

On the other hand, if the export sector pollutes, then trade liberalization will increase pollution unless the income effect in marginal damage is sufficiently strong. To see this, suppose good 1 is exported and that there is an export quota X in place. Then the domestic price of the export good is below the world price $(q < p)$ and quota rents are $(p - q)X$; and so (12) needs to be modified accordingly. Relaxing the export quota yields

$$\frac{dz}{dX} = \frac{\left[(G_{zq} - \mathrm{MD}_q) \dfrac{dq}{dX} - (p - q) \dfrac{\mathrm{MD}_R}{\beta(q)} \right]}{\Delta}.$$

In this case, we expect the domestic price q to rise towards the world price as exports are liberalized. This stimulates production in the polluting sector and causes pollution to rise via the substitution effect in production. However, both the increase in real income and the substitution effect in marginal damage cause the MD curve to shift up (which tends to reduce pollution). So whether or not pollution rises depends on whether the policy response is strong enough to offset the substitution effect on the production side. Copeland and Taylor (2003) show that a key parameter is the income elasticity of marginal damage. If the income elasticity of marginal damage is not too large (in their model, if it is less than 1), then trade liberalization will increase pollution in the country that exports the polluting good.

Overall, the effect of trade liberalization on the environment depends on the interaction between market driven forces and the policy response. With optimal policy, countries with a comparative advantage in polluting sectors will see an increase in pollution after trade liberalization unless the income effects influencing environmental policy are sufficiently strong; countries with a comparative advantage in clean sectors will generally experience a reduction in production-generated pollution.

3.2   Measuring the effects of trade on the environment

Measuring the effects of trade on the environment is challenging because it is difficult to isolate the effects of trade from other factors that determine environmental outcomes. One empirical approach is to use Computable General Equilibrium (CGE) models. These link up models of the economy with either emission coefficients or models of the natural environment and allow the researcher to run counterfactuals and thereby isolate the effects of trade. Two examples of this approach are Cole, Rayner and Bates (1998) who assess the effects of the Uruguay Round of trade liberalization on air pollution; and Perroni and Wigle (1994) who run various trade liberalization scenarios using a model benchmarked to 1986 data. Both find that the effect of trade liberalization on environmental outcomes is small. There is also an extensive literature using CGE models to assess the effects of agreements on climate change on trade and carbon leakage. See, for example, Bohringer and Rutherford (2002).

An alternative approach that can be used both for forecasting and to measure actual outcomes is to decompose the effects of trade on the environment into scale, composition and technique effects and then attempt to measure each of these component effects.[14] All else equal, pollution will rise if the economy is simply scaled up. Given the scale of production and emission intensities, pollution will fall if the composition of production and consumption shifts to activities that are less pollution intensive. And given the scale and composition of the economy, a fall in emission intensities will reduce pollution.[15]

To formalize this, I will focus on production-generated pollution.[16] Total pollution Z is the sum of emissions across sectors:

$$z = \sum_i e_i y_i,$$

where e_i is emissions per unit output in sector i. To decompose emissions into scale, technique and composition effects, we first need to define the scale S of the economy. This is a quantity index of output. Choose a base year vector of prices p^0; these will be held constant throughout any changes since their role is simply to weight outputs. Then, letting $S \equiv \sum_i p_i^0 y_i$, we have:

$$z = S \sum_i \tilde{e}_i \varphi_i$$

where $\tilde{e}_i \equiv e_i/p_i^0$ is emissions per unit value (at base prices) in sector i, and $\varphi_i \equiv p_i^0 y_i/S$ is the share of good i in the value of output at base prices. Taking logs and totally differentiating (keeping base prices constant) yields our decomposition:

$$\hat{z} = \hat{S} + \sum_i \theta_i \hat{e}_i + \sum_i \theta_i \hat{\varphi}_i,$$

where $\theta_i = z_i/z$ is the share of overall emissions generated by sector i, and where $\hat{z} \equiv dz/z$, etc. Any change in pollution can be decomposed into a sum of scale effects, weighted changes in emission intensities, and weighted changes in the composition of output. In our simple model, where sector 1 pollutes and sector 2 does not, we have

$$\hat{z} = \hat{S} + \hat{e}_1 + \hat{\varphi}_1.$$

Pollution rises if the scale of overall production rises, if emission intensity rises, and/or if the share of the polluting sector in overall output rises.

Trade liberalization will affect pollution via each of these effects. Trade liberalization will typically increase the scale of production. Emission intensities will change via imported capital equipment and knowledge, trade-induced factor price changes, and changes in abatement driven by regulatory changes or pressure from communities or consumers. Composition effects may raise or lower pollution depending on whether a country has a comparative advantage in clean or dirty industries.

These effects were estimated by Antweiler, Copeland and Taylor (2001) for sulfur dioxide pollution using an international panel of data on ambient pollution. They decompose composition effects into those driven by trade openness and those driven by changes in relative capital abundance. They do not have data on emission intensities and so use per capita income as a proxy for regulatory stringency. They find that increases in scale raise pollution; and that all else equal, increases in per capita income lower pollution (which they interpret as a technique effect).[17] The composition effect due to increases in capital abundance is positive and raises SO_2 pollution, while the effects of trade on composition vary across countries (as predicted by theory) and are small. Technique effects are found to be large relative to composition effects and for the average country in their sample, trade liberalization has a slight negative effect on SO_2 pollution. Cole and Elliott (2003) use emission data and apply this approach to four pollutants. They find results that are similar to those of Antweiler et al. for SO_2. However the net effect of scale and technique effects for nitrogen oxides (NO_X) and carbon dioxide (CO_2) were both positive, suggesting that pollution policy has not been as aggressive in targeting these pollutants as it has been for SO_2.[18] The estimated pure compositional effects of increased openness to trade for NO_X and BOD were very small. Frankel and Rose (2005) account for the endogeneity of trade and confirm the result that more open economies have lower SO_2 pollution (after controlling for per capita income, scale and other factors). Shen (2007) uses data on several pollutants for China and finds that the net effect of scale and technique on air pollution (SO_2 and dust) is positive, but negative for arsenic, cadmium and BOD. The composition effect due to increased openness to trade is positive for air pollution but negative for the other pollutants.

Levinson (2009) uses this decomposition approach to help understand the changes in air pollution from the U.S. manufacturing sector for the period 1987–2001. He has data on scale, overall pollution, and production shares at the four-digit level throughout the period; however data on emission intensities is available only for 1987 and so these are calculated as a residual using the decomposition identity. He finds that while the scale of manufacturing output increased by 24 percent, air pollution from manufacturing decreased by 25 percent over the period. Changes in technique (emission intensities) account for

78 percent of the fall in pollution over the period while changes in the composition of production account for 22 percent. His finding (using a very different methodology) of a large technique effect and relatively small composition effects is consistent with the estimates obtained by Antweiler et al. (2001).

4   Competitiveness and the pollution haven hypothesis

Perhaps the key empirical issue in the trade and environment literature has been the effects of domestic policy on international competitiveness of polluting industries. Much of the analysis and discussion of this issue has been driven by interest in the pollution haven hypothesis; however it is also important in the context of climate change, and it is a key underpinning of the political economy approach to trade policy.

The pollution haven hypothesis is that trade liberalization will cause polluting production to shift to countries with relatively weaker environmental regulation; and in most versions of this hypothesis, the weak-regulation countries are also low income countries. For the pollution haven hypothesis to be correct, two things are needed. First, tighter environmental regulation must reduce domestic competitiveness in polluting industries. I refer to this as the competitiveness hypothesis, and if it holds, then we will say that a pollution haven *effect* exists.[19] But this is not enough to ensure that trade liberalization will cause polluting industry to move to countries with weak environmental policy. A second condition is needed – weak environmental policy must also lead to a comparative advantage in polluting industry. Environmental policy must either be a key determinant of comparative advantage or else its stringency must be highly correlated with other factors that generated comparative advantage in polluting industries.

The literature in this area sometimes makes confusing reading because some papers treat the pollution haven hypothesis and competitiveness hypothesis as essentially the same issue. To see that they are different, consider the effects of country A tightening environmental policy. If the competitiveness hypothesis is correct, then at the margin we would expect to see some pollution intensive production shift out of country A. However, this does not imply that country A has a comparative disadvantage in polluting industries – it might just mean that its comparative advantage is not as strong as it was prior to the adjustment in pollution policy. Environmental policy is one of many factors determining costs and profitability. Even if at the margin, tighter environmental policy lowers competitiveness, that does not imply that it is the key determinant of production location.

Another way to think about the differences between the pollution haven hypothesis and the competitiveness hypothesis is to think of a model with many countries. Again suppose a country tightens up it environmental policy. Suppose that the competitiveness hypothesis holds and some pollution intensive production shifts out of the country. Where will that production move to? It should move to the country where overall net profitability is highest. If the pollution haven hypothesis is correct, this would be a country with weak environmental policy. But of course many other factors determine costs and profitability. The firm may instead choose to move to a country where environmental policy is more stringent because it is attracted by access to skilled labour, infrastructure, raw materials, proximity to customers and suppliers, and many other factors. Consequently, I will discuss the competitiveness hypothesis (or pollution haven effect) and the pollution haven hypothesis separately.

In the climate change literature, both the competitive hypothesis and pollution haven hypothesis figure prominently in the issue of what is in that context referred to as 'leakage' – the question is whether tightening regulations on carbon emissions will make domestic industry less competitive, and whether carbon intensive industry will shift to countries with weaker regulation.[20] Moreover, since carbon emissions are a global pollutant then if leakage is sufficiently strong, unilateral emission reductions by one country (or group of countries) need not guarantee an improvement in environmental quality if industry shifts to countries with higher emission intensities.

The theory behind the competitiveness hypothesis can be illustrated with a simple diagram. Figure 15.3 illustrates a partial-equilibrium model of an import competing industry that generates pollution during production. Domestic demand is D; initial domestic supply is S^0, and the world price is p. Initial imports are M^0. If domestic pollution regulation is tightened up, and if it raises domestic production costs, then the domestic supply curve shifts inward to S^1

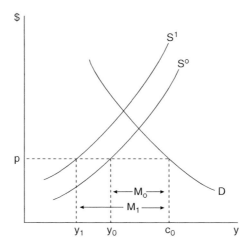

Figure 15.3   The pollution haven effect: tightening up environmental policy reduces competitiveness.

and imports rise. The key assumption needed for domestic output to fall is that environmental regulation raises costs in the polluting sector.[21] In our general-equilibrium model, the effect of reducing allowable emissions on output of the polluting good is given by equation (1):

$$-\frac{dy_1}{dz} = -G_{pz} \le 0,$$

and so output falls as regulation is tightened up. We could extend the model to include mobile capital, and it would predict that more stringent environmental policy would deter investment in the pollution intensive sector.[22]

The main alternative hypothesis (in the context of production-generated pollution) is the Porter Hypothesis (Porter and van de Linde, 1995), which proposes that pollution regulation may actually increase competitiveness in polluting sectors. Theoretical support for this hypothesis is weak, but there are some models that can generate this result.[23]

If pollution is generated by consumption, then there is no presumption that pollution regulation will reduce domestic competitiveness.[24] This is because regulations targeting consumption-generated pollution apply to all products consumed within a country, and hence apply to imported goods as well as both domestically produced goods. Again, this can be illustrated with a simple diagram (Figure 15.4). Suppose that pollution is generated only by consumption, and that the cost of complying with pollution regulation is c per unit of the good, and suppose this cost is the same for domestic and foreign producers. Then imposing the regulation shifts up the price of imports to $p + c$, and the domestic supply shifts up vertically by c. Imports fall, but there is no change in

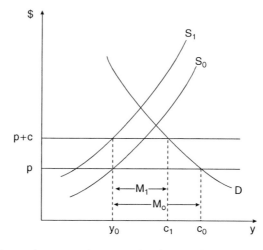

Figure 15.4   More stringent environmental policy need not reduce competitiveness when pollution is generated during consumption.

domestic output; hence, tighter policy has not reduced domestic competitiveness. Moreover, if domestic compliance costs are lower than foreign compliance costs, more stringent regulation could increase domestic competitiveness.

There has been extensive empirical work on the competitiveness hypothesis. Most of this work focuses on the manufacturing sector, and I am not aware of studies that carefully distinguish between production and consumption-generated pollution; in practice most studies focus on production-generated pollution from manufacturing. This work has been reviewed by myself and others elsewhere – (Copeland and Taylor, 2004, Brunnermeier and Levinson, 2004), and so I will not undertake a detailed review here. Early work using cross-sectional data found little or no evidence that environmental policy had a significant effect on trade and investment flows; see Jaffe et al. (1995) and Levinson (1996). However, in the past 10 or 15 years, there has been an emerging body of evidence that supports the competitive hypothesis; that is, that more stringent environmental policy increases net imports in polluting sectors (Ederington and Minier, 2003; Levinson and Taylor, 2008) and reduces new plant births in polluting industries in the United States (Becker and Henderson, 2000; List et al. 2003 and others). In the case of foreign investment, the evidence is somewhat mixed. Keller and Levinson (2002) found that that high abatement costs reduce U.S. net foreign investment inflows in polluting sectors. Eskeland and Harrison (2003) find no evidence that abatement costs explained the pattern of outward U.S. foreign investment, while Hanna (2010) finds that the Clean Air Act induced multinationals to relocate production outside the U.S. The major advances of recent work over the earlier work include the use of panel data (allowing authors to control for unobserved heterogeneity across jurisdictions), and the use of methods that account for the endogeneity of environmental policy.

There is still more work to be done – most papers have used U.S. data[25] and so there is a pressing need for more work using international data; and panel data sets with good measures of the stringency of environmental policy are rare. However, at this stage it is fair to say that there is some support for the existence of a pollution haven effect. Environmental policy reduces competiveness in sectors intensive in production-generated pollution, although the effects are not large because in most industries abatement costs are only a small fraction of overall costs. It is important to note that the result that environmental policy reduces competiveness of polluting firms does mean that it reduces welfare. If pollution is excessive, welfare improves if pollution policy is tightened up and this welfare improvement comes about in two ways – pollution regulation encourages more investment in abatement; and it causes a shift in production towards cleaner sectors and away from pollution intensive sectors.

4.1   Pollution haven hypothesis

The pollution haven hypothesis is that trade liberalization will shift polluting industry to countries with weak environmental policy. This hypothesis requires both that the competitive hypothesis be correct (so that stringent environmental policy reduces competitiveness in polluting industries), and that environmental policy differences be important to determine the pattern of trade. The first model to predict pollution havens is due to Pethig (1976). He used a Ricardian trade model and assumed that countries were identical except that one had (exogenously) more stringent environmental policy than the other. The model predicts that the country with weak environmental policy will export the polluting good.[26] Copeland and Taylor (1994) developed a pollution haven model with endogenous environmental policy. They used a Dornbusch-Fisher-Samuleson (1977) framework with a continuum of goods, each differing in pollution intensity. There were two types of countries, North and South, that differed only in that North was richer than South (Northern workers had more human capital). Because environmental quality is a normal good, and policy is assumed to be efficient, North chooses more stringent environmental policy than South. In free trade, the South exports the pollution intensive goods, and the North exports the relatively clean goods. These type of models also predict that (unless the income elasticity of marginal damage is sufficiently high) trade will increase world pollution via a global composition effect because polluting industry shifts to countries with relatively weak environmental policy.

Models that isolate the effects of pollution policy differences on trade patterns are useful because they highlight one of the forces at work in influencing trade patterns and they help us trace through the types of changes in the world economy that these forces encourage. However, many other factors also influence trade patterns. A full understanding of the logic of the pollution haven hypothesis, and an empirical strategy for testing this hypothesis, requires that we work with models that have other forces determining trade that interact with the pollution haven effect. Copeland and Taylor (1997b) and Richelle (1996) developed such a model[27]; the exposition below is based on Copeland and Taylor (2003).

Consider a special case of our competitive model; essentially a Heckscher–Ohlin model modified to take into account pollution in sector 1. Assume two primary factors, K and L. Technology is given by

$$y_1 = z^\alpha [f_1(K_1, L_1)]^{1-\alpha},$$
$$y_2 = f_2(K_2, L_2),$$

(14)

where $0 < \alpha < 1$ and where the functions f_i are linearly homogenous.[28] I assume that the polluting sector (1) is also relatively capital intensive. Assume two types of countries, North and South. North and South have identical technology and preferences as specified by (6). North is richer than South; for simplicity assume populations are identical, but Northerners each own more physical and human capital than Southerners. Pollution taxes are chosen endogenously by the government as discussed above; for simplicity, they treat goods prices as given when choosing emission policy.[29] Because North is richer than South, it will have more stringent environmental policy (more precisely, North's marginal damage curve will be above South's so that emission prices will be higher for any given z). As a simple example (not imposed in what follows), consider the following special case of preferences:

$$V(p,I,z) = \ln\left(\frac{I}{\beta(p)}\right) - \gamma z.$$

In this case marginal damage is $MD = -V_z/V_I = \gamma I$, and since emission prices are equal to marginal damage, the ratio of North's to South's emission prices is simply the ratio of national incomes:

$$\frac{\tau^N}{\tau^S} = \frac{I^N}{I^S}.$$

The richer country has more stringent pollution policy.

Relative demand and supply curves can be used to illustrate the equilibrium (see Figure 15.5). The relative demand curves (RD) are the same in North and South because preferences are separable with respect to goods consumption and environmental quality, and identical and homothetic with respect to goods consumption. The relative supply curves are the output ratios. Using the standard approach to solving Heckscher–Ohlin trade models (using full employment and free entry conditions), one can show that outputs are functions of endowments

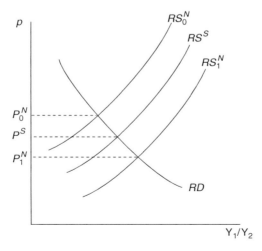

Figure 15.5   Effects of pollution policy and capital abundance on the pattern of trade.

and prices. For example, for the North, we have $y_i = y_i (p, \tau, K^N, L^N)$, where K^N and L^N are North's endowments of capital and labour. Moreover, because of constant returns to scale and the separability of environmental services and other factor services in (14), the supply functions are homogeneous of degree one in endowments. Hence we have $y_i = L^N y_i (p, \tau^N, K^N/L^N, 1)$. Relative supply in the North is therefore a function of goods prices, emission prices and North's capital–labour ratio:

$$RS^N = \frac{y_1^N(p, \tau^N, K^N/L^N, 1)}{y_2^N(p, \tau^N, K^N/L^N, 1)}.$$

The relative supply curve for the South is defined analogously:

$$RS^S = \frac{y_1^S(p, \tau^S, K^S/L^S, 1)}{y_2^S(p, \tau^S, K^S/L^S, 1)}.$$

The key issue for determining the pattern of trade is whether North's relative supply curve is above or below South's. South's relative supply is denoted RS^S in Figure 15.5, and I illustrate two possible cases for the position of North's relative supply.

Start by assuming that the capital-labour ratios are the same across countries. Then North's and South's relative supply curves differ only via the effect of emission prices; and since North has more stringent policy than South, this pushes North's relative supply up and to the left of South's.[30] This is denoted by RS_0^N in the figure. In the absence of trade, the relative price of the dirty good is higher in North than South and this means that North exports the dirty good and South exports the clean good. This is the pure pollution haven case of Copeland and Taylor (1994) because income-induced pollution policy differences are the only motive for trade.

Suppose now that North is both rich and capital abundant relative to South so that $K^N/L^N > K^S/L^S$. North's richness means that its more stringent environmental policy pushes its relative supply curve up and to the left of South's. However, its capital abundance favours the capital intensive sector, which in this case is also the polluting sector. So capital abundance pushes North's relative supply curve out and to the right. The net effect depends on which is more important in determining relative costs: capital abundance or regulatory differences. If the effect of capital abundance is stronger, then North's relative supply curve will be to the right of South's, as illustrated by RS_1^N in the figure. In this case, the relative price of the polluting good (1) is lower in North than South prior to trade. North has a comparative advantage in the polluting good, despite the fact that its environmental policy is more stringent. Trade liberalization will cause polluting industry to shift from South to North. The pollution haven hypothesis fails in this case. There is still a pollution haven effect: given the trade regime, a small tightening up of North's pollution policy will cause its relative supply curve RS_1^N to shift to the left. Its exports of the polluting good will fall; however unless the tightening up of environmental policy is sufficiently extreme, North will continue to have a comparative advantage in the dirty good.

The main point of this analysis is that the pattern of trade depends on the net effect of differences in pollution policy and other factors. The analysis above highlights the role of factor endowment differences; however other factors may also determine trade patterns. Ederington, Levinson and Minier (2005) suggest that agglomeration economies may be one of several factors that limit the mobility of polluting firms; that is, if the benefits of agglomeration outweigh the costs of relatively stringent pollution policy, a firm may prefer to remain in the jurisdiction with more stringent regulation. Zeng and Zhao (2009) formally develop an agglomeration model with this feature. Manufacturing pollutes but it also benefits from agglomeration effects. They assume that North has more stringent environmental policy than South, and show that North can export the polluting goods despite having more stringent environmental policy because of the agglomeration effect.

The theoretical case for the pollution haven hypothesis is therefore rather weak – since environmental compliance costs are small relative to other production costs in most sectors, it is plausible that trade patterns are determined mainly by other factors. There are surprising few papers that test the pollution haven hypothesis (in contrast to the large literature that tests the competitive hypothesis). Ederington, Levinson and Minier (2004) look at the pollution content of U.S. imports and exports during the period 1972–94. They find that U.S. imports have become less pollution intensive relative to U.S. exports during this time period. This result was confirmed by Levinson (2009), who took into account pollution from intermediate goods. This result is opposite to what the pollution haven hypothesis would predict. Ederington et al. (2004) also find that U.S. imports are less responsive to tariff reductions in high abatement cost industries than than low abatement cost industries, a result that is again inconsistent with the pollution haven hypothesis. Antweiler, Copeland and Taylor (2001) estimated the elasticity of ambient SO_2 pollution with respect to increased openness to trade, holding scale, capital abundance, per capita income and other factors constant. They found that this elasticity is increasing with the per capita income of the country – trade tends to increase SO_2 pollution via the composition effect more in rich countries than in poor countries (contrary to the pollution haven hypothesis), and the elasticity was negative for some poor countries. Cole and Elliot (2003) use emission data to estimate the composition effects of trade liberalization for four pollutants. They have enough data to estimate country specific trade elasticities for two of these pollutants: SO_2 and BOD. The pollution haven hypothesis predicts a negative relation between these elasticities and per capita income; they find no relationship.

These results are consistent with the hypothesis that factor abundance, agglomeration effects or other factors have been more important than pollution regulations in determining trade patterns in polluting industries. Antweiler et al. (2001) hypothesized that the lack of support for the pollution haven hypothesis in their study was because the capital abundance and environmental stringency had opposing and offsetting effects on the direction of trade flows. Cole and Elliott (2005) explicitly investigate the interaction between capital intensity and pollution intensity and find that they are positively correlated. They then hypothesize that countries that are both capital abundant and have relatively weak environmental policy would be attractive locations for pollution inten-sive production. They investigate U.S. FDI to Brazil and Mexico and find some evidence in support of this. Ederington, Levinson and Minier (2005) provide evidence that industry characteristics, such as agglomeration, transport costs or fixed costs limit the mobility of pollution intensive industries and work against the effects of environmental policy in determining trade and investment flows. Wagner and Timmins (2009) also highlight the importance of agglomeration in their study of the determinants of the destination countries for foreign direct investment from Germany. They find evidence of a pollution haven effect in the chemical industry only after controlling for FDI agglomeration spillovers.

Overall then, while there is evidence that environmental policy targeting production-generated pollution reduces competitiveness, there is as yet no compelling evidence to support the strong version of the pollution haven hypothesis.

5   Trade, renewable resources and environmental capital

In the models discussed so far, there is a tradeoff between consumption (or real income) and environmental quality. For many environmental issues this is a useful approximation of reality, but in other cases the notion that allowing increased environmental degradation will allow higher consumption is mislead-ing and will hold at best in the short run. Pollution affects human health and so can lower worker productivity. Soil erosion reduces agricultural productiv-ity, and climate change is predicted to have a variety of effects on production, especially in agriculture. Fisheries and forests can generate short-run increases in income if trade stimulates harvesting, but if harvesting occurs at rates beyond levels that are sustainable, long-run income from these sources will fall.

The standard approach to dealing with these issues is to introduce nega-tive production externalities into the models. A number of papers introduce a stock variable, which can be thought of as 'environmental capital'. Environ-mental capital is an input into production in some sectors, and degradation or depletion of the stock will lower productivity in the affected sectors. It is use-ful to distinguish between two types of production externalities; examples of each will be considered below. In one case, production from one sector lowers environmental capital in the same sector – renewable resource models have this characteristic. In the other case, production from one sector reduces environmental capital needed as an input into other sectors – for example, water pollution might damage fisheries, or air pollution could harm human health. The effects of production on biodiversity and the role of transportation of goods as a conduit for invasive species are other examples of negative production externalities that could be affected by trade.

5.1 Renewable resources

I begin with the case of negative externalities that are internal to the industry (but external to the producer). Chichilnisky (1994) and Brander and Taylor (1997a,b) both consider models with trade and renewable resources[31]; here I will use the Brander and Taylor model to discuss both. Their model combines the Ricardian trade model with the Schaeffer fisheries model. There are two goods, manufacturing (M) and the harvested good (H). M is the numeraire. Assume a representative consumer with well-behaved homothetic utility function $U(H,M)$.

There are two primary factors: Labour (L) and the stock of natural capital S. Natural capital is a common property resource. Technology exhibits constant returns to scale for given levels of S. One unit of labour produces one unit of M:

$$M = L_M. \tag{15}$$

The production function for H is:

$$H = \alpha L_H S. \tag{16}$$

In the short run, the stock of natural capital, S, is given, but in the long run it evolves over time depending on difference between the natural regeneration rate, $G(S)$, and the harvest rate. Following Schaeffer (1957) a quadratic regeneration function is assumed:

$$\frac{dS}{dt} = G(S) - H = rS\left(1 - \frac{S}{K}\right) - H,$$

where r is the intrinsic growth rate of the stock and K is the natural carrying capacity of the environment. With a fixed supply of labour (L), the full employment condition and the technology (15) and (16) yields the short-run production frontier, which is linear and depends on the current resource stock as illustrated by PPF_0 in Figure 15.6.

Outcomes in this model depend on the regulatory regime. Any individual harvester imposes an externality on others because increased harvesting lowers the stock in subsequent periods, thus reducing the productivity of other harvesters – referring to (16), a fall in S induced by harvesting reduces productivity.

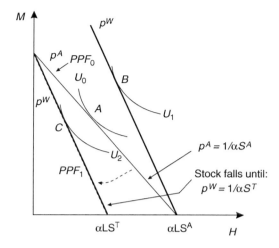

Figure 15.6   Trade leads to fall in steady state real income .

Brander and Taylor assume an open access regime in which the externality is not internalized. As is standard in fisheries models, this leads to overharvesting.[32]

First consider autarky. Open access to the harvesting sector means that entry occurs until profits are zero; hence if the harvesting sector is active, we have:

$$p\alpha L_H S - wL_H = 0. \tag{17}$$

Product markets clear at each point in time. Assume that the economy has evolved to a steady state (with $dS/dt = 0$) where harvesting just balances the natural growth of the resource stock. If the economy is diversified, then it is at a point like A in figure 15.6. In steady state, S is constant and from (17) the market clearing condition requires a relative price that satisfies[33]:

$$p^A = \frac{1}{\alpha S^A}.$$

where S^A is the steady state stock in autarky.

Suppose trade is liberalized, that the country is small so the world price of H, p^W, is given, and the country exports H: that is $p^W > p^A$. The economy specializes in H and in the short-run consumption moves to point B. However this is not sustainable because the increased harvesting causes the stock S to deplete. As the stock declines, the short-run production frontier rotates inward. Depending on parameters, it is possible for the stock to be wiped out entirely or for the economy to remain specialized in S.[34] However, suppose that the economy evolves to a new steady-state where it remains diversified in production. Then from the free entry condition (17), the new steady-state stock S^T must satisfy

$$p^W = \frac{1}{\alpha S^T}.$$

This new stock yields a new short-run production frontier which must lie below the autarky frontier. Moreover since the slope of the frontier is equal to the world price, the new consumption point is C. That is steady-state consumption (real income) must necessarily be lower in free trade than in autarky. The effect of trade on welfare depends on discount rates; however, if the discount rate is sufficiently low then welfare must fall.

The possibility that trade liberalization may lead to a decline in welfare is not surprising in a model with distortions.[35] More important for our purposes here is that the model highlights the possibility that trade-induced resource depletion can lead to real income losses if externalities are not internalized.[36] Although in the short run it may appear that there is a trade-off between real income and tightening up regulation to preserve natural capital; in the long run there is a decline in both real income and natural capital. As noted earlier, there is evidence that environmental quality is a normal good, so that increases in income lead to more pressure on governments to enact more stringent environmental regulation. However, if trade leads to real income losses, then this raises the possibility of a downward spiral where weak environmental policy leads to trade induced real income losses, which leads to a further weakening of other environmental policy, which causes more income loss, and so on.[37]

This model can be generalized in various ways.[38] One line of work focuses on the importance of the effects of trade on habitat for the resource – this is particularly important in the case of forests or endangered species. The Brander and Taylor and Chichilnisky models predict that if trade were to lead to *reduced* resource prices then pressure would be taken off the resource stock and it would recover. Reduced prices would occur if the country had a comparative disadvantage in harvesting or if, starting in a pre-existing trade regime, other countries instituted an import ban in an attempt to reduce harvesting by reducing demand. Barbier and Schultz (1997) and Jinji (2006) consider models where resources require habitat, and habitat has competing uses. A fall in resource prices may reduce the benefits of maintaining habitat and lead to resource depletion. Bans on importing tropical timber could fail to preserve forests, since it can become more attractive to convert forest land to agriculture.[39]

The outcome in renewable resource models is of course dependent on the policy regime. If externalities are fully internalized, then trade must be welfare-improving: if it is not efficient to allow the stock to decline, harvest taxes or quotas can be imposed to prevent stock depletion. There is a great deal of heterogeneity both within and across countries in the efficiency and effectiveness of renewal resource management. To fully understand the effects of trade on renewable resources it is important to account for the institutional context. Moreover, the effectiveness of resource management should be considered endogenous: it is possible that trade could have an effect on the management regime.

There has been relatively little work that explores the effects of globalization on the resource management regime.[40] Several papers build on Demsetz (1967), Cohen and Weitzman (1976) and De Meza and Gould (1992) and consider models where there is a fixed cost of managing a resource. Externalities are fully internalized once the fixed cost is paid. Francis (2001), Margolis and Shogren (2002) and Bergeron (2002) are examples of this approach. Hotte, Long and Tian (2000) develop a poaching model, which has variable enforcement costs. These papers find that if trade increases the price of the harvest good, the increased value of the resource can lead to establishment of management regimes or more intensive enforcement of existing regimes. However, while trade can encourage resource conservation, it may nevertheless still be welfare-decreasing once management and enforcement costs are taken into account. Copeland and Taylor (2009) develop a model based on imperfect monitoring and seek to explain heterogeneity in the effectiveness of resource management within and across countries, and the response of the management regime to the trade regime. Increases in the price of the harvest good (which may occur if trade is liberalized in a resource exporting country) will cause a transition to improved management in some countries but not others. All else equal, factors such as weak institutions (high monitoring costs), large numbers of agents with access to the resource, slow growing resource stocks, impatient harvesters, and efficient harvest technology all reduce the likelihood of an effective management regime and increase the likelihood that trade will lead to resource depletion and steady-state consumption declines.

The analogue of the pollution haven hypothesis has also been examined in renewable resource models – the issue here is whether trade will put increased pressure on resources in countries with weak management regimes. As in the case of pollution, the pattern of trade (that is, the countries that end up being resource exporters) depends on the interaction between resource management and many other factors, such as characteristics of the resource, capital abundance, technology and so on. However, it is nevertheless useful to focus on the case where differences in management policy are the only source of comparative advantage because this helps to highlight some differences between models with natural capital and the simple pollution models considered previously.

Chichilnisky (1994) considers a North – South model where North has fully enforced property rights and South has an open access resource regime. She argues that South's weak management gives it a 'false' comparative advantage in the harvest good. Trade benefits the North but leads to excessive harvesting, and welfare declines in the South. Brander and Taylor (1997b), however, point out that this need not be the outcome and that it is possible that both North and South may gain from trade. To see this, figure 15.7 illustrates the *long run* relative demand and supply curves implied by the renewable resource model outlined above. Assume two countries that are identical except that South

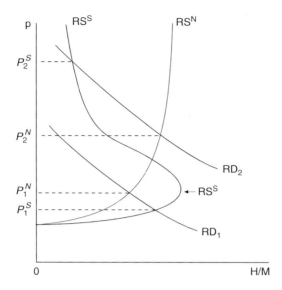

Figure 15.7   Renewable resources and the pattern of trade .

has open access resource harvesting and North fully internalizes externalities. For simplicity assume that the discount rate approaches zero so that North's manager maximizes sustained surplus from the resource.

First consider relative demand. Since preferences are homothetic and identical across countries, relative demands are downward-sloping and independent of income. Two relative demand curves are illustrated, reflecting two different possibilities for the intensity of preference for the harvest good: RD_1 is a case of low demand for the harvest good; RD_2 is a case of high demand for the harvest good. The relative supply curves depend on the management regime. In the North, because management is perfect and the discount rate approaches zero, Northern managers restrict harvesting to protect the stock. The long-run relative supply curve slopes upward and asymptotes to the maximum sustained yield from the resource stock. South's long-run relative supply curve, on the other hand, is backward-bending. When the price is low, harvesting is not very attractive and so the resource stock is high. Price increases induce entry, increasing harvesting. Hence, for low prices, the relative supply curve slopes upward. But as prices continue to rise, inducing higher sustained levels of harvesting, eventually the effects of stock depletion dominate the effects of increased harvesting effort and, hence, the sustained level of harvesting falls as the price rises.

Let us now consider the pattern of trade. First consider the case of relatively low demand for the harvest good (RD_1). The autarky prices are P_1^N and P_1^S in North and South, respectively. South's weak management gives it a comparative advantage in harvesting because, for given prices in this region, North is restricting harvesting to preserve the stock. Hence, South exports the harvest good, and North exports the manufacturing good. Trade leads to resource depletion and long-run consumption declines in South. This yields a result analogous to a pollution haven outcome. This is the case that Chichilnisky (1994) discussed.

Next, however, suppose that there is relatively high demand for the harvest good (RD$_2$). Autarky relative prices in this case are P_2^N and P_2^S. In this case, North has a comparative advantage in the harvest good. Trade causes North to export H while South exports M. North gains from trade because externalities are fully internalized; and South also gains from trade because markets reallocate Southern labour out of the harvest sector into manufacturing, thus allowing resource stocks to recover. This case illustrates the importance of natural capital as a productive input. When demand for the harvest good is high, natural capital (the resource stock) ends up depleted in an open access economy, and this leads to high production costs in the harvest sector. In contrast, North's good management ensures that natural capital is abundant even in the face of high demand for the harvest good, and this leads to relatively lower harvest cost in the North. Hence, good management (stringent harvesting regulation) can lead to a comparative advantage in natural capital intensive sectors.

5.2   Cross-sectoral production externalities

Renewable resources are examples of cases where excessive production in a sector (such as fishing) depletes natural capital in that same sector (the fish stock declines). Let us now turn to the case where production in one sector (such as manufacturing) causes pollution that depletes natural capital needed in other sectors. For example, acid rain from electric power generation or smelting can reduce productivity in agriculture or forestry; air and water pollution can harm tourism; and water pollution can kill fish.

To illustrate the implications of cross-sectoral pollution externalities for the effects of trade on the environment, again consider two sectors manufacturing (M) and the natural capital intensive sector which we will call agriculture (A).[41] There are two primary factors, Labour (L) and the stock of natural capital (N). Again we use a Ricardian framework in the short run. The production function for M is:

$$M = L_M.$$

The production function for A is:

$$A = \alpha N^\beta L_A,$$

where $0 < \beta < 1$. Natural capital is a public good, so that productivity in any firm in sector A depends on the overall stock of natural capital N. In the short run, the stock of natural capital, N, is given, but in the long run it evolves over time depending on the difference between the natural regeneration rate, and depletion caused by pollution from M. For simplicity assume a very simple linear regeneration function and assume that pollution is directly proportional to manufacturing output:

$$\frac{dN}{dt} = r\left(\bar{N} - N\right) - \lambda M.$$

If there is no manufacturing output then $\bar{N}$ is the steady-state level of natural capital; sustained increases in M lead to lower steady-state levels of natural capital, which in turn leads to lower productivity in A. Consider an open access regime where there is no pollution regulation that attempts to preserve N.

Perhaps the best way to think about the differences between a model with cross sectoral production externalities and the renewable resource model analyzed above is to note that natural capital depletion gives the renewable resource sector long-run diminishing returns, whereas in the cross sectoral externality model, natural capital depletion has an effect on manufacturing that is very similar to *increasing* returns (even though the production function in M is linear). In the resource model, increased harvesting lowers the resource stock, which lowers productivity; this is long-run diminishing returns. In the cross sectoral externality model, increased production generates pollution which destroys natural capital. This lowers productivity in agriculture. This causes sector A to contract and shed workers, thus stimulating the manufacturing sector. That is, increased manufacturing production causes the productivity of M *relative* to A to rise! Hence, the behaviour of this model shares features with that of Ethier's (1982) model of external economies of scale.[42]

One of the key features of this model is that it has an element of lock-in. Suppose there are two countries, North and South. And suppose that South has a slight comparative advantage in M. Then trade will cause South to export M, and this will amplify South's comparative advantage. Higher production of M kills off natural capital, rendering the A sector less productive, so that over time a slight comparative advantage is magnified. History matters in this model. Countries that are initially only slightly different in preferences and endowments can look very different in the long run because of the effects of trade on the evolution of natural capital.[43]

A model with cross sectoral pollution externalities exhibits very strong pollution haven effects. To see this, suppose that North and South are identical except that North has more stringent environmental policy than South. This means that North will have a higher stock of natural capital and this gives North a comparative advantage in A. North exports the environmentally sensitive clean good, which South exports the polluting good M. Moreover, via the lock-in effect, the forces making South a pollution haven are strengthened by trade as the expansion of its polluting sector destroys more of its natural capital. Recall that in the renewable resource model, severe depletion of natural capital gave South a comparative disadvantage in the harvest good and this allowed its natural capital to recover. In the cross sectoral externality model, severe depletion of natural capital locks in a comparative advantage in the polluting good, further depleting natural capital.

A relatively small number of papers on trade and the environment have considered models with cross sectoral pollution externalities. Benarroch and Thille (2001) and Unteroberdoerster (2001) extend the above model to allow for transboundary pollution. Zeng and Zhao (2009) allow for both agglomeration effects in production and cross sectoral externalities in pollution. Smulders, van Soest and Withagen (2004) and Rus (2006) consider a model where there are negative production externalities both within and across sectors.

5.3   Evidence

Lopez and Islam (2008) note the asymmetry between trends in environmental outcomes for urban pollutants (that in many cases have stabilized or improved), global pollutants (such as carbon emissions that are worsening), and rural pollutants, including natural capital (which is under increased pressure). Trends in fisheries are particularly alarming (Worm et al., 2006) where the rate of fisheries collapse has been increasing. Ineffective resource management is widely agreed to be a key part of the problem (Costello et al., 2008); the question for our purposes here is how globalization is affecting these trends.

There are relatively few empirical studies that attempt to systematically assess the effects of trade on renewable resources. Ferreira (2004) uses a panel of data on forest cover for 29 countries for the period 1961–94. She finds that openness to trade had a significant effect on deforestation only in countries where there was weak enforcement of property rights, a result that is consistent with theory. Other studies such as Deacon (1994), Bohn and Deacon (2000) and Barbier and Burgess (2001) have found that enforcement of property rights and other measures of institutional quality are important determinants of resource depletion.

There are some large studies of fisheries depletion. Costello and others (2008) show that those fisheries that have been subject to transferable quota systems have been less likely to collapse. McWhinnie (2008) has data on 200 fish stocks globally and attempts to determine factors that contribute to depletion – she finds that fisheries that are shared by more than one country are more likely to collapse. Neither of these studies, however, focused on the role of openness in influencing depletion.

There are several case studies that assess the effects of trade in specific cases of resource depletion. For example, Lopez (1997) found that trade increased the rate of deforestation in Ghana, and Taylor (2007) found that a change in technology that created markets for buffalo hide in Europe was responsible for the rapid depletion of the North American bison. Lopez (2000) provides a simulation study of the effects of trade liberalization on natural biomass in the Cote d'Ivoire. He first uses an econometric approach to estimate the extent rural farmers internalize externalities in their land allocation decisions. He finds evidence that externalities are not internalized and, hence, there is excessive land clearing. His simulation results suggest that full trade liberalization could be good for the rural biomass by encouraging a reallocation of land use away from cereal crops towards cultivated trees. This a field where more empirical work would be very fruitful.

6 Effects of environmental problems on trade policy

I now turn to policy questions. The policy literature on the interaction between trade and environment has two major themes. The first, which will be discussed in this section, is whether the possibility of environmental degradation should alter a country's stance towards trade policy. The second, which will be discussed in the next section, is whether globalization will put pressure on governments to weaken environmental policy. The theoretical and empirical work reviewed in earlier sections has found that there are cases where trade liberalization will lead to increased environmental degradation, and that there is evidence that more stringent environmental policy reduces competiveness in polluting industries. Each of these findings invites a policy response. This section considers the former; the next section the latter.

6.1 Production-generated pollution

The standard theory of distortions and policy targetting implies that if all externalities are fully internalized, then the case for free trade (in small open economies) is unaffected by environmental problems. On the other hand, if efficient environmental policy is not in place, then second-best optimal trade policy may deviate from free trade.[44] To explore these issues, consider a perfectly competitive economy with no distortions other than possibly trade barriers and externalities arising from pollution. Assume a representative consumer for simplicity. I will use the model from the previous sections, with two goods, Y_1 and Y_2. I assume that good 1 is imported and consider both the possibility that the import good is the polluting good and the possibility that the import good is clean while good 2 production pollutes. I begin with the case where pollution is generated during production.

It is convenient to work with the expenditure function, although equivalent results can be obtained by using the indirect utility function. The consumer's budget constraint is given by

$$E(p+t,v,z,u) = G(p+t,v,z) + tM \tag{18}$$

where t is a specific tariff on imports, and M is imports. Both large and small countries will be considered. In the small country case, goods prices p are determined in world markets and are treated as exogenous from the perspective of the home country. To deal with the large country case, I consider a two-country world and specify foreign export supply as $X^*(p)$. X^* will also depend on policy variables in the foreign country, but these are suppressed here because the foreign country's policy is treated as exogenous at this point. If the domestic economy uses a pollution tax to control pollution, then balanced trade requires

$$M(p, t, \tau) = X^*(p). \tag{19}$$

Totally differentiating (18), yields

$$E_u du = (\tau - E_z) dz - M dp + t dM, \tag{20}$$

To find the optimal choice of trade and environmental policy for home, choose the tariff t and pollution tax τ to maximize u subject to (18). Noting from (19) that $dM = X_p^* dp$, we can use (20) to obtain the optimal policy:

$$\tau = E_z, \tag{21}$$

$$\frac{t}{p} = \frac{1}{\varepsilon_{X^*p}}, \tag{22}$$

where $\varepsilon_{X^*p} = pX_p^*/X^*$ is the elasticity of foreign export supply.

This is the standard result from the policy targetting literature: the pollution tax should equal marginal damage to fully internalize the externality and (22) is the standard formula for an optimal tariff. If the economy is small, then $\varepsilon_{X^*p} = \infty$, and (22) implies $t = 0$. The optimal policy for a small open economy is free trade, combined with a pollution tax set equal to marginal damage. The presence of environmental problems does not affect the case for free trade.

If pollution policy is not set optimally, then trade policy can have a role to play as a second-best instrument to influence environmental outcomes. This requires, however. that trade policy can influence pollution levels. This means that the *method* of pollution policy regulation (e.g. whether taxes or emission quotas are used) as well as its stringency will matter.

For clarity, I focus on the small open economy case. Suppose that pollution policy is too weak; that is suppose that (21) is violated and we have:

$$\tau < E_z. \tag{23}$$

Referring to (20), with $dp = 0$ (because the country is small), changes in trade policy affect welfare both via the standard volume of trade effect and via the indirect effect on pollution. The effect on the volume of trade is given by

$$dM = -(G_{qq} - E_{qq})dt + (E_{qz} - G_{qz})dz + E_{qu}du$$

Substituting into (20) yields:

$$E_u(1 - tm)\frac{du}{dt} = -t(G_{qq} - E_{qq}) + |\tau - E_z + t(E_{qz} - G_{qz})|\frac{dz}{dt},\tag{24}$$

where $m \equiv E_{qu}/E_u,$[45] and where we assume $1 - tm > 0.$[46]

First suppose that pollution is regulated with binding quotas. As trade is liberalized, output of pollution intensive goods may adjust, but overall emissions do not change because of the quota – instead the shadow price of emissions adjusts. Hence, in this case, $dz/dt = 0$ and (24) reduces to

$$E_u(1 - tm)\frac{du}{dt} = -t(G_{qq} - E_{qq}) \leq 0.\tag{25}$$

Since $G_{qq} - E_{qq} > 0$ by the convexity of G and concavity of E in prices, (25) implies that trade liberalization ($dt < 0$) is unambiguously welfare-improving despite the presence of environmental distortions. This is because the presence of binding pollution quotas prevents goods prices changes induced by trade liberalization from exacerbating pollution distortions.[47] Moreover, in this case, the second-best optimal trade policy is free trade: setting $du/dt = 0$ in (25) yields $t = 0$.

If pollution is instead regulated with rigid pollution taxes, then matters are more complicated because pollution levels will adjust in response to goods price changes. To see this, treat the pollution tax as exogenous:

$$\tau = G(p + t, v, z).\tag{26}$$

The response of pollution to the change in tariffs (holding p constant) is

$$\frac{dz}{dt} = -\frac{G_{zq}}{G_{zz}}.\tag{27}$$

If good 1 is polluting then an increase in t raises pollution ($dz/dt \geq 0$); but if good 2 is polluting then $dz/dt \leq 0.$[48]

Referring to (24) a fall in tariffs is beneficial via the volume of trade effect, but the induced change in pollution may either benefit or harm welfare, depending on the level of the pollution tax and whether the import good is polluting or clean. To find the second-best optimal tariff, set $du/dt = 0$ in (24):

$$t = \frac{(\tau - E_z)dz/dt}{-dM^c/dt},\tag{28}$$

where

$$\frac{dM^c}{dt} = E_{qq} - G_{qq} + (E_{qz} - G_{qz})\frac{dz}{dt}\tag{29}$$

is the response of the compensated import demand to an increase in tariffs. This is unambiguously negative if the effects of pollution on the demand are small (i.e., if E_{qz} is small) – I assume this in what follows.

If pollution policy is too weak ($\tau < E_z$) then trade liberalization will raise welfare provided that the import-competing sector is pollution intensive. This can be thought of as a version of the double dividend argument. Trade liberalization both reduces trade distortions and reduces pollution distortions. In this case, policy should tax the import-competing sector; hence, the second-best optimal tariff is negative.

On the other hand, if the export sector is polluting and the import-competing sector is clean, then $dz/dt \leq 0$ and in this case trade liberalization will not improve welfare once tariffs are sufficiently low. The expansion of the export sector induced by trade liberalization causes an increase in pollution and the reduction of the trade distortion exacerbates the pollution distortion. The second-best optimal tariff is positive in this case.[49]

6.2   Consumption-generated pollution

Suppose now that pollution is generated during consumption of the imported good Y_1, and the emissions per unit of consumption of Y_1 differs between domestically produced and imported goods. Let α be emissions per unit of consumption of domestically produced Y_1 and let α^* denote emissions be unit of consumption of imported Y_1. To keep things clear, assume a small country so that the foreign price p^* is fixed, treat the emission intensities as exogenous, and assume there is no production-generated pollution. Again, we ask whether pollution affects the case for free trade. This question is particularly interesting in the case where foreign goods generate more pollution than domestic goods during consumption ($\alpha^* > \alpha$).

Let τ be a pollution tax imposed on pollution generated during consumption of domestic goods and let τ^* be the tax on pollution from imported goods (imposed by the domestic government). And as before we let t denote the import tariff. The domestic price to consumers of an imported good is

$$p^d = p^* + \alpha^* \tau^* + t.$$

If p denotes the domestic producer price, then domestic consumers pay $p + \alpha\tau$ for a domestic good. Arbitrage ensures that consumers are indifferent between domestically produced and imported goods, so we have

$$p = p^* + \alpha^* \tau^* - \alpha\tau + t.$$

The consumer's budget constraint is

$$E(p^* + \alpha^* \tau^* + t, z, u) = G(p^* + \alpha^* \tau^* - \alpha\tau + t, v) + tM + \tau^* \alpha^* M + \tau\alpha y, \tag{30}$$

where y is domestic output of the polluting good and where $z = \alpha^* M + \alpha y$.

Totally differentiating yields:

$$E_u du = (\tau^* - E_z)\alpha^* dM + (\tau - E_z)\alpha dy + t dM. \tag{31}$$

To find the first-best, choose τ, τ^*, and t to maximize u subject to (30). Using (31), the solution is

$$\tau = \tau^* = E_z \quad \text{and} \quad t = 0. \tag{32}$$

Once again the targeting rule applies – pollution policy is used to address environmental problems, and there is no benefit from departing from free trade. Moreover, note that the national treatment principle applies – foreign goods are taxed because they pollute in the domestic economy, but the tax rate is the same for domestic and foreign goods. The tax per unit of consumption of goods for domestic and foreign goods may differ if the emission intensities differ (the rate is $\tau\alpha$ for domestic goods and $\tau\alpha^*$ for foreign goods, but the tax per unit of *emissions* (τ) is the same across goods.

If pollution policy is too weak, then trade liberalization need not improve welfare. A tariff is equivalent to a tax on consumers combined with a subsidy to domestic producers. Since pollution policy in this case is effectively a tax on consumption of the polluting good, the consumption tax aspect of the tariff is attractive as a second-best environmental policy; however, the production subsidy component of the tariff is distortionary. To determine the second-best optimal tariff in the presence of a rigid pollution tax, use (31) to obtain:

$$t = -(\tau - E_z)\left[\alpha^* + \alpha\,\frac{dy/dt}{dM/dt}\right]. \tag{33}$$

Note that if domestically produced goods do not pollute ($\alpha = 0$) then a tariff and pollution tax are perfect substitutes: if there is no pollution tax, then $t = \alpha^* E_z$, so that the price consumers pay for an imported good would be $p^* + \alpha^* E_z$, which is the same as it would be under a fully optimal pollution tax. In this case, the fact that a tariff also stimulates domestic production is not distortionary – the first-best policy requires that consumer substitute to the good that does not pollute and, hence, domestic production should rise to accommodate this. On the other hand, if both goods pollute, then the optimal tariff does not fully internalize the pollution externality. To see this, suppose for simplicity that $\alpha = \alpha^*$. Then (33) becomes

$$t = -(\tau - E_z)\alpha\left[1 + \frac{dy/dt}{dM/dt}\right].$$

Since $dy/dt = G_{qq} > 0$ and since we expect[50] $dM/dt < 0$ this implies that for the case where the pollution tax is zero, we have $t < \alpha E_z$, which means that the consumer price is lower than it would be in the first-best. This is to mitigate the distortionary aspect of the tariff – using the tariff to fully internalize the pollution externality would excessively stimulate domestic output via the production subsidy aspect of the tariff.

7   Effects of trade liberalization on environmental policy

Much of the literature on the interaction between trade and environmental policy is concerned with how environmental policy responds to freer trade. There are three major concerns.

The first is that a country's environment may be more vulnerable in an open economy than in a closed economy. A country with a comparative advantage in environmentally sensitive industry may experience an export boom that puts significant pressure on the environment. This means that the environmental policy regime needs to be responsive to changes in the trade regime.

A second issue is policy substitution. Trade barriers are equivalent to production subsidies in the import competing sector combined with taxes on consumers of the targeted goods. Trade liberalization exposes local producers to increased competition and so the government may be pressured to look for substitutes for the production subsidy component of the trade barrier. Since weak environmental policy is in effect a production subsidy, there is a possibility that trade liberalization could lead to weaker environmental policy. In the exporting sector, there are similar concerns. Trade agreements usually ban export subsidies; consequently, weak environmental policy may be a candidate as a substitute for export subsidies.

The third concern is market access. Trade agreements open up markets to imports; previous barriers that explicitly blocked or discriminated against foreign goods are removed or weakened. Governments do, however, retain the power to regulate products sold in local markets to protect health and safety and to protect the environment. This raises the possibility that environmental policy could be designed and implemented in a way that restricts foreign access to local markets

7.1   Vulnerability of environment in open versus closed economies

Suboptimal environmental policy leads to both welfare losses and excessive environmental degradation, whether the country is relatively open or closed to trade. However, the costs of suboptimal policy can be larger in open than in closed economies. This point can be illustrated most starkly in the case when factors are mobile internationally. To see this, allow capital to be mobile in the standard model used above. Assume that the country is small and open: the goods price and the rental rate on capital are fixed by world markets at p and r respectively. The budget constraint for the representative consumer is

$$E(p, z, u) = \tilde{G}(p, \tau, v, k) - r(k - \bar{k}) + \tau z, \tag{34}$$

where $\bar{k}$ is domestically owned capital, and k is the net amount of capital (including that which is foreign owned) used in the domestic economy, and I have used the form of the national income function that depends on emission taxes as defined in (3). The amount of capital used domestically is determined by

$$r = \tilde{G}_k(p, \tau, v, k) \tag{35}$$

and the level of emissions is given by

$$z = -\tilde{G}_k(p, \tau, v, k). \tag{36}$$

Let us consider the welfare effect of a change in the pollution tax:

$$E_u du = (\tau - E_z) dz. \tag{37}$$

To find the change in pollution, totally differentiate (36):

$$dz = -\left[\tilde{G}_{\tau\tau} d\tau + \tilde{G}_{\tau k} dk\right]. \tag{38}$$

Pollution changes both because of the direct effect of the policy change and in response to changes in the supply of capital. The change in capital can be found by differentiating (35). Putting all this together yields

$$E_u \frac{du}{d\tau} = (E_z - \tau)\tilde{G}_{\tau\tau} - (E_z - \tau) \frac{\tilde{G}_{\tau k}\tilde{G}_{k\tau}}{\tilde{G}_{kk}}. \tag{39}$$

If pollution policy is too weak (i.e. if $E_z > \tau$), then not surprisingly, (39) is positive–recall that $\tilde{G}_{\tau\tau} > 0$ and $\tilde{G}_{kk} < 0$ – so that raising the pollution tax will improve welfare. More important for our purposes here is that there are two terms. The first term is the welfare effect of raising the pollution tax for a given supply of capital in the country; the second term is the welfare effect due to the induced movement of capital. Since both terms are positive, this implies that the welfare effects of tightening up pollution policy (starting from the point where it is too weak) are higher when factors are mobile internationally than when they are not. Conversely, the welfare harm caused by a deviation of pollution policy from the optimum is higher in an economy open to factor mobility than one not. The costs of environmental policy mistakes tend to be amplified in open economies.[51]

7.2 Efficient response of environmental policy to trade liberalization

Much of the concern in the policy substitution literature is that freer trade will lead to a weakening of environmental policy because of concerns about international competitiveness. However, because efficient environmental policy needs to be responsive to the trade regime, a weakening of environmental policy in response to trade liberalization is not necessarily a sign of policy failure. There are at least two reasons why efficient environmental policy may become weaker in an open economy.

Second-best environmental policy in a country with trade barriers may be higher than marginal damage prior to trade liberalization. For example, consider a small open economy with exogenous import tariffs that protect the polluting sector (and revert to the case where capital is not mobile). Then, from (5) the optimal second-best pollution tax is

$$\tau = E_z - t\frac{dM/d\tau}{dz/d\tau} > E_z. \tag{40}$$

If the import competing sector is pollution intensive, then an increase in the pollution tax will reduce local production and increase imports. Hence (with some regularity conditions) we expect $dM/d\tau > 0$; and since $dz/d\tau < 0$, the sign in (40) follows. If trade barriers promote polluting production, second-best efficient environmental policy has to be higher than marginal damage to partially offset the effects of the tariff. Once tariffs are removed, then the efficient pollution tax is simply equal to marginal damage. Hence trade liberalization could lead to a fall in the pollution tax.

Even if environmental policy is not being explicitly used to try to undo the effects of trade policy as in (40), it is important to keep in mind that environmental policy that purely targets marginal damage must still be sensitive to the trade regime. To see this, recall the analysis in Figure 15.2. Reducing protection on the import competing good shifts in the demand for emissions (pressure is taken off the environment) and also shifts the marginal damage curve via income and substitution effects. The net effect on the pollution tax is ambiguous. But if income effects are not too large, then pollution policy that internalizes marginal damage will weaken as trade liberalizes (as shown in Figure 15.2). This result is not surprising when viewed from the perspective of trade theory. A pollution tax is the price of environmental services and so can be thought of as analogous to a factor price. If trade liberalization reduces the demand for environmental services, then it is not surprising that the efficient price of these services may fall.[52]

7.3   Policy substitution

The policy substitution argument is that once protection provided by trade barriers is eliminated, governments will be persuaded to find alternative ways of supporting firms exposed to international competition; and this may lead to weaker environmental policy.[53] To explore this issue, we need to consider models where governments have a motive to impose trade protection in the first place. The literature has focused on three major motives for protection: trade policy may be used to improve the terms of trade, to give domestic firms a strategic advantage over foreign rivals or in response to lobbying.[54]

7.4   Terms-of-trade motives for protection

Consider a large country and suppose that a free trade agreement has been signed. Suppose good 1 is the polluting good and that it is the import good.

Maximizing the utility of the representative agent subject to (18) and (2) yields (5) – although with $t = 0$. Solving, we obtain the formula for the second-best optimal pollution tax:

$$\tau = E_z + M \frac{dp/d\tau}{dz/d\tau} < E_z. \tag{43}$$

Since Y_1 is the polluting good, then in the normal case, we expect an increase in the pollution tax to raise p and reduce z; hence, if Y_1 is imported, we get $\tau < E_z$. This is the classic policy substitution result: monopsony power creates an incentive to reduce imports by taxing consumers and subsidizing local producers. When tariffs are eliminated, the incentive to subsidize the import competing sector is still present and this can be achieved (albeit at some cost) by weakening environmental policy.[55]

Our result in (43) does not answer the question of whether environmental policy gets tighter or weaker when tariffs fall. One could attempt to do so by treating t as exogenous in (5) and solving for $d\tau/dt$. The result is complex for two reasons. The path of the pollution tax need not be monotonic as tariffs fall to zero because of income effects and other factors. And, as discussed above, even in the absence of strategic motives for restricting trade, the optimal pollution tax may rise or fall depending on various factors such as whether trade liberalization stimulates or depresses the polluting industry, the slope of the marginal damage curve, and income and substitution effects in the demand for environmental quality. Therefore the model does not yield strong predictions regarding whether trade liberalization leads to stronger or weaker pollution policy. However, the fundamental point is highlighted by (43). If trade policy is constrained by trade agreements, and if there are no other instruments available to the government, then trade liberalization introduces an incentive for governments to use pollution policy as a second-best trade policy instrument.

While (43) shows that governments with a terms-of-trade motive for protection have an incentive to use environmental policy to subsidize import-competing producers; it also predicts that governments have an incentive to use such policy to tax exporters. In this model, since the foreign country exports the polluting good, we have:

$$\tau^* = E_{z^*}^* - X^* \frac{dp/d\tau^*}{dz^*/d\tau^*} > E_{z^*}^*.$$

In this case, free trade would lead to environmental policy which is too stringent. This is because in this model, a country with market power in the export sector has an incentive to impose an export tax to exploit its monopoly power – if trade agreements eliminate such taxes, other domestic policies such as environmental policy can be used as second bet substitutes. Models with purely terms-of-trade motives for protection do not generally predict that governments will use export subsidies,[56] and so this model yields a potentially testable result – it predicts that trade liberalization will lead to weaker environmental policy in the import-competing sector, but not in the export sector.

A weakness of this model (and most of the literature) is that it imposes the assumption than governments have only two instruments available – trade policy and environmental policy. More generally, governments have many instruments available to subsidize or tax local firms. Each of these instruments is costly to use because distortions will be introduced. In theory, a tariff is the least distorting instrument available to target imports. However, environmental policy is unlikely to be the next best choice – production subsidies, R&D subsidies, corporate tax incentives and so fourth are all alternatives that may be both more effective and less distortionary.

7.5   Monopolistic competition

Once we move beyond perfectly competitive environments, the effects of trade on environmental policy become more complex because of the interaction between other distortions (due to agglomeration spillovers, market power and other factors) and environmental distortions. This also means that results tend to be very sensitive to assumptions about market structure.

A few papers consider the effects of free trade on environmental policy in monopolistically competitive environments.[57] Pfluger (2001) provides a useful contrast to comparative-advantage based models because countries both import and export polluting goods and so policy is not simply based on terms-of-trade issues. He considers a model where firms are internationally mobile (a unit of capital is needed for a firm and capital is mobile) and there are transport costs so that there is a home market effect (consumer prices are lower if the producer locates in their country). In the case where countries are identical, then governments have to weigh the benefits of attracting firms (which reduces consumer prices) against the costs of pollution. Depending on parameters, the outcome may be either a NIMBY (not-in-my-back-yard) equilibrium, in which case countries set pollution policy too high to chase firms out of the country; or a race-to-the-bottom equilibrium in which weak pollution policy is used to attract firms. NIMBY is more likely if firms are very pollution intensive. Haupt (2006) considers a model where the number of varieties is endogenous and there is no home market effect (because he assumes no transport costs). In his framework, more stringent environmental policy leads to fewer product varieties. Because governments do not take into account the costs to foreign consumers of a loss of product variety, he finds that environmental policy is too stringent in a trading equilibrium.

7.6 Strategic trade policy

As noted above, the terms-of-trade motive for protection does not explain why governments would subsidize exports and does not apply to small countries that do not have market power in their import or export sectors. An alternative motive for protection is based on the existence of firm level market power.[58] With market power, firms earn profits, and if there is international trade, some of these profits are extracted from foreign customers. If domestic and foreign firms are engaged in strategic competition for these profits, then there is an incentive for governments to intervene to help give their firms a strategic advantage relative to their foreign competitors.

To illustrate, consider the simple export model developed by Brander and Spencer (1985) that was applied to the pollution regulation problem by Barrett (1994).[59] Two countries (West and East) export good x to a third country (South). There is no demand in East or West for x, so all of the production is exported. Denote East variables with an asterisk so, for example, x denotes output of a West firm, while x^* is output of an East firm. We first consider a homogeneous good Cournot duopoly and then explore robustness of the results to different market structures.

Let $p(x + x^*)$ denote the inverse demand in South. Denote domestic profits for a given level of foreign output by

$$\pi(x^*, \tau, s) = \max_{x, z}\{p(x, x^*)x - c(x, z) + sx - \tau z\}, \tag{44}$$

where c is costs (increasing and convex in x and – in the relevant range – decreasing in z) and where s is an export subsidy. Let $B(x^*, \tau)$ denote the solution to the maximization problem in (44); this is the home firm's best-response function. The foreign firm solves a similar problem (although for simplicity assume that there is no foreign pollution tax) to obtain its best-response function. Let $B^*(x)$ denote Foreign's best response function. Assume that regularity conditions on demand are imposed so that best response functions slope down and (with x on the horizontal axis) B is steeper than B^*.[60] Using the best-response functions, we obtain the Cournot equilibrium outputs.

The home government chooses an export subsidy s and a pollution tax τ to maximize domestic welfare, looking ahead to the effect of its policies on the Cournot equilibrium. In our partial-equilibrium framework with no domestic consumption of x, the domestic welfare function is

$$W = \pi(x^*, \tau, s) - sx + \tau z - D(z), \tag{45}$$

where D is pollution damage. Totally differentiating W and noting that from the envelope theorem we have $\pi_s = x$ and $\pi_\tau = -z$, we have

$$dW = \pi_{x^*} dx^* - sdx + (\tau - \text{MD})dz, \tag{46}$$

where $MD \equiv D'(z)$ is marginal damage. Using the foreign best response function we have $dx^* = (dB^*/dx)dx$, and substituting into (46) yields

$$dW = \left(\pi_{x^*} \frac{dB^*}{dx} - s \right) dx + (\tau - MD)dz \tag{47}$$

If we now choose s and τ to maximize (45), then (47) implies that the solution is:

$$\tau = MD \tag{48}$$

$$s = \pi_{x^*} \frac{dB^*}{dx} > 0. \tag{49}$$
$$\underset{(-)(-)}{}$$

If export subsidies are allowed, we get a version of the targeting rule: pollution policy is used to internalize the pollution externality, and trade policy is used to promote exports. Equation (49) is the Brander/Spencer (1985) result that in an international Cournot duopoly, export subsidies can be welfare-improving because they give the home firm a strategic advantage over the foreign firm. The intuition is that the home firm could gain a strategic advantage over the foreign firm if it could act as a Stackelberg leader and pre-commit to a higher output. This, however, is not credible. The domestic government can make this commitment credible by subsidizing exports. This shifts out the domestic firm's best response function, thereby giving it a strategic advantage and allowing it to grab a bigger share of the export market. This result is particularly interesting because it is different than the usual terms-of-trade argument – the export subsidy can be shown to reduce world prices; hence, the terms-of-trade actually worsen. This effect is, however, more than offset by the increase in the home firm's market share.

Now suppose that a free-trade agreement bans the use of export subsidies. Using (47), we can find the second-best optimal pollution tax:

$$\tau = MD - \pi_{x^*} \frac{dB^*}{dx} \left[\frac{dx/d\tau}{dz/d\tau} \right] < MD.$$
$$\underset{(-)(-)}{} \qquad \underset{(+)}{}$$

The pollution tax is now less than marginal damage because the government has an incentive to subsidize the domestic firm. This is another example of how the policy substitution effect can result in pollution policy that does not fully internalize externalities. Note that as in the case of competitive markets, this result does not tell us whether policy is tighter or weaker after trade liberalization, nor does it tell us whether pollution rises or falls with trade.[61] In fact, this was a case where prior to the trade agreement, governments had an incentive to use export subsidies to promote a polluting industry. The free-trade agreement makes it more difficult to do this and so it may well lower pollution. However, it is nevertheless true that pollution is higher than it would have been relative to a free-trade benchmark where the government is fully internalizing externalities.

While the strategic trade policy motive does suggest that there are cases where using weak pollution policy to subsidize polluting firms can raise welfare in an open economy, the result is very sensitive to market structure assumptions (as Barrett 1994 noted).

First, suppose there are several domestic firms that compete with each other as well as with foreign firms. That is, generalize the model to allow for more than one domestic firm. For simplicity assume symmetry so that all domestic firms are identical. In this case one can show that as the number of domestic firms increases, the optimal policy switches from an export subsidy to an export tax.[62]

Consider a typical domestic firm with output x. Denote the output of its $n-1$ rival domestic firms by $Y = (n-1)y$. Then the profit function for a representative domestic firm is:

$$\pi[(n-1)y, x^*, \tau, s] = \max_{x,z}\{p(x + (n-1)y + x^*)x - c(x,z) + sx - \tau z\}.$$

Domestic welfare is

$$W = n[\pi - sx + \tau z] - D(nz).$$

Suppose that a free-trade agreement constrains subsidies to zero. Then the government chooses τ to maximize W. This yields:

$$\tau = \text{MD} - \pi_{x^*}\left[\frac{dx^*/d\tau}{dz/d\tau}\right] - (n-1)\pi_Y\frac{dy/d\tau}{dz/d\tau}.$$

$$\quad\quad\quad (-)\quad (-)\quad\quad\quad\quad (-)\quad (+)$$

If $n = 1$, we have the same result as above: the pollution tax is below marginal damage because the government has an incentive to shift rent from the foreign to the domestic firms. However, for $n > 1$, there is an extra term which is positive. Because all output is exported, there is an incentive for domestic firms to act as a cartel to try to extra rent from foreign consumers. When domestic firms instead act as Cournot competitors (because cartels are usually illegal), this rent is dissipated. The government can prevent the rent dissipation by taxing output of domestic firms to push up the price. Notice that this is another version of the standard argument for an export tax: the role of such a tax is to exploit a country's monopoly power by restricting domestic exports. In this model, the government faces two conflicting motives: subsidize exports to give domestic firms a strategic advantage over their foreign rival(s); and tax exports to push domestic output closer to the collusive level. In the trade literature, simulation models have shown that n need not be very large for the tax motive to be stronger than the subsidy motive; and in this case, the pollution tax would be above marginal damage. Finally, note that this result should not really be very surprising. As n goes to infinity, this model approaches perfect competition, and in that context, the standard result is that export taxes are optimal.

As another example of how the result is sensitive to market structure, Eaton and Grossman (1986) pointed out that the Brander-Spencer result is reversed if firms compete in price instead of quantities. To see this, suppose that the domestic and foreign products are imperfect substitutes and suppose that that prices (p and p^*) are the strategic variables instead of quantities.

Let $x(p, p^*)$ be the foreign demand for the domestic firm's good and define domestic profits given the foreign price as:

$$\tilde{\pi}(p^*, \tau, s) = \max_{p,z}\{px(p,p^*) - c[x(p,p^*), z] + sx(p,p^*) - \tau z\}.$$

As before, domestic welfare $\tilde{W}$ is the sum of profits and net government revenue, less pollution damage. Proceeding analogously to our derivation of (47) yields

$$d\tilde{W} = \left(\tilde{\pi}_{p^*}\frac{dp^*}{dp} - s\frac{dx}{dp}\right)dp + (\tau - MD)dz,$$

where $dp^*/dp > 0$ is the slope of the foreign best response function and $dx/dp = x_p + x_{p^*}[dp^*/dp]$. If export subsidies are allowed, then the optimal policy fully internalizes the pollution externality and sets the export subsidy as:

$$s = \tilde{\pi}_{p^*}\frac{dp^*/dp}{dx/dp} < 0.$$

$$\quad\;\; (+)\;\;\; (-)$$

In this case because domestic and foreign prices are strategic complements, the optimal export subsidy is in fact an export tax. The home firm's profits would be higher if it could precommit to a higher price; an export tax facilitates this.

If a trade agreement bans export taxes and subsidies, the second-best optimal pollution tax is now given by

$$\tau = MD - \pi_{p^*}\frac{dp^*}{dp}\left[\frac{dp/d\tau}{dz/d\tau}\right] > MD.$$

$$\quad\;\;\; (+)\;\; (+)\;\;\; (-)$$

The pollution tax is higher than marginal damage because there is an incentive to tax exports.

Overall, the strategic trade policy is based on distortions arising from market power and therefore it generates second-best arguments for using environmental policy to influence trade. However, there is no presumption that this approach would lead to either stronger or weaker environmental policy as trade is liberalized: the specific results are very sensitive to market structure.[63]

7.7 Political economy approaches to environmental policy

Governments are subject to political influence, and several authors have used a political economy approach to assess the responsiveness of governments to trade liberalization. There are a variety of models and results tend to be model specific, so I will not develop any one model in detail.[64]

Fredriksson (1999) uses a Grossman-Helpman (1994) lobbying model to consider the effects of tariff reduction in a polluting sector. He finds that the effects on the stringency of pollution policy are ambiguous. Because output in the polluting sector declines, the marginal benefits of lobbying by both industry and environmental groups falls; the net effect depends on parameters. He shows that it is possible for pollution to increase if the lobby group is successful in pressuring the government to significantly relax pollution policy in response to trade liberalization. Bommer and Schulze (1999) use a political support model in which the government maximizes an objective function that weighs the interests of different groups. Assuming that the income distribution is initially optimal from the government's perspective, the government responds to trade liberalization by using environmental policy to dampen the adverse distributional effects; that is, it manipulates environmental policy to compensate the losers from trade liberalization.[65] If the trade stimulates the polluting sector, then pollution policy will be tightened up more than in the first-best because exporters are experiencing direct gains via the export expansion, while environmentalists and those in the import-competing sector are losing. But if the import-competing sector contracts as a result of trade liberalization, the government may respond by weakening pollution policy by more than in the first-best. This effect, which is common to many political economy models, predicts that governments will face pressure to manipulate environmental policy to achieve goals previously achieved via the use of trade policy; that is, this type of model predicts policy substitution.

One of the weaknesses of the political economy approach is that it typically assumes that environmental policy is the only instrument available to help out influence groups once trade policy is constrained via the liberalization process. In reality there are many instruments available such as alterations to tax policy and various types of subsidies. It is not obvious why manipulating environmental policy would be the most cost-effective and politically appealing way to respond to interest group pressure.[66] Coate and Morris (1995) suggest that governments may use inefficient policies to help out interest groups if these are more difficult for the electorate to detect than direct policies such as subsidies or tax breaks. Sturm (2006) and Kawahara (forthcoming) apply this approach to environmental policy. In a complex world, the typical voter is unlikely to be aware of the efficient level of emissions for each pollutant and so weak environmental policy may be an attractive way of rewarding lobbyists. Of course, the argument can also work in the opposite direction as environmental groups can exploit imperfect information to push for tough standards.

7.8   Market access and product standards: consumption-generated pollution

We saw earlier that when pollution is generated by consumption the optimal policy is to use trade instruments to target the terms of trade and to impose an emission tax to internalize externalities. Moreover, the optimal emission taxes should be the same for domestic and foreign suppliers regardless of whether imports are more or less polluting than domestic goods. We now consider the effects of free trade on the incentives of governments to manipulate environmental policy in the presence of consumption-generated pollution.

Consumption-generated pollution presents governments with a broader range of options than production pollution because imported goods cause pollution at the time of consumption; and, hence, while they are under the jurisdiction of the domestic government. Governments impose taxes and regulations on products sold within their jurisdiction to influence the flow of environmental damage from consumption. This can give governments a wider range of policy options to use environmental policy to influence trade because the characteristics of foreign products can be directly targeted by domestic policy.

I first consider the effect of a free-trade agreement on the incentives for governments to manipulate policy that targets consumption-generated pollution; and then discuss some of the work on the design of trade agreements aimed at trying to constrain such behaviour.

I consider two instruments: emission taxes and product standards. Emission taxes are much less commonly used than product standards, but they serve as a useful benchmark.

I use a very simple model of product standards, which draws on work by Fischer and Serra (2000), Gulati and Roy (2008) and Copeland (2001). There are two goods, Y_1 and Y_2. Y_2 is the numeraire and does not pollute; and Y_1 pollutes during consumption. Home imports Y_1 and also produces Y_1 domestically; but it does not export Y_1. The manufacturer produces a base model of Y_1 which generates $\bar{e}$ units of emissions when consumed. Base technology is represented as before by a national income function, $G(p, v)$. The base version of Y_1 can be modified by the manufacturer to generate $e < \bar{e}$ units of emissions at a cost of $c(e)$ units of the numeraire good in the case of domestic firms (and $c^*(e)$ in the case of foreign firms). I assume that c is decreasing and convex in e.

Let p denote the price of the base version of Y_1, let t denote an import tariff and τ and τ^* be the emission taxes that the home government imposes on the domestic and foreign versions of the product. Then the price of a unit of the domestic consumable version will be

$$q = p + c(e) + \tau e.$$

The price of a unit of the foreign consumable version is

$$q^* = p^* + c^*(e^*) + \tau^* e^* + t,$$

where p^* is the price of the foreign base version. If both domestic and imported goods are consumed, arbitrage requires that $q^* = q$, and this allows us to solve for the price that domestic producers receive for the base version of the product:

$$p = p^* + t + c^*(e^*) - c(e) + \tau^* e^* - \tau e. \tag{50}$$

I first consider the optimal policy and then consider how this may change if trade is free. Given emission taxes, competition will force foreign and domestic producers to minimize the net price (inclusive of emission taxes) that consumers must pay for the good. Consequently, domestic producers set

$$c'(e) + \tau = 0. \tag{51}$$

and foreign producers set

$$c^{*\prime}(e^*) + \tau^* = 0. \tag{52}$$

The budget constraint for the representative domestic consumer is

$$E(q, z, u) = G(p, v) + \tau z^d + \tau^* z^M + tM,$$

where M is imports and total pollution z is the sum of emissions from the domestic goods z^d and imported goods z^M. Hence,

$$z = z^d + z^M = Y_1 e + M e^*.$$

Totally differentiating the budget constraint and using (51) and (52) and the balance of trade constraint ($M = X^*(p^*)$) yields

$$E_u du = (\tau - E_z) dz^d + (\tau^* - E_z) dz^M - \left(t X_{p^*}^* - X^*\right) dp^*. \tag{53}$$

Choosing emission taxes and the tariff to maximize utility yields

$$\tau = \tau^* = E_z, \tag{54}$$

$$\frac{t}{p^*} = \frac{1}{\varepsilon^*}, \tag{55}$$

where as before ε^* is the elasticity of the foreign export supply curve. This replicates our earlier results (17). The standard targeting rule applies: pollution taxes are non-discriminatory and internalize the externality, and tariffs target the terms of trade.

Suppose now that a free-trade agreement is signed so that tariffs are set equal to zero. The government has an incentive to restrict imports to improve the terms of trade and this creates an incentive to use a discriminatory emission tax. To illustrate this point clearly, consider a special case where the foreign emission standard e^* is exogenous.[67] Then since $z^M = e^*M$ and since the trade balance constraint is $M = X^*$ we can rewrite (53) (with $t = 0$) as:

$$E_u du = (\tau - E_z)\, dz^d + \left[(\tau^* - E_z)\, e^* X_{p^*}^* + X^*\right] dp^*.$$

If we now choose emission taxes to maximize utility, the above implies that the optimal taxes are:

$$\tau = E_z,$$

$$\tau^* = E_z + \frac{p^*}{e^*}.$$

The domestic emission tax internalizes the externality caused by domestic emissions. The emission tax for the foreign good has two components – the first is marginal damage; the second is the optimal tariff formula. With an exogenous foreign emission intensity, an emission tax on the imported good is equivalent to a tariff.[68] Hence, if governments are unconstrained, there is an incentive to levy a discriminatory emission tax on the imported good.

The WTO and other trade agreements have responded to the potential for discriminatory regulatory policy by imposing a National Treatment rule – this allows governments to choose their own internal regulatory policy as long as foreign firms are not treated less favourably than domestic firms. While national treatment rules play an important role in restraining protectionism (see Horn, 2006), they nevertheless do not fully eliminate the opportunity for governments to manipulate environmental policy for other purposes. To see this consider two examples: an emission tax and an emission standard.

First consider emission taxes. The National Treatment rule requires that the foreign emission tax be set no higher than the foreign emission tax. Let us therefore constrain the government to set $\tau = \tau^*$. Using (53), we can find the optimal emission tax:

$$\tau = E_z + X^* \frac{dp^*/d\tau}{dz/d\tau} > E_Z.$$
$$\phantom{\tau = E_z + X^* \frac{}{}} (+) \; (+)$$

The National Treatment rule does not prevent the government from using the emission tax to influence the terms of trade. The emission tax is set above marginal damage because there is an incentive to tax imports.

Now suppose that the government has neither consumption taxes nor emission taxes, but simply uses a product standard. This scenario has been at the heart of several trade disputes, such as the Beef hormone case, restrictions on genetically modified food, a U.S.–Canada dispute over the minimum legal size for lobsters, and others. I assume that a national treatment rule applies and consider cases in which the same standard is imposed on domestic and foreign producers. For simplicity assume that the country is small so that p^* is fixed by world markets. Rather than characterizing the optimal policy, I make a much simpler point, which is that even with the national treatment rule in place, product standards can often be manipulated to favour domestic firms over local firms. In fact depending on technology, domestic firms may have an incentive to lobby for a more stringent standard.

National Treatment must be satisfied and so we require that $e = e^*$: the government requires both local and foreign products to meet the same standard. Consider the effect of tightening the standard (a reduction in e) on domestic output of the polluting good. Using (50) we have:

$$-\frac{\partial Y_1}{\partial e} = -G_{pp}\frac{\partial p}{\partial e} = G_{pp}\left(\frac{\partial c}{\partial e} - \frac{\partial c^*}{\partial e}\right). \tag{56}$$

Two things are worth noting. First, suppose that the domestic and foreign compliance cost functions are identical. Then a tighter emission standard has no effect on domestic output. The domestic price rises by the amount of the increase in foreign compliance cost. This fully covers the increase in domestic compliance costs and so the domestic firm experiences no change in its net return at the initial output level after the emission standard is tightened. Consequently, there is no change in domestic output. Overall domestic consumption falls because consumer prices rise to cover the compliance cost, but this is fully accounted for by an adjustments in imports. This is a somewhat remarkable result because it shows that tightening up environmental policy may have no effect on the fortunes of domestic firms because they are able to fully pass the costs on to consumers without any loss in sales.

Next, note that if the foreign compliance cost function is steeper than the domestic cost function then (56) is negative.[69] This means tighter environmental policy actually increases the output of domestic firms because it is more costly for foreigners than for domestic firms to comply. Consequently, there is an incentive for domestic firms to lobby for a tighter standard to improve their competitive position with respect to their foreign rivals.

One could imagine a more general model in which the government has some flexibility in how to design the standard. The above result suggests that if there is some incentive to favour local firms, then governments will look for ways of specifying standards that are easier for domestic firms to satisfy than foreign firms. The result is a policy that is completely consistent with national treatment but effectively tends to discriminate against foreign firms. This issue has been investigated in the context of imperfectly competitive firms by Copeland (2001), Fisher and Serra (2000) and others and is an example of the well-known Salop and Scheffman (1983) result on raising rivals' costs.

I have pointed out that the National Treatment rule may not be sufficient to fully prevent governments from manipulating environmental policy to favour local producers. It is also possible that the National Treatment rule may prevent attainment of the first-best, even if governments have no incentive to deviate from the first-best. To see this, consider the following example.

Emission taxes are typically not feasible in the case of consumption-generated pollution because emissions are difficult to monitor. It is therefore useful to note that an emissions tax is equivalent to a consumption tax combined with an emission standard. Find the level of e and e^* determined by the first order conditions (51)–(54) and impose these as product standards; then use the level of τ determined by these conditions and set the consumption tax $t_c = \tau e$ and $t_c^* = \tau e^*$. This replicates the solution determined by the first order conditions when emission taxes were feasible.

While the consumption tax – emission standard combination can in principle implement the first-best, it is in general incompatible with the national treatment rule. For clarity, consider a case where there is no market power so that the optimal tariff is zero and emission taxes would be set equal to marginal damage. There is no incentive to manipulate environmental policy to influence the terms of trade, but if technology differs across countries – that is if the $c(e)$ and $c^*(e)$ functions are different – then the optimal emission standard and consumption tax that solves (51)–(54) will differ across countries. The possibility that a National Treatment rule may prevent the implementation of the first-best in cases where emission taxes are not feasible was pointed out by Gulati and Roy (2008). Horn (2006) provides a more general discussion of the merits of a National Treatment rule in situations where it may prevent implementation of the first-best. He notes that in the design of trade agreements, the choice of tariffs may be influenced by this possibility.

8   Implications for the design of trade agreements

Trade agreements are signed because in their absence governments face pressure to protect or promote domestic producers. Trade agreements eliminate some of the instruments available to governments – tariffs, import quotas, export subsidies and other overtly discriminatory policies – but they do not eliminate the pressures to protect that governments face. One of the important lessons of the work on policy substitution is that the elimination of trade barriers will create an incentive for governments (or those pressuring governments for protection) to look for alternative instruments that are unconstrained by the trade agreements;

and this can lead to outcomes where environmental policy may be manipulated to protect domestic firms.

There are relatively few empirical studies on this issue, but there is some evidence that governments do engage in policy substitution. Gawande (1999) does not focus specifically on environmental policy but finds evidence that governments substitute non-tariff barriers for tariffs and quotas as trade is liberalized. Eliste and Fredriksson (2002) report evidence from the farm sector in the U.S. that governments weaken environmental policy in response to freer trade. Ederington and Minier (2003) find that the stringency of environmental regulation (proxied by abatement costs) tends to be lower in sectors where net imports are higher.

What should we do? One option, explored in the literature on policy linkage[70] is to extend the scope of trade agreements to cover those domestic policy instruments (such as environmental policy) that can be used as substitutes for trade barriers. In our simple full information model with only two policy instruments (tariffs and pollution policy), this seems like a straightforward solution. To find the Pareto efficient solution, we choose a tariff t for the home country, an export tax t^* for the foreign country,[71] domestic and foreign pollution levels and a lump sum transfer[72] to maximize a weighted sum of domestic and foreign utilities

$$\lambda V(p+t, G(p+t, v, z) + tM - T, z)$$
$$+(1-\lambda)V^*(p-t^*, G^*(p-t^*, v^*, z^*) + t^*X^* + T, z^*)$$

subject to the balanced trade constraint:

$$M(p, t, T, z) = X^*(p, t^*, T, z).$$

With lump sum transfers available, the first-best can be obtained with free trade ($t = t^* = 0$), environmental policy that fully internalizes externalities in each country,

$$\tau = MD$$

$$\tau^* = MD^*$$

and lump sum transfers chosen to equalize the weighted marginal utilities of income:

$$\lambda V_I = (1-\lambda)V_{I^*}^*.$$

If the trade agreement is enforceable[73] and constrains both pollution policy and trade policy, then the first-best will be achieved and the 'loophole' in the trade agreement that allowed governments to substitute environmental policy for trade policy is removed.

While this approach requires that each country make binding commitments to specific environmental policies, it does *not* imply that environmental policy should be harmonized across countries (as political rhetoric about creating a 'level playing field' might suggest).[74] Efficient policy requires that externalities be fully internalized in each country.[75] This requires that the shadow price of emissions in each country be equal to marginal damage, which will vary across locations due to factors such as income, climate, population density, fragility of the local ecosystem, and so forth. There is nothing in the model that forces marginal damage to be equalized across countries.[76]

In practice, this approach has a number of drawbacks that render it impractical in many contexts. In a dynamic economy with shocks, innovation, evolving knowledge about ecosystems and other changes, marginal damage curves will shift over time and so efficient pollution policy will also change. This would require either state-contingent agreements between governments, or constant renegotiation. Moreover, environmental policy is rarely as simple as setting a pollution tax or emission quota. In practice, environmental policy is fuzzy. Pollution taxes and quotas are not commonly used in practice; instead environmental policy is often a complex set of regulations. For many environmental problems, such as land use issues, simple policies such as pollution taxes are not practical. Even in standard pollution emission problems, the characterization of efficient policy is complex when there are multiple polluters and multiple monitoring points.

In short, as Horn, Maggi and Staiger (2010) emphasize, contracting costs can be very high once trade agreements move into the realm of constraining domestic policy. And as a result of high contracting costs, trade agreements will inevitably be incomplete contracts; not all policy instruments that can affect trade flows will be convered by the agreement.

There have been several approaches to modelling trade agreements as incomplete contracts. Copeland (1990) considered a model with two instruments: trade policy and domestic policy, and assumed that contracting costs for trade policy were zero and prohibitive for domestic policy (which could be thought of as environmental policy). Trade agreements were treated as a two stage game. Governments committed to trade policy in the first stage, knowing that this would induce a second stage game in which domestic policy was used as a substitute for trade barriers. Copeland showed that as long as domestic policy was an imperfect substitute for trade policy then it still pays to enter into a trade agreement that reduces trade barriers even though it will be somewhat undermined by the manipulation of domestic policy. However, free trade need not be the second-best optimum.[77] Walz and Wellisch (1997) use this approach to show that trade liberalization raises welfare in an oligopoly model.

Bagwell and Staiger (2001) also assumed that contracting over domestic policy was prohibitively costly. However, they argued that the first-best could nevertheless be attained if governments negotiated agreements over the level of market access they will allow to foreigners, rather on instruments directly. To see this, suppose that there are two instruments, tariffs (t) and environmental policy (z) and that a binding level of imports, $\overline{M}$, has been agreed upon. Then the government will choose t and z to maximize utility subject to the balance-of-trade constraint and the import constraint:

$$\underset{\{t,z\}}{\text{Max}}\left\{V(p+t,G(p+t,v,z)+tM,z):M=\overline{M},M(p,t,z)=X^{*}(p,t^{*},z^{*})\right\}.$$

The first-order conditions for the solution imply:

$$t = \frac{\lambda}{V_I} + \frac{p}{\epsilon^*},$$
$$\tau = \text{MD},$$

where λ is the Lagrange multiplier associated with the constraint on imports. That is, tariffs are chosen to implement the import target and pollution policy is chosen to fully internalize the externality. If $\overline{M}$ is the free-trade level of imports, then the tariff that implements the target will be zero and there will be no incentive for the government to use environmental policy to influence trade flows.[78] The attractive features of this approach are both that it removes the incentive for policy substitution and it eliminates the need to negotiate directly over environmental policy (which as noted above is problematic because of its complexity). However, in practice it would fall short of implementing the first-best. Changes in technology, tastes, and other factors would alter the efficient level of imports and so the agreement would either have to be state contingent or be continually renegotiated.

Horn, Maggi and Staiger (2010) explicitly model contracting costs.[79] Their approach can explain why trade agreements constrain tariffs and import quotas but may not constrain environmental policy. If contracting costs are relatively high for environmental policy (because of complexity and lack of transparency), then it may not be covered by a trade agreement. They also show that if tariffs are not state contingent, then not constraining some domestic policy yields indirect state contingency benefits. And if trade volumes are relatively low, if countries have relatively little influence on the terms of trade, or if the political costs of weak environmental policy are high, then the benefits of constraining environmental policy are likely to be low, so in the presence of contracting costs it may not be worth including them in a trade agreement. On the other hand, if contracting costs were zero, then all policies would be constrained by state contingent agreements. Hence, their approach also predicts that the scope of trade agreements will expand to cover environmental policy in some circumstances. Countries with very high bilateral trade volumes may find that the benefits of coordinating environmental policy exceed contracting costs. And countries that are very similar in income, politics and in their approach to environmental policy will likely face relatively lower contracting costs than in countries that are very different. This can explain why the European Union has done much more to facilitate cross-country coordination of environmental policy than either the WTO or other regional trading arrangements.

9   Transboundary pollution

Now suppose that pollution spills over international borders. Let ambient pollution affecting domestic residents be $z^A = z + \gamma z^*$ and pollution affecting foreign residents be $z^{A*} = z^* + \gamma^* z$. To find the first-best policy, choose domestic and foreign emissions, trade taxes, and a lump sum transfer to maximize a weighted sum of domestic and foreign indirect utility

$$\lambda V(p+t, G(p+t, v, z) + tM - T, z^A) \\ + (1-\lambda)V^*(p - t^*, G^*(p - t^*, v^*, z^*) + t^*X^* + T, z^{A*}) \tag{57}$$

subject to the market clearing condition

$$M(p, t, T, z, z^*) = X^*(p, t^*, T, z^*, z). \tag{58}$$

The planner needs to choose policies to deal with international income distribution and environmental problems. With lump sum transfers available, the first-best can be obtained with free trade ($t = t^* = 0$) and lump sum transfers chosen to equalize the weighted marginal utilities of income:

$$\lambda V_I = (1-\lambda)V^*_{I*}. \tag{59}$$

The solution for environmental policy yields the standard Samuelson rule: pollution should be chosen so that the shadow price of emissions in each country is equal to the sum of the marginal damages:

$$\tau = MD + \gamma^* MD^*, \tag{60}$$

$$\tau^* = MD^* + \gamma MD. \tag{61}$$

If pollution has uniform effects across all countries ($\gamma = \gamma* = 1$), (60) and (61) imply that emission taxes should be the same across countries. Notice that the solution for pollution taxes is independent of the welfare weights placed on the two countries. Lump sum transfers are used to deal with distributional objectives.

If lump sum transfers across countries are not available, matters are more complex because the optimal policy is sensitive to the distribution of income and the relative weights placed upon each country. Think of Home as North and Foreign as South. If South is poorer than North, then it could be argued that North should compensate South for emission reductions. This is what occurs in the solution with lump sum transfers above. Without lump sum transfers, one might expect that a second-best solution would require North to have more stringent environmental policy than South. However, this is not necessarily the case. Choosing tariffs and emissions to maximize (57) subject to market clearing with $T = 0$ yields

$$t = -t^* \tag{62}$$

with the level of trade taxes chosen to satisfy (59) and with environmental policy determined by (60) and (61). In this case, tariffs can be used as a substitute for a lump sum transfer: (62) ensures that domestic and foreign prices are the same and so production and consumption efficiency is obtained. If South is to be favoured, then North subsidizes imports from South (and South levies an off-setting export tax).[80] Environmental policy is still determined by the Samuelson rule and in the case of a pure global public bad such as carbon emissions, the shadow price of emissions is equal across countries.

Suppose, however, that in addition to ruling out lump sum transfers, we also are constrained by a free-trade regime. That is, suppose that $T = 0$ and that $t = t^* = 0$. Then environmental policy has to play a dual role of dealing with the international distribution of income and with environmental problems.[81]

Let

$$\varphi \equiv \frac{(1 - \lambda) V_I^*}{\lambda V_I}. \tag{63}$$

Then choosing emissions to maximize (57) subject to market clearing yields:

$$\tau = \mathrm{MD} + \gamma^* \varphi \mathrm{MD}^* - M(\varphi - 1) \frac{dp}{dz}, \tag{64}$$

$$\tau^* = \mathrm{MD}^* + \frac{\gamma \mathrm{MD}}{\varphi} - X^* \left(1 - \frac{1}{\varphi}\right) \frac{dp}{dz^*}. \tag{65}$$

Suppose that the weighted marginal utility of income is higher in South than North. Then, $\varphi > 1$ and if we ignore terms-of-trade effects for a moment, (64) and (65) imply that Northern pollution taxes put a higher weight on the environmental impact of North's pollution on South than in the Samuelson rule; and, conversely, South puts a lower weight on its damage to North than in the Samuelson rule. That is, in the case of a pure public bad, and if terms of trade effects were zero, we have $\tau > \tau^*$: North has to be more aggressive in its environmental policies than South.

Moreover, when terms-of-trade effects are not zero, pollution taxes are also chosen to nudge the terms of trade in favour of South. If South's export good (North's import good) is the pollution intensive good, then we expect $dp/dz < 0$. And hence with $\varphi > 1$ the third term in both (64) and (65) is positive: pollution taxes are pushed upwards; thereby reducing the supply of South's export good and improving South's terms of trade.

9.1   Permit trade and climate change

If pollution is a pure global public bad, as in the case of carbon emissions, then our results above indicate that global efficiency requires that emission prices be equalized across countries. One approach to achieving this would be to have a global carbon tax; however, the Kyoto protocol was instead an agreement under which countries were given emission targets.[82] If these targets are binding, then allowing international trade in emission permits would lead to a convergence in permit prices and in theory could achieve efficiency.

Tradable emission permits have a great deal of appeal in a domestic context because they allow some separation between distributional objectives and efficiency. For example, if it is necessary to cut domestic SO_2 emissions by 20 percent, then a proposal that requires that all sources reduce emissions by the same percentage (20 percent) may be perceived as 'fair'; however, it is unlikely to be efficient since marginal abatement costs differ across sources. However, it sources are allocated permits on the basis of a uniform 20 percent cut, then efficiency can be achieved if they are allowed to trade permits.[83] Similarly, this could be a mechanism to deal with the international equity issues discussed above – allocations of emission permits could be determined by equity considerations and trade in those permits would then ensure efficiency.

Suppose, then, that a set of countries has been allocated binding carbon emission targets. It is tempting to argue that allowing free trade in these permits must be welfare-improving on the basis that global free trade is efficient. However, as shown by Copeland and Taylor (2005) it is possible that allowing trade in permits will lead to welfare reductions for some countries. This follows from a well-known result on the gains from trade. Starting from a world with no trade, allowing some trade is always welfare-improving. However, starting from a regime where there is free trade in some markets, opening up an additional market to free trade need not benefit all countries. Brecher and Choudri (1982) and Grossman (1984) for example show that in a world with pre-existing free trade in goods, then allowing free capital mobility may reduce welfare for some countries. This is because trade in capital will affect goods prices and some countries will suffer terms of trade losses. In our context, tradable emission permits play a similar role to mobile capital: allowing permit trade will affect goods prices and can lead to terms of trade losses.

To see this, it is useful to consider a framework where both Y_1 and Y_2 pollute, (but where Y_1 is more pollution intensive). Let Home have an endowment z of permits and consider the effect of allowing a small trade in permits. Let z^M be imports of permits, let τ^M be the price of imported permits, and let Z^W denote global pollution, which I assume is a pure global public bad. Indirect utility is $V(p, I, Z^W)$ and national income (I) is given by:

$$I = G(p, v, z + z^M) - \tau^M z^M.$$

The welfare effect for the domestic country of importing permits, starting from the position of no trade in permits, is

$$\frac{1}{V_I}\frac{dV}{dz^M}\bigg|_{z^M=0} = \left(\tau - \tau^M\right) - M\frac{dp}{dz^M} - MD\frac{dZ^W}{dz^M}.$$

There are three terms. The first is the standard gains from trade, $\tau - \tau^M$. Home gains if it can import permits at a price lower than the domestic price. The second term is the effect of permit trade on the price of traded goods. The reallocation of permits across countries will affect relative supplies of goods and this will affect the terms of trade. If Home imports the polluting intensive good and the relative price of the polluting good rises, then Home loses via the terms of trade effect. The final term is the effect of permit trade on global pollution. It is permit-trade-induced leakage. The standard concern about leakage is that if a coalition of countries commits to reducing carbon emissions, then carbon intensive industry may shift to those countries that did not join the coalition. The resulting increase in emissions from those countries is carbon leakage. The term in the expression above is an additional potential source of leakage. If permit trade leads to an increase in the price of the pollution intensive good, this will stimulate production of the pollution intensive good in countries outside the coalition and global emissions will rise. Copeland and Taylor (2005) discuss various scenarios in which permit trade can lead to welfare losses.[84] In a three-country world where all countries have agreed to limit emissions (so that the last term in the above expression is zero), then it is possible for both the importing and exporting countries to lose from allowing permit trade (the gains accrue to the third country via terms of trade effects). With carbon leakage (that is with some countries outside the coalition), the possibilities of losses are increased. These results have also been obtained in CGE simulation models. For example, McKibben and others (1999) consider a regime in which countries have been allocated fixed supplies of binding emission permits. They consider the effects of allowing free trade in permits and find that Japan losses from the transition to this regime because of increases in the price of oil (which Japan imports). Babiker, Reilly and Viguier (2004) show that international permit trading can also lead to welfare losses in some countries if there are pre-existing distortions (such as taxes and subsidies) and present CGE simulation results illustrating this possibility.

These results do not mean that trade in emission permits is a bad idea – as noted above, efficiency requires that emission prices be equalized across countries. However, the analysis does point out potential conflicts between equity and efficiency objectives; and it also illustrates the potential importance of the sequencing of reforms. If countries simultaneously agree to emission targets and an emissions trading system, then in principle the distributional effects of trading could be factored into the agreement. However, if they first agree to targets and then revisit the issue of whether to set up an international emission permit trading regime later, those countries that stand to lose from trading may be resistant.

Even in the absence of international permit trade, it is possible that trade in goods can lead to international convergence of permit prices via the same mechanism that leads to factor price equalization in the Heckscher–Ohlin model. Copeland and Taylor (2005) illustrate this result in a simple two good, two factor Heckscher–Ohlin–type model, where the two factors are labour and emission permits. If countries have identical technology, free trade in goods leads to permit-price equalization even in the absence international permit trade.[85]

9.2   Unilateral policy

Suppose now that negotiation fails and that the domestic country acts unilaterally. This was a problem studied by Markusen (1975). Assume that the foreign country is not policy-active so that Foreign emissions are an increasing function of the price of the polluting good. The Home government chooses pollution policy and trade policy to maximize

$$V(p+t, G(p+t, v, z) + tM, z + \gamma z^*)$$

subject to

$$z^* = z^*(p)$$
$$M(p, t, \tau, z^*(p)) = X^*(p, z).$$

Note that the Foreign export supply functions depend on Home pollution independently of the world price because Home pollution affects consumer utility and, hence, may shift Foreign export supply via its effect on demand.

Solving yields

$$\frac{t}{p} = \frac{1}{\varepsilon_{X^*p}} \left[1 + \gamma \frac{MDz^*}{pX^*} \varepsilon_{z^*p} \right], \tag{66}$$

$$\tau = MD - tX_z^* = MD - \gamma^* tX_{zW}^*. \tag{67}$$

Tariffs are used both to target the terms of trade and to influence Foreign pollution. If Home is not affected by transboundary pollution ($\gamma = 0$), (66) reduces to (22) which is the standard optimal tariff formula. When Home is affected by Foreign pollution ($\gamma > 0$), there is an additional term which depends on the importance of Foreign pollution relative to the value of imports from Foreign, and on the responsiveness of foreign pollution to changes in the price of its export good. This is because Home does not have direct control over Foreign pollution; its only influence in this framework is via the indirect effects resulting from its manipulation of the terms of trade.

It is tempting to think that the standard targeting rule in this context would imply that Home should use domestic pollution policy only to internalize the external damage caused at home by Home pollution. However, (67) indicates that in addition to the standard marginal damage component, the pollution tax has an additional term which reflects the direct effect of changes in Home pollution on Foreign export supply.[86] To interpret this, suppose that $X_z^* < 0$. Then from (67) we have $\tau > MD$. Increasing the pollution tax will reduce domestic pollution, which will shift out the Foreign export supply curve,[87] which will improve Home's terms of trade. Because the Foreign export supply curve is affected independently by both world prices and the pollution externality, the domestic pollution tax targets the effects of pollution on the terms of trade as well as on domestic pollution damage.

As a practical matter, the use of unilateral trade policy actions to target Foreign pollution is more complex than in the simple analysis above. Since the key channel of influence is via world prices, trade policy initiatives will have little effect unless the country is large enough to affect prices or acts with a coalition. Even if a country is large, trade policy actions may set in motion trade-diversion effects which and up increasing costs but have little effect on the environment. For example if country A restricts imports from B, then B could instead sell to C and some other country D could export to A. And, as we saw in the case of natural capital, it is possible for trade sanctions to be bad for the environment. If trade sanctions reduce the value of habitat used for producing the environmentally intensive good, then the habitat may be cleared for some alternative use (timber bans can cause conversion of forest land to agriculture).

10 Conclusion

Much of the research agenda in the area of trade and environment has been driven by concerns about policy. Good policy analysis requires a deep understanding of the interaction between the economy and environmental outcomes. There has been significant progress in this area, but there is still much that we need to know.

One of the most significant developments over the past ten to fifteen years has been the use of panel data to assess the effects of environmental policy on trade flows and production location. While earlier studies found little or no connection between environmental policy and competitiveness, many recent studies have found evidence of a linkage.

On the other hand, there is no convincing evidence that trade liberalization has caused a systematic migration of polluting industries to countries with weak environmental policy – other factors such as capital accumulation, access to markets and agglomeration are more important in determining trade patterns. And while there is evidence that growth and capital accumulation put pressure on the environment, the effects of policy responses appear to have been more important than trade in determining environmental outcomes.

There are, however, numerous gaps in our knowledge and, so, ample opportunities for further work. Much of the work on the effects of environmental policy on trade flows and plant location has used U.S. data; more work using international data is needed. Another promising line of work on the competitiveness issue would be to make increased use of firm and plant level data. In the international trade literature, there has been a major focus on the effects of trade liberalization on productivity using such data; similar work could be illuminating in increasing our understanding of how economies adjust to tighter environmental regulations.[88]

The empirical work on the effects of environmental policy on trade and plant location has important implications for the design of trade agreements because it means that pressure on policy makers regarding concerns about competitiveness need to be taken seriously. In the context of climate change, leakage issues similarly have to be addressed. The theoretical work suggests that governments have incentives to manipulate environmental policy in response to trade liberalization. However the specific results are mixed and sensitive to the modelling framework. In terms of theory, there is a need to increase our understanding of when and why policymakers may choose to adjust environmental policy for competitiveness reasons when there are many other policy instruments potentially available. And there is very little empirical work on this issue. There are only a very small number of studies that seek to determine whether, and to what extent, international competitiveness pressures have influenced environmental policy outcomes.

There is also much scope for increasing our understanding of the interaction between renewable resource depletion and globalization. While there are numerous examples of renewable resource populations that have collapsed, there are also others that are well managed. More work, especially empirical, is needed to increase our understanding of the factors that explain why some resources are managed well and others are not, and what are the roles of international trade and capital mobility in affecting outcomes.

Notes

*   Department of Economics, University of British Columbia.
1. See Siebert (1985) for an early review.
2. Several other surveys of work in this area exist. Nordstrom and Vaughan (1999) is a very useful non-technical overview of the issues and the literature up to the late 1990s. Rauscher (2005) provides a comprehensive overview of work on trade, investment and the environment. Copeland and Taylor (2004) is an expository essay on trade, growth and the environment, with a focus on theoretical and empirical work on the pollution haven hypothesis and the policy implications of that literature.

There is inevitably some overlap between that paper and the current chapter; but the present chapter has much more of an emphasis on the policy literature and covers some topics (such as trade and renewable resources) not covered in the earlier paper. Sturm (2003) reviews theoretical work on trade and environment, while Brunnermeier and Levinson (2004) review the empirical evidence on the effects of environmental policy on plant location and trade. Neary (2006) and Ulph (1997) present analytical expository reviews of some of the policy literature. Copeland (2010) provides a less technical presentation of some of the issues covered in this chapter.

3. This has its origins in Copeland (1994) and Copeland and Taylor (1994) and was influenced by McGuire (1982). Lopez (1994) and Rauscher (1997) use similar models.

4. The key assumption is that one sector is more pollution intensive than the other; for simplicity and clarity, I make the stark assumption that only one sector pollutes. For models where multiple sectors pollute, see Copeland (1994), Copeland and Taylor (1994), Rauscher (1997) and others.

5. See Woodland (1982) – he does not consider pollution, but the extension to the case of pollution is straightforward.

6. More details regarding the properties of national income functions can be found in Woodland's chapter 3 in this volume, in Copeland and Taylor (2003), and in standard international trade references such as Dixit and Norman (1980), Woodland (1982) and Feenstra (2004).

7. For more details on this approach, see Copeland (1994) and Neary (2006).

8. See for example Dasgupta et al. (2001).

9. This is based on Copeland and Taylor (2003) and a more detailed exposition can be found there.

10. That is, $-V_Z/V_I = \beta(p)h'(z)/V'(R)$.

11. This allows us to avoid the strategic motive for using trade and/or environmental policy to manipulate the terms of trade. These issues will be considered later.

12. Quotas are a little more straightforward to deal with than tariffs because (as we shall see later) the optimal pollution policy in the presence of a quota is simply to set marginal damage equal to marginal abatement cost. With tariffs, the optimal second-best policy both targets pollution and tries to offset some of the distortion from the tariff. This will be considered in a subsequent section of the chapter. As well as making the analysis more complicated, this would also raise the modelling issue of whether we want to assume that the environmental policy agency has a mandate to partially undo the protective effects of the tariff. This would distract us from the issue at hand here. We can avoid this issue by simply modelling the trade barrier as a quota. Another approach, adopted by Copeland and Taylor (2003) is to assume that trade barriers take the form of frictions such as transport costs or red tape. The basic principles are the same across instruments, although the details differ slightly.

13. This condition holds in the model of Copeland and Taylor (2003) and some authors such as Neary (2006) simply assume that this substitution effect is zero.

14. See McAusland (2010) for a review of work that estimates the effects of trade on the environment focusing on scale, composition and technique effects.

15. See Grossman and Krueger (1993) who used this approach to assess the effects of NAFTA on the environment. Copeland and Taylor (1994) derived the decomposition in a general equilibrium trade model. Levinson (2009, 2010) are recent applications.

16. It is straightforward to extend this to capture consumption-generated pollution.
17. Unlike much of the work in the related environmental Kuznets curve literature, they are able to decompose the effects of increases in income into scale and technique effects, and as expected they are opposite in sign.
18. The composition effects due to capital abundance were positive for CO_2, but close to zero for a measure of water pollution, biochemical oxygen demand (BOD) and NO_X. This is not unexpected, since a significant portion of NO_X emissions come from transportation, and industries intensive in emissions affecting BOD are much less capital intensive than those emitting SO_2.
19. This is the terminology used in Copeland and Taylor (2004).
20. There is a large literature on leakage. See Aldy and Pizer (2009) and Frankel (2008) for recent contributions.
21. To get the result that imports rise, we also need the assumption that the effect of such policy on domestic demand (if any) is smaller than the effect on production. In the diagram I implicitly assumed a negligible effect on demand.
22. Rauscher (1997; chapter 3) studies models with endogenous environmental policy and mobile capital.
23. See for example, Greaker (2006).
24. This point was stressed by McAusland (2008).
25. Recent exceptions include Dean, Lovely and Hwang (2009) on China, and Wagner and Timmins (2009) on Germany.
26. Chichilnisky (1994) analyzes a model with exogenous policy differences in a renewable resource context – in her framework, North fully internalizes externalities and South has open access.
27. Grossman and Krueger (1993) noted that trade patterns were likely to be determined mainly by factors other than pollution policy.
28. Note that I am treating pollution (environmental services) as an input here. Pollution has been modelled in the literature either as an output produced jointly with other goods, or as an input. Under some regularity conditions, the two approaches are equivalent. See Copeland and Taylor (2003; chapter 2). When modelling pollution as an input as in (14) above, some restriction must be placed on feasible levels of z to ensure that goods are not produced mainly out of environmental services. I assume that these conditions are satisfied in what follows.
29. This simplifies matters by ruling out the use of pollution policy as a second-best instrument to manipulate trade patterns; it can be justified by assuming that there are many Northern and Southern countries so that none is large enough to influence world prices.
30. This result relies on assumptions regarding the underlying pollution abatement technology; in this case as Copeland and Taylor (2003) lay out in detail, the implicit assumption here is that the factor intensity of the abatement technology is the same as that of the polluting sector. Chua (2003) considers a model where both sectors pollute and where the factor intensity of the abatement sector differs from the polluting sectors. Chua shows that the effect of an increase in the pollution tax on the relative price of the relatively pollution intensive good is ambiguous in general. This is because in addition to the direct cost-increasing effect of the pollution tax on the price of polluting goods, the induced increase in the demand for abatement will draw resources away from final goods production. This will affect factor prices and costs. If this effect is strong enough and opposite in direction to the direct effect of the tax, then (with a more general abatement technology than that in this

chapter) it is possible that the country with the more stringent environmental policy could export the polluting good.

31. McCrae (1978) develops a general equilibrium trade model with a renewable resource; he focuses on characterizing the optimal harvest policy in such an economy. See Kemp and Long (1984) for an early review of the interaction between trade and natural resources. Bulte and Barbier (2005) and Fischer (2010) provide reviews of more recent work on trade and renewable resources.

32. See the classic early treatment by Gordon (1954).

33. Note that since M is the numeraire, the zero profit condition for M implies that $w = 1$.

34. See Brander and Taylor (1997a) for details.

35. This is a standard result from the second-best literature (Lipsey and Lancaster, 1956).

36. Note that resource depletion may occur even if externalities are fully internalized if free trade leads to an increase in the price of the harvest good. The manager balances current returns from harvesting against the benefits of investing in the resource stock by limiting resource harvesting. Higher prices typically mean it is worth tipping the balance towards more harvesting. However, this would nevertheless be welfare-improving. See, e.g., Bulte and Barbier (2005).

37. This is an argument made by Daly (1993). See Copeland and Taylor (1997a) for a model with myopic governments who internalize current period externalities but not inter-temporal externalities and which can lead to a downward spiral.

38. Hannesson (2000), e.g., shows that if one moves away from linear technologies so that the short-run production frontier is strictly concave, then the result that trade *must* reduce steady-state consumption in the diversified case need not hold. Trade exacerbates the externality, but the gains from trade may or may not outweigh the costs of stock depletion.

39. See also Smulders and others (2004).

40. Ostrom (1990), Baland and Platteau (1996) and others have done extensive work that aims at explaining and documenting different resource management regimes; however relatively little of this work explicitly considers the effects of globalization in influencing these regimes.

41. This model is based on Copeland and Taylor (1999).

42. In the Ethier model, expansion of M increases relative productivity in M via the effect of external economies in M; in this model, expansion of M increases relative productivity in M by killing off natural capital and reducing productivity in A. In both cases, one can show that the long-run production frontier is convex to the origin.

43. This model predicts, for example, that trade will occur between identical countries. The no trade equilibrium is unstable because a slight increase in production of M in one country leads to natural capital depletion which leads to a comparative advantage in M, which is then magnified and locked in via trade.

44. Dixit (1985) provides a good treatment of these issues.

45. We can interpret m as the effect of an increase in income on consumption of good 1.

46. This can be shown to be necessary for stability – see Neary and Ruane (1988).

47. Falvey (1988) shows that trade policy reform in the presence of import quotas differs from tariff reform because quotas prevent exacerbation of distortions in markets not subject to reform.

48. Since G is concave in z, we have $G_{zz} < 0$. And $G_{zq} = G_{qz} = \partial y_1/\partial z$ which is the Rybczinski effect of an increase in the availability of environmental services on Y output.

49. The welfare effects of trade liberalization have been considered in models with multiple pollutants and multiple goods in Copeland (1994). This work was extended to consumption-generated pollution by Beghin et al. (1997) and transboundary pollution by Turunen-Red and Woodland (2004). See also good surveys and expository pieces by Ulph (1997) and Neary (2006).

50. Again, I assume that effects of pollution changes on demand are small so that the direct effect of the tariff change dominates.

51. This is a version of the Le Chatelier principle. See Copeland (1994) and Neary (2006).

52. Conversely, if the export good pollutes, trade liberalization will expand the export sector, increase the demand for the right to pollute and (if substitution effects in marginal damage are small) will cause the pollution tax to rise.

53. This is sometimes referred to as 'environmental dumping' or 'ecological dumping'. Rauscher (1994) provides a definition of ecological dumping in a model with a non-tradable sector and considers conditions under which governments have incentives to set weaker environmental policy in the tradable sectors than in the non-tradable sector.

54. There are many other possible motives for protection or export promotion, most of which arise from some form of market failure – such as learning spillovers, unemployment, capital market distortions, and others. One could examine the effects of trade liberalization on environmental policy in the context of these other motives for protection. The details would vary from case to case, but many of the key points would likely apply as well.

55. Second-best optimal environmental policy in large open economies with terms of trade motives for protection has been considered in a number of sources, including Markusen (1975), Krutilla (1991), Rauscher (1997), and others.

56. In models with multiple goods, export subsidies may be part of a package of optimal trade taxes. See Feenstra (1986).

57. Rauscher (1997; chapter 6) considers the effects of free trade and the effects of exogenous changes in emissions policy in a monopolistically competitive framework, but does not consider optimal policy. Gurtzgen and Rauscher (2000) consider leakage issues in a model with transboundary pollution. Benarroch and Weder (2006) consider trade in a monopolistic competition model with trade in intermediate goods that differ in pollution intensity. Pollution policy in one country alters the relative supplies of clean and dirty intermediates and so affects environmental quality in the other country.

58. See Brander and Spencer (1985).

59. See also Conrad (1993), Kennedy (1994) and Ulph (1992, 1997) for applications of the strategic trade policy approach to environmental policy. The exposition here was influenced by Neary (2006).

60. See Brander and Spencer (1985) and Barrett (1994) for assumptions that yield these results – as an example, linear demand satisfies the conditions.

61. Burguet and Sempere (2003) consider a bilateral reciprocal dumping model with Cournot competition in which environmental policy can be used as a substitute for a trade barrier. They explore the issue of whether freer trade leads to tighter or weaker environmental policy. Walz and Wellisch (1997) consider the export subsidy model

and show that trade liberalization raises welfare, despite the fact that it induces governments to use weak environmental policy as a substitute for an export subsidy.

62. This analysis is due to Dixit (1984).

63. There is also a literature that studies strategic interaction between governments to influence plant location. See Rauscher (1995), Markusen, Morey and Olewiler (1995) and Hoel (1997).

64. See Sturm and Ulph (2002) for a review of the political economy literature on trade and environment.

65. Copeland and Taylor (2003; chapter 4) also obtain a dampening result.

66. On this point see Rodrik (1995) on political economy models in general and Wilson (1996) on the race-to-the-bottom literature.

67. One could justify this by modifying our framework to include large fixed cost to producing products with different emission intensities, in which case foreign firms may not find it worthwhile to adjust their product to meet the demands of the export market. See Fischer and Serra (2001) and Copeland (2001) for an exploration of the implications of fixed costs of adjusting product specifications.

68. In the more general case where the foreign emission intensity is endogenous, the solution is more complex because the increase in the emission tax for second-best tariff purposes will introduce a distortion in the choice of e^*; however, the result that the home government has an incentive to use differential emission taxes to influence the terms of trade will continue to apply.

69. Recall that c and c^* are decreasing in e and e^* respectively.

70. See Ederington (2010) for a good discussion and overview of the literature on linkage.

71. By the Lerner symmetry theorem, an export tax on good 1 is equivalent to a tariff on good 2. It is analytically convenient to focus on trade taxes for good 1.

72. If we do not allow for lump sum transfers, then the planner will choose environmental policy both to deal with pollution but also to indirectly influence the distribution of income across countries via the effect of environmental policy on the terms of trade.

73. There is a large literature on the enforceability of trade agreements; here I simply assume that it can be enforced. Ederington (2001) considers enforcement of agreements that constrain both trade and environmental policy. On enforcement of trade agreements more generally, see Bagwell and Staiger (2002).

74. See Hoel (1997) for an overview of the harmonization issue.

75. If lump sum transfers are not available, then we are in a second-best world – other policy instruments will be used to influence the distribution of income. In our simple framework here, the only available instrument is environmental policy and so it would have to play a dual role of both influencing environmental outcomes and also indirectly influencing income distribution via its effect on the terms of trade. This means that (25) need not apply. However if we extend the model to allow for other instruments, many of these (such as tariffs for example) have a much more direct effect on the terms of trade than environmental policy and so would be better instruments to influence income distribution. And note that the second-best issue does not generate an argument for harmonization.

76. If pollution spills over borders, then there are conditions under which harmonization is efficient. This will be discussed in the next section.

77. In deciding how to set tariffs, governments have to weigh the increased average cost of trade protection (such as increased pollution distortions) that will be induced as they substitute to other instruments such as environmental policy against the

deterrence effects of removing government discretion over low cost trade policy options.

78. This can also be implemented with an agreement that require that tariffs be set to zero *and* that the level of imports be $\bar{M}$, where $\bar{M}$ is the first-best level of imports. Then any use of environmental policy that deviates from full internalization of the externality will cause the import target to be missed and the trade agreement will be violated. Bagwell and Staiger argue that the WTO rules allow 'nonviolation complaints' if market access commitments are not being met. They also note, however, that the use of this channel of trade redress has been difficult to operationalize.

79. See also Ederington (2010) for a useful discussion of their work.

80. See Mayer (1981) for this result (in the absence of environmental problems)

81. See Chichilnisky, Heal and Starrett (2000) for an exploration of this issue.

82. There is a large literature on the relative merits of taxes vs. quotas as a way to implement global emission reductions. This is beyond the scope of this paper. See Nordhaus (2007) for an overview of some of the issues.

83. This result has caveats – no transactions costs, and perfect competition is required. Hahn (1984) shows that market power in the permit market can overturn the result that the final allocation of permits will equate marginal abatement costs across sources. Also demand for a firm's products needs to be unaffected by whether a firm meets its target by buying permits or by abating emissions (in which case it might be able to market itself as being 'greener').

84. See also Ishikawa, Kiyono and Yomogida (2010) who present other scenarios under which emission trading can be welfare-reducing.

85. Ishikawa and Kiyono (2006) considered the implications of the convergence of permit prices in a free-trade regime for the choice between global pollution taxes and global pollution quotas. While it is usually expected that taxes and quotas are equivalent in a competitive market with no uncertainty, they show that they are not equivalent in a small open economy Heckscher–Ohlin framework. This is because the domestic permit demand curve is flat in the factor price equalization region; consequently, a given emission target cannot be implemented by fixing the emission price alone.

86. On this point see Panagariya et al. (2004).

87. For example if the export good is oil, a reduction in carbon emissions could lower temperatures and reduce the demand for energy to run air conditioners. This would shift out foreign export supply.

88. There is some recent promising work in this area. See Li and Sun (2009), Holladay (2010), Rodrigue and Soumonni (2010).

References

Aldy, J.E., and W. Pizer (2009) 'The competitiveness impacts of climate change mitigation policies', Pew Center on Global Climate Change.

Antweiler, W., B.R. Copeland and M.S. Taylor (2001) 'Is free trade good for the environment?' *American Economic Review* 91: 877–90.

Babiker, M., J. Reilly, and L. Viguier (2004) 'Is international emissions trading always beneficial?', *The Energy Journal* 25: 33–57.

Bagwell, K., and R.W. Staiger (2001) 'Domestic policies, national sovereignty, and international economic institutions', *Quarterly Journal of Economics* 116: 519–62.

—— (2002) *The Economics of the World Trading System.* Cambridge, MA: MIT Press.

Baland J.M., and J.P. Platteau (1996) *Halting Degradation of Natural Resources: Is There a Role for Rural Communities?* Oxford: Clarendon Press.

Barbier, E.B., and J.C. Burgess (2001) 'The economics of tropical deforestation', *Journal of Economic Surveys* 15: 413–33.

Barbier, E.B., and C.E. Schulz (1997) 'Wildlife, Biodiversity and Trade', *Environment and Development Economics* 2: 145–72.

Barrett, S. (1994) 'Strategic environmental policy and international trade', *Journal of Public Economics* 54: 325–338.

Battigalli, P., and G. Maggi (2003) 'International agreement on product standards: An incomplete contracting approach', NBER Working Paper 9533.

Baumol, W.J. (1971) *Environmental Protection, International Spillovers and Trade*. Stockholm: Almqvist and Wiksell.

Becker, R., and V. Henderson (2000) 'Effects of air quality regulations on polluting industries', *Journal of Political Economy* 108: 379–421.

Beghin, J., D. Roland-Holst and D. Van Der Mensbrugghe (1997) 'Trade and pollution linkages: Piecemeal reform and optimal intervention', *Canadian Journal of Economics* 30: 442–455.

Benarroch, M., and H. Thille (2001) 'Transboundary pollution and the gains from trade', *Journal of International Economics* 55: 139–159.

Benarroch, M., and R. Weder (2006) 'Intra-industry trade in intermediate products, pollution and internationally increasing returns', *Journal of Environmental Economics and Management* 52 (2006): 675–689.

Bergeron, N. (2002) 'International Trade and Conservation with Costly Natural Resource Management', GREEN Working Paper No. 0204, Laval University.

Bohn, H., and R.T. Deacon (2000) 'Ownership risk, investment, and the use of natural resources', *American Economic Review* 90: 526–49.

Bommer, R., and G.G. Schulze (1999) 'Environmental improvement with trade liberalization', *European Journal of Political Economy* 15: 639–61.

Bohringer, C., and T.F. Rutherford (2002) 'Carbon abatement and international spillovers', *Environmental and Resource Economics* 22: 391–417.

Brander, J.A., and B. J. Spencer (1985) 'Export subsidies and international market share rivalry', *Journal of International Economics* 18: 83–100.

Brander, J.A., and M.S. Taylor (1997a) 'International trade and open access renewable resources: The small open economy case', *Canadian Journal of Economics*, 30, 526–52.

——(1997b) 'International trade between consumer and conservationist countries', *Resource and Energy Economics* 19: 267–97.

Brecher, R.A., and E.U. Choudri (1982) 'Immiserizing investment from abroad: The Singer-Prebisch thesis reconsidered', *Quarterly Journal of Economics* 97: 181–90.

Brunnermeier, S., and A. Levinson (2004) 'Examining the evidence on environmental regulations and industry location', *Journal of the Environment and Development* 13: 6–41.

Bulte, E.H., and E.B. Barbier (2005) 'Trade and renewable resources in a second best world: An overview', *Environmental and Resource Economics* 30: 423–463.

Burguet, R., and J. Sempere (2003) 'Trade liberalization, environmental policy, and welfare', *Journal of Environmental Economics and Management* 46: 25–37.

Chichilnisky, G. (1994) 'North–south trade and the global environment', *American Economic Review* 84, 851–74.

Chichilnisky, G., G. Heal and D. Starrett (2000) 'Equity and efficiency in environmental markets: Global trade in carbon dioxide emissions', in *Environmental Markets: Equity and Efficiency*. G. Chichilnisky and G. Heal (eds), New York: Columbia University Press.

Chua, S. (2003) 'Does tighter environmental policy lead to a comparative advantage in less polluting goods?', *Oxford Economic Papers* 55: 25–35.

Coase, R.H. (1960) 'The problem of social cost', *Journal of Law and Economics* 3: 1–44.

Coate, S., and S. Morris (1995) 'On the form of transfers to special interests', *Journal of Political Economy* 103:1210–35.

Cohen, J.S., and M.L. Weitzman (1975) 'A Marxian model of enclosures', *Journal of Development Economics* 1: 287–336.

Cole, M.A., A.J. Rayner and J.M. Bates (1998) 'Trade liberalisation and the environment: The case of the Uruguay round', *The World Economy* 21: 337–47.

Cole, M.A., and R.J.R. Elliott (2003) 'Determining the trade-environment composition effect: The role of capital, labor and environmental regulations', *Journal of Environmental Economics and Management* 46: 363–83.

—— (2005) 'FDI and the capital intensity of "dirty" sectors: A missing piece of the pollution haven puzzle', *Review of Development Economics* 9: 530–48.

Conrad, K. (1993) 'Taxes and subsidies for pollution-intensive industries', *Journal of Environmental Economics and Management* 25: 121–35.

Copeland, B.R. (1990) 'Strategic interaction among nations: Negotiable and non-negotiable trade barriers', *Canadian Journal of Economics* 23: 84–108.

—— (1994) 'International trade and the environment: Policy reform in a polluted small open economy', *Journal of Environmental Economics and Management* 26: 44–65.

—— (2001)'Trade and environment: Product standards in a national treatment regim', mimeo, Dept. of Economics, UBC.

—— (2010) 'How does trade affect the environment?' in *Is Economic Growth Sustainable?* Geoffrey Heal (ed.), Palgrave Macmillan.

Copeland, B.R., and M.S. Taylor (1994) 'North-South Trade and the Environment', *Quarterly Journal of Economics* 109: 755–87.

—— (1997a) 'The trade-induced degradation hypothesis', *Resource and Energy Economics* 19: 321–44.

—— (1997b) 'A simple model of trade, capital mobility and the environment', NBER working paper 5898.

—— (1999) 'Trade, spatial separation, and the environment', *Journal of International Economics* 47: 137–68.

—— (2003) *Trade and the Environment: Theory and Evidence.* Princeton University Press.

—— (2004) 'Trade, growth and the environment', *Journal of Economic Literature* 42: 7–71.

—— (2005) 'Free trade and global warming: A trade theory view of the Kyoto Protocol', *Journal of Environmental Economics and Management* 49: 205–34.

—— (2009) 'Trade, tragedy and the commons', *American Economic Review* 99: 725–49.

Costello, C., M. Springborn, C. McAusland, and A. Solow (2007) 'Unintended biological invasions: Does risk vary by trading partner?', *Journal of Environmental Economics and Management* 54: 262–76.

Costello, C., S.D. Gaines, and J. Lynham (2008) 'Can catch shares prevent fisheries collapse?' *Science* 321: 1678–81.

Daly, Herman (1993) 'The perils of free trade', *Scientific American* 269: 2–29.

Dasgupta, S., A. Mody, S. Roy and D. Wheeler (2001) 'Environmental regulation and development: A cross-country empirical analysis', *Oxford Development Studies* 29: 173–87.

Deacon, R.T. 'Deforestation and the rule of law in a cross-section of countrie', *Land Economics* 70(4): 414–30

Dean, J.M. (2002) 'Testing the impact of trade liberalization on the environment: Theory and evidence', *Canadian Journal of Economics* 35: 819–42.

Dean, J.M., M.E. Lovely, H. Hwang (2009) 'Are foreign investors attracted to weak environmental regulations? Evaluating the evidence from China', *Journal of Development Economics* 90: 1–13.

de Meza, D., and J.R. Gould (1992) 'The social efficiency of private decisions to enforce property rights', *Journal of Political Economy* 100: 561–80.

Demsetz, H. (1967) 'Toward a theory of property rights', *American Economic Review* 57: 347–59.

Dixit, A.K. (1984) 'International trade policies for oligopolistic industries', *Economic Journal* 94: 1–16 (Supplement).

—— (1985) 'Tax policy in open economies', in *Handbook of Public Economics*. A.J. Auerbach & M. Feldstein (eds) Vol. 1. Elsevier.

Dixit, A.K., and V. Norman (1980) *Theory of International Trade*. Cambridge: Cambridge University Press.

Dornbusch, R., S. Fischer and P.A. Samuelson (1977) 'Comparative advantage, trade and payments in a Ricardian model with a continuum of goods', *American Economic Review* 67: 823–39.

Eaton, J., and G.M. Grossman (1986) 'Optimal trade and industrial policy under oligopoly', *Quarterly Journal of Economics* 101: 383–406.

Ederington, J. (2001) 'International coordination of trade and domestic policies', *American Economic Review* 91: 1580–93.

—— (2010) 'Should trade agreements include environmental policy?' *Review of Environmental Economics and Policy* 4: 84–102.

Ederington, W.J., and J. Minier (2003) 'Is environmental policy a secondary trade barrier? An empirical analysis', *Canadian Journal of Economics* 36: 137–54.

Ederington, W.J, A. Levinson and J. Minier (2004) 'Trade liberalization and pollution havens', *Advances in Economic Analysis and Policy*, 4, Article 6. Berkeley Electronic Press.

—— (2005) 'Footloose and pollution-free', *Review of Economics and Statistics* 87: 92–9.

Eliste, P., and P.G. Fredriksson (2002) 'Environmental regulations, transfers, and trade: Theory and evidence', *Journal of Environmental Economics and Management*, 43: 23450.

Eskeland, G.S., and A.E. Harrison (2003) 'Moving to greener pastures? Multinationals and the pollution haven hypothesis', *Journal of Development Economics* 70: 1–23.

Ethier, W. (1982) 'Decreasing costs in international trade and Frank Graham's argument for protection', *Econometrica* 50: 1243–68.

Falvey, R.E. (1988) 'Tariffs, quotas, and piecemeal policy reform', *Journal of International Economics* 25: 177–83.

Feenstra, R. (May 1986) 'Trade policy with several goods and "market linkages"' *Journal of International Economics* 20: 249–67.

—— (2004) *Advanced International Trade: Theory and Evidence*. Princeton University Press.

Ferreira S. (2004) 'Deforestation, openness and property rights', *Land Economics* 80: 174–93.

Fischer, C. (2010) 'Does trade help or hinder the conservation of renewable resources?' *Review of Environmental Economics and Policy* 4: 103–21.

Fischer, R., and P. Serra (2000) 'Standards and protection', *Journal of International Economics*, 52: 377–400.

Francis, M. (2005) 'Trade and the enforcement of environmental property rights', *Journal of International Trade & Economic Development* 14: 281–98.

Frankel, J.A., and A.K. Rose (2005) 'Is trade good or bad for the environment? Sorting out the causality', *Review of Economics and Statistics* 87: 85–91.

Frankel, J.A. (2009) 'Addressing the leakage/competitiveness issue in climate change policy proposals', in *Climate Change, Trade, and Competitiveness: Is a Collision Inevitable?* I. Sorkin and L. Brainard (eds), Brookings Institution Press.

Fredriksson , P.G. (1999) 'The political economy of trade liberalization and environmental policy', *Southern Economic Journal* 65: 513–25.

Gawande, K. (1999) 'Trade barriers as outcomes from two-stage games: Evidence', *Canadian Journal of Economics* 32: 1028–56.

Gordon, H.S. (1954) 'The economic theory of a common property resource: The fishery', *Journal of Political Economy*, 63: 124–42.

Greaker, M. (2006) 'Spillovers in the development of new pollution abatement technology: A new look at the Porter-hypothesis', *Journal of Environmental Economics and Management* 52: 411–20.

Greenstone, M. (2002) 'The impacts of environmental regulations on industrial activity: Evidence from the 1970 and the 1977 Clean Air Act amendments and the census of manufactures', *Journal of Political Economy* 110: 1175–219.

Grossman, G.M., and A.B. Krueger (2002) 'Environmental impacts of a North American Free Trade Agreement', in *The Mexico–U.S. Free Trade Agreement*, P.M. Garber (ed), Cambridge and London: MIT Press: 13–56.

Grossman, G.M. (1984) 'The gains from international factor movements', *Journal of International Economics* 17: 73–83.

Grossman, G.M., and E. Helpman (1994) 'Protection for sale', *American Economic Review* 84: 833–50.

Gulati, S., and D. Roy (2008) 'National treatment and the optimal regulation of environmental externalities', *Canadian Journal of Economics* 41: 1445–71.

Gurtzgen, N., and M. Rauscher (2000) 'Environmental policy, intra-industry trade and transfrontier pollution', *Environmental and Resource Economics* 17: 59–71.

Hahn, R.W. (1984) 'Market power and transferable property rights', *Quarterly Journal of Economics* 99: 753–65.

Hanna, R. (2010) 'U.S. environmental regulation and FDI: Evidence from a panel of U.S. based multinational firms', *American Economic Journal: Applied Economics* 2: 158–89.

Hannesson, R. (2000) 'Renewable resources and the gains from trade', *Canadian Journal of Economics* 33: 122–32.

Haupt, A. (2006) 'Environmental policy in open economies and monopolistic competition', *Environmental and Resource Economics* 33: 143–67.

Hoel, M. (1997) 'Environmental policy with endogenous plant locations', *Scandinavian Journal of Economics* 99: 241–59.

—— (1997) 'International coordination of environmental taxes', in *New directions in the economic theory of the environment*, C. Carraro and D. Siniscalco (eds), Cambridge University Press.

Hokby, S., and T. Soderqvist (2003) 'Elasticities of demand and willingness to pay for environmental services in Sweden', *Environmental and Resource Economics* 26: 361–83.

Holladay, J.S. (2010) 'Are exporters Mother Nature's best friends?' mimeo, NYU School of Law.

Horn, H. (2006) 'National treatment in the GATT', *American Economic Review* 96: 394–404.

Horn, H., G. Maggi, and R.W. Staiger (2010) 'Trade agreements as endogenously incomplete contracts', *American Economic Review* 100: 394–419.

Hotte L., N. Van Long, H. Tian (2000) 'International trade with endogenous enforcement of property rights', *Journal of Development Economics* 62: 25–54.

Ishikawa, J., and K. Kiyono (2006) Greenhouse-gas emission controls in an open economy', *International Economic Review* 47: 431–50.

Ishikawa, J., K. Kiyono and M. Yomogida (2010) 'Is international emission trading beneficial?' mimeo, Hitotsubashi University.

Kemp, M.C., and N. Van Long (1984) 'The role of natural resources in trade models', in *Handbook of International Economics Vol. 1*, R.W. Jones and P. B. Kenen (eds), Elsevier: 367–417.

Jaffe, A., S. Peterson, P. Portney, and R. Stavins (1995) 'Environmental regulation and the competitiveness of U.S. manufacturing: What does the evidence tell us?' *The Journal of Economic Literature* 33: 132–63.

Jinji, N. (2006) 'International trade and terrestrial open-access renewable resources in a small open economy', *Canadian Journal of Economics* 39: 790–808.

Kawahara, S. (forthcoming) 'Electoral competition with environmental policy as a second best transfer', *Resource and Energy Economics*.

Keller, W., and A. Levinson (2002) 'Pollution abatement costs and foreign direct investment inflows to US states', *Review of Economics and Statistics* 84: 691–703.

Kemp, M.C., and N.V. Long (1984) 'The role of natural resources in trade models', in *Handbook of International Economics*, Vol. I, R. Jones and P. Kenen (eds), Amsterdam: North Holland.

Kennedy, P.W. (1994) 'Equilibrium pollution taxes in open economies with imperfect competition', *Journal of Environmental Economics and Management* 27: 49–63.

Krutilla, K. (1991) 'Environmental regulation in an open economy', *Journal of Environmental Economics and Management* 10: 127–42.

Levinson, A. (1996) 'Environmental regulations and industry location: International and domestic evidence', in *Fair Trade and Harmonization: Prerequisites for Free Trade*, Jagdish N. Bhagwati and Robert E. Hudec (eds), Cambridge, MA: MIT Press, 429–57.

—— (1999) 'State taxes and interstate hazardous waste shipments', *American Economic Review* 89: 666–77.

—— (2009) 'Technology, international trade, and pollution from U.S. manufacturing', *American Economic Review* 99: 2177–92.

—— (2010) 'Offshoring pollution: Is the U.S. increasingly importing polluting goods?' *Review of Environmental Economics and Policy* 4: 63–83.

Levinson, A., and M.S. Taylor (2008) 'Trade and the environment: Unmasking the pollution haven effect', *International Economic Review* 49: 223–54.

Li, Z., and J. Sun (2009) 'Environmental policy with heterogeneous plants' mimeo, University of Toronto.

Lipsey, R.G., and K. Lancaster (1956) 'The general theory of second best', *Review of Economic Studies* 24: 11–32.

List, J.A., W.W. McHone, and D.L. Millimet (2004) 'Effects of environmental regulation on foreign and domestic plant births: Is there a home field advantage?' *Journal of Urban Economics* 56: 303–26.

List, J.A., W.W. McHone, D.L. Millimet, and P.G. Fredriksson (2003) 'Effects of environmental regulations on manufacturing plant births: Evidence from a propensity score matching estimator', *Review of Economics and Statistics* 85: 944–52.

López, R. (1994) 'The environment as a factor of production: The effects of economic growth and trade liberalization', *Journal of Environmental Economics and Management* 27: 163–84.

—— (1997) 'Environmental externalities in traditional agriculture and the impact of trade liberalization: The case of Ghana', *Journal of Development Economics* 53: 17–39.

—— (2000) 'Trade reform and environmental externalities in general equilibrium: Analysis for an archetype poor tropical country', *Environment and Development Economics* 5: 377–404.

Lopez, R., and A. Islam (2008) 'Trade and the environment' in *The Princeton Encyclopedia of the World Economy*. Princeton, New Jersey.

Margolis, M., and J.F. Shogren (2002) 'Unprotected resources and voracious world markets', Resources for the Future Discussion Paper 02–30.

Markusen, J.R. (1975) 'International externalities and optimal tax structures', *Journal of International Economics* 5: 15–29.

Markusen, J.R., E.R. Morey, and N. Olewiler (1995) 'Competition in regional environmental policies when plant locations are endogenous', *Journal of Public Economics* 56: 55–77.

Mayer, W. (1981) 'Theoretical considerations on negotiated tariff adjustments', *Oxford Economic Papers*, New Series, 33: 135–53.

McAusland, C. (2008) 'Trade, politics, and the environment: Tailpipe vs. smokestack', *Journal of Environmental Economics and Management* 55: 52–71.

McAusland, C., and C. Costello (2004) 'Avoiding invasives: Trade-related policies for controlling unintentional exotic species introductions', *Journal of Environmental Economics and Management* 48: 954–97.

McAusland, C., (2010) 'Globalization's direct and indirect effects on the environment', in*Globalisation, Transport and the Environment*, OECD.

McGuire, M.C. (1982) 'Regulation, factor rewards, and international trade', *Journal of Public Economics* 17: 335–54.

McKibbin, W.J., R. Shackleton, and P.J. Wilcoxen (1999) 'What to expect from an international system of tradable permits for carbon emissions', *Resource and Energy Economics* 21: 319–46.

McRae, J.J. (1978)'Optimal and competitive use of replenishable natural resources by open economies', *Journal of International Economics* 8: 29–54.

Neary, J.P. (2006) 'International trade and the environment: Theoretical and policy linkages', *Environmental and Resource Economics* 33: 95–118.

Neary, J.P., and F. Ruane (1988) 'International capital mobility, shadow prices, and the cost of protection', *International Economic Review* 29: 571–85.

Nordhaus, W.D. (2007) 'To tax or not to tax: Alternative approaches to slowing global warming', *Review of Environmental Economics and Policy* 1: 26–44.

Nordstrom, H., and S. Vaughan (1999) 'Trade and environment', Special Studies 4, World Trade Organization.

OECD (2010) *Globalisation, Transport and the Environment*.

Ostrom, E. (1990) 'Governing the commons: The evolution of institutions for collective action', Cambridge University Press.

Panagariya, A., K. Palmer, W.E. Oates, and A.J. Krupnick (2004) 'Toward an integrated theory of open economy environmental and trade policy', in *Environmental Policy and Fiscal Federalis*m, W.E. Oates (ed.), Cheltenham: Edward Elgar.

Perroni, C., and R.M. Wigle (1994) 'International trade and environmental quality: How important are the linkages?' *Canadian Journal of Economics* 27: 551–67.

Pethig, R.(1976) 'Pollution, welfare, and environmental policy in the theory of comparative advantage', *Journal of Environmental Economics and Management* 2: 160–9.

Pfluger, M. (2001) 'Ecological dumping under monopolistic competition', *Scandinavian Journal of Economics* 103: 689–706.

Porter, Michael E., and Claas van de Linde (1995) 'Toward a new conception of the environment-competitiveness relationship'. *Journal of Economic Perspectives* 9: 97–118.

Rauscher, M. (1994) 'On ecological dumping', *Oxford Economic Papers*, New Series, 46: 822–40.

—— (1995) 'Environmental regulation and the location of polluting industries', *International Tax and Public Finance* 2: 229–44.

—— (2005) 'International trade, foreign investment, and the environment' in *Handbook of Environmental and Resource Economics*, Vol. 3, K.-G. Mäler, J. Vincent (eds), Amsterdam: Elsevier (North-Holland Handbooks in Economics), 1403–56.

—— (1997) *International Trade, Factor Movements, and the Environment*. Oxford: Clarendon Press.

Richelle, Y. (1996) 'Trade incidence on transboundary pollution: Free trade can benefit the global environmental quality', University of Laval discussion paper 9616.

Rodrik, D. (1995) 'Political economy of trade policy' in *Handbook of International Economics*, Vol. 3, G. M. Grossman and K. Rogoff (eds), Amsterdam: Elsevier.

Rodrigue, J., and O. Soumonni (2010) 'Pollution abatement and export dynamics', mimeo, Vanderbilt University.

Rus, H.A. (2006) 'Renewable resources, pollution and trade in a small open economy', FEEM Working paper No. 140.

Salop, S.C., and D.T. Scheffman (1983) 'Raising rivals' costs', *American Economic Review Papers and Proceedings* 73: 267–71.

Schaeffer, M.B. (1957) 'Some consideration of population dynamics and economics in relation to the management of the commercial marine fisheries', *Journal of the Fisheries Research Board of Canada* 14: 669–81.

Shen, J. (2008) 'Trade liberalization and environmental degradation in China', *Applied Economics* 40: 997–1004.

Siebert, H. (1977) 'Environmental quality and the gains from trade', *Kyklos* 30: 657–73.

—— (1985) 'Spatial aspects of environmental economics', in A.V. Kneese and J. L. Sweeney (eds), *Handbook of Natural Resource and Energy Economics*, Vol. 1. Amsterdam: Elsevier: 125–64.

Smulders, S., D. van Soest, and C. Withagen (2004) 'International trade, species diversity, and habitat conservation', *Journal of Environmental Economics and Management* 48: 891–910.

Sturm, D. (2006) 'Product standards, trade disputes, and protectionism', *Canadian Journal of Economics* 39: 564–81.

—— (2003) 'Trade and the environment: A survey of the literature', in *Environmental Policy in an International Perspective*, Laura Marsiliani, Michael Rauscher, and Cees Withagen (eds), Kluwer Academic Publishers: 119–49.

Sturm, D., and A. Ulph (2002) 'Environment and trade: The implications of imperfect information and political economy', *World Trade Review* 1: 235–56.

Taylor, M.S. (2004) 'Unbundling the pollution haven hypothesis', *Advances in Economic Analysis & Policy* 4: 1–30.

—— (2007) 'Buffalo hunt: International trade and the virtual extinction of the North American bison', National Bureau of Economic Research discussion paper no. 12969.

Turunen-Red, A.H., and A. Woodland (2004) 'Multilateral reforms of trade and environmental policy', *Review of International Economics* 12: 321–36.

Ulph, A. (1992) 'The choice of environmental policy instruments and strategic international trade', in *Conflicts and Cooperation in Managing Environmental Resources*, R. Pethig (ed.), Berlin: Springer: 111–29.

—— (1997) 'Environmental policy and international trade: A survey of recent economic analysis', in *International Handbook of Environmental and Resource Economics 1997/98*, H. Folmer and T. Tietenberg (eds), Cheltenham: Edward Elgar: 205–42.

Unteroberdoerster, O. (2001) 'Trade and transboundary pollution: Spatial separation reconsidered', *Journal of Environmental Economics and Management* 41: 269–85.

Wagner, U.J., and C. Timmins (2009) 'Agglomeration effects in foreign direct investment and the "pollution havens" hypothesis', *Environmental and Resource Economics* 43: 231–56.

Walter, I. (1973) 'The pollution content of American trade', *Western Economic Journal* 11: 61–70.

Walz, U., and D. Wellisch (1997) 'Is free trade in the interest of exporting countries when there is ecological dumping?', *Journal of Public Economics* 66: 275–91.

Wilson, John D. (1996) 'Capital mobility and environmental standards: Is there a theoretical basis for a race to the bottom', in *Fair Trade and Harmonization: Prerequisites for Free Trade*, J.N. Bhagwati and R.E. Hudec (eds), Cambridge, MA: MIT Press: 393–427.

Woodland, A.D. (1982) *International Trade and Resource Allocation*. Amsterdam: North-Holland.

Worm, B., et al. (2006) 'Impacts of biodiversity loss on ocean ecosystem services', *Science* 314: 787–90.

Zeng, D.-Z., and L. Zhao (2009) 'Pollution havens and industrial agglomeration', *Journal of Environmental Economics and Management* 58: 141–53.

16

Economic Geography: A Review of the Theoretical and Empirical Literature*

Stephen J. Redding[†]

1 Introduction

The uneven distribution of economic activity across space is one of the most striking features of economic life. Perhaps the clearest visual manifestation of this is the emergence and growth of cities. The share of the world's population living in cities grew from less than one tenth in 1300, to around one sixth in 1900, and to around one half today. Even more striking is the emergence of large metropolitan areas. By 1980 there were more than two million cities with more than a hundred thousand inhabitants, and by 1995 15 cities had a population of greater than ten million.[1]

There is a long intellectual tradition in economics concerned with location choices. As is well known, Marshall (1920) highlights knowledge spillovers, locally traded intermediate inputs and the pooling of specialized skills as three potential mechanisms for the agglomeration of economic activity. Subsequently, an extensive body of research in urban and regional economics examined the origins of monocentric cities, the distribution of population concentrations across space and the organization of economic functions across these population concentrations.[2]

A key distinction in thinking about the determinants of location is that between first-nature and second-nature geography. First-nature geography is concerned with locational fundamentals, including the physical geography of coasts, mountains and natural endowments. In contrast, second-nature geography is concerned with the location of agents relative to one another in geographic space, and the role that this plays in understanding spatial disparities. While first-nature geography is largely exogenous, second-nature geography is typically endogenous, and could be influenced, at least in principle, by policy.

The sources of the uneven distribution of economic activity across space have returned to prominence over the last three decades with the emergence of the 'new economic geography' literature following Krugman (1991a).[3] This path-breaking paper was a key part of the citation for Paul Krugman's 2008 Nobel Prize, and the research to which it gave rise is the subject of this literature review.[4] A key emphasis in the new economic geography literature is the development of micro-founded models consistent with individual optimization and market clearing. The focus in this line of research is squarely on second-nature geography, in which spatially concentrated patterns of production and consumption can emerge endogenously from a featureless plain of ex ante identical locations.[5] Location choices are determined by a tension between agglomeration forces, which promote the spatial concentration of economic activity, and dispersion forces, which favor an equal distribution of economic activity. The agglomeration forces arise from pecuniary externalities due to a combination of love of variety preferences, increasing returns to scale and transport costs. The dispersion forces arise from product market competition and geographically immobile factors of production or amenities. The relative strength of these two sets of forces depends on transportation costs, so that changes in transportation costs result in endogenous changes in the distribution of economic activity across space.

A central theoretical prediction of the new economic geography literature is the so-called 'home market effect'. In neoclassical models, increases in expenditure lead to equal or less than proportionate increases in production of the good. In economic geography models, in contrast, increases in expenditure typically lead to more than proportionate increases in the production of a good. The reason is that the change in expenditure affects the location decisions of firms and/or factors of production which result, in turn, in further changes in expenditure. A related implication of the home market effect is that nominal prices of factors of production vary endogenously across locations, depending on their 'market access'. In locations with good market access, there is more value-added left after paying transportation costs to remunerate factors of production, which results in equilibrium in higher nominal factor prices. Both of these implications of the home market effect are amenable to empirical testing, and we review a growing empirical literature that has examined the production and factor price implications of economic geography models.

Another central feature of new economic geography models is that pecuniary externalities in location choices can give rise to multiple equilibria, so that the distribution of economic activity across space is not uniquely determined by locational fundamentals. While this possibility of multiple equilibria is a key feature of new economic geography models, there is much less evidence of the empirical relevance of such multiple equilibria, and this is an area in which there remains considerable scope for further empirical research.

The remainder of the chapter is structured as follows. Section 2 reviews the canonical new economic geography model, the so-called 'core and periphery' model of Krugman (1991a), and discusses other related theoretical models. Section 3 surveys the empirical evidence on the key theoretical predictions of new economic geography models. Section 4 discusses potential areas for further research and concludes.

2   Theoretical literature

In the canonical 'core and periphery' model of Krugman (1991a), the distribution of economic activity across space is determined by a tension between two agglomeration and dispersion forces. The two agglomeration forces are a 'home market effect', where increasing returns to scale and transport costs imply that firms want to concentrate production near to large markets, and a 'price index effect', in which consumer love of variety and transport costs imply a lower cost of living near to large markets. The two dispersion forces are a 'market crowding effect', where transport costs imply that firms close to large markets face a larger number of lower-priced competitors, and an immobile factor, 'agricultural labor', which together with transport costs provides an incentive for dispersed production across regions. We first outline the canonical model in its most stylized form, before discussing extensions and other related theoretical approaches.[6]

2.1   Preferences and endowments

The economy consists of two regions, 'North' and 'South', where South variables are denoted by an asterisk. While we provide expressions below for the North, analogous relationships hold for the South. There are two goods: agriculture and manufacturing. Agriculture is a homogeneous good, which is produced with a constant returns to scale production technology under conditions of perfect competition, and is subject to zero transportation costs. In contrast, the manufacturing sector consists of many differentiated varieties, which are produced with an increasing returns to scale technology under conditions of monopolistic competition, and are subject to iceberg transportation costs such that $\tau > 1$ units have to be shipped between regions in order for one unit to arrive.[7]

Consumer preferences are defined over consumption of agriculture and manufacturing, C_A and C_M respectively, and are assumed to take the Cobb–Douglas functional form:

$$U = C_M^{\mu} C_A^{1-\mu}, \qquad 0 < \mu < 1.$$

The manufacturing consumption index, C_M, is defined over horizontally differentiated varieties within the manufacturing sector, and is assumed to take the constant elasticity of substitution (CES) or Dixit and Stiglitz (1977) form:

$$C_M = \left[\sum_j c_j^{\frac{\sigma-1}{\sigma}} \right]^{\frac{\sigma}{\sigma-1}}, \quad P_M = \left[\sum_j p_j^{1-\sigma} \right]^{\frac{1}{1-\sigma}},$$

where c_j denotes consumption of each variety, $\sigma > 1$ is the elasticity of substitution between varieties, P_M is the price index dual to C_M, and p_j denotes the price of each variety.

There are two factors of production: farmers and workers. While farmers can only be employed in the agricultural sector and are geographically immobile between regions, workers can only be employed in the manufacturing sector and are geographically mobile between regions. Each region is endowed with $(1 - \mu)/2$ farmers and the economy as a whole is endowed with μ workers.[8]

2.2 Production technology

In the agricultural sector, one unit of labor is required to produce one unit of output. In contrast, in the manufacturing sector there is a fixed cost of $\alpha > 0$ units of labor to produce each variety and a constant variable cost of $\beta > 0$ units of labor. Therefore, the total labor required to produce x_j units of a manufacturing variety is:

$$l_{Mj} = \alpha + \beta x_j.$$

2.3 Producer equilibrium

The assumptions that farmers are geographically immobile and specific to the agricultural sector imply that both regions produce the agricultural good. Additionally, as the agricultural good is chosen as the numeraire, the assumptions of constant returns to scale, perfect competition and zero transport costs in the agricultural sector imply that the agricultural wage, w_A, in both regions is equal to one: $p_A = w_A = 1$.

Profit maximization in the manufacturing sector yields the standard result that the equilibrium price of each manufacturing variety is a constant markup over marginal cost, and as all varieties are symmetric, this equilibrium price is the same for all varieties:

$$p_{Mj} = p_M = \left(\frac{\sigma}{\sigma - 1} \right) \beta w_M.$$

Combining profit maximization and free entry yields the standard result that with a common constant elasticity of substitution between varieties, the equilibrium output of each variety is equal to a constant:

$$x_j = \bar{x} = \frac{\alpha(\sigma - 1)}{\beta}.$$

Finally, from the CES demand for manufacturing varieties, the 'free on board' price of each variety must be sufficiently low given demand in both regions to sell exactly $\bar{x}$ units and make zero equilibrium profits:

$$(p_M)^\sigma = \frac{\mu}{\bar{x}} \left[Y P_M^{\sigma-1} + \tau^{1-\sigma} Y^* (P_M^*)^{\sigma-1} \right],$$

where Y denotes aggregate income, which equals aggregate expenditure.

Therefore combining CES demand, zero equilibrium profits and profit maximization, we obtain the following 'wage equation', which will play a key role in the analysis below:

$$w_M = \left(\frac{\sigma-1}{\sigma\beta} \right) \left[\frac{\mu}{\bar{x}} \left(Y P_M^{\sigma-1} + \tau^{1-\sigma} Y^* (P_M^*)^{\sigma-1} \right) \right]^{\frac{1}{\sigma}}. \tag{1}$$

Intuitively, if the manufacturing sector is active in a region, the manufacturing wage must be sufficiently low given demand in both regions to sell exactly $\bar{x}$ units and make zero equilibrium profits. The right-hand side of (1) is a measure of a region's 'market access' or 'real market potential', which corresponds to a transport-cost weighted sum of market demand in each region. Therefore a key prediction of new economic geography models, which we examine further below, is that locations' nominal factor prices are systematically related to their market access.

2.4 Goods and factor markets

Another key relationship of the model relates the number of manufacturing varieties to the number of workers choosing to reside in a location. As only workers are employed in the manufacturing sector, the manufacturing production technology and factor market clearing together imply that the number of manufacturing varieties produced by a region is simply proportional to its number of manufacturing workers:

$$n = \frac{L_M}{\alpha + \beta\bar{x}} = \frac{L_M}{\alpha\sigma}. \tag{2}$$

Using the symmetry of equilibrium prices for manufacturing varieties, the manufacturing price index for each region depends on the number of varieties produced in each region, their equilibrium 'free on board' prices, and transportation costs:

$$P_M = \left[n p_M^{1-\sigma} + \tau^{1-\sigma} n (p_M^*)^{1-\sigma} \right]^{\frac{1}{1-\sigma}}. \tag{3}$$

Mobile manufacturing workers decide in which region to locate by comparing real wages. These depend on the manufacturing wage and the manufacturing price index, which can vary across regions, and the common price of the agricultural good:

$$\omega_M = \frac{w_M}{P_M^\mu P_A^{1-\mu}}. \tag{4}$$

Finally, regional aggregate income equals the number of immobile farmers times the agricultural wage of one plus the number of mobile manufacturing workers times the manufacturing wage:

$$Y = w_M L_M + \frac{1-\mu}{2}. \tag{5}$$

2.5   General equilibrium

To characterize general equilibrium, it is convenient to make a number of normalizations. Choosing units in which to measure the output of manufacturing varieties so that $\beta = (\sigma - 1)/\sigma$, we obtain $p_M = w_M$. Similarly, choosing units in which to count manufacturing varieties such that $\alpha = \mu/\sigma$, we obtain $n_M = L_M/\mu$ and $\bar{x} = \mu$. Finally, the share of the economy's endowment of manufacturing workers that choose to locate in the North is denoted by λ, with the remaining share $\lambda^* = (1 - \lambda)$ locating in the South.

Given these normalizations, general equilibrium can be represented by the following system of four simultaneous equations for the North, with four analogous equations holding in the South:

$$Y = \mu \lambda w_M + \left(\frac{1-\mu}{2}\right),$$

$$P_M = \left[\lambda (w_M)^{1-\sigma} + (1-\lambda) \tau^{1-\sigma} \left(w_M^*\right)^{1-\sigma}\right]^{\frac{1}{1-\sigma}}, \tag{6}$$

$$w_M = \left[Y (P_M)^{\sigma-1} + \tau^{1-\sigma} Y^* \left(P_M^*\right)^{\sigma-1}\right]^{\frac{1}{\sigma}},$$

$$\omega_M = \frac{w_M}{(P_M)^\mu}.$$

Together these eight equations for the two regions determine the eight endogenous variables that reference the general equilibrium: $\{Y, P_M, w_M, \omega_M\}$. All other endogenous variables can be written in terms of these elements of the equilibrium vector. As is frequently the case in the economic geography literature, the non-linearity of the model implies that closed form solutions for the equilibrium vector do not exist. Nonetheless, the properties of the general-equilibrium system (6) can be characterized analytically, and we briefly summarize them here.[9]

The combination of love of variety preferences, increasing returns to scale and transport costs gives rise to general-equilibrium forces that promote the agglomeration of all of the mobile manufacturing activity in one region. The first of these forces is the 'price index effect', whereby the location with a larger manufacturing sector has a lower manufacturing price index, because a smaller proportion of the region's manufacturing consumption bears transport costs. This price index effect provides a 'forward linkage', such that workers want to be close to abundant supplies of manufacturing goods. The second of these forces is the 'home market effect', whereby increasing returns to scale imply that firms want to concentrate production in a single location, and transport costs imply that they want to concentrate production close to a large market. This home market effect provides a 'backward linkage', such that firms want to locate proximate to large markets for manufacturing goods.

The home market effect has two important empirical implications, which will be examined in further detail below. The first of these empirical implications is evident from the right-hand side of the wage equation (1), which captures proximity to market demand in the two regions, as determined by aggregate income, Y, the price of competing varieties as summarized in the manufacturing price index, P, and transportation costs, $\tau^{1-\sigma}$. As a result of the home market effect, firms close to large markets pay higher nominal wages, because firms can charge higher 'free on board' prices and still sell enough units of output to cover fixed production costs and make zero-equilibrium profits. Therefore more value-added is left, after paying transportation costs, to remunerate factors of production. The second empirical implication of the home market effect is that an increase in manufacturing expenditure leads to a more than proportionate increase in manufacturing production. The reason is that the increase in expenditure induces firms to relocate in order to conserve transportation costs by concentrating production close to the expanded market.

While the home market effect alone implies higher nominal wages close to large markets, the home market and price index effects together imply higher real wages close to large markets. Therefore the two effects together provide an incentive for workers to locate close to large markets. While the home market and price index effects were both present in Krugman (1980), the key new element in the Krugman (1991a) model of economic geography is factor mobility. Suppose that one region initially has a larger share of manufacturing production. As a result of the home market and price index effects, the region with a larger share of manufacturing production has higher real wages, which induces more manufacturing workers to locate close to the large market. As more manufacturing workers relocate to the larger region, the resulting increase in aggregate income and expenditure makes this region an even more attractive location for manufacturing firms, which further increases the region's real wage through the home market and price index effects. The presence of factor mobility in the Krugman (1991a) model therefore gives rise to a process of 'cumulative causation', whereby the location choices of firms and worker mutually reinforce one another. Underlying this process of cumulative causation are pecuniary externalities (spillovers) between agents' location choices, whereby the decision of one agent to locate in a region increases the attractiveness of that region to other agents.

Although the home market and price index effects promote the agglomeration of manufacturing, there are two counteracting forces that promote its dispersion. The first of these is a 'market crowding effect': in the presence of transport costs, the concentration of more manufacturing firms in a region reduces the manufacturing price index in that region. From the right-hand side of the wage equation (1), this reduction in the manufacturing price index decreases demand for each manufacturing variety, which reduces the maximum price that each firm can set consistent with zero-equilibrium profits and, hence, reduces the maximum wage that each firm can afford to pay. The second of these dispersion forces is immobile agricultural laborers: the more manufacturing firms that are located in a region, the greater the incentive for a manufacturing firm to relocate to the other region in order to capture a larger share of the demand from immobile farmers in the other region by charging them a lower price net of transportation costs.

Depending on the value of the elasticity of substitution for manufacturing varieties, σ, and the share of mobile manufacturing activity in the economy, μ, there are two possible configurations of equilibria in the model. If the elasticity of substitution is sufficiently low and the share of manufacturing is sufficiently high, or more formally if $(\sigma - 1) < \mu\sigma$, agglomeration forces dominate dispersion forces for all values of transport costs. In contrast, if the elasticity of substitution is sufficiently high and the share of manufacturing activity is sufficiently low, $(\sigma - 1) > \mu\sigma$, whether agglomeration forces dominate dispersion forces depends on the value of transportation costs. (Krugman colorfully refers to the parameter condition in the above inequality as the 'no black holes condition'.)[10]

When agglomeration forces dominate dispersion forces, and regions are symmetric as considered here, the concentration of manufacturing activity in either region is a stable equilibrium. Which of these multiple equilibria is selected is not determined by model parameters, opening up a role for historical accident or forward-looking expectations in shaping the location of economic activity.[11] Furthermore, temporary policy interventions that shift the economy from one equilibrium to another can have permanent effects on the spatial distribution of economic activity.

For parameter values satisfying the 'no black holes condition', $(\sigma - 1) > \mu\sigma$, whether agglomeration or dispersion forces dominate depends on the value of transportation costs. For high values of transportation costs, there is a unique stable equilibrium, as can be seen by considering the case of infinite transportation costs, in which case manufacturing firms locate in both regions to serve immobile farmers. As transportation costs fall, both dispersion and agglomeration forces are weakened, but the dispersion forces diminish more rapidly than the agglomeration forces. As a result, for transportation costs below a critical

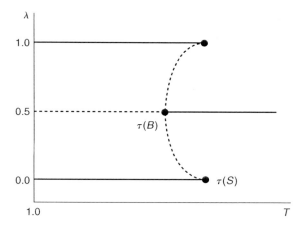

Figure 16.1   Core – periphery bifurcation

value (termed the 'sustain point'), the concentration of manufacturing activity in either region can be sustained as an equilibrium. Below the sustain point, if all manufacturing activity is concentrated in one region, there is no incentive for a firm to deviate and relocate to the other region. For transportation costs below an even lower critical value (termed the 'break point'), equilibria in which manufacturing activity is concentrated in a single region are the only stable equilibria. Below the break point, if any one firm deviates from a symmetric equilibrium and relocates to one of the two regions, all other manufacturing firms have an incentive to concentrate in that region. More formally, for parameter values satisfying the 'no black holes condition', the general equilibrium system (6) exhibits a Tomahawk Bifurcation, as shown graphically in Figure 16.1. In this region of the parameter space, small changes in transportation costs or other model parameters can have large and discontinuous effects on the spatial distribution of economic activity.

When manufacturing concentrates in one region, the other region produces only agriculture, and the resulting pattern of industrial location is described as having a 'core-periphery' structure. The historical concentrations of manufacturing on the eastern seaboard of the United States (Krugman 1991c) and in Northwestern Europe (Combes and Overman, 2004, Midelfart-Knarvik, Overman, Redding and Venables, 2000) have both been interpreted in this way. Furthermore, the potential for changes in transportation costs to induce such polarization in the distribution of economic activity has attracted considerable public policy attention. For example, manufacturing activities have been historically less spatially concentrated in the European Union than in the United States, raising the possibility that increasing European integration could prompt deindustrialization in some regions and the deepening of core-periphery patterns of the organization of economic activity (see, e.g., Kim, 1995, and Midelfart-Knarvik, Overman, Redding and Venables, 2000).

2.6   Related theoretical approaches

While the canonical core-periphery model is highly stylized, many of the forces that it highlights carry over into more general settings. An important and influential line of research follows Krugman and Venables (1995) and Venables (1996) in considering intermediate inputs as a source of cumulative causation. If the manufacturing sector uses intermediate inputs, and its production technology exhibits love of variety, increasing returns to scale and transport costs, the concentration of manufacturing activity can occur even in the absence of factor mobility. As labor is considerably less mobile across countries than within countries, models of this form are particularly applicable in a cross-country context, and the absence of labor mobility can generate equilibrium real wage differences across countries. In Puga (1999), both factor mobility and intermediate input linkages are incorporated, and the implications of different production structures in the agricultural sector are considered.

A somewhat separate but equally important and influential line of research follows Helpman (1998) in assuming complete factor mobility and introducing immobile amenities, such as housing, as an alternative dispersion force to immobile agricultural labor. This line of research has been particularly influential in empirical work, because asymmetries between regions are more easily accommodated than in Krugman (1991a), and are compatible with positive manufacturing activity in each region. In models of this form, the equilibrium distribution of population across space is determined by a population mobility condition that requires real wages to be equalized. Supposing that utility is a Cobb–Douglas function of a consumption index of manufacturing varieties and consumption of a homogeneous immobile amenity, the population mobility condition takes the following form:

$$\omega_i \equiv \frac{w_i}{\left(P_{M_i}\right)^\mu \left(P_{H_i}\right)^{1-\mu}} = \omega, \tag{7}$$

for all locations i that are populated in equilibrium, where P_H denotes the price of the immobile amenity, and μ and $(1 - \mu)$ are the expenditure shares of manufacturing and the immobile amenity respectively. Although population mobility equalizes real wages in the Helpman model, there are nominal wage differences across regions as a result of home market effect discussed above, and these nominal wage differences are offset in equilibrium by spatial variation in the nominal price of immobile amenities (such as housing). While both Krugman (1991a) and Helpman (1998) provide explanations for the spatial concentration of economic activity, their comparative statics with respect to transport costs differ. In Krugman (1991a), reductions in transport costs promote agglomeration, whereas in Helpman (1998) they have the converse effect.

While theoretical work in economic geography initially worked with CES preferences, subsequent work has considered quasi-linear preferences, as introduced by Ottaviano, Tabuchi and Thisse (2002). One of the key attractions of the quasi-linear functional form is that it permits closed-form solutions to be derived, although at the cost of imposing a constant marginal utility of income.[12] Other subsequent theoretical research has achieved greater analytical tractability by amending the core-periphery model in other ways, such as denominating the fixed and variable costs in terms of different factors of production (see, e.g., Baldwin, Forslid, Martin, Ottaviano and Robert-Nicoud, 2003). The resulting body of theoretical research is extensive in scope and rich in theoretical predictions, and general results have been derived linking the various formulations of the core and periphery model to one another (see Robert-Nicoud, 2005).

Despite these advances, the non-linearity of models of new economic geography has typically constrained their theoretical analysis to stylized settings with a limited number of regions and industries. A number of the forces highlighted in economic geography models continue to operate in more general settings, including the role of market access in influencing nominal factor prices, as analyzed empirically by Redding and Venables (2004) and discussed below. Nonetheless, as with neoclassical trade theory, the analysis of these forces in more general settings can be more nuanced, as analyzed for the home market effect in Behrens, Lamorgese, Ottaviano and Tabuchi (2004). Finally, although the theoretical literature typically draws a contrast between manufacturing and agriculture, the growth of the service sector has sometimes led manufacturing to be interpreted as a composite sector including services. Nonetheless, location choices in the service sector may well involve distinct considerations and the exploration of these considerations remains under-researched (for notable exceptions, see Arzaghi and Henderson, 2008, and Jensen and Kletzer, 2005).

3 Empirical evidence

This section reviews the empirical evidence on some of the key theoretical predictions of new economic geography models. We begin by discussing the measurement of agglomeration and generic identification problems in models with externalities. We next examine the relationship between market access and wages and the relationship between market access and industrial location. Finally, we examine the evidence on one of the central features of economic geography models, the existence of multiple equilibria.

3.1   Measurement and identification

While the very existence of cities could be viewed as evidence of agglomeration, and while there is numerous anecdotal evidence of industrial clusters, such as Silicon Valley in California and Route 128 in Massachusetts, the empirical measurement of agglomeration raises a number of challenges. Several different concepts are employed in the empirical literature. 'Agglomeration' is typically used to refer to the degree to which economic activity as a whole is geographically concentrated. In contrast, 'localization' is often used to refer to the degree to which economic activity in a particular industry is geographically concentrated after controlling for the geographic concentration of overall economic activity.[13] Both concepts are distinct from 'industrial concentration', which refers to the degree to which economic activity in a particular industry is concentrated in a small number of plants irrespective of their geographical location.

As convincingly argued by Ellison and Glaeser (1997), when measuring the degree of localization of industries, it is important to control for industrial concentration. The reason is that the number of plants in an industry is often relatively small, in which case even random location patterns cannot be expected to produce perfectly regular location patterns, For example, suppose that 75 percent of employees in the U.S. vacuum cleaner industry work in one of four main plants. In this case, even if the plants locate separately, four locations must account for at least 75 percent of the employment in the industry even in the absence of any forces of cumulative causation. This concern is all the more important given the emphasis placed on increasing returns to scale in theories of new economic geography. To address this concern, Ellison and Glaeser (1997) develop a model-based measure of geographic concentration, which can be compared against a null of random location (a 'dartboard' approach), and which controls for the degree of industrial concentration.[14]

In an important paper, Duranton and Overman (2005) argue that empirical measures of localization should exhibit five features: (a) they should be comparable across industries; (b) they should control for the overall agglomeration of economic activity; (c) they should control for industrial concentration; (d) they should be unbiased with respect to scale and aggregation; (e) they should give an indication of the significance of the results. Duranton and Overman (2005) develop an approach based on spatial point patterns that satisfies these five criteria. Using data on four-digit manufacturing industries in the United Kingdom, they find that the majority of industries are localized at the 5 percent significance level, that localization takes place mostly between 0 and 50 kilometers, the degree of localization is highly skewed across industries, and that industries that belong to the same industrial branch tend to have similar location patterns.

One of the striking features of empirical studies measuring the extent of localization across industries is that the most localized industries are not necessarily those in which one might intuitively expect the strongest forces of cumulative causation (e.g. manufacture of cutlery in the United Kingdom). These findings highlight the fact that geographical concentration can arise as a result of geographic variation in natural advantages (e.g. mineral resources) as well as forces of cumulative causation. Indeed, Ellison and Glaeser (1997) develop an observational equivalence result that the relationship between mean measured levels of concentration and industry characteristics is the same regardless of whether concentration is the result of spillovers, natural advantage or a combination of the two. This, in turn, is related to the general identification problem in the social sciences of distinguishing spillovers from correlated individual effects (see in particular Manski, 1995).

3.2 Market access and wages

As discussed above, one of the key theoretical predictions of new economic geography models is that nominal factor prices vary systematically across locations with their market access. This prediction relates to an older literature that relates spatial variation in economic activity to measures of 'market potential', defined as the distance-weighted sum of market demand:

$$\mathrm{MP}_i = \sum_j (d_{ij})^\gamma Y_j, \tag{8}$$

where MP_i is the 'market potential' of location i, d_{ij} is the bilateral distance between locations i and j, and γ is a distance-weighting parameter, traditionally set at -1.[15]

New economic geography models can be viewed as providing microeconomic foundations for empirical measures of market potential. Consider for example the right-hand side of the wage equation (1). Suppose that the impact of transportation costs on market demand, $\tau^{1-\sigma}$, is proxied by the inverse of bilateral distance, as suggested by gravity equation estimates in which the coefficient on bilateral distance is close to minus one. Suppose also that we abstract from variation in the manufacturing price index, P, across locations. In this case, the right-hand side of the wage equation is proportional to traditional empirical measures of market potential (8). However, new economic geography models themselves imply that manufacturing price indices should vary systematically across locations and, therefore, that in measuring market potential one should control for this variation in price indices. Following Redding and Venables (2004), we refer to theory-based measures of market potential that control for differences in price indices across locations as measures of 'market access'.[16]

Consider the following extension of the new economic geography model outlined in section 2. Suppose that there are many regions indexed by i, factors of production are geographically immobile and manufacturing varieties are used as intermediate inputs to production with the same CES functional form as used for consumption (see Krugman and Venables, 1995, Fujita, Krugman and Venables, 2001, and Redding and Venables, 2004). With the introduction of many regions and intermediate inputs, the wage equation (1) becomes:

$$\left(w^{\xi} P_M^{\eta} \right)^{\sigma} = \vartheta \sum_j \tau_{ij}^{1-\sigma} E_j P_{M_j}^{\sigma-1},$$

where the manufacturing cost function is assumed to have a Cobb–Douglas functional form with exponent η on intermediate inputs and ξ on labour; E_j denotes equilibrium expenditure on manufacturing varieties in location j, which now includes both final consumption and intermediate demand; ϑ absorbs earlier constants. This wage equation can be in turn rewritten in the following intuitive form:

$$w_i = \theta \mathrm{MA}_i^{\frac{1}{\xi\sigma}} \mathrm{SA}_i^{\frac{\eta}{\xi(\sigma-1)}}, \tag{9}$$

$$\mathrm{MA}_i \equiv \sum_j \tau_{ij}^{1-\sigma} E_j P_{M_j}^{\sigma-1}, \qquad \mathrm{SA}_j \equiv \sum_i n_i \left(\tau_{ij} p_i \right)^{1-\sigma} = P_{M_j}^{1-\sigma}, \tag{10}$$

where θ is again a constant. Market access, MA_i, measures a region's proximity to sources of market demand, while supplier access, SA_i, captures its proximity to sources of supply of intermediate inputs.

Redding and Venables (2004) use the structure of a new economic geography model to estimate theory-consistent measures of market access and supplier access from bilateral trade data. From the CES demand function, the aggregate value of bilateral exports of manufacturing varieties from location i to j can be written as follows:

$$n_i p_i x_{ij} = s_i \tau_{ij}^{1-\sigma} m_j, \tag{11}$$

where $s_i \equiv n_i p_i^{1-\sigma}$ is a measure of exporter i's 'supply capacity', $m_j \equiv E_j P_{M_j}^{\sigma-1}$ is a measure of importer j's 'market capacity'. From this gravity equation for bilateral trade, supply capacity can be estimated using exporter fixed effects, market capacity can be estimated using importer fixed effects, and bilateral transportation costs can be proxied with for example measures of bilateral distance and contiguity.[17] Given estimates of market and supply capacity for each exporter and importer, market and supplier access can be constructed as:

$$\mathrm{MA}_i = \sum_j \tau_{ij}^{1-\sigma} m_j, \qquad \mathrm{SA}_j = \sum_i \tau_{ij}^{1-\sigma} s_i.$$

Having used the model's predictions for bilateral trade to estimate market and supplier access, these measures can, in turn, be used to examine the empirical

relevance of the model's predictions for the relationship between spatial variation in nominal incomes and market and supplier access. Taking logarithms in
equation (9), we obtain:

$$\ln w_i = \theta + \varphi_1 \ln SA_i + \varphi_2 \ln MA_i + u_i, \tag{12}$$

where $\varphi_1 = \eta / (\xi (\sigma - 1))$, $\varphi_2 = 1/(\xi \sigma)$, and the stochastic error u_i includes cross-
country variation in the price of other factors of production that enter manu-
facturing unit costs, technical differences, and other stochastic determinants of
manufacturing wages.

Table 16.1 reports the results of estimating (12) using cross-country data with
GDP per capita as a proxy for manufacturing wages. Because of the potential
endogeneity of domestic market and supply capacity, only measures of foreign
market and supplier access are considered (i.e. own country values are ignored,
so the summations in (10) are over $j \neq i$). Column (1) presents the results using
foreign market access alone. The estimated coefficient is positive and explains
about 35 percent of the cross-country variation in income per capita. Column

Table 16.1 World market access, supplier access, and GDP per capita.

ln (GDP per capita)	(1)	(2)	(3)	(4)
Obs.	101	101	69	69
Year	1996	1996	1996	1996
η		0.5		
σ		10		
ln (FMA$_i$)	0.476	0.320	0.269	0.189
	[0.076]		[0.112]	[0.096]
ln (FSA$_i$)	–	0.178	–	–
		[0.039]		
Controls			Yes	Yes
R^2	0.346	0.360	0.669	0.654

Notes: Dependent variable is ln(GDP per capita). Independent variables are ln(Foreign
Market Access), ln(FMA$_i$), and ln(Foreign supplier access), ln(FSA$_i$). ln(FMA$_i$) and ln(FSA$_i$)
are generated from estimates of a gravity equation for bilateral trade. As these variables
are generated from a prior regression, bootstrapped standard errors are reported in square
parentheses (200 replications). The results reported in columns (1) and (2) are from tables
2 and 5 of Redding and Venables (2004), while those in columns (3) and (4) are from
table 3 of Redding and Venables (2004). The sample in columns (1) and (2) includes 101
countries, whereas the sample in columns (3) and (4) includes 69 non-OECD countries.
Columns (3) and (4) include controls for log hydrocarbons per capita, log arable land
per capita, number of mineral resources, fraction of land in the geographical tropics,
prevalence of malaria, risk of expropriation, socialist rule during 1950–95 and external war during 1960–85. Column (4) estimates the model for 69 non-OECD countries
with a measure of ln(FMA$_i$) constructed using only data on distance and OECD market
capacities.

(2) includes information on supplier access as well. Separately identifying the coefficients on these two variables is difficult given their high degree of correlation. However, choosing values for η and σ implies a linear restriction on the estimated coefficients, $\varphi_1 = \varphi_2 \eta \sigma / (\sigma - 1)$, and column (2) reports the results of estimating for values of $\eta = 0.5$ and $\sigma = 10$, both of which are broadly consistent with independent empirical estimates. Including foreign supplier access reduces the magnitude of the estimated coefficient on foreign market access, but it remains highly statistically significant.

There are a number of potential concerns about these results. Are they in fact identifying an effect of economic geography, or instead picking up that rich countries tend to be located next to rich countries, particularly within the Organization for Economic Co-operation and Development (OECD)? Or the results could in principle be driven by omitted variables (e.g., unobserved technology differences) that are correlated with both income per capita and foreign market and supplier access? To address these concerns, Redding and Venables (2004) report a number of robustness tests. For example, column (3) reports the results for non-OECD countries only, including control variables for factor endowments, physical geography, and social, political, and institutional considerations. Additionally, column (4) repeats this specification for non-OECD countries, using a measure of foreign market access based solely on distance and market capacities in OECD countries. This final specification examines the extent to which variation in income per capita across developing countries can be explained by access to OECD markets. Across each of these specifications, the effect of foreign market access remains positive and significant.

While Redding and Venables (2004) focus on cross-country variation in incomes, Hanson (2005) examines cross-county variations in wages within the United States using the Helpman (1998) model. In the absence of intermediate inputs to production, the factor mobility condition (7) together with equilibrium expenditure shares and market clearing imply that the wage equation can be written as follows:

$$
w_i = \kappa + \sigma^{-1} \ln \left(\sum_j Y_j^{\frac{\sigma(\mu-1)+1}{\mu}} H_j^{\frac{(\sigma-1)(1-\mu)}{\mu}} w_j^{\frac{\sigma-1}{\mu}} e^{-\tau(\sigma-1)d_{ij}} \right) + \varepsilon_i, \tag{13}
$$

where κ is a constant, Y_j denotes aggregate income, H_j is the stock of the non-traded amenity, and regional transport costs are modelled as an exponential function of distance: $e^{-\tau d_{ij}}$.

Columns (1) and (2) of table 16.2 report the results of estimating equation (13) time-differenced using non-linear least squares for 1970–80 and 1980–90. The estimated coefficients are signed according to economic priors and statistically significant. The estimates of the elasticity of substitution, σ, are broadly in line with independent econometric estimates of this parameter and fall between

Table 16.2   Market potential and wages across U.S. counties.

	(1)	(2)	(3)
	3705	3705	3705
	1970–80	1980–90	1980–90
Obs.			
Time period			
σ	7.597	6.562	4.935
	(1.250)	*(0.838)*	*(1.372)*
μ	0.916	0.956	0.982
	(0.015)	*(0.013)*	*(0.035)*
τ	1.970	3.219	1.634
	(0.328)	*(0.416)*	*(0.523)*
Wage controls	No	No	Yes
Adj. R^2	0.256	0.347	0.376
Log likelihood	−16698.1	−16576.9	−16479.9
Schwarz criterion	−16714.0	−16592.9	−16575.5

Notes: Reported results are from table 3 in Hanson (2005). Estimation is by non-linear least squares. Sample is all U.S. counties in the continental United States, and the equation estimated is the time-difference of equation (13). All variables are scaled relative to weighted averages for the continental United States. The dependent variable is the log change in average annual earnings from Regional Economic Information System (REIS), US BEA. Regional income is total personal income from REIS. The housing stock is measured by total housing units from the U.S. Census of Population and Housing. The specification in column (3) includes controls for human capital, demographic characteristics, and exogenous amenities. Heteroscedasticity-consistent standard errors are in parentheses. The Schwartz Criterion is written as $\ln(L) - k^* \ln(N)/2$, where k is the number of parameters.

the two time periods. The markup of price over marginal cost implied by these estimates ranges between 1.15 and 1.25. Consistent with the model, the estimated expenditure share on tradable goods, μ, lies between 0 and 1, although a value greater than 0.9 is somewhat high. The estimated value of transport costs, τ, rises between the two time periods, which is consistent with economic activity becoming more spatially concentrated in the Helpman (1998) model, and is also consistent with a shift in production away from low-transport cost manufactures to high-transport cost services. Finally, the theory-based measure of market access derived from the Helpman (1998) model outperforms the ad hoc measures of market potential discussed above, which do not control for variation across locations in the manufacturing price index.

Estimating the specification in time differences controls for unobserved heterogeneity across counties in the level of manufacturing wages. However, one potential concern is that wages have risen faster in countries with more attractive amenities (e.g., weather or natural geography) or more rapid human capital accumulation (both through the private rate of return to human capital acquisition and through any externalities), and these omitted variables could be correlated with changes in market access.[18] To address these concerns, Hanson (2005) shows that the results are robust to including controls for levels of human capital, demographic composition of the working age population, and exogenous amenities. The results including these controls are reported for 1980–90 in column (3) of table 16.2.

Subsequent research has provided further evidence of a close relationship between market access and wages. For example, using data on a panel of countries over time, Mayer (2008) finds a strong correlation between changes in income and changes in market access. Using data on regions of the European Union, and exploiting both cross-section and time-series variation, Breinlich (2006) and Head and Mayer (2006) also find a strong empirical relationship between wages and market access. Using even more finely spatially disaggregated data within Indonesia, Amiti and Cameron (2007) again find evidence that second-nature geography matters and exploit information on intermediate input use to separate market and supplier access.[19] However, while there is strong evidence of a clear association between wages and market access, a key challenge for the empirical literature has been to establish that this association is indeed causal. An important concern is the omission of other determinants of wages that are correlated with market access, such as institutions and natural endowments. A further source of concern is that theoretical models of economic geography themselves suggest that market access is endogenous. Localized shocks to income in a region will also change the region's market access both directly – as the size of the region's own market is part of its market access – and indirectly by changing neighboring regions' market access and, hence, income which, in turn, influences the region's own market access.

One strategy to address these concerns has been to use instruments for market access, which have included lagged population levels or growth rates, lagged transportation infrastructure, the distance of U.S. counties from the eastern seaboard, or the distance of countries from the United States, Europe and Japan. However, these instruments are only valid under demanding identification assumptions, which are unlikely to be satisfied in practice. For example, institutions, natural endowments and market access are all strongly persistent, and so it is unlikely that lagged population affects economic activity solely through market access. Similarly, distance from the eastern seaboard of the United States could capture a wide range of factors, including natural advantage, and is unlikely to affect only economic activity through market access.

An alternative and influential strategy to address these concerns involves the use of trade liberalizations as a source of variation in market access. In a series of important papers, Hanson (1996, 1997, 1998), has used Mexico's trade liberalization of 1985 as a natural experiment that changes the relative market access of locations within the country. Mexico's unilateral liberalization of 1985 marked a major change in the direction of trade policy, which brought to an end four decades of import–substitution industrialization and was followed by further regional integration in the guise of the North American Free Trade Agreement (NAFTA) of the early 1990s. Following the liberalization of the mid-1980s, there is evidence of a change in the distribution of economic activity within Mexico. For example, in the apparel industry, Hanson (1996) finds that prior to trade liberalization, production was concentrated around Mexico City and largely orientated towards the Mexican market. In the aftermath of trade liberalization, there is a relocation of manufacturing activity towards the U.S. border, and a shift from domestic production to offshore assembly for foreign (largely U.S.) firms. Consistent with theories of new economic geography, this change in relative market access of locations is reflected in changes in relative wages. Prior to trade liberalization, the relative wages of locations exhibit a strong wage gradient in distance from Mexico City, while between 1985 and 1988 there is a statistically significant decline in the slope of this gradient. Therefore the strong regional wage gradient centred on Mexico City prior to trade liberalization at least partially breaks as production re-orientates towards the U.S. border.[20]

While evidence based on trade liberalizations has bolstered the case for a causal interpretation of the relationship between market access and wages, there remain a number of potential concerns. In particular, a large political economy literature models trade policy as an endogenous outcome that is determined by industry characteristics, such as supply and demand elasticities, and the ratio of imports to industry output.[21] Therefore, there remains the concern that changes in trade policy may not only alter market access and so result in changes in income or production, but changes in income or production may also lead to endogenous changes in trade policy and hence market access.

To provide further evidence in support of a causal interpretation of the relationship between the distribution of economic activity and market access, Redding and Sturm (2008) examine the impact of the division of Germany in the aftermath of the Second World War and the reunification of East and West Germany in 1990 as a source of exogenous variation in the relative market access of West German cities. In the absence of intermediate inputs, the factor mobility condition (7), together with equilibrium expenditure shares and market clearing, implies that the equilibrium population of each location i can be expressed as follows:

$$L_i = \chi \, (\text{FMA}_i)^{\frac{\mu}{\sigma(1-\mu)}} \, (\text{CMA}_i)^{\frac{\mu}{(1-\mu)(\sigma-1)}} \, H_i,$$

where χ collects together constants, H_i again denotes a location's endowment of the non-traded amenity, and FMA_i and CMA_i are measures of firm and consumer market access, defined analogously to (10):

$$\text{FMA}_i \equiv \sum_j \mu Y_j \left(P_j^M\right)^{\sigma-1} \left(T_{ij}\right)^{1-\sigma}, \qquad \text{CMA}_i \equiv \sum_j n_j (p_j T_{ji})^{1-\sigma}.$$

The key idea behind the Redding and Sturm (2008) empirical approach is that German division caused West German cities close to the former border between East and West Germany ('treatment' cities) to experience a disproportionate loss of market access relative to other West German cities ('control' cities). The reason is that West German cities close to the East–West border lost nearby trading partners with whom they could interact at low transport costs prior to division. In contrast, the effect on West German cities farther from the East–West border was more muted, because they were more remote from the trading partners lost and, therefore, already faced higher transport costs prior to division.

The use of German division as a natural experiment to provide evidence of causal impact of market access has a number of attractive features. First, in contrast to cross-country studies, across cities within West Germany there is no obvious variation in institutions that could explain the differential performance of treatment and control cities. Second, as the analysis focuses on cities within West Germany, there are no obvious changes in natural advantage, such as access to navigable rivers or coasts, climatic conditions or the disease environment. Third, the change in market access following German division is much larger than typically observed in other contexts and the effects can be observed over a long period of time. Fourth, the drawing of the border dividing Germany into East and West Germany was based on military considerations that are unlikely to be correlated with pre-division characteristics of cities.

In line with the predictions of new economic geography models, Redding and Sturm (2008) find that relative to other West German cities the imposition of the East–West border led to a sharp decline in population growth of West German cities close to the border. Over the 40-year period of division, they estimate a decline in the annualized rate of population growth of 0.75 percentage points, implying a cumulative reduction in the relative size of East–West border cities of around one-third. The market access based mechanism of new economic geography models is found to account for the relative decline of East–West border cities both qualitatively and quantitatively. They also provide evidence against alternative possible explanations, such as differences in industrial structure, differences in the degree of disruption during and in the aftermath of the Second World War, western European integration, and fear of further armed conflict.

Taken together, the evidence from this line of research suggests that there is not only an association, but also a causal relationship, between market access and the spatial distribution of economic activity.

3.3   Market access and location choices

The home market effect in economic geography models has implications not only for factor prices but also for the location of production. In neoclassical trade theories, increases in expenditure lead at most to equiproportionate increases in production of a good, and typically lead to less than proportionate increases in production of a good because export supply curves are in general upward-sloping. In contrast, in new economic geography models increases in expenditure typically lead to more than proportionate increases in the production of a good (a 'magnification effect'), because of the resulting change in firms' location decisions in a model with transport costs and increasing returns to scale.

In two ground-breaking papers, Davis and Weinstein (1999, 2003) used these contrasting predictions as the basis of a discriminating test between neoclassical and increasing returns to scale trade theories in a world of positive transport costs. Their empirical specification estimates the relationship between production of a good and measures of idiosyncratic demand, and examines whether the coefficient on idiosyncratic demand is greater than or less than one, while also controlling for other determinants of production. Davis and Weinstein (2003) consider a nested specification, where factor endowments are assumed to determine production at the more aggregate level (three-digit), while economic geography effects operate in disaggregated industries. Using data for 13 OECD countries, they first construct measures of 'idiosyncratic demand' for each four-digit industry based on demand in the country and its trading partners, distance weighted. Estimating the effects of this demand variable on production in a pooled sample across countries and all four-digit industries, they find an elasticity of production with respect to demand of 1.6, indicating a strong home market effect. As industries could have different market structures, Davis and Weinstein (2003) also consider an augmented specification that allows for heterogeneity across industries. Disaggregating and running separate regressions for each three-digit industry (with the sample of countries and four-digit sub-industries), they find evidence of a home market effect (a coefficient on idiosyncratic demand of greater than unity) in a majority of industries, the estimated coefficient being significantly greater than unity in four industries, and significantly less than unity in two.

A similar pattern of results is found by Davis and Weinstein (1999) using a related specification and data for 29 sectors and 47 Japanese prefectures in 1985. Statistically significant home market effects are found in eight out of 19 manufacturing sectors, including transportation equipment, iron and steel, electrical machinery, and chemicals. These effects are not only statistically significant but also quantitatively important: for the eight sectors with statistically significant home market effects, a one standard deviation movement in idiosyncratic demand is found to move production, on average, by half a standard deviation.

Additional evidence of home market effects is found using international trade data by Feenstra, Markusen and Rose (2001), Hanson and Xiang (2004), and Head and Ries (2001).

While there is, therefore, a strong body of empirical evidence of home market effects, there is less consensus on the relative importance of natural advantages (such as factor endowments) and the forces of cumulative causation emphasized by economic geography in determining the distribution of economic activity across space. In an influential paper, Ellison and Glaeser (1999) provide evidence that a relatively parsimonious set of measures of natural advantage explains at least 20 percent of the variation in employment shares across U.S. states and four-digit manufacturing industries. Their empirical specification regresses state–industry employment shares on interaction terms between state natural advantages and measures of the extent to which industries are dependent on these natural advantages. In another influential paper, Midelfart-Knarvik, Overman and Venables (2001) develop a general equilibrium model that explicitly incorporates both natural advantage and economic geography, and present evidence on their respective contributions for the European Union.

While considerable progress has been made examining the role of natural advantage and economic geography in influencing production location, this remains an interesting area for further research. Definitely determining when a variable reflects an exogenous natural advantage as opposed to an endogenous outcome of cumulative causation is sometimes difficult. Even when a sharp distinction between these two sets of considerations is possible, they are unlikely to be orthogonal to one another. And consistently estimating the impact of measures of cumulative causation is particularly challenging, because theories of new economic geography suggest that they are inherently endogenous, and potential sources for valid instruments are often unclear, as already discussed above.[22]

3.4 Multiple equilibria

A central feature of new economic geography models is that there are ranges of parameter values for which there are multiple equilibrium distributions of economic activity across space. Which of these multiple equilibria is selected depends on historical accident or expectations.[23] This feature of new economic geography models contrasts with the predictions of neoclassical frameworks, in which locational fundamentals, such as institutions and natural endowments, are the primary determinants of location choices.

The potential existence of multiple equilibria has important policy implications. In this class of models, small and temporary policy interventions can have large and permanent effects by shifting the economy from one equilibrium to another. These ideas have reinvigorated debates about regional and industrial policy. They appear to offer the prospect that temporary subsidies or regulations can permanently alter the long-run spatial distribution of economic activity, with important consequences for the welfare of immobile factors.

While there is some anecdotal evidence of apparent examples of historical accident having long-lived effects on the distribution of economic activity across space, and an extensive theoretical literature on multiple equilibria in location, there is a surprising lack of systematic empirical evidence in favour of multiple steady-state distributions of economic activity.[24] On the contrary, in a seminal paper, Davis and Weinstein (2002) provide what appears to be strong empirical evidence against multiple evidence in industrial location. The key idea behind their empirical approach is that in a world with a unique long-run equilibrium distribution of economic activity determined by locational fundamentals, temporary shocks to the relative attractiveness of locations have purely temporary effects, as economic activity gravitates back towards its long-run equilibrium. In contrast, in a world with multiple equilibrium distributions of economic activity across space, temporary shocks can have permanent effects, because they shift the distribution of economic activity between multiple equilibria.

To examine the empirical relevance of multiple equilibria in industrial location, Davis and Weinstein (2002), therefore, consider the Allied bombing of Japanese cities during the Second World War as a large and temporary shock to the relative attractiveness of locations. Surprisingly, they find that city populations recovered very quickly from the wartime shock and cities return to their pre-war growth path within less than 20 years. If even the vast wartime devastation of cities observed in Japan cannot move the economy between multiple spatial configurations of economic activity, this appears to suggest an overwhelming role for fundamentals in determining the location of economic activity.

Following Davis and Weinstein (2002), a number of papers have examined the impact of bombing on the spatial distribution of economic activity. Davis and Weinstein (2008) show that not only the total population of Japanese cities but also the location of specific industries quickly return to their pre-war pattern. Brakman, Garretson and Schramm (2004) find that the populations of West German cities recovered rapidly from the devastation caused by the Second World War. Similarly, Miguel and Roland (2006) find that even the extensive bombing campaign in Vietnam does not seem to have had a permanent impact on the distribution of population and basic measures of economic development across the regions of Vietnam. Similarly, Bosker, Brakman, Garretson, De Jong and Schramm (2008) find apparently little evidence of major shocks, such as the plague, on the relative growth of Italian cities over several centuries. Two exceptions from this general pattern of results are Bosker, Brakman, Garretson and Schramm (2007, 2008), who find some evidence of a permanent change in the distribution of population across West German cities after the Second World War.

While war-related destruction is an ingenious source for a large and temporary shock, a potential concern is that this shock may not be sufficient to change location decisions, which are forward-looking and involve substantial sunk costs. In addition the continued existence of road networks and partially surviving commercial and residential structures may serve as focal points around which reconstruction occurs. Institutional constraints such as property rights and land-use regulations may also provide additional reasons why existing concentrations of population and industrial activity re-emerge. Finally, even if one observes changes in the location of population, as in Bosker, Brakman, Garretson and Schramm (2007, 2008), it remains unclear whether these are due to secular changes in fundamentals or a move between multiple steady-states.

To provide empirical support for the idea that location choices are not uniquely determined by locational fundamentals, Redding, Sturm and Wolf (2011) use the combination of the division of Germany after the Second World War and the reunification of East and West Germany in 1990 as a source of exogenous variation. As noted above, this natural experiment has a number of attractive features. German division, which was driven by military and strategic considerations during the Second World War and its immediate aftermath, provides a large exogenous shock to the relative attractiveness of locations. Division lasted for over 40 years and was widely expected to be permanent, which makes it likely that it had a profound influence on location choices.

In their analysis, Redding, Sturm and Wolf (2011) focus on a particular industrial activity, namely Germany's airport hub, which has a number of advantages. In particular, there are substantial sunk costs involved in creating airport hubs and large network externalities associated with their operation, which suggests that airport hubs are likely to be particularly susceptible to multiple equilibria in their location. While Germany's airport hub was located in Berlin prior to the Second World War, it relocated to Frankfurt in the aftermath of Germany's division, and there is no evidence whatsoever of a return of the airport hub to Berlin following German reunification. Redding, Sturm and Wolf (2011) provide a variety of evidence that the difference in economic fundamentals between Berlin and Frankfurt, both prior to the Second World War and in the period since German reunification, is small relative to the substantial sunk costs of creating an airport hub. This pattern of results suggests that Berlin, Frankfurt and a number of other areas within Germany are potential steady-state locations of Germany's airport hub, in the sense that if the sunk costs of creating the hub were to be incurred in those locations, there would be no incentive to relocate elsewhere.

While the attraction of focusing on a particular industrial activity susceptible to multiple steady-state locations is that it can be used to provide evidence in support of the relevance of multiple equilibria, it seems likely that other economic activities besides airport hubs have sufficiently large sunk costs and agglomeration forces for their locations not to be uniquely determined by fundamentals. Identifying the types of economic activities for which fundamentals dominate and the types of economic activities for which there are multiple steady-state locations remains an important area for future empirical research.

4   Conclusions and areas for further research

There is by now an extensive and rich theoretical literature that examines the role of love of variety, increasing returns to scale and transport costs in determining the distribution of economic activity across space. Some of the central theoretical predictions of this literature appear to receive substantial empirical support, including the importance of market access in determining factor prices and the location of economic activity. The empirical relevance of other theoretical predictions, such as multiple equilibria in industrial location and the respective contributions of natural advantage and cumulative causation in shaping location choices remain the subject of ongoing research.

Despite the considerable theoretical and empirical advances that have been made, there remain a number of areas for potential further research. One is the respective contributions of love of variety, increasing returns to scale and transport costs and other potential sources of agglomeration, such as knowledge spillovers and the pooling of specialized skills as also emphasized by Marshall (1920). In particular, there is a large and rich theoretical literature in urban and macroeconomics emphasizing knowledge spillovers and external economies, and several of the empirical predictions of these models are closely related to those of theories of new economic geography.[25] Empirical evidence on the geographical localization of knowledge spillovers using patent citations is provided by Jaffe, Henderson and Trajtenberg (1993). In an influential recent paper, Ellison, Glaeser and Kerr (2007) use information on the characteristics of co-agglomerating industries to provide evidence on the respective contributions of all Marshall's three agglomeration forces.

While new economic geography models, and theories of agglomeration more generally, provide plausible explanations for wages in densely populated areas to be higher than in sparsely populated areas, there are other possible explanations. One such possibility is the non-random selection of firms according to their productivity, as examined for example in Baldwin and Okubo (2006) and Combes, Duranton, Gobillon, Puga and Roux (2008). Another related possibility is the non-random sorting of workers according to their observed or unobserved characteristics, as examined in Combes, Duranton and Gobillon (2008). Determining the respective contributions of agglomeration and the non-random sorting of firms and workers, both theoretically and empirically, is therefore an active area of research.

Another interesting avenue for further research concerns the relationship between theories of new economic geography and the city size distribution. While city growth appears largely uncorrelated with city size ('Gibrat's Law') and a linear relationship between log population rank and log population size with a unit coefficient ('Zipf's Law') appears to provide a rough approximation towards the observed city size distribution, neither of these features is typically generated by theories of new economic geography. Recent research in urban economics has begun to explore the economic forces underlying these statistical relationships and to provide explanations for the systematic departures from Zipf's Law that are observed in the upper and lower tails of the city size distribution.[26] Although this research has largely focused on cities, in developed countries historically, and in developing countries today, much of the population is located in rural areas. Furthermore, there appear to be large and systematic departures from Gibrat's Law across both rural and urban areas, as examined by Michaels, Rauch and Redding (2008). Insofar as urbanization – the concentration of population in towns and cities – is one of the most striking features of economic development, understanding the evolution of the population distribution across both rural and urban areas remains a pressing concern.[27]

In economic geography models, one of the central forces shaping the distribution of economic activity across space is transportation costs. While transportation costs are typically thought to have fallen over time, their future evolution is perhaps unclear, since it depends on climate change and a rise in the price of oil on the one hand and the development of new transportation technologies on the other hand. Furthermore, transportation costs are likely only a small component of overall trade costs, which also depend on the costs of acquiring and communicating information at a distance as well as the contracting costs of undertaking transactions at a distance. While transportation costs are relatively easy to measure and analyze (see in particular Anderson and van Wincoop, 2004, Combes and Lafourcade, 2005, Limao and Venables, 2001, Hummels, 2007, Hummels and Skiba, 2004), far less is known about these other components of trade costs, and this is an active and exciting area of ongoing research.[28]

Finally, perhaps the most challenging issues facing empirical research in economic geography are the identification problems inherent in the study of endogenous choices of location, including, in particular, the generic problem of distinguishing spillovers from correlated individual effects. One approach to addressing these identification concerns exploits natural experiments and institutional variation, such as German division and reunification (e.g. Redding and Sturm 2008), the use of regression discontinuity design at borders to control for unobserved variation in natural advantage (e.g. Holmes, 1998;

Duranton, Gobillon and Overman, 2007), and the use of historical patterns of land allocation to estimate externalities to crop planting (e.g. Holmes and Lee, 2008). Perhaps one of the most fruitful approaches combines institutional variation with the discipline of a structural model to identify the parameters of interest (see in particular Holmes, 2005, 2008).

In summary, while great theoretical and empirical advances have been made in the field of economic geography, there remain a number of challenges and a host of interesting and important questions to be addressed.

Notes

* This chapter is produced as part of the Globalization Programme of the ESRC-funded Centre for Economic Performance. Financial support under the European Union Research Training Network grant MRTN-CT-2006-035873 is gratefully acknowledged. I am grateful to a number of co-authors and colleagues for insight, discussion and helpful comments, including in particular Tony Venables and also Gilles Duranton, Guy Michaels, Henry Overman, Esteban Rossi-Hansberg, Peter Schott, Daniel Sturm and Nikolaus Wolf. Nonetheless, I bear sole responsibility for the opinions expressed and any errors.
† Princeton University and CEPR. Department of Economics and Woodrow Wilson School, Princeton.
1. For a historical analysis of urbanization, see Bairoch (1988).
2. See in particular Alonso (1964), Christaller (1933), Harris (1954), Lösch (1954), Muth (1961) and Mills (1967).
3. For syntheses of the theoretical literature on new economic geography, see Fujita, Krugman and Venables (2001), Baldwin, Forslid, Martin, Ottaviano and Robert-Nicoud (2003), and Fujita and Thisse (2002).
4. For other complementary reviews of the new economic geography literature, see Neary (2001), Ottaviano and Puga (1998), Overman, Redding and Venables (2001), and Head and Mayer (2004). For broader theoretical and empirical reviews of the sources of agglomeration, see Duranton and Puga (2004) and Rosenthal and Strange (2004).
5. In contrast, neoclassical trade theory emphasizes first-nature geography in the form of differences in factor endowments. For a lively debate on the contribution of first-nature geography towards spatial disparities in economic development, see for example Acemoglu, Johnson and Robinson (2002), Bloom and Sachs (1998), Gallup, Mellinger and Sachs (1998), Rodrik et al. (2004).
6. Related research in regional and urban economics includes Fujita (1988), Henderson (1974, 1988) and Rivera-Batiz (1988).
7. While the assumptions of perfect competition, constant returns to scale and zero transportation costs in the agricultural sector are largely made for simplicity, they are not innocuous (see, e.g., Davis 1999), although results generalize in a number of respects (see, e.g., Fujita, Krugman and Venables 2001).
8. Choosing units in which to measure farmers and workers such that their number is proportional to the shares of sectors in consumption expenditure turns out to be a convenient normalization that simplifies expressions.
9. For a complete analysis, see Fujita, Krugman and Venables (2001) and Baldwin, Forslid, Martin, Ottaviano and Robert-Nicoud (2003).

10. While CES preferences within the manufacturing sector are in many ways a convenient simplification, they have the unattractive feature that the elasticity of substitution determines both the strength of love of variety and the equilibrium extent of increasing returns to scale. As CES preferences imply a constant markup of price over marginal cost, profit maximization and zero profits together imply that the equilibrium ratio of average cost to marginal cost is $\sigma/(\sigma-1)$.

11. Whether industrial location is determined by historical accident or forward-looking expectations cannot be determined without developing an explicitly dynamic model. Typically, the dynamics in new economic geography models are relatively ad hoc, although notable exceptions are Baldwin (2001), Krugman (1991b) and Matsuyama (1991).

12. In the quasi-linear specification, there is a downward-sloping linear demand curve for each differentiated variety. Total expenditure on differentiated varieties is determined from these demand curves given the profit-maximizing price for each differentiated variety. Once total expenditure on differentiated varieties is determined, all remaining income is spent on the homogeneous or outside good. As a result, increases in income are spent entirely on the homogeneous or outside good, and there are no income effects.

13. This terminology differs somewhat from the historical usage in Hoover (1937). While 'localization' is used in the same way, what is here termed 'agglomeration' is historically referred to as 'urbanization'.

14. In addition to the U.S. evidence in Ellison and Glaeser (1997), Devereux, Griffith and Simpson (2004) report results for the UK, while Maurel and Sedillot (1999) report results for France.

15. See, e.g., Clark et al. (1969), Dicken and Lloyd (1977), Keeble et al. (1982), Harris (1954), Hummels (1995) and Leamer (1997). For an early analysis of the role of transportation costs in influencing cross-country income, see Gallup, Mellinger and Sachs (1998).

16. Head and Mayer (2004) instead use the term 'real market potential'.

17. For an alternative approach to estimating the gravity equation that exploits expenditure minimization and market clearing to solve explicitly for price indices, see Anderson and van Wincoop (2003).

18. As human capital accumulation could be influenced in part by economic geography, it is not clear that one wants to control for this. For empirical evidence on the relationship between market access and skill acquisition, see Redding and Schott (2003).

19. Despite a large empirical literature on the effect of market access on nominal wages, there has been relatively little research examining the predictions of new economic geography models for the prices of immobile amenities such as land. A notable exception is Deckle and Eaton (1999).

20. Other studies using trade liberalization as a source of variation in market access include Overman and Winters (2006) for the United Kingdom, Tirado, Paluzie and Pons (2002) for early twentieth-century Spain, and Nikolaus Wolf (2007) for early twentieth-century Poland.

21. See for example the large literature following Grossman and Helpman (1994). The theoretical predictions of this literature receive empirical support in Goldberg and Maggi (1999) and subsequent contributions.

22. One creative source of instruments in the literature on the relationship between productivity and population density is geology, which affects the height to which

buildings can be constructed, and hence provides a plausibly exogenous source of variation in population density (see Rosenthal and Strange 2005).

23. See Krugman (1991b) and Matsuyama (1991) for an analysis of the respective role of historical accident and expectations in models featuring multiple equilibria.

24. For example, Krugman (1991c) discusses the case of carpet manufacturing in Dalton, Georgia.

25. For further discussion and analysis of external economies, see, e.g., Ciccone and Hall (1996), Combes, Duranton, Gobillon and Roux (2008), Duranton and Puga (2004), Fujita and Ogawa (1982), Greenstone, Hornbeck and Moretti (2008), Henderson (2003), Lucas and Rossi-Hansberg (2002), Rosenthal and Strange (2004, 2005), Rossi-Hansberg (2005), and Sveikauskas (1975).

26. See in particular Cordoba (2008), Duranton (2007), Eeckhout (2004), Gabaix (1999), Holmes and Lee (2007), and Rossi-Hansberg and Wright (2007).

27. See Henderson and Wang (2007) and Henderson and Venables (2008) for analyses of the emergence of new cities as a source of growth in the urban population.

28. Influential studies on non-transportation components of trade costs, include Combes, Lafourcade and Mayer (2005), Duranton and Storper (2008), Gaspar and Glaeser (1998), Grossman and Rossi-Hansberg (2008), Harrigan and Evans (2005), Harrigan and Venables (2006), Leamer and Storper (2001) and Storper and Venables (2004).

References

Acemoglu, Daron, Simon Johnson and James Robinson (2002) 'Reversal of fortune: geography and institutions in the making of the modern world income distribution', *Quarterly Journal of Economics*, 117, 1231–94.

Alonso, W. (1964) *Location and Land Use*. Cambridge, MA: Harvard University Press.

Amiti, Mary, and Lisa Cameron (2007) 'Economic geography and wages', *Review of Economics and Statistics*, 89(1), 15–29.

Anderson, James, and Eric van Wincoop (2003) 'Gravity with gravitas: a solution to the border puzzle', *American Economic Review*, 93(1), 170–92.

—— (2004) 'Trade Costs', *Journal of Economic Literature*, 42(3), September, 691–751.

Arzaghi, Mohammad, and Vernon Henderson (2008) 'Networking off Madison Avenue', *Review of Economic Studies*, forthcoming.

Bairoch, P. (1988) *Cities and Economic Development: From the Dawn of History to the Present*. Chicago: University of Chicago Press.

Baldwin, Richard E. (2001) 'Core-periphery model with forward-looking expectations', *Regional Science and Urban Economics*, 31(1), 21–49.

Baldwin, Richard, Rikard Forslid, Philippe Martin, Gianmarco Ottaviano and Frederic Robert-Nicoud (2003) *Economic Geography and Public Policy*. Princeton: Princeton University Press.

Baldwin, Richard, and Toshihiro Okubo (2006) 'Heterogeneous firms, agglomeration and economic geography: spatial selection and sorting', *Journal of Economic Geography*, 6, 323–46.

Behrens, Kristian, Andrea Lamorgese, Gianmarco I.P. Ottaviano and Takatoshi Tabuchi (2004) 'Testing the home market effect in a multi-country world: the theory', CEPR Discussion Paper, 4468.

Bloom, David E., and Jeffrey D. Sachs (1998) 'Geography, demography and economic growth in Africa', *Brookings Papers on Economic Activity*, 1998(2), 207–73.

Bosker, Maarten, Steven Brakman, Harry Garretsen and Marc Schramm (2007) 'Looking for multiple equilibria when geography matters: German city growth and the WWII shock', *Journal of Urban Economics*, 61(1), 152–69.

——(2008) 'A century of shocks: the evolution of the German city size distribution 1925–1999', *Regional Science and Urban Economics*, 38(4), 330–47.

Bosker, Martin, Steven Brakman, Harry Garretsen, Herman De Jong and Marc Schramm (2008) 'Ports, plagues and politics: explaining Italian city growth 1300–1861', *European Review of Economic History*, 12(1), 97–131.

Brakman, Steven, Harry Garretsen and Marc Schramm (2004) 'The strategic bombing of German cities during WWII and its impact on city growth', *Journal of Economic Geography*, 4(2), 201–18.

Breinlich, Holger (2006) 'The spatial income structure in the European Union – What role for economic geography?', *Journal of Economic Geography*, November.

Christaller, W. (1933) *Central Places in Southern Germany*. Jena, Germany: Fischer; English translation by C.W. Baskin; London: Prentice Hall, 1966.

Ciccone, A. and R. Hall (1996) 'Productivity and the density of economic activity', *American Economic Review*, 86(1), 54–70.

Clark, C., F. Wilson and J. Bradley (1969) 'Industrial location and economic potential in Western Europe', *Regional Studies*, 3, 197–212.

Combes, Pierre-Philippe, Gilles Duranton and Laurent Gobillon (2008) 'Spatial wage disparities: sorting matters!', *Journal of Urban Economics*, 63(2), 723–42.

Combes, Pierre-Philippe, Gilles Duranton, Laurent Gobillon and Sébastien Roux (2008) 'Estimating agglomeration economies with history, geology, and worker effects', mimeo, University of Toronto.

Combes, Pierre-Philippe, Gilles Duranton, Laurent Gobillon, Diego Puga and Sébastien Roux (2008) 'The productivity advantages of large cities: distinguishing agglomeration from firm selection', mimeo, University of Toronto.

Combes, Pierre-Philippe, and Henry G. Overman (2004) 'The spatial distribution of economic activities in the European Union', chapter 64 in J. Vernon Henderson and Jacques Thisse (eds), *Handbook of Urban and Regional Economics*, vol. 4, 2845–2909.

Combes, Pierre-Philippe, and Miren Lafourcade (2005) 'Transport costs: measures, determinants, and regional policy: implications for France', *Journal of Economic Geography*, 5(3), 319–49.

Combes, Pierre-Philippe, Miren Lafourcade and Thierry Mayer (2005) 'The trade-creating effects of business and social networks: evidence from France', *Journal of International Economics*, 66(1), 1–29.

Cordoba, Juan-Carlos (2008) 'On the distribution of city sizes', *Journal of Urban Economics*, 63(1), 177–97.

Davis, D.R. (1999) 'The home market, trade, and industrial structure', *American Economic Review*, 88(5), 1264–76.

Davis, D. and D. Weinstein (1999) 'Economic geography and regional production structure: an empirical investigation', *European Economic Review*, 43, 379–407.

Davis, Donald, and David Weinstein (2002) 'Bones, bombs, and break points: the geography of economic activity', *American Economic Review*, 92(5), 1269–89.

——(2003) 'Market access, economic geography and comparative advantage: an empirical assessment', *Journal of International Economics*, 59(1), 1–23.

——(2008) 'A search for multiple equilibria in urban industrial structure', *Journal of Regional Science*, 48(1), 29–65.

Dekle, R., and J. Eaton (1999) 'Agglomeration and land rents: evidence from the prefectures', *Journal of Urban Economics*, 46, 200–14.

Devereux, Michael P., Rachel Griffith and Helen Simpson (2004) 'The geographic distribution of production activity in the UK', *Regional Science and Urban Economics*, 35(5), 533–64.

Dicken, P., and P. Lloyd (1977) *Location in Space*. New York: Harper and Row.

Dixit, Avinash, and Joseph Stiglitz (1977) 'Monopolistic competition and optimum product diversity', *American Economic Review*, LXVII, 97–308.

Duranton, Gilles (2007) 'Urban evolutions: the fast, the slow, and the still', *American Economic Review*, 97(1), 197–221.

Duranton, Gilles, Laurent Gobillon and Henry G. Overman (2007) 'Assessing the effects of local taxation using microgeographic data', mimeo, London School of Economics.

Duranton, Gilles, and Henry G. Overman (2005) 'Testing for localization using microgeographic data', *Review of Economic Studies*, 72, 1077–1106.

Duranton, Gilles, and Diego Puga (2004) 'Micro-foundations of urban agglomeration economies', in J. Vernon Henderson and Jacques-Francois Thisse (eds), *Handbook of Regional and Urban Economics, vol. 4: Cities and Geography*. Amsterdam: Elsevier, 2063–2117.

Duranton, Gilles, and Michael Storper (2008) 'Rising trade costs? Agglomeration and trade with endogenous transaction costs', *Canadian Journal of Economics*, 41(1), 292–319.

Eeckhout, Jan (2004) 'Gibrat's Law for (all) cities', *American Economic Review*, 94(5), 1429–51.

Ellison, Glenn, and Edward Glaeser (1997) 'Geographic concentration in U.S. manufacturing industries: a dartboard approach', *Journal of Political Economy*, 105(5), 889–927.

—— (1999) 'The geographic concentration of industry: does natural advantage explain agglomeration?', *American Economic Review*, 89(2), Papers and Proceedings, 311–316.

Ellison, Glenn, Edward Glaeser and William Kerr (2007) 'What causes industry agglomeration? Evidence from coagglomeration patterns', NBER Working Paper, 13068.

Feenstra, R.C., J.A. Markusen and A.K. Rose (2001) 'Using the gravity equation to differentiate among alternative theories of trade', *Canadian Journal of Economics*, 34(2), 430–47.

Fujita, Masahisa (1988) 'A monopolistic competition model of spatial agglomeration: differentiated product approach', *Regional Science and Urban Economics*, 18(1), 87–124.

Fujita, Masahisa, Paul Krugman and Anthony Venables (2001) *The Spatial Economy: Cities, Regions and International Trade*. Cambridge, MA: MIT Press.

Fujita, M., and H. Ogawa (1982) 'Multiple equilibria and structural transition of non-monocentric urban configurations', *Regional Science and Urban Economics*, 12, 161–96.

Fujita, Masahisa, and Jacques-Francois Thisse (2002) *Economics of Agglomeration: Cities, Industrial Location and Regional Growth*. Cambridge: Cambridge University Press.

Gabaix, Xavier (1999) 'Zipf's law for cities: an explanation', *Quarterly Journal of Economics*, 114(3), 739–67.

Gallup, J.L., J. Sachs and A.D. Mellinger (1998) 'Geography and Economic Development', in B. Pleskovic and J.E. Stiglitz (eds), Annual World Bank Conference on Development Economics, World Bank, Washington D.C.

Gaspar, J., and Edward Glaeser (1998) 'Information technology and the future of cities', *Journal of Urban Economics*, 43(1), 136–56.

Goldberg, Pinelopi, and Giovanni Maggi (1999) 'Protection for sale: an empirical investigation', *American Economic Review*, 89(5), 1135–55.

Greenstone, Michael, Richard Hornbeck and Enrico Moretti (2008) 'Identifying agglomeration spillovers: evidence from million dollar plants', NBER Working Paper, 13833.

Grossman, Gene M., and Elhanan Helpman (1994) 'Protection for sale', *American Economic Review*, 84(4), 833–50.

Grossman, Gene M., and Esteban Rossi-Hansberg (2008) 'Trading tasks: a simple theory of offshoring', *American Economic Review*, 98(5), 1978–97.

Hanson, Gordon H. (1996) 'Localization economies, vertical organization, and trade', *American Economic Review*, 86(5), 1266–78.

—— (1997) 'Increasing returns, trade, and the regional structure of wages', *Economic Journal*, 107, 113–33.

—— (1998) 'Regional adjustment to trade liberalisation', *Regional Science and Urban Economics*, 28(4), 419–44.

—— (2005) 'Market potential, increasing returns, and geographic concentration', *Journal of International Economics*, 67(1), 1–24.

Hanson, Gordon H., and Chong Xiang (2004) 'The home market effect and bilateral trade patterns', *American Economic Review*, 94(4), 1108–29.

Harrigan, James, and Carolyn Evans (2005) 'Distance, time, and specialization: lean retailing in general equilibrium', *American Economic Review*, 95(1), 292–313.

Harrigan, James, and Anthony J. Venables (2006) 'Timeliness and agglomeration', *Journal of Urban Economics*, 59, 300–16.

Harris, Chauncy D. (1954) 'The market as a factor in the localization of industry in the United States', *Annals of the Association of American Geographers*, 44(4), 315–48.

Head, Keith, and Thierry Mayer (2004) 'Empirics of agglomeration and trade', in Vernon Henderson and Jacques-François Thisse (eds), *Handbook of Regional and Urban Economics*. Amsterdam: North Holland.

Head, Keith, and Thierry Mayer (2006) 'Regional wage and employment responses to market potential in the EU', *Regional Science and Urban Economics*, 36(5), 573–95.

Head, K., and J. Ries (2001) 'Increasing returns versus national product differentiation as an explanation for the pattern of US-Canada trade', *American Economic Review*, 91(4), 858–76.

Helpman, Elhanan (1998) 'The size of regions', in David Pines, Efraim Sadka and Itzhak Zilcha (eds), *Topics in Public Economics: Theoretical and Applied Analysis*. Cambridge: Cambridge University Press, 33–54.

Henderson, J. Vernon (1974) 'The sizes and types of cities', *American Economic Review*, 64(4), 640–56.

Henderson, J.V. (1988) *Urban Development: Theory, Fact and Illusion*. Oxford: Oxford University Press.

—— (2003) 'Marshall's Scale Economies', *Journal of Urban Economics*, 53, 1–28.

Henderson, J. Vernon, and Anthony J. Venables (2008) 'The dynamics of city formation', fNBER Working Paper, 13769.

Henderson, J. Vernon, and Hyoung Gun Wang (2007) 'Urbanization and city growth: the role of institutions', *Regional Science and Urban Economics*, 37(3), 283–313.

Hoover, E.M. (1937) *Location Theory and the Shoe and Leather Industries*. Cambridge, MA: Harvard University Press.

Holmes, Thomas J. (1998) 'The effects of state policies on the location of industry: evidence from state borders', *Journal of Political Economy*, 106(4), 667–705.

—— (2005) 'The location of sales offices and the attraction of cities', *Journal of Political Economy*, 113(3), 551–81.

——(2008) 'The diffusion of Wal-Mart and economies of density', NBER Working Paper, 13783.

Holmes, Thomas J., and Sanghoon Lee (2007) 'Cities as six-by-six mile squares: Zipf's Law?', mimeo, University of Minnesota.

——(2008) 'Economies of density versus natural advantage: crop choice on the back forty', mimeo, University of Minnesota.

Hummels, David (1995) 'Global income patterns: does geography play a role?' chapter 2 of Phd thesis, University of Michigan.

——(2007) 'Transportation costs and international trade in the second era of globalization', *Journal of Economic Perspectives*, 21(3), 131–54.

Hummels, David, and Alexander Skiba (2004) 'Shipping the good apples out: an empirical confirmation of the Alchian-Allen Conjecture', *Journal of Political Economy*, 112, 1384–1402.

Jaffe, Adam, Rebecca Henderson and Manuel Trajtenberg (1993) 'Geographic localization of knowledge spillovers as evidenced by patent citations', *Quarterly Journal of Economics*, 434, 578–98.

Jensen, J. Bradford, and Lori G. Kletzer (2005) 'Tradable services: understanding the scope and impact of services offshoring', in Lael Brainard and Susan M. Collins (eds), *Offshoring White-Collar Work – Issues and Implications*. Brookings Trade Forum, 75–134.

Keeble, D., P. Owens and C. Thompson, (1982) 'Regional accessibility and economic potential in the European Community', *Regional Studies*, 16, 419–32.

Kim, S. (1995) 'Expansion of markets and the geographic distribution of economic activities: the trends in US regional manufacturing structure, 1860–1987', *Quarterly Journal of Economics*, 110, 881–908.

Krugman, Paul (1980) 'Scale economies, product differentiation, and the pattern of trade', *American Economic Review*, 70, 950–59.

Krugman, Paul (1991a) 'Increasing returns and economic geography', *Journal of Political Economy*, 99(3), 483–99.

——(1991b) 'History versus expectations', *Quarterly Journal of Economics*, 106(2), 651–67.

——(1991c) *Geography and Trade*. Cambridge, MA: MIT Press.

Krugman, Paul, and Anthony J. Venables (1995) 'Globalization and the inequality of nations', *Quarterly Journal of Economics*, 857–80.

Leamer, Edward (1997) 'Access to Western markets and Eastern effort', in Zecchini, S. (ed), *Lessons from the Economic Transition, Central and Eastern Europe in the 1990s*. Dordrecht: Kluwer Academic Publishers, 503–26.

Leamer, Edward, and Michael Storper (2001) 'The economic geography of the Internet age', *Journal of International Business Studies*, 32(4), 641–55.

Limao, Nuno, and Anthony J. Venables (2001) 'Infrastructure, geographical disadvantage, transport costs and trade', *World Bank Economic Review*, 15(3), 451–79.

Lösch, A. (1954) *The Economics of Location*. Jena, Germany: Fischer.

Lucas, Robert E., and Esteban Rossi-Hansberg (2002) 'On the internal structure of cities', *Econometrica*, 70(4), 1445–76.

Manski, Charles F. (1995) *Identification Problems in the Social Sciences*. Cambridge, MA: Harvard University Press.

Marshall, Alfred (1920) *Principles of Economics*. London: Macmillan.

Matsuyama, Kiminori (1991) 'Increasing returns, industrialization, and indeterminacy of equilibrium', *Quarterly Journal of Economics*, 106(2), 617–50.

Maurel, F., and B. Sedillot (1999) 'A measure of the geographic concentration of French manufacturing industries', *Regional Science and Urban Economics*, 29(5), 575–604.

Mayer, Thierry (2008) 'Market potential and development', CEPR Discussion Paper, 6798.

Michaels, Guy, Ferdinand Rauch and Stephen J. Redding (2008) 'Urbanization and structural transformation', CEPR Discussion Paper, 7016.

Midelfart-Knarvik, Karen Helene, Henry G. Overman, Stephen Redding and Anthony J. Venables (2000) 'The location of European industry', (joint with Karen Helene Midelfart-Knarvik, Henry Overman and Anthony Venables) Economic Papers No. 142, European Commission, D-G for Economic and Financial Affairs, Brussels.

Midelfart-Knarvik, Karen Helene, Henry G. Overman and Anthony J. Venables (2001) 'Comparative advantage and economic geography: estimating the determinants of industrial location in the EU', CEPR Discussion Paper, 2618.

Miguel, Edward, and Gérard Roland (2006) 'The long run impact of bombing Vietnam', NBER Working Paper, 11954.

Mills, E.S. (1967) 'An aggregative model of resource allocation in a metropolitan area', *American Economic Review*, 57, 197–210.

Muth, R.F. (1961) 'The spatial structure of the housing market', *Papers and Proceedings of the Regional Science Association*, 7, 207–20.

Neary, J. Peter (2001) 'Of hype and hyperbolas: introducing the new economic geography', *Journal of Economic Literature*, 39(2), 536–61.

Ottaviano, Gianmarco I. P., and Diego Puga (1998) 'Agglomeration in the global economy: a survey of the "New Economic Geography"', *World Economy*, 21(6), 707–31.

Ottaviano, Gianmarco, Takatoshi Tabuchi and Jacques Thisse (2002) 'Agglomeration and trade revisited', *International Economic Review*, 43, 409–36.

Overman, Henry G., Stephen Redding and Anthony Venables (2003) 'The economic geography of trade, production and income: a survey of empirics', in James Harrigan and E. Kwan Choi (eds), *Handbook of International Trade*. Oxford: Blackwell.

Overman, Henry G., and L. Alan Winters (2006) 'Trade shocks and industrial location: the impact of EEC accession on the UK', CEP Discussion Paper No. 588, London School of Economics.

Puga, Diego (1999) 'The rise and fall of regional inequalities', *European Economic Review*, 43(2), 303–34.

Redding, Stephen J., and Peter K. Schott (2003) 'Distance, skill deepening and development: will peripheral countries ever get rich?', *Journal of Development Economics*, 72(2), 515–41.

Redding, Stephen J., and Daniel M. Sturm (2008) 'The costs of remoteness: evidence from German division and reunification', *American Economic Review*, 98(5), 1766–97.

Redding, Stephen J., Daniel M. Sturm and Nikolaus Wolf (2011) 'History and industry location: evidence from German airports', Review of Economics and Statistics, forthcoming.

Redding, Stephen J., and Anthony J. Venables (2004) 'Economic geography and international inequality', *Journal of International Economics*, 62(1), 53–82.

Rivera-Batiz, Francisco L. (1988) 'Increasing returns, monopolistic competition, and agglomeration economies in consumption and production', *Regional Science and Urban Economics*, 18(1), 125–53.

Robert-Nicoud, Frederic (2005) 'The structure of simple "New economic geography" models (or, on identical twins)', *Journal of Economic Geography*, 5(2), 201–34.

Rodrik, Dani, Arvind Subramanian, and Francesco Trebbi (2004) 'Institutions rule: the primacy of institutions over geography and integration in economic development', *Journal of Economic Growth*, 9(2): 131–65.

Rosenthal, Stuart S., and William C. Strange (2004) 'Evidence on the nature and sources of agglomeration economies', in *Handbook of Regional and Urban Economics, vol. 4: Cities and Geography*. J. Vernon Henderson and Jacques-Francois Thisse (eds), Amsterdam: Elsevier.

Rosenthal, S., and W. Strange (2005) 'The attenuation of agglomeration economies: a Manhattan skyline approach', mimeo, University of Toronto.

Rossi-Hansberg, Esteban (2005) 'A spatial theory of trade', *American Economic Review*, 95(5), 1464–91.

Rossi-Hansberg, Esteban, and Mark L.J. Wright (2007) 'Establishment size dynamics in the aggregate economy', *American Economic Review*, 97(5), 1639–66.

Storper, Michael, and Anthony J. Venables (2004) 'Buzz: face-to-face contact and the urban economy', *Journal of Economic Geography*, 4, 351–70.

Sveikauskas, L.A. (1975) 'The productivity of cities', *Quarterly Journal of Economics*, 89, 393–413.

Tirado, Daniel A., Elisenda Paluzie and Jordi Pons (2002) 'Economic integration and industrial location: the case of Spain before WWI', *Journal of Economic Geography*, 2(3), 343–63.

Venables, A.J. (1996) 'Equilibrium locations of vertically linked industries', *International Economic Review*, 37, 341–59.

Wolf, Nikolaus (2007) 'Endowments vs. market potential: what explains the relocation of industry after the Polish reunification in 1918?', *Explorations in Economic History*, 44(1): 22–42.

17
Gravity Equations and Economic Frictions in the World Economy

Jeffrey H. Bergstrand* and Peter Egger[†]

1 Introduction

At the same time that the modern theory of international trade due to comparative advantage developed in the post–World War II era to explain the patterns of international trade using $2 \times 2 \times 2$ general equilibrium models, a small and separate line of empirical research in international trade emerged to 'explain' statistically actual aggregate bilateral trade flows among large numbers of countries. Drawing upon analogy to Isaac Newton's Law of Gravitation, these international trade economists noted that observed bilateral aggregate trade flows between any pair of countries i and j could be explained very well using statistical methods by the product of the economic sizes of the two countries ($GDP_i GDP_j$) divided by the distance between the country pair's major economic centers ($DIST_{ij}$). Specifically, these researchers conjectured that:

$$PX_{ij} = \beta_0 (GDP_i)^{\beta_1} (GDP_j)^{\beta_2} (DIST_{ij})^{\beta_3} \varepsilon_{ij} \tag{1}$$

or

$$\ln PX_{ij} = \ln \beta_0 + \beta_1 \ln GDP_i + \beta_2 \ln GDP_j + \beta_3 \ln DIST_{ij} + \ln \varepsilon_{ij}, \tag{2}$$

where PX_{ij} is the value (in current prices) of the merchandise trade flow from exporter i to importer j, GDP_i (GDP_j) is the level of nominal gross domestic product in country i (j), $DIST_{ij}$ is the bilateral physical distance between the economic centers of countries i and j, and ε_{ij} is assumed to be a log normally distributed error term. In equation (2), $\ln$ refers to the natural logarithm. Intuition suggested that $\beta_1 > 0$, $\beta_2 > 0$, and $\beta_3 < 0$. In the 1960s, equations (1) and (2) came to be known among international trade economists as the 'gravity equation' – owing to its obvious similarity to Newton's gravity equation in physics. Two notable aspects of equations (1) or (2) were that (i) actual bilateral trade flows could be explained quite well by this specific and simple multiplicative or log linear equation and (ii) bilateral trade flows were actually strongly influenced by economic trade 'frictions' (or trade 'costs') – such as distance – which had played a very minor role in the traditional theory of international trade.[1]

This chapter examines both the role of frictions in international trade and the contribution of the gravity equation towards understanding international trade flows. The gravity equation has also been used extensively for understanding the determinants of observed bilateral foreign direct investment and migration flows, although to an extent less than for trade flows; we will address these flows also but not as extensively, due to space constraints. We organize this chapter into five parts. Section 2 discusses the role of frictions inhibiting the flows of goods, services, capital, and labour in the world economy. While distance has long been recognized as a prominent friction impeding trade, foreign direct investment (FDI) and migration flows, there are numerous other impediments to these flows, some of which are also 'natural' – such as being landlocked – and some of which are 'unnatural' (or 'man-made') – such as government policy based impediments.

In the remainder of the paper, we discuss the gravity equation. Section 3 discusses the historical evolution of the literature on and contribution of the 'traditional' gravity equation, including some important empirical applications. However, starting in 1979, rigorous theoretical general-equilibrium foundations surfaced for the gravity equation for trade. Section 4 discusses the state of the art in theoretical foundations for the gravity equation for trade and econometric implications of these developments since 1979. Yet, in a world with multinational enterprises, international trade flows are not independent of FDI and migration flows. Section 5 discusses very recent developments in the theoretical foundations for the gravity equation in a world with national *and* multinational firms, and econometric implications of these developments for understanding trade, FDI and migration flows. Section 6 concludes.

2 Frictions in the World Economy

Contrary to the popular notion that globalization has proceeded so rapidly due to technological advance and trade policy liberalizations, frictions to international trade, FDI and migration flows are still prominent and play an important role in explaining the levels of such flows. Section 2.1 discusses important frictions to international trade flows. Section 2.2 discusses frictions to FDI flows. Section 2.3 discusses those frictions associated with migration flows.

2.1 Trade frictions

Frictions that impede international trade flows are often called 'trade costs'. Trade costs can be decomposed into two main sources: 'natural' trade costs and 'unnatural' (or policy based) trade costs. Natural trade costs refer to those costs incurred largely – though not exclusively – by geography. Distance between a pair of countries is an example of a natural trade cost. Unnatural trade costs refer to those additional costs impeding trade if physical distances (or other natural costs) were absent. These costs are largely 'man-made' or 'artificial', and are mainly attributable to policy decisions of governments. A tax imposed by one nation's (j's) government on imports from another country (i) – typically called a tariff – is an example of a policy based (or man-made) trade cost.

2.1.1   Natural trade frictions

Natural trade costs can be decomposed into transport costs and other related costs. The most common measure of transport costs is referred to commonly as the 'CIF FOB factor'. Trade flows from one country to another are often measured 'free on board' (FOB), which refers to the value of a shipment of goods delivered to and put 'on board' an overseas vessel for potential shipment. The same trade flows are often also measured reflecting 'cost insurance freight' (CIF), which refers to the value of the same shipment at the destination port (or airport), including the cost of insurance and freight charges. The ratio of these two values minus unity provides an ad valorem 'rate' for the add on associated with international transport. Baier and Bergstrand (2001) report that average CIF FOB factors for 16 Organization for Economic Co-operation and Development (OECD) countries in 1958 and 1988 were 8.2 percent and 4.3 percent, respectively. Moreover, they show that the decline in such costs explain about 8 percent of the increase in world trade from the late 1950s to the late 1980s, after accounting for expanding GDPs and falling tariffs. Hummels (1999) finds that freight rates in 1994 vary dramatically across countries with average transport costs ranging from 3.8 percent for the United States to 13.3 percent for landlocked Paraguay. Such costs vary even more across commodities within countries. An excellent early study defining the major issues with respect to CIF FOB measurements is Moneta (1959). Data on CIF FOB factors is obtainable from the International Monetary Fund, either through the *International Financial Statistics* or the *Direction of Trade Statistics*.

Intuitively, one would expect that geographic variables – such as distances between two countries' economic centers and sharing a common land border (often termed in the literature 'adjacency') – would be important factors explaining trade costs; such intuition is correct, although other factors matter as well. Two excellent studies that have examined systematically the geographic (and miscellaneous) factors explaining variation in CIF FOB factors (and other measures of shipping costs) are Hummels (1999) and Limão and Venables (2001). Hummels (1999) finds robust evidence that the transport cost factor's elasticity with respect to distance is approximately 0.25; this implies a 4 percent increase in distance raises the transport cost factor by 1 percent. Hummels (2007) found that fuel costs matter also in explaining transport cost factors.

Limão and Venables (2001) also examined the determinants of transport cost factors. Using a unique data set on shipments from Baltimore, Maryland, in the United States to various destinations and also using CIF FOB factors to over 100 countries, these authors found that transport cost factors were influenced by both marginal and fixed cost factors. Regarding marginal costs, Limão and Venables (2001) found that the distance between and adjacency of two countries had economically and statistically significant effects on transport cost factors, with distance increasing costs and adjacency (representing better transit networks) reducing costs. Regarding fixed trade costs, the authors found that – for coastal economies – the higher the level/quality of infrastructure of both the exporting and importing countries the lower the cost, and – for landlocked countries – the higher the level or quality of infrastructure of the 'transit' exporting or importing country (the one used for its ocean port) the lower the cost. Since the level of infrastructure in economies is endogenous to the level of government expenditures, consequently infrastructure may be considered a 'policy based' factor by some researchers.

While CIF FOB factors are the most common method for estimating the costs associated with transit of a good from country *i* to country *j*, this measure is not without flaws. Hummels (2007) raises the concern that this measure may underestimate the true transport costs. He finds that the average level (and variances) of CIF FOB factors in disaggregated data is much higher than that in aggregate data. He interprets the lower CIF FOB factors for aggregate data as reflecting that importers minimize transport costs; thus, trade costs have an allocative effect on trade flows.

Time also is a natural trade cost. It takes longer on average for the same good to move between countries than within countries (of course, it could take longer for a good to move between two cities in the United States than between Brussels, Belgium, and Amsterdam, the Netherlands). Hummels (2001) found that every additional day in ocean travel for a shipment to arrive reduces the probability of outsourcing manufactures by 1 percent. Moreover, he found that, conditional upon shipping, firms are willing to pay approximately 1 percent more for a shipment for each day saved in ocean shipping. Declines in air shipment costs relative to ocean shipment costs have likely increased the relative share of shipments by air versus ocean over the last 40 years.

The level and quality of communications in and between countries also plays a role in enhancing trade. Goods must move *within* countries often to reach a port (although this is less essential as air shipment increasingly replaces ocean transport). Anderson and van Wincoop (2004), in a comprehensive discussion of trade costs, estimate that the average cost of delivering a good from the point of manufacture to the destination (including international tariff and non-tariff policy barriers) is about a 170 percent addon to the cost of producing the good. They decompose this into 74 percent international trade costs (21 percent natural and 44 percent international border related) and 55 percent associated with domestic retail and wholesale distribution costs. Also, Limão and Venables (2001) remind us that many countries are landlocked, imposing additional costs to international trade.

2.1.2   Unnatural trade frictions

Unnatural trade costs refer to those costs associated with policy (hence, artificial or man-made costs). Unnatural trade costs can be decomposed into the exhaustive categories of 'tariffs' – taxes on goods crossing international borders – and 'nontariff barriers' on international trade.[2] Nontariff barriers refer to such restrictions on trade associated with customs procedures as well as 'behind the border' measures such as domestic laws and regulations that alter international trade relative to domestic trade.

Tariffs on goods that flow across national borders – essentially, border taxes – as a means of protection have a long history in international trade. Due to numerous rounds of reductions in tariff rates of developed and developing countries, first under the Generalized Agreement on Tariffs and Trade (GATT), then under the World Trade Organization (WTO), and more recently due to the spread of regional economic integration agreements (EIAs), levels of tariffs are much lower now than, say, immediately after World War II. Because several other chapters in this handbook on trade policy deal with tariffs in considerable detail, we need not explore the rationale for tariffs in detail here. However, tariffs still play a considerable role in explaining trade flows empirically using the gravity equation (to be discussed later), so some discussion of their measurement is important here. Systematic data on bilateral tariff rates has been difficult to obtain until fairly recently. The best source for a broad range of bilateral tariff rates by industrial sector and pairs of countries is the World Integrated Trade Solution (WITS), available at the World Bank website. This data set reports tariff rates for developed countries that are generally less than 5 percent. For developing countries, average tariff rates range between 10 and 25 percent.

While measures of tariff rates are available, nontariff barriers, or measures, (NTBs) are even more difficult to quantify. One method of measurement of the importance of NTBs is to calculate the share of industries in a country that are subject to NTBs in that country; this is typically referred to as the 'NTB coverage ratio'. Using a broad definition, it ranges from 10 to 75 percent; see also Anderson and van Wincoop (2004, table 3). Such ratios have been used frequently in gravity equations to estimate the impact of NTBs on trade flows; see also Lee and Swagel (1997).

2.2 Frictions to foreign direct investment

While empirical researchers have often been frustrated by the absence of systematic and comprehensively constructed data sets on tariff rates and NTBs on goods trade, data for foreign direct investment (FDI) frictions are even worse. As with goods, a useful decomposition of FDI frictions is natural and unnatural frictions. In empirical analysis, researchers have often found bilateral distance to be a significant impediment to bilateral FDI flows. This result has tended to raise questions about the economic interpretation of distance. For many years, distance was considered to be a proxy for transport costs. However, most trade and FDI flows – which are among developed countries – tend to be viewed as substitutes. If distance between two countries is high, then trade costs are high, and exports (and exporting firms) should diminish, with multinational firms replacing them and FDI increase (see also Markusen, 2002); hence, distance and FDI would be positively related. However, distance and FDI are negatively related in the data, suggesting that distance is likely reflecting trade and FDI 'costs' different from transport costs. A common interpretation of distance's role as an impediment to trade and FDI is that distance captures information costs.

Since a consistently negative effect of distance on FDI flows has been found, other factors influencing information flows have been sought. As for trade flows, many studies have used binary indicator (dummy) variables capturing the presence or absence of a common language to explain FDI flows with success; a common language reduces information costs.

Policy variables also influence FDI frictions. One of the most common policy variables examined that potentially influence FDI is tax policy. Higher taxes on corporate profits in host countries have long been argued to reduce FDI; however, evidence is mixed on tax rates' effects on FDI. See Swenson (1994) and Desai and others (2004) for some recent representative studies.

Another important policy variable influencing FDI behaviour is tariff rates on *goods*. Since tariffs on goods impose a tax on imports, firms in exporting countries may switch their provision of goods to production in the foreign market via FDI. Consequently, tariffs may increase FDI; this is called 'tariff jumping.' Both Belderbos (1997) and Blonigen (2002) find evidence of tariff jumping FDI.

2.3 Migration frictions

As with trade and FDI flows, natural and unnatural frictions also impede migration flows. The literature on impediments to migration is also broad; migration issues are addressed more fully in the chapter by Gaston and Nelson. Among natural impediments, bilateral distance, of course, plays a significant role. Most studies of migration find that distance has an economically significant effect on such flows. Being a landlocked country reduces migration flows significantly.

The presence of a common language has a significant effect on reducing migration costs. Also, immigrants are aided significantly by a large stock of previous migrants into the destination country, as the latter provide an infrastructure that reduces the costs to migrants of establishing themselves, cf., Hatton and Williamson (2002, 2005). Policies also play a significant role in that most countries have quotas on the number of immigrants and other selection policies to determine the economic characteristics of immigrants. For more on the policy debate, see Borjas (1994, 1999), Freeman (1996), Hatton and Williamson (2002, 2005), Hanson (2006), and Grogger and Hanson (2008).

3   Historical Roots of the Gravity Equation

In this section, we discuss the literature concerning historical gravity equations of international trade. The gravity equation actually has quite a rich history in social science applications, dating back to the nineteenth century. Section 3.1 provides a brief general overview of the traditional gravity equation and discusses the early social science roots of it.

The empirical literature on the gravity equation for international trade began in earnest around 1962, as discussed in section 3.2; from 1962 to 1979, the 'traditional' gravity equation (2) became more popular. In international trade, the gravity equation primarily surfaced as a statistical model to 'explain' variation in aggregate bilateral trade flows among pairs of countries for cross sections using OLS.

3.1   Overview and early social science roots

The empirical explanation and prediction of interregional commodity or factor flows has been captured for over 100 years by the gravity equation.[3] Consequently, the social science literature addressing the gravity equation is enormous. Hence, we narrow our discussion to approaches relevant primarily to international trade flows, with some reference to FDI flows and only minimal reference to migration flows (owing to the vastness of the migration literature).

The naming of equation (1) as the 'gravity equation' in the social sciences descends, according to Olsen (1971), from the 'social physics school' at Princeton University. John Q. Stewart, a school member who familiarized the school's name, 'found it rewarding to regard members of a social group as the individual molecules of a physical mass and to analyze the interaction between social groups in the same way as the physicists analyze interaction between masses' (Olsen, 1971, 14). In fact, Stewart (1948) noted that a gravity equation is more closely related to Newton's equation for the *energy* between two masses, rather than its *force*; force is related to the inverse of the square of bilateral distance, while energy is related to the inverse of distance (with an exponent of unity).

This led Stewart to formalize demographic 'energy' into the equation:

$$E_{ij} = \beta_0(POP_i)(POP_j)/(DIST_{ij}), \tag{3}$$

where E_{ij} is the 'demographic energy' between two countries i and j and POP_i (POP_j) is the population in i (j). Equation (3) is interesting because – much later – most international trade applications have found empirically that the elasticities of trade flows with respect to GDPs (bilateral distance) are approximately one, as equation (3) suggests. While there has been no meta-analysis of GDP elasticities, Disdier and Head (2008), using a meta-analysis of distance elasticities for trade flows, found that the average elasticity is 0.9.

Stewart's 'social physics school' is often considered the motivating force behind the development of the spatial interaction/regional science literature in the 1950s; see also Sen and Smith (1995). For the purposes ultimately of understanding the international trade flow literature on the gravity equation, it is useful to know that this school diverged into two fundamental paths. Sen and Smith (1995) call one the 'Deterministic Approach' and the other the 'Probabilistic Approach.'

3.1.1 Deterministic approaches

For international trade, economists have largely followed the Deterministic Approach. In the 'spatial interaction' literature, this approach was used as a foundation for one theory for explaining commodity trade flows. Niedercorn and Moorehead (1974) assumed the existence of a firm (monopolist) k in region i maximizing total revenue subject to a constraint embodying an assumption that the firm's total transportation cost budget and total output are fixed. The firm, according to Niedercorn and Moorehead, faces the problem of how to allocate its given total product over N different markets, such that revenue is maximized for a given budget $_kY_i$. For instance, Niedercorn and Moorehead assumed a logarithmic revenue function, $_kR_i = \sum_{j=1}^{N} POP_j \ln (_kq_{ij}/POP_j)$ where $_kR_i$ is total revenue of firm k in origin i and $_kq_{ij}$ is output sold by firm k in origin i shipped to destination j. Assuming the transport budget constraint $_kY_i = r\sum_{j=1}^{N}(DIST_{ij}^{\alpha})(_kq_{ij})$, where r is the exogenous cost per mile to ship firm k's good and α is a parameter, maximizing revenue subject to the transport budget constraint yields the following gravity equation:

$$q_{ij} = [(Y_i)(POP_j)]/[(rDIST_{ij}^{\alpha})(\sum_{j=1}^{N} POP_j)] \tag{4}$$

There are several limitations of the approach; we mention just some. First, there are several restrictive assumptions to the approach, such as that all firms are monopolists. Second, this yields a gravity equation with a measure of income for the origin region, but a measure of population for the destination. Third, *relative* prices play no role. Fourth, as earlier, no other region's factors play a role (with the exception of other regions' populations). While restrictive in nature, 'spatial interaction' models such as these were early precursors of the modern theoretical foundations for international trade gravity equations. However, before we explore those, we mention briefly some influential papers in the other thread of the spatial interaction approach, that is, the 'Probabilistic Approach'.

3.1.2 Probabilistic approaches

This approach concerned explaining flows using a statistical methodology. While this literature is also extensive, with regard to international trade flows one of the earliest models was Savage and Deutsch (1960). The purpose of the paper was to generate a framework for 'predicting' bilateral trade flows, given information on multilateral trade (exports and imports). They intentionally avoided specifying economic behaviour, and referred to their model as the 'null model'.

Leamer and Stern (1970) used the Savage Deutsch model as the basis for a 'theory' of the gravity equation. In their model, the value of the trade flow from i to j was determined by:

$$PX_{ij} = Mbp_iq_jg(R_{ij}) + \varepsilon_{ij}, \tag{5}$$

where b is the exogenous size of every transaction (a constant), M is the exogenous number of transactions (a constant), R_{ij} measures trade resistances (or enhancements), and p_i and q_j would each be determined by GDPs and populations in the respective countries. While the approach provided a grounding for the multiplicative form of the gravity equation, it did not explain the unity elasticities for GDPs, why populations should be included, the specification for $g(R_{ij})$, or the determinants of M or b. Leamer and Stern (1970), however, did raise econometric concerns about heteroskedasticity in estimating a log linear version of gravity equation (5) by ordinary least squares, concerns that would surface prominently more than 30 years later.

3.2 The gravity equation in international trade: 1962–1979

The gravity equation, most commonly specified as equation (2), became a popular tool beginning in the early 1960s to explain actual *aggregate gross bilateral* trade flows. This equation did not evolve from the mainstream theory of international trade, discussed in Part A of this volume. The mainstream theory – and empirical evaluation of it – in the 1960s was concerned instead with explaining the pattern and commodity composition of trade. Ricardo's theory of comparative advantage and the Heckscher–Ohlin model were basically silent on *aggregate gross bilateral* trade flows (especially in empirical 'multi country' settings – that is, with the number of countries N exceeding two). By contrast, the study of aggregate gross bilateral trade flows has been referred to as the analysis of the 'volume' of trade.

In the international trade literature, Nobel laureate Jan Tinbergen is credited as the first to specify econometrically what has become a benchmark 'traditional' gravity equation for studying international trade flows; see also Tinbergen (1962). Using a specification similar to equation (2), Tinbergen estimated:

$$lnPX_{ij} = ln\beta_0 + \beta_1 ln\,GDP_i + \beta_2 ln\,GDP_j + \beta_3 ln\,DIST_{ij} + \beta_4 ADJ_{ij}$$
$$+ \beta_5 EIA1_{ij} + \beta_6 EIA2_{ij} + ln\,\varepsilon_{ij}, \tag{6}$$

where ADJ, EIA1, and EIA2 are dummy variables with values of one if two countries share a common land border, are members of the British Commonwealth, and are members of the BENELUX free trade agreements, respectively (and zero otherwise).[4] Tinbergen found GDP elasticities of 0.7 and 0.6 for i and j, respectively, a distance elasticity of 0.6, and a small but statistically significant effect of Commonwealth membership of 5 percent (0.05). In fact, the motivation for Tinbergen's use of the gravity equation was to determine the 'normal pattern' of international trade in the absence of 'discriminatory trade impediments' (such as the Commonwealth or BENELUX) and to estimate the effect of such agreements (see also Tinbergen, 1962, 262), a central motivation for using the gravity equation to this day.

Tinbergen's work is important also in spurring more studies by his students. Pöyhönen (1963 a,b), Pulliainen (1963) and Linnemann (1966) developed further the theoretical and empirical foundations for the gravity equation. Especially noteworthy was Linnemann (1966), the first monograph to use the gravity equation in an extensive empirical analysis. In international trade, many empirical applications of the gravity equation to aggregate bilateral trade flows appealed to a third approach, an economic model described in Linnemann (1966). The Linnemann model was based upon the following approach: Suppose importer j's demand for the trade flow from i to j (PX_{ij}^D) is a function of j's GDP, the price of the product in i (p_i), and distance from i to j. Suppose exporter i's supply of goods (PX_i^S) is a function of i's GDP and p_i. Market clearing would require county i's export supply to equal the sum of the N-1 bilateral import demands (in an N country world). This generates a system of $N+1$ equations in $N+1$ endogenous variables: N-1 bilateral import demands PX_{ij}^D ($j = 1, \ldots, N$ with $j \neq i$), supply variable PX_i^S, and price variable p_i. This system could be solved for a bilateral trade flow equation for PX_{ij} that is a function of the GDPs of i and j and their bilateral distance. Then p_i is endogenous and excluded from the reduced form bilateral trade flow gravity equation.

There are several shortcomings of this approach; we mention a few. First, the model cannot explain the multiplicative form of the gravity equation. Second, to eliminate all other N-2 countries' prices, Linnemann (1966) assumed a 'general world price level' due to arbitrage and perfect product substitutability (cf., p. 41). Third, microeconomic foundations for including GDPs (and, in some studies, populations of countries) are absent. Nevertheless, in one of the earliest surveys of the gravity equation in trade, Leamer and Stern (1970) considered Linnemann's theory as one of three alternative approaches, alongside the spatial interaction deterministic and the probability approaches.

Linnemann's book provided a major breakthrough in terms of empirical analysis of aggregate bilateral trade flows, and remains a useful resource. Among empirical contributions, Linnemann found:

(1) half of world trade flows are measured as zeros (under $100,000 technically), creating econometric problems, an issue only addressed systematically 30 years later in Felbermayr and Kohler (2006), Santos Silva and Tenreyro (2006), Helpman, Melitz and Rubenstein (2008), and Egger, Larch, Staub and Winkelmann (2009),

(2) measurements of the 'economic centers' of countries to calculate economic distance (sea and land) for a large number of countries, used by subsequent researchers,

(3) identification of a large sample of economic integration agreements potentially causing trade creation and diversion and the first economically and statistically significant ex post trade creation effects of preferential trade agreements,

(4) potential effects of heteroskedasticity identified,

(5) the first estimates suggesting that trade diversion from preferential trade agreements is quite limited.

The empirical success of Linnemann's work led to other researchers looking to find ex post estimates of economic integration agreements (EIAs) on trade flows. Aitken (1973) provided one of the first sets of a time series of cross sections to try to estimate the effects of the original six-member European Economic Community (EEC) and original seven-member European Free Trade Agreement (EFTA) on trade flows. He found no economically or statistically significant effect of the agreements prior to the date of entry, and economically and statistically significant effects on trade of the EEC (EFTA) in 1963 (1966) and later years. Aitken then used coefficient estimates to generate gross and net trade creation effects of membership for each country. Sapir (1981) used the same methodology to estimate effects of the Generalized System of Preferences (GSP) for developing countries.

These two studies provided the first economically plausible and statistically significant effects of EIAs on trade, providing guidance for numerous subsequent empirical analyses using the traditional gravity equation. The traditional gravity equation was subsequently used to model the effects of numerous other economic, political, cultural, and social variables on trade flows. For instance, Dunlevy and Hutchinson (1999) estimate the impact of immigration flows on international trade, Abrams (1980) and Thursby and Thursby (1987) the effect of exchange rate variability on trade, Rose (2000) and Frankel and Rose (2002) the effect of currency unions on trade, Pollins (1989) and Reuveny and Kang (2003) the effect of international political conflicts on trade, Gowa and Mansfield (1993) and Mansfield and Bronson (1997) the effect of military alliances on trade, van Beers (1998) the effect of labour standards on trade, and McCallum (1995) national political borders on trade; these are only a few of the numerous studies.

4 Gravity Equations of Trade Based on General-equilibrium Models: 1979 to Present

Prior to 1979, the absence of rigorous theoretical microeconomic foundations for the gravity equation in international trade inhibited its use for policy work and left the equation on the periphery of mainstream international trade research. Beginning in 1979, theoretical rationales for the gravity equation in trade surfaced based upon general-equilibrium frameworks. The models tended to take either of two paths. One approach assumed 'separability' of production and consumption decisions from the decision concerning with which country to trade (henceforth, the 'trade separability' assumption). The separability of the bilateral trade decision from production and consumption decisions implied a two stage budgeting process, and the gravity equation assumed an 'endowment economy' to ignore the first stage decision regarding production and consumption in countries. These 'conditional general-equilibrium' (or conditional GE) models are discussed in section 4.1. Theoretical foundations also surfaced in the absence of the 'trade separability' assumption. These formulations – henceforth, 'unconditional' GE models – will be addressed in section 4.2. Finally, section 4.3 will address advances in empirical implementations of the gravity equation.

4.1 Conditional general-equilibrium (GE) approaches

Anderson (1979) is generally recognized as the first formal conditional GE model of the gravity equation for trade. The model is based upon three assumptions. First, assume that each country specializes completely in the production of its own good, and there is one good for each country produced exogenously (i.e., an 'endowment economy'). Second, assume identical, homothetic preferences. Third, assume a frictionless world with zero transport costs, tariffs, and distribution costs; with no frictions, all prices can be normalized to unity. In this world, the value of trade from i to j (PX_{ij}) can be represented by:

$$PX_{ij} = \theta_i Y_j,$$ (7)

where θ_i is the fraction of a country's income spent on i's product (same for every country due to identical homothetic tastes) and Y_j is nominal GDP in j. Since production of every country i must equal the volume of exports and domestic consumption of the good, market clearing implies:

$$Y_i = \sum_{j=1}^{N} PX_{ij} = \sum_{j=1}^{N} \theta_i Y_j = \theta_i \left(\sum_{j=1}^{N} Y_j \right) \tag{8a}$$

or

$$\theta_i = Y_i \Big/ \left(\sum_{j=1}^{N} Y_j \right) = Y_i / Y^W, \tag{8b}$$

where $Y^W = \sum_{j=1}^{N} Y_j =$ is world GDP, which is constant across country pairs. Substituting equation (8b) into equation (7) yields:

$$PX_{ij} = Y_i Y_j \Big/ \left(\sum_{j=1}^{N} Y_j \right) = Y_i Y_j / Y^W. \tag{9}$$

This simple frictionless gravity equation relies only upon the (adding up) constraints of an expenditure system combined with identical homothetic preferences and the production specialization of each country in one good.

In reality, of course, the world is not frictionless. Anderson (1979) extended the simple frictionless gravity equation for one sector into allowing tradable vs. non-tradable goods, multiple sectors, tariffs, distance, and constant-elasticity-of-substitution (CES) utility functions, deriving alternative gravity equations. With Cobb–Douglas preferences, distance as the only trade cost, and no non-tradables, Anderson's gravity equation is:

$$PX_{ij} = \left[Y_i Y_j \Big/ \left(\sum_{j=1}^{N} Y_j \right) \right] [1/f(DIST_{ij})] \left(\sum_{j=1}^{N} (Y_j/Y^W)[1/f(DIST_{ij})] \right)^{-1} \tag{10}$$

where $f(DIST_{ij})$ represents trade costs – a function of distance. This equation is close in specification to equation (1), assuming little variation across exporters i in the third term in brackets (which is a distance-weighted measure of the economic size of the rest of the world), a potential source of omitted variables bias. One limiting aspect of equation (10) is that it is not derived from a CES utility function, which became the norm in international trade to reflect the notion of 'love of variety'. With CES preferences, equation (10) becomes more complicated, and slightly less transparent to the popular specification of gravity equation (1) or (2).[5] A second limitation of Anderson's approach is an assumption that all prices are assumed unity (using the convention that 'free trade prices are unity'). This assumption is fine in a frictionless world; however, with asymmetric trade costs, prices differ across producers. These limitations of the theory motivated subsequent theoretical refinements by others – as well as by Anderson himself.

The absence of price terms in Anderson's gravity equation above (10) motivated another conditional GE theory for the gravity equation in Bergstrand (1985). First, starting from a 'nested' CES utility function in an endowment economy, Bergstrand derived an import demand function for goods from i to j, allowing the elasticity of substitution among imported goods (σ) to be different potentially from that between imported and domestic goods, μ (i.e. two stage allocation process). Second, motivated by the assumption that goods are tailored to foreign markets (and incorporate increasing marginal costs of distribution and marketing as developed in rigorous detail in Arkolakis, 2008), Bergstrand assumed that output by exporter i is not costlessly substituted among foreign markets; in Anderson (1979), goods are costlessly substitutable across destination markets. Representing the exporter's allocation among markets by a constant elasticity of transformation (CET) function (the elasticity given by γ) – the production analogue to the CES utility function – Bergstrand derived an export supply function for goods from i to j.[6] Third, assuming the aggregate trade flow from i to j is 'small' relative to other flows and assuming identical CES and CET functions across countries generated gravity equation:

$$PX_{ij} = Y_i^{(\sigma-1)/(\gamma+\sigma)} Y_j^{(\gamma+1)/(\gamma+\sigma)} C_{ij}^{-\sigma(\gamma+1)/(\gamma+\sigma)} T_{ij}^{-\sigma(\gamma+1)/(\gamma+\sigma)} E_{ij}^{\sigma(\gamma+1)/(\gamma+\sigma)}$$

$$\times \left(\sum_{k=1,k\neq i}^{N} P_{ik}^{1+\gamma} \right)^{-(\sigma-1)(\gamma-\eta)/(1+\gamma)(\gamma+\sigma)} \left(\sum_{k=1,k\neq j}^{N} \overline{P}_{kj}^{1-\sigma} \right)^{(\gamma+1)(\sigma-\mu)/(1-\sigma)(\gamma+\sigma)}$$

$$\times \left[\left(\sum_{k=1,k\neq i}^{N} P_{ik}^{1+\gamma} \right)^{(1+\eta)/(1+\gamma)} + P_{ii}^{1+\eta} \right]^{-(\sigma-1)/(\gamma+\sigma)}$$

$$\times \left[\left(\sum_{k=1,k\neq j}^{N} \overline{P}_{kj}^{1-\sigma} \right)^{(1-\mu)/(1-\sigma)} + P_{jj}^{1-\mu} \right]^{-(\gamma+1)/(\gamma+\sigma)}, \tag{11}$$

where C_{ij} is the CIF FOB factor on goods from i to j, T_{ij} is the gross tariff rate on i's products to j, E_{ij} is the value of j's currency in terms of i's currency, and P_{ij} is the price of i's product in country j. The distinguishing feature of Bergstrand's gravity equation was the explicit presence of prices, which differed across countries owing to trade costs; under an additional assumption that the CES (CET) between home and foreign goods were the same, the two price terms in the second line above both simplify to unity, leaving two 'multilateral' price terms (one for exporter and one for importer).

Bergstrand then evaluated his gravity equation using conventional published price 'indexes.'

$$\left(\sum_{k=1,k\neq i}^{N} P_{ik}^{1+\gamma}\right)^{1/(1+\gamma)}$$ was approximated by i's export price index,

$$\left(\sum_{k=1,k\neq j}^{N} \overline{P}_{kj}^{1-\sigma}\right)^{1/(1-\sigma)}$$ was approximated by j's import price index,

and the last two RHS terms in (11) were approximated by i's and j's GDP deflators, respectively.

Using these indexes – measured relative to a base period – Bergstrand found that the price indexes influenced bilateral trade flows, with the coefficient estimates for the price variables implying that the elasticity of substitution among importables (σ) exceeded unity, the elasticity of substitution between domestic and imported products (μ) is below unity, and the elasticity of transformation of production among export markets (γ) exceeded that between production for domestic markets and foreign markets (η), which were all economically plausible inferences.

However, cross-section empirical estimation of Bergstrand's gravity model was compromised by using crude indexes for multilateral price levels. GDP deflators, import price indexes, and export price indexes measure changes in price levels relative to a base period, and consequently are much more suitable for time series analysis than for cross-section analysis. Since the gravity equation had typically been used for evaluating cross-section data and long-run equilibrium relationships between trade flows and various RHS variables, such price indexes provide only a rough approximation to their cross-sectional values; see also Feenstra (2004).

Over the years until 2003, many empirical gravity applications cited the (conditional GE) models of Anderson (1979) and Bergstrand (1985) as theoretical foundations for the gravity equation. However, such studies usually either ignored the role of multilateral prices or included readily available price indexes. For instance, McCallum (1995) found that – due to the Canadian – U.S. national border – inter-provincial Canadian trade flows were *22 times* (2100 percent) higher than trade between Canadian provinces and U.S. states, but treated multilateral prices using an ad hoc 'remoteness' index.' Motivated by McCallum (1995), Anderson and van Wincoop (2003) (A-vW) enhanced the conditional GE theoretical foundations for estimating gravity equations, using a system of equations to allow for the endogeneity of prices in estimation and then to conduct appropriate comparative statics. The starting point for the theory was the (by now) standard assumption of CES preferences for every country's representative consumer j:

$$\left(\sum_{i=1}^{N} \beta_i^{(1-\sigma)/\sigma} c_{ij}^{(1-\sigma)/\sigma} \right)^{\sigma/(\sigma-1)}, \tag{12}$$

where β_i is an exogenous arbitrary parameter reflecting relative preference for country i's product and c_{ij} is consumption of i's product by the representative consumer in j.

Maximizing (12) subject to a standard budget constraint yields the nominal demand for region i goods in region j:

$$PX_{ij} = \left(\frac{\beta_i p_i t_{ij}}{P_j} \right)^{1-\sigma} Y_j, \tag{13}$$

where p_i is the price of country i's product, t_{ij} is the gross trade cost of goods from i to j, and P_j is the consumer price index of j:

$$P_j = \left[\sum_{k=1}^{N} (\beta_k p_k t_{kj})^{(1-\sigma)} \right]^{\frac{1}{(1-\sigma)}}. \tag{14}$$

Assuming market clearance, one can then solve for the gravity equation:

$$PX_{ij} = \frac{Y_i Y_j}{Y^w} \left(\frac{t_{ij}}{\Pi_i P_j} \right)^{1-\sigma}, \tag{15}$$

where

$$\Pi_i = \left(\sum_{i=1}^{N} \left(\frac{t_{ij}}{P_j} \right)^{1-\sigma} \theta_j \right)^{\frac{1}{(1-\sigma)}}, \tag{16}$$

$$P_j = \left(\sum_{i=1}^{N} \left(\frac{t_{ij}}{\Pi_i} \right)^{1-\sigma} \theta_i \right)^{\frac{1}{(1-\sigma)}}. \tag{17}$$

Together, equations (15)–(17) define the gravity equation, which can be solved in terms of income shares (θ_i), bilateral trade costs, and the elasticity of substitution in consumption (σ). In the special case of symmetric bilateral trade costs, equation (15) becomes:

$$P_j^{1-\sigma} = \sum_{i=1}^{N} P_i^{\sigma-1} \theta_i t_{ij}^{1-\sigma}, \tag{18}$$

where

$$PX_{ij} = \frac{Y_i Y_j}{Y^w} \left(\frac{t_{ij}}{P_i P_j} \right)^{1-\sigma} \tag{19}$$

In A-vW, the authors show that estimation of equations (18) and (19) using non-linear least squares (NLS) yields considerably different estimates of gravity equation parameters than those from estimating the traditional gravity equation ignoring the multilateral price terms. However, as A-vW and others have found since, gravity equation parameters may still be biased if the multilateral price terms are not the only country specific variables influencing trade flows. An alternative approach to estimating equations (18) and (19) by NLS is to estimate equation (18) alone using country specific fixed effects to generate unbiased gravity equation parameters, and then use a non-linear solver with the system of equations (18) and (19) to conduct GE comparative statics.

While most researchers using the gravity equation have recognized the importance of accounting for the multilateral price terms in estimation using country specific fixed effects, few have actually gone further to compute the full comparative static effects of a bilateral trade cost change on the bilateral trade flow. To see the importance of this issue, return to equations (15)–(17). A reduction in the bilateral trade cost from i to j (t_{ij}) will have a positive partial (or direct) impact on the bilateral trade flow PX_{ij}. However, a fall in t_{ij} also lowers multilateral resistance in j, causing an increase in imports from all countries, and potentially decreasing trade from i to j as other countries' products substitute for i's goods. The fall in P_j reduces PX_{ij}. Another GE effect is that the fall in t_{ij} also puts downward pressure on i's multilateral price index, Π_i, tending to reduce PX_{ij} as well. These two GE effects tend to offset the trade enhancing direct effect of a lower t_{ij}. Moreover, the theory implies that the effect of a national barrier is larger on internal trade for a small country (such as Canada) relative to that for a large country (such as the United States), which is borne out empirically. These GE effects are the second contribution of A vW, which helped to reduce substantively the estimated effect of the Canadian–U.S. border on international trade between Canadian provinces and U.S. states. For instance, A-vW found that – ignoring the GE effects – the Canadian–U.S. border reduced international trade by 80 percent. However, once GE effects were accounted for, the border reduced Canadian–U.S. trade by only 44 percent.

While empirical researchers since 2003 have cited increasingly A-vW as theoretical foundations for the gravity equation, and applied country fixed effects to capture the multilateral price terms in estimation, few researchers have explored the full GE comparative static effects of trade cost changes.[7] One reason for this is the lack of effort to simulate the trade flows and multilateral price terms with and without barriers using a non-linear solver. To offer one partial remedy for this, Baier and Bergstrand (2009a) provided a method for 'approximating' the GE comparative static effects without having to use non-linear solvers. Baier and Bergstrand (2009a) use a first order log linear Taylor series expansion of the multilateral price terms (16) and (17) above to solve for multilateral 'resistance' terms – GDP share weighted (or simple) averages of the 'exogenous' components of the endogenous multilateral price terms – allowing estimation of a reduced form gravity equation and providing a simple method to approximate the multilateral price terms for comparative statics. Specifically, applying the Baier-Bergstrand technique to equations (15)–(17) – even allowing for *asymmetric* bilateral trade costs – yields the gravity equation:

$$\frac{PX_{ij}}{Y_i Y_j / Y^T} = \left(\frac{t_{ij}}{t_i(\theta) t_j(\theta) / t^T(\theta)} \right)^{-(\sigma-1)},$$

(20)

where

$$t_i(\theta) = \prod_{k=1}^{N} t_{ik}^{\theta_k}, t_j(\theta) = \prod_{k=1}^{N} t_{kj}^{\theta_k}, t^T(\theta) = \prod_{k=1}^{N} \prod_{m=1}^{N} t_{km}^{\theta_k \theta_m},$$

and recall $\theta_i = Y_i / Y^T$. Using a Monte Carlo analysis, Baier and Bergstrand (2009a) show that virtually identical coefficient estimates (relative to fixed effects estimates) can be obtained using their approximation method in a gravity equation. Moreover, using another Monte Carlo exercise for world trade flows among 88 countries, they show that 74 percent of GE comparative static effects of forming the European Economic Area are within 5 percent of the comparative statics estimated using the A vW technique; see also Bergstrand, Egger, and Larch (2008a).

4.2 Unconditional general-equilibrium approaches

The fundamental difference between unconditional GE approaches and conditional GE ones is the *absence of separability* of decisions to produce and consume from decisions to allocate goods across national borders in unconditional GE models. The conditional GE models described above assume 'endowment economies'; in unconditional GE models, the roles of technology and market structure become explicit. A consequence of unconditional models is that they can be more closely tied to prevailing theories of trade, where production functions and market structure are explicit.

The three most prominent unconditional GE approaches in international trade are the Ricardian, Heckscher–Ohlin (H-O), and Helpman-Krugman (H-K) approaches. The Ricardian approach emphasizes labour productivity differentials, the H-O approach relative factor endowment differentials, and the H-K monopolistic competition approach internal economies of scale with tastes for variety as the source of trade. Interestingly, the unconditional GE approaches toward gravity began with H-K's monopolistic competition model, then a H-O approach, and most recently a Ricardian approach.

4.2.1 Krugman approach

The first (unconditional) GE approach surfaced in Krugman (1979). Assume a one sector economy with one factor of production, labour (l), and assume

CES preferences, like equation (12), but where each exporting country has a (endogenously determined) number of varieties of goods to offer instead of an arbitrary taste parameter, β_i, as assumed in A vW:

$$\left(\sum_{i=1}^{N} \sum_{k=1}^{n_i} c_{ijk}^{(1-\sigma)/\sigma} \right)^{\frac{\sigma}{(\sigma-1)}}, \tag{21}$$

where c_{ijk} is the consumption of households in country j of variety k from country i and n_i is the (endogenous) number of varieties produced in country i of the product. Assuming for convenience that all products of an exporter enter symmetrically in utility, utility function (21) simplifies to:

$$\left(\sum_{i=1}^{N} n_i c_{ijk}^{(1-\sigma)/\sigma} \right)^{\frac{\sigma}{(\sigma-1)}}. \tag{22}$$

Note the similarity of utility function (22) versus (12); the only difference is that consumption levels in equation (22) (in equation (12)) are weighted by the number of varieties (an arbitrary taste parameter). Maximizing (22) subject to a standard budget constraint yields a demand function for country j's imports from country i:

$$PX_{ij} = n_i \left(\frac{p_i t_{ij}}{P_j} \right)^{1-\sigma} Y_j, \tag{23}$$

where P_j is the consumer price index of j:

$$P_j = \left[\sum_{i=1}^{N} (n_i p_i t_{ij})^{(1-\sigma)} \right]^{\frac{1}{(1-\sigma)}}. \tag{24}$$

Equations (23) and (24) bear strong resemblance to equations (13) and (14). The difference is that the arbitrary 'taste' parameter, β_i, in equations (13) and (14) has been replaced by the (potentially endogenous) number of varieties of goods produced in (exporting) country i, n_i; hence, relative preferences for various exporters' goods are linked to the endogenous number of varieties available to consumers in j from country i, which itself may be related to the level of economic activity in i.

Krugman (1979) and Helpman and Krugman (1985) assume a monopolistically competitive market structure with increasing returns to scale in production (internal to the firm) and a single factor (labour); this production/market structure is a simple and parsimonious way to (sufficiently) identify the numbers of varieties in equations (23) and (24), although at a cost of imposing more assumptions on the model than in a simple conditional GE endowment economy.

The representative firm in country i is assumed to maximize profits subject to the workhorse linear cost function:

$$l_i = \alpha + \phi g_i, \tag{25}$$

where l_i denotes labour used by the representative firm in country i and g_i denotes the level of goods output of each firm; α reflects the consumption of labour to 'set up' a firm (the fixed cost) and ϕ denotes the marginal amount of labour required per unit of output. Following Dixit and Stiglitz (1977), two conditions characterize equilibrium in this class of models. First, profit maximization ensures that prices are a markup over marginal costs, ensuring:

$$p_i = |\sigma/\sigma 1|\phi w_i, \tag{26}$$

where w_i denotes the wage rate per unit of labour in country i, determining the marginal cost of production. Second, under monopolistic competition, zero economic profits in equilibrium ensures that output of the representative firm is a constant (g):

$$g_i = (\alpha/\phi)(\sigma 1) = g. \tag{27}$$

An assumption of full employment of labour in each country ensures that the size of the exogenous factor endowment (and population), L_i, determines the number of varieties:

$$n_i = L_i/(\alpha + \phi g). \tag{28}$$

With labour the one factor of production, $Y_i = w_i L_i$ or $w_i = Y_i/L_i$. Using equations (26) and (28), one can substitute $|\sigma/(\sigma - 1)|\phi w_i$ for p_i and $L_i/(\alpha + \phi g)$ for n_i in equations (23) and (24) and substitute Y_i/L_i for w_i in the resulting equation to yield:

$$PX_{ij} = \frac{Y_i Y_j}{Y^w} \frac{(Y_i/L_i)^{-\sigma} t_{ij}^{1-\sigma}}{\sum\limits_{k=1}^{N} Y_k (Y_k/L_k)^{-\sigma} t_{ij}^{1-\sigma}}. \tag{29}$$

Combining equation (29) with market clearing condition:

$$\sum_{j=1}^{N} PX_{ij} = \sum_{j=1}^{N} PX_{ji} \tag{30}$$

yields a system of $N(N-1)$ bilateral trade equations (29) and N market clearing conditions (30) in $N(N-1)$ unknown PX_{ij}s and N unknown Y_is.

Although one of the costs of the unconditional general-equilibrium approach is imposing more structure on the model, a potential gain is more accurate (i.e. closer to the true value) estimated general-equilibrium comparative statics when the parameter of the elasticity of substitution is not known. Bergstrand, Egger and Larch (2008a) provide two results that extend Anderson and van Wincoop (2003). Empirical evidence suggests that many countries' industries (though not all) are better represented by a Krugman model with many differentiated varieties produced under economies of scale than by an Armington (endowment economy) approach; see also Head and Ries (2001), Feenstra, Markusen and Rose (2001), and Feenstra (2004). Using the Anderson and van Wincoop technique (allowing bilateral asymmetry), U.S. welfare falls because of the convergence of prices and wages between the countries. However, in the Krugman model *both* countries incur positive welfare gains. This is due to the difference between the assumed elasticity of substitution in A-vW and the estimated one in Bergstrand, Egger and Larch (2008a).

4.2.2 Ricardian approach

An alternative unconditional general-equilibrium approach to the H-K model is one that focuses more on the production side, in the spirit of Ricardo's Law of Comparative Advantage. Eaton and Kortum (2002) built upon the Dornbusch, Fischer and Samuelson (1977) model of Ricardian trade with a continuum of goods. Countries are assumed to have differential access to technology, so that efficiency varies across commodities and countries, treating the cost of a bundle of inputs identically across commodities in each country (owing to internal factor mobility) and assuming perfect competition. Allowing CES preferences for goods in utility, and assuming each country's distribution of levels of Ricardian 'efficiency' is a Frechet distribution, Eaton and Kortum solve for a gravity equation:

$$X_{ij} = T_i Y_j \frac{(c_i t_{ij})^{-\theta}}{\sum\limits_{k=1}^{N} T_k (c_k t_{kj})^{-\theta}}, \tag{31}$$

where T_i denotes the exporter's 'efficiency' level (or i's 'state of technology,' which influences the exporter's overall sales) and c_i denotes the unit cost of inputs (say, labour). They use the model then to compute several general-equilibrium comparative statics. Equation (31) bears striking resemblance to equations (13) cum (14) – based upon the A-vW endowment economy approach with the trade flow positively related to the taste parameter for exporter i, β_i – and to equation (29) – based upon the Helpman-Krugman monopolistic competition approach with the trade flow positively related to the number of producers/varieties for exporter i, n_i. In all three approaches, the trade flow from i to j is a function of importer j's overall economic activity and the price of exporter i's output *relative to* a measure of the overall level of prices of goods facing importer j. However, all three approaches have different economic interpretations of the exporter i 'activity' variable and the interpretation of the sole parameter (the elasticity of substitution in consumption in A-vW and

H-K and an index of Ricardian heterogeneity in production in Eaton and Kortum); see also Eaton and Kortum (2002, note 20). See Alvarez and Lucas (2007) for an example of using the Eaton-Kortum framework to motivate general-equilibrium comparative static effects of a worldwide elimination of remaining tariffs.

4.2.3 *Hetergeneous firms, endogenous varieties, and 'margins of trade'*

Due to space limitations, we cannot discuss in much detail the most recent developments in models of bilateral trade that incorporate 'heterogeneity' among firms and various new 'margins' of trade. The empirical motivation for recent enhancements of the foundations for gravity equation is summarized well in Bernard, Jensen, Redding and Schott (2009). The authors discuss – using a detailed panel data set of firm level and transaction level observations for U.S. exporters and importers (including multinational firms) – the main sources of cross sectional and time series variation in U.S. bilateral trade flows. The data set decomposes, for instance, aggregate bilateral U.S. exports (and imports from) to some country *j* into four components: (1) number of U.S. export firms to *j*, or 'extensive margin of firms'; (2) number of products each firm exports to *j*, or 'extensive margin of products'; the 'density' of trade (i.e. the share of the number of firm product observations for which trade is positive); and the 'intensive margin' (i.e. the average value of a firm product observation). It turns out that – across pairings of countries in a given year – the vast bulk of variation (about 70 percent) is explained by the extensive margin of *firms*. Put simply, larger trade flows are explained predominantly by *large countries* (in terms of GDP or populations), which have a large number of firms. Hence, the Helpman-Krugman framework described above is suitable to explain the vast bulk of variation *cross sectionally* in trade flows. Most of the rest of the cross sectional variation is explained by the 'intensive margin', that is, variation in average sales per firm product. However, in the short run (say, annually), most of the variation in trade flows is explained by the intensive margin. Consequently, shocks over time – such as changing trade policies – may well explain changes in average values of firm product observations, also consistent with the frameworks above. Nevertheless, newly explored margins – such as new products per firm or new consumers per product firm destination – play some role. Their exploration is emphasized in papers such as Melitz (2003), Chaney (2008), Helpman, Melitz and Rubinstein (2008), Arkolakis (2008), and Egger, Larch, Staub and Winkelmann (2009), among others, which 'nest' these features into gravity equations.

4.3 Empirical applications

As gravity equations have been estimated using regression techniques for nearly fifty years, the number of empirical studies is immense. We discuss mostly some recent estimates that have become useful and whose specifications are based upon rigorous theoretical and econometric foundations.

4.3.1   Effects of economic integration agreements

One of the oldest and most prominent uses of the gravity equation has been to estimate the impacts of economic integration agreements (EIAs) – notably, free trade agreements (FTAs), customs unions and other forms of preferential trade agreements (PTAs) – on trade. Tinbergen (1962), in the first gravity equation application to trade, evaluated the effect of (membership in) the BENELUX FTA and the British Commonwealth on members' trade. Most studies have examined the trade creation effects, while a few have also attempted to measure the effects of trade diversion. Some early influential partial EIA estimates using traditional gravity equations can be found in Linnemann (1966), Aitken (1973), Sapir (1978), Bergstrand (1985), Brada and Mendez (1985), and Frankel (1997). Partial – or direct – effects reflect the coefficient estimates on EIA dummies. Such estimates ignore feedback effects on trade flows from other price changes; we discuss estimation of general-equilibrium (GE) effects of EIAs later. Moreover, Ghosh and Yamarik (2004) use extreme bounds analysis to find that coefficient estimates of EIA effects using traditional cross section gravity equations are quite 'fragile'.

In the last decade, researchers have turned more to panel data to estimate the partial effects of EIAs on trade flows in order to avoid unobservable heterogeneity across country pairs. In a series of papers, Egger (2000, 2002, 2004) finds overwhelming evidence of fixed effects specifications over random effects specifications (as well as over traditional specifications ignoring unobserved heterogeneity). However, there are numerous possible fixed effects specifications. Mátyás (1997) proposes including an exporter fixed effect, an importer fixed effect and a time fixed effect (i.e. a set of time dummies). Egger (2000) finds that a random effects specification is rejected in favor of such a fixed effect specification. Egger and Pfaffermayr (2003) and Cheng and Wall (2005) reject a fixed effect specification with exporter effect, importer effect and time effect in favor of a specification with a country pair fixed effect and a time effect; Cheng and Wall (2005) also reject symmetry in the country pair effect, which was used in Glick and Rose (2001). Baltagi, Egger and Pfaffermayr (2003) suggest estimating models with fixed country pair and also fixed exporter year and fixed importer year effects. In models à la Eaton and Kortum (2002), Anderson and van Wincoop (2003), or Bergstrand, Egger and Larch (2008a) and applications with panel data, fixed exporter year and fixed importer year ensure that the coefficients of bilateral trade costs are not biased by omitted general-equilibrium effects. In a panel (endogenous) unobservable multilateral price terms for each country vary over time; consequently, panel estimation requires exporter time (it) and importer time (jt) effects, rather than exporter (i) and importer (*j*) effects. Moreover, unobserved heterogeneity in country pairs suggests the inclusion of country pair fixed effects (*ij*), as Cheng and Wall (2005) recommended.

Several recent studies have consequently investigated the effects of EIAs on trade flows motivated by these theoretical and econometric considerations. Baier and Bergstrand (2007) investigated the average partial (treatment) effect of numerous EIAs using these country time and country pair effects, finding that the average partial effect of an EIA between a pair of countries on their bilateral trade was approximately 100 percent after 10–15 years, with little further effect after that (and no permanent 'growth' effects). Baier, Bergstrand and Vidal (2007) used this technique to find credible effects of various Latin American EIAs on members' trade flows. Baldwin and Taglioni (2007) employed exporter time, importer time and country pair fixed effects and found smaller EU integration effects and no effect of Eurozone membership on members' trade. Baier, Bergstrand, Egger and McLaughlin (2008) used the same technique to find plausible effects of various Western European agreements on members' trade flows. Gil, Llorca and Martinez Serrano (2008) used the same methodology to examine the partial trade creation and trade diversion effects of European Community/Union enlargements as well as various other agreements (including monetary agreements) on members' trade flows, finding credible estimates.

Two other issues have been raised as important for estimating properly the effects of EIAs on trade flows. First, the formation of an EIA is not *exogenous* to trade flows; in fact, most economic factors that explain trade flows also explain FTA formations; see also Baier and Bergstrand (2002, 2004). Since unobservable variables which influence selection into EIAs by pairs of countries' governments may also influence trade flows themselves, endogeneity bias arises which may tend to overstate or understate the true (partial) effect of an EIA in a regression. One method to address this potential endogeneity issue is the use of instrumental variables (two stage) estimation, requiring estimation in the first stage of the likelihood of an EIA between a country pair and then using an instrument for the EIA dummy in the second stage; see also Baier and Bergstrand (2002), Carrère (2006), and Egger, Larch, Staub and Winkelmann (2009). Such a method can be used potentially with cross section data. A second method to address this endogeneity bias requires panel data. If decisions to form or enlarge EIAs are slow moving relative to trade flows, estimation of EIAs' effects on trade using exporter time, importer time, and country pair fixed effects can eliminate potentially the endogeneity bias; see also Baier and Bergstrand (2007), Baldwin and Taglioni (2007), and the other studies cited in the previous paragraph.

Second, as noted as early as Linnemann (1966), *half* of the world's bilateral trade flows are zero. Given recent developments in the theory of international trade to examine firm 'heterogeneity' (Melitz, 2003) and the existence of national data sets of international trade flows of countries' firms/plants, theories have surfaced to explain which countries select into international trade and consequently why half of the world's bilateral trade flows are zero. Helpman, Melitz, and Rubinstein (2008) use the Melitz (2003) model to set up a two stage system for estimating gravity models. The first stage is predicting which country pairs trade, given the existence of fixed costs to trade in the Melitz model and selection issues. Conditioned upon a positive trade flow, the second stage provides a Helpman-Krugman based model of economic determinants of trade flows. The zeros issue was also addressed in Santos Silva and Tenreyro (2006) using a Poisson quasi maximum likelihood estimator in their effort to eliminate bias arising from hetereoskedasticity in the error terms in typical gravity equations; Westerlund and Wilhelmsson (2009) also use a Poisson estimator to address the zeros issue in gravity models and Felbermayr and Kohler (2004) a Tobit estimator. Baldwin and Harrigan (2007) address the zeros issue in terms of examining divergent predictions of various trade models for explaining observed trade prices and offer a modified Melitz model of heterogeneous firm behavior. Both zero trade flows and bias arising from endogeneity of EIA dummies were addressed simultaneously in Egger, Larch, Staub and Winkelmann (2009). They find that ignoring endogeneity bias of EIAs is relatively more important than ignoring selection bias into trading (the zero trade flow issue). Accounting for endogeneity of EIAs raises the estimated long run, general-equilibrium impact of an EIA on members' trade by about 40 percentage points, doubling the GE effect of assuming exogenous EIAs. Accounting for 'selection' into trade flows raises the estimated impact of an EIA by only 10 percentage points.

4.3.2 Trade and growth

The gravity equation has found an important use in helping to understand the effects of trade on economic growth. There is a large literature examining the effects of trade and 'openness' on countries' levels of per capita income – alongside the influences of institutions and geography. However, unlike geography, trade and per capita incomes are determined simultaneously, so coefficient estimates of regressions of per capita incomes on measures of trade (alongside other determinants) are potentially biased by endogeneity issues. One important paper addressing this issue is Frankel and Romer (1999). Since trade is endogenous, they needed an instrument for trade that is exogenous to per capita incomes. Since gravity equations using populations (instead of GDPs), distance, and other exogenous variables can predict well bilateral trade flows, the predicted values of these flows could generate an (exogenous) instrumental variable for trade openness. Using this technique, they demonstrated that trade has an economically and statistically significant effect on per capita income, raising per capita GDP by almost 1 percent for every 1 percent higher trade relative to GDP. Alcala and Ciccone (2004) used the Frankel-Romer procedure along with instruments to account for the endogeneity of the 'institutions' variable to show that – accounting for institutions properly – trade openness retained its economically and statistically significant effect on per capita income.

Badinger (2008) extended this type of analysis further to show the positive impacts of EIAs on productivity levels across countries (which then raise per capita incomes). Following Baier and Bergstrand (2004), Badinger predicted bilateral trade flows to construct an instrument for trade openness, accounting for the endogeneity between EIAs and trade flows discussed earlier. Using instruments for EIAs to help predict trade flows, Badinger (2008) found that trade openness – alongside institutions and geography – has an economically and statistically significant effect on productivity levels (and by extension per capita incomes).

4.3.3 Infrastructure, currency unions, political and institutional factors, and immigrant stocks

As noted earlier, the gravity equation has been used extensively to estimate the impact of numerous other factors on the volume of trade; another entire survey would be needed to discuss comprehensively all of these efforts. Hence, the remainder of this section addresses each of four other important areas of application of the gravity equation briefly.

Traditionally, the gravity equation has included variables associated with *marginal* trade costs, such as distance representing maritime and air transport costs. However, as recent developments in trade theory to account for firm heterogeneity (see also Melitz, 2003, Yeaple, 2005) suggest, fixed costs play a role in determining both selection into international trade as well as its volume. Infrastructure for trade is a likely important factor in influencing both the existence as well as the level of trade. Recently, several studies have examined the impact of trade infrastructure on bilateral trade flows using gravity equations. One of the earliest papers addressing the importance of infrastructure for trade was Limão and Venables (2001). For instance, using a gravity framework, Limão and Venables (2001) found that reducing the quality and degree of infrastructure from the median to the seventy-fifth percentile increased trade costs by 12 percent and reduced the volume of trade by 28 percent. Guided by an Eaton-Kortum based general-equilibrium model, Donaldson (2009) finds that the railroad system in India decreased trade costs, increased interregional and international trade, and improved productivity significantly. Other papers finding significant effects of infrastructure on trade flows include Francois and Manchin (2007), Grigoriou (2007), Shepherd and Wilson (2007) and De (2008).

Beginning with Abrams (1980) and Thursby and Thursby (1987), the gravity equation has been used for decades to examine the effects of exchange rate variability and – more recently – of currency unions on international trade flows. Rose (2000) started a cottage industry in the literature on monetary arrangements, finding using a gravity equation that membership in a common currency union increased bilateral trade (the partial effect) of *235 percent*. The large size of this effect spurred considerable debate and a large number of critiques. Baldwin (2005) summarized several of the arguments that have been offered to explain this large estimated effect, which was associated with very small, poor and open economies. Among the concerns were potential biases arising from pro-trade effects that were omitted and likely correlated with the currency union dummy, a concern about reverse causality (big trade flows causing formation of currency unions), and possible model misspecification.

The gravity equation has been used extensively in political science circles as well. For instance, early applications of the traditional gravity equation to examine the influences of conflict, political cooperation, detente and so forth on trade flows include Summary (1989), Pollins (1989), van Bergijk and Oldersma (1990), Gowa and Mansfield (1993) and Mansfield and Bronson (1997). Polachek (1980) was one of the first to examine formally the relationship between conflict and trade, and Polachek has worked extensively on the simultaneity between conflict and trade; see also Polachek and Seiglie (2006). Reuveny and Kang (2003) extended analysis of simultaneous determination of conflicts and trade using gravity equations. Mansfield, Milner and Rosendorff (2000) examine the roles of democratic institution and governments' choice of trade policies for influencing trade flows and cite many related articles. Anderson and Marcouiller (2002) explore the role of government institutions regarding 'insecurity' and trade flows in a gravity framework. More recently, the gravity equation has been used with general-equilibrium theoretical foundations to explore violence, war and trade flows; see also Blomberg and Hess (2006), Martin, Mayer and Thoenig (2008), and Glick and Taylor (2009).

The gravity equation has also been used to link trade and migration flows. Gould (1994) extended the theoretical foundations for the gravity equation in Bergstrand (1985) to examine the role of immigrant stocks in home and host countries for influencing trade flows, which is motivated by the role that immigrant stocks play in providing informational advantages. Supporting evidence for this is found in Head and Ries (1998), Dunlevy and Hutchinson (1999), Rauch (1999, 2001), Rauch and Trindade (2002) and Girma and Yu (2002).

5   General-equilibrium Motivated Gravity Models of Trade, Investment and Migration

Although the gravity equation has been used more extensively to study patterns of international trade, it has also been used prominently to study foreign direct investment (FDI) flows as well as migration flows. As mentioned earlier, the gravity equation was first used to study migration patterns long before studying trade and FDI flows, but space constraints prevent much discussion here of the study of migration flows. However, the prominence of multinational firms in the world economy – which by nature have foreign investments, affiliates, and operations – suggests some discussion of the complementarity and substitutability of trade and FDI flows. Moreover, the gravity equation has gained increasing popularity in the study of FDI flows.

5.1   General-equilibrium foundations for the gravity of trade, FDI, and skilled migration

Blonigen (2005) noted two important facts regarding the use of the gravity equation for modelling bilateral FDI flows. First, the empirical specification most frequently used in the study of economic determinants of FDI flows is the gravity equation. Second, theoretical justification for using the gravity equation has been usually *by analogy* to trade flows. Unlike the extensive general-equilibrium theoretical foundations for gravity equations of trade flows, there has been no general-equilibrium theoretical foundation provided for FDI flows until very recently.

At the same time that gravity equations have flourished in the empirical analysis of FDI flows over the past twenty years, general-equilibrium theoretical foundations for the existence of multinational firms and foreign affiliate operations surfaced quite separately. However, only recently have the general-equilibrium foundations broadened to provide a theoretical foundation for FDI flows *and* trade flows *simultaneously.* Since we will discuss empirical applications later, we focus in this section on a general-equilibrium theoretical foundation for gravity equations of FDI and trade.

The starting point for general-equilibrium analysis of national and multinational enterprises (NEs and MNEs, respectively) is summarized by Markusen in chapter 8, the details of which are comprehensively discussed in Markusen (2002). Much of Markusen (2002) is based upon earlier papers; see also Markusen (1984), Markusen and Venables (1998), Markusen and Venables (2000) and Carr, Markusen and Maskus (2001). Consequently, we discuss only some recent advances that build upon these $2 \times 2 \times 2$ models of MNEs that provide theoretical foundations for estimating gravity equations of FDI and foreign affiliate sales (FAS).

Only a few recent papers have attempted to provide theoretical foundations for the gravity equation of FDI and FAS flows. Motivated by the puzzle in the Markusen-Venables (M-V) $2 \times 2 \times 2$ GE model of NEs and MNEs that two countries with identical relative factor endowments maximize their bilateral FAS when their absolute factor endowments (and hence GDPs) are identical but have *zero* (intra industry) bilateral trade, Bergstrand and Egger (2004, 2007) introduced a third factor (internationally mobile physical capital) and a third country (Rest of World, or ROW) to resolve this puzzle and motivate a rationale for estimating gravity equations of FDI *and trade* simultaneously. First, the reason for the M-V puzzle can be attributed to only two factors in the M-V model. With headquarter *and* plant setups requiring skilled labour, when two countries are identical in absolute and relative factor endowments (for given bilateral trade and investment costs), both countries tend to be more efficiently served by horizontal MNEs with headquarters in their home countries but plants in home and foreign countries, rather than ship large volumes via trade.[8] Since MNEs require more skilled labour than national firms for setups, the higher relative price of skilled (to unskilled) labour when the countries are equally sized 'crowds out' entirely national exporting firms, yielding large FDI but zero intra-industry trade in equally sized economies. The addition of (imperfectly internationally mobile) physical capital to the $2 \times 2 \times 2$ M-V model – along with the assumption that plant setups require *physical* capital and headquarter setups require *human* capital – easily resolves this puzzle. As two countries become identical in economic size (for given trade and investment costs), the higher relative demand for MNEs over NEs increases the relative price of physical to human capital due to the shift from single plant NEs to multi-plant MNEs. The rise in the relative price of physical to human capital dampens the increase in MNEs and the decrease in NEs, allowing NEs to coexist with MNEs even if the two countries are *identical* in every aspect. However, in the Bergstrand-Egger model, intra-industry trade is not maximized when the two countries are identical, when only two countries are allowed. However, further extension of the model to three countries leads to an even stronger dampening of the shift from single plant NEs to multi-plant MNEs, such that the relationships between bilateral FDI (and FAS) *and trade* with economic size and similarity can be approximated by the 'gravity equation'. A further extension of the Bergstrand-Egger model to allow imperfectly internationally immobile skilled labour yields simultaneous theoretical gravity equations for bilateral international trade, FDI *and* skilled migration flows; see also Bergstrand, Egger and Larch (2008b).

Only a few other papers have attempted to motivate gravity equations for FAS. Grazalian and Furtan (2005), Kleinert and Toubal (2005) and Lai and Zhu (2006) assume models with exogenously heterogeneous productivities to generate coexistence of MNEs and NEs, in the spirit of the model in Helpman, Melitz, and Yeaple (2004), but do not address simultaneously FDI and trade. Shim (2005) extends the Anderson and van Wincoop (2003) conditional GE model of trade to include FAS to further explain the McCallum 'border puzzle', but must assume exogenously the unique equilibrium in Markusen and Venables (2000) to generate the coexistence of NEs and MNEs (attributable to the two factor limitation in the M-V model). Head and Ries (2008) extend the theoretical foundations for a gravity equation of FDI in order to explore the motive of 'corporate control' for determining FDI flows.

5.2 Empirical applications

The most common tool to analyze observed bilateral FDI flows is the gravity equation. As for trade flows, the gravity model has been applied to analyze empirically the effects on FDI flows of various economic and political considerations. A complete review of such studies is beyond the scope of this chapter; however, some more recent applications are indicative of its usefulness.

As for trade flows, gravity equations have been used to analyze the effects of natural impediments to FDI. One of the earliest applications of the gravity equation to FDI flows is Eaton and Tamura (1994). This study was one of the first to identify that both trade and FDI flows have positive relationships with market size and similarity using similar specifications. While Eaton and Tamura (1994) used regional dummies instead of bilateral distance, most studies have found that distance has a significant negative impact on FDI flows. Since most FDI tends to be horizontal in nature, and a substitute for trade, this negative impact implies that distance may not be representing transport costs of goods, as the 'proximity concentration' ratio hypothesis would suggest; see also Brainard (1993) and Markusen (2002). Schatz and Venables (2000) confirmed that, 'Distance and market size are extremely important in determining where firms establish their foreign affiliates'. In an extension of the proximity concentration ratio hypothesis, Irac (2004) suggests that distance may have a negative effect if the fixed cost of a new plant outweighs transport costs; she shows that cultural differences are a large impediment for FDI. While most gravity equations include distance and GDPs, recent work has looked at 'spatial' lag models; see also Blonigen, Davies, Waddell and Naughton (2007). For instance, regions/countries with large GDPs and surrounded by large markets tend to have more FDI, suggesting export platform FDI, which has been uncovered using spatial lag models. Also, natural costs to FDI are not limited to distance. For instance, Stein and Duade (2007) use a gravity equation to estimate the negative effects of time on FDI and trade. They find that time zones have a strong effect on both, but is relatively stronger on FDI than trade.

As with trade, the gravity equation has been used to examine the impacts of (man-made) investment policies on FDI flows. Blonigen and Davies (2004) estimate that bilateral tax treaties have increased FDI flows by 2–8 percent for each year of the treaty. Moreover, they find that, while treaties have an immediate impact on FDI, there is a substantial lag before treaty adoptions positively affect FDI stocks and foreign affiliate sales. Egger and Pfaffermayr (2004) also find evidence of bilateral investment treaties on FDI. Mutti and Grubert (2004) use a gravity equation to examine tax rates explicitly on types of MNE FDI decisions. Smith (2001) used a gravity equation to examine whether foreign patent rights affect U.S. exports, affiliate sales and licenses. She found that strong foreign patent rights increase U.S. affiliate sales and licenses, particularly across countries with strong imitative abilities. Globerman and Shapiro (2002) and Bénassy Quéré, Coupet and Mayer (2007) find that the quality of governance institutions is important for FDI flows.

Some researchers have even examined the impact of *trade* policies on FDI flows (and then, subsequently, investment policies on trade flows) using gravity equations. For instance, Baltagi, Egger and Pfaffermayr (2008) use a spatial lag model to isolate the effects of regional trade agreements on FDI flows. Trade liberalization of a set of parent countries with some host markets leads to a relocation of FDI from other hosts into the liberalizing ones. Amiti and Wakelin (2003) estimate the cross price elasticity of exports with respect to investment liberalizations. When countries' differences in relative factor endowments are large and levels of trade costs are small, investment liberalization stimulates exports, but when the reverse conditions hold investment liberalization reduces exports. Two other recent studies examining the effects of trade agreements on FDI are Levy Yeyati, Stein and Daude (2002a, b). Finally, Norbäck, Urban and Westerberg (2007) find evidence that accession to the World Trade Organization significantly increases the export intensity of foreign affiliates of MNEs.

6 Conclusion

The gravity equation has been used for over fifty years in examining empirically the economic, political, and cultural determinants of bilateral trade, FDI and migration flows – that is, of globalization. Theoretical foundations have been developed over the last thirty years that provide a rigorous, logical economic rationale for its econometric use, although such foundations are not yet complete. However, the advancement of our theoretical understanding of the gravity equation – specifically, the roles of frictions, economic size and similarity and relative factor endowments – have certainly enhanced the equation's usefulness as a tool for policymakers in determining the effects of various policies on the flows that comprise globalization. Nevertheless, much theoretical and empirical analysis is still needed to further help our understanding of the determinants of trade, FDI and migration flows, which will consequently help policy makers institute welfare improving policies in a global economy.

Notes

* University of Notre Dame.
† ETH University.
1. A common measure of a good statistical fit is the R^2 measure. Gravity equations often produce R^2 values of 80–90 percent. This suggests that 80–90 percent of the variation across country pairs in observed trade flows could be explained the variation in GDPs and bilateral distance – using the logarithmic version in ordinary linear least squares (OLS).

2. Recently, international economists have been replacing the term nontariff 'barriers' with nontariff 'measures' (where the latter can be interpreted as either impeding or aiding international trade flows); thus, some nontariff measures impose additional trade costs whereas others reduce such costs. Also, some economists consider nontariff measures to apply to nonprice, *nonquantity* measures (thus, excluding quantitative 'quotas'); however, we will consider nontariff measures to include 'quotas'.
3. See, for instance, Carey (1865) and Ravenstein (1885, 1889).
4. EIA denotes 'economic integration agreement'. Note that Walter Isard's work had a substantive influence on Tinbergen's work; see also Isard (1954; 1960) and Isard and Peck (1954), which built upon the work of Stewart (1948) and Reilly (1929).
5. See the appendix in Anderson (1979) for derivations.
6. See Feenstra (2009) for recent developments on this issue.
7. Recently, Anderson and Yotov (2009) extended Anderson and van Wincoop (2003) to examine the relatively larger impact of exporter multilateral resistance (π_i) relative to importer multilateral resistance (P_j), as defined in equations (16) and (17), respectively.
8. If one country is much larger than the other, the larger country can more efficiently serve the foreign market by exporting to it.

References

Abrams, Richard K. (1980) 'International trade flows under flexible exchange rates.' *Economic Review*, Federal Reserve Bank of Kansas City, March, 3–10.

Aitken, Norman D. (1973) 'The effect of EEC and EFTA on European trade: a temporal cross section analysis', *American Economic Review*, vol. 63, No. 5, December, 881–92.

Alcala, Francisco, and Antonio Ciccone (2004) 'Trade and productivity', *Quarterly Journal of Economics*, vol. 119, No. 2, May, 613–46.

Alvarez, Fernando, and Robert E. Lucas, Jr. (2007) 'General equilibrium analysis of the Eaton Kortum model of international trade', *Journal of Monetary Economics*, vol. 54, 1726–68.

Amiti, Mary, and Katherine Wakelin (2003) 'Investment liberalization and international trade', *Journal of International Economics*, vol. 61, No. 1, October, 101–26.

Anderson, James E. (1979) 'A theoretical foundation for the gravity equation', *American Economic Review*, vol. 69, No. 1, March, 106–16.

Anderson, James E., and Douglas Marcouiller (2002) 'Insecurity and the pattern of trade: an empirical investigation', *Review of Economics and Statistics*, vol. 84, No. 2, May, 342–52.

Anderson, James E., and Eric van Wincoop (2003) 'Gravity with gravitas', *American Economic Review*, vol. 93, No. 1, March, 170–92.

—— (2004) 'Trade costs', *Journal of Economic Literature*, vol. 42, September, 691–751.

Anderson, James E., and Yoto V. Yotov (2009) 'The changing incidence of geography', Working Paper, Boston College.

Arkolakis, Costas (2008) 'Market penetration and the new consumers margin in international trade', Working Paper, Yale University.

Badinger, Harald (2008) 'Trade policy and productivity', *European Economic Review*, vol. 52, July, 867–91.

Baier, Scott L., and Jeffrey H. Bergstrand (2001) 'The growth of world trade: tariffs, transport costs, and income similarity', vol. 53, No. 1, February, 1–27.

—— (2002) 'On the endogeneity of international trade flows and free trade agreements', Working Paper, University of Notre Dame.

——(2004) 'Economic determinants of free trade agreements', *Journal of International Economics*, vol. 64, No. 1, October, 29–63.

——(2007) 'Do free trade agreements actually increase members' international trade?' *Journal of International Economics*, vol. 71, No. 1, March, 72–95.

Baier, Scott L., Jeffrey H. Bergstrand and Erika Vidal (2007) 'Free trade agreements *in* the Americas: are the trade effects larger than anticipated?', *The World Economy*, vol. 30, No. 9, September, 1347–77.

Baier, Scott L., Jeffrey H. Bergstrand, Peter Egger and Patrick McLaughlin (2008) 'Do economic integration agreements actually work? Issues in understanding the causes and consequences of the growth of regionalism', *The World Economy*, vol. 31, No. 4, April, 461–97.

Baier, Scott L., and Jeffrey H. Bergstrand (2009a) '*Bonus vetus* OLS: a simple method for approximating international trade cost effects using the Gravity Equation', *Journal of International Economics*, vol. 77, No. 1, February, 77–85.

——(2009b) 'Estimating the effects of free trade agreements on international trade flows using matching econometrics', *Journal of International Economics*, vol. 77, No. 1, February, 63–76.

Baldwin, Richard E. (2005) 'The Euro's trade effect', paper prepared for a European Central Bank workshop.

Baldwin, Richard E., and James Harrigan (2007) 'Zeros, quality and space: trade theory and trade evidence', National Bureau of Economic Research Working Paper 13214, July.

Baldwin, Richard E., and Daria Taglioni (2007) 'Trade effects of the Euro: a comparison of estimators', *Journal of Economic Integration*, vol. 22, No. 4, December, 780.

Baltagi, Badi H., Peter Egger and Michael Pfaffermayr (2003) 'A generalized design for bilateral trade flow models', *Economics Letters*, vol. 80, 391–97.

——(2008) 'Estimating regional trade agreement effects on FDI in an interdependent world', *Journal of Econometrics*, vol. 145, 194–208.

Belderbos, Rene (1997) 'Antidumping and tariff jumping Japanese firms' DFI in the European Union and United States', *Weltwirtschaftliches Archiv*, vol. 133, 419–57.

Bénassy Quéré, Agnès, Maylis Coupet and Thierry Mayer (2007) 'Institutional determinants of foreign direct investment', *The World Economy*, vol. 30, No. 5, May, 764–82.

Bergstrand, Jeffrey H. (1981) *The Gravity Equation in International Trade*. Ph.D. dissertation, Department of Economics, University of Wisconsin at Madison.

——(1985) 'The Gravity Equation in international trade: some microeconomic foundations and empirical evidence', *Review of Economics and Statistics*, vol. 67, No. 3, August, 474–81.

Bergstrand, Jeffrey H., and Peter Egger (2004) 'A theoretical and empirical model of international trade and foreign direct investment with outsourcing: part 1, developed countries', Working Paper, University of Notre Dame.

——(2007) 'A knowledge and physical capital model of international trade flows, foreign direct investment, and multinational enterprises', *Journal of International Economics*, vol. 73, No. 2, 278–308.

——(2009) 'A general equilibrium theory for estimating gravity equations of bilateral FDI, final goods trade, and intermediate goods trade', in S. Brakman and P. van Bergeijk (eds), *The Gravity Model in International Trade: Advances and Applications*. Cambridge: Cambridge University Press, forthcoming.

Bergstrand Jeffrey H., Peter Egger and Mario Larch (2008a) 'Gravity *redux*: structural estimation of gravity equations, elasticities of substitution, and economic welfare under asymmetric bilateral trade costs', Working Paper, University of Notre Dame.

—— (2008b) '*The New Expats*: economic determinants of bilateral expatriate, FDI, and international trade flows', Working Paper, University of Notre Dame.

Bernard, Andrew B., J. Bradford Jensen, Stephen J. Redding and Peter K. Schott (2009) 'The margins of U.S. trade (long version)', Working Paper CES 09 18, U.S. Census Bureau.

Blomberg, S., and Gregory D. Hess (2006) 'How much does violence tax trade?' *Review of Economics and Statistics*, vol. 88, No. 4, 599–612.

Blonigen, Bruce A. (2002) 'Tariff jumping antidumping duties', *Journal of International Economics*, vol. 57, No. 1, 31–50.

Blonigen, Bruce A., and Ronald Davies (2004) 'The effects of bilateral tax treaties on U.S. FDI activity', *International Tax and Public Finance*, vol. 11, 601–22.

Blonigen, Bruce A., Ronald Davies, Glen R. Waddell and Helen Naughton (2007) 'FDI in space: spatial autoregressive relationships in foreign direct investment', *European Economic Review*, vol. 51, No. 5, July, 1303–25.

Borjas, George J. (1994) 'The economics of immigration', *Journal of Economic Literature*, vol. 32, No. 4, December, 1667–1717.

—— (1999) The economic analysis of immigration', in O.C. Ashenfelter and David Card (eds), *Handbook of Labour Economics*. Amsterdam: Elsevier Science.

Brada, Josef C., and Jose A. Mendez (1985) 'Economic integration among developed, developing, and centrally planned economies: a comparative analysis', *Review of Economics and Statistics*, vol. 67, No. 4, November, 549–56.

Brainard, Lael S. (1997) 'An empirical assessment of the Proximity Concentration Hypothesis trade off between multinational sales and trade', *American Economic Review*, vol. 87, No. 4, September, 520–44.

Carey, H.C. (1865) *Principles of Social Science*. Philadelphia: J.B. Lippincott and Company.

Carr, David, James R. Markusen and Keith E. Maskus (2001) 'Estimating the knowledge capital model of the multinational enterprise', *American Economic Review*, vol. 91, No. 3, June, 693–708.

Carrère, Céline (2006) 'Revisiting the effects of regional trade agreements on trade flows with proper specification of the Gravity Model', *European Economic Review*, vol. 50, 223–47.

Chaney, Thomas (2008) 'Distorted gravity: the intensive and extensive margins of international trade', *American Economic Review*, vol. 98, No. 4, September, 1707–21.

Cheng, I. Hui, and Howard J. Wall (2005) 'Controlling for heterogeneity in gravity models of trade', Federal Reserve Bank of St. Louis *Review*, January/February, 49–63.

De, Prahir (2008) 'Trade Costs and Infrastructure: Analysis of the effects of trade impediments in Asia', *Integration and Trade*, No. 28, January-June, 241–65.

Desai, Mihir A., Fritz C. Foley and James R. Hines, Jr. (2004) 'Foreign direct investment in a world of multiple taxes', *Journal of Public Economics*, vol. 88, No. 12, 2727–44.

Disdier, Anne Celia, and Keith Head (2008) 'The puzzling persistence of the distance effect on bilateral trade', *Review of Economics and Statistics*, vol. 90, No. 1, February, 37–48.

Dixit, Avinash, and Joseph E. (1977) 'Monopolistic competition and optimum product diversity', *American Economic Review*, vol. 67, No. 3, June, 297–308.

Donaldson, David (2009) 'Railroads of the Raj: estimating the impact of transportation infrastructure', London School of Economics Working Paper, June.

Dornbusch, Rudiger, Stanley Fischer, and Paul A. Samuelson (1977) 'Comparative advantage, trade, and payments in a Ricardian model with a continuum of goods', *American Economic Review*, vol. 67, 823–39.

Dunlevy, James A., and William K. Hutchinson (1999) 'The impact of immigration on American import trade in the late nineteenth and early twentieth centuries', *The Journal of Economic History*, vol. 59, 1043–62.

Eaton, Jonathan, and Akiko Tamura (1994) 'Bilateralism and regionalism in Japanese and U.S. trade and direct foreign investment patterns', *Journal of the Japanese and International Economies*, vol. 8, No. 4, December, 478–510.

Eaton, Jonathan, and Samuel Kortum (2002) 'Technology, geography, and trade', *Econometrica*, vol. 70, 1741–80.

Egger, Peter (2000) 'A note on the proper econometric specification of the Gravity Equation', *Economics Letters*, vol. 66, 25–31.

—— (2002) 'An econometric view on the estimation of gravity models and the calculation of trade potentials', *The World Economy*, vol. 25, 297–312.

—— (2004) 'On the problem of endogenous unobserved effects in the estimation of gravity models', *Journal of Economic Integration*, vol. 19, 182–91.

Egger, Peter, and Michael Pfaffermayr (2003) 'The proper panel econometric specification of the Gravity Equation: a three way model with bilateral interaction effects', *Empirical Economics*, vol. 28, 571–80.

—— (2004) 'The impact of bilateral investment treaties on foreign direct investment', *Journal of Comparative Economics*, vol. 32, 788–804.

Egger, Peter, Mario Larch, Kevin E. Staub and Rainer Winkelmann (2009) 'The trade effects of endogenous preferential trade agreements', Working Paper, University of Zurich.

Feenstra, Robert C. (2004) *Advanced International Trade*. Princeton: Princeton University Press.

—— (2009) 'Measuring the gains from trade under manopolistic competition', National Bureau of Economic Research Working Paper No. 15593.

Feenstra, Robert C., James R. Markusen and Andrew K. Rose (2001) 'Using the Gravity Equation to differentiate among alternative theories of trade', *Canadian Journal of Economics*, vol. 34, No. 2, May, 430–47.

Felbermayr, Gabriel, and Wilhelm Kohler (2006) 'Exploring the intensive and extensive margins of world trade', *Review of World Economics*, vol. 142, 642–74.

Francois, Joseph, and Miriam Manchin (2007) 'Institutions, infrastructure, and trade', World Bank Policy Research Working Paper 4152, March.

Frankel, Jeffrey H. (1997) *Regional Trading Blocs in the World Economic System*. Washington, D.C.: Institute for International Economics.

Frankel, Jeffrey, and David Romer 'Does trade cause growth?' *American Economic Review*, vol. 89, No. 3, June, 379–99.

Frankel, Jeffrey, and Andrew K. Rose (2002) 'An estimate of the effect of common currencies on trade and income', *Quarterly Journal of Economics*, vol. 117, No. 2, May, 437–66.

Freeman, Richard B. (2006) 'People flows in globalization', *Journal of Economic Perspectives*, vol. 20, No. 2, Spring, 145–70.

Ghosh, Sucharita, and Steven Yamarik (2004) 'Are regional trading arrangements trade creating? An application of extreme bounds analysis', *Journal of International Economics*, vol. 63, No. 2, July, 369–95.

Gil, Salvador, Rafael Llorca and J. Antonio Martinez Serrano (2008) 'Assessing the enlargement and deepening of the European Union', *The World Economy*, vol. 31, No. 9, September, 1253–72.

Girma, Sourafel, and Zhihao Yu (2002) 'The link between immigration and trade: evidence from the United Kingdom', *Weltwirtschaftliches Archiv*, vol. 138, No. 1, 115–30.

Glick, Reuven, and Andrew K. Rose (2001) 'Does a currency union affect trade? The Time Series evidence', National Bureau of Economic Research Working Paper No. 8396, July.

Glick, Reuven, and Alan M. Taylor (2009) 'Collateral damage: trade disruption and the economic impact of war', *Review of Economics and Statistics*, forthcoming.

Globerman, Steven, and Daniel Shapiro (2002) 'Global foreign direct investment flows: the role of governance infrastructure', *World Development*, vol. 30, No. 11, 1899–1919.

Gould, David (1994) 'Immigrant links to the home country: empirical implications for U.S. bilateral trade flows', *Review of Economics and Statistics*, vol. 76, No. 2, May, 302–16.

Gowa, Joanne, and Edward D. Mansfield 'Power politics and international trade', *American Political Science Review*, vol. 87, No. 2, June, 408–20.

Grazalian, Pascal L., and W. Hartley Furtan (2005) 'The border effects: recognizing the role of FDI', Working Paper, University of Saskatchewan.

Grigoriou, Christopher (2007) 'Landlockedness, infrastructure, and trade: new estimates for central Asian countries', World Bank Policy Research Working Paper 4335, August.

Grogger, Jeffrey, and Gordon H. Hanson (2008) 'Income maximization and the selection and sorting of international migrants', National Bureau of Economic Research Working Paper No. 13821.

Hanson, Gordon H. (2006) 'Illegal migration from Mexico to the United States', *Journal of Economic Literature*, vol. 44, No. 4, December, 869–924.

Hatton, Timothy J., and Jeffrey G. Williamson (2002) 'What fundamentals drive world migration?' National Bureau of Economic Research Working Paper No. 9159.

—— (2005) *Global Migration and the World Economy*. Cambridge, MA: MIT Press,.

Head, Keith, and John Ries (1998) 'Immigration and trade creation: econometric evidence from Canada', *Canadian Journal of Economics*, vol. 31, No. 1, February, 47–62.

—— (2001) 'Increasing returns versus national product differentiation as an explanation for the patter of U.S.–Canada Trade', *American Economic Review*, vol. 91, No. 4, September, 858–76.

—— (2008) 'FDI as an outcome of the market for corporate control: theory and evidence', *Journal of International Economics*, vol. 74, No. 1, January 2–20.

Helpman, Elhanan, and Paul Krugman (1985) *Market Structure and Foreign Trade*. Cambridge, MA: MIT Press.

Helpman, Elhanan, Marc J. Melitz and Yona Rubinstein (2008) 'Estimating trade flows: trading partners and trading volumes', *Quarterly Journal of Economics,* vol. 123, No. 2, May.

Helpman, Elhanan, Marc J. Melitz and Stephen R. Yeaple (2004) 'Export versus FDI with heterogeneous firms', *American Economic Review*, vol. 94, No. 1, March, 300–16.

Hummels, David (1999) 'Toward a geography of trade costs', Working Paper, University of Chicago.

—— (2001) 'Time as a barrier to trade', Working Paper, Purdue University.

—— (2007) 'Transportation costs and international trade in the second era of globalization', *Journal of Economic Perspectives*, vol. 21, No. 3, 131–54.

Irac, Delphine (2004) 'Distance and foreign direct investment: evidence from OECD countries', Working Paper, Columbia University, March.

Isard, Walter (1954) 'Location theory and trade theory: short run analysis', *Quarterly Journal of Economics*, vol. 68, No. 2, May, 305–20.

Isard, Walter (1960) *Methods of Regional Analysis: An Introduction to Regional Science*. New York: John Wiley and Sons.

Isard, Walter, and Merton J. Peck (1954) 'Location theory and international and interregional trade theory', *Quarterly Journal of Economics*, vol. 68, No. 1, February, 97–114.

Kleinert, Jorn, and Farid Toubal (2005) 'Gravity for FDI', Working Paper, Georg August Universitat Gottingen.

Krugman, Paul (1979) 'Increasing returns, monopolistic competition, and international trade', *Journal of International Economics*, vol. 9, 469–79.

Lai, Huiwen, and Susan Chun (2006) 'U.S. exports and multinational production', *Review of Economics and Statistics*, vol. 88, No. 3, August, 531–48.

Leamer, Edward E., and Robert M. Stern (1970) *Quantitative International Economics*. Chicago: Aldine.

Lee, Jong Wha, and Philip Swagel (1997) 'Trade barriers and trade flows', *Review of Economics and Statistics*, vol. 79, 372–82.

Levy Yeyati, Eduardo, Ernesto Stein and Christian Daude (2002a) 'Regional integration and the location of FDI', Inter American Development Bank Working Paper.

—— (2002b) 'The FTAA and the location of foreign direct investment', Inter American Development Bank Working Paper.

Limão, Nuno, and Anthony J. Venables (2001) 'Infrastructure, geographical disadvantage, transport costs, and trade, *The World Bank Economic Review*, vol. 15, No. 3, 451–79.

Linnemann, Hans (1966) *An Econometric Study of International Trade Flows*. Amsterdam: North Holland.

Markusen, James R. (1984) 'Multinationals, multi plant economies, and the gains from trade', *Journal of International Economics*, vol. 16, 206–26.

—— (2002) *Multinational Firms and the Theory of International Trade*. Cambridge, MA: MIT Press.

Markusen, James R., and Anthony J. Venables (1998) 'Multinational firms and the new trade theory', *Journal of International Economics*, vol. 46, 183–203.

—— (2000) 'The theory of endowment, intra industry and multinational trade', *Journal of International Economics*, vol. 52, December 209–34.

Mansfield, Edward D., and Rachel Bronson (1997) 'Alliances, preferential trading arrangements, and international trade', *American Political Science Review*, vol. 91, No. 1, 94–107.

Mansfield, Edward D., Helen V. Milner and B. Peter Rosendorff (2000) 'Free to trade: democracies, autocracies, and international trade', *American Political Science Review*, vol. 94, No. 2, June, 305–21.

Martin, Phillipe, Thierry Mayer and Mathias Thoenig (2008) 'Make trade, not war', *Review of Economic Studies*, vol. 75, No. 3, 865–900.

Mátyás, László (1997) 'Proper econometric specification of the Gravity Model', *The World Economy*, vol. 20, No. 3, 363–68.

McCallum, John (1995) 'National borders matter: Canada–US regional trade patterns', *American Economic Review*, vol. 85, No. 3, September, 615–23.

Melitz, Marc J. (2003) 'The impact of trade on intra industry reallocations and aggregate industry productivity', *Econometrica*, vol. 71, No. 6, November, 1695–1725.

Moneta, Carmellah (1959) 'The estimation of transport costs in international trade', *Journal of Political Economy*, vol. 67, No. 1, February, 41–58.

Mutti, John, and Harry Grubert (2004) 'Empirical asymmetries in foreign direct investment and taxation', *Journal of International Economics*, vol. 62, 337–58.

Niedercorn, John H., and Burley V. Bechdolt, Jr. (1969) 'An economic derivation of the "Gravity Law" of spatial interaction', *Journal of Regional Science*, vol. 9, 273–82.

Niedercorn, John H., and Josef D. Moorehead (1974) 'The commodity flow gravity model: a theoretical reassessment', *Regional and Urban Economics*, vol. 4, 69–75.

Norbäck, Pehr Johan, Dieter Urban and Stefan Westerberg (2007) 'The economics of multinational firms', CESifo Working Paper, June.

Olsen, Erling (1971) *International Trade Theory and Regional Income Differences: United States 1880–1950*. Amsterdam: North Holland.

Polachek, Solomon W. (1980) 'Conflict and trade', *Journal of Conflict Resolution*, vol. 24, No. 1, March, 55–78.

Polachek, Solomon W., and Carlos Seiglie (2006) 'Trade, peace, and democracy: an analysis of dyadic dispute', Institute for the Study of Labour (IZA) Working Paper 2170, June.

Pollins, Brian M. (1989) 'Conflict, cooperation, and commerce: the effect of international political interactions on bilateral trade flows', *American Journal of Political Science*, vol. 33, No. 3, August, 737–61.

Pöyhönen, Pentti (1963a) 'A tentative model for the volume of trade between countries', *Weltwirtschaftliches Archiv*, Band 90, Heft 1, 93–100.

—— (1963b) 'Toward a general theory of the international trade', *Economiska Samfundets Tidskrift*, vol. 16, 69–77.

Pulliainen, Kyosti (1963) 'A world trade study: an econometric model of the pattern of the commodity flows of international trade in 1948–60', *Economiska Samfundets Tidskrift*, vol. 16, 78–91.

Rauch, James E. (1999) 'Networks versus markets in international trade', *Journal of International Economics*, vol. 48, 7–35.

—— (2001) 'Business and social networks in international trade', *Journal of Economic Literature*, vol. 39, December, 1177–1203.

Rauch, James E., and Vitor Trindade (2002) 'Ethnic Chinese networks in international trade', *Review of Economics and Statistics*, vol. 84, No. 1, February, 116–30.

Ravenstein, Ernest G. (1885) 'The laws of migration: part 1', *Journal of the Royal Statistical Society*, vol. 48, 167–227.

—— (1889) 'The laws of migration: part 2', *Journal of the Royal Statistical Society*, vol. 52, 241–301.

Reuveny, Rafael, and Heejoon Kang (2003) 'A simultaneous equations model of trade, conflict, and cooperation', *Review of International Economics*, vol. 11, No. 2, May, 279–95.

Rose, Andrew K. (2000) 'One money, one market: estimating the effect of common currencies trade', *Economic Policy*, vol. 30, 7–46.

Santos Silva, J.M.C., and Silvana Tenreyro (2006) 'The log of gravity', *Review of Economics and Statistics*, vol. 88, No. 4, 641–58.

Sapir, André (1981) 'Trade benefits under the EEC Generalized System of Preferences', *European Economic Review*, 15, 339–55.

Savage, I. Richard, and Karl W. Deutsch (1960) 'A statistical model of the gross analysis of transaction flows', *Econometrica*, vol. 28, 551–72.

Schatz, Howard J., and Anthony J. Venables (2000) 'The geography of international investment', World Bank Policy Research Working Paper 2338, May.

Sen, Ashish, and Tony E. Smith (1995) *Gravity Models of Spatial Interaction Behavior*. Berlin: Springer.

Shepherd, Ben, and John S. Wilson (2007) 'Trade, infrastructure, and roadways in Europe and Central Asia: new empirical evidence', *Journal of Economic Integration*, vol. 22, No. 4, December, 723–47.

Shim, Kieun (2005) 'Border effects and FDI: can FDI explain the border puzzle?' Working Paper, University of Virginia.

Smith, Pamela J. (2001) 'How do foreign patent rights affect U.S. exports, affiliate sales, and licenses?' *Journal of International Economics*, vol. 55, 411–39.

Summary, Rebecca (1989) 'A political economic model of U.S. bilateral trade', *Review of Economics and Statistics*, vol. 71, No. 1, February, 179–82.

Stein, Ernesto, and Christian Daude (2007) 'Longitude matters: time zones and the location of foreign direct investment', *Journal of International Economics*, vol. 71, 96–112.

Stewart, John Q. (1948) 'Demographic gravitation: evidence and applications', *Sociometry*, vol. 11, No. 1/2, February/May, 31–58.

Swenson, Deborah L. (1994) 'The impact of U.S. tax reform on foreign direct investment in the United States', *Journal of Public Economics*, vol. 54, No. 2, 243–66.

Thursby, Jerry G., and Marie C. Thursby 'Bilateral trade flows, the Linder Hypothesis, and exchange risk', *Review of Economics and Statistics*, vol. 69, No. 3, August, 488–95.

Tinbergen, Jan (1962) *Shaping the World Economy: Suggestions for an International Economic Policy*. New York: The Twentieth Century Fund.

Van Beers, Cees (1998) 'Labour standards and trade flows of OECD countries', *The World Economy*, vol. 21, No. 1, January, 57–73.

Van Bergeijk, Peter, and Harry Oldersma (1990) 'Detente, market oriented reform, and German unification: potential consequences for the world trade system', *Kyklos*, vol. 43, No. 4, 599–609.

Westerlund, Joakim, and Fredrik Wilhelmsson (2009) 'Estimating the gravity model without gravity using panel data', *Applied Economics*, vol. 41, 1–9.

Yeaple, Stephen Ross (2005) 'A simple model of firm heterogeneity', *Journal of International Economics*, vol. 65, No. 1, January, 1–20.

18
Computational General Equilibrium Modelling of International Trade

Joseph Francois* and Will Martin†

1 Introduction

When we focus on empirical assessments of the linkages between trade and economic performance, two approaches stand out. One follows the path of application of econometric techniques to examine the historical record. In the area of international economics and growth, this includes, for example, the now extensive cross-country growth literature. It also includes the literature on globalization and labour markets, the literature on technology spillovers and the literature on linkages between international capital markets and national performance. The second path involves the use of calibration models. Small calibrated computable general-equilibrium (CGE) models (often with a only single goods sector, and almost exclusively without intermediate linkages) are applied extensively in the real business cycle literature. Large calibrated general-equilibrium models are used in the assessment of issues ranging from global trade liberalization to domestic tax reform and global-warming related emissions taxes. This second set of models is characterized by more complexity on the real side of the economy, usually with sector interaction through both intermediate goods and competition for primary factors of production.

In this chapter, we provide an overview of large scale, computational modelling of trade with models that feature intermediate linkages and many sectors. As we focus on the shape taken by the existing literature, we do not highlight the early history of the literature, though overviews can be found in Shoven and Whalley (1984); Robinson (1989); and Gunning and Keyzer (1995). The chapter is organized as follows. Section 2 provides an overview of functional specification of production, demand side issues like Armington preferences and macroeconomic closure. Section 3 discusses labour market closures in CGE models. Section 4 discusses market structure, while section 5 discusses both dynamic closures linked to investment and the related question of adjustment costs. Section 6 focuses on public finance aspects of tariffs. Section 8 discusses parameter estimation. There is much that is not covered in this chapter, given space limitations. This includes, for example, measurement and modelling of non-tariff barriers, application of tariff formulas, database issues and linkages of trade policy to climate change. However, the applied papers surveyed do touch on these issues, and so are a good starting point for additional reading.

2   Basic Concepts – Data and Theory

Applied general-equilibrium modelling combines detailed, theoretical specification of the full structure of an economy with balanced national accounts data. The data requirements themselves require a mapping of imports, exports and final expenditures at the sector level with the structure of production feeding final demand. This includes the flow of intermediate inputs between sectors, as well as the allocation of primary factors of production (value added) across sectors. The data requirements for such an exercise can be quite substantial (Reinert and Roland-Holst, 1997; Robinson et al., 2001; Dimaranan and McDougall, 2002; Badri and Walmsley, 2008). Depending on the goal of the exercise, supplementary data requirements can range from tax data (production and trade taxes for example) to estimates of the greenhouse gas emissions linked to activity across sectors.

In this section, we examine basic issues linked to the merging of data and theory. This includes typical assumptions about technology, issues linked to the determinacy or determinacy of equilibrium in multi-sector models (see Woodland, chapter 3 in this volume, as well as Ethier, 1984; and Keyzer, 1997), and the problem of macroeconomic closure. Resources for obtaining balanced data meeting the requirements of a full general-equilibrium system, or of minimizing the pain when constructing such data, are also discussed.

2.1   Production

In CGE models, the 'whole' economy, for the relevant aggregation of economic agents, is modelled simultaneously. This means that the entire economy is classified into production and consumption sectors. These sectors are then modelled collectively. Production sectors are explicitly linked together in value-added chains from primary goods, through higher stages of processing, to the final assembly of consumption goods for households and governments. These links span borders as well as industries. The link between sectors is both direct, such as the input of steel into the production of transport equipment, and also indirect, as with the link between chemicals and agriculture through the production of fertilizers and pesticides. Sectors are also linked through their competition for resources in capital and labour markets.

We start here with production, specifying production technologies using a basic, constant returns to scale specification. Assume that output q^j in sector j

can be produced with a combination of intermediate inputs z^j and value added services (capital, labour, land, etc.) v^j. This is formalized in equation (1).

$$q^j = f^j\left(z^j, v^j\right).\tag{1}$$

Assuming homothetic cost functions and separability, we can define the cost of a representative bundle of intermediate inputs z^j for the firm producing q^j and similarly the cost of a representative bundle of value added services v^j. This will depend on the vector of goods prices P and primary factor prices ω.

$$P_z = g\left(P\right),\tag{2}$$

$$P_v = h\left(\omega\right).\tag{3}$$

Unit costs for q then depend on the mix of technology and prices embodied in equations (1), (2), and (3). We represent this in equation (4).

$$\zeta^j = c\left(P_z, P_v\right).\tag{4}$$

In the absence of taxes, in competitive sectors ζ^j will represent both marginal cost and price. On the other hand, with imperfect competition on the output side (an issue we focus on in one of the following sections) ζ^j can be viewed as measuring the marginal cost side of the optimal markup equation, with markups driving a wedge between ζ^j and P.

To combine this rudimentary representation of production technologies with data, we need to move from general to specific functional forms. The dominant functional forms involve CES (constant elasticity of substitution) production functions. These can be nested, with a CES representation of value added activities v^j, a CES representation of a composite intermediate z^j made up of intermediate inputs, and an upper CES nest that then combines these to yield the final good q^j. Such a setup is illustrated in figure 18.1, on the assumption we have two primary factors, capital k and labour l, as well as n production sectors that may (or may not, depending on the goods involved) be used as intermediate

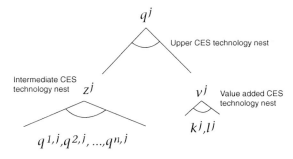

Figure 18.1   Representative nested production technology.

inputs. Abstracting for the moment from the implications of taxes, total value added G will be the sum of labour and capital income, as in (5).

$$G = wL + rK. \tag{5}$$

In (5), w represents wages, r represents the price of capital services, and L and K represent the full stock of labour and capital services employed in production. (We will admit at this point that we are not looking explicitly at unemployment; we will discuss, briefly, the issues of inequality, unemployment, and adjustment costs later in this chapter.)

Given an assumption of CES technologies, we can represent value added in sector j as a function of capital k^j and labour l^j employed in the sector, as well as the elasticity of substitution in value added σ^j.

$$v^j = \left[\alpha_{lj} l^{j \frac{\sigma^j-1}{\sigma^j}} + \alpha_{kj} k^{j \frac{\sigma^j-1}{\sigma^j}} \right]^{\frac{\sigma^j}{\sigma^j-1}} \quad \text{where } 0 < \frac{\sigma^j-1}{\sigma^j} < 1. \tag{6}$$

Equation 6 has an associated CES price index.

$$P_{vj} = \left[\alpha_{lj}^{\sigma^j} w^{1-\sigma^j} + \alpha_{kj}^{\sigma^j} r^{1-\sigma^j} \right]^{\frac{1}{1-\sigma^j}}. \tag{7}$$

Similarly, we can specify a CES technology for intermediates with its associated CES price index, as in equation (8).

$$P_{zj} = \left(\sum_{i=1}^{n} \beta_{ij}^{\phi^j} P_i^{1-\phi^j} \right)^{\frac{1}{1-\phi^j}}. \tag{8}$$

In equation (8), the coefficient ϕ^j is the elasticity of substitution between intermediate inputs. This is often assumed to be Leontief (i.e. $\phi^j = 0$), though an important issue in the recent literature on trade-based carbon leakage in CGE models that include CO_2 emission targets is the degree of substitution between energy, primary inputs and other intermediates (Burniaux and Truong, 2002). From the first order conditions for minimizing the cost of production, we can map the allocation of primary factors to the level of value added across sectors. This is formalized in equations (9) and (10).

$$\bar{L} = \sum_i v^i \left(\frac{\alpha_{li}}{w} \right)^{\sigma^j} P_{vi}^{\sigma^j}, \tag{9}$$

$$\bar{K} = \sum_i v^i \left(\frac{\alpha_{ki}}{r} \right)^{\sigma^j} P_{vi}^{\sigma^j}. \tag{10}$$

We can also specify the allocation of intermediate goods across sectors as a function of the producer price of composite intermediates P_{zi}, the scale of intermediate demand across sectors z^j, and prices of individual goods P_i.

$$\bar{q}^i = \sum_j z^j \left(\frac{\beta_{ij}}{P_i} \right)^{\phi^j} P_{zj}^{\phi^j}. \tag{11}$$

Finally, with the upper next CES for goods we can also map value added v^j and intermediate demand z^j in terms of equations (7) and (8), output q^j and the elasticity of substitution ψ^j between inputs and value added.

$$\bar{v}^j = q^j \left(\frac{\gamma_{vi}}{P_{vj}} \right)^{\eta^j} P_j^{\eta^j},\tag{12}$$

$$\bar{z}^j = q^j \left(\frac{\gamma_{zi}}{P_{zj}} \right)^{\eta^j} P_j^{\eta^j}.\tag{13}$$

In (13) and (12), the terms γ are the CES weights – similar to those in (6) – while η^j is the upper nest elasticity of substitution in the production function.

At this point, we may have enough structure to determine output and GDP uniquely as a function of goods prices. For example, consider the classic Heckscher–Ohlin model. In particular, assume we have $n = 2$ goods sectors, and both goods are final goods without any intermediate demand. In this case $v^j = q^j$, and (5) and (7) give us exactly three equations determining three unknowns: G, w, r,. We can also determine factor allocations by manipulation of the first order conditions for cost minimization. This yields (14) and (15). Combined with the first order conditions for input demands, we can also link value added levels to prices and endowments as in (16) and (17).

$$\bar{K} = \sum_i \left(\frac{w}{r} \right)^{\sigma^i} \left(\frac{\alpha_{ki}}{\alpha_{li}} \right)^{\sigma^i} l^i,\tag{14}$$

$$\bar{L} = \sum_i \left(\frac{r}{w} \right)^{\sigma^i} \left(\frac{\alpha_{li}}{\alpha_{ki}} \right)^{\sigma^i} k^i,\tag{15}$$

$$l^j = v^j \left(\frac{\alpha_{lj}}{w} \right)^{\sigma^j} P_{vj}^{\sigma_j},\tag{16}$$

$$k^j = v^j \left(\frac{\alpha_{kj}}{r} \right)^{\sigma^j} P_{vj}^{\sigma_j}.\tag{17}$$

Together, (14), (15), (16), and (17) give us six equations defined over six unknowns: v^j, k^j, l^j where $j = 1, 2$. Combined with equation (7) we have a total of eight equations and eight unknowns (a version of the 2×2 Heckscher–Ohlin model). As we have specific functional forms, we can solve these numerically as a simple applied general-equilibrium system, where we impose final goods prices and solve for factor allocations and value added. Things become more complicated as we admit intermediate linkages through (8) and (13). Even so, we can still solve the system numerically, mapping GDP, output, and factor incomes to goods prices.

We need more structure when we add more sectors. To see this, look again at our full system of equations (5), (7), (14), (15), (16), and (17).If we add one more sector, we get two additional equations through (16) and (17). However, we have three new unknowns: v^3, l^3, k^3. We can still determine GDP and factor incomes, but we have lost determinacy in the allocation of resources across sectors (see Ethier, 1984, and Woodland, in this volume).

Establishing determinacy in multi-sector general equilibrium, or in other words to introduce sufficient convexity to the economy so that resource allocations and production can also be determined requires departures from the classical Heckscher–Ohlin setup, with or without intermediate linkages. Standard solutions involve a mix of supply and demand side features. For example, in some versions of the Michigan CGE model, capital is assumed to be sector specific (Brown, 1994; Brown, Deardorff and Stern, 1999). In the GTAP (Global Trade Analysis Project) model (Hertel 1997) there is scope to make all factors somewhat sector specific (technically with the introduction of an elasticity of transformation across sectors). Both of these supply side specifications add sufficient structure (convexity) to the supply side of the economy to determine output. An additional source of stability in resource allocation follows from demand side features found in many CGE models. In particular, if national goods are imperfect substitutes for foreign goods (known as the Armington assumption), then demand side forces will also drive the full general equilibrium system toward stability and determinacy.

In the system we have spelled out so far, we can close the system with a simple demand specification. For example, if we assume that we have a representative household with a well defined utility function defined over goods q, then from the first order conditions for utility maximization, we can derived the price of utility P_u as a function of prices P. In the case of CES preferences, this will be as follows:

$$P_u = \left(\sum_{i=1}^{n} \alpha_i^{\psi} P_i^{1-\psi} \right)^{\frac{1}{1-\psi}} \quad \text{where } 0 < \frac{\psi - 1}{\psi} < 1. \tag{18}$$

The expenditure function is then $E = WP_u$ where W is the level of utility or welfare. Taking national income as our budget constraint, then combining equation (5) with the expenditure function yields the following:

$$\left(\sum_{i=1}^{n} \alpha_i^{\psi} P_i^{1-\psi} \right)^{\frac{1}{1-\psi}} = wL + rK. \tag{19}$$

We can also define welfare from the expenditure function and incomes.

$$W = \left(\sum_{i=1}^{n} \alpha_i^{\psi} P_i^{1-\psi} \right)^{\frac{1}{\psi - 1}} (wL + rK). \tag{20}$$

Finally, we can also recover quantities from the expenditure function using the envelope theorem.

$$q^d = \frac{1}{1-\psi} \left(\sum_{i=1}^{n} \alpha_i^{\psi} P_i^{1-\psi} \right)^{\frac{\psi}{1-\psi}} \alpha_i^{\psi-1} (1-\psi) P_i^{-\psi}. \tag{21}$$

We can combine equation (19) with equations (14), (15), (16), and (17) to give us the closed economy solutions to final prices P from the demand side of the economy. The set of prices from this block of equations can be used to solve for welfare and consumption quantities through equations (20) and (21). If we instead also introduce trade at world prices $P*$, then the difference between production q^i and consumption $q^{d,i}$ in equilibrium will be imports (where a negative value denotes exports):

$$M^i = q^{d,i} - q^i. \tag{22}$$

2.2 Issues related to demand and macroeconomic closure

In the previous section, we provided an overview of issues linked to specifying production in CGE models or trade. The other side of these models, logically, rests on specifying the demand side. For a great deal of applied work, a common approach is to specify a composite household (see Francois and Reinert, 1997). This household receives income from taxes, profits and primary factor income, and allocates it across private consumption, government spending, and savings and investment. Recently, there has been a great deal of applied work that highlights the impact of trade on household inequality. Much of this has been sponsored by the World Bank. It involves dropping the single household assumption in favor of multiple households, often linking CGE models to detailed household survey data. See Edwards (1997); Spilimbergo, Londoño and Székely (1999); Barro (2000); Higging and Williamson (1999), Winters (2004), Winters (2002); Hertel and others Hertel et al., Ivanic and Martin (2008), Topalova (2007); Valenzuela (2009); and Do and Levchenko (2009). Whether we have a single representative household or many households, private demand is derived from utility maximization at the household level, which can follow form simple homothetic demand systems or more complex non-homothetic systems that emphasize expenditure shifts linked to Engel curvers. (This includes the GTAP model, for example, which by construction emphasizes income driven changes in demand for food and other consumer goods.)

Nesting household demand, numerical general equilibrium models require a further functional mapping of total income across public and private consumption and investment. The latter of these, investment, raises the question of macroeconomic closure, or the specification of a sufficient set of conditions to determine aggregate consumption and savings-investment allocations. The term macroeconomic closure originates with Sen (1963), and was first applied to CGE models by Taylor and Lysy (1979). A problem with comparative static models (like static CGE models) is that the savings-investment decision is a fundamentally dynamic problem. Static closure options include alternatively fixing savings or investment, and allowing adjustment to occur through the remaining endogenous channels. For example, if savings rates are fixed and savings levels adjust in response to changes in income, then investment (foreign and domestic) will also adjust to reflect these changes. Hertel and others and Taylor (1990) provide further discussion on this point. Macroeconomic closure is important as it provides a link between policy and investment. An extension to dynamic closures, as an alternative to static macroeconomic closures, is reserved for a later section in this chapter.

Another demand-related issue involves specification of demand for imports. While classical trade theory highlights homogenous goods and inter-industry trade, most trade is actually intra-industry. For example, a great deal of world trade involves countries at similar levels of income (the OECD) trading similar goods back and forth. Since CGE models involve mapping theoretically based numerical systems of equations to actual data, most models implement CES-based demand for traded goods and services to accommodate such two-way trade. For industrial goods, this is often done through monopolistic competition. With monopolistic competition, products differ between firms as well as between countries. As a result, Hondas are treated as being different from Toyotas, even when both are produced in Japan. Both may be specified as competing directly with Chryslers and Fiats produced in other countries. This approach raises questions about the relevant market structure. If products are differentiated at the level of the firm, individual firms will have some degree of market power, allowing them to control their own prices. This implies imperfect competition, which requires estimates of parameters measuring market power and scale economies. The available estimates are crude at best, causing a great deal of uncertainty about their values. (See Francois and Roland-Holst, 1997, for a discussion of this problem.)

A standard alternative to monopolistic competition is perfect competition and 'Armington' preferences. Under this approach, two-way trade is explained by assuming products within the same product category, but originating in different nations, are imperfect substitutes (the so-called Armington assumption). This is the structure of the basic GTAP model (Hertel, 1997), for example. German automobiles, hence, are treated as different from U.S. automobiles. As a result, Germany and the United States will trade with each other for automobiles. The Armington assumption is consistent with perfect competition, making estimates of scale economies unnecessary. However, there is instead a need for econometric estimates of trade substitution elasticities as an input to the modelling process. Technically, these elasticities measure the similarity of domestic and imported goods. Like market power measures, there is a good deal of uncertainty in the economic literature about 'correct' parameter values.

There are important differences between the two approaches. Models with Armington specifications usually yield smaller trade and output effects than models with either homogeneous goods or models with firm level product differentiation. The implied adjustment costs of trade liberalization are, hence, much greater in both homogenous goods models and firm level product differentiation models than in Armington models.

2.3 Calibration and computation

The combination of supply side and demand side functional forms gives us the basic setup for a computational general equilibrium model. For policy applications, this theoretical superstructure then needs to be fit to data (calibrated) to yield an actual numerical model with some links to real world data. Because CGE models are specified with specific functional forms, calibration means finding the set of constants, such as CES weights in production functions (the α, β, and γ terms in our discussion above), expenditure shares and related parameters needed to fit the model to the data. A second issue is then external parameters like substitution elasticities. These are often based on econometric estimates, such as gravity based estimates of trade substitution elasticities.

A well calibrated model, when solved numerically, yields the structure of the base data set when nothing is changed in terms of policy levers or parameters. Policy experiments then involve counterfactual experiments, where policy parameters of other exogenous parameters (like projected population changes or exogenous trends in innovation) are changes, and the model is resolved. There are different schools, and different software associated with those schools, for solving these large non-linear systems. GAMS (2010), for example, offers a number of numerical solvers, employing quite different solution algorithms, for optimization problems involving very large non-linear systems of equations subject to equality and inequality constraints. GAMS based models, therefore, are focused on explicit solution of the non-linear systems that make up the demand and supply side of an economy. An alternative is to employ local linearization with stepwise solution and updating of share coefficients. This is the strategy followed with GEMPACK. As described by Harrison and Pearson (1994) and Pearson (2002), GEMPACK allows for a range of choices, all based on stepwise solution of locally linearized versions of non-linear systems. Smaller models can be solved with less demanding software. The numerical version of the 123 model of de Melo and Robinson (1989) is implemented in Excel, for example. However, large scale modelling increasingly relies on more computationally powerful software packages such as GAMS and GEMPACK. Rutherford (1992a, b) has also pioneered both a programming meta-language specifically designed for CGE models, MPSGE, as well as mixed complementary problems (MCP) within large numerical models. MCP programming has become increasingly important as it allows both for explicit modelling of quota-based trade policy regimes, as well as switching between technologies in energy models. Though originally an independent package, MPSGE and the related MILES solver have since been fully integrated into the GAMS suite of numerical solvers and related programming packages (Rutherford, 2010). Indeed, while early CGE modelling led to development of a range of solution methods for non-linear economic systems (e.g. Robinson, 1975, and Mathiesen, 1985), many have been subsumed in the GAMS and GEMPACK packages.

3   Labor Market Closure

The most common specification in CGE-based studies focusing on trade reform is a relatively neutral one such as assuming that employment, or total unemployment, is unchanged as a consequence of trade reforms. This approach has been challenged – e.g. by Ackerman (2005) – with a call for approaches such as determining employment endogenously in the presence of a fixed real consumer wage. Indeed, the specification of a fixed real consumer wage has been widely used in many applications of the ORANI model in Australia (Dixon, Parmenter, Sutton and Vincent, 1982) and its descendants the MONASH model (Dixon and Rimmer, 2002) and GTAP (Hertel, 1997). (In the GTAP model this is an option but not the default). This approach made considerable sense in the Australian institutional environment, where informal employment was relatively uncommon, wages tended to be indexed for movements in the consumer price index, and unemployment benefits were readily available to those unable to find employment at institutionally determined wages. There seems little evident justification for adopting such a specification in economy-wide models of developing countries, where none of these conditions are satisfied. Maechler and Roland-Holst (1997) and Thierfelder and Shiells (1997) also provide an overview of alternatives, including efficiency wages and search cost models.

Ideally, modelling of labour market behaviour should be based more closely on the institutional features of individual countries in order to capture the impacts of trade reform and other shocks on the labour market outcomes. For developing countries, this is likely to require careful analysis of both formal and informal labour markets, and of the links between them. When there is substantial reported unemployment in the formal sector, the inadequacies of social safety nets in most developing countries typically force workers excluded from the formal-sector workforce to participate in informal labour markets. Even with an ideal specification of labour markets, considerable care needs to be given to the interpretation of the results. Is it appropriate to identify the welfare effects of trade reform in the presence of labour market distortions with the trade reforms themselves? If one follows standard rules on policy assignment (Muldell, 1962), then responsibility for trade policy would be assigned to one set of actors, and labour market policy to another, such as the labour ministry. If changes in trade policies require adjustments in the labour market, the responsibility for making the adjustments needed to restore balance in that market would fall on the labour ministry. Under this assignment, only the direct costs associated with trade distortions need to be attributed to trade policy. Any adverse outcomes in the labour market are the responsibility of the labour ministry and require adjustments in labour market policies.

One surprising feature of the specification of labour markets in most studies of global trade reform is that the supply of labour is exogenous. While the uncompensated labour supply elasticity of prime working-age males is widely thought to be close to zero, the compensated supply of most categories of labour, including prime working age males, is generally thought to be price responsive. Adding labour supply responsiveness would introduce an additional channel of response to the change in tax rates, and this is the elasticity of relevance for welfare impacts (Anderson and Martin 2011). If labour market distortions were also introduced, it might be expected to introduce substantial welfare changes, since the distortions prevailing in labour markets, including taxes on earnings, and wage interventions such as minimum wages, are frequently very large relative to average tariff rates. At the same time, Harrison and Leamer (1997) provide evidence that the impact of trade reforms on aggregate employment might be smaller than many have suspected. Their country studies for Morocco and Mexico suggest's that the effects of trade reform on overall employment, and even on sectoral employment, were quite modest. They also point out that fixed minimum wages, even where they exist, do not typically determine total employment. If minimum wages become binding, their effect is typically to transfer employment from the formal labour market to informal labour markets, where wages are lower and more flexible.

4 Market Structure

Market structure has been an important area in explaining differences in otherwise seemingly identical CGE-based policy assessment exercises (see for example Francois, 2000; Baldwin and Venables, 1995; Gilbert and Wahl, 2002; as well as the survey by Francois and Roland-Holst, 1997). In the first generation of CGE models, production structure was based strictly on constant returns to scale technology as outlined above, with competitive markets and unchanging levels of factor productivity. Important departures from this approach in the subsequent literature have included changes in firm and industry level efficiency for a variety of reasons. The move away from the constant returns to scale, perfect competition CGE models began in the 1980s. It was inspired by the Dixit–Stiglitz formulation of preferences, which takes into account the number of different varieties available to purchasers of intermediate inputs of goods and/or services (see Harris, 1984; Brown, 1994; Francois and Roland-Holst, 1997; Jensen, Rutherford and Tarr, 2007). Important path-breaking work in this area involved the Michigan model (Brown, 1994). Productivity and efficiency effects linked to imperfect competition are known, collectively, as 'pro-competitive effects.' The more recent trade and geography literature (Fujita, Venables and Krugman, 2000) explores, theoretically and numerically, the equilibrium properties of the class of multi-sector CGE model with monopolistic competition first introduced in the early 1980s.

A new agenda item for the CGE model relates to models of firm-level productivity. These have been embedded in theoretical and econometric models of monopolistic competition so that firm and industry effects both are now part of the same complex analytical mix. It is well established that pro-competitive effects, in their various guises, can have dramatic implications for the linkages between trade policy and economic performance. The econometric evidence supports the importance of this aspect of firm and market structure. However, there is a great deal of work remaining to be done to properly integrate recent advances in this area, from the theoretical and econometric literature, into computational models. The extension to include Melitz (2003) type firm heterogeneity looms as one of the next challenges in this branch of the literature (Baldwin, 2005).

Monopolistic competition has been an important feature in multi-region CGE models of the Doha and Uruguay rounds, and can be traced to earlier CGE work on U.S.–Canada trade in the 1980s, including Reinert and Shiells (1993) and Francois and Shiells (1994) and the literature on deeper integration in the European Community (Smith and Venables, 1988). These models integrate firm level differentiation of intermediate and final goods with intermediate good linkages and input–output linkages. Typically, in this homogenous firm type of variety models, it is assumed that the individual varieties are symmetric in terms of selling at the same price and quantity, but that increases in the number of varieties yield benefits because they are perceived by their purchasers to be different. In terms of our system of equations above, one can reduce Ethier and Krugman type monopolistic competition models to Armington-type demand systems with external scale economies linked to variety effects (Francois and Roland-Holst, 1997; Francois and Nelson, 2002). In this case, final variety scaled goods $\tilde{q}$ are linked to the scale of inputs q:

$$\tilde{q} = q^{\xi} \quad \text{where } 2 < \xi \leq 1. \tag{23}$$

Here we have reinterpreted q above as a mix of physical inputs (value added, intermediates) fed into the industry. As monopolistic competition involves average cost pricing, we can also link the price of input bundles P to variety scaled prices $\tilde{P}$ as follows:

$$\tilde{P} = Pq^{1-\xi}. \tag{24}$$

A common approach in CGE models is to mix Armington sectors and monopolistic competition using versions of equations (23) and (24), which allow otherwise identical CES-based model code to reflect either competitive markets, monopolistic competition, or variations of external scale economies Francois (1998). A challenge on incorporating more information on the population of firms with heterogeneous cost structure will be to find relatively parsimonious reduced forms like equations (23) and (24) that avoid geometric explosion in the computational complexity of the models.

The use of Dixit–Stiglitz preferences for intermediate and final goods can result in larger estimates of the overall welfare benefits of trade reform by expanding the range of varieties available to consumers who prefer variety. Broadly speaking, in this class of models, effects are much larger with firm-based variety effects than with models based on the Armington specification. The love-of-variety specification is widely used for non-agricultural sectors, but rarely used for agriculture, and this difference in specification can bring about large differences in the measured welfare implications of reform from different sectors, with the Michigan Model, for example, generating much larger gains from reform of the manufacturing sector relative to the agricultural sector. (Brown, Deardorff and Stern, 1999). An important question about the Dixt-Stiglitz class of models has been raised by Hummels and Klenow (2005), who note that the pure Dixit–Stiglitz model attributes all export expansion to increases in varieties exported. However, they find that only around 60 percent of the increase in exports in growing economies comes from increases in product variety, with the remainder coming from increases in both the quantity and quality of goods exported. Ardelean (2006) estimates a model of export expansion that nests the conventional Armington model and the Dixit–Stiglitz model and finds that consumers love of variety is roughly 40 percent less than would be suggested by a pure Dixit–Stiglitz model. Fan (2006) found in a simulation model context that full love of variety resulted in an apparently excessive preference for variety and obtained more plausible results in a model that was intermediated between the Armington and Dixit–Stiglitz type models.

While models of firm based variety have led to major substantive changes in the representation of industrial structure in CGE models, these models actually sterilize strategic interaction between firms. While this is done for reasons of tractability, a different strand of the CGE literature has instead emphasized explicit interaction between firms under various forms of oligopoly. This can actually lead to substantively different sets of results for the same policy assessment exercise, and as such can substantially affect the estimated static welfare implications of trade reform and related measures such as the productivity implications of trade reform (Harrison, 1994). Reductions in trade barriers can reduce price-cost margins in oligopolistic industries, and result in gains to national income from output expansion and greater exploitation of scale economies as well as those from increased imports (see Cox and Harris, 1985; Baggs, Head and Ries, 2002; Francois and Roland-Holst, 1997).

Market structure is also an important, unanswered question for CGE models of trade, where carbon leakage and climate change policy are addressed. This is because different market structures imply a different propensity for trade and industry location to adjust (and in some cases to essentially offset) policy changes (Francois, McDonald and Nordstrom, 1995). This question of industry relocation has always been important to the literature on economic geography and location of industry. An important insight of that literature is that, in a world with firm rather than national determinants of product variety, production is more easily relocated between regions. The vast bulk of computational assessments of climate change mitigation policies have draw on relatively pedestrian, Armington-based demand structures (Burniaux and Truong, 2002). This may point to a very real need to assess the sensitivity of carbon leakage estimates under regional emission schemes to underlying market structures (Boehringer et al., 2004). It also reinforces the need to link econometric specification testing to the construction of CGE models. We touch on this point briefly in section 8.

5   Dynamics and Investment

Investment-based dynamic effects feature prominently in a number of CGE-based studies of trade liberalization and regional integration. This includes models of the Uruguay Round (surveyed in Francois, McDonald and Nordstrom, 1995), EU Enlargement (Baldwin, Francois and Portes, 1997) and the Doha Round (Francois, van Meijl and van Tongeren, 2005). Recent approaches vary, including recursive dynamics, overlapping generation models, and Ramsey-type models with inter-temporal optimization examples. Often, the numerical policy literature focuses on steady-state dynamics in a competitive setting, either in the form of comparative steady-states, or in the calculation of transition paths starting from initial steady states. However, recent work with stylized, fully dynamic models suggests that, for small countries, combining accumulation effects with variety effects may lead to far greater gains than in the competitive case (Rutherford and Tarr, 2002).

Identification of policy-induced investment in CGE models does not support the claim that policy should target investment. Indeed, if we have no policy distortions to begin with, then a policy-induced increase in investment provides no benefit. This is because savers are then acting optimally, and are indifferent between current and future consumption. However, by its nature, policy reform is motivated by distortions that means the private and social returns to investment are not equal. In such cases, the welfare effects, like the effect on income paths, can be quite substantial. What all of this suggests is that proper, intertemporal multi-sector modeling should yield larger income gains for developing countries than frameworks that focus on steady-state comparisons would suggest. There can be other reasons, apart from policy distortions, for a gap between private and social returns. This can follow, for example, from scale economies and related agglomeration effects, from labour market distortions, or from market power that varies across sectors (Rutherford and Tarr, 2002). All such cases point to potential welfare gains greater than static analysis would suggest, as long as investment levels increase, and as long as social returns exceed private returns. For small countries, they can be particularly large.

In addition to capital market adjustment, other dynamic issues that receive much less attention in CGE-based policy assessments are labour market transition mechanisms and related adjustment costs. These combine issues linked to heterogeneous household impacts, the time path of wages and capital income and the speed with which labour is able to adjust to policy shocks. The absence of adjustment costs from most trade-focused CGE models has received a great deal of criticism (see, e.g., Ackerman, 2005). These can be added to the dynamic framework outlined above by incorporating increasing costs of adjusting stock variables, such as sectoral capital stocks, as is done by McKibbon and Sachs (1991) and McKibbon and Wilcoxin (1999). The presence of adjustment costs raises the costs of achieving the benefits associated with reforms, and delays the full receipt of these benefits. Along the adjustment path from the initial equilibrium, agents are seeking to minimize, not just adjustment costs, but the combined costs of adjustment and being out of equilibrium, so that minimization of adjustment costs alone is an inadequate guide to policy formulation.

The presence of adjustment costs raises three important questions: (a) how large are these costs; (b) what influence do they have on the timing of reform; and (c) what policies might be used to reduce them. Matusz and Tarr (2000) examine the first question, using several case studies, and conclude that the social costs are generally very small relative to the benefits obtainable from trade reform, even when the benefits are measured using conventional procedures that generate small benefits. They note, also, that the private costs to individuals may frequently be greater than the social costs as, for example, when people are earning rents in employment from which they are displaced by trade reform.

6 Tariff Revenues and Public Finance Constraints

A standard approach in CGE models is to treat changes in tariff revenues as lump sum transfers. This has been criticized by Ackerman (2005) and others for assuming that lost revenues are either replaced by a lump sum tax, or accommodated by reducing a lump sum transfer. This is a valid criticism of the usual presentation of results in CGE models, especially given the early development of CGE modelling to look explicitly at public finance issues (see, e.g., Ballard et al., 1985). Yet in a modelling context, the lump sum approach has the advantage of neutrality given that we do not, in general, know what choices governments will make in replacing these revenues. The choices include raising alternative taxes, and reducing government expenditures. Once the choices are known, the costs of raising government revenues, or of government expenditures foregone, can be combined with the estimated gains from trade reform to make an assessment of the overall implications. If a specific choice about how revenues are to be replaced is made, and a single net estimate of benefits or costs is provided, there will not be enough information to allow analysis of alternative choices.

One plausible approach to dealing with this problem is to assume that the government will raise any lost revenues through adjustments to the rates of an alternative tax. This effectively augments the income-expenditure condition for the economy with a government budget constraint. A more general framework would incorporate the benefits to the economy of the goods provided by governments as well as the budget constraint (Anderson and Martin 2011). This broader approach allows for a wider range of adjustments to the change in revenues.

Harrison, Harrison, Rutherford and Tarr (2002) show that incorporating tariff revenue replacement can make a large difference to the results. While, in principle, a Value-Added Tax (VAT) should be uniform across sectors and, hence, much less distorting than a typical tariff regime, they found that the Chilean VAT varied considerably across sectors. They found that the marginal cost of funds for the existing VAT was 7.6 percent, as against 18.5 percent for the customs tariff, suggesting that replacing tariff revenues by a VAT increase would reduce the measured welfare gains from trade reform by roughly 40 percent.

7   Econometric Foundations and Validation

We next turn to an important area for future research, parameter estimation and model validation. The growing use of calibrated models, without measures of confidence, and of goodness of fit (in short without measuring the models up against reality) has been accompanied by heavy criticism, especially from the econometrics community. Calibration modelers, in turn, criticize the more recent body of econometric exercises for sometimes steering clear of, or over-simplifying, important, but empirically complex policy issues. The general-equilibrium literature thrives on computational complexity, and parameters are drawn from outside sources, while data are massaged (a two-step process involving 'construction of social accounting matrices' and also 'calibration') to eliminate inconvenient incompatibilities between data and theory. One branch of the general-equilibrium literature well along the path to incorporating econometric techniques is the real business cycle literature (see Kim and Pagan, 1995). However, this literature deals with a much smaller, and analytically different, set of models than those used in the international trade, public finance and development research communities. Given the complexity of multi-sector models, and the complexity inherent in their results, some creativity is called for. Jorgenson, with various co-authors, has employed non-linear econometric methods to estimate parameters within subsystems, making up the production side of a general-equilibrium model emphasizing energy use (Jorgensen, 1998). More recently, work along the lines of Eaton and Kortum (2002), as well as Francois (2001) and Arndt (1996), represents a move in the direction of full system-based econometric estimation within the structure of computational general equilibrium models. There is also need not only for estimating parameters and testing specifications, but for improved methods of sensitivity analysis. This has been reinforced by the marriage of CGE models with climate models, which has led to a class of numerical models in which the time needed for a single set of model runs precludes Monte Carlo methods (see Arndt, 1996, as well as Kehoe, 2003).

Closely related to the question of parameter estimation and specification testing is the need for benchmarking of ex ante assessments against ex post results. In general, the use of econometrics in this context has been driven by a need for parameters with which to feed the CGE models. Ex post assessments have been almost an afterthought, in reaction to critical questions by the policy community (a major consumer of these models) about how well the models actually perform. Yet given the role of these models in policy formation, this is clearly an area that merits more mainstream focus. While there is some literature on this area, it is more occasional than mainstream (Hertel et al., 2007; Francois, 2004). Some of the research along these lines has focused on matching the projected impact of NAFTA implementation to what has actually happened, including Fox (1999) and Kehoe (2003).

8 Conclusion

In this chapter, we have provided an overview of the field of large scale, multi-sector modelling of trade policy. CGE modelling has emerged as an important tool in guiding and informing the public debate on trade policy formation, including regional and multilateral trade agreements. It brings together, in a computational format, structure guided by trade theory, parameters from the econometric literature, and detailed information on economic policy from a range of sources, again including econometric estimates but also large scale database projects funded by by the UN, OECD, and research consortia like GTAP.

Indeed, since the prominent role CGE studies played in the public policy debate over the US–Canada FTA and NAFTA, this set of economic tools has been a basic input to assessments of regional integration schemes (like EU enlargement), multilateral initiatives (like the Uruguay and Doha rounds of WTO negotiations), and in assessing the impact of globalization on wages, inequality and poverty. Such models also provide a mechanism, through inclusion as subsystems, for representing global human activity (the global economy) in large scale climate models. CGE models of trade have evolved in parallel and sometimes ahead of the trade theory literature (key features of theoretical multi-sector geography models were introduced to multi-region CGE models in the mid-1980s and early 1990s). They have also emerged as a bridgehead, a point for dialogue where academic trade economists can interact with the machinery of policy formation. There are, of course, key questions and doubts about how these tools are sometimes used, and how well their limitations are recognized. This is one reason for our identification of lines for further research in this chapter. Yet one should also keep in mind that one reason this class of tools is open to criticism is relative transparency of structure and strict data mapping. This can be considered a strength rather than a weakness. As computing power increases and data sources improve, and as numerically based theory and theory-based numerics move closer in future, research in this area promises high scientific and social returns.

Notes

* University of Linz and CEPR.
† World Bank.

References

Ackerman, F. (2005) 'The shrinking gains from trade: a critical assessment of Doha Round projections'. Global Development and Environment Institute Working Paper No. 05-01, Medford, MA: Tufts University.

Ardelean, A. (2006) 'How strong is the love of variety?' Paper presented to the European Trade Study Group Conference, Vienna, September. www.etsg.org.

Arndt, C. (1996) 'An introduction to systematic sensitivity analysis via Gaussian Quadrature'. Purdue University: GTAP technical paper No. 2.

Arndt, C., S. Robinson and F. Tarp (1999) 'Parameter estimation for a computable general equilibrium model: a maximum entropy approach'. International Food and Trade Policy Institute TMD discussion paper No. 40.

Baggs, J., K. Head, and J. Ries (2002) 'Free trade, firm heterogeneity and Canadian productivity'. mimeo, University of British Columbia, www.sauder.ubc.ca.

Baldwin, R.E. (1992) ' Measurable dynamic gains from trade'. *Journal of Political Economy* 100(1): 162–74.

Baldwin, R.E. (2005) 'Heterogeneous firms and trade: testable and untestable properties of the Melitz model'. NBER Working Paper No. 11471, Cambridge, MA: National Bureau of Economic Research.

Baldwin, R.E., and Venables (1995) 'Regional economic integration', in Grossman, G., and K. Rogoff (eds), *Handbook of International Economics*, vol III. Amsterdam: North Holland.

Baldwin, R.E., J. Francois and R. Portes (1997) 'Costs and benefits of Eastern enlargement: the impact on the EU and Central Europe'. *Economic Policy*. 12(24): 125–70.

Baldwin, R., and J. Harrigan (2007) 'Zeros, quality and space: trade theory and trade evidence'. CEPR discussion paper No. 6368.

Badri, N.G., and T.L. Walmsley (eds), (2008) *Global Trade, Assistance, and Production: The GTAP 7 Data Base*. West Lafayette: Center for Global Trade Analysis, Purdue University.

Ballard, C.L., D. Fullerton, J.B. Shoven and J. Whalley (1985) *A General Equilibirum Model for Tax Policy Evaluation*. Chicago: University of Chicago Press.

Barro, R. (2000) 'Inequality and growth in a panel of countries', *Journal of Economic Growth*, 5(1): 5–32.

Boehringer, C., A. Loeschel, and J. Francois (2004) 'A Computational General Equilibrium Model for Climate Change'. In C. Boehringer and A. Loeschel (eds), *Climate Change Policy and Global Trade*. Berlin: Springer-Verlag.

Brown, D. (1994) 'Properties of applied general equilibrium trade models with monopolistic competition and foreign direct investment', In J. Francois and C. Shiells (eds), *Modeling Trade Policy: Applied General Equilibrium Assessments of North American Free Trade*, Cambridge: Cambridge University Press.

Brown, D., A. Deardorff, and R. Stern (1999) *The Michigan Model of World Production and Trade*. University of Michigan, School of Public Policy/Department of Economics.

Burniaux, J-M, and T.P. Truong (2002) 'GTAP-E: An energy-environmental version of the GTAP model'. GTAP Technical Paper No. 16, January.

Cox, D., and R. Harris (1985) 'Trade liberalization and industrial organization: some estimates for Canada'. *Journal of Political Economy* 93(1): 115–45.

Ethier, W. (1984) 'Higher dimensional issues in trade theory', in R.W. Jones and P.B. Kenen (eds), *Handbook of International Economics*, North Holland: Elsevier.

Dimaranan, B.V., and R.A. McDougall (2002) *Global Trade, Assistance, and Production: The GTAP Data Base*. Center for Global Trade Analysis, Purdue University.

Dixon, P., B. Parmenter, J. Sutton and D. Vincent (1982) *ORANI: a Multisectoral Model of the Australian Economy*. Amsterdam: North Holland.

Dixon, P., and M. Rimmer (2002) *Dynamic, General Equilibrium Modelling for Forecasting and Policy: a Practical Guide and Documentation of MONASH*. Contributions to Economic Analysis 256. Amsterdam: North Holland.

Do, Q-T, and A.A. Levchenko (2009) 'Trade, inequality, and the political economy of institutions', *Journal of Economic Theory* 144(4): 1489–1520.

Eaton, Jonathan, and Samuel Kortum (2002) 'Technology, geography, and trade', *Econometrica* 70(5), 1741–79.

Edwards, S. (1997) 'Trade policy, growth and income distribution', *American Economic Review* 87(2): 205–10.

Fan, Z. (2006) 'Preferential trade agreements in Asia: alternative scenarios of hub and spoke'. Paper presented to the Conference on Global Economic Analysis, Addis Ababa, June. www.gtap.org

Fox, A.K. (1999) 'Evaluating the success of a CGE model of the Canada–U.S. Free Trade Agreement', presented at the Second Annual Conference in Global Economic Analysis, 20Ð22 June.

Francois, J., B. McDonald and H. Nordstrom (1995) 'Assessing the Uruguay Round', In W. Martin and L. Alan Winters (eds), *The Uruguay Round and the Developing Economies.* Cambridge: Cambridge University Press.

Francois, J.F., and K.A. Reinert (eds) (1997) *Applied Methods for Trade Policy Analysis: a Handbook.* New York: Cambridge University Press.

Francois, J.F., and D. Roland-Holst (1997) 'Scale economies and imperfect competition', in J. Francois and K. Reinert (eds), *Applied Methods for Trade Policy Analysis: A Handbook.* Cambridge: Cambridge University Press.

Francois, J.F., and C.R. Shiells (eds) (1994) *Modelling Trade Policy: Applied General. Equilibrium Assessments of North American Free Trade.* Cambridge: Cambridge University Press.

Francois, J.F. (2000) 'Assessing the results of general equilibrium studies of mutilateral trade negotiations'. Policy Issues in International Trade and Commodities Study Series No. 3, UNCTAD: Geneva. UNCTAD/ITCD/TAB/4.

——(2001) 'Flexible estimation and inference within general equilibrium systems', CIES working paper No. 129.

Francois, J.F., F. van H. van Meijl and F. van Tongeren (2005) 'Trade liberalization in the Doha Development Round'. *Economic Policy* 20(42): 349–91.

Francois, J.F. (2004) 'General equilibrium studies of multilateral trade negotiations: Do they really help?' In D. Nelson (ed.), *The Political Economy of Policy Reform: Essays in Honor of J. Michael Finger.* Amsterdam: Elsevier.

——(1998) 'Scale economies and imperfect competition in the GTAP Model', GTAP Technical Papers 317, Center for Global Trade Analysis, Department of Agricultural Economics, Purdue University.

Fujita, M., A. Venables and P. Krugman (2000) *The Spatial Economy: Cities, Regions and International Trade.* Cambridge, MA: MIT Press.

Francois, J.F., and D. Nelson (2002) 'A geometry of specialization', *The Economic Journal* 112(July): 649–78.

GAMS corporation (2010) *GAMS: The Solver Manuals*, GAMS corporation, Washington, D.C.

Gilbert, John, and T.I. Wahl (2002) 'Applied general equilibrium assessments of trade liberalisation in China', *The World Economy* 25: 697–731.

Gunning, J.W., and M.A. Keyzer (1995) 'Applied general equilibrium models for policy analysis'. In J. Behrman and T.N. Srinivasan (eds), *Handbook of Development Economics, Vol. III.* Amsterdam: Elsevier Science BV.

Harris, R.G. (1984) 'Applied general equilibrium analysis of small open economies with scale economies and imperfect competition'. *American Economic Review* 74(5): 1016–32.

Harrison, A., and E. Leamer (1997) 'Labor markets in developing countries: an agenda for research'. *Journal of Labor Economics* 15: S1–S19.

Harrison, W.J., and K.R. Pearson (1994). 'Computing solutions for large general equilibrium models using GEMPACK'. Centre of Policy Studies/IMPACT Centre, Melbourne University.

Harrison, A. (1994) 'Productivity, imperfect competition and trade reform'. *Journal of International Economics* 36: 53–76.

Harrison, G.W., T.F. Rutherford and D.G. Tarr (1995) 'Quantifying the Uruguay round'. In W. Martin and L.A. Winters (eds), *The Uruguay Round and the Developing Economies*, World Bank Discussion Paper 307. Washington, D.C.

Harrison, G., T. Rutherford and D. Tarr (2002) 'Trade policy options for Chile: the importance of market access'. *World Bank Economic Review* 16(1): 49–79.

Hertel, T., D. Hummels, M. Ivanic, and R. Keeney (2007) 'How confident can we be in CGE-based assessments of free trade agreements?' *Economic Modelling* 24(4): 611–6

Hertel, T.W., W. Martin, K. Yanagishima and B. Dimaranan (1995) 'Liberalizing manufactures in a changing world economy'. In W. Martin and L.A. Winters (eds), *The Uruguay Round and the Developing Economies*. World Bank Discussion Paper 307. Washington, D.C.

Hertel, T., ed. (1997) *Global Trade Analysis: Modeling and Applications*. New York: Cambridge University Press.

Hertel, T.W., E. Ianchovichina and B.J. McDonald (1997) 'Multi-region general equilibrium modeling'. Chapter 9 in J.F. Francois and K.A. Reinert (eds), *Applied Methods for Trade Policy Analysis: a Handbook*. Cambridge: Cambridge University Press.

Hertel, T.W., M. Ivanic, P.V. Preckel and J. A. Cranfield (2004) 'The earnings effects of multilateral trade liberalization: implications for poverty in developing countries', *World Bank Economic Review* 18(2): 205–36.

Higgins, M., and J. Williamson. (1999) 'Explaining inequality the World Round: cohort size, Kuznets Curves and openness', NBER Working Paper No. 7224.

Hummels, D., and P. Klenow (2005) 'The variety and quality of a nation's exports'. *American Economic Review* 95(3): 704–23.

Ivanic, M. and Martin, W. (2008), 'Implications of higher global food prices for poverty in low-income countries' *Agricultural Economics* 39: 405–16.

Jensen, J., T. Rutherford and D. Tarr (2007) 'The impact of liberalizing barriers to foreign direct investment in services: the case of Russian accession to the World Trade Organization'. *Review of Development Economics* 11(3): 482–506.

Jorgenson, D.W. (1998) *Growth: Vol. 1, Econometric General Equilibrium Modelling*. Cambridge MA: MIT Press.

Kehoe, T.J. (2003) 'An evaluation of the performance of applied general equilibrium models of the impact of NAFTA'. Research development staff report No. 320, Federal Reserve Bank of Minneapolis, August.

Keyzer, M. (1997) *The Structure of Applied General Equilibrium Models*. Cambridge, MA: MIT Press.

Kim, K., and A.R. Pagan (1995) 'The econometric analysis of calibrated macroeconomic models'. *Handbook of Applied Econometrics*. Basil-Blackwell.

Maechler, A., and D.W. Roland-Holst (1997) 'Labor market structure and content'. In J. Francois and K. Reinert (eds), *Applied Methods for Trade Policy Analysis: A Handbook*. Cambridge: Cambridge University Press.

Mathiesen, L. (1985) 'Computation of economic equilibria by a sequence of linear complementarity problems', *Mathematical Programming Study* 23: 144–162.

Matusz, S., and D. Tarr (2000) 'Adjusting to trade policy reform'. In Krueger, A. (ed.) *Economic Policy Reform: The Second Stage*. Chicago: University of Chicago Press.

McKibbin, W., and J. Sachs (1991) *Global Linkages: Macroeconomic Interdependence and Cooperation in the Global Economy*. Washington, D.C.: The Brookings Institution.

McKibbin, W., and P. Wilcoxen (1999) 'The theoretical and empirical structure of the G- cubed model'. *Economic Modelling* 16: 123–48. Also, *Brookings Discussion Papers in International Economics* No. 118, December 1995.

Melitz, M. (2003) 'The impact of trade on intra-industry reallocations and aggregate industry productivity'. *Econometrica* 71(6): 1695–725.

de Melo, J., and S. Robinson (1989) 'Product differentiation and the treatment of foreign trade in computable general equilibrium models of small economies'. *Journal of International Economics* 27: 47–67.

Mundell, R. (1962) 'The appropriate use of monetary and fiscal policy for internal and external stability'. *IMF Staff Papers* 9: 70–79.

Pearson, K. (2002) 'Solving nonlinear economic models accurately via a linear representation', Centre of Policy Studies working paper IP-55, Melbourne: Monash University.

Reinert, K.A., and D.W. Roland-Holst (1997) 'Social accounting matrices'. In J.F. Francois and K.A. Reinert (eds), *Applied Methods for Trade Policy Analysis: A Handbook*. Cambridge: Cambridge University Press.

Reinert, K., and C.R. Shiells (1993) 'Armington Models and terms-of-trade effects: some econometric evidence for North America'. *The Canadian Journal of Economics* 26(2): 299–316.

Robinson, S. (1975) 'A quadratically-convergent algorithm for general nonlinear programming problems', *Mathematical Programming* 3(1): 145–156.

—— (1989) 'Multisectoral models'. In *the Handbook of Development Economics, Vol. II*, Amsterdam: North Holland.

Robinson, S, A. Cattaneo and M. El-Said (2001) 'Updating and estimating a social accounting matrix using cross entropy methods'. *Economic Systems Research* 13(1): 49–64.

Rutherford, T., and D. Tarr (2002) 'Trade liberalization, product variety and growth in a small open economy: a quantitative assessment'. *Journal of International Economics* 56: 247–72.

Rutherford, T.F. (1992a) ' Extensions of GAMS for variational and complementarity problems with applications in economic equilibrium analysis'. Working Paper 92-7, Department of Economics, University of Colorado.

—— (2010) ' MILES'. In *GAMS: The Solver Manuals*. Washington, D.C.: GAMS Corporation.

—— (1992b) 'Applied general equilibrium modeling using MPS/GE as a GAMS subsystem'. Working Paper 92-15, Department of Economics, University of Colorado.

Sen, A.K. (1963) 'Neo-classical and Neo-Keynsian theories of distribution'. *Economic Record* 39: 54–64.

Shiells, C.R. (1991) 'Errors in import-demand estimates based upon unit-value indexes'. *The Review of Economics and Statistics* 73(2): 378–82.

Shoven, J., and J. Whalley (1984) 'Applied general-equilibrium models of taxation and international trade: an introduction and survey'. *Journal of Economic Literature* 22(3).

Smith, A., and A. Venables (1988) ' Completing the internal market in the European Community'. *European Economic Review* 32: 1501–25.

Spilimbergo, A., J. Londoño, and M. Székely (1999) 'Income distribution, factor endowments, and trade openness', *Journal of Development Economics* 59: 77–101.

Taylor, L. (ed.) (1990) *Socially Relevant Policy Analysis: Structural Computable General Equilibrium Models for the Developing World*. Cambridge, MA: MIT Press.

Taylor, L., and F.J. Lysy (1979) 'Vanishing income redistributions: Keynesian clues about model surprises in the short run'. *Journal of Development Economics* 6: 11–29.

Thierfelder, K.E., and C.R. Shiells (1997) 'Trade and labor market behavior'. In J. Francois and K. Reinert (eds), *Applied Methods for Trade Policy Analysis: A Handbook*. Cambridge: Cambridge University Press.

Topalova, P. (2007) 'Trade liberalization, poverty, and inequality: evidence from Indian districts', in A. Harris (ed.), *Globalization and Poverty*. National Bureau of Economic Research Conference Report, University of Chicago Press.

Valenzuela, E. (2009) *Poverty, Vulnerability, and Trade Policy*. General Equilibrium Modelling Issues, Berlin: VDM Verlag.

Winters, L.A., N. McCulloch and A. McKay (2004) 'Trade liberalization and poverty: the empirical evidence', *Journal of Economic Literature* XLII: 72–115.

Winters, L.A. (2002) 'Trade, trade policy, and poverty: what are the links?' *World Economy* 25(9): 1339–67.

Woodland, A. (2011) 'General equilibrium trade theory'. In D. Bernhofen, R. Falvey, D. Greenaway and U. Kreickemeier (eds), *Palgrave Handbook of International Trade*. Palgrave.

19
Trade and Economic Growth
*Paul S. Segerstrom**

1 Introduction

In the widely used textbook *International Economics: Theory and Policy* by Paul Krugman and Maurice Obstfeld (2009), a case is made for why free trade is better than protectionism. It is argued that the conventionally measured costs of deviating from free trade are large, that there are additional benefits from free trade that add to the costs of protectionist policies when there are economies of scale in production, and that any attempt to pursue sophisticated deviations from free trade is likely to be subverted by the political process. While all of these arguments are important, one of the potentially most important reasons for favouring free trade is not presented in standard textbooks like Krugman and Obstfeld: namely, that trade liberalization promotes technological change.

The argument is fairly easy to state. When trade barriers between countries are lowered, firms earn higher profits from exporting their products and, consequently, higher overall profits. Because these profits represent a reward for innovating and developing new products or lower cost ways of producing existing products, firms have a stronger incentive to innovate when there are lower trade barriers between countries. They devote more resources to research and development (R&D) and innovate more often. People living in these liberalizing countries benefit from faster technological change.

More than any other development, what has led economists to take this argument seriously is the experience of the East Asian 'tigers': Hong Kong, Taiwan, South Korea and Singapore. While other developing economies pursued the strategy of import-substituting industrialization and experienced relatively low rates of economic growth, the East Asian 'tigers' adopted much more open trade policies and experienced 'miracle' rates of economic growth. Real Gross Domestic Product (GDP) in the 'tiger' economies grew at an average annual rate of 8–9 percent from the mid-1960s until the 1997 Asian financial crisis. This compares with 2–3 percent growth rates in the United States and Western Europe during the same time period.

Since the East Asian 'tigers' were much more export-oriented than other developing economies, and they experienced much higher rates of economic growth, the connection between trade policy and technological change could be very important – indeed, it could be more important for welfare than the static welfare gains from trade liberalization that are emphasized in standard economics textbooks. Thinking about the East Asian growth miracle lead Robert Lucas (1988, 5) to write:

> I do not see how one can look at figures like these without seeing them as representing *possibilities*. Is there some action a government of India could take that would lead the Indian economy to grow like [South Korea's]? If so, what, exactly? ... The consequences for human welfare involved in questions like these are simply staggering: Once one starts to think about them, it is hard to think about anything else.

The rest of this chapter is organized as follows: In section 2, I provide an overview of the literature on trade and growth. I discuss the different types of models that have been developed, the results that have been obtained and also the evidence that there is a connection between trade policy and economic growth. The literature on trade and growth is challenging to read because even the simplest models take many steps to solve. To help the reader get into this literature, I present in section 3 a relatively simple model of trade and growth. I spell out in considerable detail how this model is solved so it can serve as a useful entry point for readers into the rest of the literature. I also discuss what happens when some of the strong assumptions in the model are relaxed. Finally, I offer some concluding comments in section 4.

2   An Overview of the Literature

In discussing the literature on trade and growth, it is natural to begin with the earliest models of endogenous growth. Before endogenous growth models were introduced in the late 1980s, there were only growth models in which the rate of technological change was assumed to be exogenously given (i.e., Solow, 1956). These exogenous growth models could not explain how public policies like trade liberalization could have any effect on technological change. But with the development of endogenous growth models, economists finally had a theoretical framework where public policies could influence the rate of technological change and consequently, the rate of economic growth.

2.1   First-generation endogenous growth models

The earliest endogenous growth models were developed in papers by Romer (1990), Segerstrom, Anant and Dinopoulos (1990), Grossman and Helpman (1991) and Aghion and Howitt (1992). These models explored the incentives firms have to engage in R&D activities aimed at discovering new products or processes (that is to say, developing new ideas). A key feature which distinguishes these models from earlier exogenous growth models is that the assumption of perfectly competitive product markets is relaxed. In all four papers, firms that innovate earn monopoly profits, at least temporarily, as a reward for their past R&D efforts. The incentives that profit-maximizing firms have to engage in R&D help to determine the equilibrium rate of technological change and because public policy choices can affect these incentives, they can influence the long-run (or steady-state) rate of economic growth.

The papers by Romer (1990), Grossman and Helpman (1991) and Aghion and Howitt (1992) do not directly address trade policy issues and instead study closed-economy models in which there is no international trade. In Romer (1990), firms do R&D to develop new varieties of intermediate inputs used in production of a final good. When Romer solves his model, he finds that the steady-state equilibrium rate of economic growth without government intervention is unambiguously lower than the welfare-maximizing (or optimal) economic growth rate and that by appropriately subsidizing R&D investment the optimal outcome can be achieved as a steady-state equilibrium outcome. In Grossman and Helpman (1991) and Aghion and Howitt (1992), firms do R&D to develop new ideas that are not just different (like new varieties of intermediate inputs in Romer) but are better in some sense (higher quality products in Grossman and Helpman, lower cost technologies for producing existing products in Aghion and Howitt). As a result, there is an additional 'business-stealing' externality associated with R&D investment in these models, since innovating firms are able to drive other firms out of business and the equilibrium economic growth rate without government intervention can be either greater or less than the optimal economic growth rate. These papers make a case for either subsidizing or taxing R&D expenditures depending on the size of innovations and other parameter values.

Even though Romer (1990), Grossman and Helpman (1991) and Aghion and Howitt (1992) do not directly address trade policy issues, these papers do have interesting implications for international trade. All three models imply that the long-run rate of economic growth is an increasing function of factor endowments, which has subsequently become known as the 'scale effect' property. In Romer (1990), the economic growth rate is higher when the economy has more human capital and, in the other two papers, the economic growth rate is higher when the economy has more labour. What this means is that if two such identical closed economies suddenly become fully integrated through free trade in goods, it is as if one of the economies suddenly became twice as large. Going from autarky to free trade in these types of models increases the long-run rate of economic growth by stimulating firms to devote more resources to R&D.

The first paper on endogenous growth to directly address trade policy issues is Segerstrom, Anant and Dinopoulos (1990). This paper presents a North–South trade model where firms do R&D to develop higher quality products. These products are initially discovered and produced by firms in the North (developed countries) and are exported to the South (developing countries). Northern firms that innovate receive patent protection for their products and earn monopoly profits until their patents expire. Then production shifts to the South where wages are lower and the products are exported back to the North. The paper studies the steady-state equilibrium effects of tariffs designed to protect dying industries in the North from southern competition. It is shown that when more northern industries are protected from southern competition using prohibitive tariffs, this leads to higher relative wages for northern workers and a lower rate of innovation in the North. Because a lower rate of innovation results in a lower rate of economic growth, this paper links protectionist trade policies with lower economic growth.

Instead of studying trade policy in a North–South trade context, Rivera-Batiz and Romer (1991a) study trade policy in a model with two perfectly symmetric countries that impose the same tariff on all imported goods. They build directly on the earlier paper by Romer (1990) when it comes to the preferences and technology of each country. Focusing on the steady-state equilibrium effects of trade policy choices, Rivera-Batiz and Romer find a U-shaped relationship between the common tariff and economic growth. Starting from the point where the tariff rate equals zero, the economic growth rate decreases as the tariff rate increases. As the tariff rate continues to increase, the economic growth rate eventually reaches a minimum, and then increases from then on. However, the economic growth rate does not return all the way back to the free-trade economic growth rate. Thus, Rivera-Batiz and Romer can conclude that, compared with free trade, trade restrictions reduce the global rate of economic growth.

In Rivera-Batiz and Romer (1991a), integration in the sense of full communication of ideas is assumed throughout. Thus, the entire stock of ideas in the world is available for researchers in each country to use in the development of new ideas. This assumption is relaxed in the companion paper Rivera-Batiz and Romer (1991b). Using a knowledge-driven specification for R&D, where human capital and knowledge are used as inputs to produce new ideas, they find that integration that involves free trade in goods alone (without flows of ideas) has no effect on the long-run rate of economic growth. But if integration involves both free trade in goods and free flow of ideas, such integration results in permanently faster economic growth. Rivera-Batiz and Romer also study a lab-equipment specification for R&D in which ideas are produced using the same technology as goods. In this case, free flow of ideas is not important and integration that involves free trade in goods alone results in a permanently higher economic growth rate.

2.2   Second-generation endogenous growth models

All of the above-mentioned endogenous growth models have a 'scale effect' property, namely, that the steady-state rate of economic growth is an increasing function of population size. Indeed, the scale effect property is highlighted by Rivera-Batiz and Romer (1991b) as being the key to why economic integration is growth-promoting in endogenous growth models. However, this very property was called into question in an important paper by Jones (1995a).

To see that the scale effect property represents a problem for endogenous growth theory, it suffices to consider the U.S. evidence using the endogenous growth model developed by Grossman and Helpman (1991). During the time period 1950–87, the number of scientists and engineers engaged in R&D in the United States grew from less than 200,000 to almost one million, a more than five-fold increase. The steady-state economic growth rate is proportional to the R&D employment level in Grossman and Helpman (1991), so an increase in population size that leads to a five-fold increase in R&D employment should also lead to a five-fold increase in economic growth. But, as Jones (1995a) points out, there has been no upward trends in the economic growth rates of the United States, France, Germany or Japan since 1950 in spite of substantial increases in population size and R&D employment. The scale effect property is clearly in conflict with empirical evidence.

In response to the Jones critique of first-generation endogenous growth models, a variety of second-generation endogenous growth models have been developed that do not have the scale effect property, including Jones (1995b), Kortum (1997), Segerstrom (1998), Young (1998) and Howitt (1999). All of these papers get rid of the scale effect property by making different assumptions about R&D. Jones (1995b) modifies the R&D technology in Romer (1990) by assuming that existing knowledge does not contribute as much to the creation of new knowledge, that is, by assuming weaker knowledge spillovers in R&D activities. Kortum (1997) and Segerstrom (1998) modify the R&D technology in Grossman and Helpman (1991) so that innovating becomes progressively more difficult over time. Young (1998) and Howitt (1999) study models where there are two types of R&D: horizontal R&D aimed at developing new product varieties, and vertical R&D aimed at developing improved versions of existing products. With just vertical R&D, these models would have the scale effect property but with both types of R&D taking place, the product proliferation resulting from horizontal R&D serves to nullify the scale effect.

All of the above-mentioned second-generation models are closed-economy models that look at a single economy in isolation. Significant progress has been made at extending these models to allow for international trade. I present two examples of papers that yield important insights using second-generation models of trade and growth.

The first example is Dinopoulos and Segerstrom (1999) and is particularly worth discussing for its trade policy implications. They present a model with two perfectly symmetric countries that impose the same tariff on all imported goods, as in Rivera-Batiz and Romer (1991a). But unlike in this earlier work, there are two factors (unskilled and skilled labour) that are used in both production and R&D activities. Furthermore, there is endogenous skill acquisition: workers are born with different ability levels and they choose whether or not to spend time training to become skilled. Dinopoulos and Segerstrom focus on the effects of trade liberalization, that is, a reduction in the common tariff rate. Assuming that R&D is the skill-intensive activity (compared to production), they find that trade liberalization increases the relative wage of skilled workers, induces more workers to choose to acquire skills, and increases the rate of technological change (either temporarily or permanently, depending on the R&D specification). This paper is interesting because it helps to explain the large increase in wage inequality that was observed in the 1980s. This was a time period when many countries were reducing their import tariffs and opening up to international trade. In the model, trade liberalization not only promotes technological change, it also increases wage inequality within countries (and wage dispersion within industries).

The second example is Dinopoulos and Segerstrom (2010) and illustrates the usefulness of trade and growth models for thinking about intellectual property rights (IPR) issues. They present a model of North–South trade where firms do innovative R&D to develop higher-quality products in the North and then do adaptive R&D to learn how to transfer their production to the South. The profit flows earned by firms jump up when they are successful in transferring their production to the South and each production transfer is associated with a royalty payment from the foreign affiliate to its parent for the use of the parent firm's technology. When firms are successful in transferring their production to the South, they also become exposed to a positive rate of imitation by southern firms. Dinopoulos and Segerstrom show that stronger IPR protection in the South leads to an increase in the rate of technology transfer to the South within multinational firms and an increase in R&D employment by southern affiliates of northern multinationals. Empirical support for these properties has been found in Branstetter, Fisman and Foley (2006), who conclude that improvements in IPR protection resulted in significant increases in technology transfer from U.S.–based multinationals to their affiliates in developing countries.

2.3   Trade and growth with firm-level productivity differences

All of the previously mentioned models of trade and growth have representative firms and assume away any firm level differences. This modelling approach has been called into question by empirical research showing that there are large and persistent productivity differences among firms in narrowly defined industries and that these productivity differences are important for understanding both trade and growth. In Clerides, Lach and Tybout (1998) and later papers, researchers have found that many firms do not export their products and it is the most productive firms that tend to export. Trade liberalization induces the least productive firms to exit and induces more productive non-exporting firms to become exporters, market share reallocations that contribute in a significant way to productivity growth.

In a seminal contribution to trade theory, Melitz (2003) developed the first model of international trade with firm level productivity differences that can account for this empirical evidence. Melitz's model is particularly interesting because it highlights a new mechanism linking trade liberalization with productivity growth. In the model, each firm incurs a fixed cost to develop a new product variety. Then the firm draws from a productivity distribution and learns how productive it is at producing the new variety. With this knowledge, the firm decides whether to exit, just produce for the local market, or incur an additional fixed cost to enter each export market. Melitz solves this symmetric country model for a steady-state equilibrium and he finds that only the more productive firms export, less productive firms choosing to only produce for the domestic market. Solving for the steady-state equilibrium effects of lowering trade costs between countries, he finds that such trade liberalization permanently increases overall productivity in the world economy by inducing the least productive firms to exit and more productive non-exporting firms to become exporters.

The model by Melitz (2003) has a stationary steady-state equilibrium with zero productivity growth and, thus, is not really an endogenous growth model. Trade liberalization leads to a one-time increase in productivity. But endogenous growth models with Melitz-type properties have recently been developed. One such model is Gustafsson and Segerstrom (2010), in which firms develop new product varieties, and another such model is Haruyama and Zhao (2008), in which firms develop higher quality products. In both models, trade liberalization induces the least productive firms to exit and more productive non-exporting firms to become exporters, resulting in faster productivity growth.

2.4   Empirical evidence

While all of the previously discussed models of trade and growth have the property that trade liberalization promotes growth (at least temporarily), this is not a general conclusion in the theoretical literature. For example, in a model with asymmetric countries that builds on Romer (1990), Grossman and Helpman (1990) find when a country reduces its tariff on imports of final goods this decreases the long-run rate of economic growth in the world economy if the country has a comparative disadvantage in R&D. And even in the symmetric country case, trade liberalization does not have to promote growth. Baldwin and Forslid (2000) present a symmetric two-country model where lower trade costs increase the profits that firms earn from exporting, but this is exactly offset by the lower profits that firms earn from selling domestically, given the assumption of CES preferences. Lower trade costs have no effect on overall firm profits and, consequently, no effect on the long-run rate of economic growth. Also Baldwin and Robert-Nicoud (2008) present a symmetric two-country model with firm level productivity differences in which, in two out of five R&D specifications, trade liberalization permanently lowers the economic growth rate.

I turn now to discussing what empirical researchers have found about this issue. Is there empirical support for the property that trade liberalization promotes growth? Do countries that open up to international trade grow more rapidly?

In the empirical literature on trade and growth, perhaps the most influential early paper is Sachs and Warner (1995). They study 79 countries during the time period 1970–89 and categorize each country as 'open' or 'closed'. A country is categorized as being 'open' if: for the duration of the 1970s and 1980s, the country's average tariff rate was less than 40 percent; non-tariff barriers covered less than 40 percent of trade; its black market exchange rate premium was less than 20 percent; there was no state monopoly on major exports; and there was no socialist economic system. If any of these five conditions is not satisfied, a country is categorized as 'closed'. Using this categorization, Sachs and Warner examine whether the real annual per capita growth in GDP over the time period 1970–89 was higher for open countries than for closed countries. They find a surprisingly large and statistically significant effect: the average rate of economic growth for the open countries was 2.2 percent higher than for the closed countries (regression 7 in table 11). Sachs and Warner conclude that there is strong evidence that protectionist trade policies reduce overall growth when controlling for other variables.

Sachs and Warner's conclusions have been called into question in a paper by Rodriguez and Rodrik (2000). They argue that the Sachs-Warner findings are less robust than claimed, because of difficulties in measuring openness, the statistical sensitivity of the specifications, the collinearity of protectionist policies with other bad policies, and other econometric difficulties. For example, Rodriguez and Rodrik point out that the Sachs-Warner dummy variable for openness derives its strength mainly from the combination of the black market premium (BMP) and the state monopoly of exports (XMB) variables. Very little of the dummy's statistical power would be lost if it were constructed using only these two indicators. In particular, there is little action in the two variables that are the most direct measures of trade policy: tariff and non-tariff barriers. The Rodriguez-Rodrik paper has led many economists to be skeptical that open trade policies are significantly associated with economic growth.

The latest word on this issue is an important paper by Wacziarg and Welch (2008). They study a larger sample of 136 countries during the longer time period from 1950 to 2000. Wacziarg and Welch use the same five-part criterion for openness as in Sachs and Warner (1995) but instead of categorizing a country as being 'open' if it satisfies the openness criterion during the entire time period, they use the data to identify dates of trade liberalization. During the time period from 1950 to 2000, there are unique dates of trade liberalization for many countries, years when specific countries switched from being closed to being open. For example, the United Kingdom and the United States were already open in 1950, Sweden became open in 1960, Japan became open in 1964, Chile became open in 1976, Mexico became open in 1986, and both China and India were still closed in 2000. Responding to the Rodriguez-Rodrik critique, Wacziarg and Welch check that the dates of trade liberalization do not just capture changes in the black market premium or state monopoly of exports variables, but also reflect broader liberalization.

Since dates of trade liberalization can be identified for many countries in the world, it is conceptually straightforward to ask the question: Do countries tend to experience faster or slower economic growth rates after trade liberalization? Using standard statistical techniques for analyzing panel data, Wacziarg and Welch provide an answer to this question. They find that trade-centered reform has, on average, robust positive effects on economic growth rates within countries. For the typical country that switches from being closed to being open, the growth rate of real per capita GDP (income per person) increases by 1.4 percent (see table 5). This estimate of 1.4 percent is both highly statistically significant and economically significant. It means that for a typical country growing at an average annual rate of 1.1 percent before trade liberalization, its average annual growth rate jumps up to 1.1 percent + 1.4 percent = 2.5 percent after trade liberalization.

3   A Simple Model of Trade and Growth

In this section, I present a relatively simple two-country model of trade and growth. The two countries are structurally identical, so everything that happens in one country happens in the other country as well. Trade between the two countries is not free and is subject to positive trade costs. The model is a modified and simplified version of Dinopoulos and Segerstrom (1999).

3.1 Household behavior

There is a continuum of households in each country indexed by ability $\theta \in [0, 1]$. All members of household θ have the same ability level equal to θ, and all households have the same number of members at each point in time. Each household is modelled as a dynastic family whose size grows over time at an exogenously given rate $n > 0$. Each individual member of a household lives forever. Letting N_0 denote the number of members of each household at time $t = 0$, the population size in each country at time t is $N(t) = N_0 e^{nt}$.

Family-optimization considerations determine the allocation of income across final goods, the evolution of consumption expenditure over time, and the decision whether to become skilled or enter the labour force as unskilled workers. In making these decisions, each family takes prices of final products, wages and the interest rate as given.

Each individual knows her own ability level θ, as do all the firms that might potentially hire her. An individual can enter the labour force as unskilled and earn the wage w_L from then on. Alternatively, an individual with ability θ can enter the labour force after spending an exogenously given period of time T in 'training' to become skilled. A skilled worker with ability θ earns a wage θw_H from then on and does not earn any income during her period of training or apprenticeship. Thus skilled workers with higher ability levels earn higher wages. I assume for simplicity that the training process does not require any real resources (other than the time of the trainee), and therefore the opportunity cost of becoming a skilled worker equals the discounted value of forgone unskilled wage income. I also assume that income is evenly shared within each family (between employed and trainees) so that, at each point in time, consumption expenditure is the same for each member of a family.

The optimization problem of a family with ability θ is

$$\max_{q_\theta} U_\theta \equiv \int_0^\infty N_0 e^{-(\rho-n)t} \ln u_\theta(t)\, dt \tag{1}$$

subject to the following constraints:

$$\ln u_\theta(t) \equiv \int_0^1 \ln \left[\sum_j \lambda^j q_\theta(j, \omega, t) \right] d\omega, \tag{2}$$

$$c_\theta(t) \equiv \int_0^1 \left[\sum_j p(j, \omega, t) q_\theta(j, \omega, t) \right] d\omega, \tag{3}$$

$$W_\theta + Z_\theta = \int_0^\infty N_0 c_\theta(t) e^{nt} e^{-R(t)}\, dt. \tag{4}$$

Equation (1) is the discounted utility of a household with ability θ, where $\rho > 0$ is the constant subjective discount rate, $n > 0$ is the exogenous population growth rate, and $\rho - n > 0$ will be assumed to guarantee that the integral in (1) converges. Equation (2) defines the static utility function of each household member, where $q_\theta(j, \omega, t)$ denotes the quantity consumed by an individual with ability θ of a good with j improvements (innovations) in its quality in industry $\omega \in [0, 1]$ at time t. The parameter $\lambda > 1$ captures the size of each quality improvement and λ^j denotes the total quality of a good after j innovations. Since λ^j is increasing in j, (2) captures in a simple way the idea that consumers prefer higher quality products. This static utility function with a finite number of industries was introduced in Segerstrom, Anant and Dinopoulos (1990). Equation (3) states that per capita consumption expenditure $c_\theta(t)$ at time t must equal the value of all final goods consumed, where $p(j, \omega, t)$ and $q_\theta(j, \omega, t)$ denote the price and quantity of a final product with j improvements in its quality in industry ω at time t. Finally, equation (4) is the standard inter-temporal budget constraint. From the perspective of time $t = 0$, W_θ is the family's discounted wage income and Z_θ is the value of the family's financial assets. The right-hand side (RHS) of (4) equals the discounted value of the family's consumption and $R(t) \equiv \int_0^t r(s)\,ds$ is the market discount factor with $\dot{R}(t) = r(t)$ denoting the market interest rate at time t.

The formal derivation of the solution to the family's dynamic optimization problem is presented in the appendix. This problem can be solved in four steps. First, solving for the utility-maximizing allocation of consumer expenditure across products within an industry ω at time t yields that consumers only buy the product(s) in each industry with the lowest quality-adjusted price $p(j, \omega, t)/\lambda^j$. Second, maximizing static utility (2) subject to the expenditure constraint (3) yields a unit elastic demand function $q_\theta(j, \omega, t) = c_\theta(t)/p(j, \omega, t)$ for the product(s) in each industry with the lowest quality-adjusted price. A unit elastic demand function is the simplest type of demand function. Third, maximizing discounted utility (1) subject to the inter-temporal budget constraint (4) yields the usual inter-temporal optimization condition

$$\frac{\dot{c}_\theta(t)}{c_\theta(t)} = r(t) - \rho. \tag{5}$$

The differential equation (5) states that per capita consumption expenditure grows over time if and only if the market interest rate exceeds the subjective discount rate. When the market interest rate is relatively high, consumers want to save more now and spend more later, resulting on positive growth in per capita consumption expenditure over time. Fourth, training/employment decisions are made to maximize each family's discounted wage income, which is equivalent to maximizing each member's discounted wage income. The latter depends on whether the individual member earns the unskilled wage or becomes a skilled worker and then earns the skilled wage. It is optimal for an individual with ability θ born at time t to train and become a skilled worker if and only if

$$\int_t^\infty e^{-[R(s)-R(t)]} w_L(s)\,ds < \int_{t+T}^\infty e^{-[R(s)-R(t)]} \theta w_H(s)\,ds. \tag{6}$$

The left-hand side (LHS) of inequality (6) equals the discounted wage income of an individual from being employed as an unskilled worker and earning the wage w_L from time t on. The RHS of (6) is the lifetime income of a skilled worker, who earns zero income during her training period and θw_H from time $t+T$ on.

I focus on the model's steady-state equilibrium properties where w_L, w_H and c_θ are all constants over time. Then (5) implies that $r(t) = \rho$ for all t. Condition (6) can be used to determine endogenously the steady-state supply of unskilled labor. Because the RHS of (6) is increasing in θ, whereas the LHS is independent of θ, there exists a level of ability denoted by θ_0 such that (6) holds as an equality. All individuals with ability lower than θ_0 choose to remain unskilled, and all individuals with ability greater than θ_0 undergo training and then enter the labour force as skilled workers. Setting (6) to hold as an equality yields $\int_t^\infty e^{-\rho(s-t)} w_L\,ds = \int_{t+T}^\infty e^{-\rho(s-t)} \theta_0 w_H\,ds$, which simplifies to $w_L/\rho = e^{-\rho T} \theta_0 w_H/\rho$. Solving for the steady-state value of θ_0 then yields

$$\theta_0 = \frac{w_L}{w_H} e^{\rho T}. \tag{7}$$

Equation (7) implies that the wage of a skilled worker θw_H must always be higher than the wage of any unskilled worker w_L. An increase in the duration of training T or in the relative wage of unskilled labour w_L/w_H increases the fraction of the population that chooses to remain unskilled θ_0. The supply of unskilled labour in each country at time t, $L(t)$, equals the number of individuals in the population that choose to remain unskilled:

$$L(t) = \theta_0 N(t). \tag{8}$$

The derivation of the steady-state supply of skilled labour at time t is slightly more complicated. A fraction $(1 - \theta_0)$ of each country's population train and become skilled workers, and therefore $(1 - \theta_0)N(t)$ individuals either work as skilled workers or are training to become skilled workers in each country at time t. In this sub-population, the skilled workers are the older individuals, namely, those individuals who were born before $t - T$:

$$\int_{-\infty}^{t-T} n(1 - \theta_0)N(s)\,ds = n(1 - \theta_0)\int_{-\infty}^{t-T} N_0 e^{ns}\,ds = (1 - \theta_0)e^{-nT}N(t). \tag{9}$$

The average skill level of workers $\theta \in [\theta_0, 1]$ that have finished training equals $(\theta_0 + 1)/2$ and therefore the supply of skilled labour at time t, measured in efficiency units of human capital, is given by $H(t) = \frac{(\theta_0+1)(1-\theta_0)}{2}e^{-nT}N(t)$ or more simply

$$H(t) = \frac{[1-(\theta_0)^2]}{2}e^{-nT}N(t). \tag{10}$$

It is obvious from equations (7), (8) and (10) that a decline in the relative wage of unskilled workers decreases θ_0 and $L(t)$, and increases $H(t)$, resulting in a rise of skilled labour abundance $H(t)/L(t)$ in each country. In the steady-state equilibrium, each country's factor supplies grow at the same rate as the population because θ_0 is constant over time: $\frac{\dot{H}(t)}{H(t)} = \frac{\dot{L}(t)}{L(t)} = \frac{\dot{N}(t)}{N(t)} = n$.

3.2   Product markets

There is a continuum of industries in each country indexed by $\omega \in [0, 1]$. In each industry, firms produce final consumption goods using unskilled labour. Firms compete in prices and maximize their expected discounted profits. For every firm that knows how to produce a good, one unit of unskilled labour produces one unit of output and production is characterized by constant returns to scale. Thus, each firm has a constant marginal cost of production equal to w_L. There are also trade costs separating the two countries that take the 'iceberg' form: $\tau > 1$ units of a good must be produced and exported in order to have one unit arriving at its destination. Thus, the marginal cost of a firm serving the domestic market is w_L and the marginal cost of a firm serving the foreign market is τw_L. I treat the unskilled wage as the numeraire price ($w_L = 1$), that is, I measure all prices relative to the price of unskilled labour.

In each industry, I will refer to the firms that produce the state-of-the-art quality product as 'quality leaders' and I will use the term 'quality followers' to refer to firms producing a product one quality step below the highest-quality product. When a firm wins a R&D race and becomes a quality leader, it receives a patent to exclusively produce the new product and sell it to all consumers in the world. This patent expires (or ceases to be enforced) when further innovation occurs in the industry. All products that are not protected by patents can be produced competitively in both countries.

I will refer to the two countries as Home and Foreign. Consider a Home quality leader that exports its product to the Foreign market (the analysis of the exporting behaviour of a Foreign quality leader is identical because of structural symmetry between the two countries). Because unit costs of all Foreign quality followers are identical ($w_L = 1$) and Home quality followers have higher unit costs when serving the Foreign market ($\tau w_L > w_L$), Home leaders compete against a competitive fringe of Foreign followers in the Foreign market (and against a competitive fringe of Home followers in the Home market).

Let Q_ℓ^* denote the output that the Home leader sells to Foreign consumers, let P_ℓ^* denote the price that Foreign consumers pay for the state-of-the-art quality product, let Q_f^* denote the output of Foreign followers, and let P_f^* denote the price that Foreign followers charge Foreign consumers. With the competitive fringe of Foreign followers charging the competitive price $P_f^* = 1$, the profit flow earned by the Home leader from selling to Foreign consumers is

$$\pi_\ell^* = \begin{cases} P_\ell^* Q_\ell^* - \tau Q_\ell^* & \text{if } P_\ell^* \leq \lambda \\ 0 & \text{if } P_\ell^* > \lambda. \end{cases}$$

If the price charged by the Home leader is too high ($P_\ell^* > \lambda$), then all Foreign consumers buy from Foreign followers. The Home leader has to charge a sufficiently low price to attract Foreign consumers ($P_\ell^* \leq \lambda$) and I assume that in the borderline case ($P_\ell^* = \lambda$) where consumers are indifferent, they only buy from the firm selling the higher quality product (the Home leader). Taking into account that consumer demand is unit elastic, the profit flow earned by the Home leader becomes

$$\pi_\ell^* = \begin{cases} P_\ell^* \frac{c^* N^*(t)}{P_\ell^*} - \tau \frac{c^* N^*(t)}{P_\ell^*} & \text{if } P_\ell^* \leq \lambda \\ 0 & \text{if } P_\ell^* > \lambda, \end{cases}$$

where c^* is the per capita consumption expenditure in the Foreign country and $N^*(t)$ is the number of consumers in the Foreign country. Assuming that $\tau \in (1, \lambda)$, this profit flow is maximized by charging the limit price $P_\ell^* = \lambda > 1$. In equilibrium the Home leader sells $Q_\ell^* = c^* N^*(t)/\lambda$, Foreign followers sell $Q_f^* = 0$ and the Home leader earns the profit flow

$$\pi_\ell^* = c^* N^*(t) \left[1 - \frac{\tau}{\lambda}\right].$$

Note that trade liberalization ($\tau \downarrow$) contributes to increasing the profits earned from exporting.

Because a Home quality leader faces segmented markets and does not incur the trade cost τ when selling to Home consumers, the analysis of price competition in the Home market is identical to the analysis in the Foreign market when $\tau = 1$. The Home quality leader charges the limit price $P_\ell = \lambda > 1$ to Home consumers, the Home leader sells $Q_\ell = cN(t)/\lambda$ to Home consumers, Home followers sell $Q_f = 0$ to Home consumers and the Home leader earns the profit flow

$$\pi_\ell = cN(t) \left[1 - \frac{1}{\lambda}\right],$$

where c and $N(t)$ are per capita consumption expenditure and population in the Home country. Structural symmetry across the two countries implies that $c = c^*$ and $N(t) = N^*(t)$. Therefore, each quality leader (Home or Foreign) exports the state-of-the-art quality product as well as sells to domestic consumers and earns the global profit flow

$$\pi \equiv \pi_\ell + \pi_\ell^* = cN(t) \left[2 - \frac{1 + \tau}{\lambda}\right]. \tag{11}$$

The product market equilibrium has three interesting features. First, only the state-of-the-art quality products are produced and traded. Second, all followers charge the same price $P_f = P_f^* = 1$ which is used as the numeraire, and all quality leaders charge the same price $P_\ell = P_\ell^* = \lambda > 1$ since they are price-constrained by domestic follower firms selling inferior quality goods. Third, trade liberalization ($\tau \downarrow$) does not have any effect on relative prices (of domestically produced goods versus imported ones) but increases the global profit flows of quality leaders [$\tau \downarrow \Longrightarrow \pi \uparrow$].

Because trade liberalization has no effect on domestic relative prices in either country, any effect that trade liberalization has on relative wages (w_H/w_L) must operate through some channel other than the traditional Stolper–Samuelson mechanism. The previously established property that a reduction in τ directly increases the global profit flows of quality leaders will turn out to be significant.

3.3   R&D

There are sequential and stochastic R&D races in each industry $\omega \in [0, 1]$. These races result in the discovery of higher-quality products. Only skilled workers can engage in R&D activities, unskilled workers being employed in production activities. All firms participating in a R&D race use the same R&D technology and there is free entry into each race.

A firm i that hires $h_i(\omega, t)$ skilled workers to engage in R&D in industry ω at time t is successful in discovering the next higher quality product with instantaneous probability

$$I_i(\omega, t) = \frac{h_i(\omega, t)}{X(\omega, t)}, \tag{12}$$

where $X(\omega, t)$ is a function that captures the difficulty of conducting R&D. By instantaneous probability (or Poisson arrival rate), I mean that $I_i(\omega, t)\,dt$ is the probability that the firm will innovate by time $t + dt$ conditional on not having innovated by time t, where dt is an infinitesimal increment of time. This R&D technology was introduced in Segerstrom (1998).

The returns to R&D investment are independently distributed across firms, across industries, and over time. Thus the industry-wide instantaneous probability of success in industry ω at time t is $I(\omega, t) = \sum_i I_i(\omega, t)$ in the Home country and $I^*(\omega, t) = \sum_i I_i^*(\omega, t)$ in the Foreign country. The global arrival of innovations in each industry is governed by a Poisson process whose intensity equals $I(\omega, t) + I^*(\omega, t)$. Higher levels of R&D investment increase the expected frequency of innovations and result in a higher rate of technological change.

Concerning the function $X(\omega, t)$, I assume that R&D starts off being equally difficult in all industries [$X(\omega, 0) = X_0$ for all ω where $X_0 > 0$ is a constant] and the level of R&D difficulty grows over time according to

$$\frac{\dot{X}(\omega, t)}{X(\omega, t)} = \mu[I(\omega, t) + I^*(\omega, t)], \tag{13}$$

where $\mu > 0$ is a constant. This differential equation captures the notion that ideas that are easier to discover tend to be discovered earlier in time. The assumption $\mu > 0$ is the reason why the model does not have the scale effect property. In the first-generation endogenous growth model by Grossman and Helpman (1991), $\mu = 0$ is assumed and consequently the long-run economic growth rate is an increasing function of population size in their model.

I solve the model for a symmetric steady-state equilibrium where both Home and Foreign innovation rates are constant over time and do not vary across industries, that is, $I(\omega, t) = I = I^*(\omega, t) = I^*$ for all ω and t. It immediately follows from (13) that X does not vary across industries, that is, $X(\omega, t) = X(t)$ for all ω and t. Furthermore, I solve for a steady-state equilibrium where relative R&D difficulty $x(t) \equiv X(t)/N(t)$ is constant over time. Thus $X(t)$ grows over time at the constant population growth rate n and it follows that $\dot{X}(t)/X(t) = \mu[I + I^*] = \mu 2I = n$ fully determines the steady-state innovation rate

$$I = I^* = \frac{n}{2\mu}. \tag{14}$$

Given the steady-state innovation rate, I can solve for the corresponding steady-state growth rate of consumer utility. By substituting for consumer demand $q_\theta = c_\theta/\lambda$ into the representative consumer's static utility function (2), I obtain

$$\ln u_\theta(t) = \int_0^1 \ln\left[\lambda^{j(\omega,t)} \frac{c_\theta}{\lambda}\right] d\omega$$

$$= \ln c_\theta - \ln \lambda + \int_0^1 \ln \lambda^{j(\omega,t)} d\omega,$$

where $j(\omega, t)$ is the number of quality improvements in industry ω from time 0 to time t. The last integral in this expression grows over time in the steady-state equilibrium as new higher-quality products are continuously being introduced. The value of this integral equals $(I + I^*)t \ln \lambda$ or $2It \ln \lambda$. Thus, in the steady-state equilibrium, each consumer's utility grows at the deterministic rate

$$g_u \equiv \frac{\dot{u}_\theta(t)}{u_\theta(t)} = 2I \ln \lambda = \frac{n}{\mu} \ln \lambda. \tag{15}$$

The utility growth rate g_u is completely determined by the exogenous rate of population growth n, the R&D difficulty growth parameter μ and the innovation size parameter λ. Utility growth is higher when the population of consumers grows more rapidly, when R&D difficulty increases more slowly over time and when innovations are of larger size. Since this utility growth rate is also the real wage growth rate, it is the proper measure of economic growth in the model.

Equations (14) and (15) have two important implications. First, they imply that public policy changes like trade liberalization (a decrease in τ) have no effect on the steady-state rate of innovation I and hence the steady-state rate of economic growth g_u. In this model, growth is 'semi-endogenous.' I view this as a virtue of the model because both total factor productivity and per capita GDP growth rates have been remarkably stable over time in spite of many public policy changes that one might think would be growth-promoting. For example, plotting data on per capita GDP (in logs) for the United States from 1880 to 1987, Jones (1995a) shows that a simple linear trend fits the data extremely well. This data leads me to be skeptical about models in which public policy changes have large long-run growth effects. Second, they imply that the level of per capita income in the long run is an increasing function of the size of the economy (because positive population growth is associated with positive economic growth). Jones (2005) has a lengthy discussion of this 'weak scale effect' property and cites Alcala and Ciccone (2004) as providing the best empirical support. Controlling for both trade and institutional quality, Alcala and Ciccone (2004) find that a 10 percent increase in the size of the workforce in the long run is associated with 2.5 percent higher GDP per worker.[1]

3.4   R&D incentives

There is a global stock market that channels consumer savings to firms that engage in R&D. Because there is a continuum of industries with simultaneous R&D races, consumers can diversify completely the industry-specific risk and earn the risk-free interest rate $r = \rho$. Each firm engaged in R&D issues a security that pays the flow of monopoly profits if the firm wins the R&D race and zero if it does not win the race. Let $v(t)$ denote the expected discounted profits of a successful firm (i.e. quality leader) in each industry at time t. Because each quality leader is targeted by R&D firms in both countries that try to discover the next higher quality product, the shareholder suffers a loss $v(t)$ if further innovation occurs.[2] This event occurs with probability $[I + I^*]dt$ during the time interval dt, whereas the event of no innovation occurs with probability $1 - [I + I^*]dt$. Over the time interval dt, the shareholder of a stock issued by a successful R&D firm receives a dividend $\pi(t)dt$ and the value of the firm appreciates by $\dot{v}(t)dt$. The stock market values the firm so that its expected rate of return just equals the riskless rate of return r:

$$\frac{\dot{v}(t)}{v(t)}[1 - (I + I^*)dt]dt - \frac{v(t) - 0}{v(t)}[I + I^*]dt + \frac{\pi(t)}{v(t)}dt = r\,dt.$$

Dividing both sides by dt and then taking the limit as $dt \to 0$ yields $\frac{\dot{v}(t)}{v(t)} - [I + I^*] + \frac{\pi(t)}{v(t)} = r$, which can be rewritten as

$$v(t) = \frac{\pi(t)}{r + I + I^* - \dot{v}(t)/v(t)}. \tag{16}$$

The global profit flow π earned by a quality leader is appropriately discounted using the instantaneous market interest rate r and the instantaneous probability $I + I^*$ of being driven out of business by further innovation (the creative-destruction effect). Also taken into account in (16) are the capital gains $\dot{v}/v$ that accrue to the firm as the world economy grows.

Consider a firm i that is located in the Home country and engages in R&D. This firm chooses its R&D intensity I_i to maximize its expected discounted profits, that is, it solves the problem

$$\max_{I_i} v(t)I_i\, dt - w_H X(t)I_i\, dt.$$

Free entry into each R&D race drives these expected discounted profits down to zero and implies that $v(t) = w_H X(t)$, which can be rewritten as

$$\frac{v(t)}{X(t)} = \frac{w_H}{w_L}. \tag{17}$$

In steady-state equilibrium, the reward for innovating $v(t)$ increases over time as the economy grows but $X(t)$ also increases over time as innovating becomes progressively more difficult. The ratio $v(t)/X(t)$ measures the reward for innovating relative to its cost and can be thought of as the 'relative price of innovation'. Equation (17) implies that there is a direct relationship between the relative price of innovation $v(t)/X(t)$ and the relative wage of skilled workers w_H/w_L. This is a Schumpeterian version of the Stolper–Samuelson mechanism. I will show that trade liberalization increases the relative price of innovation and consequently the relative wage of skilled workers.

Since $X(t)$ grows at the constant rate n, the free entry condition $v(t) = w_H X(t)$ implies that $v(t)$ also grows at the constant rate n. Using (11) and (14), it follows that the free entry condition becomes

$$v(t) = \frac{cN(t)\left[2 - \frac{1+\tau}{\lambda}\right]}{\rho + I + I^* - \dot{v}/v} = w_H X(t).$$

Dividing both sides by $N(t)$, I obtain the steady-state R&D condition:

$$\frac{c\left[2 - \frac{1+\tau}{\lambda}\right]}{\rho + 2I - n} = w_H x. \tag{18}$$

The LHS is the market size-adjusted benefit from innovating and the RHS is the market size-adjusted cost of innovating. In steady-state calculations, I need to adjust for market size because market size changes over time. The market size-adjusted benefit from innovating is higher when the average consumer buys more ($c \uparrow$), there are lower trade costs associated with exporting ($\tau \downarrow$), future profits are less heavily discounted ($\rho \downarrow$), quality leaders are less threatened by further innovation ($I \downarrow$) and quality leaders experience larger capital gains over time

($n \uparrow$). The market size-adjusted cost of innovating is higher when skilled workers earn a higher wage ($w_H \uparrow$), and innovating is relatively more difficult ($x \uparrow$).

3.5 Labour markets

Labour markets are perfectly competitive, workers are perfectly mobile across industries and wages adjust instantaneously to equate labour demand and labour supply. Because both countries are structurally identical, I concentrate on the derivation of equilibrium for the Home country.

The demand for unskilled labour comes from production by quality leaders since only quality leaders produce in equilibrium and only skilled labour is employed in R&D activities. The assumption of structurally identical countries implies that 50 percent of the world's quality leaders are Home firms and 50 percent are Foreign firms. In industries with a Home quality leader (exporting industries), total output produced equals $Q_\ell + \tau Q_\ell^*$. The Home quality leader produces output Q_ℓ for the Home market and, taking into account trade costs, the Home quality leader needs to produce output τQ_ℓ^* at Home in order to sell output Q_ℓ^* in the Foreign market. In industries with a Foreign quality leader, total Home output is zero. Therefore, the total output produced in the Home country is

$$q \equiv \frac{Q_\ell + \tau Q_\ell^*}{2} = \frac{cN(t)(1+\tau)}{2\lambda},$$

where q is the average quantity of final output produced in each industry. The Home demand for unskilled labour is given by q and the supply of unskilled labour is given by equation (8). Full employment of unskilled labour implies that $L(t) = \theta_0 N(t) = cN(t)(1+\tau)/2\lambda$. Dividing both sides by $N(t)$ yields a market size-adjusted version of the full-employment condition for unskilled labour:

$$\theta_0 = \frac{c(1+\tau)}{2\lambda}.$$

This equation can be rewritten in a more convenient form by substituting for the unknown c. Equation (7) implies that $w_H = e^{\rho T}/\theta_0$ and then equation (18) implies that

$$c = \frac{(\rho + 2I - n)e^{\rho T} x}{\left[2 - \frac{1+\tau}{\lambda}\right]\theta_0}.$$

Substituting for c yields the *steady-state unskilled labour condition* in (x, θ_0) space:

$$(\theta_0)^2 = \frac{(\rho + 2I - n)e^{\rho T}(1+\tau)}{\left[2 - \frac{1+\tau}{\lambda}\right]2\lambda} x. \tag{19}$$

Equation (19) is a full employment condition for unskilled labour that takes into account the implications of profit-maximizing R&D behaviour by firms. An increase in θ_0 increases the LHS, so x must increase on the RHS to restore equality in (19), given that I is pinned down by (14). It follows that the steady-state unskilled labour condition is upward-sloping in (x, θ_0) space.

The intuition behind the upward slope is as follows: Suppose that there is a decline in the skilled wage w_H, making it less attractive for workers to acquire skills and increasing the supply of unskilled labour ($\theta_0 \uparrow$). In steady-state equilibrium, any increase in the supply of unskilled labour must be matched by an increase in the demand for unskilled labour. But firms only want to hire more unskilled workers in production (the only activity where they are employed by assumption) if there is stronger consumer demand for their products. Stronger consumer demand increases the benefit from innovating and the initial fall in the skilled wage w_H decreases the cost of innovating. Profit-maximizing firms respond to these incentives by devoting more resources to R&D, resulting in a long-run increase in relative R&D difficulty x. Thus, to satisfy both labour-market clearing and R&D optimization conditions, any increase in the supply of unskilled labour ($\theta_0 \uparrow$) must be matched by an increase in consumer expenditure, which stimulates R&D investment and serves to raise the long-run level of relative R&D difficulty x.

The demand for skilled labour comes from R&D since only unskilled labour is employed in production activities. The Home demand for skilled labour in industry ω at time t is $X(t)I$. Since there is a measure one of industries where Home firms do R&D, the country-wide demand for skilled labour is also $X(t)I$. The Home supply of skilled labour is given by equation (10). Full employment of skilled labour then implies that $H(t) = \frac{[1-(\theta_0)^2]}{2} e^{-nT} N(t) = X(t)I$. Dividing both sides by $N(t)$, I obtain a market size-adjusted version of the full-employment condition for skilled labour:

$$\frac{[1 - (\theta_0)^2]}{2} e^{-nT} = xI,$$

where I have used the steady-state property that relative R&D difficulty $x \equiv X(t)/N(t)$ is constant over time. Rearranging terms yields the *steady-state skilled labour condition* in (x, θ_0) space:

$$1 - (\theta_0)^2 = [2Ie^{nT}]x. \tag{20}$$

Equation (20) is a full employment condition for skilled labour that takes into account the skill acquisition process. An increase in θ_0 decreases the LHS, so x must decrease on the RHS to restore equality in (19), given that I is pinned down by (14). It follows that the steady-state skilled labour condition is downward-sloping in (x, θ_0) space.

The intuition behind the downward slope is straightforward: Suppose that there is a decline in the skilled wage w_H, making it less attractive for workers to acquire skills and decreasing the supply of skilled labour ($\theta_0 \uparrow$). In steady-state equilibrium, any decrease in the supply of skilled labour must be matched by a decrease in the demand for skilled labour. Since the steady-state innovation rate $I = n/2\mu$ is constant and given by parameter values, firms only hire less skilled workers in R&D (the only activity where they are employed by assumption) if R&D becomes relatively less difficult ($x \downarrow$). Thus, to satisfy market clearing for skilled labour, any decrease in the supply of skilled labour ($\theta_0 \uparrow$) must be matched by a decrease in the demand for skilled labour in R&D and this only occurs if R&D becomes relatively less difficult ($x \downarrow$).

3.6 Steady-state equilibrium properties

Taking into account that $I = n/2\mu$ determines the steady-state innovation rate in each country, solving the model for a symmetric steady-state equilibrium reduces to solving the system of two equations (19) and (20) in two unknowns $[x, \theta_0]$. These equations are illustrated in figure 19.1 and are labeled 'Unskilled' and 'Skilled', respectively. Given that the steady-state unskilled labour condition is globally upward-sloping and goes through the origin, and the steady-state skilled labour condition is globally downward-sloping with strictly positive intercepts, these two curves must have a unique intersection. Thus, the steady-state equilibrium values of x and θ_0 are uniquely determined and are given by point A in figure 19.1. Since (7) then uniquely determines w_H, I have fully solved the model and have established.

Theorem 1 *The model has a unique symmetric steady-state equilibrium.*

It is now straightforward to determine the steady-state equilibrium effects of trade liberalization that takes the form of a permanent reduction in trade costs τ. A decrease in τ has no effect on the skilled labour condition (20) but causes

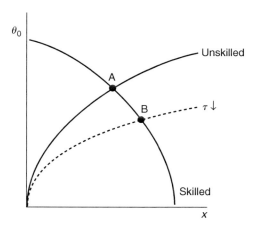

Figure 19.1   Steady-state equilibrium properties.

the RHS of the unskilled labour condition (19) to decrease for any given value of x. Thus, the unskilled labour condition shifts down as illustrated in figure 19.1 and there is a new intersection of the two curves given by point B. A decrease in τ leads to a permanent decrease in θ_0 and a permanent increase in x.

From (7), the permanent decrease in θ_0 is associated with a permanent increase in w_H. To see the implications of the permanent increase in x, I take logs and differentiate the definition $x(t) \equiv X(t)/N(t)$ to obtain

$$\frac{\dot{x}(t)}{x(t)} = \frac{\dot{X}(t)}{X(t)} - \frac{\dot{N}(t)}{N(t)} = 2I\mu - n. \tag{21}$$

In any steady-state equilibrium, $I = n/2\mu$ implies that x is constant over time ($\dot{x}(t) = 0$). Thus, for x to permanently increase, the global innovation rate in each industry $2I$ must temporarily increase above its steady-state level $2I = \frac{n}{\mu}$. I have established

Theorem 2 *Trade liberalization that takes the form of a permanent reduction in trade costs ($\tau \downarrow$) leads to*

(1) a permanent increase in the relative wage of skilled labour ($w_H/w_L \uparrow$),
(2) a permanent increase in the fraction of the population that chooses to acquire skills ($\theta_0 \downarrow$), and
(3) a temporary increase in the global innovation rate in each industry ($2I \uparrow$).

Although it has taken a good deal of work to solve this model, its properties are quite intuitive. When trade costs fall, firms earn higher profits from exporting their products and consequently their overall profits increase [$\tau \downarrow \Longrightarrow \pi \uparrow$ from equation (11)]. Because these profits are a reward for developing better products, it follows that when trade costs fall, firms have a stronger incentive to develop better products [$\tau \downarrow \Longrightarrow v(t) \uparrow$ from equation (16)]. The demand by firms for skilled workers capable of doing R&D increases, bidding up the relative wage of skilled labour [$w_H/w_L \uparrow$]. When workers see that the reward for becoming skilled has gone up, more workers choose to undergo the training needed to acquire skills [$w_H/w_L \uparrow \Longrightarrow \theta_0 \downarrow$ from equation (7)], R&D employment increases [$\theta_0 \downarrow \Longrightarrow (1 - \theta_0)e^{-nT}N(t) \uparrow$ from equation (9)] and the global economy experiences a faster rate of technological change [$x \uparrow \Longrightarrow 2I \uparrow$ from equation (21)]. The model highlights a potentially very important benefit of trade liberalization, namely, that it promotes technological change.

3.7 Robustness of results

The above-described model has some strong assumptions and the question naturally arises, how do the results change when these assumptions are relaxed? In this subsection, I discuss the robustness of the results obtained in Theorem 2.

Several of the strong assumptions are made to keep the model as simple as possible and are not critical to driving the results in Theorem 2. As shown in

Dinopoulos and Segerstrom (1999), the results in Theorem 2 continue to hold when iceberg trade costs are replaced by tariffs and when firms set quantities instead of prices. The strong assumption that production uses only unskilled labour and R&D uses only skilled labour is relaxed in Dinopoulos and Segerstrom (1999), who study the general case where both activities (production and R&D) uses both factors as inputs (unskilled and skilled labour). They find that Theorem 2 continues to hold under the reasonable assumption that R&D is the skill-intensive activity (for given factor prices, R&D uses a higher ratio of skilled to unskilled labour than the production of goods). They also show that the issue of whether economic growth is 'semi-endogenous' (public policies have no long-run growth effects) or 'fully-endogenous' (public policies have long-run growth effects) is not critical in driving their results. When the assumption that leads to semi-endogenous growth $[\dot{X}(\omega,t)/X(\omega,t)=\mu(I(\omega,t)+I^*(\omega,t))$ where $\mu > 0]$ is replaced by an assumption that leads to fully endogenous growth $[X(\omega,t)=\mu N(t)$ where $\mu > 0]$, the only change in Theorem 2 is that trade liberalization leads to a permanent (instead of temporary) increase in the innovation rate.

One strong assumption that is not relaxed in Dinopoulos and Segerstrom (1999) is the assumption that the elasticity of substitution in consumption equals one. This assumption is implicit in equation (2) and results in unit elastic consumer demand. It is a useful exercise (left to the reader) to solve the model when the static utility function in (2) is replaced by the more general CES utility function

$$u_\theta(t) \equiv \left\{ \int\limits_0^1 \left[\sum_j \lambda^j q_\theta(j,\omega,t) \right]^\alpha d\omega \right\}^{1/\alpha},$$

where $\alpha \in (0,1)$ is a preference parameter and $\sigma \equiv \frac{1}{1-\alpha} > 1$ is the constant elasticity of substitution in consumption.[3] To obtain that a steady-state equilibrium exists, the R&D technology must be modified when $\sigma > 1$. Following Li (2003), suppose that (12) is replaced by the more general R&D technology

$$I_i(\omega,t) = \frac{h_i(\omega,t)}{X(\omega,t)q(\omega,t)},$$

where $q(\omega,t) \equiv \lambda^{(\sigma-1)j(\omega,t)}$ is an alternative measure of product quality in industry ω at time t and $j(\omega,t)$ is the number of innovations in industry ω from time 0 to time t. Then R&D difficulty increases over time in each industry because of research failures (increases in X) and also because of research successes (increases in q).

Solving this modified model, I find that the results depend on whether or not innovative firms face effective competition in product markets. When innovative firms face effective competition and practice limit-pricing $[\tau/\alpha > \lambda]$, then trade liberalization increases the overall profits earned by innovative firms [$\tau \downarrow \Longrightarrow \pi \uparrow$] and consequently, has the same effects as in Theorem 2 [$\tau \downarrow \Longrightarrow w_H/w_L \uparrow, \theta_0 \downarrow, 2I \uparrow$]. However, when innovative firms do not face effective competition and charge monopoly prices [$\tau/\alpha < \lambda$], then trade liberalization has no effect on the overall profits earned by innovative firms [$\tau \downarrow \Longrightarrow \pi$ unchanged] and consequently, has no effect on the relative wage of skilled labour, skill-acquisition choices or the rate of technological change [$\tau \downarrow \Longrightarrow w_H/w_L, \theta_0, 2I$ unchanged]. The case $\tau/\alpha > \lambda$ has to hold if τ is sufficiently high but the case $\tau/\alpha < \lambda$ can occur if τ is low. Thus, trade liberalization definitely promotes technological change in the modified model when trade costs are high but can have no effect on the innovation rate when trade costs are low.

The above-mentioned analysis helps to shed light on the otherwise puzzling results in Baldwin and Forslid (2000). They present a model with increasing product variety and find that trade liberalization has no effect on the rate of technological change. In the Baldwin-Forslid model, firms charge monopoly prices in all product markets and never face effective competition since no product is ever improved upon by other firms or copied. Because monopoly pricing always prevails in product markets, trade liberalization has no effect on the overall profits earned by innovative firms [$\tau \downarrow \Longrightarrow \pi$ unchanged]. Effective competition in product markets is crucial to the results derived in Theorem 2.

4 Conclusion

This chapter provides an introduction to the literature on trade and growth. I discuss a variety of models where trade liberalization promotes technological change. Since the literature on trade and growth is challenging to read, I also present a fully worked out model of trade and growth. My reason for focusing on models where trade liberalization is growth-promoting is that such models have better empirical support than models where trade liberalization is growth-retarding. In the most careful study of the evidence to date, Wacziarg and Welch (2008) find that the typical country grows at an average annual rate of 1.1 percent before trade liberalization and its average annual growth rate jumps up to 2.5 percent after trade liberalization. Countries experience significantly higher growth rates after opening up to international trade.

Appendix

In this appendix, household optimization calculations are spelled out in more detail. In what follows, I omit the subscript θ for notational simplicity. The household's optimization problem can be solved in four steps.

The first step is to solve for the allocation of consumer expenditure across products within a particular industry ω at time t. Since all products in an industry are perfect substitutes by assumption (equation 2) and only differ in their quality, consumers only buy the product(s) with the lowest quality adjusted price $p(j, \omega, t)/\lambda^j$. The easiest way to see this is to solve the simple consumer optimization problem $\max_{q_1, q_2} q_1 + \lambda q_2$ subject to $p_1 q_1 + p_2 q_2 = c$, $q_1 \geq 0$ and $q_2 \geq 0$. The solution is to only buy good 1 if $p_1 < p_2/\lambda$ and only buy good 2 if $p_1 > p_2/\lambda$.

The second step is to solve for the allocation of individual consumer expenditure $c(t)$ across industries at time t. For the set of products with the lowest quality-adjusted price in industry ω at time t, let $p(\omega, t)$ denote the price of the highest quality product and let $q(\omega, t)$ denote the quality-weighted quantity consumed of products, measured in units of the highest quality product. Then the static problem of allocating consumer expenditure across industries becomes

$$\max_{q(\cdot)} \int_0^1 \ln\left[\lambda^{j(\omega,t)} q(\omega, t)\right] d\omega \quad \text{s.t.} \quad c(t) = \int_0^1 p(\omega, t) q(\omega, t) d\omega,$$

where $j(\omega, t)$ equals the number of innovations in industry ω from time 0 at time t. This problem can be rewritten as the optimal control problem

$$\max_{q(\cdot)} \int_0^1 \ln\left[\lambda^{j(\omega,t)} q(\omega, t)\right] d\omega \ \text{s.t.} \ \frac{\partial y(\omega, t)}{\partial \omega} = p(\omega, t) q(\omega, t), \ y(0, t) = 0, \ y(1, t) = c(t),$$

where $y(\omega, t)$ is a new state variable. The Hamiltonian function for this optimal control problem is

$$H \equiv \ln\left[\lambda^{j(\omega,t)} q(\omega, t)\right] + \mu(\omega, t) p(\omega, t) q(\omega, t),$$

where $\mu(\omega, t)$ is the costate variable. The costate equation $\frac{\partial H}{\partial y} = 0 = -\frac{\partial \mu(\omega,t)}{\partial \omega}$ implies that $\mu(\omega, t)$ is constant across ω. Taking this into account, the first-order condition $\frac{\partial H}{\partial q} = \frac{1}{q(\omega,t)} + \mu(t) p(\omega, t) = 0$ implies that

$$q(\omega, t) = \frac{-1}{\mu(t) p(\omega, t)}.$$

Substituting this back into the budget constraint yields

$$c(t) = \int_0^1 p(\omega, t) q(\omega, t) d\omega = \int_0^1 p_t(\omega) \left[\frac{-1}{\mu(t) p(\omega, t)}\right] d\omega = \frac{-1}{\mu(t)}.$$

It immediately follows that the consumer demand function is unit elastic:

$$q(\omega, t) = \frac{c(t)}{p(\omega, t)}.$$

The third step is to maximize discounted utility (1) subject to the intertemporal budget constraint (4). Now

$$\ln u(t) = \int_0^1 \ln\left[\lambda^{j(\omega,t)}\frac{c(t)}{p(\omega,t)}\right]d\omega$$

$$= \int_0^1 \{\ln\lambda^{j(\omega,t)} + \ln c(t) - \ln p(\omega,t)\}d\omega$$

$$= \int_0^1 \ln\lambda^{j(\omega,t)}d\omega + \ln c(t) - \int_0^1 \ln p(\omega,t)d\omega.$$

The individual household takes both the innovation rate and the prices of all products as given, so the two integrals can be ignored in solving the household's dynamic optimization problem. This problem simplifies to

$$\max_{c(\cdot)} U \equiv \int_0^\infty N_0 e^{-(\rho-n)t}\ln c(t)\,dt$$

$$\text{s.t.} \quad y(0) = 0, \ \lim_{t\to+\infty} y(t) = W_\theta + Z_\theta, \ \dot{y}(t) = c(t)e^{[nt-R(t)]},$$

where $y(t)$ is a new state variable. The Hamiltonian function for this optimal control problem is

$$H \equiv N_0 e^{-(\rho-n)t}\ln c(t) + \mu(t)c(t)e^{[nt-R(t)]},$$

where $\mu(t)$ is the relevant costate variable. The costate equation $-\dot{\mu}(t) = \frac{\partial H}{\partial y} = 0$ implies that $\mu(t)$ is constant over time. Taking this into account, the first order condition is

$$\frac{\partial H}{\partial c} = N_0 e^{-(\rho-n)t}\frac{1}{c(t)} + \mu e^{[nt-R(t)]} = 0,$$

or $N_0 e^{-(\rho-n)t}/c(t) = -\mu e^{[nt-R(t)]}$. Taking logs of both sides yields $\ln N_0 - (\rho-n)t - \ln c(t) = \ln(-\mu) + [nt - R(t)]$ and then differentiating with respect to time yields $-(\rho-n) - \frac{\dot{c}(t)}{c(t)} = n - r(t)$ or

$$\frac{\dot{c}(t)}{c(t)} = r(t) - \rho. \tag{5}$$

The fourth step, making the training/employment decisions that maximize each household's discounted wage income, is described in the main text. Since each household's discounted utility is increasing in consumer expenditure and there is no disutility associated with training or working, each household maximizes its discounted utility by maximizing its discounted wage income.

Notes

* Stockholm School of Economics, Department of Economics.
This research was financially supported by the Wallander Foundation.

1. In spite of the arguments in Jones (2005), the issue of whether economic growth is 'semi-endogenous' (public policies have no long-run growth effects) or 'fully-endogenous' (public policies have long-run growth effects) remains controversial. For example, Ha and Howitt (2007) present evidence that fully endogenous growth models have better empirical support than semi-endogenous growth models. I think that their analysis has an important limitation. Ha and Howitt implicitly assume that convergence to steady-state is fast, so that with 50 years of data, they can just focus on the steady-state implications of growth models. This assumption is called into question in Steger (2003), who calibrates a semi-endogenous growth model using U.S. data and finds that convergence to steady-state is slow: it takes almost 40 years to go half the distance to the steady-state. With such slow convergence, I think that future tests of semi-endogenous growth theory should take into account the transition path implications of the models.

2. Because industry leaders have less to gain from innovating than follower firms, all R&D is done by follower firms in equilibrium. For a model in which industry leaders have cost advantages and thus engage in R&D, see Segerstrom (2007).

3. The static utility function in (2) emerges as the limiting special case when α converges to zero.

References

Aghion, Philippe, and Peter Howitt (1992) 'A model of growth through creative destruction', *Econometrica*, 60, 323–51.

Alcala, Francisco, and Antonio Ciccone (2004) 'Trade and productivity', *Quarterly Journal of Economics*, 199, 613–46.

Baldwin, Richard E., and Rikard Forslid (2000) 'Trade liberalization and endogenous growth: a q-Theory approach', *Journal of International Economics*, 50, 497–517.

Baldwin, Richard E., and Frederic Robert-Nicoud (2008) 'Trade and Growth with Heterogeneous Firms', *Journal of International Economics*, 74, 21–34.

Branstetter, Lee G., Raymond Fisman and C. Fritz Foley (2006) 'Does stronger intellectual property rights increase international technology transfer? Empirical evidence from U.S. firm-level panel data', *Quarterly Journal of Economics*, 121, 321–49.

Clerides, Sofronis K., Saul Lach and James R. Tybout (1998) 'Is learning by exporting important? Micro-dynamic evidence from Colombia, Mexico and Morocco', *Quarterly Journal of Economics*, 113, 903–47.

Dinopoulos, Elias, and Paul S. Segerstrom (1999) 'A Schumpeterian model of protection and relative wages', *American Economic Review*, 89, 450–72.

—— (2010) 'Intellectual property rights, multinational firms and economic growth', *Journal of Development Economics*, 92, 13–27.

Grossman, Gene M., and Elhanan Helpman (1990) 'Comparative advantage and long-run growth', *American Economic Review*, 80, 796–815.

—— (1991) 'Quality ladders in the theory of growth', *Review of Economic Studies*, 58, 43–61.

Gustafsson, Peter, and Paul S. Segerstrom (2010) 'Trade liberalization and productivity growth', *Review of International Economics*, 18, 207–228.

Ha, Joonkyung, and Peter Howitt (2007) 'Accounting for trends in productivity and R&D: A Schumpeterian critique of semi-endogenous growth theory', *Journal of Money Credit and Banking*, 33, 733–74.

Haruyama, Tetsugen, and Laixun Zhao (2008) 'Trade and firm heterogeneity in a quality-ladder model of growth', mimeo, Kobe University, Japan.

Howitt, Peter (1999) 'Steady endogenous growth with population and R&D inputs growing', *Journal of Political Economy*, 107, 715–30.

Jones, Charles I. (1995a) 'Time series tests of endogenous growth models', *Quarterly Journal of Economics*, 110, 495–525.

——(1995b) 'R&D-based models of economic growth', *Journal of Political Economy*, 103, 759–84.

——(2005) 'Growth and Ideas', in Aghion, P., and S. Durlauf (eds), *Handbook of Economic Growth*, Elsevier, 1063–111.

Kortum, Samuel (1997) 'Research, patenting and technological change', *Econometrica*, 65, 1389–419.

Krugman, Paul, and Maurice Obstfeld (2009) *International Economics: Theory and Policy*, 8th ed., Boston: Pearson/Addison-Wesley.

Li, Chol-Won (2003) 'Endogenous growth without scale effects: comment', *American Economic Review*, 93, 1009–17.

Lucas, Robert (1998) 'On the mechanics of economic development', *Journal of Monetary Economics*, 22, 3–42.

Melitz, Marc (2003) 'The impact of trade on intra-industry reallocations and aggregate industry productivity', *Econometrica*, 71, 1695–725.

Rivera-Batiz, Luis A., and Paul M. Romer (1991a) 'International trade with endogenous change', *European Economic Review*, 35, 971–1004.

——(1991b) 'Economic integration and endogenous growth', *Quarterly Journal of Economics*, 106, 531–55.

Rodriguez, Francisco, and Dani Rodrik (2000) 'Trade policy and economic growth: a skeptics guide to the cross-national evidence', in Ben Bernanke and Kenneth Rogoff (eds), *NBER Macroeconomics Annual 2000*, Cambridge, MA: MIT Press.

Romer, Paul M. (1990) 'Endogenous technological change', *Journal of Political Economy*, 98, S71–S102.

Sachs, Jeffrey D., and Andrew Warner (1995) 'Economic reform and the process of global integration', *Brookings Papers on Economic Activity*, 1, 1–118.

Segerstrom, Paul S. (1998) 'Endogenous growth without scale effects', *American Economic Review*, 88, 1290–1310.

——(2007) 'Intel economics', *International Economic Review*, 48, 247–80.

Segerstrom, Paul S., T.C.A. Anant and Elias Dinopoulos (1990) 'A Schumpeterian model of the product life cycle', *American Economic Review*, 80, 1077–92.

Solow, Robert M. (1956) 'A contribution to the theory of growth', *Quarterly Journal of Economics*, 70, 65–94.

Steger, Thomas (2003) 'The Segerstrom Model: stability, speed of convergence and policy implications', *Economics Bulletin*, 15, 1–8.

Wacziarg, Romain, and Karen H. Welch (2008) 'Trade liberalization and economic growth: new evidence', *World Bank Economic Review*, 22, 187–231.

Young, Alwyn (1998) 'Growth without scale effects', *Journal of Political Economy*, 106, 41–63.

20
Trade, Trade Policy and Development
*Chris Milner**

1 Introduction

Although the consensus has changed over time, the present consensus (in particular among those with a neoclassical training) is that openness to international
trade and outward-oriented trade strategies are in general beneficial for countries, including developing countries. Nonetheless, the underpinning of that
consensus by theory and empirical evidence gives rise to considerably more
controversy than might be inferred from the consensus on the net or overall
evaluation. In this chapter we seek to review the individual issues and controversies that exist in the theoretical and empirical literatures on the roles of trade
and trade policy in economic development.

In section 2 we explore why some economists have viewed trade as a potential source of impoverishment, while others emphasize the possible sources of
enrichment arising from increased international trade. One strand emphasizes
the effects of trade in the presence of pervasive market failures and structural
rigidities, while the other emphasizes the static and dynamic benefits of competition and market-led processes (and the dangers of policy failure). As we show
in section 3, and irrespective of the extent of market failure, the neoclassical
defence for liberal trade policies is the non-optimality of trade policy interventions in general to remedy domestic market failures. Interestingly, the criticism
of this position made by supporters of active or interventionist trade policies in
developing countries is that optimal intervention analysis calls for policy capacity and coordination beyond the administrative capability of most developing
countries. They also point to what they view as the selectively interventionist
trade and industrial policies of some of the successful East Asia exporters as providing empirical justification for their position. In section 4, therefore, we review
the issues around the selection of trade strategies, and whether export promotion can and should be achieved through import liberalization and by means of
mixed trade interventions in the export and import-substitution sectors. While

in section 5 we review the empirical evidence on the trade policy-development relationship, exploring also into the factors that seem to condition the effectiveness of trade policy reform to generate positive growth benefits. It is evident that the impacts of trade and trade policy reform are not, and should not be, divorced from a whole gamut of complementary policies. These are considered in section 6. Finally, the summary conclusions of the chapter are set out in section 7.

2   Role of Trade in Development

As explained in the previous section, the role of trade in development has generated considerable differences of opinion among economists. The aim of this section is to highlight the basis of this controversy, that is to understand why and under what conditions trade might be viewed as a source of impoverishment as opposed to a source of enrichment. Both the theoretical and empirical basis of each view will be investigated and evaluated.

2.1   Trade as a source of impoverishment

'Structuralism' has been an influential body of thought in the development literature in the period since the 1950s. Two key aspects of structuralist thinking are the viewing of developing countries as inflexible and the world as being subject to a 'core-periphery' dichotomy between the industrialized countries of the 'North' (producing income-elastic and technologically intensive goods subject to scale economies) and low productivity (relatively income-inelastic primary producing or low-tech manufacturing) developing countries of the 'South'. This representation of the world and developing countries was particularly influential in the post-independence stage of many developing countries in the 1950s and 1960s and in the policy stance and prescriptions of some of the new United Nations institutions of this period (e.g. United Nations Economic Commission for Latin America, whose first director was Raul Prebisch). These fundamental structural characteristics were viewed as steering the gains from trade towards the North and creating a dependency in the South on types of trade that would not allow structural change and technological development. The logic of this view was that interventionist government policies were required to deal with the pervasive market failures and to remove the bottlenecks and constraints on domestic structural change, and that dependence on traditional trade patterns needed to be reduced through inward-oriented industrialization strategies.

Terms of trade decline?

The idea that developing countries are faced with a secular tendency towards declining terms of trade can be traced back to the influential contributions of Singer (1950) and Prebisch (1950).

The argument is grounded in a simple North–South model of the world economy. Southern developing countries are labour abundant and primary products are labour intensive, thus southern countries specialize in and export primary products. In contrast northern countries are relatively capital abundant and manufactures are relatively capital intensive, thus the North specializes in and exports manufactures. So far this is simply a description of the simple H O S model. The tendency for the terms of trade to deteriorate is explained by the structural characteristics of world markets for primary commodities and manufactures. It is claimed that demand for primary commodities is income inelastic. In the case of 'soft' commodities this is simply an application of Engel's Law; in the case of 'hard' commodities it follows from the emergence of fabricated substitutes for natural products. Thus, as income grows in the North, the demand for primary products grows less proportionately. This places downward pressure on relative prices which is exacerbated by the fact that world markets in these products are highly competitive. The presence of surplus labour ensures that productivity gains are passed forward in the form of lower prices. In contrast world markets in manufactures are dominated by international firms and imperfectly competitive markets. The fruits of any productivity gains are captured by firms and organised labour. Moreover demand for manufactures is income elastic. Thus income growth keeps upward pressure on their prices.

The initial support for this thesis was provided by Prebisch (1950). His examination of the British net barter terms of trade over the period 1870–1930 led him to a belief in the chronic tendency to secularly declining terms of trade. The subsequent empirical evidence is less clear-cut. A review of the evidence by Spraos (Spraos, 1980) concluded that there was no discernable evidence of a decline in the terms of trade of developing countries. This is contested by Sapsford (1985), and Bleaney and Greenaway (1993) confirm a downward trend (see also a number of essays on this topic in Sapsford and Chen, 1998). It is clear, however, that the pattern is sensitive to the time period taken, and that there is considerable heterogeneity across developing countries, depending on the composition of their primary and manufactured exports. Further, the welfare implications of terms of trade changes are ambiguous in a time period when the quality of imported goods is also rapidly changing.

Export instability

The potential problem of export instability is often confused with that of a decline in the terms of trade, although conceptually it is quite separate. It has the same starting point, namely dependence on primary commodity exports and the structural characteristics emphasised are different here, namely price elasticities of supply and demand which are highly inelastic over the relevant range, and supply and demand schedules which are subject to random and unpredictable shocks. Thus (North) demand for soft commodities is price inelastic (since we are dealing primarily with foodstuffs), and these products are particularly susceptible to supply side shocks (due for instance to pestilence, adverse weather conditions and so on). Demand for hard commodities is also price inelastic. In this case, however, the problem is demand side shocks driven largely by cyclical movements in output in the North.

When demand and supply schedules are inelastic over the relevant range, small perturbations to supply and/or demand can result in relatively large perturbations to price. Moreover, if elasticities have the appropriate values, once the initial equilibrium is disturbed the adjustment path to a new equilibrium may be protracted and/or divergent. In some circumstances the classic 'cobweb adjustment' is possible. The essential point is that even if a cobweb does not result there may nevertheless be price instability which is then transmitted through to export earnings instability. One can certainly often find spectacular examples of this phenomenon. For example, the change in coffee prices in 1975 following the late frost in Brazil, the increase and decrease in hard commodity prices following the commodity price boom of the early 1970s, the aftermath of the oil shock of 1973–74 and so on. Concerns about this were influential in creating pressures for inward orientation. The argument is quite simple – to ameliorate the effects of export instability one must reduce dependence upon primary product exports. A means of accomplishing this is via planned diversification. But one might ask why producers need to be directed into the manufacturing sector. Why does this not come about naturally? The structuralist answer to this question is market failure. Many branches of manufacturing activity are infant industries. As such they require state support to nurture them. Of course the truth is that many developing countries have now diversified their production and exports, and it is difficult to say with confidence whether market forces or government intervention were more important in bringing this about.

Infant-industry protection?

The infant industry argument has been central to the policy debate in academic circles and in developing countries. It is an argument which is compatible with a range of market imperfections, and it has a very obvious and very seductive appeal in a developing country context.

The crudest infant industry arguments are framed by reference to scale economies. Established, mature producers benefit fully from scale economies. As a result they produce at minimum efficient scale and supply at minimum unit cost. So long as the scale curve is declining over the relevant range, developing countries are unable to compete. They do not have the market share required to compete, nor are there any immediate prospects of acquiring that share. Thus temporary protection serves to raise the selling price of mature competitors. This allows the new entrant to expand capacity, gain market share and move down the scale curve. In time the infant matures and the protection can be removed. However, as Johnson (1970), Baldwin (1969) and others have argued, scale economies in themselves do not constitute a defensible argument for infant-industry protection. After all, scale economies are a pervasive feature of manufacturing activity in industrialized countries and the capital market has a mechanism for dealing with them: all 'infant' producers have to do is demonstrate that once scale economies are fully exploited, profits will be sufficient to offset initial losses and guarantee a rate of return at least equivalent to what could be earned elsewhere. However, in a developing country the capital market may be missing or underdeveloped. For example, the inability to satisfactorily insure against possibly inappropriable returns to investment in physical and/or human capital can result in first-mover disadvantages. Alternatively, private discount rates may be significantly in excess of social discount rates. In such circumstances it is argued that infant industry protection is required. Since manufacturing activity is a key element in the industrial sector, and since the entire manufacturing sector may potentially be in its infancy, a structuralist perspective argues for widespread protection of manufacturing.

Even if there is a case for government intervention because there is a market failure deterring new entrant firms and/or the move to maturity of infant firms, then the issue of the optimal form and level of government intervention arises. Protection from imports by taxing or restricting imports is a possible means of infant industry support, but not necessarily the optimal form of government intervention; an issue discussed further in section 3 below. There is, however, a danger that the political economy pressures will be for governments to intervene where there are not market failures, or to give more and longer support than is required to deal with the market failure. Certainly there is a considerable amount of evidence of rent-seeking behaviour during the import-substitution periods of many developing countries, and of many infants not appearing to reach maturity (Bell, Ross-Larson and Westphal, 1984). Protection appears to have provided infants with access to rents and limited incentive to raise efficiency and capacity utilization in sheltered markets. The protection in turn becomes difficult for governments to remove. There is some evidence that the governments of South Korea and Taiwan were able to precommit and deliver on temporary protection (Lee, 1997; Pack, 1988). But the existence of a few such cases does not constitute a general defence of infant industry support, nor for giving infant industries an important role in trade policy design.

2.2   Trade as a source of enrichment

Most neoclassical economists tend to acknowledge the presence of market rigidities and failures, but typically do not view the problems as severe as structuralist economists nor view the remedy as requiring major departure from liberal trade policies. The greater influence of neoclassical thinking on policy formulation in developing countries from the 1980s onwards reflected the growing empirical evidence on, the costs of poorly designed interventionist and trade-restricting policies, the associated poor performance in developing countries, and on optimizing behaviour by economic agents in developing countries (Stern, 1989). It also reflected, however, renewed intellectual underpinning of the neoclassical basis for traditional gains from trade (Lal, 1983), and evidence of success in some of the outward-oriented developing countries in Asia (though the basis of this success is open to alternative interpretations). Of course some of the greater influence was also imposed on developing countries as part of their policy-conditioned lending from the World Bank and IMF.

Consumption and specialization gains

The lowering of trade barriers gives rise to opportunities for the standard (static) gains from trade in terms of consumption opportunities and the allocation of resources. Consumers face lower prices and increased choice and, although these are typically viewed as a source of net gains for an economy irrespective of the income levels of consumers affected, it is difficult not to view this as being a possible source of gain for poor consumers in many developing countries. Indeed the gross gains for consumers will be much larger than the net gains (which are often small relative to GDP), given that the lowering of trade barriers will tend to redistribute away from protected producers and government (in the form of reduced tariff revenue) or import licence holders (in the form of reduced import quota rents).

The production specialization gains associated with trade expansion may take longer to reap, given that an adjustment process is required. Indeed in the short term there may be no specialization gains if factors released from the more open, import-competing sector remain unemployed. (The issue of adjustment support policies is discussed in section 6.) However the releasing of resources from activities of comparative disadvantage creates the potential for expanding activities of comparative advantage, in particular exportable activities for which the market potential is much greater in the case of the many small developing countries than the domestic market for importables. With completely free trade, then, there may also be gains from the uniformity of incentives across activities (compared with the non-uniform trade policy interventions that are in place in developing countries). This removes the large allocative distortions or biases against exportables production, or specific sectors (e.g. against agricultural activities when trade policy was previously used to give particular support for industrial activity). But it also reduces the biases within sectors and across different stages of production, for example giving equal incentive to produce intermediate as final goods. This may become a more important consideration with the fragmentation of international production, and associated need for developing countries to specialize on specific stages of production. With the escalating tariff structures often in place, developing countries have tended to give higher effective protection for final than intermediate goods production (Greenaway and Milner, 1993). Indeed the distortionary effects of a non-uniform and escalating tariff structure tend to be compounded in many developing countries by other (non-trade policy) sources of trade costs. Poor transport infrastructure, uncompetitive transport services and inefficient ports in many low income and remote developing countries serve to exaggerate the resource misallocation effects of trade policy (Milner, 1997).

Scale and pro-competitive effects

Much standard trade analysis assumes competitive markets and production subject to constant or decreasing returns to scale. These may be appropriate assumptions often for activities in tradeable agricultural sectors, but for many manufacturing activities there may be a relatively high minimum scale of efficiency and correspondingly more concentrated markets. Advocates of open markets often argue, therefore, that one of the cases for the lowering of trade barriers is that openness to foreign competition limits the power of domestic monopolists or oligopolists to exercise market power and that, if there is scope for firm entry and exit, domestic industries have the scope to reorganize in the face of foreign competition in order to fully exploit scale economies. This type of argument is to be found extensively in the literature (Corden, 1974; Krueger, 1991; Dornbusch, 1992; and Krugman, 1993). The theoretical defence for this argument is in fact not as strong as it appears. As Buffie (2001) demonstrates, the impact of trade liberalization on the output and efficiency of oligopolistic industries depends on a number of factors – the precise form of trade policy instrument involved, the demand and technology characteristics facing industries, the scope for firm entry, whether markets are segmented or not, and the factor intensity rankings of industries. This conclusion is widely found in the theoretical literature (Flam and Helpman, 1987; Markusen and Venables, 1988). There is not a general case, therefore, for claiming precompetitive benefits of trade on the basis of theory, but the possibility does exist.

How important this is in practice is also difficult to gauge because the empirical evidence is thin. What there is on the extent of scale economies in the form of decreasing marginal costs in the manufacturing sectors of many developing countries may in fact be quite limited; see plant level evidence for example for Mexico and Chile (Tybout and Westbrook, 1995; Tybout, de Melo and Corbo, 1991). This type of plant level analysis is not, however, capable of detecting fixed cost sources of scale benefits. As for the output response to trade liberalization the simulation modelling of trade liberalization show large potential gains from pro-competitive and scale effects; see for example the CGE modelling of Cox and Harris (1985) which shows gains of several percentage points of GDP and much larger ones than for a perfect competition model approach. But of course these follow from the properties of the model and elasticity parameters assumed.

The limited evidence on the average plant size in import-competing sectors following trade reform is not consistent with the simulation evidence (Tybout, 1996).

Reducing x-inefficiency and rent-seeking

Openness of the domestic economy, in contrast to the protected conditions that many developing countries experienced pre-trade liberalization, is often viewed as providing a stimulus to productivity by reducing x-inefficiency and reducing the effort going into unproductive activities in search of economic rents. The effects of this stimulus can be viewed as coming both through a direct effect on import-competing firms and an indirect, compositional effect as a greater share of economic activity is driven into the export sector.

There is theoretical analysis of the direct effect of trade on the pressure for importable firms to achieve technical efficiency, which establishes an ambiguity of effect; greater trade openness not only reducing the incentive or opportunity for entrepreneurs to be idle, but also reducing the return to effort (Martin, 1978) or to investments in achieving cost reductions (Rodrik, 1988). There is, however, a substantial amount of empirical evidence that suggests that x-inefficiencies were high and costly under many developing countries' protectionist trade regimes (Little, Scitovsky and Scott, 1970). The recent empirical evidence on the effects of the move into exporting at the firm or plant level is also shown to be associated with the need to raise productivity (Tybout and Roberts, 1997). Further there is also recent analysis showing that increased trade policy openness has tended to reduce aggregate or economy-wide x-inefficiency (Henry, Kneller and Milner, 2009). Similarly there is a substantial amount of evidence that the highly protectionist, pre-trade reform period in many developing countries was typified by much and costly rent-seeking activity (Bhagwati, 1978). By contrast there is no contradictory evidence in favour of the restriction of trade increasing x-efficiency and reducing rent-seeking.

Technology transfer and trade

Disentangling the contributing sources of economic growth and their relative importance is notoriously difficult. Some of the factors already discussed (e.g. pro-competitive and scale effects) no doubt are potential dynamic sources of trade-induced productivity growth, but many analysts would argue that the principal driver of growth is technical change. The complex forces, such as education, research capacity and investment in R&D, which influence technical change, are not precisely understood nor easily analysed theoretically and empirically. It is evident, and for understandable reasons, however, that developing countries do not in general have a comparative advantage in bringing about technological change. For most developing countries the enhancing of growth potential through technological improvements requires the transfer of new ideas and technologies from developed countries and their absorption and effective adoption in developing countries (Blomström, Lipsey and Zejan, 1994). One can envisage a number of ways in which greater openness and exposure to trade can support technology transfer. More contact with or exposure to foreign firms (either through competition in the domestic market for import-competing firms or in international markets for exporting firms) creates opportunities to learn about new products and processes or technologies developed abroad. Greater competition from foreign producers, again in a less protected domestic market or with a shift of production away from more protected domestic to unprotected export markets, in turn gives a greater stimulus to adopt new products and processes. Further, many technical improvements are embodied in intermediate and capital goods. In which case, the opening up of domestic markets to imports and reducing the 'tax' on and cost of imported goods increases the opportunity and capacity of domestic firms to acquire this 'embodied' technology.

The theoretical underpinning for this type of representation of the role of trade in affecting both the location of R&D/innovation activity and the influence of knowledge spillovers can be found in Grossman and Helpman (1991), Rivera-Batiz and Romer (1991) and Feenstra (1996). Output is modelled as increasing when firms have access to a wide range of specialised intermediate inputs, which are supplied (in blueprint form) by the R&D sector. The cost of developing new products is represented as declining as the stock of general knowledge and cumulative R&D experience grows. There are therefore dynamic scale economies and sustained technical progress in this type of 'endogenous' growth model; the precise mechanism for this spillover effect for developing countries depending on whether knowledge spillovers are national or international and on endowments conducive to the R&D sector development. If there are international spillovers of knowledge or factor requirements conducive to R&D sectors in developing countries, the rate technological progress (and even innovation rate) will rise in developing countries. In the more likely case (at present at least) of the existing national stocks of knowledge and other relevant endowments (human capital and education, research capital, etc.) giving developing countries a comparative disadvantage in R&D activity and with knowledge not speedily or freely spilling across national boundaries, then greater trade openness will cause domestic R&D capacity to contract (even disappear) in developing countries and to reduce the domestic innovation rate. The growth rate, however, will increase because greater openness to trade allows the developing country to purchase a wider array of more technologically advanced intermediate inputs.

There is a body of empirical research now that gives credence to the importance of technology transfer through trade for developing countries. Coe, Helpman and Hoffmaister (1997) estimate that a 1 percent increase in the R&D

capital stock of the industrialised countries raises output by 0.06 percent in developing countries. The literature identifies a number of possible channels for this transfer or spillover effect to developing countries, including FDI and dis-embodied R&D spillovers such as international patenting. The main focus has, however, been on the trade (import) embodiment channel. Coe and Helpman (1995), for instance, estimate an equation of the following form:

$$\log \text{TFP}_{it} = \alpha_i + \alpha_t + \beta_1 \log R_{it} + \beta_2 \log S_{it} + \varepsilon_{it}, \tag{1}$$

where TFP is total factor productivity, R is the domestic R&D stock, S is the accessible, foreign R&D stock, α_i and α_t are country (i) and time (t) fixed effects and ε is an error term.

The accessible, foreign R&D stock is measured by:

$$S_i = \sum_{h \neq i} \frac{M_{ih}}{M_i} S_h,$$

where M_{ih} is i's manufactured imports from h and M_i is i's total manufactured imports. This is a bilateral imports share-weighted sum of the R&D stocks of capital of a country's trading partners. Coe and Helpman (1995) find that the more a country imports from countries with large R&D capital stocks the more productivity increases in the importing country. Keller (1998) and Lichtenberg and van Pottelsberghe de la Protterie (1998) challenge this finding, but later work has confirmed the effect when foreign R&D is weighted by capital goods imports rather than total manufacturing imports (Coe, Helpman and Hoffmaister, 1997; Mayer, 2001).

3   Trade Policy, Distortions and Development

For a small country (and most developing countries are small in the sense of being unable to affect world prices) and first-best conditions (perfect competition, market clearing and no externalities) free trade is Pareto-efficient. It is also sustainable if non-distortionary domestic redistribution is feasible. Free trade is optimal under these conditions because it allows the marginal conditions for efficient resource allocation to be satisfied; efficient patterns of expenditure and production are achieved where the marginal rate of (consumer) substitution and marginal rate of transformation (in production) are equal to relative world prices.

3.1   Distortions and optimal intervention

Clearly, the assumption of first-best conditions is a heroic one, especially in a developing country context. Without first-best conditions free trade is not opti-mal, and trade policy interventions may be welfare-improving. But going back to the classic articles on distortions by Johnson (1965), Bhagwati and Srinivason (1969), and Bhagwati (1971), the presence of distortions has been shown not to be sufficient to justify interventionist trade policy. Trade taxes will not be optimal in general to correct for the allocative efficiencies induced by distortions. Rather the principle of targeting requires that some combination of free trade and appropriate tax or subsidy that directly deals with the source of the market failure will be the optimal form of intervention. (These ideas are more fully reviewed in the chapter on trade policy in this volume – chapter 9.)

The fundamental theorems of welfare economics set out above are in effect an alternative way of expressing the gains from trade in a distortionless world where lump-sum transfers are feasible; all individuals in an economy can be made better off from free trade and compensating transfers. This is the case for both gains from trade in a static context (Samuelson, 1962; Kemp, 1962) and for inter-temporal gains from trade (e.g. Smith, 1979). In this latter context, free trade with first best conditions allows higher steady-state levels of consumption and welfare, though not necessarily higher long-run growth rates. In exogenous growth models the long-run growth rate is determined by factors such as population growth or technological progress, though more policy openness may raise the growth rate in the transition to new steady states. By contrast, in endogenous growth models the removal of trade policy-induced distortions may have a positive effect on the long-run growth rate, though the influence of trade policy is sensitive to the way in which the decision to innovate and the impact of innovation is modelled. (For further discussion of this issue, see Grossman and Helpman, 1991). In both a static and dynamic setting the treatment of distortions as exogenously given leads liberal economists in general to point to the principles of optimal intervention, and the superiority of using domestic taxes and subsidies over trade taxes for achieving Pareto-optimality.

3.2   Limitations of the Analysis?

One obvious limitation of the analysis in this section to date is that the distortion may lie in the international market itself. There may be international buyer or seller power that will make the use of trade policy optimal. This is not an issue we will dwell on long here, given that developing countries can rarely be viewed as 'large' countries or to be exporting products where the strategic use of trade policy is possible. Of much greater relevance in a developing country context are concerns about the exogeneity of, and degree of information about, distortions in developing countries, and about the administrative costs and feasibility of implementing lump-sum transfers and corrective tax/subsidy interventions.

The optimal intervention framework is criticized (e.g. Rodriguez, 2008) for presuming a high level of information or certainty about the nature and extent of market distortions and a high level of competence or institutional and administrative capacity on the part of government to evaluate and correct distortions. In a world of pervasive distortions, uncertainty and constrained capacity to intervene one might argue that trade policy reform may not be the reform one should initially focus on (with other distortions still in place). Indeed with other distortions remaining the sign on the welfare effect of a tariff increase may be positive. But the presence of uncertainty and complexity equally implies that the degree of tariff increase and direction of this welfare effect is uncertain. Given the political economy pressures for protection and role of reciprocity in international trade negotiations, this may argue against raising tariffs and moving away from the long term, first best optimum (even if it does not provide a rationale for further or rapid liberalization.)

In arguing above that a production subsidy was superior to a tariff in correcting for a production distortion, it was assumed that the subsidy could be financed by a lump-sum tax. Clearly in practice lump-sum taxation is not available, and a subsidy will have to be funded by a distortionary tax. In which case it is less clear that a subsidy-cum-distortionary tax is superior to a tariff, since now both measures induce by-product distortions. Unbundling a tariff, however, allows one to think of it is as an equivalent to a production subsidy and consumption tax on importables at an equal rate. The tax component of the unbundling of the tariff is, however, more revenue-raising than is required to fund the production subsidy. An actual production subsidy can be paired with a lower consumption tax the equivalent (subsidy-cum-consumption) of the tariff. In which case a tariff is inferior to an appropriately set subsidy/tax policy.

In making the continued defence of domestic tax/subsidy (relative to trade policy) interventions, one is continuing to abstract from administrative costs. It may, however, be the case that trade taxes, especially in a developing country context, entail lower administrative costs because they raise tax revenue and 'disburse' implicit subsidies at the customs authority at the port or border rather than requiring an administrative capacity to raise domestic taxes and to distribute (explicit) subsidies domestically.

There certainly is evidence of higher collection costs for consumption taxes than tariffs in developing countries (World Development Report, 1988), though some diversification of the tax base has taken place in recent decades with the development of non-trade taxes. The cost of disbursing subsidies and the scope for fraud/corruption are also likely to be high. In which case it is legitimate to worry that administration costs may be a constraint on the implementation of first-best policies (Rodrik, 1992).

Another criticism that has been raised about optimal intervention analysis is that it represents distortions as exogenously given. This may be appropriate in many cases. For example, minimum wage laws may be viewed as imposing a wage above the market-clearing rate and inducing underemployment in the industrial sectors of many developing countries. If tariffs are as costly (or not sufficiently more costly) to administer as non-trade taxes, then the first-best intervention remains an appropriate wage subsidy (cum tax). But what if high wages reflect the power of trade unions in the formal, industrial sector *and* the strategic behaviour of unions is influenced by the policy instrument used by government to remedy the labour market distortion. A wage subsidy may induce more aggressive behaviour in its wage demands, and the optimal subsidy be larger than in the 'exogenous' case. Now the optimal wage subsidy may, *but only may*, not dominate the optimal tariff, even without administrative cost differences.

The possible endogeneity of distortions does not necessarily offer a major undermining of the traditional ranking of policy instruments. It is not obvious that a wage subsidy is necessarily a more transparent or targetable instrument than tariffs, and of course governments can affect also the nature of the strategic game through precommitment to subsidy levels. Besides which, the choice should not only be between a wage or employment subsidy and a tariff. The case for the active use of trade policy requires that the tariff is first-best.

3.3 Taking stock

The argument that free trade is *always* first-best is difficult to sustain from theory, when one allows for both differential administrative costs between trade taxes and domestic tax/subsidy schemes and for the 'endogeneity' of distortions arising out of the strategic response of economic agents to the choice of policy instruments. (See Dixit and Norman, 1980 for a discussion of whether trade protection may be justified on theoretical or normative grounds.) But, equally, one cannot claim a general case for more restricted trade as being desirable on theoretical grounds. The targeting of all policies (trade and non-trade) with appropriate allowance for administrative costs and strategic behaviour is called for. One has to recognize, however, that there is a long term rationale for the pursuit of first-best conditions and that nonintervention may be superior to poor or non-optimal intervention. In which case one might argue that the extent and pace of trade policy liberalization should be fashioned in part at least by developing countries' capacity to implement alternative and uncostly domestic policies. This capacity, no doubt, should include the development of effective and efficient domestic expenditure taxation systems. Finally, it should be emphasized that the significance of the theoretical literature on distortions and optimal intervention analysis for the overall policy approach of developing countries depends on how pervasive market failure is in fact. As we saw in section 2, perceptions of the pervasiveness of market failure differ among development economists!

4 Trade Strategies for Development

There is now little or no intellectual support for the extreme pessimistic views of the role of trade referred to in section 3, nor for explicit and general import-substitution (IS) strategies that many developing countries adopted in the first decades of their post-independence development. The need for more outward-oriented and export-promoting trade strategies is now widely acknowledged, and by economists from a range of schools of thought. There is, however, controversy and disagreement about the precise alternative to an IS strategy and how to achieve export promotion (EP).

4.1 Export promotion through import liberalization

The neoclassical analysis of trade strategy in industrialization, especially in its 'strong' version, emphasizes neutrality across tradeables as an export-promoting strategy (with free trade the extreme version of this).[1] Bhagwati (1990) represents export promotion as involving the lowering of the bias against exports. The idea of an import substitution (IS) strategy involving a net incentive on average to produce importables rather than exportables (relative to what international relative prices dictate) can be found throughout the empirical literature of the costs and distortions associated with the IS era (Krueger, 1978; Balassa, 1982; Bhagwati, 1978). Different measures of relative incentives (real exchange rates or effective rates of protection) may be used, but the bottom line was the same: the bias in favour of importables and against exportables production needed to be substantially lowered, even eliminated, in order to implement an EP strategy.[2] Of course, greater neutrality in this two sector (importables and exportables) representation of economies could be achieved when shifting from an IS strategy either by reducing the incentives for importables (by lowering tariffs and non-tariff barriers on imports) or by increasing the incentives to exportables (by implicit and explicit subsidizing of exports or exportables production). There are deterrents to the latter route, given that there may be international trade rules or threats of retaliation by other countries which constrain the use of export incentives, and that many developing countries may have a fiscal constraint on the funding of subsidies. But neoclassical economists would also be concerned that there may be equivalent distortionary effects and embedded pressures for intensifying government intervention induced in the exportables sector analogous to those associated with IS measures.

The rationale for emphasizing trade liberalization as a means of promoting exportables production and exports was particularly obvious when faced with the extreme 'anti-export bias' that typified many developing countries in their pre-liberalization era. But does the logic apply at lesser levels of anti-export bias, and is there a danger of representing all relative neutral and outward-oriented trade regimes as being effectively very similar? One could argue that the reason

Table 20.1   Average[1] effective[2] rates of protection for importables[3] and exportables[4] and trade regime bias indices for a selection of countries.

	Effective rates of protection (%)		Trade regime bias
	e_M	e_X	(B)
Barbados (1988/9)	221	10	2.92
Trinidad (1991)	154	−21	3.22
Mauritius (1990)	79	−3	1.85
Uganda (1992)	62	−15	1.91
South Korea (1968)	−12	−9	0.97
South Korea (1978)	33	14	1.17
Israel (1968)	14	−18	1.39
Argentina (1969)	41	−60	3.53
Singapore (1967)	2	−6	1.09
Taiwan (1969)	18	−13	1.36
Colombia (1969)	5	26	0.83

Notes:
[1] Unweighted for Barbados, Trinidad, Mauritius and Uganda, otherwise weighted by shares in value-added.
[2] Net rates adjusted for currency overvaluation.
[3] Strictly protection in domestic sales and exports.
[4] Manufacturing sectors but for consumer goods industries only for Trinidad and non-traditional for Israel.
[5] $B = (1 + e_M)/(1 + e_X)$.
Source: Milner and McKay (1996), table 5.1.

for the success of Asian countries such as Hong Kong, Singapore, South Korea and Taiwan in promoting exports is that they all avoided anti-export bias, that is the balance of the relative incentives they gave to importables and exportables were similar and that relative neutrality was a common feature across them. In table 20.1 some average effective rates of protection for importables (e_m) and exportables (e_x) in some developing countries (in the period from the late 1960s to early 1990s and including for Singapore, South Korea and Taiwan) are reproduced. The 'free trade' (or approximately so) regime of Singapore (with effective protection rates of 2 and 6 percent for importables and exportables) is very similar in terms of relative incentives (as represented by a trade regime index) as that of South Korea; the trade regime index for Singapore is 1.09, while it is 0.97 or 1.17 for South Korea in 1968 and 1978, respectively. Many commentators would, despite the similarity in terms of relative incentives, view South Korea as differing from Singapore because of the former's more active and selective industrial policies and generally more interventionist government policies in the tradeable goods sector. Indeed, some would criticize (e.g. Singer, 1988) the use of only average relative incentives as a means of classifying trade regimes. Even the World Bank (World Bank, 1993) has revised its interpretation somewhat of the policy basis of the East Asian countries' growth based on export growth, but it continues to place an emphasis on openness to trade and reliance on markets as fundamental to their success story. However others (e.g. Wade, 2003) view the form of government intervention (active and selective industrial policies to support import substitution and export promotion) as more critical to the success of some of these countries, and as a model for others.

4.2 On mixed and selective trade strategies

In the traditional, static two sector (importables and exportables) model, there is only one long-run relative price, the price of importables relative to exportables. Uniform, mixed trade intervention of export promotion and import substitution will not alter this relative price. This is the corollary of the Lerner-symmetry theorem. But if we extend the dimensions of the model in terms of sectors and time periods, then we can conceive of the possibility of pro-tradeables strategies and of selective and temporary intervention. This allows us to explore the issue of neutrality in a more useful context for policy purposes. Further, if we subsequently allow for the possibility of externalities, then we will also be able to consider the implications of temporary and permanent trade policy interventions with and without market distortions.[3]

Consider a small, open and undistorted economy producing two types of each tradeable (exportables X_1 and X_2 and importables M_3 and M_4) and one composite non-tradeable good (N). We allow for inter-temporal effects by using a two-period framework. (Simple dynamic models of this kind can be found in Edwards, 1989, and Chen and Devereux, 1994, and further discussion of the properties of this type of general equilibrium model can be found in chapter 3 of this volume). Consumption (C) preferences are represented by an aggregate utility (U) function defined over the consumption levels of each of the goods over the two periods. An inter-temporal trade expenditure function (E) can then be used to represent equilibrium as follows:

$$E\left(P_T, P_N, \delta P_{\tilde{T}}, \delta P_{\tilde{N}}, U, F\right) = C\left(P_T, P_N, \delta P_{\tilde{T}}, \delta P_{\tilde{N}}, U\right) - R^1(P_T, P_N, F) - R^2(\delta P_{\tilde{T}}, \delta P_{\tilde{N}}, F),$$

$$(2)$$

where
$C(\cdot) =$ the expenditure function,
$R^t(\cdot) =$ the revenue from production function for time period t,
$F =$ fixed factor supplies,
$P_T =$ vector of prices of tradeable goods T, (X_1, X_2, M_3, M_4),
$P_N =$ price of non-tradeable good N, and
$\delta =$ discount factor.
(The addition of tilde ($\sim$) denotes the variable in the second period).

World prices of tradeables (P^*) are treated as given in line with the small country assumption, and policy interventions take the form of ad valorem import tariffs (t) or export subsidies (s) which cause domestic prices of tradeables (P_T) to deviate from world prices. (Non-distortionary redistribution or taxation is assumed to be possible.)

The equilibrium conditions for this economy are set out in equations (3), (4) and (5); a balance of payments constraint (equation (3)) that discounted income must equal discounted expenditure.[4] Excess demand for non-tradeables must be equal to zero in both period one (equation (4)) and period two (equation (5)).

$$E(\cdot) = \sum s_X P_X^* E_X + \sum t_X P_M^* E_M + \sum \delta s_{\tilde{X}} P_{\tilde{X}}^* E_{\tilde{X}} + \sum \delta t_{\tilde{M}} P_{\tilde{M}}^* E_{\tilde{M}}, \tag{3}$$

$$E_N(\cdot) = 0, \tag{4}$$

$$E_{\tilde{N}}(\cdot) = 0. \tag{5}$$

Totally differentiating the equilibrium conditions we can identify the change in the pattern of relative incentives or real exchange rates ($e_i = P_i/P_N$) for each tradeable good in either of the time periods associated with a particular pattern of trade policy interventions. Below we solve for the first time period, assuming that world prices are constant and for simplicity do not (at this stage) fully endogenize income (y). We assume also that trade policy interventions are used only in the first period, with all tariffs and subsidies being set to zero in the second period ($t_{\tilde{m}} = s_{\tilde{x}} = 0$). Thus, with world prices and the initial non-tradeables price set equal to unity (for simplicity), this gives us that:

$$\hat{e}_i = \hat{P}_i - (w_1 ds_1 + w_2 ds_2 + w_3 dt_3 + w_4 dt_4) - (\mu dy), \tag{6}$$

where w_i coefficients are the intra- and inter-temporal substitution/complementarity relationships of each tradeable with non-tradeables, μ is the income effect on the real exchange rate of any trade policy-induced income change, and $\hat{}$ denotes proportionate change.

The effects of uniform and non-uniform interventions in the absence of externalities on the (first period) individual and average real exchange rates are summarized in table 20.2.

Permanent interventions

Consider first the effect of introducing uniform import tariffs and export subsidies across all tradeables, $s_1 = s_2 = t_3 = t_4 > 0$, when there had previously been free trade and when the measures are viewed as permanently set at this level. By implication the introduction of trade taxes will involve no income effects ($\mu = 0$) *and there will be no inter-temporal substitution effects so that each w_i term in* equation (6) will involve intra-temporal substitution effects only. Thus, given the assumption that each of the tradeable goods is a substitute rather than a complement for the non-tradeable, each w_i term in equation (6) will be positive

Table 20.2 A summary of real exchange rate responses to trade policy interventions (no externalities effects).

Change[a] in Real Exchange Rate for:	Permanent[b] Interventions				Temporary[c] Interventions			
	Uniform[d]		Non-uniform[e]		Uniform		Non-uniform	
		With income effects		With income effects		With income effects		With income effects
	(1)	(2)	(3)	(4)	(5)	(6)	(7)	(8)
X_1	0	0	←	←	?	?	?	?
X_2	0	0	→	?	?	?	→	?
Exportables ($\sum X$)	0	0	?	?	?	?	?	?
M_3	0	0	←	←	?	?	?	?
M_4	0	0	→	?	?	?	→	?
Importables ($\sum M$)	0	0	?	?	?	?	?	?
Tradeables ($\sum X + \sum M$)	0	0	?	?	?	?	?	?

[a] 0 denotes constant, direction of arrow shows rise or fall and ? denotes ambiguous response.
[b] Commitment to use of trade measure in both time periods.
[c] Announced use of trade measure; in first time period only.
[d] Uniform ad valorem tariffs and subsidies across all tradeables (i.e., $s_1 = s_2 = t_3 = t_4 > 0$).
[e] $s_1 = t_3 > 0$ but $s_2 = t_4 = 0$.
Source: McKay and Milner (1997a), table 1.

but less than unity (i.e. $0 < w_i < l$), as homogeneity requires that $\sum w_i = 1$. The proportionate rise in the price of non-tradeables ($\hat{P}_N$) will be the same as the uni-form (nominal) rate of promotion of each tradeable. All individual and aggregate real exchange rates are unaltered and the corollary of Lerner-symmetry holds in the presence of non-tradeables. (All e_i values are shown to be unaltered in column one of table 20.2.)

With non-uniform intervention, selective promotion of particular tradeables is, however, possible. In table 20.2 (column four) we report on selective and uniform (i.e. $s_l = t_3 > 0$) promotion of, let us say, a non-traditional exportable (X_1) and competing importables (M_3). If we rule out complementarities both w_1 and w_3 lie between zero and unity. Thus $\hat{P}_N$ must be greater than $\hat{P}_2$ and $\hat{P}_4$ and less than $\hat{P}_1$ and $\hat{P}_3$; in other words the real exchange rate rises for the protected tradeables and falls for the unprotected tradeable sectors.[5] Of course, what happens to an average real exchange rate (importables, exportables or tradeables as a whole) is still ambiguous, depending on the relative magnitude of the substitution coefficients for the promoted sectors and the corresponding weights of these sectors in the relevant basket of tradeables.

With non-uniform selective intervention (say $t_3 > s_1 > 0$ with $s_2 = t_4 = 0$) the situation is more complex. The real exchange rate for the most protected sector (importable M_3) must rise, while that for the non-protected sectors must fall. But, the real exchange rate for exportable X_1 could rise or fall, depending *inter alia*, on the relative levels of the tariff and subsidy and on the magnitude of the substitution coefficients relating to the nominally promoted sectors (i.e. w_1 and w_3).

How are the above conclusions affected by the incorporation of income effects, (which will arise if trade policies are adjusted from a non–free trade position)? On the face of it the conclusions that uniform interventions will be neutral does not appear to be robust. If all $\hat{e}_i = 0$ when there is no income effect (i.e. $\mu \hat{y} = 0$), then it would seem that $\hat{e}_i \neq 0$ if $\hat{y} \neq 0$. But this interpretation applies only if the change in income is treated as exogenous, which it is explicitly not. If we fully endogenize the trade policy-induced change in the price of non-tradeables, we would identify revised w_i' coefficients (which embody both the substitution and income effects of a change in the price of a specific tradeable on the price of non-tradeables). Homogeneity properties of the general equilibrium framework still require, however, that $\sum w_i' = 1$ (McKay and Milner, 1997b). In which case permanent uniform intervention across all tradeables still leaves all real exchange rates unaltered. But now the effect of the trade policy-induced change in income on any individual w_i' coefficient is ambiguous. Some coeffi-cients must be positive if $\sum w_i' = 1$, but one or more may be negative in instances where the income effect dominates the substitution effect. Selective interven-tion may now drive the price of non-tradeables up or down depending upon the value of the w_i' coefficients for the promoted sectors. In these circumstances all real exchange rate responses, for promoted sectors, non-protected sectors and any subset or aggregation, are ambiguous. Indeed, it is possible that judicious use of selective trade policy intervention causes the price of non-tradeables to fall, so that all real exchange rates will rise. In this case the burden of selective protection/promotion of tradeables is shifted entirely onto the non-tradeables sector. But, equally, non-judicious use of selective trade policy measures could bring about precisely the reverse effect, with price of non-tradeables rising by more than even the nominally promoted sectors.

Temporary interventions

The incorporation of inter-temporal substitution possibilities serves to increase the complexity of the impact of trade policy interventions on the price of the non-tradeable good. Temporary promotion measures from initial free trade in period one which raise the price of tradeables tend to switch supply of tradeables to the first period and demand for tradeables to the second. The substitution effect of these measures serves to raise the price of non-tradeables in both periods. In particular, all the w_i in equation (6) will continue to be positive. Now, however, even in the absence of income effects (i.e. intervening from undistorted free trade) homogeneity does not imply that $\sum w_i = 1$, rather $\sum w_i \lessgtr 1$. In which case the individual and aggregate real exchange rate adjustments in the first period to uniform (temporary and nominal) promotion of all tradeables is strictly ambiguous; all $e_i \lessgtr 0$ as $\sum w_i \lessgtr 1$. (This ambiguity is recorded in column five of table 20.2.) Uniform intervention can lead to an appreciation (or depreciation) of the real exchange rate for each tradeable.

A similar result holds for the uniform intervention case where we allow for income effects. Although income is not endogenized in equation (6), the intuition is clear. Trade policy measures which increase income levels will tend to push the non-tradeable price up and above the increase generated by the substitution effect. As we are now explicitly in a second-best world, with the initial level of some tariffs and/or subsidies at non-zero levels, it cannot be unambiguously determined whether further increases in trade policy interventions will raise or lower income. But, irrespective of this, as in the pure substitution case, we cannot appeal to homogeneity to draw conclusions about whether $\sum w_i' \lessgtr 1$ and so about whether the real exchange rate will appreciate or depreciate given uniform intervention. This is what is recorded in column six in table 20.2.

The move from a one-period to a two-period model has generated greater ambiguity or uncertainty about the revealed or ex post pattern of relative prices. Certainly pro-tradeables bias is far from being the necessary outcome of uniform promotion of all tradeables. Is the same increase in ambiguity generated by considering selective or non-uniform temporary protection of tradeables? The answer to this question is, yes. The only unambiguous conclusion is that the real exchange rate for the unpromoted sectors will fall (appreciate) in the absence of income effects. In this case each of the w_i coefficients for the promoted sectors must be greater than zero (i.e. substitution effects only), P_N must rise if $s_1 > 0$ and $t_3 > 0$, and e_2 and e_4 must appreciate (fall).

Table 20.2 shows that the pattern of actual or ex post protection or promotion of tradeables may not necessarily be in line with the intended or ex ante pattern of promotion. Information requirements about the general-equilibrium characteristics of the economy are high, even of the relatively simple economy modelled here.

Allowing for externalities

In the analysis so far it has been assumed that there is no market failure. As a result trade policy interventions move the economy from first-best conditions. In short, there is no justification for trade policy, at least not relative to the first-best equilibrium. Let us assume instead, therefore, that learning-by-doing effects exist for all tradeables and can be represented in our two-period model by letting the second period revenue function depend positively on the output of tradable goods in the first period. In other words, the fact that more tradeables are produced in the first period makes it more profitable to produce tradeables in the second. The trade expenditure function thus becomes:

$$
E(P_N, P_T, \delta P_{\tilde{N}}, \delta P_{\tilde{T}}, U, R_T^1) \equiv C(P_N, P_T, \delta P_{\tilde{N}}, \delta P_{\tilde{T}}, U) - R^1(P_N, P_T, F)
$$
$$
- R^2(\delta P_{\tilde{N}}, \delta P_{\tilde{T}}, F, R_T^1), \tag{7}
$$

where R_T^1 represents the derivative of the first period revenue function with respect to the price vector of the tradable good(s). The equilibrium conditions for this model are represented as before, but now using the revised definition of the trade expenditure function capturing learning by doing effects. The model can be solved as before.

We focus here only on the intuition of the results. Temporary intervention, even if it is uniform across all tradeable goods, will generate a real exchange rate change; and again the direction of change is ambiguous. However, the learning-by-doing effects do not by themselves make a real exchange rate depreciation more or less likely, they affect only the magnitude of the response. Though, now even marginal trade policy interventions about an initial free-trade equilibrium have welfare effects.

In fact, if we retain the assumption of initial free trade there is a clear relationship between the welfare impact of introducing trade policy measures and the real exchange rate response. Specifically, a necessary and sufficient condition for uniform trade policy measures to be welfare-improving is that they cause the real exchange rate to depreciate; to increase the incentive to produce tradeables in period one. As a result of the learning-by-doing effect, the increased output of tradeables in period one also makes period two production more profitable, thus raising income/welfare levels relative to what they would be in the absence of intervention. The critical point, though, is that the first period real exchange rate depreciation must be achieved; if it is not, the above argument works in reverse and trade policy reduces, rather than increases, welfare.

Finally, this clear relationship between the real exchange rate response and the welfare response unfortunately does not carry over to the more complex case of an initial equilibrium with trade policy measures in place. In such circumstances it is even more difficult to be confident that trade policy measures will raise welfare.

All of this has been considered under the assumption that trade policy intervention is uniform across all tradable goods. A similar analysis, however, could be applied to the case in which only one tradeable good is subject to a learning-by-doing externality and to trade policy intervention. A similar analysis would apply, except that what has been considered above as the real exchange rate for all tradeables would only be the relative price applying to the tradeable good in question. Again, such policy measures, even though they may discriminate against other tradeables, could be welfare-improving, though this is not necessarily the case.

Overall assessment

Changes in trade policy interventions have general-equilibrium consequences affecting protected and unprotected sectors as well as welfare. The desired or intended movement in relative prices (real exchange rates) may not actually be achieved under the fairly wide range of circumstances relating to the mix of trade policies and of substitution and income effects.

Starting from an initial situation in which trade policy interventions are already present, changes in these trade policy interventions will inevitably have welfare consequences. Even if trade policy becomes more protectionist on average, however, welfare need not necessarily fall; this is a standard second-best result. But in the absence of market failures, no equilibrium characterized by trade policy interventions will be welfare-superior to the free trade equilibrium. In short, in such a world free trade is a better strategy than pursuing active trade policy intervention.

The case may be different if there are learning-by-doing effects or other externalities, however. Where these are present in the tradeable goods sector, then it is possible that an equilibrium characterized by trade policy interventions in favour of the sectors characterized by learning by doing will be superior (though not necessarily optimal) in welfare terms to the free-trade equilibrium. But this is by no means necessarily the case, because such interventions may in fact be welfare-lowering. Even in this world, trade policy interventions need to be very carefully designed, based on relatively detailed information about the economy, if they are not to lead to a reduction in welfare. The type of information required includes knowledge of the strength of the learning-by-doing effects in the different sectors, and knowledge of the degree of substitution between different goods at a point in time and intertemporally. In practice, such information may be very difficult to come by. Recall also the earlier discussion in section 4 on optimal intervention, that other forms of policy intervention besides trade policy are likely to be more efficient forms of policy intervention.

5   Empirical Evidence on the Trade Policy–Development Relationship

The relationship between trade policy openness, or strategy, and growth is a contentious empirical issue, as well as a contentious theoretical issue. A number of issues lie at the heart of the controversy.

Measurement of trade policy openness

The suitability of the indices commonly used in empirical studies to proxy a country's trade regime is one major area of concern. Rodrik (1995) argues that in most studies of openness and growth, the trade regime indicator is typically measured very badly and 'openness in the sense of lack of trade restrictions is often confused with macroeconomic aspects of the policy regime' (Rodrik, 1995, 2941). The inherent problem of summarizing trade policy across multiple trade policy instruments (when tariff and non-tariff measures may simultaneously apply) and across many products (typically for up to several thousand different tariffs) is compounded in the case of developing countries by data unavailability or quality that often restricts the country and time period coverage of the empirical estimation. One response to this problem has been to adopt a range of alternative partial and imperfect proxy indicators of trade policy stance. Edwards (1998), for example, uses nine alternative proxies, including the average tariff, coverage of NTBs, black market foreign exchange premium, collected trade tax revenue as a share of the value of trade, and various subjective (e.g. Sachs-Warner index of openness) and estimated indices. But if, as Pritchett (1996) shows, the correlation between such commonly used proxies of overall trade policy is low, then the confidence in the meaning and robustness of any finding of a positive association between some or all of these proxies and economic growth is undermined.

Many studies fall back on the use of an 'output' rather than direct policy or 'input' measure, taking a country's trade (value of exports plus imports) to GDP ratio as the measure of trade policy. It has the convenient property of requiring data that is widely available and the index is easily calculated across countries and over time. Cross-sectional (country) variation in this trade openness indicator is, however, likely to be driven at least as much by functional differences between countries (e.g. differences in country size and location) as by trade policy differences. Policy changes may be more reasonably viewed as a driver of changes in the index over time, but may not be the only driver. Herein lies a link with the discussion in section 4 about the interpretation of different trade regimes. Should one interpret increased trade openness (as indicated by the trade-GDP ratio) in the East Asian exporting countries as indicating more liberal and open trade policies or as being brought about by successful industrial policies which have promoted export activities? Alternatively, one might be concerned about whether we can view this output or outcome measure of trade policy as an exogenous, independent variable in a growth regression, since it may be that either growth itself is fostering greater trade (e.g. driving the import of consumer and investment goods) or improved trade performance is allowing more liberal trade policies. This gives arise to econometric modelling issues to which we return below.

Econometric modelling issues

Theory gives limited precise guidance as to the specification of the empirical growth model that should be estimated. As a result there is a danger that any estimated growth model will not be robust, either because there are omitted influences or inappropriately modelled conditioning factors (e.g., interactions between trade policy and other characteristics of the economy or policy environment). Further the estimated model may be sensitive to the properties of the sampled countries (e.g. to outlier and heteroskedasticity problems), and to the estimation method.

Edwards (1998) estimates the following model for a cross-section of up to 73 countries (j) (depending on the proxy of trade policy used):

$$\text{TFP growth}_j = \beta_0 + \beta_1 \text{GDP}_j^{65} + \beta_2 \text{HC}_j + \beta_3 \text{Open}_j + e_j, \tag{8}$$

where

TFP growth = average total factor productivity growth for the period 1980–90,

GDP^{65} = log of initial GDP per capita (i.e. for the year 1965),

HC = initial level of human capital (mean years of schooling in 1965),

Open = trade policy openness (proxied by nine alternative indicators).

Using a weighted least squares estimation method to deal with heterogeneity (and with and without instrumented variables to control for endogeneity), Edwards finds for 17 of the 18 estimated models that there is a significant positive relationship between openness and productivity growth. Further, he reports that this finding is robust to the exclusion of outliers and to the inclusion of other potentially omitted variables (institutional quality, political instability and macroeconomic instability). This would seem to offer strong evidence of the growth benefits of trade policy openness. However, this and other papers (e.g. Dollar, 1992; Sachs and Warner, 1995) have been subject to very critical scrutiny by Rodriguez and Rodrik (2000), who emphasize the measurement of trade policy issue and the sensitivity of the results to specification and sample (country coverage and time period).

Recent panel evidence

Other cross-section work (e.g. Frankel and Romer, 1999), which treats the issue of endogeneity and other influences (e.g. geography and institutions) seriously finds a positive influence of trade share on growth. But ultimately the most convincing evidence on this topic comes from more recent research using panel data methods, which allow for cross-country and time effects. This allows country fixed effects to be modelled, and thereby reduces concerns about omitted variables. It also allows the modelling of the dynamics of the openness and growth relationship, and thereby reduces concerns about causality. The problem remains of measuring trade policy. A solution to this problem awaits the extension of recent work on for instance more comprehensive measurement of summary trade restrictiveness indices (Kee, Nicita and Olarreaga, 2009), in particular in extending the measurement over time.

An example of panel evidence is to be found in Henry and Milner (2005). They adopt a similar model as (8) above, but with country and time period fixed effects terms included and indicators of alternative aspects of openness simultaneously included – trade shares, Sachs-Warner openness index and a measure of the deviation of domestic prices from purchasing power parity. The sample used for the estimation comprises a maximum of 79 developed and developing countries and covers six (five-year) time periods between 1960 and 1990. Estimates for a fixed effects (within) estimator and then allowing for the endogeneity of trade shares using a GMM (Instrumental variables – IV) estimator. In each case alternative measures of country TFP growth (TFPG) are used; TFPG (AMG) allows for heterogeneity in production parameters across countries and homogeneity in factor elasticities and TFPG (HET) which allows for heterogeneity in both. The fixed effects results give clear support for a positive trade share and openness effect on TFP growth and some support for lower price distortions increasing TFP growth. When, however, allowance is made for the endogeneity of trade share and trade policy the trade share effect is no longer significant, but the findings on openness indicators hold up. Based on their GMMIV estimation with TFPG (HET) as the dependent variable it can be argued that countries that are open have on average a TFP growth rate of about 1.3 percent higher than countries that are closed – based on the Sachs-Warner classification.

Significant, positive per capita GDP growth effects are also found by Greenaway and others (2002), again using panel econometric methods but now using the trade liberalization evidence or episodes to explore the post-liberalization responses of growth (having controlled for other standard influences on growth). The dynamic approach to exploring before and after (and simultaneously with and without) liberalization effects is not unproblematic – see Greenaway and Haque (2005) – but it offers an obvious way of confronting the direction of causation issue. Greenaway and others (2002) report results (GMM estimates that confront the endogeneity concerns) for a panel of 73 countries over the period 1979–93, using alternative indicators of the liberalization events to check for robustness. Although there are differences across the indicators of liberalization, with the indicators of actual liberalization (based on the use, again, of the Sachs-Warner index) finding stronger growth effects than those based on intended or planned liberalization. They also find differences in the short- and long-term growth effects, with often short-term negative effects and long-run positive growth effects (as one might expect during the adjustment between trade policy regimes).[6]

Exploring conditioning factors

One criticism that might levelled against the empirical approaches discussed above is that they have not considered whether the effects of trade policy or openness on growth or other aspects of performance are conditioned by characteristics of the economy; this might be endowments of the economy (e.g., human capital levels), the institutional or policy characteristics of the country or aspects of geography or the infrastructure. A growing body of evidence points towards historical events having long-term effects on current economic development or performance (see, e.g. Nunn, 2009). A number of recent trade policy studies also suggest that this may be a fruitful area of research.

Miller and Upadhyay (2000) model, for instance, the determinants of aggregate total factor productivity (TFP), in particular exploring the influence of openness, trade orientation and human capital on TFP for pooled cross-section (83 developed and developing countries) and time series (averaged five-year periods from 1960 to 1989) data. Besides incorporating separate effects of a country's human capital level and export (to GDP) share on TFP (and other control variables), they also include an interaction term (interacting the export share and human capital variables). The effect of export share or openness is shown for the whole sample of countries to be leveraged by human capital; more human capital implying a larger (positive) effect of openness on TFP. But when they separate their sample of countries into low, middle and high income countries, the (significant) positive interaction effect is only found for the low income countries. In other words the leverage influence of human capital on the openness-TFP relationship is conditioned by the level of development. This suggests a need for further exploration of what characteristics of low income countries fashion or condition the effect of trade openness or trade policy.

Some studies (Wacziarg, 1998; Ades and Glaeser, 1999; Alesina et al., 2000) have examined how a country's geography affects the trade openness-growth relationship. Again using interaction terms in their estimating equations, they generally find that the benefits of trade openness are smaller for larger countries. Using a different methodology which allows for endogenous thresholds (above and below which there may be differential effects of trade openness on growth, depending on the threshold or conditioning variable), Girma and others (2009) find that countries with higher 'natural' barriers (more remote or poorer infrastructure countries) receive greater benefits from trade policy liberalization. By contrast, Chang, Kaltoni and Loayza (2008) examine the interaction between trade openness and institutional and other policy or regulatory characteristics of countries (e.g. labour market flexibility). They consistently find from their panel data estimates of this non-linear growth model that the positive growth effects of trade openness can be enhanced by complementary institutional and policy reforms.

6   Complementary Policies to Trade Reform

6.1   Adjustment to trade reform in developing countries

Trade policy reform requires economies to adjust. Indeed the more smoothly and quickly adjustment occurs, the more quickly countries may be able to gain in income, productivity and overall growth terms. As identified in the previous section, differences in initial policy and economic conditions appear to affect countries' abilities to cope and adapt to increased globalization and openness.

The textbook model of adjustment to trade liberalization often abstracts from or downplays the rigidities, especially in developing countries that slow down adjustment and increase the costs of adjustment. In the stylized representation of adjustment, import liberalization encourages restructuring of the import-competing sector which smoothly allows the release of resources (capital and labour) for the expansion of the export sector. Restructuring in the import-competing sector may in practice mean factory closure and unemployment, or at least firm level restructuring. New working and managerial methods and new skills and technologies are likely to be required in both the contracting and expanding sectors. These changes in turn require investment in physical and human capital. Indeed, this will generally involve new or additional investments for what in the case of developing countries are capital-poor countries. The existing capital (including private investment in production and public investment in infrastructure) in the import-competing sector is unlikely to be transferable to other sectors.[7]

The recent theoretical (e.g. Eaton and Kortum, 1996) and empirical (e.g. Pavcnik, 2002 for Chile) modelling of firm level adjustment to trade liberalization now recognizes that the capacity of firms within the same sector is likely to vary. More technologically advanced firms, and those firms in regions where the business environment and flexible labour markets are conducive to change and risk-taking, are more likely to be willing and able to adapt and increase productivity. Some research on India's liberalization experience (Aghion et al., 2004) shows that the response of manufacturing firms even within the same industry can be very heterogeneous. The capacity of the export sector to expand may be constrained by a variety of domestic and external bottlenecks – shortage of capital, infrastructure deficiencies, bureaucratic or institutional hindrances and technical barriers to export market access. Adjustment is likely to be smoother and quicker where the export sector can expand more quickly. In many developing countries with high dependence on traditional exports, the smallness and undiversified nature of their export sector may limit the capacity for rapid expansion of export supply.

Production and employment adjustment

The issue of adjustment support is not uncontroversial. Many industrialized countries themselves have had schemes of assistance relating to trade-induced adjustment experienced by workers (compensation for unemployment, support for relocation and retraining) and by firms (closure, production line restructuring, etc). It is probably unwise for governments to seek to directly compensate all factors of production (owners of capital and workers) for all shocks (irrespective of whether they are caused by policy change or by exogenous factors). There are a many potential sources of such need for adjustment, and the existence of mechanisms of compensation is likely to encourage a general resistance by governments to policy change and it would be rather unfair to develop adjustment assistance schemes that are directed at compensating dislocation or assisting relocation from only one specific source. The experience of trade adjustment assistance schemes in the developed countries has been mixed at best, with limited evidence of facilitating adjustment and of cost effectiveness (e.g. Trebilcock, Chandler and Howse, 1990). The development of institutional structures that increase the willingness to adjust (e.g. through the provision of social safety nets for all dislocated workers or improved employment services – see Rodrik, 1999) may be a better means of supporting adjustment to greater openness.

Skills development and productivity enhancement

Adjustment costs will be reduced if competitiveness and productivity can be increased quickly, through the enhancement of workers' skills, the improvement of firm's organization and improvements in management, financial and marketing methods, and enhancements in human capital and skills. The shift of resources is likely to require new employment skills and the entry of new businesses into these markets. Enhancement of public and private sector capacity to deliver training for workers and managers and to induce greater private sector involvement in training and the innovation process may be required if more open domestic markets are to bring the benefits of increased growth.

Trade facilitation and export diversification

Actual and potential exporters in developing countries are likely to need support with developing export products and gaining knowledge about export market opportunities. Accumulated experience of exporting across a wide range of export products is usually viewed as indicating that countries have institutions (private and public sector) and an infrastructure that are conducive to exporting. Many developing countries have an undiversified export structures, having acquired experience and understanding of exporting in only a narrow range of traditional exports (from natural resources or land-based activities). The diversification of exports into non-traditional manufacturing activities may require knowledge of different markets (new commercial contacts, etc.) and market access conditions (e.g. product standard requirements), and require improved customs procedures (e.g. to speed up access to intermediate inputs) and changes in transport facilities (e.g. refrigeration facilitates at airports). The actual requirements will vary across countries as the pattern of comparative advantage and export potential and initial conditions vary. What is required is a broad view of trade facilitation, not simply concern for the speed and efficiency of border/customs procedures (Milner, 2006). Major infrastructure developments to improve transportation systems may require much larger and more comprehensive trade facilitation programmes.

Other adjustment issues

Many developing countries may need support in the process of negotiating and implementing trade reform, and with understanding the implications for legislative reform and administrative change. There may also be a tax revenue or fiscal adjustment issue arising out of trade reform for many, in particular low income, developing countries. Where tariff revenue declines are associated with trade reform a country will need to either revise or reform the structure of taxation from non-trade tax sources in order to increase revenue from these alternative sources (see Baunsgaard and Keen, 2005). The amount of direct fiscal loss for any specific country resulting from the lowering of tariffs on imports will depend on a range of factors. These will include the pattern (average and spread) of current tariffs on imports and the amount of imports prior to the tariff reforms. However, it is not the revenue effect itself that captures the cost of fiscal adjustment. The decline in customs revenue is a domestic redistribution from the government to consumers of imported goods. For the governments of some countries any decline in customs revenue can be relatively easily offset by increasing tax collection from other sources (e.g. sales and income taxes). For others the absence or underdevelopment of the tax regime makes this switch of revenue generation more difficult and more costly to resolve. The adjustment costs will be associated with a range of legislative and administrative changes, hiring and retraining costs, or infrastructure developments required in order to extend or develop tax revenue generating capacity in the non-trade tax domain.

6.2   Complementary Policies

Measures to increase developing countries capacity to adjust to trade openness and policies to increase export supply capability are not separable from each other. Creating new jobs in the export sector facilitates adjustment, while more adaptable economies are more likely to create new jobs. A policy agenda beyond adjustment policies is relevant, and forms part of what has become known as 'aid for trade'. An integrated approach to trade and development, nationally and internationally, is required (UNCTAD, 2004). Pro-development measures can help developing countries cope with the challenges of increased trade and international integration, but also allow them to take advantage of new opportunities, while pro-integration measures seek to raise the effectiveness of measures that promote trade and international engagement. The mix of measures will vary across developing countries as they vary in size, location, economic structures, institutional arrangements and existing policies.

To sustain development, greater openness to international competition and trade expansion, developing countries must be able to efficiently absorb capital and intermediate goods, new ideas and new technologies, and to produce goods and services that can compete on price and quality in domestic and international markets. Developing these capacities requires greater accumulation of physical, human and organizational capital and enhanced technological capacity.

Trade liberalization itself can contribute to accumulating capital and improving technology. If it allows the expansion of exports and reduces the balance of payments constraint, it permits more capital goods imports that embody technological improvements. Access to cheaper imported intermediate goods and increases in competition resulting from increased openness can raise returns on investment and increase incentives to invest. However, a range of other industrial, sectoral, public sector and microeconomic policies may also be required.

In many developing countries many poor live in rural areas and work in agriculture, often with limited or no engagement with tradeable goods sectors. The capacity of producers and consumers to access supplies of imported goods efficiently and to deliver exports to foreign markets is not only influenced by its own and its trade partner's trade policies. It is critically dependent also on the scale and quality of the infrastructure affecting domestic and international transport and related services, such as communications, and the quality of its institutions supporting trade (see Milner, 2004).

For many countries the costs of imported goods and the competitiveness of their products in export markets depends more on international transport and other natural trade costs than on their own or other countries' trade policies. If trade costs are broadly measured to include policy barriers, international transport costs, information and contract enforcement costs, costs of currency conversions, legal and regulatory costs and local distribution costs, these are still much higher than one might imagine. Poor countries are likely to experience substantially higher costs; see Anderson and van Wincoop (2004). Some countries are remote or landlocked. There may be a weak transport infrastructure and uncompetitive transport services. Further, the relatively small scale of trade may be more important than the distance to markets or from suppliers. There is growing recognition that trade policy, narrowly defined, has been over-emphasized at the expense of complementary trade-related measures. Africa-wide information can be found in Limao and Venables (2001). For detailed country-specific information on Uganda, see Milner and others (2000), and on Malawi see Milner and Zgovu (2006). Such measures include domestic and international transport policy reforms, national or regional infrastructure developments, or reforms to improve business services (e.g. insurance, banking) affecting the cost of international transactions. Manufacturing is transactions-intensive, and with the growing fragmentation of international production and creation of international production networks it is important that developing countries have access to competitive trade and trade-related services if they are to be able to be a part of such networks.

7 Conclusion

The judgement that trade economists reach about the role of trade policy in the development process tends to be fashioned by their view of whether trade is generally a source of enrichment or a source of impoverishment. The view that trade is, in general, a source of impoverishment in a world of pervasive structural rigidities, and market failure is now much less influential in the trade and development literature than it used to be. There is little intellectual support for the type of inward-looking and import-substituting trade policies that were witnessed in the 1950s and 1960s. The experience and evidence of high costs of protection from resource misallocation, under-utilization of capacity and of potential scale economies arising from uncompetitive domestic markets, and of incentives to produce for often, small domestic markets, resulting in x-inefficiencies and rent-seeking behaviour, and from constrained access and exposure to competitive intermediate inputs and capital goods embodying technological innovations, undermined the case for highly interventionist and inward-oriented trade strategies. The demonstration effect of the East Asian economies in successfully supporting industrialisation through outward-oriented and exporting trade strategies also added (initially at least) further impetus to the case for more liberal trade policies.

There is, however, still considerable controversy to be found in the literature on trade, trade policy and economic development. It is possible to represent in a credible fashion trade as having asymmetries, with smaller dynamic gains (even losses) for the less technologically advanced nations or with effects that reduce these countries capacity to conduct domestic R&D and be a source of future innovation. There are associated fears in developing countries that they are destined to be producers of natural-resource based or low skill, labour-intensive goods. In the absence of market failures, the optimal trade policy is still free trade which maximizes the developing countries' access to the most technologically advanced intermediate and capital goods imports. Although perhaps less pervasive than perceived by structuralist thinking, there are often many market imperfections and other sources of market (and policy) failures in developing countries that may provide a case for intervention. The debate about the need for intervention and capacity of developing country governments to intervene effectively and efficiently remains. Liberal trade economists continue to point to the non-optimality in general of trade policy to correct for domestic market failures, even if trade policy is appropriately targeted and set. Constraints (including fiscal administrative and information ones) on the use of optimal, non-trade policies are cited by opponents of the liberal stance, as is what they would view as the inappropriate treatment of distortions as exogenous. These opponents of liberal trade policies tend, as a result, to advocate more interventionist policies, including interventionist trade policies. Indeed they look for empirical support for their case from the experience of the East Asian exporting countries, for whom they offer the revised view that a number of these countries succeeded through the use of active and selective trade and industrial policies to support both import-substitution and export promotion. We reviewed this argument in some depth (section 4). Although there clearly were differences in the policy regimes of the relatively free-trade Asian exporters (Hong Kong and Singapore) and countries such as South Korea, it is evident that incentives in all these countries produced relatively neutral trade regimes. Further, we point to the technical and political economy dangers of encouraging the less-developed economies (with less policy and administrative capacity) to pursue effective mixed and selective trade policies.

The sceptical assessment offered here of the revisionist assessment of the basis of the successful Asian exporters goes along with a revised assessment of the fairly influential sceptic's view of the empirical evidence on the growth benefits of trade openness. The sceptics are correct in pointing to the problems of measuring and comparing summary trade policy indicators across countries, and to the dangers of misinterpreting cross-sectional (country) evidence of a positive growth-openness relationship. The more recent panel estimation of growth models across countries and time, which controls for fixed and other effects more appropriately and which confronts endogeneity issues, provides more robust support for a positive growth benefit of trade openness and trade reform. This recent literature also points to factors that may condition the trade policy–growth relationship; that is the related policies or conditions (human capital, institutional and/or infrastructure conditions) that may make trade policy openness more beneficial in growth terms. This empirical evidence points to the insufficiency of trade policy reform in supporting development, and the associated need for complementary policies. Section 6 reviews a range of adjustment support and complementary (pro-development and pro-integration) measures. Trade policy design is important for development, but it is certainly not the only policy that matters for development!

Notes

* GEP and School of Economics, University of Nottingham.
1. It is also typically views the avoidance of excessive and selective government intervention in factor and product markets as desirable, but this has been discussed in section 3.
2. Indeed, Bhagwati (1988) refers to relative incentives which favour exportables relative to importables as an 'ultra-EP' strategy.
3. The analysis below draws heavily on McKay and Milner (1997a). For a less technical treatment of the issues, see McKay and Milner (1998).
4. Allowing also for saving and/or borrowing between the two periods and summing over each type of exportable and importable good.
5. The larger the increase in the price of non-tradeables induced by selective intervention, the greater the share of the burden of protection that is borne by unprotected tradeables rather than by non-tradeables. For a discussion of the idea of shifting the burden and incidence of protection, see Greenaway and Milner (1987).
6. Yanikkaya (2003) finds long-run growth effects of liberalization based on trade-volume based indicators that are generally consistent with Greenaway et al. (2002) for a larger panel of countries (100) and longer time period (1970–97), but not when based on trade barrier indicators.
7. There is some case study evidence on labour market adjustment to trade liberalization in developing countries but data limitations have restricted systematic cross country analysis. There is indirect evidence (see Santos-Paulino and Thirlwall, 2004) of potential adjustment problems arising from the more rapid response of imports than exports to trade liberalization.

References

Adnes, A.F., and E. Glaeser (1999) 'Evidence on growth, increasing returns and the extent of the market', *Quarterly Journal of Economics* 114: 1025–45.

Aghion, P., R. Burgess, S. Redding and F. Zilibolt (2004) 'Entry, liberalization and inequality in economic performance', *Journal of the European Economic Association* 3: 291–302.

Alesina, A.E., E. Spolaore and R. Wacziarg (2000) 'Economic integration and political disintegration', *American Economic Review* 90: 1276–96.

Anderson, J.E., and E. van Wincoop (2004) 'Trade costs', *Journal of Economic Literature* 42: 691–751.

Balassa, B. (1982) *Development Strategies in Semi-Industrialised Countries*. Washington, D.C.: World Bank.

Baldwin, R.E. (1969) 'The case against infant industry protection', *Journal of Political Economy* 77: 295–305.

Baunsgaard, T., and M. Keen (2005) 'Tax Revenue and (or?) Trade Liberalisation', IMF Working Paper, 05/112, Washington, D.C.

Bell, M.B., B. Ross-Larsin and L. Westphal (1984) 'Assessing the performance of infant industries', *Journal of Development Economics* 16: 101–28.

Bhagwati, J.N. (1988) 'Export promoting trade strategy: issues and evidence', *World Bank Research Observer* 3: 22–58.

—— (1978) *Anatomy and Consequences of Exchange Control Regimes*. Cambridge, MA: Ballinger Publishing Co.

—— (1978) *Foreign Trade Regimes and Economic Development*. Cambridge, MA: Ballinger.

—— (1971) 'The generalised theory of distortions and welfare', in J. Bhagwati et al. (eds), *Trade, Balance of Payments and Growth*. Amsterdam: North Holland.

—— (1990) 'Export promoting trade strategy: issues and evidence', in C. Milner (ed.), *Export Promotion Strategies: Theory and Evidence from Developing Countries*. New York: New York University Press.

Bhagwati, J.N., and T.N. Srinivason (1969) 'Optimal intervention to achieve non-economic objectives', *Review of Economic Studies* 36: 27–38.

Bleaney, M.F., and D. Greenaway (1993) 'Long run trends in the relative price of primary commodities and in the terms of trade of developing countries', *Oxford Economic Papers*, 45: 349–63.

Blomström, M., R.E. Lipsey and M. Zejan (1994) 'What explains developing country growth?', in W. Baumol, R. Nelson and E. Wolff (eds), *Convergence of Productivity: Cross-National Studies and Historical Evidence*. London: Oxford University Press.

Buffie, E.F. (2001) *Trade Policy in Developing Countries*. Cambridge: Cambridge University Press.

Corden, M. (1974) *Trade Policy and Economic Welfare*. Oxford: Clarendon Press.

Chang, R., L. Kaltoui and N.J. Loayza (2008) 'Openness can be good for growth: the role of policy complementarities', *Journal of Development Economics* (in press).

Chen, L.L., and J. Devereux (1991) 'Protection, export promotion and development', *Journal of Development Economics* 40: 387–95.

Coe, D., and E. Helpman (1995) 'International R&D spillovers', *European Economic Review* 39: 859–87.

Coe, D., E. Helpman and A. Hoffmaister (1997) 'North-south R&D spillovers', *Economic Journal* 107: 134–49.

Cox, D., and R.G. Harris (1985) 'Trade liberalisation and industrial organisation: some estimates for Canada', *Journal of Political Economy* 93: 115–45.

Dixit, A., and V. Norman (1980) *Theory of International Trade*, London: Cambridge University Press.

Dollar, D. (1992) 'Outward-oriented developing countries really do grow more rapidly: evidence from 95 LDCs, 1976–1985', *Economic Development and Cultural Change* 40: 523–44.

Dornbusch, R. (1992) 'The case for trade liberalization in developing countries', *Journal of Economic Perspectives* 6: 69–86.

Eaton, J., and S. Kortum (1996) 'Trade in ideas: productivity and patenting in the OECD', *Journal of International Economics* 40: 251–78.

Edwards, S. (1998) 'Openness, productivity and growth: what do we really know', *Economic Journal* 108: 383–98.

——(1989) *Real Exchange Rates, Devaluation and Adjustment: Exchange Rate Policy in Developing Countries*. Cambridge, MA: MIT Press.

Feenstra, R. (1996) 'Trade and uneven growth', *Journal of Development Economics* 49: 229–56.

Flam, H., and E. Helpman (1987) 'Industrial policy under monopolistic competition', *Journal of International Economics* 22: 79–102.

Franbel, J.A., and D. Romer (1999) 'Does trade cause growth?' *American Economic Review* 89: 379–99.

Girma, S., M. Henry, R. Kneller and C.R. Milner (2009) 'Thresholds in the trade liberalisation – productivity growth relationship: the role of natural barriers', *Oxford Bulletin of Economics and Statistics* (forthcoming).

Greenaway, D., and C.R. Milner (1993) *Trade and Industrial Policy in Developing Countries*. Basingstoke: Macmillan.

——(1987) 'True protection concepts and their use in evaluating commercial policy in developing countries', *Journal of Development Studies* 23: 200–19.

Greenaway, D., and M.E. Haque (2005) 'Liberalisation and aggregate productivity growth', in H. Gorg, D. Greenaway and R. Kneller (eds), *Globalisation and Productivity Growth: Theory and Evidence*. Basingstoke: Palgrave Macmillan.

Greenaway, D., C.W. Morgan and P. Wright (2002) 'Trade liberalisation and growth in developing countries', *Journal of Development Economics* 67: 229–44.

Grossman, G.M., and E. Helpman (1991) *Innovation and Growth in the Global Economy*. Cambridge: MIT Press.

Henry, M., R. Kneller and C.R. Milner (2009) 'Trade, technology transfer and national efficiency in developing countries', *European Economic Review* 53: 237–54.

Henry, M., and C.R. Milner (2005) 'Globalisation and aggregate productivity growth', in H. Gorg, D. Greenaway and R. Kneller (eds), *Globalisation and Productivity Growth: Theory and Evidence*. Basingstoke: Palgrave Macmillan.

Johnson, H.G. (1965) 'Optimal trade intervention in the presence of domestic distortions', in R. Baldwin et al. (eds), *Trade, Growth and the Balance of Payments'*. Chicago: Rand McNally.

——(1970) 'A new view of the infant industry argument', in I.A. McDougall and R.H. Snape (eds), *Studies in International Economics*. Amsterdam: North Holland.

Kee, H.L., A. Nicita and M. Olarreaga (2009) 'Estimating trade restrictiveness indices', *Economic Journal* 119: 172–99.

Keller, W. (1998) 'Are international R&D spillovers trade-related? Analyzing spillovers among randomly matched trade partners', *European Economic Review* 42: 1469–81.

Kemp, M. (1962) 'The gains from international trade', *Review of Economic Studies* 72: 803–19.

Krueger, A. (1991) 'Industrial development and liberalization', in L. Krause and K. Kihwan (eds), *Liberalization in the Process of Economic Development*. Berkeley: University of California Press.

Krueger, A.D. (1978) *Liberalisation Attempts and Consequences*. New York: National Bureau of Economic Research.

Krugman, P.R. (1993) 'Protection in developing countries', in R. Dornbusch (ed), *Policy-making in the Open Economy*. New York: Oxford University Press.

Lal, D. (1983) 'The Poverty of Development Economics', Hobart Paper No. 16, Institute of Economic Affairs, London.

Lee, J. (1997) 'The maturation and growth of infant industries: the case of Korea', *World Development* 25: 1271–81.

Lichtenberg, F.R., and B. Van Pottelsberghe de la Potteri (1998) 'International R&D spillovers: A comment', *European Economic Review* 42: 1483–91.

Limao, N., and A.J. Venables (2001) 'Infrastructure, geographical disadvantage, transport costs and trade', *World Bank Economic Review* 5: 451–79.

Little, I., T. Scitovsky and M. Scott (1970) *Industry and Trade in Some Developing Countries*. London: Oxford University Press.

Markussen, J., and A.J. Venables (1988) 'Trade policy with increasing reforms and imperfect competition: contradictory results from competing assumptions', *Journal of International Economics* 24: 299–316.

Martin, J. (1978) 'X-inefficiency, managerial effort and protection', *Economica* 45: 273–86.

Mayer, J. (2001) 'Technology diffusion, human capital and economic growth in developing countries', UNCTAD Discussion Paper No. 154; Geneva: UNCTAD.

McKay, A., and C.R. Milner (1998) 'The strategic use of trade policies for development: some general equilibrium issues', in Sapsford and Chen (eds), opp cit.

—— (1997b) 'Defining and measuring trade strategy: theory and some evidence for the Caribbean', *Journal of Development Studies* 33: 658–74.

—— (1997a) 'Strategic trade policy, learning by doing effects and economic development', *World Development* 25: 1893–99.

Miller, S.M., and M.P. Upadhyay (2000) 'The effects of openness, trade orientation and human capital on total factor productivity', *Journal of Development Economics* 63: 399–423.

Milner, C.R. (2006) 'Making NAMA Work: Supporting adjustment and development', *The World Economy* 29: 1409–22.

—— (1997) 'On natural and policy-induced sources of trade regime bias', *Review of World Economics* 132: 740–52.

Milner, C., and A. McKay (1996) 'Neutrality and export promotion: issues, evidence and policy implications', in V.N. Balasubramanyam and D. Greenaway, *Trade and Development: Essays in Honour of Jagdish Bhagwati*. London: Macmillan.

Milner, C.R., W.O. Morrissey and N. Rudaheranwa (2000) 'Policy and non-policy barriers to trade and implicit taxation of exports in Uganda', *Journal of Development Studies* 37: 67–90.

Milner, C.R., and E. Zgovu (2006) 'A natural experiment for identifying the impact of "natural" barriers on exports', *Journal of Development Economics* 80: 251–68.

Nunn, N. (2009) 'The importance of history for economic development', *Annual Review of Economics* 1: 65–92.

Pack, H. (1988) 'Industrialization and trade', in H. Chenery and T.N. Srinivason (eds), *Handbook of Development Economics*, vol 1 Amsterdam: North Holland.

Pavcnik, N. (2002) 'Trade liberalisation, exit and productivity improvements: evidence from Chilean plants', *Review of Economic Studies* 69: 245–76.

Prebisch, R. (1950) *The Economic Development of Latin America and its Principle Problems*. New York: United Nations.

Pritchett, L. (1996) 'Measuring outward orientation in developing countries', *Journal of Development Economics* 49: 307–35.

Rivera-Batiz, L., and P. Romer (1991) 'Economic integration and endogenous growth', *Quarterly Journal of Economics* 106: 531–55.

Rodriguez (2008) 'Trade and development', in A. Dutt and J. Ros (eds), *International Handbook of Development Economics*. Cheltenham: Edward Elgar.

Rodrik, D. (1999) 'The New Global Economy and Developing Countries: Making Openness Work', Policy Essay 24, Overseas Development Council, Washington, D.C.

Rodrik, D. (1995) 'Trade policy and industrial policy reform', in J. Bereman and T.N. Srinivason (eds) *Handbook of Development Economics*. Amsterdam: North Holland.

—— (1992) 'Conceptual issues in the design of trade policy for industrialization', *World Development* 20: 309–20.

—— (1988) 'Imperfect competition, scale economies and trade policy in developing countries', in R. Baldwin (ed.), *Trade Policy Issues and Empirical Analysis*. Chicago: University of Chicago Press.

Rodrik, D., and F. Rodriguez (2000) 'Trade policy and economic growth: a skeptic's guide to the cross national evidence', mimeo.

Sachs, J., and A. Warner (1995) 'Economic reform and the process of global integration', *Brookings Papers on Economic Activity* 1: 1–118.

Samuelson, P.A. (1962) 'The gains from international trade once again', *Economic Journal* 37: 47–61.

Santos-Paulino, A., and Thirlwall, A.P. (2004) 'The impact of trade liberalisation on exports, imports and balance of payments of developing countries', *Economic Journal* 114: F50–F72.

Sapsford, D. (1985) 'The statistical debate on the net barter terms of trade: a comment and some additional information', *Economic Journal* 95: 781–8.

Sapsford, D., and J.-R. Chen (1998) (eds) *Development Economics and Policy*. Basingstoke: Macmillan.

Singer, H.W. (1988) 'The World Development Report 1987 on the blessings of outward orientation: a necessary correction', *Journal of Development Studies* 24: 232–6.

—— (1950) 'The distribution of the gains between borrowing and investing countries', *American Economic Review* 40: 473–85.

Smith, M.A. (1979) 'Intertemporal gains from trade', *Journal of International Economics* 9: 239–48.

Spraos, J. (1980) 'The statistical debate on the net barter terms of trade', *Economic Journal* 90: 107–28.

Stern, N. (1989) 'The economics of development: a survey', *Economic Journal* 99: 597–685.

Trebilcock, M.J., M.A. Chandler and R. Howse (1990) *Trade and Transitions: A Comparative Analysis of Adjustment Policies*. London: Routledge.

Tybout, J. (1996) 'Scale economies as a source of efficiency gains', in M. Roberts and J. Tybout (eds), *Industrial Evolution in Developing Countries*. New York: Oxford University Press.

Tybout, J., J. de Melo and V. Corbo (1991) 'The effects of trade reforms on scale and technical efficiency: new evidence from Chile', *Journal of International Economics* 31: 231–50.

Tybout, J., and D. Westbrook (1995) 'Trade liberalization and dimensions of efficiency change in Mexican manufacturing industries', *Journal of International Economics* 39: 53–78.

Tybout, J., and M. Roberts (1997) 'The decision to export to Colombia: an empirical model of entry with sunk costs', *American Economic Review* 87: 545–63.

UNCTAD (2004) *The Least Developed Countries Report, 2004: Linking International Trade with Poverty*. Geneva: UNCTAD.

Wacziarg, R. (1998) 'Measuring the dynamic gains from trade', *World Bank Economic Review* 15: 393–429.

Wade, R. (2003) *Governing the Market: Economic Theory and the Role of Government in East Asian Industrialization*. Princeton: Princeton University Press.

World Bank (1993) *The East Asian Miracle: Economic Growth and Public Policy*. Washington: The World Bank.

World Bank (1988) *World Development Report*. Washington, D.C.: The World Bank.

Yanikkaya, H. (2003) 'Trade openness and economic growth', *Journal of Development Economics* 72: 55–79.

21
International Migration*

Noel Gaston† and Doug Nelson‡

Like migration itself, economic research on migration seems to come in waves. The large scale of current global migration, and the sometimes quite ugly politics associated with immigration, have produced just such a wave of research. Theoretical and empirical research on migration, in particular, occurs across the social sciences, with particularly large bodies in economics, demography/sociology and political science. Within economics, the study of migration falls between trade and labour economics, with sizable bodies of both theoretical and econometric work. To limit the field of coverage and maintain consistency with the other chapters in the volume, we will focus on a set of questions framed by standard trade theoretic models and the empirical research that bears on those questions. As with the bulk of the recent literature, we pay particular attention to how migration impacts labour market outcomes. The popular perception that these outcomes may be adverse for native workers constitutes an important ingredient in the political economy of immigration.

We begin our analysis with two sorts of background: section 1 provides a brief overview of data on the scale and distribution of global migration; while section 2 provides an overview of the main theoretical models that will be used in this chapter. The substantive core of the chapter is the analysis of a set of questions that treat migration as a straightforward case of international factor arbitrage. We consider two broad types of questions: those that are essentially international questions; and those that are essentially domestic questions. With respect to the first type, we consider the effect of migration on comparative advantage and trade patterns, and whether immigration and trade are complements or substitutes. Turning to essentially national questions, we will focus on aggregate level effects on production structure and labour markets. All of these topics treat migration as straightforward factor arbitrage. That is, nothing essential would be lost by switching the theoretical analysis from labour to capital migration. Section 3 reviews the empirical literature on the labour market effects of immigration. In section 4, we turn to two issues which are fundamentally about the international equilibrium: comparative advantage and the pattern of trade and the relationship between trade and labour mobility. In section 5, we examine an issue in which the analysis really is about labour in an essential way: the role of networks. In the final section, we conclude the chapter with some observations on the political economy of immigration policy.

1 Some Basic Data on International Migration

Migration is not a recent phenomenon: people have always migrated in search of food, shelter and fortune (e.g. the gold rushes in California, Victoria, etc.). They have left the mother country for the colonies; have fled their countries during wartime, times of persecution, famine and political chaos. Historically, much migration was involuntary: African slaves were transported to the United States, convicts transported to Australian penal colonies and bonded labour was transported to East Africa and other places. Most modern day migration, however, is voluntary and is driven by the search for a better life.

In 2010, the number of international migrants in the world reached almost 214 million, which represents 3.1 percent of the world population. In the last two decades, the world has had 59 million more international migrants (see table 21.1). While 3 percent seems a trifling amount, there are considerable differences across regions and individual countries. Developed countries have

Table 21.1 Estimated number of international migrants, 1990–2010.

Development group and major area	Number of international migrants (millions)		Percentage of total population		Percentage distribution of international migrants	
	1990	2010	1990	2010	1990	2010
World	154.8	213.9	2.9	3.1	100.0	100.0
More developed regions	82.4	127.7	7.2	10.3	53.2	59.7
Less developed regions	72.5	86.2	1.8	1.5	46.8	40.3
Africa	16.4	19.3	2.5	1.9	10.6	9.0
Asia	49.8	61.3	1.6	1.5	32.2	28.7
Latin America and the Caribbean	7.0	7.5	1.6	1.3	4.5	3.5
Northern America	27.6	50.0	9.8	14.2	17.8	23.4
Europe	49.4	69.8	6.9	9.5	31.9	32.6
Oceania	4.8	6.0	16.2	16.8	3.1	2.8

Source: United Nations, Department of Economic and Social Affairs, Population Division, *Trends in the International Migration Stock: The 2008 Revision.*
Notes: 2010 figures are estimates. *More developed regions* comprise all regions of Europe plus Northern America, Australia/New Zealand and Japan. *Less developed regions* are Africa, Asia (excluding Japan), Latin America, the Caribbean, plus Melanesia, Micronesia and Polynesia. *International migrant stock*: Mid-year estimate of the number of people living in a country or area other than that in which they were born. If the number of foreign-born was not available, the estimate is the number of people living in a country other than that of their citizenship.

absorbed about three-quarters of the increase in the number of international migrants in the past two decades. The major increases in the number of international migrants occurred in North America (22.4 million) and Europe (20.4 million). The proportion of migrants in the total population between 1990 and 2010 increased in all the more developed regions and declined in the less developed regions. Lowell (2007) notes that these trends actually extend back to at least 1975.

At the present time, the countries with at least 20 million inhabitants, where international migrants will constitute more than 20 percent of the population, are Australia, Canada and Saudi Arabia (table 21.2). Countries with increases in the last two decades of international migrants of greater than 60 percent include Canada, Germany, the United Kingdom and the United States. The most dramatic change has been experienced by Spain, where the number of international migrants grew by a remarkable 686 percent. A relatively small number of countries host the majority of the world's international migrants. The United States accepts by far the largest number of international migrants.

During most of the 1990s, while there was no significant increase in legal immigration flows, illegal immigration increased steadily. On the one hand, this fact points to the effectiveness of policies aimed at restricting immigration (Hanson, 2009). On the other hand, the difficulty in controlling illegal flows has elevated immigration to an important place on the political stage in many countries. Migration and population policies are driven by different considerations in source, transit and eventual host countries. However, migration policies

Table 21.2   International migration, by country.

Country	Total (millions)	Percentage of total population	Total (millions)	Percentage of total population
	2010		1990	
Saudi Arabia	7.3	27.8	4.7	29.2
Australia	4.7	21.9	3.6	21.0
Canada	7.2	21.3	4.5	16.2
Spain	6.4	14.1	0.8	2.1
United States of America	42.8	13.5	23.3	9.1
Germany	10.8	13.1	5.9	7.5
Ukraine	5.3	11.6	6.9	13.4
Côte d'Ivoire	2.4	11.2	1.8	14.4
France	6.7	10.7	5.9	7.5
United Kingdom	6.5	10.4	3.7	6.5

Source: United Nations, Department of Economic and Social Affairs, Population Division. *International Migration, 2009 Wallchart.*
Notes: Countries with populations greater than 20 million and migrant stock proportions greater than 10 percent in 2010.

have changed most notably in many developed countries: from an almost open policy (for whites, at least) to much more targeted programs favouring migrants with higher levels of education, skills and human capital. In reality, this policy shift may be illusory. Hatton and Williamson (2006) suggest that any changes in targeting the number of 'high quality' immigrants, relative to 'low quality' immigrants, has more to do with the countries and regions from which the new residents are emigrating.

More than two-thirds of the immigrants in OECD countries come from low-income regions of the world (Hanson, 2009). Lowell (2007) shows that there was a net increase of just less than 7.5 million non-tertiary educated migrants from less developed and into more developed nations during the 1990s (an increase of 64 percent). In fact, in the year 2000 almost 96 percent of all adult migrants with less than a tertiary education settled in North America, Europe or Oceania.[1] The most heated debates are undoubtedly concerned with the immigration of unskilled labour and its impact on labour market performance. While immigration is generally thought to have had a relatively minor impact on national wage levels, there may be, however, unwanted effects on the wages of certain occupations or skill groups. As with trade liberalization, these distributional issues are very prominent in the debate about the desirability of immigration.

2   The Basic General-equilibrium Framework: Factor Mobility and Factor Returns

Most research on immigration begins by abstracting from both preference heterogeneity and technology heterogeneity to focus on endowment heterogeneity. Immigration is simply a transfer of some foreign factors of production from one country to another. When discussing migration, these factors will be called labour; but in these models there is nothing in particular to distinguish different sorts of labour from one another, or to distinguish labour as a class from other types of factors of production.

For most trade economists, the 2-factor × 2-good model of general competitive equilibrium, with the Heckscher–Ohlin–Samuelson (HOS) assumptions, is the first stop for developing intuition on real (as opposed to monetary) international questions. By contrast, most labour economists start with some version of the many-factor × 1-good model of general equilibrium. As we shall see, these models, as well as higher dimensional trade models, involve quite different adjustment processes following endowment changes.

2.1   Factor mobility in the 2-factor × 2-good, Heckscher–Ohlin–Samuelson model

In the HOS model, the equilibrium factor prices can be solved for using only the zero profit conditions. Moreover, as long as both goods continue to be produced, the factor endowments do not enter into the determination of relative factor prices. Leamer (1995) calls this important result the *factor price insensitivity theorem*. This is the one-country version of the more well-known, but empirically more dubious, *factor price equalization theorem*. The maintained assumption of an unchanged production technology before and after an immigration shock seems more empirically plausible than the assumption that technology is common across countries.

At this point, we simply note that instead of adjustment in relative factor prices, adjustment to the immigration shock occurs on the output margin, with one sector (the labour intensive sector) expanding and the other sector contracting. Adjustment being all on the output margin is captured by the *Rybczynski theorem*: 'At constant relative commodity prices, and under the full set of HOS assumptions, an increase in the endowment of one factor, holding the other endowment constant, will cause an increase in the output of the commodity whose production uses that factor intensively, proportionally greater in magnitude than the change in endowment; and a decrease in the output of the other commodity' (Rybczynski, 1955).

Factor price insensitivity (FPI) needs to be qualified in at least two ways. First, if the country is large, so that a change in its pattern of production changes the world relative prices, then standard Stolper–Samuelson effects also apply. The second qualification refers to an endowment change sufficiently large as to move the endowment point outside the cone of diversification.

2.2   Factor mobility in the *m*-factor × 1-good model

The $m \times 1$ model is the most common framework applied by labour economists working on estimating the effects of immigration, as well as the basis of the two-country model widely used for discussion of international equilibrium of migration. For this model, the commodity is interpreted as gross domestic product.

Here the relative endowments enter into the determination of relative factor prices. This is most transparent in the two factor case. If a country permits an increase in the stock of the mobile factor, say by increasing the immigration quota, it is easy to see that the consequent change in relative factor supplies means that all units of the mobile factor previously resident in the country experience a reduction their return, while all units of the internationally immobile factor experience an increase in their return. Generalizing this result to the case of multiple immobile factors requires that all immobile factors be substitutes for the internationally mobile factor.[2]

2.3   Factor mobility in *m*-factor × *n*-good models

In the general case, *m* factors are used to produce *n* final goods. When $m = n$ (the 'even' case used extensively in the literature), endowment change has no effect on factor prices. If $m > n$, FPI will not generally hold and immigration will reduce wages which, of course, is what our intuition tells us should be the effect of immigration on wages. Note, however, that it depends on the *prima facie* least plausible assumption about the relative dimensionality of endowments *versus* produced commodities. Most empirical work seems to find support for a world in which there are many more commodities than factors and multiple cones of diversification.[3] The empirically plausible case of $m < n$ is tricky because the production structure is indeterminate (see Bhagwati et al., 1998, 187–88). However, at least for FPI, this is not so dire. As is often pointed out, if prices are parametrically given (the small country case), however many goods there are in the world, the small open economy will generally produce only $m = n$. That is, if an endowment change remains within the original cone of diversification and commodity prices are unchanged, then factor prices are unchanged.

We have spent time on FPI in the standard Heckscher–Ohlin (HO) environment because there seems to be quite a bit of misinterpretation. It is worth noting for future reference that the sole relevant difference between the basic frameworks in use by labour and trade economists is dimensionality. Dimensionality is not nearly so damaging of FPI as it is of factor price equalization (FPE). But it seems that, on any but fairly short-term interpretations of the concepts of commodity and factor, there are massively more commodities than factors, and in this case the *logic* of FPI holds quite straightforwardly. Note that we are not arguing that FPI actually obtains, but that, within the parameters that are commonly agreed in the basic labour and trade theoretic traditions, $m \leq n$ seems a more plausible assumption, from which FPI follows. We should generally expect adjustment at the output-mix margin to play a considerable role in responding to factor immigration. If the mechanism breaks down, it must be as a result of deviations from those elements of the basic model that are shared between trade and labour economists, and not on dimensionality.[4]

3   Core Empirical Results Based on Standard Models

The preceding section considered two main comparative static questions: the effect of endowment changes on output; and the effect of endowment changes on factor wages. Perhaps not surprisingly, the second question has attracted by far the majority of systematic research with specific reference to the migration of labour. Nonetheless, there has been some research seeking to estimate Rybczynski effects. While most of this research does not specifically consider migration, the causal factors are closely related, so following a review of the literature on the labour market effects of immigration, this section turns to a brief discussion of empirical research on the Rybczynski theorem.

In turning to the relevant empirical research, it is important to keep in mind the two common ways of organizing or interpreting empirical analysis. On the one hand, the referent of the analysis can be a single country, observed before and after a comparative static shock. Alternatively, the referents can be two (or more) countries, differing only in the comparative static shock. We have already seen this distinction in the discussion of FPI *versus* FPE. There we noted that the auxiliary assumptions supporting empirical interpretation (specifically, identical technological opportunities before and after the shock) are more plausible across relatively short periods of time (for FPI) than across countries (for FPE), and that this difference helps explain the greater scepticism as to the empirical content of FPE relative to that of FPI. In the next subsection, we consider empirical work on immigration and wages. In the context of immigration, it makes sense to focus on this relationship in the national context, but it should be noted that testing for FPE is formally the same question. Then we turn briefly to empirical work on output changes and immigration. In the one country case, for the HOS model, this concerns the Rybczynski theorem. However, the empirical literature has also considered cross-country analyses of the relationship between the endowment vector and the structure of output that is formally identical.

3.1   Empirics of immigration and wages

Our primary focus here is on the contribution of immigration to the growing inequality experienced in many OECD countries during the 1980s, and the implications of that experience for future policy. In this section we consider in some detail empirical research by labour economists on the link between immigration and labour market outcomes (primarily wages). Contemporary empirical research on the labour market effects of immigration has grown quite large since its development in the early 1980s. We will divide this research into two broad categories: production function based studies; and cross-sectional wage or unemployment studies.

Whether or not the implementation takes a structural form, the structure that drives both the econometric specification and the intuition for interpreting that analysis is generally a one-sector, perfectly competitive model. The labour economists' standard approach to wage inequality and income distribution is firmly rooted to an analysis of 'supply, demand and institutions' (Freeman, 1993, 444–49). To evaluate the labour market effects of immigration, identifying how the immigration of workers with differing skills affects the relative supply of labour can be viewed as necessary first step. In turn, the skill group characteristics of new immigrants are affected by the returns to skill as well as the distribution of earnings in both the source and host countries. Finally, labour market institutions are important because they affect the degree of wage inequality, the structure of wages and the labour market response to shocks.

Before proceeding, we comment briefly on a well-known gross distinction used to characterize this literature: area studies *versus* factor content studies. The problem is that the label is misleading. Most labour theoretic frameworks apply a factor content based approach, that is, it is the change in relative supply that generates the change in labour market outcomes. The issue is actually about *level of analysis*. That is, how large must the geographic unit be such that observations on supplies and prices of various classes of labour are independent? As we shall see, there are good reasons for believing that geographic units like standard metropolitan statistical areas (SMSAs), or states, are linked in ways that are inconsistent with cross-sectional observations being independent draws from some distribution; however, it is not at all clear that the statistically optimal level of analysis is the nation. There is considerable evidence that national borders have economic effects but, by the same token, there is also considerable evidence that quite local labour markets take significant periods of time to adjust fully to macro shocks. On balance, it is not clear to us that there is a good reason to prefer one level of analysis to another. Level of analysis is always an important research decision, but this does not strike us as an essential distinguishing aspect in this body of research.

In addition to the issue of the appropriate level of analysis, another essential research question is the manner in which the common theoretical framework structures the research. We can thus make another broad distinction between structural (or 'production function') methods and regression based methods. We start with the former for the case of local labour market data.

3.1.1   Production function based methods

The first method to be developed in the current wave of research on the labour market effects of immigration involves selecting a specific functional form for the aggregate production function. That function is estimated, and hypotheses on the degree of substitutability or complementarity between inputs are tested. In addition, elasticities of derived demand can then be used to carry out policy experiments.

In carrying out work of this sort, investigators must select a functional form that does not prejudice the conclusion from the start. Thus, the commonly used Cobb–Douglas and CES forms are inappropriate for any input vector with more than two arguments. As a result, investigators have generally used one or another of the flexible functional forms.[5] In addition to selecting a specific functional form, the other major choice in this body of research involves the definition of the input vector. Broadly speaking, there are two approaches here: one defines the input vector in terms of observable characteristics (e.g. gender, age, immigrant status, etc.); while the other seeks to identify production relevant characteristics (e.g. quantity of human capital). As Borjas (1990) notes, regardless of the approach adopted, this research consistently finds little evidence that immigrants have a sizable adverse impact on the earnings or employment opportunities of natives in the United States.

While most of this research considers essentially closed economies, some papers develop analyses of immigration in the context of economies that are open to trade. For example, Wong (1988) works with an indirect trade utility function estimated on prices for home produced durable goods, home produced nondurable goods and services, and imported goods and services, and endowments of capital, land and labour, for a number of years between 1948 and 1983. Foreign capital and labour are taken to be perfect substitutes for the domestic factors, so the comparative statics on the indirect utility function can be used to generate elasticities. These elasticities are all small. In a number of papers, Kohli develops this sort of analysis in considerably greater detail. For example, using annual Swiss data from 1950 to 1986, Kohli (1999, 2002) estimates the translog cost function associated with the primal GNP function and a vector containing capital, home labour, immigrant labour and imports. Thus, where Wong treats home and immigrant labour as perfect substitutes, Kohli is able to test this relationship. In fact, Kohli finds that home and immigrant labour are substitutes, though not perfect substitutes. Commodity imports and immigrant labour are found to be complements. The magnitude of the estimated effect of immigration on native wages is negative, but quite small. However, Kohli simulates a short-run model in which the wage is downward inflexible, and finds the effect on home labour displacement to be large. Hijzen and Wright (2010) estimate a translog function with two types of domestic and immigrant labour, skilled and unskilled, along with capital and traded intermediates and two types of output. Like a number of other production function based studies, Hijzen and Wright find that the largest effect of unskilled immigrants is on unskilled immigrants already in the labour force, and that it is small. The impact on native unskilled workers is also negative, but even smaller. Skilled immigrants have little effect on the structure of factor payments at all.

Overall, econometric research which explicitly exploits production theoretic structure tends to find strong substitutability between immigrants and other immigrants of the same vintage and national origin and, otherwise, widely varying patterns of complementarity and substitutability between immigrants and natives. More importantly, the elasticities between immigrant and native labour are consistently small, and are smaller yet when channels of adjustment other than the wage are explicitly permitted in the analysis. That is, natives and immigrants are consistently found to be quite imperfect substitutes in production.

3.1.2   *The regression based approach to estimating wage effects of immigration*

While the production theoretic framework directly implements the theory that forms the basis for much of the labour theoretic research on the labour market effects of immigration, its requirements are demanding. To be set against the advantage of directly estimating cross elasticities of substitution is the reliance on functional form assumptions to identify the parameters of interest. Structural estimation invariably needs to trade off the requirements of functional form flexibility and strict adherence to the restrictions implied by the theory. In addition, while human capital variables can relatively easily be accommodated in the production theoretic framework, the incorporation of a wide range of standard control variables does not fit easily within this framework. Thus, as a result of the relative ease of application, greater similarity to existing techniques in labour econometrics and the desirability of including a richer set of controls, the majority of the research on the labour market effects of immigration has taken place within a regression framework. The latter approach generally involves reduced form regression analysis or the use of natural experiments to examine the empirical regularities.

What has become known as the 'aggregate factor proportions approach' involves regressing the ratio of skilled wages to unskilled wages in year t, on the relative labour supply of the two types of labour. Borjas et al. (1997) find that immigration was responsible for the decline in the earnings of unskilled native workers that occurred during the 1980s. Their paper has contributed to the view that, relative to the effects of growing international trade with less developed countries, immigration may have had a proportionately larger negative impact on the earnings of unskilled U.S. workers. A qualitatively similar approach is used to derive estimating equations for regional unemployment or wages. For example,

$$w_j = \gamma \lambda_j + \beta X_j + \varepsilon_j, \tag{1}$$

where j indexes the local labour market, w is the logarithm of the wage for a particular skill group, X is a vector of control variables and λ is the proportion of immigrants in the jth local labour market.[6] Altonji and Card (1991) and LaLonde and Topel (1991) use this approach and find scant evidence that immigration has disadvantaged U.S. workers.

Of course, regression specifications based on equation (1) have widespread application. For instance, there have been many studies using the regression framework that have focused on the importance of the large increase in the relative supply of workers during the 1970s to the increasing wage inequality that occurred throughout the later 1980s and early 1990s. The increase in the U.S. workforce caused by the labour force entry of the 'baby boomers' easily dwarfs the increase in the labour force caused by immigration. A common finding of a wide range of studies is that changes in cohort size associated with the baby-boom generation did not have a significant impact on cohort earnings. In the debate about the causes of rising earnings inequality during the 1980s, supply side changes were discounted as a candidate explanation for the increased dispersion in the income distribution in the United States during that period.

Notwithstanding, such findings do not necessarily imply that all supply side shocks are unimportant. As noted, some authors claim that immigration may have been responsible for the decline in the earnings of unskilled native workers that occurred during the 1980s. The immigration issue has been increasingly seen as one driven by distributional concerns. Freeman (Freeman, 1998, 110) argues that immigration may have had substantially larger effects on native unskilled workers than increased international trade with low-income countries, for instance. During the 1980s, a period during which wage inequality rapidly increased in the United States, immigration raised the supply of high school dropouts by approximately 25 percent, which exceeds the increase in the 'effective' labour supply, or factor content, of such workers attributable to trade.

The use of regressions to uncover the wage effects of immigration by regressing immigrant shares and other controls on wages or relative wages poses familiar problems. Among the more prominent concerns with regression analysis is the omission of important right-hand side variables. Biased estimates result if relevant characteristics or controls are not included in the regression equation. Similarly, how do various characteristics that are included in a model specification interact with one another? More generally, empirical work usually forces researchers to assume an appropriate functional form in order to reduce the problem at hand to one of estimating the parameters of interest. For example, would a linear function involve a serious misspecification loss? As the previous section revealed, there is a wide range of functional forms from which to choose and so the robustness of parameter estimates is invariably an issue that needs to be confronted.

Variable (mis)measurement and interpretation also pose problems. For instance, when does a migrant finally assimilate and become a native? The latter problem is particularly obvious in those countries that are essentially composed of older generations of immigrants (e.g. Australia and the United States).[7] More formally, there is the issue of weak separability of the various types of labour – not just of skilled versus unskilled labour, but also of native workers versus immigrant workers as well as first generation migrants versus second and later generations of migrants.

One of the more important difficulties in the empirical literature is the possibility that labour supply functions may not be independent of wages. Workers with high earnings potential are likely to migrate from a country with an egalitarian wage structure, while workers with low earnings potential are especially likely to migrate from a country with great wage inequality. In terms of source country characteristics, equality of the income distribution encourages what is termed 'positive selection bias'. Negative selection bias results when source countries have unequal income distributions and, therefore, migrants are likely to be the least skilled.

Addressing the endogeneity problem is the motivation for the use of instrumental variables and the quasi-experimental approach in the empirical labour literature. Due to the substantial difficulties associated with choosing 'good' instruments, considerably more weight in this branch of the literature has been attached to the results of the latter approach. Natural experiments occur when exogenous variation in independent variables (that determine 'treatment assignment') is created by abrupt exogenous shocks to labour markets. For example, natural experiments can arise due to institutional peculiarities (e.g. Vietnam era draft lotteries) or due to exogenous policy changes that affect some groups but not other groups. In the latter case, Hanson and Spilimbergo (2001) examine how enforcement of the U.S.–Mexico border is affected by changes in illegal immigration. They find that the equilibrium level of border enforcement varies inversely with relative demand shocks (and consequently, demand for undocumented labour). In other words, the authorities relax border enforcement when the demand for undocumented workers is high.

Without question, the most cited natural experiment paper is Card (1990) which examines the impact of the 'Mariel Boatlift' on Miami's labour market. As is well known, despite the dramatic and sudden 7 percent increase in the size of Miami's work force, Card is unable to detect any adverse impact on the wages or unemployment of less-skilled workers. Recently, Glitz (2006) uses the large migration associated with reunification of Germany to examine the labour market effects of migration. While he finds no evidence of wage effects, he does find that immigration increases unemployment. This is consistent with other findings that immigration in the context of labour market inflexibility can result in unemployment (e.g. Angrist and Kugler, 2003; D'Amuri et al., 2010).

Although subject to varying interpretations, the most common finding is that the wage effects of immigration are 'quantitatively unimportant'. However, one potential problem is the possibility that immigrants locate to areas where jobs are expanding anyway. Given the continuing significance of a small number of immigrant gateway cities (consistent with the major role played by networks in channelling immigration), it is not surprising that there is little evidence supporting this conjecture. A potentially more serious problem is that the internal migration by natives offsets the increased supply of immigrants. Consider the case of the Mariel Boatlift: natives who were considering moving to Miami might now foresee lower wages as a result of the increased labour force (or even decide to avoid Miami for racist or other social reasons); they will now try to identify a similar city as their new migration target; but those cities are likely to be precisely the cities used by Card as ideal untreated units (i.e. similar on all dimensions to Miami, but not receiving the immigrant shock). The new native immigrants to those cities will have a similar effect on the labour markets there to the effect of the *Marielitos* on the Miami labour market, thus biasing the analysis towards a finding of no effect. Card (2001; see also Kritz and Gurak, 2001) examined this conjecture and found that the inter-city migration decisions of natives and older immigrants are largely unaffected by inflows of new immigrants. However, using census data from 1960 to 2000, Borjas (2006) presents evidence consistent with a large effect of foreign migration on internal migration, and of the internal migration on estimates of the wage effect of foreign migration. Finally, while Cortes (2008) finds evidence of some offsetting native migration in her study of the effect of immigration on prices of non-traded goods and services in local markets, she concludes that this effect is not sufficient to arbitrage away the effect of migrants on prices. Overall, it remains a puzzle that regional economies should adjust so quickly to immigrant shocks, but so slowly to most other shocks studied by regional and labour economists.

One possibility, suggested by FPI, is that adjustment occurs on the output margin rather than on the wage margin. That is, the composition of output may change in response to an endowment shock, in such a way that factor prices are unchanged. The evidence on this is mixed: as we discuss in the next section, there is evidence of the sorts of Rybczynski effects needed to support this adjustment mechanism, as well as some (weak) direct evidence directly related to immigration shocks. Specifically, Hanson and Slaughter (2002) document the rapid growth in apparel, textiles, food products and other labour intensive industries in California after the arrival of Mexican migrants. They focus on state-specific endowment shocks and state-specific wage responses. They show that the state output-mix changes broadly match state endowment changes and that variation in state unit factor requirements is consistent with FPE across states. States absorb regional endowment shocks through mechanisms other than changes in regional relative factor price changes. This is consistent with the findings of Blanchard and Katz (1992) which indicate that wages and income per capita converge for American states. However, Blanchard and Katz also find that employment performance diverges, that is, shocks to employment grow and persist.[8] Overall, this is consistent with the view that small local labour market effects may be consistent with somewhat larger aggregate labour market effects.

3.1.3 *'Factor proportions', skill-cells and national data*

The approaches we have considered to this point, both production function and regression based, primarily identify labour market effects from variance across regions. We have just noted that internal migration of natives, and even of earlier waves of migrants, could interfere with inference in analyses based on local labour market data. As a response to this potential problem, Borjas has argued that analysis of the effect of migration on labour markets should proceed at the level of the national economy (Borjas et al., 1992; Borjas, Freeman and Katz, 1997; Borjas, 2003, 2006).

A first approach to this problem was taken by Borjas, Freeman and Katz (BFK 1992, 1997). The idea here was to use a standard, partial-equilibrium framework to calculate the effect of a fixed increase in inelastically supplied labour implied by empirical immigration. Specifically, BFK focus on the effect of a change in the supply of one factor relative to another on the relative wages of those factors.

Factors are taken to be inelastically supplied while the relative demand for labour is downward-sloping. If every factor i's supply is made up of a domestic component and an immigrant component, and if we let the ratio of immigrant to domestic labour be $m_i = M_i/N_i$, then the aggregate supply of factor i is $N_i(1 + m_i)$. Then, with labour aggregated into either skilled (S) or unskilled (U) categories, the effect of a change in relative supplies on relative wages is

$$\Delta \ln\left(\frac{w_U}{w_S}\right) = -\frac{1}{\sigma_{SU}} \Delta \ln\left(\frac{1+m_U}{1+m_S}\right), \tag{2}$$

where σ_{SU} is the elasticity of substitution between S and U and Δ denotes that the change is taken between fixed dates. The effort using this method goes mostly into constructing the aggregates. In addition, by focusing on a one sector model, all adjustment to immigration is forced through the wage margin. As our discussion of the relevant general-equilibrium theory suggests, this virtually guarantees overestimates of wage effects.

BFK construct two pairs of aggregate labour terms: {high school dropouts, high school grads} and {high school equivalent, college equivalent}, and apply the Katz and Murphy (1992) estimates of σ_{SU} to make the calculations of the effect of immigration on relative wages.[9] BFK conclude that the immigration-induced change in the relative supply of high school dropouts accounted for about 44 percent of the total decline in their relative wage.

For studies with a national-level empirical focus, the key to identifying the effect of immigrants on wages is the assumption that the individuals in the 'skill cells' are perfect substitutes for one another, but are imperfect substitutes across cells. In this case, it seems perfectly plausible to assume that individuals cannot switch cells in response to differentials in wages. As with research based on spatial relationships, there are both regression based and production function based variants on the skill cell approach.

The first step in applying this approach is to exploit variance in immigrant presence across skill cells to identify the effect of immigration on wages. Borjas (2003) aggregates on age cohort ('experience') and education. That is, he assumes that workers (whether native or immigrant) with the same level of schooling and experience are perfect substitutes, but that workers with the same level of schooling, but different experience are imperfect substitutes (similarly for same experience but different schooling). For this strategy to work, we must be confident that the definitions of the cells are such that workers in different cells really are imperfect substitutes and that workers in the same cell really are perfect substitutes.[10] For his analysis, Borjas works with four education groups (high school dropouts, high school grads, some college, college grads) and eight labour market experience groups (five-year bands for workers with one–40 years of experience), for a total of 32 age-experience cells. Data from five U.S. censuses (1960, 1970, 1980, 1990, and 2000) gives Borjas a data set of 160 observations on male workers. Borjas finds that the elasticity of the wage with respect to the ratio of immigrants to natives in a given cell is −0.40, that is, an increase of immigrants in education-experience cell by 10 percent is estimated to cause a 4 percent fall in weekly earnings. The effect on annual earnings is estimated to be −6.4 percent and on labour supply −3.7 percent. As Borjas notes, these estimates are much higher than in other immigration studies.

In addition to this reduced form approach, Borjas also considers a more structural approach based on estimation of (a) production functions defined on labour defined in skill/experience terms. Unlike the production function approach based on spatial variation and a limited set of labour types (often just {native, immigrant} or native/immigrant crossed with racial categories), Borjas has a large number of schooling/experience types and a relatively small number of annual observations, so he requires a technology that has a relatively small number of parameters that must be estimated. For this purpose, he uses a nested CES function.[11]

Borjas then applies the same methods as those applied in analyzing production functions using regional data (see section 3.1.1) to simulate the effects of immigration shocks on wages. Using this framework, Borjas calculates that U.S. immigration in the 1980s and 1990s resulted in a 9 percent reduction in the wages of high school dropouts and a 4.9 percent reduction in the wages of college graduates. These are the two education categories with the highest shares of immigrants. For high school graduates wages fell by 2.6 percent and workers with some college were only minimally affected.

There have been a number of applications of the methods from this paper, and none have produced estimates of equivalent magnitude.[12] The most explicitly critical work is contained in a pair of papers by Ottaviano and Peri (OP, 2008; 2010). The core of OP's criticism is an argument that three of Borjas's simplifying assumptions – high school dropouts and high school grads are imperfect substitutes, natives and migrants are perfect substitutes and that capital is a fixed endowment – end up biasing his results towards finding larger negative effects of immigration. OP work with the structural approach developed in Borjas, but extend his approach to embed, and test for, two versus four skill groups and perfect versus imperfect substitutability of immigrants and native. To deal with the potential perfect substitutability between types of skilled and types of unskilled labour, OP consider an aggregate of two types of labour – L_S (skilled) and L_U (unskilled). In turn, each of the types is itself a CES aggregate of two subtypes: L_S is an aggregate of college dropouts and college grads and L_U an aggregate of high school dropouts and high school grads. This specification nests the four skill–group structure and can be used to test Borjas' specification. To deal with the assumption that migrants and natives might be imperfect substitutes, they develop a fourth aggregate that produces each of the four skill groups, L_{ijt}, using home and native workers with education level i and experience level j in time t.

Finally, OP introduce an explicit model of sluggish capital adjustment derived from earlier empirical work on economic growth.

The empirical implementation finds two broad results: first, while high school dropouts/high school grads and college dropouts/college grads are very good (essentially perfect) substitutes for one another, their aggregates are very imperfect substitutes; and, second, immigrants and natives are imperfect substitutes for one another. That is, OP produce strong evidence that a model using two education groups and distinguishing between natives and immigrants dominates the Borjas model. In addition, OP develop a framework in which, assuming international capital mobility or capital accumulation, capital adjusts to immigration shocks to maintain a constant real return to capital and a constant capital–output ratio. Under these two adjustments to Borjas' structural model, OP calculate that immigration has had a small negative effect on high school dropouts, positive effects on other groups and a positive aggregate effect on the average wage of U.S. workers overall.

Overall, then, the broad conclusion from all four approaches – regional versus skill-based observations by structural vs. reduced form methods – to estimating the effect of immigrants on native labour market performance come to essentially the same conclusion: at worst, immigration has small negative effects on native wages and employment prospects, with the largest negative effects falling on previous waves of immigrants with the same labour market traits. There is some evidence that, consistent with a loose interpretation of Samuelson's Le Châtelier principle, the negative effects are more severe in the short run than in the long run. For an area of research that is often seen as riven by deep debates between rival schools, this level of overall agreement seems surprising.

3.2   Empirical links between endowment changes and output changes

Once again, the most direct approach to evaluating the Rybczynski theorem is one that directly exploits the model structure, extending the production-theoretic approach to the simultaneous existence of trade in goods and factors. Empirical trade economists have exploited duality theory to estimate comparative static effects of trade by treating trade as a direct argument in a GNP function.[13] The marriage of this approach to trade modelling to the production-theoretic modelling of immigration seems obvious, but has only rarely been done. As we noted above, Kohli develops this sort of analysis in considerable detail. With particular reference to the Rybczynski relations, most of Kohli's work analyses a single output economy and cannot really speak to Rybczynski effects. However, the economy in Kohli (2002) has two final outputs (exports and domestically consumed goods) and here there is evidence that immigration is associated with increased production of the domestic good, but not the exportable. Hijzen and Wright (2010) explicitly evaluate Rybczynski effects in a production-theoretic framework with two final outputs (high and low skill-intensive goods) and six factors (high and low skilled domestic and foreign workers, capital and imports) for UK data from 1975 to 1996. Loosely consistent with the Rybczynski theorem, Hijzen and Wright find a (small) positive effect of immigration on output quantities. Taken together with evidence of a (small) negative effect on own wages, it seems sensible to interpret the overall results as suggesting that economies adjust to an immigration shock on both the wage and output margins.

Additional evidence on Rybczynski-like effects is found in the literature (often seeking to 'test' HO theory) examining the empirical link between endowments and production structures. The most straightforward approach exploits the fact that, under HOV assumptions and assuming $m = n$, there is a linear relationship between outputs and endowments. In work explicitly focused on both Rybczynski effects and technological differences, Harrigan (1997) estimates a translog GDP function with seven manufacturing sectors and six factors (arable land, two types of capital and three types of labour), for ten industrial countries over the years 1970–88. Importantly, technology in sectors is permitted to vary across countries and time in Hicks neutral fashion. The results are consistent with significant effects of endowments on sectoral outputs.[14]

Related to this work, and explicitly about immigration, is a pair of important papers by Hanson and Slaughter (2002) and Gandal et al. (2004), the first dealing with the United States, the second with Israel. These papers are based on a clever accounting decomposition that seeks to identify the contributions of output-mix change and technological change in adjusting to endowment shocks. In the U.S. case, Hanson and Slaughter present results consistent with productivity-adjusted FPE across states and, further, present evidence suggesting that states have absorbed changes in labour endowments primarily via skill-biased technological change which is common across all states and, secondarily, via changes in output mix. That there should be evidence of output-mix adjustment in a period of rapid and substantial technological change strikes us as important. However, such evidence does not exist in the Israel case, where Gandal et al. find that global changes in technology were (more than) sufficient to absorb the huge, relatively skilled influx of immigrants from Russia. In addition to the finding that output-mix adjustment was playing a role, there are two important implications of this work for the discussion to follow. First, there is some suggestion that, at least among relatively developed economies, the assumption of a common technology across countries may be less of a distortion than assuming a common technology across a finite period of time. Second, while appropriately constructed comparative static analyses may identify important forces operating at the level of the economy, dynamic forces might well overwhelm the static forces. On the other hand, since these forces are both less well understood and less controllable, their relevance for policy analysis is very unclear.

3.3 Increasing returns, agglomeration and immigration

To this point, we have stressed the fundamental theoretical consistency of the frameworks in use by trade and labour economists is dimensionality, and here we have argued for a presumption that the number of goods is at least as large as the number of factors of production. Under this assumption, we have seen that FPI generally obtains. This seems broadly consistent with the overwhelming majority of studies which find, at most, small wage/employment effects. At a minimum, something other than wage adjustment is going on – it might be adjustment on the output margin (as implied by FPI), or endogenous technological adjustment, or something else, but there just is not much evidence of major adjustment on the wage margin.

This said, the apparent existence of quite distinct local economies is problematic for either approach. Bernard and Jensen (2000) note that although the United States as a whole experienced increasing wage inequality, this fact disguised very different patterns of wage inequality at the state level. In fact, some states experiencing sharp declines in inequality. This fact argues against the view of a well-oiled, highly-integrated U.S. economy – at least in the short-to-medium terms. In response to employment shocks, Blanchard and Katz (1992) found that labour markets were integrated after a period of ten years. Interstate migration does indeed act to smooth shocks, but it only does so very slowly. Wage adjustments were also extremely sluggish, with some effects often lingering beyond ten years. In other words, shocks to regions are not rapidly transmitted to other regions. This suggests that even the most carefully crafted research, for example, such as Borjas's, which divides workers into industry, occupation, education, experience, race and sex, may be biased because it does not also distinguish between locations – or separate labour markets. There are at least two further implications of this research. First, the measured effects on local labour markets are genuinely indicative of the small adverse impact that new immigrants have on native workers and second, that the skating rink hypothesis, in which each new foreign unskilled worker forces a native off the ice (i.e. to migrate to another region), is dubious.

In more recent work, (Bernard et al., 2008; 2009) show that relative wages vary across regions in the United States and the United Kingdom. They also show that the type of industry varies with the skill wage premium and that skill-abundant regions exhibit lower skill premia than skill-scarce regions. Hence, firms adjust production across and within regions in response to relative wage differences. In an HOS model with multiple cones of diversification one implication is that different regions with different skill endowments have different relative wages. In equilibrium, regions abundant in skilled workers offer lower skill premia.

The existence of multiple cones suggests that economic activity, as well as factors of production, tend to agglomerate. When factors are immobile, regions specialise in the good that uses most intensively their abundant factor. In turn, the 'lumpiness' of factor endowments can constitute a basis for trade. The point of course is that regions within countries may often differ more than they do with comparable regions overseas. The lumpiness can be sustained by lower prices for non-tradeables or by locational amenities, such as nice weather. In the latter case, real wages would not equalize, although sunshine-adjusted real wages would. Hence, there would be no FPE. In a similar vein, Overman and Puga (2002) show the existence of regional unemployment clusters in the EU which often span national borders. These neighbourhood effects are important, regardless of whether the neighbours happen to be domestic or foreign. They argue that the clustering reflects the agglomeration effects of economic integration. Interestingly, the polarization into high unemployment regions and low unemployment regions cannot be being driven by migration because intra-regional migration has been falling in Western Europe.

4   Global Effects of International Migration

To this point we have looked at the issue of migration primarily from the perspective of a single, immigrant-receiving country. We now turn to two issues which are fundamentally about the international equilibrium: comparative advantage and the pattern of trade and the relationship between trade and factor mobility.

4.1   International equilibrium and comparative advantage with (some) mobile factors

Immigration has an interesting effect on comparative advantage in the Ricardian model. Free migration equalizes wages, but in the Ricardian model this means that absolute advantage will determine the location of production (rather than comparative cost differences). If either country has an absolute advantage in the production of both goods, the technologically disadvantaged country will simply empty out. In the intermediate case, in which each country has an absolute advantage in the production of one of the goods, the world economy functions like a single Ricardian economy, so relative commodity prices are determined by the technology (i.e. tastes play no role). Tastes do, however, play a role in the determination of the pattern of labour flows between the two countries. Specifically, if world demand is such that, at the technologically determined prices, the demand for the good produced in, say, the Home country exceeds the capacity of the initial Home labour endowment to produce that good, migration will flow from Foreign to Home.

Factor mobility in the basic HOS model is also quite straightforward. As we discuss in the next section, factor mobility is at least a partial substitute for commodity mobility. One way of seeing this is that free trade without factor mobility can produce the same equilibrium (in the sense of goods prices and allocations) as free factor mobility without trade. The key here is that the endowments of the two countries must fall within the same FPE region. Where specialization can interfere with complete equalization of factor prices, if one of the factors is mobile as well, there must be complete equalization of factor prices. In the absence of trade, mobility of one factor will move the national economies toward the integrated equilibrium.[15] Furthermore, the directions of trade and migration are predictable based on initial endowments and knowledge of the common technologies.

Beginning with important papers by Kemp (1966) and Jones (1967), the focus of much of the literature on trade and migration in general equilibrium shifted to models in which countries differ in their technologies. The HOS model with mobile capital under international differences in technology is often referred to as the *Kemp–Jones model*. Jones argued that, with technological differences, there was a presumption that international factor mobility would lead to specialization of at least one economy. Markusen and Svensson (1985) study the $m \times n$ case. Assuming a specific form of technology difference, these authors show that factor mobility strengthens the relationship between trade and endowments in the no-factor-mobility case; and are able to show that countries will import factors that are used intensively in the sectors with technological advantage. As in the Kemp–Jones case, international factor mobility pushes countries to specialize more strongly and induces a Ricardian element in the model.

4.2 Are factor mobility and commodity mobility complements or substitutes?

An issue of theoretical, empirical and policy interest is the degree to which trade and migration are substitutes or complements. As a policy matter, it is often argued that countries have a choice between admitting goods and admitting people. During the NAFTA debates, proponents of NAFTA often argued that the United States could reduce immigration pressure by increasing its trade with Mexico. Similar arguments have been made about the EU's eastern enlargement. The default position for most people seems to be that trade should be expected to substitute for immigration. The logic is clear enough, and derives directly from the HOS model: commodities are simply bundles of factors of production, so trade along HOS comparative advantage lines should cause factor prices to become more similar, reducing pressure for migration.

4.2.1   Complements and substitutes in theory

Mundell's (1957) classic develops precisely this logic. In the context of a standard 2-factor × 2-good × 2-country HOS model, Mundell proves a converse to the FPE theorem. Samuelson (1949) showed that, under the full set of HOS assumptions and as long as both countries remained unspecialized after the opening of trade, free trade between countries that differ only in their endowments of productive factors, in addition to equalizing commodity prices, must equalize the real prices of factors even though they are not internationally mobile. Furthermore, even if one country specializes before factor prices are completely equalized, commodity trade must cause factor prices to move toward equalization. The key to understanding this result is that, in the HOS model, there is a one-to-one, technologically determined relationship between relative commodity prices and relative factor prices. As Mundell argued, under the same conditions (in particular, non-specialization) that guaranteed FPE, if a wedge is driven between commodity prices (say, by a tariff) but factor mobility is permitted, that factor mobility will support the same allocations as in the free-trade equilibrium. Furthermore, given the assumptions on technology and demand, this must be the same relative commodity price and relative factor price as in the free-trade case. Thus, as the public logic maintains, in this case trade and immigration are substitutes.

However, it turns out that most movements away from the strict HOS framework open the door to complementarity (or, at least, greater complexity) in the relationship between commodity trade and factor trade. It is important to be clear on just what we will mean by 'substitutes' and 'complements'. We can focus on the relationship between: physical movement of commodities and factors; commodity and factor prices as a function of such movements; and final allocations under commodity or factor movements. Each of these is made up of two comparisons: the effect of commodity trade on immigration flows, prices and allocations; and the effect of immigration on commodity trade, prices and allocations. We follow Wong (1986) in referring to

1. *Quantity substitutes*: if an increase in the volume of trade reduces the volume of migration (trade substitutes for migration); and if an increase in the volume of migration reduces trade in commodities (migration substitutes for trade). If the relationship is symmetric, we will say that trade and migration are quantity equivalent. If an increase in the volume of one increases the volume of the other, we will say they are quantity complements.
2. *Price substitutes*: if an increase in the volume of trade reduces the difference in factor prices between countries (trade substitutes for migration); and if an increase in the volume of migration reduces the difference in prices between countries (migration substitutes for trade). If the relationship is symmetric, we will say that trade and migration are price equivalent. If an increase in the volume of one causes the prices of the other to move further apart between countries, we will say they are price complements.
3. *Allocation equivalence*: if trade is sufficient to reproduce the integrated equilibrium; and if migration is sufficient to reproduce the integrated equilibrium. If trade and migration are individually allocation equivalent, we say that trade and migration are allocation substitutes. If both are required to reproduce the integrated equilibrium, they are allocation complements.

With these definitions in hand, it is easy to see that in the HOS model trade and migration are quantity equivalent, price equivalent and allocation equivalent. If both countries produce both goods in all equilibria (i.e. under free commodity trade, free trade in factors, and free mobility of both) these equivalences are perfect. The existence of a technologically determined, one-to-one relationship between commodity prices and factor prices is an essentially 2×2 phenomenon.[16] However, as long as there are at least as many final commodities as factors, it is once again the case that, if country endowments are relatively similar (as defined by sharing the same cone of diversification), trade and migration are price, quantity and allocation equivalent. The situation becomes harder to interpret in a world that involves some mobile factors as well as mobile goods. When we consider substitutability of commodity for factor trade, under any of the definitions, are we interested in mobility of the previously immobile factors, or are we interested in the already mobile factors. Svensson (1984) focuses on trade in the mobile factors and finds that whether mobility of these factors and trade in goods are (quantity) substitutes or complements depends on whether immobile factors and mobile factors are cooperative (substitutes) or competitive (complements) in production.

As discussed above, in the HOS model there is a one-to-one relationship between relative commodity prices and relative factor prices. Figure 21.1 illustrates this fact.[17] For example, consider an initial equilibrium in which both countries are in autarchy, so that they are at different points on a *given P–ω* schedule. If there is factor mobility so that factor prices are equalized, it must be the

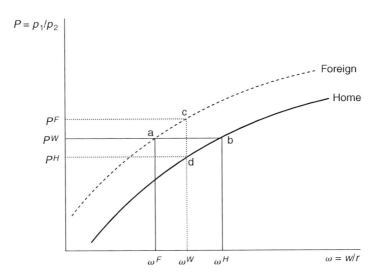

Figure 21.1 Commodity and factor prices

case that commodity prices are also equalized. Furthermore, given the assumptions on technology and demand, this must be the same relative commodity price and relative factor price as in the free-trade case.

Now suppose that we retain all of the HOS assumptions except that we suppose countries have identical initial endowments and that one country ('Home') has a Hicks neutral superior technology in the production of good 1. The Home country is represented by a curve that lies uniformly below that of the Foreign country. Now suppose that free trade results in the equalization of commodity prices at P^W. Note that national factor prices are different, at points a and b. Specifically, as drawn, the return to labour in Home exceeds the return to labour in Foreign. In this trading environment, Home exports good 1. If we now permit migration, labour flows to Home, increasing its comparative advantage in standard Rybczynski fashion and, thus, increasing trade. So factor mobility is both price and quantity complementary to free trade in goods. Now suppose, instead, that free migration is permitted following the technical change. Labour will move until real wages are equalised, at points c and d. If both countries continue to produce both goods, the factor price ratio will be equalized but commodity prices will move apart. If trade is now permitted, there will be increased production of each country's comparative advantage good, which should result in increased migration. Thus, trade is price and quantity complementary to migration.

It is easy to see that the migration only and trade only equilibria involve very different commodity and factor prices. Thus, neither alone moves the economy to the integrated equilibrium. Rather, trade and migration must be allocation complements as well. There are a variety of other sources of comparative advantage, including taxes, economies of scale, imperfect competition and factor market distortions. As for these other cases: 'There is a strong presumption that intra-industry trade and trade due to aggregative economies of scale or to international differences in the degree of imperfect competition are strongly complementary to migration. There is also a strong presumption that inter-industry trade due to disaggregative economies of scale or to monopolistic competition relates to migration in the same ways as does comparative advantage trade' (Ethier, 1996, 65).

It is interesting to note that research on the foundations of comparative advantage over the last couple of decades has stressed precisely the factors that imply a presumption of complementarity (i.e. technological differences and monopolistic competition as a foundation for intra-industry trade). This leads us to the empirical evidence on the relationship between trade and immigration.

4.2.2   *Empirical research on complements and substitutes*

The theoretical work we have discussed to this point considers the question of whether trade and migration are substitutes or complements in terms of factor arbitrage. That is, the source of any relationship is taken to be the way factors respond to differences in wages between countries. Early empirical work on this question was motivated in precisely this fashion. Horiba and Kirkpatrick (1983) looked at interregional trade and migration between regions (South and non-South) in the United States in the 1960s. They looked at quantity flows of people (considering heterogeneity of labour) between regions and (using standard input–output techniques) the flows of labour embodied in trade. Under the maintained assumption of an $m \times n$ HO-type economy, it is predicted that labour should flow from a region relatively well-endowed with labour to regions relatively poorly endowed with labour; and, in standard HOV fashion, embodied trade in factors should follow the same pattern. For our purposes, the key finding was that both of these predictions are borne out. In addition, there was some evidence of a tendency toward FPE. These results would seem to be broadly consistent with a substitutive relationship between trade and labour mobility. These results are closely related to a growing body of trade research whose results suggest that the HO model, under various plausible extensions (e.g. the presence of trading costs or Hicks neutral international differences in technology) and generalization of the Rybczynski theorem, does a reasonably good job of accounting for production patterns; and research on growth which fails to find a link between migration and convergence.

A more direct approach to evaluating the relationship between trade and migration involves introducing migration into a theoretically well-grounded model of international trade. We have already seen this methodology applied to the question of the relationship between immigration and wages (see section 3.2.1). Kohli (2002) explicitly considers domestic output and exports as outputs in a joint revenue function and finds immigration and imports to be quantity complements, but essentially no relationship between immigration and exports. As discussed previously, Hijzen and Wright (2010) divide UK immigrants (and the endowments of domestic labour) into skilled and unskilled labour – thus, production involves capital, domestic skilled labour, domestic unskilled labour, immigrant skilled labour, immigrant unskilled labour and imports. In addition, because they want to permit output adjustment, they consider two outputs – skilled-intensive and unskilled-intensive outputs. The results here are interesting: skilled immigrants are quantity complements with trade; but unskilled workers are, if anything, quantity substitutes.

5   The Social Structure of Migration: Networks, Migration and Trade

In the research which treats migration as an instance of factor arbitrage, there is no essential difference between capital and labour: both generate income for households and can be used to produce outputs under given production functions. To the extent that there is any difference, it is not uncommon to treat the income from internationally mobile capital as consumed in its Home country, while the income from mobile labour is consumed in the Host country. This is an extremely useful simplification for many analytical purposes; however, it is also the case that, in many ways, capital and labour are fundamentally different things. In the words of the Swiss writer Max Frisch commenting on guest worker programs: '*We wanted workers, we got people*'. Capital, by contrast, is fundamentally separable from its human owners.[18] Thus, in addition to differences in the skill mix (and possibly taste differences) of migrants relative to natives, immigrants also carry cultural differences that might affect their willingness to cooperate with natives in unions (and vice versa). Perceptions of social/citizenship difference might affect the legitimacy of state transfer programs or participation in reciprocal arrangements with natives in the labour market. These perceptions of difference even go to economically important social values like fairness. Sociologists and political scientists have dealt with many of these issues. In this section, we will focus on an issue that deals with social institutions – networks.[19]

In section 1 we discussed how emigration and immigration are far from uniformly distributed across the globe. This heterogeneity becomes even more pronounced as one takes account of individual-level variation (e.g. by age, gender, education, etc.). Accounting for this heterogeneity in aggregate patterns has been, and continues to be, an active area of research. For economists, the essential starting point for such analysis is the notion that emigration emerges from a utility maximising choice. That is, immigrants compare the benefits of staying in their home country to the benefits (net of costs) of moving to some new country. Because this decision involves comparison of returns to various choices that occur in time, it is convenient to conceive of the choice as one of investment in human capital. In making such a comparison, a potential emigrant compares the origin country wage to that in alternative destination countries. For each destination country, the potential emigrant must deduct the costs of migrating to that country. Since all of this must be done in expectation, one might also want to include a measure of the likelihood of finding a job (e.g. a comparison of unemployment rates). An important advance in the theoretical and empirical analysis of immigration flows was Borjas's (1987) adaptation of Roy's (1951) model of occupational selection to the case of selection among emigrant destinations. While Borjas was primarily interested in identifying the causes and consequences of differences in immigrant 'quality' across source countries to the United States, he also argues that the same analytical framework predicts emigration patterns across those source countries.

Taking per capita GDP as a proxy for wages and distance as a proxy for costs, one can represent the Roy-Borjas selection model, loosely speaking, by a gravity equation.[20] Gravity modelling of migration generally takes the form

$$m_{ijt} = \beta G_{ijt} + f_{ijt} + \varepsilon_{ijt}, \tag{3}$$

where m_{ijt} is the migration from origin country i to destination country j at time t; G_{ijt} is a matrix of standard gravity variables (e.g. origin and destination GDP, distance and other 'migration cost' variables), f_{ijt} is a matrix of fixed effects and ε is an error term. More recently, a number of papers have sought to make the link between the Roy-Borjas model and the gravity framework more explicit. For example, Grogger and Hanson (2008) find that destination GDP is positively and distance is negatively associated with migration flows. Unexpectedly, origin GDP (which should be negatively associated with migration) is generally not significantly different from zero, and even sometimes of the wrong sign.[21] In addition to such standard gravity variables, immigration policy variables in the destination country have been found to have a significant effect. We note, for later reference, that a small number of papers introduce some trade variable into the migration gravity model and that all find the trade variable is positive and, usually, significant.

Stories about immigration, whether contemporary or historical, journalistic, academic or fictional, have long stressed the role of social relations as an essential element in the decision to engage in migratory behaviour. Migrants are linked to both their home and host countries by networks that provide information, resources and comfort, all in a variety of forms. Where economists have tended to analyze immigration as reflecting optimization by individuals or households, sociologists/demographers have been very successful building network models of the immigration decision.[22] More recently, as economists have developed sophisticated models of networks, these considerations have increasingly been built into migration analysis. Empirical work seeking to explain migration patterns now commonly includes variables intended to capture network effects – usually some measure of the stock of immigrants from a given home country in a given host country. The key here is not that networks substitute for rational choice of destinations by migrants, but that networks affect the costs of migrating to one market *versus* another.

Just as networks play a fundamental role in getting migrants from one country to another, and helping determine the allocation of migrants from home to host countries, networks also play a fundamental role in organizing the social and economic life of migrants once they arrive in a given host country. Of particular interest for us is the way that networks affect the relationship between migration and trade. Broadly speaking, networks of migrants might affect international trade by responding to two sources of transaction costs: uncertainty/incomplete information and asymmetric information/opportunism. With respect to the first, the idea is that trade in some commodities requires search, and that the cost of such search varies systematically across countries. Especially for the case of specialized/differentiated goods, the lack of a deep, well-developed arms-length market can require costly search. When this search must occur across international borders, especially between countries with very different social and/or political structures, those costs can be quite high (Rauch, 1999; Rauch and Casella, 2003; Portes and Rey, 2005). In this situation, migrants can act as 'weak ties' in Granovetter's (Granovetter, 1973, 1983, 2005) sense of providing an information bridge between two dense networks (in this case, suppliers in the home market and demanders in the host market). That is, because migrants possess economic, cultural and institutional knowledge about both the home and the host markets, they are able to mediate economic exchange between those markets, thus increasing trade above what it would be in the absence of such migration. In this case, migrants engage in market *creation*. Because such information problems are expected to be more severe for differentiated products, we would expect to find strong positive effects for trade in such products, especially between countries with very different economic, cultural and political environments. In some sense, once such a bridge has been constructed, the need for additional migrants might well be expected to decline.

Unlike transactions costs that emerge through simple lack of knowledge, those related to asymmetric information, imperfect enforcement of contracts and opportunism create a more fundamental role for networks. In an environment characterized by these problems, the opportunity for mutually beneficial trades may be foregone. In the limit, these problems can cause the collapse of markets. This, in turn, creates an opportunity for non-market (or 'market replacing') institutions; which, of course, is the opening wedge for Williamson's (Williamson, 1975, 1985, 1996) Nobel prize-winning development of transaction cost economics. However, independently of transaction cost economics' emphasis on the role of asymmetric information and opportunistic behaviour in understanding the creation and operation of firms; anthropologists, sociologists and historians used essentially the same factors in explaining the role of ethnic networks and diasporas in the organization of trade across political jurisdictions or, more generally, in the absence of effective protection of contractual/property rights. More recently the analytical structures of transaction cost economics and game theory have provided more formal frameworks for examining these relationship-based trade links. The basic idea here is that ties of trust, and social capital more generally, built up among coethnics in the migration process can substitute for imperfect contract enforcement (whether a function of incomplete contracts or lack of effective judicial systems). The enforcement mechanism in this case is exclusion from the social and economic benefits of the community/network.[23] As with the case of transaction costs deriving from informational problems, where migrants engage in market creation, we would expect contracting problems to be most severe in the case of goods for which a deep, arms-length market does not exist. However, unlike that case, where we might expect the need for a weak-link to decline once the information bridge has been built; as long as the contracting problem remains in a given market, the need for the contract enforcement role of the network will remain in place. Furthermore, to the extent that the role of the ethnic community declines with successive generations, we might even expect a need for continuing flows of migrants to support that role.

Before turning to a discussion of the empirical work on the role of immigrant networks in reducing trade costs, we should note that, in addition to the role of networks, the most straightforward way that immigrant differences might affect trade patterns runs through preferences – immigrants may have a preference for their own goods that they bring with them when they emigrate.[24] Not only does this have a direct effect on demand for the immigrant-preferred goods, but we would also expect that demonstration effects would increase the demand for these goods among natives as well. Given that nonimmigrants from a given country (i.e. natives and immigrants from other countries) will generally dramatically outnumber immigrants from a given country, we might expect the indirect effect to be larger than the direct effect. It is conventional in the empirical literature to assert that taste effects should affect only imports, and among imports only consumer goods. While this may be a plausible approximation, it is surely the case that information gleaned by immigrants from consuming in the host country can be transferred to the home country in a variety of ways. Thus, the common inference in the gravity literature that a positive estimated effect of immigrant stock on imports is evidence of a preference effect, while a positive effect on exports is evidence of network effects, seems less than strong. By contrast, the presumption that the preference effect should be seen in consumer goods seems quite well founded. In either case, when evaluating the link between immigration and trade, we surely need to account for the effect of differences in preferences between immigrants and natives.

Empirical work suggesting the presence of large border effects (McCallum, 1995; Helliwell, 1998) and missing trade (Trefler, 1995) has spurred extensive research on the role of trade costs as a source of these findings and networks as a response to these costs. Once again, a standard tool for evaluating the effects of such trade costs is the gravity model. Analysis using gravity models has provided strong support for the notion that social and political differences, and poor enforcement of contractual rights, act as barriers to trade. We are particularly interested here in the evidence of the role of immigrant networks in alleviating these transaction costs. Gravity modelling of trade, with the variables extended to include a migration variable, takes the form

$$X_{ijt} = \alpha m_{ijt} + \beta G_{ijt} + f_{ijt} + \varepsilon_{ijt}, \tag{4}$$

where X_{ijt} is the value of dyadic trade (exports or imports) between partner country i and reference country j at time t, G_{ijt} the matrix of gravity variables (e.g. reference and target country GDP, distance and other 'trade cost' variables). The parameter of interest in this work is α.

The seminal paper here is Gould's (1994) study of the effect of immigrants on trade between the United States and 47 trading partners that were also sources immigrants, for the years 1970–86. In addition to estimating a gravity model, extended to include stocks of immigrants from the foreign country residing in the United States, for bilateral aggregate imports and exports; Gould also estimated separate regressions for imports and exports of producer and consumer goods. With respect to aggregate imports and exports, Gould found immigrants increased trade (though at lower levels than much of the later literature); and, somewhat unusually given later results, found a larger effect on exports than on imports. The usual inference from this pattern is that preference effects explain the difference between the import effect and the export effect (since the network effects are apparently taken to be symmetric). Thus, this is taken as evidence against a significant role for preference effects. When the analysis was done on consumer and producer goods separately, Gould found the effect on consumer goods was larger for both imports and exports. Gould's presumption was that consumer goods are more differentiated than producer goods, and took this as evidence of network effects.

Building on Gould's work, a sizable literature of gravity-based estimates of the effect of migration on trade has developed.[25] Very broadly, and with very few exceptions, these papers consistently find significant positive effects of immigration on trade – whether measured as imports or exports. Furthermore, of the papers that report results for both imports and exports, it is about twice as common to find the estimated effect of immigration on imports to be greater than that on exports. Again, this is taken as evidence that preference effects and network effects are both operating.

A number of papers have taken advantage of the existence of trade and migration data collected at sub-national levels. A benefit of using sub-national data is that they permit the analysis to focus on more specifically defined geographic regions, thus achieving greater precision in estimation. A related benefit is that analysts can control for national level common determinants of trade and migration using country-level fixed effects, but still retaining sub-national level variation for identifying the effect of migrants. A particularly interesting paper is Herander and Saavedra (2005), which attempts to identify the relative effects of both state- and national-level migrant stocks. The authors find strong evidence that the local effects are larger than the national effects. This suggests that, whether they are mainly market creating or market replacing, network links are all about proximity. Herander and Saavedra also test for whether size of previous immigrant stock reduces the effect of current immigrants on trade flows. Consistent with Gould's result, they find that the previous immigrant stock does reduce the effect of current immigrants. Given the discussion above (i.e. that market creating networks should experience such a decline, while market replacing links do not), this would appear to be strong evidence in favour of the greater importance of market creation.

To summarize: there is strong and consistent support for immigration having a positive effect on trade. That link appears to be stronger: for commodities whose trade is likely to involve informational problems; for trade with countries that are different from the reference country on a number of dimensions; and when the partner country is characterized by institutional problems (such as corruption). This would seem to be strong evidence for the network story. However, since these analyses are never carried out in the context of a structural analysis that permits an evaluation of the relative price effects that drive the general-equilibrium analysis standard in the trade theoretic accounts, these results neither permit comparison with the trade theoretic claims, nor do they speak directly (or unambiguously) to the issues of whether trade and migration are substitutes or complements.

6 Conclusion: The Peculiar Political Economy of Immigration

When it comes to the impact of immigration, trade theory yields a tight prior on an essentially zero labour market impact. As for the empirical literature, it is widely agreed that there are non-trivial negative effects on migrants of the same origin and vintage, and, perhaps not quite so widely held, agreement that the small, and shrinking, group of native high school dropouts experience statistically significant, but economically modest, negative consequences from contemporary immigration. Otherwise, evidence of negative effects is largely absent.

To the extent that there is a dispute in the immigration case, it revolves around the framework to be used for evaluating the results of the empirical work. The main substantive difference between labour and trade economists relates to the dimensionality of the model used to evaluate the results – with labour economists preferring an m-factor $\times$ 1-final good model and trade economists preferring an $m \times n$ good model (with a modal preference for the 2×2 model). As long as $m \geq 2$ and $n \leq 2$, output-mix adjustment will play a role in adjusting to an immigration shock, and the failure to account for that role will produce overestimates of the wage (or unemployment) effects of any given shock. Furthermore, we have also argued for the fundamental plausibility of the m-factor n-good model on essentially *a priori* grounds. If this argument is accepted, there is some presumption that output-mix adjustment fully absorbs the immigration shock and that factor price insensitivity holds.

This inevitably leads us to the most difficult question: if immigration is *really* not relevant to the long-run economic life of citizens, why does it occasionally become such a large political issue?[26]

Fundamental to the political economy of immigration are the social relations between the community of immigrants and that of natives. For example, the 'foreignness' of immigrants affects natives' sense of who they are as a community; the act of fixing legal limits on the number of immigrants requires real resources to enforce those limits and creates a class of illegal immigrants; and the presence of a redistributive welfare state in all major immigrant host countries creates yet another margin on which immigration might affect native welfare. Given their potential impact on native welfare, each of these forms the basis of political mobilization on the immigration question.

The emergence of radical right parties in Europe has been strongly associated with anti-immigrant politics that can only very partially be explained by economic effects of that immigration. 'Foreigners' make a particularly attractive target for more-or-less unfocussed anger in the context of general economic difficulties. Thus, while it is surely true that attitudes towards immigrants are affected by an understanding of labour market effects, as argued in this chapter, recent research suggests that these effects are dwarfed by social concerns. Card et al. (2009) refer to these social concerns as 'compositional amenities'. Given the overall conclusions of empirical research on the labour market effects of migration, and the increasingly heated public politics of immigration, the centrality of such compositional amenities should not surprise us.

While nothing like as extensive as research on the political economy of trade, there is a very lively literature on the political economy of immigration. Much, perhaps most, of the recent work has focused on identifying the preferences of citizens, a small amount has sought to model equilibrium outcomes as a function of factor price effects, and a larger sub-literature has focused on the political economic link between immigration and welfare state provision. The basic question addressed by this body of research is clear: does admitting immigrants (especially poor immigrants) lead to a reduction in welfare state effort? What systematic research exists on this topic tends to find that increased immigration from relatively poor countries is associated with lower public support for the welfare state and lower welfare state effort (Razin et al., 2002; Hanson et al., 2007; Facchini and Mayda, 2008; Eger, 2010). However, the interpretation of these results is open to considerable question (Hainmueller and Hiscox, 2010).

Unlike the case of trade, it turns out to be considerably more difficult to rationalize immigration policy in terms of straightforward models that run from factor ownership to preferences over policy to policy outcomes. It seems an unavoidable conclusion that the economic impact of immigration is dominated by the social fact of immigrant differences from the native community as a driver of individual attitudes toward, and politics about, immigration.

Notes

* This chapter is dramatically shorter than the working paper version, which contains substantially more analytical detail and references. The working paper version can be downloaded from the Bond University Globalisation and Development Centre's web page. The authors are grateful to Rod Falvey and two anonymous referees for detailed comments and advice.

† Globalisation and Development Centre and School of Business, Bond University, Australia.

‡ Murphy Institute of Political Economy, Tulane University. Centre for Research on Globalisation and Economic Policy, School of Economics, University of Nottingham.

1. The fact that most migrants flow to a relatively small number of wealthy OECD countries is in stark contrast to the effects of liberalized trade which are not so geographically concentrated.

2. Most empirical studies find quite complicated relations between immigrant labour and other national factors (see below). This fact will have important implications for conclusions about the distributional effects of immigration.

3. See Bernstein and Weinstein (2002), for example, The presence of multiple cones holds out the prospect that $m = n$ is an empirically plausible maintained assumption from which to begin. Of course, in a sufficiently short period of time factors are specific to industries and the assumption of $m > n$ becomes more reasonable.

4. For a discussion of immigration in $m \times n$ economies with non-traded and intermediate goods, see Gaston and Nelson (2010).

5. A functional form is *flexible* if it can approximate any arbitrary, twice continuously differentiable function in the sense that its parameters can be chosen such that its value, gradient and Hessian equal the corresponding magnitudes for the arbitrary function at a given point. See Lau (1986).

6. See Gaston and Nelson (2010) for the theory underlying equation (1).

7. Zimmermann (1995) notes that the European research on immigration has more to do with the effects of possessing citizenship. Unlike the U.S. literature, which has tended to focus on the effects of newly arrived immigrants on native workers as well as on earlier generations of immigrants, the European data do not distinguish individuals as foreign-born or not.

8. Decressin and Fatás (1995) have similar findings for the regions of Europe. However, they show that changes in labour force participation rates bear proportionately more of the burden of adjustment in response to labour market disturbances.

9. It is interesting to note that BFK were interested in evaluating the effects of both trade and immigration on relative wages. Their estimate of the effect of trade on labour supply applied input–output methods to identify the implicit imports and exports of labour via trade. At the time, immigration had not generally been considered in the set of major factors taken to explain the rapid rise of the skill premium in the 1980s (i.e. technological change, trade, shifts in product demand, and erosion of institutions supporting higher wages such as unions and minimum wages). As a result, BFK's conclusion that immigration played a major role in accounting for the change in the skill premium was all the more striking.

10. Both of these turn out to be tricky. For instance, Card (2009, section III B) argues that 'workers with less than a high school education are *perfect substitutes* for those with a high school education' (p. 2, our emphasis). The issue of whether or not immigrants and natives are perfect substitutes is a matter of ongoing dispute. The argument for

treating any worker with the same labour market-relevant attributes (i.e. education and experience) as identical to any other worker is strong on *a priori* grounds. Antidiscrimination law even tries to mandate this as an outcome when gender or race is the discriminating factor. Not surprisingly, aggregating workers (characterized by many forms of heterogeneity) into age/experience cells is a standard approach in labour economics. This has certainly been a common strategy in research on the labour market effects of immigration in virtually every sort of method: factor proportions, production function, regression analysis of local labour markets, and, of course, the regression analysis of skill cells in national labour markets. It is notable that given the range of outcomes reported in this literature, that the perfect substitutes assumption alone cannot account for findings of large or small effects.

11. See Gaston and Nelson (2010) for details.
12. The list of papers – for the United States as well as a number of other countries – here is large. The reader is referred to Gaston and Nelson (2010).
13. The underlying idea is to treat trade as an input to final GNP under the argument that virtually all goods in trade must be processed further for final sale. See Kohli (1991) for a development of the theory, econometrics and results from this research.
14. The work discussed in this paragraph interprets technological difference as a function of differing degrees of technological progress across countries (and, possibly, sectors). An alternative, and complementary, approach sees technological difference as a function of selecting technologies from common sets in the face of differing prices. For further discussion, see Bernhofen's chapter 4 in this volume.
15. The integrated equilibrium is the equilibrium of the single global economy in which all factors and goods are perfectly and costlessly mobile, i.e. before Samuelson's angel (Samuelson, 1949, 194) divides the world into separate countries. This integrated equilibrium has proved a highly useful baseline.
16. Global univalence, the generalization of the no-factor intensity reversal condition which underwrites the one-to-one mapping between the commodity price vector and the factor price vector, is not generally a property of higher dimensional versions of the Heckscher–Ohlin model.
17. Note that we have drawn the figure under the assumption that good 1 is labour intensive. Thus, if $P = p_1/p_2$ and $\omega = w/r$, we know from the Stolper–Samuelson theorem that the P-ω relationship is positively sloped.
18. Human capital is, of course, inseparable from humans. That is why, legally and socially, immigration of human capital is treated as labour, not as capital. It is also worth noting that modern research on foreign direct investment emphasises firm-theoretic factors rather than capital arbitrage.
19. In Gaston and Nelson (2010) we also deal with two other issues that deal with social institutions – illegality and welfare states. Specifically, we discuss the political structuring of migration: community, illegality and welfare state effort.
20. Immigration, and related issues of inter-regional travel, has been a focus of research using the gravity model for virtually as long as the gravity model has been applied. For a general overview of gravity modelling, with a primary focus on international trade see Bergstrand and Egger's chapter 17 in this volume.
21. In this literature, destination GDP is a 'pull factor' and origin GDP is a 'push factor'. In theory, what matters to the potential migrant is income net of costs, so the ultimate comparison is $[(w_D - w_O) - C]$ where the w's are wages in origin and destination and C is the cost of migration from O to D. Since the effects of the first two terms enter

this analysis symmetrically, the asymmetry in the results is a puzzle. See Gaston and Nelson (2010) for further discussion.

22. Beginning with the modern classic *Return to Aztlan* (Massey et al., 1987), Douglas Massey and his colleagues have developed an impressive body of research focusing on these networks between Mexico and the United States. In addition to the massive literature on Mexican migration to the United States, the importance of networks to the migration decision have been found for many other countries as well, see Gaston and Nelson (2010).

23. While economists tend to stress exclusion from economic benefits (e.g. Greif, 1993), one of the reasons that *ethnic* communities play such an important role here (rather than simply repeated interaction of more-or-less randomly generated networks) is the broader role of social solidarity. This social solidarity is often linked to distinctiveness relative to the native community induced via common language and religion, as well as ghetto-ization and endogamy. Thus, to be excluded from the community implies substantially higher costs than simple exclusion from trading networks.

24. Most of the theoretical research on the complements versus substitutes questions abstracts from taste differences by assuming globally common, homothetic preferences. Once we permit systematically different preferences or heterogeneity/monopolistic competition, the analysis becomes more complex. In the HOS world, the obvious assumption is that natives have a strong preference for their exportable commodity (thus, immigrants carry a stronger preference for the exports of their home country, increasing the host country's demand for imports from the immigrant's home); but this pattern of preferences can yield the Opp et al. (2009) 'reverse Rybczynski' effect. Similarly, once we enter the world of country-specific varieties of goods, we are in a world where results are sensitive to details of market structure (Ethier, 1996).

25. See Gaston and Nelson (2010).

26. This question is raised in Gaston and Nelson (2000) and analyzed in more detail in Greenaway and Nelson (2010).

References

Altonji, Joseph, and David Card (1991) 'The effects of immigration on the labor market outcomes of less-skilled natives', in J.M. Abowd and R.B. Freeman (eds.), *Immigration, Trade and Labor Market*. Chicago: University of Chicago Press/NBER.

Angrist, Joshua D., and Adriana D. Kugler (2003) 'Protective or counter-productive? Labour market institutions and the effect of immigration on EU natives', *Economic Journal* 113(488): F302–F31.

Bernard, Andrew B., and J. Bradford Jensen (2000) 'Understanding increasing and decreasing wage inequality', in R.C. Feenstra (ed.), *Impact of International Trade Wages*. Chicago: University of Chicago Press, 227–61.

Bernard, Andrew B., Stephen J. Redding and Peter K. Schott (2009) 'Testing for factor price equality in the presence of unobserved factor quality differences', NBER Working Paper No. 8068.

Bernard, Andrew B., Stephen J. Redding, Peter K. Schott and Helen Simpson (2008) 'Relative wage variation and industry location in the United Kingdom', *Oxford Bulletin of Economics and Statistics* 70(4): 431–59.

Bernstein, Jeffrey R., and David E. Weinstein (2002) 'Do endowments predict the location of production? Evidence from national and international data', *Journal of International Economics* 56(1): 55–76.

Bhagwati, Jagdish N., Arvind Panagariya and T.N. Srinivasan (1998) *Lectures on International Trade*, 2nd edition. Cambridge, MA: MIT Press.

Blanchard, Olivier J., and Lawrence F. Katz (1992) 'Regional evolutions', *Brookings Papers on Economic Activity* (1): 1–61.

Borjas, George J. (1987) 'Self-selection and the earnings of immigrants', *American Economic Review* 77(4): 531–53.

____. (1990) *Friends or Strangers: The Impact of Immigrants on the U.S. Economy*. New York: Basic Books.

____. (2003) 'The labor demand curve is downward sloping: reexamining the impact of immigration on the labor market', *Quarterly Journal of Economics* 118(4): 1335–74.

____. (2006) 'Native internal migration and the labor market impact of immigration', *Journal of Human Resources* 41(2): 221–58.

Borjas, George J., Richard B. Freeman and Lawrence F. Katz (1992) 'On the labor market effects of immigration and trade', in G. J. Borjas and R. B. Freeman (eds.), *Immigration and the Work Force*, 213–44. Chicago: University of Chicago Press/NBER.

____. (1997) 'How much do immigration and trade affect labor market outcomes?', *Brookings Papers on Economic Activity* (1): 1–90.

Card, David (1990) 'The impact of the mariel boatlift on the Miami labor-market', *Industrial & Labor Relations Review* 43(2): 245–57.

____. (2001) 'Immigrant inflows, native outflows, and the local labor market impacts of higher immigration', *Journal of Labor Economics* 19(1): 22–64.

____. (2009) 'Immigration and inequality', *American Economic Review* 99(2): 1–21.

Card, David, Christian Dustmann and Ian Preston (2009) 'Immigration, wages, and compositional amenities', NBER Working Paper No. 15521.

Cortes, Patricia (2008) 'The effect of low-skilled immigration on U.S. prices: evidence from CPI data', *Journal of Political Economy* 116(3): 381–422.

D'Amuri, Francesco, Gianmarco, I.P. Ottaviano and Giovanni Peri (2010) 'The labor market impact of immigration in Western Germany in the 1990s', *European Economic Review*, 54(4): 550–70.

Decressin, Jörg, and Antonio Fatás (1995) 'Regional labor market dynamics in Europe', *European Economic Review* 39(9): 1627–55.

Eger, Maureen A. (2010) 'Even in Sweden: the effect of immigration on support for welfare state spending', *European Sociological Review* 26(2): 203–17.

Ethier, Wilfred J. (1996) 'Theories about trade liberalisation and migration: substitutes or complements?', in P.J. Lloyd and L. Williams (eds.), *International Trade and Migration in the Apec Region*. Melbourne: Oxford University Press, 50–68.

Facchini, Giovanni, and Anna Maria Mayda (2008) 'From individual attitudes towards migrants to migration policy outcomes: theory and evidence', *Economic Policy* (56): 65–713.

Freeman, Richard B. (1993) 'Immigration from poor to wealthy countries: experience of the United States', *European Economic Review* 37(2–3): 443–51.

____. (1998) 'Will globalization dominate U.S. labor market outcomes?', in S.M. Collins (ed.), *Imports, Exports and the American Worker*. Washington, D.C.: Brookings Institution Press, 101–31.

Gandal, Neil, Gordon H. Hanson and Matthew J. Slaughter (2004) 'Technology, trade, and adjustment to immigration in Israel', *European Economic Review* 48(2): 403–28.

Gaston, Noel, and Douglas Nelson (2000) 'Immigration and labour market outcomes in the United States: a political-economy puzzle', *Oxford Review of Economic Policy* 16(3): 104–14.

Gaston, Noel, and Douglas R. Nelson (2010) 'International migration', Bond University Globalisation and Development Centre Working Paper No. 39.

Glitz, Albrecht (2006) 'The labour market impact of immigration: quasi-experimental evidence', CReAM Discussion Paper No. 0612.

Gould, David M. (1994) 'Immigrant links to the home country: empirical implications for United States bilateral trade flows', *Review of Economics and Statistics* 76(2): 302–16.

Granovetter, Mark (1973) 'Strength of weak ties', *American Journal of Sociology* 78(6): 1360–80.

____. (1983) 'The strength of weak ties revisited', in R. Collins (ed.), *Sociological Theory – 1983*, 201–33.

____. (2005) 'The impact of social structure on economic outcomes', *Journal of Economic Perspectives* 19(1): 33–50.

Greenaway, David, and Douglas R. Nelson (2010) 'The politics of (anti-) globalization: what do we learn from simple models?', in N. Gaston and A. Khalid (eds.), *Globalization and Economic Integration: Winners and Losers in the Asia-Pacific*. Cheltenham: Edward Elgar, 69–92.

Greif, Avner (1993) 'Contract enforceability and economic institutions in early trade: the Maghribi traders coalition', *American Economic Review* 83(3): 525–48.

Grogger, Jeffrey, and Gordon H. Hanson (2008) 'Income maximization and the selection and sorting of international migrants', NBER Working Paper No. 13821.

Hainmueller, Jens, and Michael J. Hiscox (2010) 'Attitudes toward highly skilled and low skilled immigration: evidence from a survey experiment', *American Political Science Review* 104(1): 61–84.

Hanson, Gordon H. (2009) 'The economic consequences of international migration', *Annual Review of Economics* 1: 179–208.

Hanson, Gordon H., Kenneth Scheve and Matthew J. Slaughter (2007) 'Public finance and individual preferences over globalization strategies', *Economics and Politics* 19(1): 1–33.

Hanson, Gordon H., and Matthew J. Slaughter (2002) 'Labor market adjustment in open economies: evidence from US states', *Journal of International Economics* 57(1): 3–29.

Hanson, Gordon H., and Antonio Spilimbergo (2001) 'Political economy, sectoral shocks, and border enforcement', *Canadian Journal of Economics* 34(3): 612–38.

Harrigan, James (1997) 'Technology, factor supplies, and international specialization: estimating the neoclassical model', *American Economic Review* 87(4): 475–94.

Hatton, Timothy J., and Jeffrey G. Williamson (2006) 'International migration in the long-run: positive selection, negative selection and policy', in F. Foders and R.J. Langhammer, (eds.) *Labour Mobility and the World Economy* Kiel: Springer.

Helliwell, John F. (1998) *How Much Do National Borders Matter?* Washington, D.C.: Brookings Institution Press.

Herander, Mark G., and Luz A. Saavedra (2005) 'Exports and the structure of immigrant-based networks: the role of geographic proximity', *Review of Economics and Statistics* 87(2): 323–35.

Hijzen, Alexander, and Peter W. Wright (2010) 'Migration, trade and wages', *Journal of Population Economics*, 23(4), 1189-211.

Horiba, Yutaka, and Rickey C. Kirkpatrick (1983) 'United States North–South labor migration and trade', *Journal of Regional Science* 23(1): 93–103.

Jones, Ronald W. (1967) 'International capital movements and theory of tariffs and trade', *Quarterly Journal of Economics* 81(1): 1–38.

Katz, Lawrence F., and Kevin M. Murphy (1992) 'Changes in relative wages, 1963–1987: supply and demand factors', *Quarterly Journal of Economics* 107(1): 35–78.

Kemp, Murray C. (1966) 'Gain from international trade and investment: a neo-Heckscher–Ohlin approach', *American Economic Review* 56(4): 788–809.

Kohli, Ulrich (1991) *Technology, Duality, and Foreign Trade: The Gnp Function Approach to Modeling Imports and Exports*. Ann Arbor: University of Michigan Press.

____. (1999) 'Trade and migration: a production theory approach', in R. Faini, J. de Melo and K.F. Zimmermann (eds.), *Migration: The Controversies and the Evidence*. Cambridge: Cambridge University Press.

____. (2002) 'Migration and foreign trade: further results', *Journal of Population Economics* 15(2): 381–87.

Kritz, Mary M., and Douglas T. Gurak (2001) 'The impact of immigration on the internal migration of natives and immigrants', *Demography* 38(1): 133–45.

Lalonde, Robert J., and Robert H. Topel (1991) 'Labor market adjustments to increased migration', in J.M. Abowd and R.B. Freeman (eds.), *Immigration, Trade and the Labor Market*, 167–99. Chicago: University of Chicago Press/NBER.

Lau, Lawrence (1986) 'Functional forms in econometric model building', in Z. Griliches and M. Intriligator (eds.), *Handbook of Econometrics*, 1515–66. Amsterdam: Elsevier.

Leamer, Edward E. (1995) *The Heckscher–Ohlin Model in Theory and Practice*. Princeton: International Finance Section, Department of Economics, Princeton University.

Lowell, B. Lindsay (2007) 'Trends in international migration flows and stocks, 1975–2005', OECD Social, Employment and Migration Working Paper No. 58.

Markusen, James R., and Lars E.O. Svensson (1985) 'Trade in goods and factors with international differences in technology', *International Economic Review* 26(1): 175–92.

Massey, Douglas S., Rafael Alarcón, Jorge Durand and Humberto Gonzalez (1987) *Return to Aztlan: The Social Process of International Migration from Western Mexico*. Berkeley: University of California Press.

McCallum, John (1995) 'National borders matter: Canada–US regional trade patterns', *American Economic Review* 85(3): 615–23.

Mundell, Robert A. (1957) 'International trade and factor mobility', *American Economic Review* 47(3): 321–35.

Opp, Marcus M., Hugo F. Sonnenschein and Christis G. Tombazos (2009) 'Rybczynski's Theorem in the Heckscher–Ohlin world: anything goes', *Journal of International Economics* 79(1): 137–42.

Ottaviano, Gianmarco I.P., and Giovanni Peri (2011) 'Rethinking the effects of immigration on wages', *Journal of the European Economic Association*, forthcoming.

____. (2008) 'Immigration and national wages: clarifying the theory and the empirics', NBER Working Paper No. 14188.

Overman, Henry G., and Diego Puga (2002) 'Unemployment clusters across Europe's regions and countries', *Economic Policy* (34): 115–47.

Portes, Richard, and Helene Rey (2005) 'The determinants of cross-border equity flows', *Journal of International Economics* 65(2): 269–96.

Rauch, James E. (1999) 'Networks versus markets in international trade', *Journal of International Economics* 48(1): 7–35.

Rauch, James E., and Alessandra Casella (2003) 'Overcoming informational barriers to international resource allocation: prices and ties', *Economic Journal* 113(484): 21–42.

Razin, Assaf, Efraim Sadka and Phillip Swagel (2002) 'Tax burden and migration: a political economy theory and evidence', *Journal of Public Economics* 85(2): 167–90.

Roy, A.D. (1951) 'Some thoughts on the distribution of earnings', *Oxford Economic Papers* 3(2): 135–46.

Rybczynski, T.M. (1955) 'Factor endowments and relative commodity prices', *Economica* 22: 336–41.

Samuelson, Paul A. (1949) 'International factor price equalization once again', *Economic Journal* 59(234): 181–97.

Trefler, Daniel (1995) 'The case of the missing trade and other mysteries', *American Economic Review* 85(5): 1029–46.

Williamson, Oliver E. (1975) *Markets and Hierarchies: Analysis and Antitrust Implications: A Study in the Economics of Internal Organization.* New York: Free Press.

____. (1985) *The Economic Institutions of Capitalism: Firms, Markets, Relational Contracting.* New York: Free Press.

____. (1996) *The Mechanisms of Governance.* New York: Oxford University Press.

Wong, Kar-yiu (1986) 'Are international trade and factor mobility substitutes', *Journal of International Economics* 21(1–2): 25–43.

____. (1988) 'International factor mobility and the volume of trade: an empirical study', in R.C. Feenstra (ed.), *Empirical Methods for International Trade.* Cambridge: MIT Press, 231–50.

Zimmermann, Klaus F. (1995) 'Tackling the European Migration Problem', *Journal of Economic Perspectives* 9(2): 45–62.

Index